Questions for America

To solve its multiple challenges post-2024, America must act with intelligence and wisdom, which can only come from an active and well-informed citizenry. The issues that confront us post-2024 are profound: climate change, inequality, artificial intelligence, an unstable geopolitical global order, existential threats from unfriendly nations, just to name a few. A democracy needs an educated citizenry which requires not just information, but knowledge and understanding.

As the dust settles from the 2024 presidential election, we are faced with several philosophical issues. How we act post-2024 will affect our America and our children's America. Our future depends on the proactive action that we take now, which is influenced by how much we understand today's issues. This is a book about today's America.

Jack Reardon is Senior Lecturer of Economics at the University of Wisconsin—Eau Claire. He is the founding editor of *International Journal of Pluralism and Economics Education*, passionately advocating for a reconceptualized, inclusive, and pluralist economics and economics education so that we all can reach our potential. Author of several books on economics and a novel, Jack has taught and lectured across the globe, including in China, India, the Soviet Union, Latvia, Lithuania, the UK, Germany, France, Italy, and Mexico.

David Wheat is Emeritus Professor of System Dynamics at the University of Bergen in Norway. During the 1972–1975 period, he served as White House Staff Assistant to Presidents Nixon and Ford, working on economic and energy policy issues. Later, he headed a private consulting firm in Texas. Professor Wheat's current projects include collaboration with Ukrainian economists to build dynamic modeling capacity at universities in Kyiv and Lviv and working with policymakers on a post-war reconstruction planning model for Ukraine.

Questions for America

2024 and Beyond

Jack Reardon *with* David Wheat

Routledge
Taylor & Francis Group

NEW YORK AND LONDON

Designed cover image: Getty Images

First published 2025
by Routledge
605 Third Avenue, New York, NY 10158

and by Routledge
4 Park Square, Milton Park, Abingdon, Oxon, OX14 4RN

Routledge is an imprint of the Taylor & Francis Group, an informa business

Library of Congress Cataloging-in-Publication Data
Names: Reardon, Jack, author. | Wheat, David (Professor of system dynamics), author.
Title: Post-2024 : questions for America / Jack Reardon ; with David Wheat.
Description: New York : Routledge, 2025. | Includes bibliographical references and index.
Identifiers: LCCN 2024043055 (print) | LCCN 2024043056 (ebook) | ISBN 9781032970400 (hardback) | ISBN 9781032769097 (paperback) | ISBN 9781003591856 (ebook)
Subjects: LCSH: United States--Economic conditions--2009- | United States--Politics and government--2021- | United States--Environmental conditions--21st century.
Classification: LCC HC106.84 .R4325 20025 (print) | LCC HC106.84 (ebook) | DDC 330.973--dc23/eng/20250130
LC record available at https://lccn.loc.gov/2024043055
LC ebook record available at https://lccn.loc.gov/2024043056

ISBN: 978-1-032-97040-0 (hbk)
ISBN: 978-1-032-76909-7 (pbk)
ISBN: 978-1-003-59185-6 (ebk)

DOI: 10.4324/9781003591856

Typeset in Times New Roman
by KnowledgeWorks Global Ltd.

Contents

Introduction

0.1 What This Book Is About

The issues that confront us post-2024 are profound: Climate change, inequality, artificial intelligence, an unstable geopolitical global order, existential threats from unfriendly nations, just to name a few. To solve our multiple challenges, America must act with intelligence and wisdom, which can only come from an active and well-informed citizenry. A democracy[1] needs an educated citizenry. And an educated citizenry needs not just information, but knowledge and understanding. How we act post-2024 will affect *our* America and *our* children's America. How our future unfolds depends on the proactive action we take now, which, in turn, will be influenced by how much we understand today's issues.

This a book about America and America's role in the world. It is a book about how we see ourselves, about the America that we want to bequeath to our children and to our children's children.

As Americans, we dialogue and debate with our friends (sometimes just at the corner bar) which is critical in forming our collective intelligence and establishing a rich and flourishing social capital, so vital for our nation. We intend this book to promote understanding, to jumpstart dialogue, ideas, and action, and to clarify who we are and what America means. We hope that this book provides a spark for further thought and dialogue, recognizing that "each new area of knowledge, each fresh idea has to be viewed as a seed of power placed within people's grasp" (de Tocqueville, 1840 [2003], p. 13). After all, dialoging, listening, and debating on the basis of knowledgeable understanding is what democracy is all about. Hopefully, this book will shed light on what America is and what America can become, while emphasizing the fruitful benefits of democratic participation.

0.2 The Book's Nuts and Bolts

0.2.1 The Importance of Asking Questions

When my (Jack) children were young, I told them that there was no such thing as a stupid question; that the only stupid question was the one unasked. Today, I say the same to my university students. Students and children typically question a specific thing, what it means, or even to clarify. The answers help build confidence. But in writing this book, we had in mind a different type of question—a generative question, which is "asked to develop new understanding…that neither entrenches current understanding nor creates misunderstanding. A good generative question leads to more answers and more questions in unexpected ways" (Boyd and Reardon, 2020, p. 27). A generative question is a tad more sophisticated than a clarifying question, but at the same time no less important.

Having 'question' in the title attenuates any presumed arrogance on the part of the author toward the reader. Yes, as social scientists we have spent a good deal of our working lives researching and teaching these issues; and yes we know a great deal and have a lot to offer, but to paraphrase the late Edward Said, one of world's foremost intellectuals, we want "to put our matter…before the… reader…not as something watertight and finished, but as something to be thought through, tried out, engaged with…" (Said, 1992, p. xii). After all, "the rays of human ability do not radiate from one central point but crisscross each other in every direction" (de Tocqueville, 1840 [2003], p. 214).

0.2.2 The Issues

Of course we cannot ask questions without issues. Our book presents the issues that define today's America and will define America post-2024. How we respond to the challenges raised by these issues will determine what America becomes post-2024. No claim is made to present all the issues (space precludes us) but taken together, we feel they paint a picture of who we are as a people and what America is.

Not only do these issues affect us individually but many are game changers, requiring thoughtful and participatory action from all of us. For example, the Transition to **Net Zero** (i.e., net zero emissions of Global Warming Gases by 2050), already underway, is "the biggest transformation project in human history…requiring \$275 trillion of cumulative investments in physical assets *alone* by 2025 (Montgomery and Van Clieaf, 2023, p. 3; emphasis added). Where and how will we get the funds? How will decisions be made as to how we transition? Who will make these decisions? How are the specific goals and the means to be selected? Should we "rely on a vertical conception of public policy and the common interest [where policy makers] arrogate to themselves, without restraint, the monopoly on expertise and information that accompanies it?" (Piketty, 2022, pp. 180–181). Or should such decisions be made democratically based on full understanding by all stakeholders? We much prefer the latter. The most effective way, at least for us, is to present the issues 'to be tried out' and 'engaged with.' Which in turn requires knowledge and understanding. This is our America. These are our issues that are (and will be) affecting all of us. Hence, we all should all have a hand in how they play out. Isn't this the essence of democracy?

The issues discussed in this book are grouped into six units:

- **Introduction:** Discussed here are metrics frequently in the news such as Inflation, Unemployment, Recessions, GDP, and the Dow Jones Industrial Average.
- **Domestic Issues:** Abortion and Reproductive Rights, Guns and Gun Violence, the Supreme Court, Student Debt, the Minimum Wage, Inequality, Labor Unions, the Federal Reserve, and LGBTQ.
- **Power and Technology**: Big Tech, Artificial Intelligence, Corporate Power, and Antitrust.
- **International Governance:** The United Nations, NATO, the EU, Tariffs and Trade, the BRICS, Bretton Woods, and the Gold Standard.
- **International Trouble Spots**: China; North Korea, Iran, and Russia; the Question of Palestine.
- **Energy and Climate Change**: Fossil Fuels, the Oil Industry, Net Zero, and Climate Change.

In writing this book, we found that issues often overlapped, e.g., **Antitrust**, **Big Tech**, and **AI**; and **Fossil Fuels** and **Climate Change**; nevertheless, we thought it best to present each issue separately, while of course acknowledging any and all interconnections. To fully understand an issue, it is not just enough to present it as it is today, but how and why it became important. An issue does not arise out of nowhere; understanding its provenance can enable us to understand its evolution and its significance both for today and post-2024. Issues in bold will be discussed in various chapters. And post-2024, refers to America after the 2024 presidential election.

Finally, in a book about issues/questions, it is natural to ask if we have an axe to grind, and/or if we support a particular political party. The answer to both questions is no. Yes, we do have values—everyone does—and it is our values that energize our writing and give us passion. That doesn't mean that we are partisan; for there is a significant difference between being partisan and passionate. We are passionate about fairness, justice, equality, individual rights, and the right of self-determination. We are passionate about this special nation of ours. We are passionate about democracy.

Note

1 Of course, we are cognizant of the difference between a democracy as a form of government and a republic. As James Madison explains, "by democracy I mean a society consisting of a small number of citizens who assemble and administer the government in person…whereas a republic delegates the government to a small group of citizens elected by the rest" (Hamilton et al., 2003 [1787–1788], #10, p. 55). Here, we refer to democracy as a beacon of hope, a clarion call for equality both in representation and decision making. And more specifically, "as a system of government with regular, free and fair elections, in which all adult citizens have the right to vote and possess basic civil liberties such as freedom of speech and association" (Levitsky and Ziblatt, 2018, p. 9).

References

Boyd, Graham and Jack Reardon (2020) *Rebuild the Economy, Leadership, and You: A Toolkit for Builders of Better World*, Evolutesix, London.

Hamilton, Alexander, James Madison, and John Jay (2003 [1787–1788]) *The Federalist Papers*, Bantam Books, New York.

Levitsky, Steven and Ziblatt, Daniel (2018) *How Democracies Die*, Broadway Books, New York.

Montgomery, John and Mark Van Clieaf (2023) *Net Zero Business Models: Winning in the Global Net Zero Economy*, Wiley, New York.

Piketty, Thomas (2022) *A Brief History of Equality*, Belknap Press, Harvard University.

Said, Edward W. (1992) *The Question of Palestine*, Vintage, New York.

Tocqueville, Alexis de (1835 [2003]) *Democracy in America*, Penguin, New York.

Part I

Basic Economic Indicators

The Issue: In order to achieve our goals, we need an indicator/measurement of our success/failure. Then, based on the data, we can adjust our strategy. This unit will discuss the most important indicators of economic performance: The **Dow Jones Industrial Average, Gross Domestic Product** (how much the economy is producing), the **Unemployment Rate** (the percentage of people looking for work), **Inflation (increase in the average level of prices),** and **the Business Cycle** (whether the economy is in a recession or expansion). While no indicator can be devised that is perfect and all-encompassing, the indicators discussed in this issue were all developed much earlier, when the economy was so different, which raises questions on their current efficacy. If public policy is to be effective, then our indicators must accurately reflect and measure what we ask of them. Each indicator has significant intrinsic shortcomings which must be adequately understood to use them properly; but, unfortunately the indicators used today are inadequate to conceptualize, measure, and assess the 'great transformations' underway, including **Artificial Intelligence**, **Climate Change**, and the **Transition to Net Zero**. To re-conceptualize our indicators to meet the challenges of a new age is a high-priority task, post-2024.

DOI: 10.4324/9781003591856-1

1 The Dow Jones Industrial Average

The Issue: The Dow Jones Industrial Average, 'the Dow' is everywhere. It is reported constantly in every form of media, giving it an exaggerated sense of self-importance. Understanding the Dow, and stock market prices in general, is critical to becoming economically literate. And being economically literate is critical for a well-functioning democracy.

1.1 Introduction

When I (Jack) was younger, I had the good fortune of teaching in the Union of Soviet Socialist Republics (USSR), a nation that no longer exists.[1] I taught during the latter stages of glasnost (openness) and perestroika (market restructuring), two initiatives launched by the USSR's last premier, Mikhail Gorbachev. His intent was to save and even resuscitate the moribund USSR. But, alas, his reforms set in motion irrevocable centrifugal forces, leading to the USSR's quick dissolution.

My first lecture in the USSR was exciting for me, as it was for my students—their first-time meeting someone from the United States. I had been asked to deliver a series of lectures on the origins of American capitalism. After introducing ourselves, and before getting down to work, I decided to open the floor for any questions either about me or the United States. To my surprise, the very first question was 'what is the Dow Jones Industrial Average?' At the time, the students were able to access CNN Weekly, which frequently mentioned the Dow, how much it gained/lost, but never explained what it was. Being that this was before the internet, the students wanted to hear it from me. I happily obliged.

Here in the United States, the DJIA is ubiquitous: It is mentioned on every newscast, night and day, but seldom is the Index explained; nor what an increase/decrease means for ordinary Americans. To do so is the purpose of this issue.

1.2 Origin of the DJIA

The DJIA was constructed in 1896. It was conceived by Charles Dow (1851–1902), Edward Jones (1856–1920), and Charles Bergstresser (1858–1923); three financial news reporters/journalists working on Wall Street.[2] Charles Dow was originally

DOI: 10.4324/9781003591856-2

based in Providence, Rhode Island, working at the *Providence Journal*, which to-day bills itself as the oldest continuous daily newspaper in the USA. While at the *Journal*, he began succinctly summarizing the day's news, which provided the inspiration for the eventual DJIA, in Providence, he met Edward Jones, who worked at the rival *Providence Evening Press*. The two moved to New York City (which like now, was the place to be for a financial journalist) to work at the Kiernan News Agency, where they met Mr. Bergstresser. Dissatisfied with Kiernan, in November 1882, the three left to form the Dow Jones Company, which went on to become one of the most iconic names in American business. While Dow and Jones were active managers, Bergstresser was mostly a silent, fund-providing partner.

In 1882, the company began publishing the *Customers' Afternoon Letter*. Thanks to Bergstresser's suggestion, the publication was renamed *The Wall Street Journal* and is now one of America's most important and influential news publications. In 1903, Clarence Barron, a Boston-based financial news reporter, bought out Mr. Dow's shares, and eventually formed *Barron's*, an influential and highly regarded financial weekly. The DJIA was officially launched on May 26, 1896.

1.3   The Nuts and Bolts of the DJIA

Dow, Jones, and Bergstresser wanted their Index to succinctly summarize the day's economic news by capturing in one number the performance of the USA's most important firms. While there are many ways to do so, e.g., profits, revenue, productivity, patents, number of employees, etc., the DJIA focused on only one: The price of a share of stock.[3]

A corporation might issue a share(s) of stock as one possible way of raising money (other ways include issuing bonds, using retained earnings, taking a loan from a bank). Once issued, a share could then be bought/sold on exchanges.[4] Conversely, an investor has several choices where to invest his/her money: Banks (which at the time did not have a reserve guarantee like today, so they were not exactly risk-free), government bonds, corporate bonds, real estate, entrepreneurial deals, or even under the mattress.

By purchasing a stock whose price is expected to rise, the investor hopes to reap a capital gain (i.e., a positive difference between the buying and selling price) and/or receive dividends[5] (i.e., money distributed to shareholders out of a firm's revenue). Expecting a pecuniary gain, however, is not the only motivation to buy stock: Some investors might enjoy owning a part of America, while others might want to strategically influence a particular corporation.

Since a stock's shares are limited, if more investors purchase a stock's shares, then ceteris paribus, its price should increase, and vice versa. The key here is expectations, i.e., how well investors think a firm will do: The more positive, the greater will be the demand for shares, all else equal. Given that expectations are subjective, the DJIA and stock prices are often driven by emotion and animal spirits, as much as by hard-core empirical data forecasting.[6]

The Dow's founders envisioned it as a gateway to the larger world of stock investing: An increasing index would hopefully entice more individuals to invest in stocks. Then, as now, the Index components had to be carefully chosen to accurately reflect the economy. The components, i.e., corporations,[7] were selected to meet the double standards of consistently making profits and being representative of the American economy.

The original 1896 DJIA was comprised of twelve of America's best-known companies, (although not necessarily the twelve largest). The twelve were industrial companies, i.e., producing physical goods like rubber, lead, cotton, as opposed to providing a service. They were American Cotton Oil Company, American Sugar Company, American Tobacco Company, Chicago Gas Company, Distilling & Cattle Feeding Company, General Electric, Laclede Gas Company, National Lead Company, North American Utility Company, Tennessee Coal & Iron, US Leather Company, and US Rubber Company. General Electric, by the way, was the longest lasting company on the DJIA (1896–1988), testimony to how GE constantly reinvented itself—not so much to remain on the Index but to continually evolve as a profitable and significant player.

In 1916, the Index was increased to 20 corporations, and in 1928 to its present-day 30. Since 1896, the Index's composition has changed 57 times, about once every four years. Reading these changes over time gives an unparalleled evolution of the American economy, providing a veritable who's who of American business (Wikipedia, 2023).

The most recent change occurred on August 31, 2020, when Amgen, Salesforce, and Honeywell replaced Exxon Mobil, Pfizer, and Raytheon Technologies. It is not clear at this point when the Index will be next revised, although it is certain that it will. (Of course, if the Index were to remain as the original, it would have quickly fallen out of favor.)

Currently, the 30 Index members are: American Express, 3-M, Amgen, Salesforce, Honeywell, Microsoft, Goldman Sachs, Home Depot, United Health, McDonald's, Caterpillar, VISA, Boeing, The Travelers Companies, Apple, IBM, Johnson & Johnson, Walmart, Procter & Gamble, J.P. Morgan, Chevron, Merck & Co., Nike, Walt Disney, Coca Cola, Dow[8] Inc., Cisco Systems, Intel, Verizon, and Walgreens & Boots Alliance. While these thirty are large by any measure, they are not America's largest.[9]

The original index was just that—an index. The numerator summed the closing prices of the twelve shares, which was then divided by 12. Since the denominator remained fixed, an increased numerator (i.e., the sum of the twelve share prices) would increase the DJIA. But, over time, as companies became more successful, the demand for their stock would increase, causing the share price to increase, all else equal. This made it less affordable for the average investor. So corporations began splitting their stocks (i.e., stock splits) by reducing the price while increasing the number of shares.

A split maintained constant the stock's overall capitalization (price x # shares). A typical stock split is two-for-one[10] (i.e., double the shares and halve the price). For example, I own five shares of stock, each valued at $4/share. If the company executes a 2-for-1 stock split, then the number of shares doubles to 10, while the price per share falls to $2, maintaining my total capitalization of $20.

By reducing the share price, stock splits make the share price more afford-able, broadening the ownership base. And if the firm is interested in buying back its stock, perhaps to regain control, as some of today's corporations are wont to do, a stock split will cheapen the price.

If the denominator in the DJIA remained at the original 12 (or now 30), then stock splits would have continuously decreased the average, especially as splits became more widespread. This would have given a false and misleading per-spective on corporate performance. To solve this problem, a numerical 'divisor' is substituted for 30, which gives the same value to the Index as if no companies engaged in splits. As this manuscript goes to press (October 2024), the divisor is 0.1517275259384.

To see how the movement of any one stock affects the Index, let's use In-vestopedia's example (Segal, 2021): Divide the stock's price change by the cur-rent divisor. For example, if Walmart is up $5, divide five by the current [at the time] divisor (0.147), which equals 34.01. Thus, if the DJIA was up 100 points on the day, Walmart was responsible for 34.01 of those points. And from *The Wall Street Journal*, explaining more or less the same thing for the second week of January 2024, "The DJIA gained 126.87 points, or 0.34%, on the week. A $1 change in the price of any DJIA stock = 6.59-point change in the average" (January 16, 2024, p. B8).

Originally, the Dow Jones Corporation decided both the number of firms in the Index and the firms themselves. But today, thanks to a corporate ownership change, it no longer does. In 2008, News Corporation acquired the Dow Jones Corporation, and the DJIA now is operated by S&P Dow Jones Indices, a joint venture launched in 2012 between News Corporation, S&P Global, and the CME Group (which operates the Chicago Mercan-tile Exchange, the Chicago Board of Trade, and the New York Mercantile Exchange).

1.4   Does Movement in the DJIA Affect the Average American?

Keep in mind that the DJIA calculates the performance of the average of thirty stock prices. Nothing more and nothing less. The Index increases/decreases when the average of the 30 share prices increase/decrease. The key driver of change is expectations of firm profits. Any number of factors can affect profit expectations: The economy's overall growth; innovations/new technological developments; and ironically layoffs. For example, if a corporation lays off part of its workforce, all else equal, its costs will decrease, potentially increasing profit expectations.[11]

A rising Dow exudes a sense of overall confidence in the economy, that things are going well, which may or may not directly affect the individual—since the individual, unless actively investing, is too far removed.

1.5   The DJIA and the Macroeconomy

In August 1929, a recession hit the USA economy, largely caused by the Federal Reserve increasing interest rates in order to subdue overly optimistic stock purchasing.[12] The latter had in turn, "increased the DJIA six-fold from 63 in August 1921 to 381 in September 1929" (Richardson et al., 2011). The effusive stock purchasing was enabled by

> A new industry of brokerage houses, investment trusts, and margin accounts [which] enabled ordinary people to purchase corporate equities with borrowed funds. Purchasers put down a fraction of the price, typically 10 percent, and borrowed the rest. The stocks that they bought served as collateral for the loan. Borrowed money poured into equity markets, and stock prices soared.
>
> (Richardson et al., 2011)

Not surprisingly, it didn't take that much to burst the stock price bubble,

> A soaring, overheated economy that was destined to one day fall, likely played a large role. Equally relevant issues, such as overpriced shares, public panic, rising bank loans, an agriculture crisis, higher interest rates and a cynical press added to the disarray.
>
> (Marks, 2021)

As the Federal Reserve writes,

> The epic boom ended in a cataclysmic bust. On Black Monday, October 28, 1929, the Dow declined nearly 13 percent. On the following day, Black Tuesday, the market dropped nearly 12 percent. By mid-November, the Dow had lost almost half of its value. The slide continued through the summer of 1932, when the Dow closed at 41.22, its lowest value of the twentieth century, 89 percent below its peak. The Dow did not return to its pre-crash heights until November 1954.
>
> (Richardson et al., 2011)

The 1929 stock market crash was a symptom rather than a direct cause, although the lost wealth in turn reduced consumer spending, and hence business investment, which exacerbated the recession's severity.

Increased inflation, ceteris paribus, tends to reduce stock purchases and hence the DJIA, because inflation tends to eat away at corporate profits, especially for more indebted firms. In addition, inflation usually causes the Federal Reserve to increase interest rates, which in turn will reduce corporate profits, all else equal. Higher interest rates make it more difficult to borrow and hence more difficult to invest. Conversely, reduced inflation could set in motion the opposite chain of events.

Today, domestic consumer spending accounts for approximately two-thirds of USA economic activity. Economists understand very well why consumption increases/decreases. A key factor is wealth. Greater wealth fueled by increased stock prices, or increased real estate prices, will increase current spending, ceteris paribus; thus increasing economic activity as measured by **GDP**. Conversely, decreased stock prices set in motion the opposite chain of events.

1.6   The DJIA's Strengths and Weaknesses

Strengths

- It succinctly summarizes corporate performance in one number.
- The Dow represents 25% of the value of all stocks traded in the USA.
- Continuously in use since 1896, it gives useful trend information, both short and long term.

Weaknesses

- Of America's 3000+ stocks, the DJIA only includes 30, albeit among the biggest and best known, i.e., the blue chips.[13]
- The Dow doesn't represent the smaller, high-growth, entrepreneurial companies, especially those from the technological sector.
- The American economy is complex and ever-changing. It is impossible to construct one number to effectively capture all aspects of our economy. Hence, "trying to choose just 30 stocks to represent the economy naturally makes the selection committee resist putting in new members until they have been doing so well for so long that it can't be avoided" (Mackintosh, 2024, p. B3). Thus, a lag between a company's performance and its inclusion in the Dow.
- The Dow "is a badly designed index that gives outsize weight to certain stocks based on the share price, rather than the market value used by almost all other large indexes" (Mackintosh, 2024, p. B3).

1.7   Alternatives to the DJIA

Not surprisingly, given the above criticisms, alternatives to the DJIA abound. The three most important are: (1) the S & P 500; (2) the Nasdaq Composite Index; and (3) the Wilshire 500 (Banton 2023).

The S & P 500: Formerly known as the Standard and Poor's 500. As its name indicates,[14] it is comprised of 500 stocks and, thus, is a much broader measure of stock market activity. Unlike the DIJA, which is weighted by share price, the S&P 500 is weighted by market capitalization, i.e., share price x #shares outstanding.[15] Given its broader base, the S&P 500 is included in the Conference Board's Index of Leading Indicators, which is used to forecast our economy's future movements,[16] whereas the Dow "is a measure of companies that used to be considered great, … the S&P is dominated by companies that are currently considered great. In times of change, the two move apart, as the S&P rebalances toward the newest companies, and the Dow doesn't" (Mackintosh, 2024, p. B3).

The Nasdaq Composite Index: An index of 2500 stocks listed on the Nasdaq Stock Exchange. The acronym Nasdaq stands for the National Association of Securities Dealers Automated Quotations. Both the Exchange and Index were founded in February 1971. The Index is heavily weighted toward technology stocks, which comprise 55.32% of Nasdaq's total value. In comparison, the next two largest sectors are consumer discretionary (18.8%) and healthcare (8.08%). Some of the best-known technology companies are listed on the Nasdaq, e.g., Microsoft, Apple, Telsa, Alphabet, and Nvidia.[17] Unlike the DJIA, the S&P 500 and the Nasdaq include international stocks.

The Wilshire 5000: Created in 1974 by Wilshire Associates. It includes all publicly traded stocks in the USA, with no minimum requirement for capitalization. Despite its much broader base, it is not as popular and well-known as the other indices cited here.[18]

Many investors will look at all three indices, as well as assiduously study the company's fundamentals before making any investment choice.

1.8 Conclusion

In terms of its narrow, purported function, the DJIA succeeds, but it is a creature of an earlier age, the 19th century. This is not to suggest that the Index has worn out its usefulness; only that we need not place too much/overdue emphasis on it. The Index doesn't tell us anything about how these corporations are transitioning to **Net Zero**, their technological or environmental prowess, nor the wellbeing of a corporation's other stakeholders. But that was never Dow's intention. As our economy evolves toward **Net Zero**, more pertinent information might be of interest to investors, such as how the corporation is adhering to its plan to reach zero emissions.

Notes

1 Formed in the tumult of the Russian Revolution, the USSR formally disbanded in December 1991. The USSR (capital, Moscow) comprised 15 republics which then became independent nations, the largest in area and population being **Russia**.

2   While it is assumed that Wall Street is named for its tall buildings, the name however refers to an earlier large fort protecting the area from marauders coming from the north.

3   According to Investopedia, "A stock, also known as an equity, is a security that represents the ownership of a fraction of the issuing corporation. Units of stock are called 'shares' which entitle the owner to a proportion of the corporation's assets and profits equal to how much stock they own" (Hayes, 2023).

4   The USA's first stock exchange was the Philadelphia Stock Exchange in 1790 (now owned by the NASDAQ, see the text below). The world's oldest stock exchange is the Amsterdam Stock Exchange, established in 1602 by the East India Tea Company. It has since merged with competitors and is now part of Euronext. For a fascinating discussion of the Amsterdam Stock Exchange, see *Confusion of Confusions* (1688 [2006]). Still in print, it is considered a financial classic.

5   There is no formal requirement for a stock-issuing corporation to issue dividends. Some do as this a way of rewarding shareholders, but others invest the money back into the company, thus (hopefully) rewarding the investor over the long term with a capital gain.

6   For an interesting discussion of emotions run amuck on Wall Street, see Keynes (1936 [2010], pp. 147–164).

7   A corporation, from the Latin corpus (i.e., body), is "a group of individuals incorporated by law into a single body" (Magnuson, 2022, p. 4). A corporation's investors are shielded from any lawsuits. In fact, limited liability is an important attribute of a corporation. While other business forms, e.g., the entrepreneur, the partnership, are limited by the initial owners' funds, there is no limit as to a corporation's size, at least theoretically. While only corporations issue stock, not all corporations are large, but conversely, all large companies tend to be corporations. A notable exception is mining and construction companies: Many small forms incorporate to limit/shield from lawsuits filed over accidents/injuries.

8   While sometimes confused with the Dow Jones Co., especially since it is part of the DJIA, the two are separate. Dow, Inc., is a Midland Michigan-based holding company for The Dow Chemical Co., founded by Henry Hebert Dow, and no relation to Charles Dow.

9   See the Fortune 500 at (fortune.org).

10 Of course, stock splits can be three-for-one, four-for-one, or any such combination. The bottom line is that total capitalization remains the same.

11 The Dow doesn't differentiate between domestic and foreign profits, even though domestic citizens might be affected by the latter. So, for example, if MacDonald's is expected to make profits in Europe, this doesn't directly benefit American citizens, but nonetheless, the Index will increase.

12 For a detailed account see Studenski and Kroos (1963, pp. 327–352).

13 A term borrowed from poker: the blue chips have the highest value. Perhaps fitting, since investing in stocks is never safe; there is always a risk, i.e., a gamble, if you will.

14 In 1860, Henry Poor, published his *History of Railroads and Canals in the United States*, a very influential contemporary book. Later in the decade he together with his son, co-founded H.W. Poor Co. In 1941, the company merged with the Standard Statistics Bureau (founded in 1906) to become Standard & Poor's.

15 For the S&P 500, market capitalization is the main criteria for membership. As of January 2024, the minimum market capitalization for inclusion is $14.5b (S&P Press Release, 2024).

16 The Conference Board's other indicators are as follows: average weekly hours in manufacturing, average weekly initial unemployment claims, manufacturers' new

orders, ISM index of new orders, manufacturers' new orders for non-defense capital goods, building permits for new private housing, leading credit index, interest rate spread, and average consumer expectations.

17 An interesting company that we discuss is **Nvidia.** Founded on April 5, 1993, in Santa Clara, California, it makes computer chips to process AI algorithms.

18 As this manuscript goes to press (October 2024), there were 3427 stocks listed on the Wilshire 5000; for a full listing, see (Ciura 2024).

References

Banton, Caroline (2023) 'Top 3 US Stock Market Indices,' *Investopedia* Top 3 U.S. Stock Market Indexes (investopedia.com).

Ciura, Bob (2024) 'Updated List of All Wilshire 5000 Stocks,' January 11, 2024 (sure-dividend.com).

de la Vega, Joseph (2006 [1688]) *Confusion of Confusions*, Sonsbeek Publishing, Arnhem Netherlands.

Hayes, Adam (2023) 'Stocks: What They Are, Main Types, How They Differ From Bonds,' *Investopedia*, (investopedia.com).

Keynes, John Maynard (1936 [2010]) *The General Theory of Employment, Interest, and Money*, Martino Publishing, Mansfield, Centre, Connecticut.

Mackintosh, James (2024) 'The Dow is a Terrible Index. But it is Telling Us Something Important,' *The Wall Street Journal*, May 11–12, p. B3.

Magnuson, William (2022) *For Profit: A History of Corporations*, Basic Books, New York.

Marks, Julie (2021) 'What Caused the Stock Market Crash of 1929, *History* (April 27) https://www.history.com/

Richardson, Gary, Alejandro Komai, Michael Gou, and Daniel Park (2011) 'Stock Market Crash of 1929', *Federal Reserve History*, https://www.federalreservehistory.org/

S&P Press Release (2024) 'Dow Jones Indices Announces Update to S&P Composite 1500 Market Cap Guidelines,' January 2, (spglobal.com).

Segal, Troy (2021) 'How Does the Dow Jones Work' *Investopedia*, (investopedia.com).

Studenski, Paul and Herman E. Kroos (1963) *Financial History of the United States*, 2nd ed., McGraw Hill, New York.

Wikipedia (2023) 'Historical components of the Dow Jones Industrial Average,' In *Wikipedia, The Free Encyclopedia*, December 3 https://en.wikipedia.org/w/index.

2 Inflation

The Issue: Probably, no American has escaped the recent ravages of inflation. Most of us have an intuitive feel for its definition: An increase in prices. Inflation hits us where it hurts most: Our pocketbooks. It is as if we are taxed, effectively reducing our budget and constricting our economic choices. Given that inflation affects all of us, it is paramount to know how it happens and how to solve it.

2.1 Preface: A Lesson in History

We all know that the South lost the Civil War (1861–1865). What we might not know is that inflation played a key role. A critical decision in fighting any war is financing, which ideally should cause the lease amount of disruption and discomfort. Several options:

- Increase taxes on citizens. But since war is already imposing a burden on society (conscription, shortage of goods/services, day-to-day angst, wariness, etc.) taxing will reduce living standards, and perhaps if severe enough, erode the will to continue.
- Borrow from citizens and/or citizens of other nations, promising to repay, i.e., issue bonds (an IOU promising future repayment with interest). However, to do this, a nation must have a workable financial system in place.
- Keep the nation's industries running in order to earn revenue both at home and abroad.
- Print money. This is usually chosen by default when the others are not available. While ostensibly the easiest, it is the most destructive, since war-time shortages coupled with more money will increase inflation, thereby reducing living standards.

During the Civil War, the North was able to keep its industries running, while also issuing bonds. The South, however, being a slave-based agricultural society, principally producing cotton and tobacco, was only able to print money. [1]Making matters worse: On April 16, 1861 (four days after the fighting began at

DOI: 10.4324/9781003591856-3

Fort Sumter, Charleston, South Carolina), President Lincoln ordered a blockade of all southern ports which crippled the cotton trade, depriving the South of much-needed export revenue. During the Civil War, inflation increased by 80% in the North, but 9000% in the South, making it almost impossible for the Confederacy to adequately provide for its army and its citizens. Such high inflation also increased overall angst and desperation.

History teaches us that inflation, if severe enough, can topple governments and even lead to revolution. Think of the French Revolution (begun 1789) where poor harvests caused the price of bread to soar; the Russian Revolution when rising prices caused widespread insecurity; and Weimar Germany (during the 1920s) with inflation so confiscatory that people had to carry their money in wheelbarrows to make everyday purchases. Incidentally, they were more concerned about having their wheelbarrow stolen, which was far more valuable than the worthless paper currency that filled it. And Tiananmen Square in 1989, when the Chinese government opened fire on protesting students and workers; in addition to demanding democracy, free speech, and a free press, a major student complaint (and others on a fixed income) was sharply rising prices. Of course, this is not to say that inflation always and everywhere will cause a revolution or even an uprising; rather, that inflation is one factor among several.

2.2 Defining Inflation

Inflation is defined as an increase in the average level of prices. Inflation is caused by a disconnect between the amount of money circulating in an economy *relative* to the goods/services available. It is the relative amounts of each that matter, and not the absolute amount. For example, if there is an inadequate supply of a good/service relative to the amount of money, but everyone wants it, its price will increase. In this situation, more money becomes the enabler, just like pouring gasoline on a fire.

Wait a minute you might say, if everyone needs money to buy goods and services, but few people have enough, then how can we have too much money? Why can't the government give everyone whatever money they need? No more worries, right? Wrong. Remember the scene from the movie *Bruce Almighty*, when 'God' (Bruce) decides to grant everyone's prayers in one computer click. Since everyone who had asked to win the lottery won, each 'winner' hardly won any money at all, so no one really won. In our economy, giving everyone money without correspondingly increasing the available goods and services, would effectively make everyone worse off, since the prices of those goods/services would increase.

Prices tend to increase because the buyers most anxious to obtain a good bid up its price, and human nature being what it is, some firms, sensing that they are in the driver's seat, will jack up prices. I (Jack) remember being in central London several years ago during a record-breaking heat wave. Walking in the central city was hot and uncomfortable. Sweaty and thirsty, I stopped in a shop, and asked for a bottled water; of which I noticed, only a few were left. The proprietor, sizing me up, offered a price triple the usual. Despite my thirst, I left, angry that I was being ripped off.

To counter the rising cost of resources, some firms have engaged in 'price pack architecture,' or what most of us call shrinkflation, i.e., reducing the size of the good sold or shrinking the contents therein without changing its price. This has been frustrating consumers, so much so that Senator Elizabeth Waren (D. Mass.) and Senator Bob Casey (D. Pennsylvania) introduced a bill in February 2024 to crack down on this invidious practice (Moreno, 2024, p. 4). As this manuscript goes to press, it is not clear how this bill (or perhaps other similar ones) will turn out.

The influential doctrine of monetarism, however, lays the preponderant responsibility for inflation on the money supply, "money has a major influence on economic activity, so much so that the [economy's] price level and that the objectives of monetary policy are best achieved by targeting its rate of growth" (Carlin and Soskice, 2015, p. 472). If the money supply is the most preponderant variable, this suggests the need for a limited state, and a limited role for fiscal policy. Thus, "the only thing necessary was a well-run Federal Reserve…[monetarism] fostered suspicion of the ever-growing state and created the intellectual climate in which the conservative revolution of 1979-1980 became possible" (Piketty, 2014, pp. 712–713).

Monetarism was tried in the UK, the USA, and Canada during conservative revolutions of the 1970s and 1980s, and was not successful, causing Friedman himself to lose his enthusiasm (Carlin and Soskice, 2015, p. 473).

While it is easier to see the monetary cause (too much money) vis-à-vis to the economic (too few goods), it might be easy to miss the political cause: Why did the government allow/tolerate a lack of production, and/or excessive money increases? Inflation always has a political component.

Defining inflation as a disconnect between the amount of money and the available goods/services immediately suggests solutions: Decrease the money supply and/or increase the available goods. We will return to this discussion later in this chapter in the context of the recent bout of inflation.

2.3   How Inflation Is Measured

Here in the USA, the rate of inflation is calculated by the Bureau of Labor Statistics (BLS), housed within the Department of Labor. Several methods are used[2]:

- **The Consumer Price Index (CPI):** The BLS selects a sample of goods that consumers will most likely purchase and tracks their prices over time. The basket is held constant while only the prices can change. If the average level of prices increases, then we have inflation. And conversely, if the average level of prices decreases, then we have deflation, which will be explained in the next section. A problem with this method is that it assumes that the sample of goods/service will not change until the next sample is obtained.[3] But this ignores the law of demand: As a good's price increases/decreases, consumers will substitute away/toward it.[4]

- **The Producer Price Index (PPI):** Its methodology is similar to that of the CPI, except that it focuses on typical goods/services bought by producers. The same methodological criticism applies. Changes in the PPI are often a harbinger of changes in the CPI.
- **The Personal Consumption Expenditures Price Index (PCE):** As its name implies, this index focuses only on personal consumption expenditures, the largest **GDP** component, accounting for approximately 69% of US economic activity. The PCE measures the average increase in prices for all domestic personal consumption. The PCE accounts for consumer substitution behavior, whereas the CPI does not, rendering it a tad more accurate, and it is for this reason that the Fed prefers the PCE (Bullard, 2013).

2.4   What About Deflation: Is This Preferable to Inflation?

Deflation is defined as a decrease in the average level of prices. If inflation is harmful, wouldn't deflation be desirable, and even welcome? Aren't inflation and deflation more or less opposites? Unfortunately, deflation is even worse than inflation.[5] To see why put yourself in the position of a business owner, where prices are falling all around you. Since your output prices are falling, that means so too are your profits, all else equal. You'll probably lay off some of your employees and postpone any investment plans. The more severe the deflation, the greater the adverse effects. If enough firms suffer, then the entire economy will slow, resulting in a **recession**. And if the recession is severe enough then we have a **depression**, like the USA had during the 1930s (aka, The Great Depression) and during the 1870s.

During deflation, consumers expect prices to decrease. This incentivizes consumers/firms to postpone consumption and investment: why buy/invest now, given that future prices will be lower? Postponed spending/investment results in unemployment, declining economic activity, and if not corrected, a **depression**. Due to falling price expectations, deflation can easily downward spiral.[6]

But wait, it gets worse: Falling prices tend to put downward pressure on wages, which combined with layoffs, is a recipe for increased labor unrest. The American Federation of Labor, for example, was formed in 1886, in the middle of a deflationary depression; likewise, the Congress of Industrial Organizations (CIO) formed during the deflationary depression of the 1930s.[7]

Just like inflation, deflation always has a cause—it never just happens. Very typical is an artificial restriction/reduction in the money supply, as during the 19th century **gold standard**. Or an inadvertent (or even intentional) reduction in the money supply, like happened during the second half of 1929 which turned an 'ordinary' recession into a full-blown depression.[8]

2.5   Understanding the USA's Most Recent Bout of Inflation[9]

If we understand how inflation occurs and how to solve it, then why does it happen? This is a difficult question to answer, for it is tantamount to asking if we know how we get a common cold, and we understand its remedies, then why do we let ourselves get sick? The easy answer (although not necessarily a cop-out) is that stuff happens, often beyond our control and even beyond our foresight. If, for example, you knew that on a certain day, you would find yourself sitting next to a person on the bus sneezing and coughing, then you wouldn't take that bus, or if you had too, you would do your best to avoid that person. But unfortunately, we cannot predict the future.

The most recent bout of inflation, which saw the steepest price increases since 1979–1981, officially began in March 2021.[10] It peaked in June 2022 at 9.1% and has since gradually decreased. As this manuscript goes to press, the CPI-measured rate of inflation was 3.4% in April 2024, still stubbornly high and still above the Fed's acceptable threshold of two percent.[11]

Even though inflation has decreased since peaking at 9.1%, it is the cumulative changes that matter and hit one's pocketbook: In 2021, inflation increased by 4.7%; in 2022 by 8.0%; in 2023 by 4.1%; and as this manuscript goes to press 3.4% in April 2024. So, from 2021 to 2024, prices on average increased by 20.2%.[12] For many Americans, it is small consolation that the inflation rate has decreased to only 3.4%, since the cumulative effect 20.2% is felt by many, especially higher food and energy prices, higher costs for loans, mortgages, and rents, higher insurance cost, etc. This especially resonates with voters, remembering that inflation rates in 2019 and 2020 were 1.8% and 1.2%, respectively (Historical Inflation Rates, 2024).

Most people were surprised by this recent burst of inflation, or perhaps more accurately, had been lulled into complacency, since inflation had been so low for so long; well, at least since the early 1980s.

The causes of the post-COVID inflation: (1) a sharp increase of 420% in the money supply[13] from January 2020 (one month before the beginning of the 2020 recession) to April 2022 (St. Louis Federal Reserve, 2024); (2) a sharp recession-induced reduction in output and aggregate demand; (3) a COVID-induced interruption in global supply chains; and (4) massive government stimulus payments by both the Trump and the Biden administrations.

Even though economists understood the side effects (i.e., higher inflation) of increased spending, it was felt by many policy officials (especially at the Fed) that ending the COVID-induced recession mattered most and that inflation would be dealt with later. Aggressive fiscal/monetary action explains why the COVID **recession** (February 2020–April 2020) lasted only two months, making it the shortest on record.

Given the causes of inflation, the solutions are/were obvious: (1) fix/mend the supply chains, while even questioning overreliance on globalization; (2) reduce the money supply; (3) reduce demand for goods and services by increasing interest rates, making it more difficult and expensive for firms/individuals to borrow; (4) eliminate the stimuli; and (5) increase the production of goods and services. Easier said than done. This, by the way, is a recipe to prevent future inflation, although once again, easier said than done, especially when unforeseen events happen, and their solutions necessarily take precedence.

The above five solutions have been actively undertaken: The money supply has decreased by 14% percent since peaking in April 2022; the last stimuli were enacted as part of the American Rescue Plan Act (enacted March 11, 2021). The supply-side restrictions have eased. Yet, inflation remains stubbornly high, abetted by the Russian/Ukraine invasion, and the Hamas/Israel war.

The **Federal Reserve**, using its well-tried responses/solutions to inflation, has since March 2022 raised its benchmark federal funds rate by 5 percentage points, the fastest and steepest increase since the late 1970s/early 1980s. In turn, other interest rates like those on mortgages, credit cards, etc., have increased, which by making borrowing more expensive, decreases consumer spending.

2.6   Conclusion

A preponderant point of this chapter is that the inflation's causes are often multi-faceted with enough blame to go around, although starting with the Fed. But Americans tend to blame the captain of the ship, i.e., the president. Not only this is short-sighted—actually, the foundation for inflation was laid during the Trump administration—but it obfuscates the real causes, and the necessity for multiple solutions.

Notes

1 For a good discussion see Ball (1991), and Nugent (1967).
2 For an in-depth discussion, see BLS (2023), and Salwati and Wessel (2021).
3 Although directly felt by consumers and business firms, higher interest rates per se are not included in the official calculation of inflation. Thus, American consumers are hit with a double whammy. See Bolhuis et al. (2024).
4 Social security benefits are directly tied to the rate of inflation as measured by the CPI. So, if inflation increases annually by let's say 5%, then so will the annual Social Security benefits. Likewise, many collective bargaining agreements are often linked to changes in the CPI.
5 The worst three-year period for deflation in the USA was 1930–1932, when prices declined by 26%. And not coincidentally, in 1932, **the rate of unemployment** reached 24.9%, a record for the USA. During the period 1866–1899, the USA experienced either annual deflation or a 0% change every year.
6 Of course, this argument works in reverse to explain spiraling inflation. For example, if one expects the price of gasoline to double in two weeks' time one would (most likely) buy gas now, which of course, exacerbates price increases.
7 These two organizations merged in 1955 to form the AFL-CIO.
8 For an in-depth discussion, see Freidman and Schwartz (1963).
9 See the Bureau of Labor Statistics 'Overview of BLS Statistics on Inflation and Pricing (BLS.gov) for in-depth discussion of inflation data bases and methodology.

10 The late 1970s and the early 1980s saw exceptionally high inflation rates in the USA. During the period 1979–1981, prices increased by 35.13%, a USA record for any three-year period. Unless one's wages/salary increased by the same amount, then the standard of living declines. In addition, higher inflation increases uncertainty, which in turn reduces both consumption and investment. High inflation was a major reason why President Jimmy Carter lost his bid for reelection in 1980. (In 1980, the inflation rate was 13.55%.) We will return to this in our chapter, **The Federal Reserve**.

11 For an understanding of the significance of the two percent threshold, see our chapter on the **Federal Reserve**.

12 Data source: Historical Inflation Rates (2024).

13 According to the Fed, the money supply (M1) is defined as the sum of currency held by the public, along with checking accounts and savings accounts. M1 is the most liquid definition of money, meaning that it can be used immediately to make purchases. M2, slightly less liquid than M1, includes all of M1, plus M1 plus small-denomination time deposits (issued in amounts of less than $100,000) and retail money market mutual fund shares. Source: Federal Reserve Board (2024).

References

Ball, Douglas B. (1991) *Financial Failure and Confederate Defeat*, University of Illinois Press, Urbana.

Bolhuis, Marijn A, Judd N. L. Cramer, Karl Oskar Schulz, and Lawrence H. Summers (2024) 'New Evidence on the Consumer Sentiment Anomaly,' Brookings Institution, Working Paper 32163, February, https://www.nber.org/

Bullard, James (2013) 'President's Message: CPI vs. PCE Inflation: Choosing a Standard Measure,' *The Federal Reserve Bank of St. Louis*, July 1, (stlouisfed.org).

Bureau of Labor Statistics (2023) 'Consumer Price Index' Handbook of Methods, Overview: Handbook of Methods: U.S. Bureau of Labor Statistics (bls.gov).

Carlin, Wendy and David Soskice (2015) *Macroeconomics: Institutions, Instability, and the Financial System*, Oxford University Press, Oxford, UK.

Federal Reserve Board (2024) 'Money Stock Measures,' May 28, https://www.federal-reserve.gov/release

Freidman, Milton and Anna J. Schwartz (1963) *A Monetary History of the United States, 1857-1960*, Princeton University Press, Princeton.

'Historical Inflation Rates: 1914-2024' (2024) Historical Inflation Rates: 1914-2024 (usinflationcalculator.com).

Moreno, J. Edward (2024) 'Price Pack Architecture' *The New York Times*, June 2, p. BU 4.

Nugent, Walter, T.K. (1967) *The Money Question During Reconstruction*, W.W. Norton, New York.

Piketty, Thomas (2014) *Capital in the Twenty-First Century*, Belknap Press of Harvard University Press, Cambridge, Massachusetts; translated by Arthur Goldhammer.

Salwati, Nasiha and David Wessel (2021) 'How Does the Government Measure Inflation?' Brookings Institution, Washington DC, https://www.brookings.edu/

St. Louis Federal Reserve (2024) 'M1' (stlouisfed.org).

3 Gross Domestic Product (GDP)

3.1 Introduction

3.1.1 GDP's Genesis

During the 1930s, it was obvious that the economy had broken down and was no longer functioning: Millions were out of work, and millions of farms had been foreclosed forcing a migration west to find the elusive American dream,[1] with "breadlines, shanty towns, and hobos hoping freights...everywhere" (Gruner, 2022, p. 64). While it was obvious that the economy was not functioning, the full extent of its breakdown was not known. There was no adequate measure or indicator. And there were no data.

Simon Kuznets (1901–1985) of the National Bureau of Economic Research was tasked by the Commerce Department to develop an adequate measure. The result was a set of national income accounts, which eventually became known as Gross Domestic Product (GDP). Kuznets, a Russia émigré (with his family) during the Russian Revolution of 1917, was awarded the Nobel Prize in Economics in 1971 for his efforts. Today, the Bureau of Economic Analysis calculates GDP.[2]

3.1.2 Defining GDP

Based on the work of Kuznets,[3] we define GDP as: 'The market value of all final goods and services produced within a country's borders in a given period of time.' Four things to note about this definition:

- GPD effectively sums up prices, i.e., 'market value.' This is much easier (and of course more meaningful) than summing up physical quantities.
- 'Final' or what Kuznets called 'ultimate consumption' (Kuznets, 1941, pp. 36–41) refers to the ultimate or final user, as opposed to intermediate goods (like steel, aluminum, rubber, etc.,) used to produce a final good.

DOI: 10.4324/9781003591856-4

- 'Within a country's borders' means whoever produces on American soil, regardless of national origin. If Toyota produces automobiles in Tennessee, for example, the value added of the production on USA soil is included in USA GDP.
- A 'given period of time' is usually a quarter, or a year.

Today, GDP is used by every country in the world with precisely the same definition. GDP has been called one of the "best" inventions of the 20th century (GDP, 2000). Here in the USA, GDP was central in the USA's victory effort during World War II,

> the capacity to escalate the speed at which the civilian economy could be effectively converted into a war machine without hampering internal consumption turned out to be one of the most critical advantages of the US vis-à-vis other nations, especially Nazi Germany.
>
> (Fioramonti, 2013, p. 18)

3.1.3   What GDP Is Not

First and foremost, GDP excludes any activity that does not have a price, i.e., does not take place in the market. For example, when my (Jack) daughter was born, I took some time off to help raise her. I considered this to be one of the most important things I could have done for her, but this activity/endeavor was excluded from GDP. If instead, I had enrolled her in a day care center, with a specific agreed-upon price, that activity would have been included in GDP.

A preponderant reason for excluding non-market activities is that during the 1930s, most such activities were performed by women. This is not to disparage Mr. Kuznets (after all, he was a product of his time; of which he emphasized several times in his writings[4]). At the same nevertheless, since domestic and caring work is primarily done by women, especially in developing nations, it diminishes the significance of their economic contribution (Reardon et al., 2018, p. 205). And today, given that more and more activities are taking place in the commons (Rifkin, 2014, pp. 17–25), this suggests that "the GDP metric will likely decline in significance as an indicator of economic performance" (Rifkin, 2014, p. 21).

GDP says nothing about how well the economy is, nor how well off the individuals are within the economy. Just like visiting the doctor, stepping on a scale is the most rudiment measure of health, but it says nothing about one's condition. Finding out how much the economy is producing at a given moment is only the first (and very rudimentary) step in a more vigorous and comprehensive diagnosis.

GDP excludes all negative costs like air pollution, global warming, water pollution, and climate change that are incurred to produce goods and services.

Since such negatives reduce our quality of life, along with those of future generations, GDP will overestimate the economy's performance.

Since only human-made capital (e.g., factories, automobiles, computers, etc.) is included in GDP, while ignoring environmental, social, and intellectual capital, then only depreciation (i.e., normal wear and tear over time) of human-made capital is included. This is a severe shortcoming since we need other capitals and especially environmental capital in order to construct human-made capital. Excluding depreciation on all capitals lends a false sense of security and over-measures performance.

To redress these deficiencies, alternative measures of GDP have been constructed, e.g., the Human Development Index, and the Happy Planet Index.[5] But given that GDP, in its current form, is thoroughly ensconced in policy-making throughout the world, it is difficult for all nations to agree to use a different measure. After all, it took the world's nations 60 years to adopt today's uniform GDP definition (thanks to the prodding of the **United Nations**).[6]

3.1.4 Concluding Thoughts

GDP was developed during a specific time (the 1930s) to do a specific job in a specific time/place. Its construction and measurement were based on the day's value judgments, as Kuznets himself acknowledged, "For those not intimately acquainted with this type of work it is difficult to realize the degree to which estimates of national income have been and must be affected by implicit or explicit value judgments" (Kuznets, 1941, p. 5). But as the economy and its attendant values change, so should GDP, the economy's most basic measure. Kuznets expected it to change. But it has not. This is problematic since it impugns GDP's function/mission and delegitimizes the public policy upon which it is based. Not to change GDP is itself a value judgment.

As we progress toward **Net Zero** and the widespread adoption of the 17 UN Sustainability Goals, we need a new system of national accounts, i.e., a new GDP. It is impossible to accurately track our progress using an old and outdated indicator. If Mr. Kuznets were alive today, he would be the biggest cheerleader, and the first to roll up his sleeves, so to speak.

Notes

1 John Steinbeck superbly documents this trek in his *The Grapes of Wrath* (1936 [1996]), fully capturing the dominant power structures, the poverty and inequality of America in the 1930s, and with an environmental focus.
2 See their web page at (BEA.org).
3 We recommend reading Kuznets' very thoughtful and enlightening rationalization/ explanation of his construction of GDP (Kuznets, 1941). Also see (Dickinson 2011)
4 For example: "The statistician who supposes that he [sic] can make a purely objective estimate of national income, not influenced by preconceptions concerning the

'facts', is deluding himself; for whenever he includes one item or excludes another, he is implicitly accepting some standard of judgment" (Kuznets, 1941, p. 3). These facts, of course, are determined by the specifics of time and place.

5 For a discussion see Reardon et al. (2018, pp. 209–211).

6 Incidentally, the USA was the last nation to adopt the current definition of GDP, preferring to use Gross National Product, which is the same as the GDP except that it measures the output of domestic firms no matter their location, whereas GDP measures domestic production, irrespective of national origin.

References

Dickinson, Elizabeth (2011) 'GDP: A brief history: One stat to rule them all,' *Foreign Policy*, www.foreignpolicy.com.

Gruner, Ronald (2022) *We the Presidents: How American Presidents Shaped the Last Century*, Libratum Press, Naples, Florida.

Kuznets, Simon (1941) *National Income and Its Composition, 1919-1938, Volume 1*, (assisted by Lillian Epstein and Elizabeth Jenks) NBER, Washington, DC.

Fioramonti, Lorenzo (2013) *Gross Domestic Problem: The Politics Behind the World's Most Powerful Number*, Zed Books, London.

Reardon, Jack, Maria Madi, and Cato, Molly Scott (2018) *Introducing a New Economics*, Routledge, London.

Rifkin, Jeremy (2014) *The Zero Marginal Cost Society*, Palgrave MacMillan, New York.

Steinbeck, John (1936 [1996]) *The Grapes of Wrath*, Penguin, New York.

4 Unemployment

4.1 Introduction

During the USA's longest recession, from October 1873 to March 1879 (65 months), a new phenomenon became visible: Numerous people not working, despite their intentions otherwise. They were economically idled by something beyond their control, deprived of their self-ability to provision. Although there had always been people not working, to see so many on such a large scale was new—so new that a word had to be invented: Unemployment.

During the period 1870s–1930s, the specifics of the definition of unemployment were debated: Should we include all able-bodied individuals available for work? Or only those actively searching for work? The Great Depression of the 1930s mandated a universally accepted definition.

4.1.1 Defining Unemployment and Employment

It is the job of the Bureau of Labor Statistics (BLS) to conceptualize the definition of unemployment, and then to obtain the data (in conjunction with the US Dept. of the Census) to calculate the respective rates (see below for an example). The BLS was first created in 1884 and housed within the Department of Interior before being transferred to the newly created Department of Labor in 1913.[1] In addition to the unemployment rate, the BLS also calculates the employment rate, the labor force participation rate, productivity, health and safety indices, and the **inflation rate**, among others.

The definition of *unemployment* constructed during the 1930s is still in use today: A person is unemployed if she/he:

- Was not employed during the survey reference week (typically, the survey is monthly).
- Was available for work (except for temporary illness).
- Had made a specific, active effort to find employment sometime during the 4-week period ending with the survey reference week.
- If none of the above, but the individual was waiting to be recalled to work while temporarily laid off.

DOI: 10.4324/9781003591856-5

This definition was chosen for ideological reasons, in order not to fully blame unemployment solely on the economy. This definition shares the burden between the individual and the economy.

If person is employed if he/she:

- Worked at least one hour as a paid employee.
- Worked in their own business, profession, or farm; unpaid.
- Worked 15 or more hours as an unpaid worker in a family business.
- Was temporarily absent due to illness, vacation, bad weather, or labor dispute.

4.1.2   *The Methodology of Calculating*

The BLS obtains its data (working with the Census) from two sources:

- The household survey administered by mail/telephone. The sample contains 60,000 households, approximately 110,000 individuals.[2] The survey is conducted during the second week of the month. It is administered via a series of questions designed to weed out any inadvertent incorrect answers. The unemployment rate, one of the economy's most important indicators, depends for its accuracy on the respondents' honesty. Problematic with any such survey is that an individual's perception of their situation might differ from reality.
- The payroll establishment survey, which targets 119,000 business and government agencies, which approximates 629,000 workers. Unlike the household survey, it excludes the self-employed, unpaid family members, and workers in private households.

The BLS prefers using both surveys, since each gives a slightly different picture of the labor market.

Adding the number of employed plus the unemployed gives us the *labor force*, sometimes called the civilian labor force since it excludes Americans serving in the armed forces. Since by definition they are fully employed, any ameliorative measures to reduce unemployment need not be targeted to the armed forces. The labor force also excludes everyone under the age of 16, in prison, full-time correctional facilities, nursing homes, and mental healthcare facilities.

To calculate the rate of unemployment, we divide the number of unemployed by the labor force; then multiply by 100:

$$\text{Un. Rate} = \left(\text{unemployed} \div \text{labor force}\right) \times 100$$

Saying the same thing:

$$\text{Un. Rate} = \left(\text{unemployed} \div \left(\text{unemployed} + \text{employed}\right)\right) \times 100$$

And notice we divide by the labor force and not by the total population.

The labor force participation rate (LFPR) is calculated by dividing the number of people in the labor force by the civilian noninstitutional population. The latter is defined as individuals older than 16, and not in an institution such as a prison, hospital, or the military. The LFPR captures the percent of the economy's population actually participating in the labor force (i.e., either employed or unemployed). The employment rate measures the percent of the labor force that is employed (based on the above definition).

The official unemployment rate doesn't distinguish between those who work part-time and those who do not; and between those who prefer to work full-time but can only get part-time work. Although the BLS maintains data on these distinctive categories, it is not entered into the official definitions and hence the official rates.

The record for the highest USA unemployment rate is 24.9% in 1933 which just eclipsed the previous record of 23.6% in 1932. The record for the lowest unemployment rate is 1.4% in 1944, during WWII. The unemployment rate tends to increase during recessions and decrease during expansions.

Is there an ideal/optimal unemployment rate that policymakers should strive for? Economists like to say that the ideal rate is consistent with low **inflation**, but the problem here is that economists don't exactly know what that rate is; and even if they did know, it changes over time. Nevertheless, everyone agrees that the optimal rate is not zero. This is due to the definition of unemployment: Out of work but searching. Paradoxically, the more vibrant the economy, the more people will be actively searching for work (i.e., unemployed). Such people could either enter the labor force (perhaps previously retired) or quit their job in order to search for work. This means that as an economy recovers from a recession and the economy is looking better, more people would want to search for work, all else equal, causing the unemployment rate to not decrease as much as it would otherwise. And conversely, as a recession begins, fewer people will search for work, all else equal, causing the unemployment rate to not increase as much as it would otherwise.

There are three broad categories of unemployment: (1) permanent job loss; (2) temporarily job loss, with the affected individual awaiting recall; (3) a mismatch between labor market and actuality, e.g., I quit my job assuming that I can easily find another. Individuals who have permanently lost their jobs are the most serious, while those who voluntary quit are the least problematic since they are in a good position anyway and will have the least difficulty landing a position. So public policy tends to focus on a mix of retraining (assuming we know what to train for[3]) and streamlining information to align job searchers with employers looking to hire. A perennial question is whether the private or public sector should effectuate solutions; and if the latter, whether state or federal. Another perennial question (and very much related) is who pays.

Over the last twenty years, the unemployed who have permanently lost their jobs has held steady at about one-third, rising a tad during recessions but then falling with expansions. This is largely due to technological change and the economy's dynamic vitality. But as **Artificial Intelligence** looms, Americans are increasingly concerned over its effects on unemployment. We return to this important issue later in our book.

4.1.3   Concluding Thoughts

Being unemployed is costly for both the individual and society. For the former, it entails loss of prestige and income, and possibly health. For the latter, society loses potential output and income, which, in turn, is exacerbated by the multiplier effect: If I am no longer working, then I cut back on my own spending, which negatively affects the incomes of the shops/stores that I used to frequent. And, if the effect is severe enough, then the economy could slip into a **recession**, or even a **depression**.

Like GDP, the methodology of calculating unemployment and the definition itself was constructed during the 1930s. Back then, the labor force was comprised mostly of men; and most firms were large and relatively stable, and it was relatively easy to differentiate between the employed and unemployed. There was little active searching for work while still employed. But today's economy is much different thanks to the internet, so that with

> subcontracting, consultancies, multiple job-holding, youth internships, and working out of the home, as well as multiple wage earning families and early retirees… [such] workers do not easily fit into the traditional categories of the unemployed, employed, or those out of the labor force…[Their] income is ever more decoupled from traditional employment relationships.
> (Baxandall, 2004, pp. 234–235)

As Baxandall notes, "unemployment is a socially constructed benchmark used for evaluating the competency of economic rule" (Baxandall, 2004, p. 4). So, as the economy changes so should the unemployment rate. It has not done so. If unemployment is "mis-conceptualized and incorrectly defined, we will fail to understand its root causes and hence offer ineffective solutions" (Reardon et al., 2018, p. 118). However, until a new methodology is developed that is more attuned to our current economy, we are stuck with the old.

4.2   Time for a Re-assessment of Both GDP and the Unemployment Rate

Our choice of indicators is just as important as how they are constructed and what they measure. Given that the choice "is an eminently political one: No indicator should be regarded as sacred, and the nature of the indicators chosen must be at the heart of public debate and democratic confrontation" (Piketty, 2022, p. 21). As our economy transitions to **Net Zero**, as renewable energy becomes more important; and as **Artificial Intelligence** looms ever larger over more aspects of our lives, we must dialogue over what type of economy we want and how best to measure it, realizing of course, that we need a multiplicity of indicators, that no single indicator can do the trick. All of us must dialogue, and not just the elites; if not, "we must not be surprised if the indicators selected reflect priorities other than the ones we care about" (Piketty, 2022, pp. 27–28).

Notes

1 See their web page at www.bls.gov.
2 For more specific information on how the BLS obtains the data and calculates the rate of unemployment, see 'How the Government Measures Unemployment' (2024); and the *BLS Handbook of Methods* (2024).
3 The BLS provides a very detailed prognosis for just about every job and every industry in their annual *Occupational Outlook Handbook.*

References

Baxandall, Phineas (2004) *Constructing Unemployment: The Politics of Joblessness in East and West*, Ashgate, Aldershot, UK.
Bureau of Labor Statistics (2024) *BLS Handbook of Methods* Handbook of Methods: U.S. Bureau of Labor Statistics (bls.gov).
Bureau of Labor Statistics (2024) 'How the Government Measures Unemployment', U.S. Bureau of Labor Statistics (bls.gov).
Piketty, Thomas (2022) *A Brief History of Equality*, Belknap Press of Harvard University, Cambridge, Massachusetts, translated by Steven Rendall.
Reardon, Jack, Maria Madi, and Cato, Molly Scott (2018) *Introducing a New Economics*, Routledge, London.

5 The Business Cycle: Recessions/Depressions

5.1 Introduction

Most of us have experienced the common cold, and when we do, we feel run down, sluggish, not our normal selves; and if severe enough we might have to miss work or school. Eventually, however, we recover and resume our normal lives. As we all know, a common cold can be short, long, mild, or severe. We also know that, unfortunately, we can't predict its occurrence beforehand, for if so, we could take preventive action. Nevertheless, once a cold sets in, we understand the remedy, and at least for most of us, we take the ameliorative medicine, and quickly return to normal.

In a sense, a recession is like a cold for the economy: Demand for goods and services falls, profits fall, workers are laid off; the economy is not its normal self: It is sluggish and run down. And just like a cold, we cannot predict a recession's occurrence, for if we could, we could prevent.

5.2 Defining a Recession

Although the cold analogy is a good one, for purposes of public policy we need a more formal definition.[1] A recession is 'a significant decline in economic activity that is spread across the economy, lasting more than a few months.' Notice the subjectivity in the key terms 'significant,' 'economic activity,' 'spread across,' 'decline,' and 'a few months.'

Deciding when the economy is in a recession is important, since corrective action cannot be taken without knowledge. The job is tasked to the National Bureau of Economic Research (NBER),[2] which despite its name, isn't a government organization (the word 'national' refers to its purview rather than its ownership). Imagine if a government agency was tasked with this important job—we might never have a recession! Within the NBER, the Business Cycle Dating Committee will sift through the data and try to objectify the subjective words/phrases listed above. This important committee is comprised of eight

DOI: 10.4324/9781003591856-6

bigwigs from the economics profession, all selected for their expertise in macroeconomics.[3] While lots of non-NBER people/organizations do their best to predict when a recession begins/ends, only the NBER's Business Cycle Dating Committee has the official imprimatur.

5.3   Recession Facts

The Dating Committee's database extends back to 1854. Since then, the USA has suffered 33 recessions, or one every 4.2 years (on average), suggesting that recessions are relatively common,[4] or at least more common than most people would assume. In fact, since 1854, only two presidents have escaped a recession: Lyndon Baines Johnson (1963–1968) and Bill Clinton (1992–2000). Remarkable about the latter is that he was a two-term president.[5]

Before 1854, the data are murky, resulting in disagreement over the recession start/end dates as well as the severity. Nevertheless, a rough consensus is that between 1785 and 1854, there were 17 recessions. No president during that time was immune.

Sticking to the data from the modern era (i.e., post-1854), for which we can be absolutely sure, we can offer these facts/generalizations:

- Recessions have been getting shorter. During the period 1854–1919, for example, recessions lasted on average 21.6 months, while since 1945, recessions have lasted 10.3 months. The preponderant reason is that before the Great Depression, it was assumed that the economy could heal itself; and that the federal government was too incompetent to enact a cure.
- The Great Depression taught us that recessions do not heal themselves and that to end them, we must take action. Also, during the 1930s, the economics profession developed the public policy tools to effectuate a solution, giving the public much-needed confidence (well, almost).
- Not surprisingly, the record for the longest recession occurred during the late 19th century: October 1873 to March 1879 (65 months). Imagine a recession today lasting over six years? And, incidentally, it was during this long, seemingly unending recession, with lots of people out of work, that the concept of unemployment was developed.
- The record for the shortest recession was the most recent: February 2020–April 2020, lasting only two months. The reason: Active and expansive bipartisan cooperation to end the recession quickly and to prevent it from getting worse. As COVID hit, the federal government and the **Federal Reserve** (our central bank) used all the means at its disposal (e.g., reducing interest rates, giving money to consumers, cutting taxes, increasing federal spending) to end the recession and get the economy back to normal.[6] Another example of immediate federal action to end a recession

was in 2001. This recession lasted only eight months (March–November) despite the economic impact of 9/11. The brevity was due to very stimulative monetary policy and significant increases in federal government spending.

- We cannot pinpoint the start/end of a recession to an exact day or even week. The best we can do is the month. So, for example, the most recent recession began in February 2020 and ended in April 2020. (And before 1854, given the murkiness of the data, we can't even pinpoint the month.)

- At a particular point in time, we say that the economy is either in a recession or it is not. When the economy is not in a recession, it is in a recovery (also called an expansion). And once the recession ends, the expansion begins, sharing the same month. Thus, the current expansion began in April 2020 with the ending of the most recession. As this manuscript goes to press, we are in an expansion.

- Except for one italicized word, the definition of an expansion is almost identical to that of a recession: 'a significant *increase* in economic activity that is spread across the economy, lasting more than a few months.' For an expansion to begin (and like a recession, its beginning/end is determined by the NBER[7]), it is not necessary for the economy to return to its full potential or even to normalcy. All that matters is that economic activity is increasing and that the increase is 'significant.' Since the two definitions only differ by one word, the same subjectivity plagues both.

- Since 1854, expansions have been increasing in length (concomitant with recessions decreasing in length). Specifically, from 1854 to WWII, an expansion, on average, lasted 26.6 months, compared to 64.2 months, post-1945. Not surprisingly, the record for the longest expansion was recent: June 2009–February 2020 (128 months). And the two previous records for were also post-WWII: March 1991–March 2001 (120 months) and February 1961–December 1969 (106 months).

- The reason for the longer expansions (and shorter recessions) is that the federal government has taken quick and effective action (based on economic theory) which nowadays mostly means **deficit** spending and induced consumer spending (e.g., a stimulus). Surprisingly, quick and effective ameliorative action is bipartisan.

- A recession occurring during a presidential election year can and often does influence the outcome. Three recent examples: (1) the 1932 election between the incumbent Hebert Hoover and Franklin Roosevelt. Hoover was heavily criticized for not only 'causing' the recession, which, as measured by the **unemployment rate**, was the most severe in American history, but for not doing enough to end it (Gruner, 2022, p. 64). Not surprisingly, Hoover lost in a landslide; (2) in 1960, John F. Kennedy defeated Richard M. Nixon, the vice president during Eisenhower's two terms, in the closest popular vote margin in American history, with Nixon only losing by 112,827 votes. A recession had begun, April 1960 (under Eisenhower's watch), and was not officially over until February 1961, one month after Kennedy was inaugurated; and (3) in 1980, Ronald Reagan resoundingly defeated Jimmy Carter who was running for reelection. A recession had begun in January of 1980 (the election year) ending in July 1980, which, by the way, is the second shortest recession on record. While certainly other factors were present in all three elections, the state of the economy palpably played a role.[8]

5.4   The Conditions Necessary for a Depression: A Perfect Storm

If conditions during a recession are severe enough, it is labeled a depression, which is circuitously defined as 'a severe recession.' Unlike the determination of a recession, there is no authoritative agency tasked with deciding when a recession becomes a depression. In addition, we lack a universal consensus on its definition. Nevertheless, *all* of the following elements must be present:

- Longevity, i.e., lasting longer than what is considered a normal recession.
- The economic deterioration is more severe than a normal recession measured by the rate of unemployment, the level of poverty, and the decline in GDP. Keep in mind that the words 'severe' and 'normal' are subjective.
- **Deflation** exists, i.e., the average level of prices decreases.
- The rate of **unemployment** tops 10%.
- There is a pervasive sense of pessimism, with an absence of immediate hope.

So for example, with the most recent recession (February 2020–April 2020) despite the unemployment rate reaching 14.7%, the highest since the 1930s, the federal government and the **Federal Reserve** quickly implemented policies to end the COVID-induced recession, resulting in a quick recovery. If the federal government did not actively intervene, it is a safe bet that the unemployment rate would have increased even more, and the recession of 2020 would have been a lot longer, and maybe even becoming a depression, with little hope of immediate amelioration.[9]

While everyone agrees that a depression occurred during the 1930s, disagreement exists as to its ending. Some argue that the recession beginning in August 1929 (which we all agree) and ending in March 1933, should have been labeled a depression[10] since it lasted 48 months, with the unemployment rate hitting a record 23.6% in 1933, topping the previous year's record of 23.6%. But then, in March 1933, economic activity began to increase, and conditions began to improve, so the economy was officially labeled to be in an expansion, i.e., a recovery.[11] On the other hand, some economists contend that the whole decade up until the advent of WWII should have been labeled a depression, since the unemployment rate never dipped below 14.7%, hardly normal even for a recession.[12]

During the 19th century, there were two depressions. Many economists label the USA's longest recession (October 1873–March 1879) as a depression. October 1873 is agreed as the start date, with the ending either in 1890 or 1896 depending on which data is used. We endorse 1896 since after the economy 're-covered' in 1879, it slipped into recession in March 1882 lasting until May 1885 (38 months)—the third longest recession; followed by four recessions in succession until 1896, each lasting on average 15.2 months. Pessimism abounded as the economy was besieged by successive recessions.

Data also suggest a depression during the period 1839–1843, which was characterized by sharp declines in economic activity, although the precise start/end is not clear due to the murkiness of the data.[13]

5.5   What Causes Recessions?

Of the goods and services that our economy produces (i.e., **GDP**), consumers buy more than two-thirds (specifically 69%), while the rest is purchased by the USA government (federal, state, and local), firms, and foreigners. Given its preponderant size, if consumers decrease their spending for whatever reason, then economic activity will decline, all else equal; and if steep enough a recession ensues. Any number of factors can cause consumer spending to decrease, such as more personal debt, angst about the future, increasing interest rates which makes it more expensive to borrow, increased taxes, increased commodity prices (such as oil), cutback in federal spending, higher unemployment; and of course, unanticipated events like COVID, which was the principal cause of the February 2020–April 2020 recession. And likewise, if the economy is in recession, significant increases in consumer spending can pull the economy through. Hence, the importance of government stimulus packages.

Firm investment is also a significant driver: If firms reduce investment spending, increased layoffs and depressed consumer confidence can ensue. Consumer spending and business investment are mutually reinforcing: As consumer spending decreases, the motivation for business investment decreases—why invest if no one is buying? And conversely, as consumer spending increases, so does the motivation for increased investment.

Once a recession is underway, the most effective solution is to incentivize consumer spending. This can be done via stimulus checks, reduced tax rates, higher unemployment compensation, more job creation, all of which increase disposable income and hence investment. In addition, decreased interest rates will make it easier to borrow, increasing the demand for big-ticket items like housing and automobiles, which in turn will incentivize firms to invest. As the severity of the 2020 recession became evident, the federal government did all of the above quickly and forcefully, ending the recession. But unfortunately, the increased spending and increased money supply sowed the seeds for future **inflation.**

5.6   Conclusion

While it is interesting to ask whether Democrats or Republicans have had more recessions during their watch, we believe such an exercise is futile for the following reasons:

- There is often a lag between the causes of a recession and its actual effects.
- The causes are varied and multi-dimensional, with extraneous events often playing a critical role, i.e., COVID; 9/11; and during the 1970s, increased oil prices.
- The **Federal Reserve** has abetted many recessions by raising interest rates. The 2001 recession, and the 2007–2009 recession are good recent examples. (Technically the Fed is non-political and structured to make itself immune from political pressure.)
- Once a recession begins, the overall thrust to end it is bipartisan, although Democrats and Republicans often disagree over the specific solutions, e.g., Democrats favor more federal spending, whereas Republicans favor tax cuts. Such a bipartisan effort was visible during the two most recent recessions: February–April 2020 and December 2007–June 2009.

We can say with certainty that a future recession is inevitable. Although we cannot predict when it will occur, in hindsight we know the reasons; and once begun, we can implement policies to end it. Here, we might ask that if we know the reasons why a recession occurs, then can't we take extra care to prevent the reasons from actualizing? Easier said than done, especially when exogenous events often play a key role.

However, I think we can say with some confidence (although not 100%) that given the bipartisan commitment to end a recession almost immediately, the odds of another depression are slim, but certainly not zero.[14]

Finally, we should mention that economists have a notoriously poor track record of predicting when (and if) a recession will occur. A well-known example was Irving Fisher, the president of the American Economic Association, who on October 15, 1929, boasted to a gathering of the Purchasing Agents in New York City, that 'stock prices appear to have reached a permanently high plateau.' Two weeks later the stock market crashed.[15] Unbeknownst to Mr. Fisher, a severe recession was already underway (beginning August 1929), largely caused by the macroeconomic policies of the late 1920s and the actions of the **Federal Reserve**, which we will discuss later in this book.[16]

Perhaps the reason for our inability to predict recessions is that economists just don't understand human nature, despite protestations otherwise. The economy, after all, is comprised of people, and we just don't understand human nature well enough to predict when they will change their spending behavior. (If we could predict, we could prevent.) Perhaps someday we will, but most likely by then the economy will be very different.

Notes

1   As recently as the 1980s, the definition was more streamlined: 'a recession occurs when real **GDP** declines for at least six months.' Whereas GDP measures the market value (i.e., prices) of goods and services produced by an economy in a certain time period; real GDP, however, holds prices constant, effectively measuring how much stuff the economy actually produces. On the one hand, the main attraction of this definition was its one-variable focus, which was also its preponderant weakness. Compare the old definition to the new which literally incorporates hundreds of variables.

2   The NBER, established in 1920, is based in Washington. For further discussion of its objectives, see its webpage, National Bureau of Economic Research (nber.org).

3   Economics is divided into two main branches: macroeconomics which studies the overall big picture of the economy, and microeconomics which studies the individual units that comprise the economy, like firms and consumers.

4   Data on recessions before 1854 were obtained from 'List of Recessions' (2023), and data on recessions post-1854 were obtained from Business Cycle Dates (2023).

5   James Garfield, the 20th president of the United States, began his term in March 1881 and was assassinated in September 1881; seven months without a recession. John F. Kennedy, the 35th president, took office in January 1961 while a recession was underway (begun in April 1960) and certainly not his doing; the recession ended in February 1961.

6   The word 'normal' is also subjective; its interpretation largely influenced by what comes before and after.

7   A business cycle combines recession and expansion; in turn each of these is known as a phase of the business cycle. Since no two recessions (or expansions) are alike—they differ in length and severity—no two business cycles are alike.

8   Interestingly, one would have assumed that Al Gore, the vice-president under Bill Clinton (1992–2000) would have been a shoo-in in the 2000 election against the Republican challenger George W. Bush. As mentioned earlier, the Clinton administration was only one of two administrations never to have experienced a recession. In addition, the macro numbers looked good: low inflation, the lowest unemployment rates since the late 1960s, federal budget surpluses in 1997–2001 (yes, surpluses!), strong overall economic growth, and a general feeling of optimism. Yet Al Gore lost. There were lots of problems with both his campaign and his attractiveness as a candidate (e.g., Gore failed to win his home state of Tennessee) which we really cannot delve into here.

9   In February 2020, there was speculation (and even predictions) that the unemployment rate would top 25%.

10 Gruner offers a most convincing argument (2022, pp. 101–102).

11 A recession occurred May 1937–June 1938; thus the 1930s experienced two business cycles.
12 For an interesting discussion of America during the 1930s recession, see Goldston (1968).
13 We discuss this depression in our chapter on **The Federal Reserve**.
14 For a good discussion of the pros/cons, see Minsky (2016).
15 On the 1929 crash, see the highly readable Galbraith (1954).
16 It is a pity that this one remark tarnished his image, since Irving Fisher was one of the most thoughtful and influential economists of his day (Dimand and Geanakoplos, 2005). His macro theories have helped us to understand why depressions occur, i.e., increased consumer debt reduces spending, which if severe enough can lead to a depression (Dimand, 1994).

References

'Business Cycle Dating' (2023) Business Cycle Dating | NBER.

Dimand, Robert W. (1994) 'Irving Fisher's Debt–Deflation Theory of Great Depressions,' *Review of Social Economy*, Vol. 52, No. 1, pp. 92–107.

Dimand, Robert W., and Geanakoplos, John (2005) 'Celebrating Irving Fisher: The Legacy of a Great Economist,' *American Journal of Economics & Sociology*, Vol. 64, No. 1, pp. 3–18.

Goldston, Robert (1968) *The Great Depression: The United States in the Thirties*, Fawcett Publications, Greenwich, Connecticut.

Gruner, Ronald (2022) *We the Presidents: How American Presidents Shaped the Last Century*, Libratum Press, Naples, Florida.

'List of Recessions in the United States' (2023) Wikipedia.

Minsky, Hyman (2016) *Can "It" Happen Again?* Routledge, London.

Part II

Domestic Cultural and Political Issues

6   The USA Supreme Court

The Issue: Recent Supreme Court decisions have affected a wide range of American life, from abortion to gun control to the bureaucracy to climate change, to giving a former president immunity, to dismantling the administrative state, to voting and campaign finance. At the sametime, however, among the G-7 nations, the USA is tied with Italy with the lowest trust in their judicial system. Losing trust in a major political institution is dangerous for a democracy, and the first step (among many) in a slippery slope toward autocracy. How did this come to be? How can trust be restored to this major political institution, which should be a bastion of democracy? This chapter will discuss the Court's constitutional origins and its critical role in our democracy.

6.1   Introduction

Fundamental to our structure of government is the separation of powers into three co-equal branches: The presidency (executive), the legislature, and the judiciary. Key to a well-functioning democracy is a system of checks and balances deliberately designed to prevent one branch from usurping the functions of the other two. In this issue, we will discuss the role and importance of the judiciary, with special focus on the Supreme Court.

6.2   The Judiciary Is the Weakest of the Three Branches

Alexander Hamilton, co-author of *The Federalist Papers*,[1] argued that the judiciary is the weakest of the three branches of government,

> The executive not only dispenses the honors, but holds the sword of the community. The legislature not only commands the purse, but prescribes the rules by which the duties and rights of every citizen are to be regulated. The judiciary on the contrary has no influence over either the sword or the purse, no direction either of the strength or of the wealth of the society, and can take no active resolution whatever. It may truly be said to have neither Force nor Will but merely judgement.
>
> (The Federalist # 78, p. 472)[2]

DOI: 10.4324/9781003591856-8

Perhaps to underscore this relative weakness, in 1800, when the federal government moved the nation's capital from Philadelphia to Washington DC,[3] no provision was made to house the justices of the Supreme Court, since "priority was given to housing the President and executive offices" (Smith, 1996, pp. 284–285). John Marshall, serving as John Adams' Secretary of State, and the overseer of the construction of Washington, D.C., wrote "[I] neither noted the need nor made arrangements for space to house the Court" (Smith, 1996, p. 285). Ironically, Marshall would become Chief Justice in 1801 (see our discussion below). In 1801, John Jay, co-author of *The Federalist Papers*, and the nation's first Chief Justice of the Supreme Court,[4] explained to John Marshall why he didn't want to return,

> I left the bench perfectly convinced that under a system so defective it would not obtain the energy, weight, and dignity, which was essential… nor acquire the public confidence and respect which, as the last resort of the justice of the nation, it should possess.
>
> (quoted in Smith p. 531 note #73)

Today, the Supreme Court is housed in a neoclassical building, constructed in 1935, on First Street in Washington, one block from the US Capital. Beforehand, the Supreme Court was housed in various buildings in Washington, including the Old Senate Chamber from 1860 to 1935,[5] once again underscoring its relative unimportance, at least symbolically.

The Supreme Court first met February 1, 1790, but given that only three of six justices were present, the Court reconvened the next day for its first official session.

6.3   For the Supreme Court, the Constitution Is Fundamental

Alexis de Tocqueville, an astute observer of early 19th-century America, wrote of the Constitution, "The dominant power rests with it alone…it is the primary law and cannot be modified by a law" (Tocqueville, 2003 [1835, 1840], p. 119). And Alexander Hamilton,

> A constitution is in fact, and must be, regarded by the judges as a fundamental law…Until the people have by some solemn and authoritative act annulled or changed the established form, it is binding upon themselves collectively, as well as individually; and no presumption, or even knowledge of their sentiments, can warrant their representatives in a departure from it.
>
> (The Federalist #78, pp. 474 and 477)

Of course, this doesn't mean that the Constitution is forever unalterable, as Hamilton noted, "[The people] have a right to alter or abolish the established constitution whenever they find it inconsistent with their happiness" (Tocqueville,

2003 [1835, 1840], p. 476).[6] Given the primacy of the Constitution, it is the Judiciary's prerogative to "declare all acts contrary to the manifest tenor of the constitution void" (Tocqueville, 2003 [1835, 1840], p. 473). Indeed, "the power granted to American courts to pronounce on the constitutionality of laws remains still one of the most powerful barriers ever erected against the tyranny of political assemblies" (Tocqueville, 2003 [1835, 1840], p. 122). In addition, de Tocqueville noted,

> the peace, prosperity and very existence of the Union lie continually in the hands of the …justices. Without them, the Constitution would be a dead letter; it is to them that the executive authority appeals against the encroachments of the legislature; the legislature, to defend itself against the assaults of the executive; the Union to enforce obedience from the states; the states to rebuff the impertinent onslaughts of the Union; public interest against private interest; the spirit of conservation against the destabilizing effects of democracy. Their power is immense…
>
> (Tocqueville, 2003 [1835, 1840], p. 176)

Later, in this chapter, we will discuss this 'immense power.'

6.4   What Does the Constitution Say About the Judiciary?

Article III of the US Constitution, which details the role of the judiciary, is by far the briefest of the three articles describing each of the government's three branches. Nevertheless, the Judiciary's general functions/objectives are clear. Article III, Section I opens with the sentence, "The judicial power of the United States shall be vested in one supreme court, and in such inferior courts as the congress may from time to time ordain and establish." Here, 'inferior' means lower in rank/authority, not in competence/quality.

On this constitutional basis, in 1789, Congress passed the Judiciary Act to put some meat on the bare bones of this constitutional provision. A reason for just the bare bones was visceral disagreement during the Constitutional Convention (May 25–September 17, 1787) over the specific roles/functions of the Court,

> the drafters of the Constitution had been unable to agree on key points—most importantly, whether to create inferior federal courts, what types of cases the federal courts would be able to hear, and what sort of relationship the Supreme Court would have with the state courts. The Constitution was also silent on the number of Justices who would sit on the Court. The drafters therefore left to Congress the task of addressing many of these questions as it saw fit, subject to the boundaries set forth in Article III.
>
> (Presidential Commission, 2021, p. 19)

Among other features, the Act gives us the three-level federal court system as it exists today:

- At the top, the US Supreme Court.
- Next, the circuit[7] courts, where presiding judges literally travel throughout the specified geographic area to hear cases, also known as the court of appeals of which there are 13.
- US district courts of which today there are 94. The latter are not to be confused with the state courts, which hear cases pertinent to only state law.

The three levels of federal courts only hear cases related to federal law, i.e., the Constitution. This fits the Founding Fathers' vision to limit the role of the federal government by delegating to the judiciary only the roles/obligations as mentioned in Article III, Section Two (see below).

The Supreme Court has original jurisdiction (meaning the case bypasses the inferior courts), in "all cases affecting ambassadors, other public ministers and consuls, and those in which a state shall be party." As Hamilton noted,

> In all other causes of federal cognizance[8]... [i.e.] those which arise out of the laws of the United States, passed in pursuance of their just and constitutional powers of legislation...the original jurisdiction would appertain to the inferior tribunals, and the supreme court would have nothing more than an appellate [i.e., appeal] jurisdiction.
> (The Federalist #81, p. 497; and #80, p. 483)

Inferior courts were created to "obviate the necessity of having recourse to the supreme court in every case of federal cognizance" (The Federalist #81, p. 494). Today, other than cases for which it has supreme authority, the Supreme Court will not take a case unless it originates in the inferior courts, or ambiguity exists over its constitutional meaning, or it is of interest for the whole nation, or if the inferior courts disagree over interpretation.[9]

This limits the Judiciary's purview while also limiting its ability to encroach on the other two branches of government. Alexis de Tocqueville expands on this very important point:

> For there to be court intervention, rights must be contested. For there to be a judge, an action must be brought to court... as long as a law does not challenge a right, judges have no occasion to consider the matter... [such that] whenever he [sic] pronounces upon a law without reference to a particular case, he steps right outside his sphere and invades that of the legislature...[the judge] is to pronounce upon individual cases and not general principles (Tocqueville (2003 [1835, 1840], p. 117)).

Thus, "judicial power can only act when summoned, or when it is seized of the matter…By its nature, judicial power is not active; it has to be triggered into action" Tocqueville (2003 [1835, 1840], p. 117).

While this is ideal, we find it problematic that the Roberts Court (2005—present) has unprecedently "shown a greater willingness to exercise its authority earlier in the litigation, by making its preference known…and not having the patience to wait for cases to first come up through the courts" (Davenport, 2024, p. 9). Does this mean that the Court has overstepped its bounds? While we are not legal experts, we feel that the Court is covered by Section 25 of the 1789 Judiciary Act, although the Court's specific behavior seems unprecedented.

A central concern of the drafters of the Constitution was that if the Supreme Court is to 'declare all acts contrary to the tenor of the constitution void,' then the justices must be independent of the other two branches of the government. This follows a widely held notion that "there is no liberty, if the power of judging be not separated from the legislative and executive powers" (The Federalist #78, p. 473). To ensure this needed separation, Article III (Section 1, 2nd sentence) says "The judges…shall hold their offices during good behavior…" While it is not explicitly mentioned that justices hold their tenure for 'life,' as is commonly understood, the phrase 'during good behavior' implicitly means "if they behave properly, they will be secured in their places for life" (*The Federalist* #79, p. 481).

Given the recent ethical transgressions of several justices (see below), one wonders exactly what 'good behavior' means. According to Article III (Section 3, 1st sentence), only treason against the United States warrants a transgression, whereby treason is defined as "levying war against the [US] or in adhering to their enemies, giving them aid and comfort."

Interestingly, Hamilton discussed the possibility of including some measure of ability as a barometer of good behavior but dismissed this, and for good reason since, "any attempt to fix the boundary between the regions of ability and inability, would much oftener give scope to personal and party attachments and enmities, than advance the interests of justice, or the public good" (*The Federalist* #79, p. 482).

Another requirement to secure the independence of judges is to fix their salaries, so that the latter is independent of discretion. This is necessary since "a power over a man's [sic] subsistence amounts to a power over his will" (*The Federalist* #79, p. 480). Thus, according to Article III (Section 1, sentence 2), the justices, "shall at stated times, receive for their services a compensation, which shall not be diminished during their continuance in office." Since the tenure will be held during good behavior (i.e., potentially for life), it is necessary to adjust the salary from time to time (to offset the insidious effects of inflation) but never to diminish it.

While we understand that longevity in office is necessary to develop an expertise in the sea of legal rules and precedents, which can only be "acquired by long and laborious study" (*The Federalist* #81, p. 492) and that having to leave another job only to take a temporary position in the Court would diminish the expertise and the quality of potential applicants, we don't understand how this would make the Court any less political. Alexander Hamilton commented on this, while suggesting that permanent appointments would lessen the chance of a poor choice,

> Periodical appointments, however regulated, or by whomever made, would in some way or another be fatal to their necessary independence. If the power of making them was committed either to the executive or legislature, there would be danger of an improper compliance to the branch which possessed it.
>
> (*The Federalist* #78, p. 478)

It was assumed that this constitutional provision would extirpate any biases. But today, even a casual observer of the Court would easily see that this is not true, an issue we will return to below.

Hamilton had great confidence (although, perhaps a tad naïve) in the efficacy of the Constitution's provisions to prevent a miscarriage of public sentiment, as well as to minimize any overt bias that would obfuscate an individual's true merits. Starting with the president, Hamilton assumed that there would always be "great probability of having the place supplied by a man [sic] of abilities, at least respectable" (*The Federalist* #76, p. 461).

Today, that is a big assumption to make, but perhaps it was true then, when George Washington was all but certain to become the USA's first president. Hamilton assumed that the president would be careful to "to investigate with care the qualities requisite to the stations to be filled, and to prefer with impartibility the persons who may have the fairest pretensions to them" (*The Federalist* #76, p. 461). This is especially true knowing that his [sic] choice would be public knowledge for all to see, and then to be either extolled or disparaged.

The president then chooses a candidate with the advice and consent of the senate as delineated in Article II, Section 2, par. 2, "He shall have power, by and with the advice and consent of the senate…to appoint…judges of the supreme court." The senate would provide an "excellent check upon a spirit of favoritism in the President" (*The Federalist* #76, p. 463). Unfortunately, Hamilton's idealization doesn't seem to comport with today's Court[10] (see below).

6.5   A Brief Note on John Marshall (1755–1835)

6.5.1   *Introduction*

Space does not allow for a historical discussion of the Supreme Court's evolution, nor of individual cases, nor of the inferior courts. While there have been many well-abled chief justices (and many well-abled associate justices), and admitting that everyone has their favorites, for us, one person stands out and should be mentioned in this chapter: John Marshall, the nation's fourth Chief Justice (1801–1835) and the longest serving.[11] It was Marshall, more than anyone else, who "asserted the authority of the Supreme Court to interpret the Constitution" (Smith, 1996, p. 2).

There is a plethora of cases that we could discuss from the Marshall Court, and we wish we had space to discuss them all, but doing so would require a book. But two cases deserve mention here: Marbury v. Madison and McCulloch v. Maryland.

6.5.2   *Marbury v. Madison (1803)*

Marbury v. Madison[12] might be the most important in the Court's history, for it was this case that established the concept of judicial review—a cornerstone of constitutional law—i.e., that the Court can strike down laws that are repugnant to the Constitution. Indeed, had

> Marshall not confirmed review power at the outset…it is entirely possible it would have never been insisted upon [and that over time] given judicial acquiescence in congressional supremacy, it is probable that [any] opposition then would have been futile.
>
> (Schwartz, 1993, p. 41)

Briefly, Marbury's background: In the hard-fought election of 1800, Thomas Jefferson defeated the incumbent John Adams. Adams, determined to frustrate the incoming administration, nominated 44 individuals for justices of the peace. All but four commissions were confirmed, only because John Marshall, at the time the Secretary of State, simply ran out of time. Upon taking office, Thomas Jefferson refused to acknowledge the four unfulfilled commissions. One, to be held by William Marbury, sued James Madison, the new Secretary of State.[13]

In his ruling, John Marshall,

> interposed the Court as a check against legislative omnipotence and affirmed the principles that lie at the root of constitutional government. The people, not the government, are sovereign, and the constitution reflects their will. By exercising judicial review, the Court was merely enforcing the will of the people as expressed in the Constitution, over the desire of the government as expressed in the statue.
>
> (Smith, 1996, p. 326)

Although back then, as now, not everyone accepted the supremacy of judicial review, arguing that it contravened democracy, and the much-heralded separation of powers. James Madison, for one, argued that it "would make the Judiciary Department paramount in fact to the Legislature, which was never intended and can never be proper" (Bouie, 2022, p. 9). At least in theory, judicial review comports with Hamilton's assertion that "a constitution is in fact, and must be, regarded by the judges as a fundamental law." But as we discuss below, this principle can often be abused.

6.5.3 *McCulloch v. Maryland (1819)*

In McCulloch v. Maryland the issue was the constitutionality of the Second Bank of the United States,[14] established in 1816. Critics of the Bank, which included Thomas Jefferson and James Madison, among the more notable, argued that since the Constitution did not mention anything about a central bank, then its very existence was unconstitutional. When the state of Maryland taxed the Bank's Maryland branch, "one of several measures designed to curtail the Bank's activities" (Smith, 1996, p. 441), the Maryland branch manager, James McCulloch, refused to pay.

Given the widely understood importance of the case, it was heard before the Supreme Court. The plaintiffs for Maryland argued for the preponderance of states' rights and that since the Constitution was silent on a central bank, then the Constitution's 10th Amendment became relevant, "The powers not delegated to the United States by the Constitution, nor prohibited by it to the states, are reserved to the states respectively, or to the people." The bank's critics argued,

> The Constitution was framed and adopted, not by the people of the United States at large, but by the people of the respective states…It is therefore a compact between the states, and all the powers not expressly relinquished by it, are reserved to the states.
>
> (Smith, 1996, p. 442)

Marshall vehemently disagreed,

> The government of the Union…is emphatically and truly, a government of the people. In form and substance, it emanates from them. Its powers are granted by them, and are to be exercised directly on them, and for their benefit…the power to tax involves the power to destroy…[If the states could tax the bank] they may tax the mail; they may tax the mint; they may tax patent rights; they may tax the judicial process; they may tax all the means employed by the government…This was not intended by the American people. They did not design to make their government dependent on the states.
>
> (Smith, 1996, p. 444)

One of Marshall's biographers, Jean Edward Smith, noted that,

> McCulloch v. Maryland may be the most important case in the history of the Supreme Court. The questions Marshall addressed—the extent of federal power, the limits of state sovereignty, the nature of the Union, and the principles by which the Constitution should be interpreted—are of continuing relevance, and the answers he provided have shaped the nation's growth for almost two centuries. McCulloch did not so much expand federal sovereignty as restrict state sovereignty.
>
> (Smith, 1996, p. 441, p. 445)

6.6 Today's Supreme Court

6.6.1 *The Most Conservative in 90 Years*

Today's court is demographically the most diverse ever, with four women, two blacks, and one Latino.[15] Ideologically, today the Court has three liberals (Elena Kagan, Ketanji Brown Jackson, and Sonia Sotomayor) and six conservatives[16] (Chief Justice John Roberts,[17] Neil Gorsuch, Amy Coney Barrett, Clarance Thomas, Samuel Alito, and Brett Kavanaugh). Roberts has been Chief Justice since 2005 and currently presides over "the most conservative court in 90 years" (Totenberg, 2022). Of the six conservatives, three are centrist conservatives: Roberts, Barret, and Kavanaugh; while the other three are arch-conservatives: Thomas, Alito, and Gorsuch.[18]

But why should the Court, so important in the lives of ordinary Americans (as de Tocqueville noted), be peopled by justices who are conservative or liberal? Why not neutrals, who can somehow rise above the pettiness of politics? Sure, everyone has their own values, their own vision of how the world works and how it should work, but why can't justices—the very word suggests fairness, lawful, fact-finding—put the interests of the nation first and foremost, above the interests of competing factions, while jettisoning any and all ideology?

Unfortunately, this "has never been the case" (Zirin, 2020). During the John Adams administration (1797–1801), for example,

> When the Federalists were defeated in 1800, the lame-duck Congress contracted the size of the court from six to five—spitefully, to deprive Democratic-Republican President Thomas Jefferson of an appointment. [Nevertheless], the incoming…Congress repealed the Federalist legislation and increased the roster to seven to give Jefferson an additional appointment.
>
> (Zirin, 2020)[19]

As Richard Posner notes, "there is no way to purge political principles from constitutional decision-making, but they do not have to be liberal or conservative principles. A preference for judicial modesty—for less interference by the Supreme Court with the other branches of government...would be a wise choice" (Posner, 2008).

We agree.

Given that the power of 'justices is immense,' de Tocqueville (although, perhaps a tad naively) fully expected that,

> the federal judges [to] not only be upright citizens, learned men [sic] of integrity, and possess[ing] the qualities necessary for all magistrates, but they must also display statesmanship. They must be able to perceive the spirit of their age, to confront obstacles that need to be overcome, steer out of the current whenever the wave threatens to carry them away, and with them the sovereignty of the Union and the obedience to its laws.
> (Tocqueville, 2003 [1835, 1840], p. 176)

Certainly, today's justices fall far short of this ideal, so much so that it seems naïve and even a tad quixotic to think that we would have ever required such characteristics of justices. Today, there is a palpable disconnect between standards of any kind and the behavior and performance of the Court justices. In a survey of G-7 nations, "Americans are tied with Italians in having the lowest trust in their judicial system" (Busted Trust, 2024, p. 20). This is worrisome because "the immense power of the Justices rests upon *public opinion*" (Tocqueville, 2003[1835, 1840], p. 176; emphasis added) while at the same time "strong and credible institutions count among the best guarantors of a country's long-term stability" (Busted Trust, 2024, p. 20). What does this say about a democracy when the Supreme Court cannot be trusted? This is a significant problem that warrants immediate post-2024 attention.

Rather than being able to 'perceive the spirit of their age,' during the last 50 years "the votes of Supreme Court Justices have become more predictable just about all of the time"[20] (Carter, 2023). Ideologically, the temperament of the Court has "swayed significantly from that of most Americans, [that is, to the right] even from most Republicans" (Seung and Long, 2022). Not surprisingly, today's court is viewed "as a vehicle for the conservative movement" (Bouie, 2022, p. 9).[21] Any case that comes before the Court, one can more or less predict its outcome on the basis of ideology alone.

6.6.2 Originalism

In addition to the Roberts Court being the most conservative in 90 years, it is "the most originalist in American history" (Gass, 2021). Originalists believe that the Constitution should be interpreted to comport with original meaning, i.e., "what the public would have understood [the framers'] words to mean at the time,[22] using contemporary dictionaries and news coverage, among other sources" (Gass, 2021). Justices Thomas, Gorsuch, and Barrett[23] are strong originalists, while Justices Alito and Kavanaugh seem to be originalist-inclined (Gass, 2021).

A preponderant argument in favor of originalism is that by focusing on meaning, overt bias in rendering a decision is reduced. Originalism,

> purports to constrain judges by requiring them to follow a written text even when they dislike the outcomes that text commands. At least in theory, originalism prevents judges from [subsidizing their own judicial bias/predilections] by lashing them to the unchanging meaning of a written document.
>
> (Millhiser, 2020)

After all, as Alexander Hamilton said, 'a constitution is in fact, and must be, regarded by the judges as a fundamental law.'

Critics of originalism argue that the Constitution's words/phrases are often ambiguous,[24] and that the framers themselves often disagreed over specific meaning. In addition, the framers were driven by ideology and economic interests of their own (Beard, 1986[1935]). And, finally, and perhaps most importantly, originalism is de facto exclusionary, by excluding the voices who were, at the time, political non-entities.

In our chapter on **Abortion and Reproductive Rights**, we discuss *Dobbs v Jackson Women's Health* (2022) in full detail, in which the Court, in a 6-3 majority utilized originalist arguments to overturn *Roe v. Wade* (1971), effectively making abortion illegal.

Part and parcel of the Roberts' Court conservative bent is that states, rather than the federal government, should decide our laws, at least, whenever appropriate. But ironically, this is occurring at the same time that Republicans have made it more difficult for citizens at the state level to vote, and where "gerrymandering [has] put extremists in control. State houses [have] passed draconian abortion laws, passed extreme gun laws, and wrote laws prohibiting public school teachers from teaching divisive concepts" (Richardson, 2023, p. 159).

The Supreme Court for the first two-thirds of its existence generally focused on the relation between the federal government and the states (i.e., federalism) (Levinson, 1991, p. 1052) an important task given the widespread fear of the newly created federal government's usurpation of state power. Then, the focus shifted to "the limits of governmental power on individual rights [and] the duties of government to provide resources necessary to the individual's full enjoyment of these rights" (Levinson, 1991, p. 1052). And now today, the Roberts Court has shifted to a broad-based attack on the administrative state, challenging and even repudiating these earlier judicial-given rights, using originalism whenever it can.

6.6.3   *Summary and Conclusion*

The Roberts Court in its pursuit of an active conservative agenda has overall been quite successful. Since 2021, the Court "has ticked the three boxes of the conservative legal movement: ending abortion rights, overturing affirmative action, and constraining the administrative state—along with bolstering the Second Amendment" ('Supremely Controversial', July 6, 2024, p. 21).

   In addition to the cases already discussed in this chapter, two more deserve mention as indicators/barometers of the Court's thinking:

- **Loper Bright v. Raimondo**[25]: The Court's 6-3 conservative majority overturned the 1983 Chevron doctrine[26] which in effect said that if a law is ambiguous, then "the federal courts had to defer to a regulatory agency so long as the interpretation of the law seemed to be a permissible construction of the statute" ('What the Chevron Ruling Means', 2024, p. 22). The Court didn't like that Chevron afforded the federal bureaucracy too much power (Savage, 2024, p. 16). Loper builds on West Virginia v. EPA[27] in which the Court required a higher standard of clear congressional authorization if agencies asserted new powers with economic and political significance, i.e., the 'major questions doctrine.'[28] On the one hand, Loper and West Virgina will tame the bureaucracy's overarching penetration into the three branches of government; as *The Economist* admitted, "the bureaucracy performs a legislative function in crafting rules and regulations, they mirror courts by interpreting their own authorities, and they exercise power in the name of the president" ('What the Chevron Ruling Means', 2024, p. 22). On the other hand, Loper will force Congress to update its legislation and to be very specific and forceful in what it wants. But alas, this assumes a workable functional Congress (Davenport, 2024, p. 9).

- **Trump v. the United States**[29]: The 6-3 conservative majority effectively ruled that Trump was largely immune from his subversive actions on January 6, 2022, since these could be categorized as official acts. The Court distinguished between private acts (where the president is liable for wrongdoing) and public/official acts where the president is immune. Chief Justice Roberts, who wrote the majority, argued that presidents would not be able to conduct their duties if they were constantly under fear of prosecution once they left office. But Roberts did not offer any examples, nor present a helpful guide as to which is which. In reading this case, it is hard not to disagree that "the majority's opinion …is not so much a legal decision as it a political one" (Bouie, 2024). A political decision, not just ideological, in the sense that "nothing is more natural to men [sic] in office, than to look with peculiar deference towards that authority to which they owe their official existence" The Federalist, #22, p. 131). Does this mean that trying to subvert democracy by overturning election results is now allowable and under the Court's protection, given that it is considered an official act? What antidemocratic behavior will future presidents be able to get away with? After all, "the hope of immunity is a strong incitement to sedition—the dread of punishment—a proportionately strong discouragement to it" Hamilton et al. (2009 [1787–1788], # 27, p. 157). What about the rights of ordinary citizens to be protected against such blatant usurpations of democracy? The Constitution clearly states, "No title of nobility should be granted by the United States…" (Article I Section 9). While no title has been granted ipso facto but by issuing a "stay out of jail card" ('Supremely Controversial', 2024, p. 20), isn't this the epitome of royalty?

6.7   Conclusion

As this manuscript goes to press (October 2024), President Biden promised to call for legislation that would reform the Supreme Court, motivated to appease the left-leaning members of his Party, hoping to solidify his renomination (Restuccia, 2024). But on July 21, 2024, President Biden withdrew from the race, rendering his motivation moot. Nevertheless, his calls for reform tap a deeper unease, a disconnect between the lofty ideals of judges being "able to perceive the spirit of their age, to confront obstacles that need to be overcome, steer out of the current whenever the wave threatens to carry them away," and today's judges' highly ideological decision making.

The average American wants a judge to be impartial, bereft of ideology; to look at the facts and make a decision for what is best for the nation; to decide each case based on its merits; to root the decision in law and not according to ideological predilection; and the thought process not to be influenced by gratuitous gifts. It is no wonder that Americans are tied with Italians (among the G-7 nations) in having the lowest trust in their judicial system. Losing trust in a major political institution is dangerous for a democracy and the first step (among many) in a slippery slope toward autocracy. Richard Posner's call for judicial modesty would

> go some distance toward de-politicizing the Supreme Court. It would lower the temperature of judicial confirmation hearings, widen the field of selection of justices, and enable the Supreme Court to attend to the many important non-constitutional issues that it is inclined to neglect.
>
> (Posner, 2008)

Such a call, would, however, as Posner admits have to imposed.

Passage of President Biden's specific reforms, or something similar,[30] passage would be difficult even in the best of times, and this is certainly not the best of times. Nevertheless, a quick look is warranted:

- **Term limits**: In *The Federalist Papers*, Alexander Hamilton provided cogent reasons in favor of life tenure given good behavior, which we have already discussed. On the hand, perhaps we could look to the Federal Reserve whose members are appointed for a staggered 14 years, which seems to us more than adequate. Having staggered appointments assures that there is a (relatively) new appointment, whose views/policies are more in tune with the current state of the union. This would encourage/enable the judges,

> to perceive the spirit of their age, to confront obstacles that need to be overcome, steer out of the current whenever the wave threatens to carry them away, and with them the sovereignty of the Union and the obedience to its laws.
>
> (Tocqueville, 2003[1835, 1840], p. 176)

Gabe Roth offers a similar proposal,

> Congress would pass a law whereby future justices would maintain the office of federal judge for life, per Art. III, §1, but after 18 years, they would move into senior status and either rotate to a lower court, retire or stand by to fill in at the high court should there be an unexpected vacancy. The math works out that a new justice would be added every two years; nine times two is an 18-year term.
>
> (Roth, 2021, p. 9)

This is fine for us. As Roth admits "Eighteen is not a magic number, but I would argue there's value in ensuring that the justices serve for a time, not (seemingly) for all time" (Roth, 2021, p. 9). We agree. Nor is there nothing magical about '14,' nor 'good behavior,' except that the latter is ensconced in Art. III, §1, requiring an amendment to change. But there is nothing wrong with this. The Founding Fathers recognized that the conditions would change and wisely implemented an amendment process, albeit a deliberately difficult one to effectuate change (see below). We like the idea of rotating justices out of direct case hearing after 18 years, but we go one step further: Why not elect four justices, say for terms of 10 years each, with the other five appointed for 18 years? This would mimic the bicameral nature of the legislature: Four judges receptive to the popular mood with five taking a broader view of the issues (just like the Senate was expected to do). Finally, this proposal comports very nicely with the Robert's Court emphasis on originalism, since an obvious disconnect exists between the ideal expectations of the justices (albeit a tad naïve), and their behavior today, no matter what metric we use,

> A term limits statute would make high court appointments part of regular Senate business. It would move the appointment process away from a gross misapplication of the Founders' attempt to bolster judicial independence toward something our founding generation would more recognize—and a policy our current generation would approve.
>
> (Roth, 2021, p. 11)

- **Code of ethics**: The Court's self-imposed 2023 code of ethics was heavily criticized for its lack of enforcement and self-reference over case recusal. Any code of ethics would have to be passed by Congress, and we don't see this highly partisan Congress agreeing on a workable set of rules.
- **Overturn the immunity granted to presidents for official acts**: Presumably, this would be accomplished by a Constitutional Amendment, but the amendment process was purposively made exceptionally difficult to "guard equally against that extreme facility which would render the constitution too mutable; and that extreme difficulty which might perpetuate its discovered faults" (Hamilton et al., 2003 [1787–1788], #78, p. 474). And, as mentioned earlier, passing an amendment is almost impossible in our highly partisan Congress.

None of these proposals would completely solve the problem at hand—a lack of trust—but cumulatively would constitute a big step forward. Restoring trust in one of our most important institutions which currently severely lacks in trust, should be a top priority of post-2024, "public officials in a democracy need public scrutiny, and since federal judges and justices are public officials, they should not be exempt from it. That scrutiny…will build trust in these officials, in their rulings and in the third branch as a whole" (Roth, 2021, p. 1).

6.8 Appendix: A Brief Note on William Howard Taft

Taft, the 20th president of the USA (1909–1913) merits a brief note as the only president ever to serve as Supreme Court Chief Justice. As his biographer notes, the day he was appointed Chief Justice by President Warren Harding (October 3, 1921) Taft exclaimed, "This is the greatest day of my life" (Goodwin, 2013, p. 748). An interesting tidbit is that Chief Justice William Howard Taft was on the winning side of 89.5% of 5-4 cases, the highest of any justice in the court's history (Carter, 2023). Overall, Taft, a Republican, and a conservative one at that, brought a decidedly conservative bent to the Court, with a strong anti-labor bias.[31]

Notes

1 We discuss Alexander Hamilton, as well as *The Federalist Papers*, in our **Budget Deficit and the Debt.**
2 The upper-cased words are in the original, which typified the writing of the day. In the same paper, Hamilton, quotes Montesquieu, the 17th century political thinker, that "the Judiciary is next to nothing" (The Federalist, #78, p. 473, note #1).
3 New York served as the nation's capital from 1785 to 1790; Philadelphia from 1790 to 1800; and Washington DC since.

4   George Washington appointed John Jay on September 26, 1789. In 1795, Jay resigned to become governor of New York.

5   We find this ironic now—working out of the old Senate building—although it is not clear that at the time, there was any intended irony. Hamilton strongly objected to a contemporary argument that the Supreme Court should be constitutionally part of the Legislature branch. (See Hamilton's arguments in *The Federalist* #81.)

6   Article V of the Constitution allows "the Congress, whenever two-thirds of both houses shall deem it necessary, shall propose amendments to this constitution or, on the application of the legislatures of two-thirds of the several states, shall call a convention for proposing amendments…" Hamilton noted, "The words of this article are peremptory. The Congress 'shall call a convention.' Nothing in this particular is left to the discretion of that body." (Hamilton et al., 2003 [1787–1788], # 85, p. 537).

7   The word 'circuit' is derived from the Latin word 'circumire,' i.e., to go around. The United States has 13 circuit courts: one for each of the nation's 11 geographical region, and one for the District of Columbia.

8   These areas of federal cognizance are delineated in Article III, Section 2. In addition, Hamilton clearly explains in Federalist #81.

9   Only a fraction of the cases petitioned to be heard by the Court are chosen, "The Court receives approximately 7,000–8,000 petitions for a writ of certiorari each term. The Court grants and hears oral argument in about 80 cases" (FAQs n.d.), approximately 1% of the total.

10   The *Presidential Commission on the Supreme Court of the United States* (2021) provides a good historical foundation.

11   Marshall died July 6, 1835, and two days later, July 8, during Marshall's funeral procession in Philadelphia, the Liberty Bell cracked, never to ring again (Smith, 1996, p. 20).

12   The citation: Marbury v. Madison, 5 US (1 Cranch) 137 (1803).

13   Madison was the United States' fourth president (1809–1817), and the architect of the Constitution and the Bill of Rights.

14   For a more in-depth discussion of the United States' central banks, and especially the relationship between the first two, and the current, see the **Federal Reserve.**

15   Thurgood Marshall was the nation's first black justice (1967–1991). Ketanji Brown Jackson is the first black woman on the Court (2022). Sandra Day O'Connor was the Court's first woman (1981–2006). Louis Brandeis was the first Jewish American to be appointed to the Court (1916–1939).

16   The 6-3 conservative majority occurred when Trump nominated Amy Coney Barrett in 2020, transforming from a 5-4 majority. Mimicking the 1800 shenanigans (see text), Senator Majority Leader, Mitch McConnell, had hurriedly shepherded Ms. Barret through the nomination process to ensure that she would be on the bench at the expiration of Trump's term in 2020.

17   Of the 17 Supreme Court Chief Justices dating back to John Jay (1789–1795), all have been white male, including Mr. Roberts.

18   The liberals have not been further delineated.

19   After several changes, Congress settled at nine justices in 1868, during the administration of Ulysses Grant. It has since remained at nine, although FDR, worried that much of his New Deal legislation would be overturned by an increasingly conservative court, tried unsuccessfully to augment the number of justices during his second term to guarantee a liberal majority. See Leuchtenburg (2005) and Schwartz (1993, pp. 236–236).

20   An important exception was Sandra Day O'Connor, the Court's first woman, "who was often a swing voter, [she] listened to both sides of an argument and based her decision on merit" (Carter, 2023).

21 Bouie (2022, p. 9) notes that today "large corporations, right-wing activists and conservative religious groups [can] approach the court knowing that a majority of justices are almost certainly on their side."

22 Justice Antonin Scalia shifted originalism from original intent to original meaning; the latter more easily to ascertain than the former (Gass, 2021).

23 For a good discussion of originalism in the context of Justice Barrett, see Millhiser (2020).

24 Millhiser (2020) lists a few ambiguities: "What are the 'privileges or immunities' of citizens of the United States? What makes a search or seizure 'unreasonable'? If the government wants to deny liberty, how much 'process' is 'due'? What's a 'public use' of private property? What is the general welfare of the United States?'

25 The citation: Loper Bright Enterprises v. Raimondo, 603 US ___ (2024). *The Economist* noted that this "may turn out to be the most important of the lot" ('What the Chevron Ruling Means,' 2024, p. 22).

26 The citation: Chevron USA, Inc. v. Natural Resources Defense Council, Inc., 467 US 837 (1984).

27 The citation: West Virginia v. Environmental Protection Agency, 597 US 697 (2022).

28 The Court used this doctrine to invalidate the Biden administration's attempt to cancel student debt.

29 The citation: Trump v. United States, 603 US ___ (2024).

30 For elaboration, see Biden (2024).

31 For a pithy discussion of the Taft Court 1921–1930, see Schwartz (1993, pp. 213–224). We discuss one such labor case in **The Minimum Wage**.

References

Beard, Charles A. (1986 [1935]) *An Economic Interpretation of the Constitution of the United States*, The Free Press, New York.

Bouie, Jamelle (2022) 'The Trouble with Judicial Review,' *The New York Times,* April 10, Sunday Opinion, p. 9.

Bouie, Jamelle (2024) *The New York Times*, July 14, Sunday Opinion, p. 3.

'Busted Trust' (2024) *The Economist*, April 20, p. 20.

Carter, Stephen L. (2023) 'A Justice's Legacy of Listening,' *Bloomberg Opinion*, December 2, https://www.bloomberg.com/opinion

Davenport, Coral (2024) 'Justices' Rulings Sharply Curtail E.P.A. Authority,' *The New York Times*, June 30, p. 1 and p. 9.

Gass, Henry (2021) 'Originalism Moves from Theory to High Court: What that Means for US,' *The Christian Science Monitor*, December 21.

Goodwin, Doris Kearns (2013) *The Bully Pulpit: Theodore Roosevelt, William Howard Taft, and the Golden Age of Journalism*, Simon and Schuster, New York.

Hamilton, Alexander, James Madison, and John Jay (2003 [1787–1788]) *The Federalist Papers*, Bantam Books, New York.

Leuchtenburg, William E. (2005) 'When Franklin Roosevelt Clashed with the Supreme Court—and Lost,' *Smithsonian Magazine*, (May), https://www.smithsonianmag.com/history

Levinson, Sanford (1991) 'The Supreme Court,' *The Reader's Companion to American History*, Eds. Eric Foner and John Garraty, Houghton Mifflin, pp. 1050–1052.

Millhiser, Ian (2020) 'Originalism, Amy Coney Barrett' Approach to the Constitution Explained, *Vox*, October 12, https://www.vox.com/21497317

Posner, R. A. (2008) 'In Defense of Looseness: The Supreme Court and gun control,' *The New Republic*, August 27, https://newrepublic.com/article/62124/defense-looseness

Presidential Commission on the Supreme Court of the United States (2021) SCOTUS-Report-Final-12.8.21-1.pdf (whitehouse.gov).

Restuccia, Andrew (2024) 'Biden Seeks Changes for High Court,' *The Wall Street Journal*, July 17, p. A5.

Roth, Gabe (2021) 'Statement: Fix the Court Presidential Commission on the Supreme Court of the United States,' To the members of the Presidential Commission on the Supreme Court of the Unit, July 20, Roth-Testimony.pdf (whitehouse.gov).

Savage, Charlie (2024) 'Weakening Agencies will be a Legacy of the Roberts Court,' *The New York Times*, June 30, p. 16.

Schwartz, Bernard (1993) *A History of the Supreme Court*, Oxford University Press, New York.

Seung, Min Kim, and Collen Long (2022) 'Biden Outpacing Trump, Obama with Diverse Judicial nominees' *AP News* (December 30), https://apnews.com/article

Smith, Jean Edward (1996) *John Marshall: Definer of a Nation*, Henry Holt, New York.

'Supremely Controversial' (2024) *The Economist*, July 6, pp. 20–21.

Tocqueville, Alexis de (2003 [1835, 1840]) *Democracy in America*, Penguin Books, New York.

Totenberg, Nina (2022) 'The Supreme Court is the most conservative in 90 years,' NPR, July 5, https://www.npr.org/2022/07/05

'What the Chevron Ruling Means,' (2024) *The Economist,* July 6, p. 22–23.

Zirin, James D. (2020) 'Beyond Court Packing: The Supreme Court Has Always been Political,' (December 2), https://time.com/5906442/

7 The Budget Deficit, The Debt, and The Debt Ceiling

The Issue: America last ran a budget surplus in 2001. No reputable forecast is calling for a budget surplus in the near future. The federal debt has increased five-fold since 2000. If nothing is done, by 2053, interest on the federal debt will become the federal government's largest expenditure, surpassing Social Security, Defense, and Medicare. Many Americans feel that federal spending is out of control but feel powerless to do anything. As this manuscript goes to press (October 2024) reducing the deficit/debt is a non-issue among the presidential candidates. Nevertheless, continuing deficits are unsustainable. This chapter explores why deficits/debt are problematic and potential solutions.

7.1 Introduction

As this manuscript goes to press (October 2024), the White House is projecting budget deficits at least until 2030. That means that in 2028, unless something changes, the United States will break its own record for the longest era of successive federal budget deficits (previously, 1970–1996). This is not necessarily a record worth celebrating. Since 1970, the United States has only run a budget surplus in four years (1997, 1998, 1999, 2000, and 2001). And, unless something changes, the 2001 budget surplus might be the last, at least for a while.

In the 19th century, the United States consistently ran budget surpluses, with a record-setting string of consecutive budget surpluses (1869–1993). What is going on here? Why are budget surpluses becoming extinct, and why are budget deficits the norm?

7.2 Defining the Budget Deficit and the Debt

In any given year, the federal government can either

- Balance its budget (i.e., outlays = receipts).
- Run a budget deficit (outlays > receipts).
- Run a budget surplus (outlays < receipts).

DOI: 10.4324/9781003591856-9

If the government runs a deficit, then just like you and I, it must come up with the differential. So if, for example, the government spends $150 (hypothetical yes, but simple math) in a fiscal year, but its receipts are only $100, then it must come up with the $50 differential; if not, it has no choice but to declare bankruptcy. The government can pay the differential in one of two ways:

- Ask/demand/cajole/inveigle the **Federal Reserve** (The Fed) to print money. Today, the Fed refuses, given the potential for **inflation**.
- Borrow from the public. Doing so will increase the federal debt (sometimes called the public debt), defined here as the sum of outstanding loans lent by the public (both domestic and international) to the US government (specifically the Treasury) to finance budget deficits.

If the federal government never ran a budget deficit, then there would be no federal debt. And, as budget deficits increase/accumulate, given the current mode of financing, so will the federal debt, ceteris paribus. And, as we shall see later in this issue, the federal debt can only be reduced by budget surpluses. Since there aren't any budget surpluses on the horizon (near or far), we expect the debt to continue to increase.

7.3   The 19th Century: Budget Surpluses the Norm

7.3.1   Introduction

Since George Washington's administration (1789–1797), every administration until the **Great Depression** (1930s) wanted to either balance its budget or run a budget surplus. There was no practical reason, other than it was assumed that a balanced budget exemplified prudency; while conversely, deficit spending exemplified profligacy; and a profligate government sets a bad example for everyone else. The only exception was war, when the government should prudently borrow, then pay back the debt when the war ended by running budget surpluses.

7.3.2   The United States Was Born with a Debt

The United States was born with a sizable debt of 75 million. Before the USA Constitution was adopted in 1787, the federal government under the Articles of Confederation was weak and ineffectual, lacking the power to tax. But it still needed money to function, which it tried to raise by issuing paper Continentals which soon became worthless due to over-printing, and by borrowing from both domestic and foreign sources. Neither method was effective, nor it became clear to most that a new constitution with the ability to tax and hence raise revenue was needed.[1]

The new Constitution was formally ratified June 1788 (and became operational March 4, 1789). The Constitution transformed the federation of 13 colonies into the United States of America. It strengthened the central government by giving it the power to tax and hence raise revenue for its needed functions. But the accumulated debts from the federation still had to be paid. (Or perhaps not? Perhaps the creditors—most of whom lived in Europe—would have understood: A new nation; a revolution creating a new government, jettisoning the debt while starting anew? Wouldn't that have been expected?) However, Article VI of the Constitution explicitly states that "All debts contracted and engagements entered into, before the adoption of this constitution, shall be as valid against the United States under this constitution, as under the confederation." Hence, the new government had no option. According to James Madison, this constitutional phrase,

> may have been inserted, among other reasons, for the satisfaction of the foreign creditors of the United States, who cannot be strangers to the pretender doctrine that a change in the political form of civil society, has the magical effect of dissolving its moral obligations.
>
> (Madison, *The Federalist* #43, p. 268)

Indeed, it was estimated that in 1790, the United States owed "$11.7 million to foreigners, mostly to Dutch bankers and the French government, and about $42 million to domestic creditors. The [13 states] also had a ton of debt (about $25 million) which the Federal government assumed" (Phillips, 2012). Altogether, the debt represented 30% of **GDP**, a sizable sum.[2]

7.3.3   *Alexander Hamilton Puts the Young United States on a Sound Financial Path*

Alexander Hamilton, the first Secretary of the Treasury (and some would say perhaps the most able and the most astute), made it a top priority to begin immediately paying off the debt (Ellis, 2000, pp. 48–80). In his first 'Report to Congress,' Hamilton argued that "an adequate provision for the support of the public credit is a matter of high importance to the honor and prosperity of the United States" (Hamilton, 1790). And to further assuage the financial markets, Hamilton decided that the creditors would be paid back in gold with a substantial premium, and at par. Consequently,

> From a position where the US government was nearly bankrupt in the 1780s, in 1803 it had no trouble borrowing $11.25 million on short notice mostly from foreign subscribers ($6.25 million made payable in London, and $5 million in Amsterdam) to finance the Louisiana Purchase, which doubled the size of the nation,
>
> (Sylla, 1991, p. 773)[3]

Hamilton effectively got the United States' finances off to a solid start; although today, sadly, we seemed to have lost his purposive wisdom. Before we move on, we must mention Hamilton's life-ending duel with the Aaron Burr, Thomas Jefferson's vice-president; although thanks to the eponymous musical, Hamilton's life is somewhat familiar.

Hamilton and Burr were long-time political enemies, with a mutual and intolerable dislike. Hamilton effectively nudged the 1800 presidential nomination in favor of Jefferson, while slighting Burr. In 1804, Hamilton defeated Burr for governor of New York, while slandering Burr's capability. Apparently, that was the straw that broke the camel's back, so to speak: Burr, to defend his honor challenged Hamilton to a duel, and on July 11, 1804, in Weehawken, New Jersey, Burr shot Hamilton who died the next day.

For a duel, the guns were loaded (or whatever the weapon of choice) with no blank bullets, but that didn't mean that one had to shoot to kill. One could deliberately miss (or accidentally miss, as the case may be) or shoot to wound; of course, hoping that one's opponent would do the same, and then get on with the business of living, honor restored, more or less.

In their duel, Hamilton missed (we are not sure if accidental or deliberate, although apparently, he had slipped), but Burr directly hit (not sure if accidental or deliberate). Back then, a duel was an accepted and widespread way of settling an affront to one's dignity (Hamilton had earlier lost a son to a duel). After Hamilton's death, public outrage forced combatants to find other ways of settling. A good thing, because if duels were still in vogue, then today there might not be anyone left in the federal government.

Throughout the 19th century, a strong, consistent, and successful effort was made to reduce the Federal debt by running budget surpluses, only interrupted by major wars: The War of 1812, the Civil War, and the Spanish American War.[4]

7.3.4   Andrew Jackson: The Only USA President to Eliminate the Debt

Only Andrew Jackson (1767–1845), the nation's seventh president (1829–1837) was able to eliminate the debt. His motivation is interesting and stems more from his personal character (or some would say lack thereof). Despite being a general and having made a name for himself in the War of 1812, Jackson detested elites, and particularly central bankers.[5] This dislike stems from when Jackson, as a young man, got saddled with a friend's debt after he had declared bankruptcy. As Gordon tells the story,

> In 1795, in Philadelphia, [Jackson] sold 68,000 acres to a David Allison, taking the latter's promissory notes in payment [which] he used in turn to purchase supplies for a trading post. Allison's bankruptcy in 1797 rendered Jackson liable for Allison's notes. This affair would haunt Jackson

for the next [15 years] before it was finally settled in its entirety. And it would give Jackson a lifelong horror of debt and the use of paper money to finance, or even facilitate transactions.

(Gordon, 1998, pp. 58–59)

In 1828, when Jackson was being considered for the presidency,[6] he promised to pay off the national debt (not an insignificant sum at $58.4 million) as a way of "ridding the nation of paper money" (Gordon, 1998, pp. 59). And very much related, he promised not to renew the 20-year charter of the Second Bank of the United States, which, for Jackson, represented the epitome "of moneyed aristocracy dealing in paper money and not real wealth such as land and manufacturing facilities" (Gordon, 1998, pp. 59–60).[7]

Jackson kept both promises. By 1836, the federal debt was completely eliminated, accomplished by paying off the Treasury's creditors. Jackson was the only USA president to ever eliminate the debt during his tenure,[8] a feat which remains,

unique in the history of modern nations and one that arose far more from the personality and history of Andrew Jackson than from economic theory. Indeed, it would contribute in no small way to [the] country's first great depression.

(Gordon, 1998, p. 57)

More specifically, Jackson's payoff meant that a substantial amount of money left the United States for Europe; in turn, this left the United States with insufficient cash to support its economy. As recession clouds were brewing during the last year of Jackson's administration, he was reported to have said that he was thrilled to be leaving Washington and could not get out fast enough. Jackon's deliberate elimination of the debt handed his predecessor, Martin Van Buren (1837–1841) a bona fide **depression**, the nation's first.

Jackson was re-elected in 1836, and in the last year of his term, he kept his promise to not renew the charter of the Second Central Bank,[9] largely for personal reasons mentioned earlier. It was not until the Federal Reserve Act of 1913 that our third and current central bank—the **Federal Reserve System** (Fed)—was created. So, from 1836, until 1913 the United States was without a central bank.

Interestingly, the Fed's architects decided to put Andrew Jackson's portrait on the 20-dollar bill to make a statement: Here's the guy who dismantled the United States' second central bank, but because of the Fed's new structure, there's no way that anyone will be able to dismantle it.

There have been repeated attempts to replace Jackson's portrait on the 20-dollar bill with someone more palatable; although as this manuscript goes to press (October 2024), it looks like no decision until 2030.

The 19th-century budget surpluses were financed by **tariffs**. Running annual surpluses was the method of choice to systematically reduce the federal debt, which accumulated during war. During the Civil War, for example, the federal debt increased four-fold, breaking the psychological barrier of $1 million (in nominal dollars) in 1863 (Gordon, 1998, p. 208). But immediately after the war, the government persistently ran budget surpluses from 1866 to 1893; a record which still stands, and one that we can safely say will not soon be broken. The string of budget surpluses decreased the debt to $961 million by 1893, and to 6.97% of GDP (Gordon, 1998, p. 208). The deficit, in nominal terms, nor as a percentage of GDP, would never again be this low (Phillips, 2012).

7.4   About Face in the 20th Century

During the 19th century, especially after the Civil War, the federal government actively constructed the nation's infrastructure (roads, highways, canals) which were largely financed via tariff revenue. But the federal government did nothing to stimulate the economy when there was a slowdown, i.e., there was no fiscal policy. This is why **recessions** during the 19th century were long and frequent, including the nation's longest (1873–1879).

However, the severity of the Great Depression, with a record-setting **unemployment** rate of 24.5%, activated the federal government. While President Roosevelt implemented policies to get the American economy up and running,[10] John Maynard Keynes' *The General Theory* (1936) provided the supporting intellectual basis. Keynes, no fan of big government, but a strong advocate of workable capitalism, exhorted that during recessions the federal government should run budget deficits in order to stimulate aggregate demand. No one else could: Not consumers, not firms, and certainly not foreigners. But once the recession was over, the government should run budget surpluses to return to fiscal solvency and reduce the debt.

In theory, this symmetry appeals, but it did not work in practice. In an important book, *Democracy in Deficit* (1977 [2000]), Joe Buchanan and Richard Wagner argued that democracy and budget surpluses are incongruent: The Keynesian prescription is biased toward deficit expansion and that the political process is not equipped to churn out budget surpluses. In plain English, it is easy and tempting to increase spending and reduce tax rates, whereas reducing spending and increasing taxes can be politically costly.

From 1946 to 1996, the government ran a budget surplus in only ten years, with all but two before 1953.[11] The federal government established a record of consecutive budget deficits from 1970 to 1997; a record that will (most likely) soon be broken. Not surprisingly, the debt increased five-fold during this period, crossing the psychological threshold barrier of $1 trillion (in nominal dollars) in 1981/1982.

7.5   Budget Deficits Today

As this manuscript goes to press (October 2024), the federal deficit is $1.7 trillion, albeit a considerable decrease from the COVID-induced record deficit of $3.1tr in 2020 and down from $2.8tr in 2021 (CBO, 2023a). There is no reputable forecast calling for an annual deficit below $1.5tr, at least in the near term; nor any forecasts predicting a significant debt reduction. The Congressional Budget Office (CBO, 2023a) forecasts annual budget deficits of $2.0tr from 2024 until 2033.

While these numbers seem quite large, perhaps a better way to understand the deficit's burden is to express it as a percentage of the nation's income. Just like if you go to a bank, requesting a loan, the first thing that the banker asks is your income. If, for example, your requested loan is $10,000, but your income is only $30,000, servicing the loan (i.e., repayment) will be problematic. But if your income is $100,000, the debt becomes much more manageable.

We can express the deficit as a percent of **GDP** (i.e., deficit/GDP). As we explain in our issue on **Economic Indicators**, GDP measures a nation's annual output of goods and services and, equivalently, its annual income. In 2024, this ratio was 6.3%, meaning that if we wanted to balance the budget, we could do so with 6.3% of the nation's income.[12] Although this is not recommended since a severe recession would result, caused by reduced consumer spending and investment.

Today (July 2024), the debt stands at $33.2tr, a record in absolute terms. As a percentage of GDP, the total debt is 128%, meaning that if we chose to eliminate the debt, we could do so with 100% of our income this year and 28% next year (although more due to interest). Also not recommended, since a complete elimination of the debt in just two years would result in an unprecedented depression.

As of 2024, 22% of the debt is intra-government owned (i.e., one branch has borrowed from the other, e.g., Treasury from Social Security), while 78% is held by the public (DHBP).[13] To those who loan the Treasury money, the loan is an asset, since they receive interest and the principal at a future date. Economists,

generally view the DHBP as the most meaningful measure of debt, because it reflects the amount that the Treasury has borrowed from outside lenders through financial markets to support government activities. At high levels, DHBP can crowd out private investments in the economy, making it more difficult to respond to economic crises, and increase volatility within the economy.

('The Federal Government has Borrowed Trillions,
but who owns all that debt?' 2023)

Currently, the DHBP/GDP is 99%. It is expected to increase to 118% in 2033 and then 195% in 2053 (CBO, 2023a). This is due to the growth in interest and spending, outpacing the growth in revenues.

The DHBP is further distinguished by domestic holders and foreign holders. Of the former, the largest are (as a % of domestic DHBP):

The Federal Reserve	35%
Mutual Funds	15%
Depository Institutions	10%
State/local gov.	9%
Pension Funds	6%
Insurance Companies	2%
Other	22%

Since the 2008 recession, the Fed has increased its Treasury bond holdings five-fold. This was done in order to stimulate the economy.[14] When the Fed purchases Treasury bonds from banks, it pays for them by depositing funds in their accounts. The banks can then use these deposits in order to make loans. Whenever a loan is made, the money supply is increased, which in turn reduces the federal funds rate—the Fed's main interest rate, which has been continuously in the news since 2022. Beginning in mid-2023, the Fed began selling bonds in order to reduce inflation. When it sells bonds, banks pay for the bonds by reducing their cash, which in turn reduces their ability to make loans, thus decreasing the money supply, ceteris paribus, while increasing the federal funds rate.

Foreign holdings of DHBP have increased significantly since 1970, from 5% to 30%. The latter figure would have been much higher if not for **the Federal Reserve's** stimulative actions (see the preceding paragraph). The top five foreign holders of the federal debt are (as a percent of total DHBP)[15]:

Japan	5.5%
China	3.7%
UK	2.7%
Belgium	1.3%
Cayman Islands	1.2%

Given that ownership of US Treasury bonds is considered by most investors as a safe haven, it is not surprising that over 30 nations have invested in USA debt.

The following domestic institutions are the largest owners of intra-government debt (as a percent of total intra-government debt):

Social Security	38.0%
Federal Employees Retirement Funds	14.7%
Medicare	5.8%
Deposit Insurance Trust Fund	1.8%
Highway Trust Fund	1.7%

7.6 Why Deficits Occur

The federal budget (like any budget) is a relationship between outlays and receipts. Understanding this relationship explains how deficits/surpluses occur. Generally speaking, increases/decreases in spending will increase/decrease the deficit, while decreases/increases in revenue will result in a budget deficit/surplus (or a reduced surplus), all else equal. Deficit spending tends to increase during a recession. The more severe a recession, the greater federal outlays and the lower government tax revenue as more people are out of work, and firm profits decrease.

In 2023, the federal government's top five outlays were as follows:

Social Security	22.0 (% of total federal outlays)
Medicare	13.8%
Defense	12.7%
Net Interest on debt	11.5%
Medicaid	10.0%

Source: CBO, 2023b

The big five accounted for 70% of federal total outlays. In 2023, Net Interest overtook Medicaid for the 4th spot. Net Interest is the fastest growing federal expenditure, increasing 33% from just 2022 to 2023, while doubling since 2000.

The big three federal receipts are as follows:

Income taxes	51.1% (of total receipts)
Social Security taxes	24.4%
Corporate taxes	9.1%

Source: OMB, 2023

The big three account for 84.6% of total revenue. The remainder (15.4%) includes excise taxes, miscellaneous taxes, and tariffs. Tariffs, the 19th century's largest federal receipt, today oscillates annually between 1 and 2% of total revenues.

7.7 How to Reduce the Deficit

7.7.1 Pass a Balanced Budget Act

Or a balanced budget amendment that would mandate an annual equalization of outlays and receipts. Although balanced budgets are currently mandated at the state level, the chances of such legislation being passed at the federal level are nil, given the lack of interest. (Several unsuccessful attempts have been made in the past.)

Proponents argue that a balanced budget is the only sure way to rein in a profligate government. Opponents argue that a balanced budget amendment would straightjacket the federal government, rendering it impotent to handle emergencies, or even normal exigencies. For example, if a balanced budget law/amendment had been in effect in 2001, the federal government would not have been to increase defense spending to counter international terrorism. Nor could the federal government have passed ameliorative measures during the 2007–2009 recession, and it would have been powerless to combat the COVID-induced recession of 2020. A balanced budget law would have made each recession longer and much deeper. Of course, escape clauses could have been implemented, allowing discretionary spending due to exigencies, but this would have eviscerated the essence of the balanced budget law, rendering it ineffectual.

7.7.2   Balance the Budget Over the Business Cycle

This is a more nuanced version of the first solution, and perhaps slightly more politically palatable. Specifically, the objective would be to run deficits during **recessions** (by increasing federal spending and/or cutting taxes) and run budget surpluses during **expansions** by raising taxes and/or cutting spending. For this to work, however, one must be able to predict with reasonable accuracy the two phases of the business cycle (i.e., recession and expansion). But alas, the economics profession is unable to do so, nor anyone else. Additionally, it is politically more difficult to run a budget surplus (especially by raising taxes) than a deficit, especially during elections.

7.7.3   Reduce Federal Government Expenditures

To do successfully, it is necessary to tackle the big five. While theoretically possible, practically speaking, i.e., politically, it is not:

- **Social Security:** Is the largest federal expenditure. As we explain in our chapter on **Social Security,** it is politically difficult (although certainly not impossible) to increase SS taxes or to reduce SS benefits.
- **Medicare**: Similarly, recipients are politically active and would not tolerate sharp benefit reductions.
- **Defense:** Today, in a seemingly increasing hostile world, with several wars ongoing, it is difficult to reduce defense spending. No political candidate wants to be portrayed as weak on defense.[16]
- **Medicaid:** Is jointly run by the state governments, leaving the federal government with less discretion. However, significant reductions in Medicaid would open the government (both federal and state) to charges of callousness, disregarding the neediest.
- **Interest:** Reducing the interest on the debt is non-negotiable. Incidentally, the interest on the debt is the fastest growing federal expenditure: Since 2020, it has doubled, now at $659 billion (1.9% of GDP).[17] If nothing is done, then

by 2033, net interest will double to $1.4tr; and by 2053, to $5.4tr (6.7% of GDP) making it the largest federal expenditure. The reason is two-fold: (1) With continued deficits, the debt increases; and (2) with the Fed increasing interest rates, the Treasury is forced to pay higher rates to borrow (4.5–5.5%).

Sure, we could systematically reduce all remaining government programs (e.g., energy, welfare, and agriculture) and even attempt to eliminate them without touching the big five, but this would be quixotic at best, given expected formidable vested interests.

7.7.4   *Increase Federal Revenue*

One or all of the big three would have to be increased, and especially income taxes, by increasing the rates of taxation. Doing so would reduce consumption spending (all else equal) and investment spending, since investment is buoyed by expected consumer spending. Increasing taxes would also increase the probability of a recession, all else equal. Today, no politician wants to be on record for deliberating causing a recession. Nor is today's political climate conducive to increasing taxes of any kind (except on the very wealthy, although not every agrees that this is the most efficacious). Likewise for taxes on **Social Security**. Only small, gradual increases can be politically palatable, which by itself will not be enough to reduce the deficit. Corporate income tax rates have been systematically declining here in the United States as a percentage of total federal revenue, which has been due to their increased bargaining clout.

Furthermore, increased revenue via increased tax rates might not be as much as optimistically anticipated. Evidence suggests that when taxed, or threatened to be taxed, those to be taxed will modify their behavior to minimize exposure.

7.7.5   *Reduce Spending and Increase Revenue*

A little of each might be more politically palatable than exclusively doing one or the other. President Clinton did this in 1996 somewhat successfully. Spurred by the Fed's argument that if nothing was done to reduce the deficit, then interest rates would rise, as the federal government competed with private sector borrowers. The end result would be a recession, caused by decreased consumption and investment. Interestingly, no Republican voted for the legislation.

The same combination, however, didn't work for FDR during the 1930s. The Roosevelt administration increased taxes to pay for the extensive New Deal programs (income taxes in 1934, a wealth tax in 1935, a corporate profits tax in 1936; and in 1937, closure of tax loopholes and the first Social Security taxes). In addition, it cut federal spending to balance the budget; while the Federal Reserve tightened the money supply and increased interest rates.[18] The result was a recession: May 1937–June 1938.

But today, with Congress even more dysfunctional than it was in the 1990s, it is highly improbable that the two Parties could work out a deal to reduce the deficit/debt by any means.

7.7.6   *Economic Growth*

Given the political difficulties of the above solutions, this leaves economic growth. As the economy grows, federal receipts automatically increase, all else equal, since more people are working and paying more taxes, even if tax rates do not change. Likewise, as the economy grows, so do corporate profits, increasing federal coffers. With more people working, welfare spending will decrease, all else equal, further reducing the deficit (or increasing the surplus, as the case may be). It was no coincidence that during the late 1990s, as the economy grew annually at 4%, and with labor force participation rates reaching record levels, the federal government ran a budget surplus four years (1997–2001).

But economic growth doesn't just happen; rather, the federal government must take an active role incentivizing (and minimizing disincentives) firms and consumers, while establishing the necessary ground rules for the market system to do its stuff. A functional Congress is needed to make economic growth happen. Obviously missing today.

7.8   Should We Worry About the Deficit/Debt?

There is no debt threshold above which the debt is harmful and below, benign. The threshold will differ for each nation (and over time) depending on a host of factors. For example, can a nation attract funding? Doing so depends on the nation's own fiscal and monetary policies. Will the nation be able to pay back its debt? This is determined by how the debt is used. If used to increase investment, then all else equal, future revenue should increase, enabling the debt to be repaid. Increasing the debt to increase consumption (usually done by decreasing taxation rates) makes paying the debt back more problematic.

We argue that an increasing deficit/debt, is problematic for the following reasons:

- As anyone who is in debt knows, the more debt, the less discretion to add expenditures. A high/increasing debt renders the government less likely to meet any contingencies that might arise. In addition, a high debt represents a taboo against increased further spending. In 2023, for example, the preponderant argument against the Inflation Reduction Act, was that it would add to an already significant debt. The criticism ultimately led to less money being allocated.
- As debt increases, so do interest payments, which tend to transfer the burden of debt to future generations, while higher interest rates crowd out other types of spending.

- If an increasing percent of the debt is owned by foreigners, an increasing amount of interest payments will leave the United States. (Indeed, this was a preponderant factor in the depression of 1837–1843, just as Andrew Jackson was leaving office.) More specifically,

> more income sent abroad means less for domestic investors, more foreign-owned debt reduces the control of financial markets in the U.S. Yet on the other hand, foreign investment may help increase U.S. economic activity if the money borrowed from such investors is used for productive purposes, such as stimulating recovery from a recession or funding investments in the nation's economy.
>
> ('The Federal Government has Borrowed Trillions, but who owns all that debt?' 2023)

This is especially so if domestic savings is low, which is typical in the United States during non-recession years.

Even if we substantially cut the deficit, say from $1.6tr to $600b (extremely unlikely given the reasons cited in the previous section), the federal debt will continue to increase since we have to borrow money to finance the still-existing deficit. The only way to reduce the debt is to run budget surpluses. But alas, the probability of doing so today, is zero.

7.9   How About a Federal Debt Ceiling?

Authorized by Congress, a debt ceiling is the maximum limit that the government (Treasury) can borrow. It is not a cap on total spending, but only a cap on the amount that can be borrowed. In 1917, Congress passed the Second Liberty Bond Act, which created the inaugural federal debt ceiling. This enabled the Treasury to borrow (as long as the funds were under the imposed ceiling) without seeking Congress' approval, thus saving time.

Since 1917, the debt ceiling limit has been raised/modified/temporarily suspended 98 times[19] (Elving, 2021). But until recently,

> Congress always (after a bit of posturing) increased the debt ceiling, and created the expectation that debt-limit fights were a seasonal Washington ritual, like the Cherry blossoms, or the Marine Corps Marathon, of no existential importance. [And once lifted, Congress could continue to borrow funds to pay the already incurred bills.] But lifting the debt is no longer routine.
>
> (Lofgren, 2023)

The debt ceiling is analogous to a couple agreeing to limit how much borrowing in a given year. But contingencies/emergencies always arise, sometimes forcing the couple to borrow beyond the agreed-to limit. Inevitably, they will agree to increase the debt ceiling and hence their debt. The couple will also recognize that the debt must be repaid and that subsequently, active measures must be taken to reduce the debt by either increasing revenue and/or reducing expenditures. Breaching the pre-agreed borrowing limit will not incur sanctions/ punishments other than higher interest payments. If the couple refuses to take the necessary steps, to borrow to pay the expenses, or even to forego the debt, it suggests nothing more than a dysfunctional relationship.

If raising the ceiling has been so routine (at least until now), then why not jettison the agreement to limit the debt altogether? But in so doing,

> Voters might just take that as fiscal irresponsibility…They also don't like the idea of a government with no limits on its borrowing. And it's important to say that there are plenty of legislators who like the debt ceiling, both as a restraint on the growth of federal spending and as a chance to tie controversial stuff they want done to something that people, in the end, have to vote for.
>
> (Elving, 2021)

Today, federal spending is held hostage to political posturing. However, we would argue that the best way to prevent these squabbles is to reduce the deficit/ debt. But Congress has become so dysfunctional that it cannot compromise/ dialogue to reach a solution in the nation's best interest. By refusing to raise the ceiling in order to pay debts already incurred, Congress is playing with fire. The most recent such tantrum occurred on January 19, 2023, when the federal government reached its maximum debt limit. Congressional Republicans threatened not to raise the ceiling unless Democrats agreed to significant spending cuts. Democrats countered that the Constitution's 14th Amendment (Section 4), left the government no choice, "The validity of the public debt of the United States, authorized by law…shall not be questioned." Incidentally, during the Trump administration, the ceiling was routinely raised three times, each with bi-partisan support.

Today, tax revenue only covers four-fifths of government spending, with borrowing needed to cover the remainder. If the government were to default, then "abruptly halting the 1/5 would be akin to ripping out 5% of GDP overnight pushing America to a crushing recession" (*The Economist,* January 28, 2023). And "the poor would invariably bear the burden with spending cuts focused on programs that help the least well-off such as Head Start, and assistance for food, childcare, and housing" (Dionne, 2023).

A refusal to lift the debt ceiling would unleash an economic Armageddon: Interest rates would soar, stocks would crash, investment would cease as would consumption; and capital would flee the United States. And if this wasn't bad enough, the dollar might be replaced as the world's dominant currency with something more reliable and dependable. The **BRICS** are already leaning in that direction; one more debt ceiling fiasco could push them over the edge.

7.10   Who Is to Blame for Profligate Spending?

An interesting question to ask. Democrats? Republicans? Actually, both,

> America's ballooning debt is the result of choices made by both Republicans and Democrats. Since 2000, politicians from both parties have made a habit of borrowing money to finance wars, tax cuts, expanded federal spending for baby boomers, and emergency measures to help the nation endure two debilitating recessions…there have been bipartisan tax cuts and bipartisan spending increases…It's not a simple case of Republicans cut taxes and Democrats increase spending. They each have been doing a little of both…By one crude measure, the debt has been a bi-partisan pursuit: it grew by $12.7tr when Mr. Bush and Mr. Trump were in office and $13tr under Mr. Obama and Biden.
>
> (Tankersley, 2023)

(Perhaps this is why the deficit/debt was not an issue during the 2024 presidential campaign?) Conversely, a lack of a workable relationship between the two parties can cause increasing deficits/debt. In fact, research shows that a factor in the decline of global superpowers is a dysfunctional government awash in debt, although the causation can work both ways (Phillips, 2002, pp. 171–200).

7.11   Conclusion

Today's fiscal irresponsibility cannot be sustained. Its continuance is an abnegation of responsibility. Two strategies are necessary to reverse this profligacy and reign in the deficit/debt:

- A functional Congress (at the very least, one whose members listen to each other) that can map out an effective strategy.
- A broad appeal to restructure the American economy based on sustained and accelerated growth. This recognizes that economic growth is the only practical method to reduce the deficit/debt. As we discuss in our chapter on **Net Zero**, a transition to renewable energy and sustainability is already underway; and a full transition is inevitable. So why not invest now in order to contour the transition so that it is favorable to the public interest?

The fact that neither solution is in the cards right now underscores the abnegation of the public interest, which in turn is a hallmark of bad government, irrespective of ideology.

Notes

1 This motivated publication of *The Federalist Papers,* originally a series of newspaper articles published between 1787 and 1788, to sway Americans in favor of adopting the newly proposed Constitution. Co-authored by Alexander Hamilton, a Revolutionary War aide to General George Washington, and the nation's first Treasury Secretary; James Madison, the principal architect of the Constitution, elected as the United States' fourth president; and John Jay, president under the Articles of Confederation, and the nation's first Supreme Court Chief Justice. The causal effect on contemporaries, however, was tenuous, "If the first aim of the series was to persuade New Yorkers to elect friends of the Constitution to the ratifying convention, then Hamilton failed. The [New York] delegation opposed the Constitution two to one" (Wills, 2003, p. xi). (Note: each of *The Federalist's* 85 papers begins with, 'To the People of the State of New York.') Nevertheless, *The Federalist Papers* is a masterful commentary on the USA Constitution. Reading this, especially today as the USA teeters toward autocracy, is essential to understand how the USA Constitution was designed to work.

2 Indeed, it was sizeable, "a debt/GDP ratio that high was not seen again in US history until the 1930s when the Great Depression led to large deficits and increases in the debt at the same time that the GDP was collapsing" (Sylla, 1991, p. 773).

3 For the specifics of Hamilton's debt funding, as well as domestic opposition see Studenski and Kross (1951, pp. 51–56).

4 While Washington was revered by most, he was bluntly criticized for running deficits during four of his eight years in office. Back in those days (thanks to the new USA constitution), the main source of federal revenue was the **tariff**, but tariff revenue in the early days was not sufficient to balance the budget, never mind run a budget surplus. Today, few people look back at his administration to criticize his four budget deficits. In fact, some might laud him for running four budget surpluses!

5 Indeed, as one of his biographers wrote, Jackson "was the most contradictory of men" (Meacham, 2008, p. xxi).

6 Back in those days it wasn't considered cool for a presidential candidate to personally campaign; rather his supporters would do the lion's share of the work. William Harrison broke tradition in the 1840 election. Before 1840, presidential candidates presented a "Cincinnatus-like fiction that they harbored no personal ambition for power--[although] limiting voters' ability to get to know them" (Levitsky and Ziblatt, 2018, p. 194).

7 We discuss this further in our chapter on the **Federal Reserve**.

8 In his 1834 State of the Union message (presented to Congress in written form rather than spoken, following the lead of Thomas Jefferson), Jackson noted that "the last of the debt was discharged, and the Treasury would have a positive balance on January 1, 1835" (Gordon, 1998, pp. 60–61).

9 We briefly discuss the First and Second central bank in our issue on the **Federal Reserve**. Here, we mention that the First Central Bank (1791–1811) was proposed and founded by Alexander Hamilton. Before the Civil War, all corporations (central banks included) were granted fixed-term charters (typically, twenty years) and upon expiration, its performance was assessed, and a renew/not renew decision was rendered.

10 See Gruner (2022, pp. 75–106). In sifting through the criticism against Roosevelt, Gruner noted that "Roosevelt treaded a middle ground between the laissez faire capitalism of Harding and Coolidge and the massive government programs radicals were

advocating. Rather than destroying American Capitalism, Roosevelt may well have saved it" (2022, p. 106).

11 During a press conference upon taking office, President Eisenhower urged that "the objective of tax reduction is an absolutely essential one and must be attained in its proper order…there must be balanced budgets before we are again on a safe and sound system in our economy. That means, to my mind, that we cannot afford to reduce taxes…until we have in sight a program of expenditures that shows that the factors of income and outgo will be balanced" (Gruner, 2022 p. 195). It seemed that Gruner was reading my mind, when in the very next sentence he wrote, "Imagine a President today leveling with the public as Eisenhower did" (Gruner, 2022, p. 195). Yes, imagine.

12 As the CBO notes, the 50-year average of the deficit/GDP ratio is 3.7%, which has been exceeded six times since 1946 (the years during 2009–2012; and 2020, 2021) (CBO, 2023b).

13 'The article 'The Federal Government has Borrowed Trillions, but who owns all that debt?' (2023) provides the statistics on debt ownership in this paragraph and the next.

14 If this paragraph seems like a lot to digest here, we will return to it the **Federal Reserve**.

15 The debt statistics presented here are taken from Congressional Budget Office (2023b).

16 During the late 1990s, defense spending was reduced since "the USA believed it would never have to invest as much in defense as when the USSR was a threat" (Tankersley, 2023). In retrospect, that was ill-advised.

17 Luhby (2023) provides the stats on interest rates.

18 See Gruner (2022, pp. 99–101).

19 Add one more, in 2024 to this tally, making it 99 times.

References

Congressional Budget Office (2023a) 'The Budget and Economics Outlook: 2023 to 2033,' (February) The Budget and Economic Outlook: 2023 to 2033 | (cbo.gov).

Congressional Budget Office (2023b) 'Monthly Budget Review: Summary for Fiscal Year 2023' November 8, Monthly Budget Review: Summary for Fiscal Year 2023 | (cbo.gov).

Dionne, E.J. (2023) 'Poor are Being Held Hostage in the Debt Ceiling Standoff,' *The Washington Post,* (May 21), https://www.washingtonpost.com/opinions

Ellis, Joseph (2000) *The Founding Brothers: The Revolutionary Generation,* Vintage, New York.

Elving, Ron (2021) 'Congress is seeking (its own) permission to borrow another trillion or two,' National Public Radio, September 24, https://www.npr.org

Gordon, John Steele (1998) *Hamilton's Blessing: The Extraordinary Life and Times of Our National Debt,* Penguin, New York.

Gruner, Ronald (2022) *We the Presidents: How American Presidents Shaped the Last Century,* Libratum Books, Naples, Florida.

Hamilton, Alexander (1790) 'First Report on the Public Credit,' communicated to the House of Representatives, National Archives, January 14, (schillerinstitute.com).

Levitsky, Steven and Ziblatt, Daniel (2018) *How Democracies Die,* Broadway Books, New York.

Lofgren, Mike (2023) 'Republicans are Putting our Standard of Living at Risk,' *The New York Times,* May 14, p. 5 (Opinion section).

Luhby, Tami (2023) 'Interest Payments on the Nation's Debt are Soaring, adding pressure to Congress' Spending battle,' (November 16) https://www.cnn.com/2023.

Keynes, John Maynard (1936 [2010]) *The General Theory of Employment, Interest, and Money*, Martino Publishing, Mansfield Centre, Connecticut.

Meacham, Jon (2008) *American Lion: Andrew Jackson in the White House*, Random House, New York.

Office of Management and Budget (2023) *Budget of the US Government*, Budget of the United States Government, Fiscal Year 2023 (whitehouse.gov).

Phillips, Kevin (2002) *Wealth and Democracy*, Broadway Books, New York.

Phillips, Matt (2012) 'The Long Story of U.S. Debt, from 1790 to 2011, in 1 Little Chart,' *The Atlantic,* (November 13). https://www.theatlantic.com/business

Reardon, Jack, Maria Madi, and Molly Scott Cato (2018) *Introducing a New Economics*, Pluto Press, London.

Studenski, Paul and Herman Edward Kross (1951) *Financial History of the United States* BeardBooks, Washington, DC.

Sylla, Richard (1991) 'National Debt' in *The Reader's Companion to American History*, (Eds.) Eric Foner and John A. Garraty, Houghton Mifflin, Boston, pp. 771–776.

Tankersley, Jim (2023) 'How the US Amassed Debt of $31 Trillion, *The New York Times*, January 22, p. 1 and p. 18.

'The Federal Government has Borrowed Trillions, but who owns all that debt?' (2023) Peter G. Peterson Foundation, May 11, (pgpf.org).

Wills, Gary (2003) 'Introduction' in Hamilton, Alexander, James Madison, and John Jay (2003 [1787–1788]) *The Federalist Papers*, Bantam Books, New York, pp. vi–xxvii.

8 The Federal Reserve System: America's Third (and Final?) Central Bank

The Issue: The Federal Reserve's preponderant function is to conduct monetary policy, i.e., use the money supply and interest rates to affect the business cycle (recession/expansion). More specifically during a recession, the Fed stimulates the economy by reducing interest rates; and conversely, during bouts of inflation (like the one we have been experiencing), the Fed increases interest rates to slow down the economy by reducing demand. The Fed's decisions affect us all; and thus, how monetary policy is conducted here in the United States needs to be understood by all.

8.1 Introduction

Thanks to the musical *Hamilton*, most of us know at least a little about Alexander Hamilton: A principal aid to George Washington during the Revolutionary War[1]; co-author of *The Federalist Papers* (the definitive account of our Constitution and highly recommended, by the way); the first Secretary of the Treasury; and more directly related to our purposes here, the architect of the United States' first central bank.[2] These achievements justify a well-deserved membership in America's Founding Fathers (Ellis, 2000).

8.2 The United States' First Two Central Banks[3]

Alexander Hamilton (among others) called for creating a central bank in order for the young nation to stabilize and improve its credit, and to act as a funding source for the federal government. But not everyone agreed. The Bank of England's abuses during the colonial era were still fresh in the minds of many Americans, tilting the opinion away from a central bank of any kind. Sifting through the competing for/against arguments, President George Washington made the affirmative decision, largely persuaded by Hamilton.

The **First Bank of the United States** was established in Philadelphia, Pennsylvania,[4] opening for business, December 12, 1791. It was given a 20-year

DOI: 10.4324/9781003591856-10

charter. This was typical for all corporations in the early 19th century: State governments would issue a charter, usually for 20 years, then renew (or not renew) based on performance,[5] i.e., how closely the firm adhered to its founding principles. In addition, the First Central Bank was the nation's first national chartering. Not surprisingly, it fueled much debate, especially over whether the federal government could charter any corporation, not just a central bank (see **The Judiciary**).

Indeed, "The question of constitutionality had split Washington's cabinet ascribing the formation of political parties to the division that occurred. Federalists favored [it]; Republicans opposed it" (Smith, 1996, p. 441). Although the Federalist position prevailed, when the Bank's charter expired in 1811, the Republicans blocked its renewal (Smith, 1996, p. 441).

Despite the Bank being run efficiently and making a profit, its charter was not renewed. The reasons were as follows:

- The bank was stingy in making loans, thus not fully satisfying the demand for money by entrepreneurs and business owners, even though the state governments at the time issued 80% of the circulating currency.
- The Bank focused on the regional interests of New England, New York, and the mid-Atlantic states, while largely ignoring the rest of the country.
- It was largely dominated by the eastern moneyed and financial interests.
- A visceral distrust by many of the federal government's intrusive role.
- Southern agrarian interests were worried that a national bank would weaken/abolish slavery.

However, the War of 1812 (with England) left the federal government's finances in disarray, not to mention a significant debt, convincing many (even those formally opposed) of the need for a new central bank. The Second Bank of the USA opened in 1816 with a 20-year charter; and like the first, it was located in Philadelphia.

But deeper trouble was brewing. Critics of the Bank (including Thomas Jefferson and James Madison, among the most notable) argued that since the Constitution did not mention a central bank, then its existence was unconstitutional and hence illegal.[6] In the US Supreme Court case McCulloch vs. Maryland (1819), the Court examined this argument and upheld Congress' power to charter the Second Bank.[7]

Despite the Constitutional protection, the Second Bank was not renewed, largely for the same reasons as the First. And, in addition, as we explain in our issue on the **Deficit and the Federal Debt**, President Andrew Jackson's (the United States' seventh president, 1829–1837) idiosyncrasies also played a key role. Briefly: Running for president, Jackson vowed that if elected president, he would not renew the bank's charter, and he would eliminate the entire **federal debt**.[8] President Jackson kept both promises.

From 1836 until 1913, the United States was without a central bank—the longest span in our history.[9] The United States was on the **gold standard** for most of this time, which, as we later explain, limited the amount of money in circulation. This resulted in a semi-permanent state of **deflation,** peppered **by recessions** and **unemployment,** especially after the Civil War.

The nation also experienced frequent bank panics during this time. (The federal government's guarantee of bank deposits, i.e., The Federal Deposit Insurance Corporation, would not be implemented until 1933.) Thus, if a bank was experiencing problems, i.e., short of cash, and word got out, a stampede of anxious customers would camp out at the bank, hoping to be the first to get their money, hence a bank panic. And since bank panics effectively withdrew money from the economy, they often precipitated a **recession**.

8.3   The Federal Reserve System

Such a panic happened in October 1907, with a run on the Knickerbocker Trust Company, which, in turn, contracted the money supply, sending the economy into a recession. The federal government was forced to borrow from some America's richest citizens in order to pay its bills. The distasteful spectacle (at least to some) created a hullabaloo (yes, people still use this word) Imagine today, if the federal government, short on cash, tried to borrow from Bill Gates or Warren Buffet. As a reaction, Congress passed the Federal Reserve Act (December 23, 1913) creating the Federal Reserve System. This was the United States' third central bank; still in existence today, and easily the longest.[10]

The architects of the Fed assiduously studied the failures of the first two central banks to ensure that the failures would not repeat. So instead of just one central bank (remember the regional interests of the first two central banks), the 1913 Act created 12 central banks—one for each geographical region of the United States.[11] Each of the 12 is semi-autonomous, basing money supply decisions on regional needs; but at the same time, each is part of a system—the Federal Reserve System.

Take a look at the face of a one-dollar bill. To the left of George Washington is a circle centered with an upper-case letter, designating one of the 12 banks (starting from the east, Boston, i.e., A; and ending in the west, San Francisco, i.e., L). Notice the wording encircling the letter: 'The Federal Reserve Bank of…'. So, for example, for A, we have the Federal Reserve Bank of Boston, indicating that the Boston bank (one of the 12) is part of a system—the Federal Reserve System.

When the Federal Reserve was created in 1913, each of the 12 banks was given a 20-year charter, with the option of renewal upon expiration. But, given the favorable macro-economic conditions during the early 1920s, especially the inflation rate,[12] and remembering that the first two banks were not renewed, Congress decided to take the initiative. Buoyed by the public's relatively positive view of the Fed, Congress passed the McFadden Act, February 25, 1927. The Act[13] recharted each of the 12 banks seven years ahead of schedule and into perpetuity. And, interestingly, "if Congress had waited to renew the Federal Reserve's charters [in 1934], the debate over renewal would have occurred during the Great Depression. The decision may have been different, and the Federal Reserve as we know it today may not exist" (Richardson et al., 2013).

Overseeing the 12 banks is the Board of Directors (comprised of seven members).[14] The Board's chair does not necessarily have to come from Board, but like other Board members, he/she[15] is nominated by the United States president and confirmed by the Senate.[16] The Chair serves a four-year term, with option for renewal, while the other Board members serve staggered 14-year terms. Jerome Powell, currently chair, was appointed in 2018 and then re-appointed in 2022. His term expires in 2026, with option for renewal.[17]

In terms of race and gender, today's Board is the most diversified, although ideologically, all members (past and present) are restricted to the center, with a concomitant expertise in law, economics, and/or banking.

While the Board provides an overall vision for monetary policy (i.e., whether it should be expansive or restrictive), the Federal Open Market Committee (FOMC) conducts the day-to-day monetary policy. Based at the Federal Reserve Bank of New York, it is comprised of the seven members of the Board of Directors, plus five of the presidents of the 12 central banks, selected on a rotating basis (for a one-year term). The president of the Federal Reserve Bank of New York is accorded a permanent position on the FOMC, given the importance of Wall Street and the financial sector. Currently, the FOMC's chair is Jerome Powell.

The Fed is a creature of Congress. It was created in 1913 and Congress can amend/abolish it. Congress does not interfere in the Fed's day-to-day operations. Nevertheless, presidents sometimes cajole and influence the Fed, especially if increasing interest rates threatens a recession. Presidents Nixon and Trump come to mind; the latter stating that he will not reappoint Jerome Powell if elected when his term expires in 2026.

8.4   Monetary Policy

Monetary policy is conducted by the FOMC and the Fed's Board of Directors. Without getting too technical, it consists of raising/lowering interest rates (i.e., the cost of borrowing money) and reducing/increasing the amount of money, to influence the economy. More specifically, the Fed targets the federal funds rate (FFR), i.e., the interest rate on a loan from one bank to another.[18] As the FFR increases/decreases so do all other interest rates that affect you and I (at least those that are not fixed) such as mortgage rates, rates on automobile loans, and credit cards.

To stimulate the economy, the Fed will lower the FFR, which reduces the cost of borrowing between banks, and which reduces other interest rates. Lower rates will encourage the purchase of 'big ticket' items like automobiles, real estate, and housing and will encourage businesses to invest since the cost of borrowing has decreased. In addition, increased domestic demand will increase business optimism, incentivizing businesses to invest. As interest rates are lowered, the money supply increases.

Conversely, if the Fed wants to reduce inflation, it will increase the FFR, which in turn increases the costs of inter-bank borrowing, and the public's borrowing costs, thus reducing the demand for big ticket items, and disincentivizing business investment. Increasing interest rates acts like a brake on the economy, slowing it down, while reducing interest rates lets loose the brake, stimulating the economy.

If you think that raising interest rates is a blunt and callous stick to wield against **inflation**—after all, the newly unemployed had nothing to do causing the inflation, but they obviously suffer the brunt—then you are right. At least for us, it underscores the importance of taking special care to prevent the occurrence of inflation in the first place.

The Fed's annual target for the inflation rate is not 0%, as most people would assume, but 2%. This is because the Consumer Price Index (CPI), the methodology commonly used to calculate the rate of **inflation,** overestimates the actual rate. More specifically, the CPI assumes a fixed basket of goods and services over a period of years that the average consumer will buy. Prices are then tracked, and if the average level of prices increases from one year to the next, then we have inflation; and likewise, if the average level of prices decreases, then we have deflation. But as a good's price increases, usually, consumers would substitute away; and conversely, substitute toward if the good's price decreases. However, the CPI methodology doesn't account for any substitution. Thus, the inflation methodology overestimates the rate of inflation. In addition, since the Fed considers **deflation** to be a worse problem than inflation (once begun, deflation is more difficult to extricate from), a two percent goal gives the Fed a bit of a cushion.[19]

In addition to its preponderant objective of conducting monetary policy, the Fed also conducts several other key functions,[20] all designed to ensure that the United States monetary system runs smoothly: Maintain accounts for depository institutions; transfer funds electronically, foster financial payments and settlements safely and efficiently; collect checks; distribute and receive currency and coin; and act as the U.S. government's fiscal agent, i.e., the 'government's bank.'

8.5   The Difference between Fiscal and Monetary Policy

Fiscal policy is using government spending and/or tax rates to affect the business cycle. Given a recession, government spending can be increased, and tax rates can be decreased. Fiscal policy is conducted by Congress (the Senate and the House of Representatives) and the president. A preponderant difference between fiscal and monetary policy is that citizens directly elect the people conducting fiscal policy, whereas officials conducting the latter are not directly elected by the voters. Perhaps this is why the members of the Board are not exactly household names, and most Americans are not able to name the Fed chair, never mind the other Board members. The Fed offers the following reasons for this asymmetry.

- Monetary policy is complex and thus, the purview of expertise.
- Since inflation-reducing policies are painful for most citizens, not directly electing members of the Fed insulates them from political pressure.
- Directly electing members would create a pro-cyclical monetary policy around elections, i.e., lowering interest rates and increasing the money supply, creating an inflationary bias. (But the same argument could also be made that fiscal policy creates an election cycle pro-cyclical bias, resulting in ever-increasing deficits.) [21]
- Officials conducting fiscal policy will campaign on what they promise to do (or against that of others) rather than on their knowledge and expertise. However, officials conducting monetary policy are appointed for their monetary expertise and (usually) not on the basis of what they will or will not do.
- Officials conducting fiscal policy need no qualification other than the age/citizenship requirements specificized in the Constitution,[22] whereas monetary officials typically need to have demonstrated subject proficiency. Requiring any set of credentials to conduct the business of government by elected representatives was rejected as fomenting an elitism, something that the Constitution was designed to prevent.[23]

8.6   Recent Monetary Policy

To combat the recent bout of **inflation,** which began in March 2021, the Fed began raising the federal funds rate in March 2022, which, as explained earlier, increased other interest rates. The Fed hoped that higher borrowing costs would reduce the demand for goods/services, turn slowing the economy. Since March 2022, the Fed has increased the FFR 11 times, to 5.25–5.50%, the highest level since the early late 1970s/early1980s. As this manuscript goes to press, the inflation rate has decreased to 2.4%, still higher than the Fed's preferred optimal of 2%.

The Fed's objective in conducting monetary policy during **inflation** is to engineer a 'soft landing,' i.e., raise interest rates just enough to reduce economic activity so that inflation is subdued without causing a **recession**. This is very tricky, and quite often the Fed will overshoot, causing significant unemployment and a recession, as happened in 2001 and 2007.

The Fed's massive stimulus during the two most recent recessions (December 2007–June 2009 and February 2020–April 2020) has increased its size and importance.[24] This is evidenced by the explosion of the Fed's balance sheet

(Board of Governors of the Federal Reserve System 2024b). Due to the severity of the 2007–2009 recession, the Fed engaged in quantitative easing (QE), an unconventional[25] monetary policy, "largely untested (outside of Japan) ... never before been used on a such a widespread scale" (Carlin and Soskice, 2015, p. 486). Under QE, the Fed would purchase assets (at par value), especially more risky assets, such as mortgage-backed securities (MBS),[26] along with more traditional assets, such as mortgages.[27] The Fed would assume ownership of the assets while crediting electronically the reserves of the banks and individuals, i.e., the sellers.

The following reasons explain why the Fed implemented QE:

- It was thought that the traditional tools of monetary policy (reducing interest rates and increasing the money supply) would not work, given each recession's severity. (Actually by 2008, the Fed had reduced the FFR to practically zero.)
- Purchasing MBS would increase their value and help rescue the balance sheets of banks who bought these bonds liberally and foolishly. Specifically, increased purchases would increase their price, which, in turn, would increase the value of the bank's assets. Similarly, asset purchases from individuals would increase their income which would help stimulate aggregate demand. For individuals/banks who did not sell, the increased asset prices would increase wealth, thus bolstering their balance sheet. (Economic theory posits that wealth is positively correlated to consumer spending.) And finally, since an MBS is a bond, interest rates should decrease as prices increase (bond prices and interest rates are inversely correlated). Lower interest rates, it was assumed, would stimulate both consumption and investment.

A direct (and important) consequence of QE was an explosion in the Fed's balance sheet,[28] from just under $1 trillion in 2001 to $9 trillion in June 2022 (Federal Reserve System 2024b). Given the easing of inflation, in June 2022, the Fed has ceased QE, while implementing QT (i.e., quantitative tightening) which essentially works the opposite of QE. QT policy is conducted to reduce the Fed's balance sheet. It is now at $7 trillion as the manuscript goes to press,[29] still significantly more than in 2001. It is not clear how much more the Fed's balance sheet will be reduced.

For some, the exploding balance sheet is an inevitable result of the necessity of ending two recessions; for others, it is unpalatable.

8.7 Time to Reconceptualize the Central Bank's Role

In this book, we have consistently argued that the great transformational changes that are upon us now (**Artificial Intelligence**, sustainability, and the transition to **Net Zero**) will radically change how we live, how we work, and what/how we produce and consume. This will require a revolution in our thinking to develop workable solutions that transcend traditional silo-based thinking.

One potential change that we should take seriously is a reconceptualized central bank. Heretofore, in most Western countries, the central bank has been tasked with regulating the money supply and interest rates in order to achieve a limited set of objectives. Monetary policy is inserted into "a conservative schema" whose decision makers "decide among themselves the best way to use immense amounts of public resources" (Piketty, 2022, p. 241 and p. 242).

But the transition to **Net Zero** alone is expected to cost $275 trillion of cumulative investments just in physical assets by 2050 (Montgomery and Van Clieaf, 2023, p. 3). Where is the money to come from?

A central bank (e.g., our Fed) is the most logical supplier. Our money supply isn't chained to any physical commodity like gold, and as we argued in our chapter on **gold standard**, neither should it be. Creating money is all done electronically, which the central bank can create without limits. To bolster such thinking, Stephanie Kelton in her book (2020) presents Modern Monetary Theory (MMT), whose central tenet is that a sovereign nation (i.e., a money issuer, like the USA) "doesn't have to manage [its] budgets as a household would. They can use their currency-issuing capacity to pursue policies aimed at maintaining a full employment economy" (Kelton, 2020, p. 19).

That doesn't mean that we should always maintain an open spigot, for inflation is an important economic and social problem that we should always guard against. As we argued in our chapter on **inflation**, inflation is determined by the relationship between the money supply *and* the amount of goods and services. If the latter is increasing more than the former, then inflation will not be problematic; if the former is increasing more than the latter, then it is time to stop the money creation. Thus,

> so long as there is no substantial increase in consumer prices, there is no solid reason not to increase the money supply if it enables us to finance useful policies such as the struggle for full employment, a guaranteed job, the thermal insulation of buildings, or public investments in health care, education, and renewable energy.
>
> (Piketty, 2022, p. 240)

Indeed, imagine,

> A just and more prosperous world—one that combines ecological sustainability with full employment, human well-being, a lower degree of inequality, and excellent public services that meets the needs of all of—is within reach. As we collectively expand our understanding of public money…we can build a better economy, one that works for all of our people.
>
> (Kelton, 2020, p. 260)

Granted, the obstacles to reconceptualizing the Fed's role are formidable, especially given the assiduous effort made by many Western central banks to cultivate a reputation of independence, steering away from governmental pressure (Carlin and Soskice, 2015, p. 175). But keep in mind that Congress has twice abolished our central bank. There is no reason that the Fed could not be reconceptualized to comport with the recommendations of Piketty/Kelton.[30] Perhaps for starters, we can rethink the composition of the Fed's Board of Governors. Yes, we want expertise, but also a broader membership with an interest in solving the formidable transformations that lie ahead, so that all can benefit.

Notes

1 We are tempted to add that he was born illegitimate, which he was, but that invidiously sullies Hamilton. Obviously, he cannot control when he was born or who his parents were, but he can control (somewhat) what happens later.

2 We tell the story of Hamilton's untimely death in a duel with Aaron Burr, Thomas Jefferson's vice-president, in our chapter on **The Deficit and the Debt.**

3 These two central banks merit discussion since the architects of the current Federal Reserve had learned from their failures, and designed the Fed so that the failures would not repeat.

4 Philadelphia was the nation's capital from 1790 to 1800; after which Washington DC became the capital. New York City served as the nation's capital from 1785 to 1790.

5 This would change in the second half of the 19th century, as state governments responsible for the issuing of charters were more wont (due to business lobbying) to grant charters in perpetuity, rendering corporations largely free from state oversight. For a discussion see (Korten, 1996). Also see our **Big Tech** chapter for a discussion of resuscitating this notion of state/federal chartering.

6 Although Article One, Section 8, of the USA Constitution gives Congress "the right to coin money and regulate the value thereof," the Constitution does not mention anything about a central bank. Here, Article #10 of the Bill of Rights is apropos: "The powers not delegated to the United States by the Constitution, nor prohibited by it to the States, are reserved to the States respectively, or to the people." In the above case, the state of Maryland decided to tax the Bank, which the Supreme Court eventually ruled unconstitutional.

7 We discuss this case in our chapter, **the Judiciary**.

8 The two decisions are intricately related and will be discussed in our issue on the **Deficit and the Debt.**

9 For a detailed history, see Studenski and Krooss (1951).

10 For a history of the Fed, see (Wheellock, 2021).

11 It was assumed that each region's economy significantly differed from the others. The location of the twelve central banks was also a function of the density of population at the time. Only three banks: Kansas City, Dallas, and San Francisco are west of the Mississippi River, while Minneapolis, more or less, straddles it.

12 Inflation annually increased in double digits from 1917 to 1920, followed by deflation in 1921 and 1922. Then, in 1923 the inflation rate stabilized at 1.8%, dipping to 0.0% in 1924 (hinting at deflation), 2.3% in 1924, and 1.1% in 1926. Stable prices helped sway public opinion in favor of the newly formed Fed, helping to pass the McFadden Act Source: ('Historical Inflation Rates: 1914–2024' (2024).

13 The Act permitted national banks to operate multiple branches, while prohibiting interstate banking. For a full discussion see Preston (1927), Rajan and Ramcharan (2012), and Studenski and Krooss (1951, p. 336).

14 For an overview, see Federal Reserve System (2021).

15 Of the 16 Fed chairs since 1913, only one was a woman: Janet Yellen (2014–2018) who is currently the United States' Treasury Secretary, as this manuscript goes to press in July 2024. Yellen was nominated as Chair by President Obama, February 3, 2014. Trump did not re-appoint her when her term expired in 2018—unusual given that chairs are (or, at least have been) routinely reappointed regardless of the administration's ideology. No good reason existed, other than that Trump did not get along with her personally, and that the Fed's raising interest rates jeopardized his economic policies. She was replaced by the current chair Jerome Powell, who was re-appointed by President Biden in 2022. Source: Board of Governors of the Federal Reserve System (2024a.)

16 This is intended to provide "a measure of political control" (Piketty, 2014, p. 724).

17 The chair serves concurrently as a member of the Board. Mr. Powell initially was appointed to the Board on May 25, 2012, to fill an unexpired term. He was reappointed and sworn in on June 16, 2014, for a term ending January 31, 2028.

18 The Fed maintains a target for the FFR using open market operations (i.e., the buying/selling of government debt). In a sense, the FFR measures the availability of funds that banks can use to make loans. If the FFR falls beneath the target, the Fed can reduce the amount of funds, thereby raising the FFR. The Fed reduces the amount of funds by selling government bonds to the largest banks, which decreases their reserves. Conversely, if the FFR rises above the targeted range, the Fed will do the opposite.

19 We will discuss this in our **Inflation** chapter.

20 Source: Federal Reserve System (2021).

21 We make this argument in our chapter on the **Deficit/Debt.**

22 According to the US Constitution (Article I, Section 3, par. 3) no direct qualifications for the Senate are imposed except "a senator…shall have attained to the age of thirty years, and been nine years a citizen of the United States…and when elected, be an inhabitant of that state for which he shall be chosen." And likewise for a member of House of Representatives (who from the get-go were directly elected by the people): "a representative …shall have attained the age of twenty-five years, and been seven years a citizen of the United States" (Article I, Section 1, par. 2). Pertaining to the latter, Alexander Hamilton urged "the door ought to be equally open to all" Hamilton et al. (2003 [1787–1788], #36, p. 203).

23 The 17th Amendment passed May 13, 1913, enabled the people to vote for their senators. Before passage, the senators were selected by their respective state legislatures. The Founding Fathers assumed that this would offset the potential irrationality and exuberance in the House of Representatives, whose members would be directly elected by the people.

24 One wonders of a maximum limit to what the Fed could purchase, and thus its ultimate size. Piketty answers: "the central banks could decide to buy all of a country's firms and real estate, finance the transition to renewable energy, invest in universities, and take control of the entire economy. Clearly the problem is that the central banks are not well suited to such activities and lack the democratic legitimacy to try them" (Piketty, 2014, p. 717).

25 QE is unconventional because, "the policy lever it uses is different to that used in modern-inflation targeting regimes, which adjust short-term interest rates to influence aggregate demand" (Carlin and Soskice, 2015, p. 486).

26 A MBS is a bond with "cash flows tied to the principal and interest payments on a pool of underlying mortgages" (Fuster et al., 2022, p. 1).

27 Most of us are familiar with how a traditional mortgage works: Once approved, the bank will set the terms with the borrower, i.e., principal, repayment schedule, and interest rate, based on the borrower's risk. If any changes occur with the borrower, then the lender can adjust the terms as necessary, even foreclosing, if need be. A MBS works differently: it combines groupings of mortgages into one saleable asset. In so doing it "decouples mortgage lending from mortgage investing" (Fuster et al., 2022, p. 1). Problematically, an MBS obscures the underlying risk of individual mortgages by tying them together. This was done, at least theoretically, to reduce the asset's overall risk. The Fed began raising interest rates in December 2005, increasing the vulnerability of the most marginal borrowers. As word and knowledge spread, demand for MBS plunged, reducing the balance sheets of banks who had purchased such assets; and the wealth of individuals who had done so. The effects cascaded into widespread reduced demand and falling prices, which plunged the United States into recession. There were lots of blames to go around: government policies, Wall Street, rating agencies, the mortgage industry, and mortgage borrowers. For a good discussion of the connection between the MBS, the housing crisis, and the 2007–2009 recession, see Gruner (2022, pp. 454–475).

28 See Federal Reserve Board (2024).

29 For a helpful discussion of QE and QT see (Wessel, 2024).

30 The Fed in its current form, certainly has its detractors. See Paul (2010), Greider (1989), Griffin (2010), and Rothbard (2021). For a good discussion of the criticism against the Fed since its inception, see Wikipedia contributors (2024).

References

Board of Governors of the Federal Reserve System (2024a) 'Board of Governors Members, 1914- Present,' (federalreserve.gov).

Board of Governors of the Federal Reserve System (2024b) 'Credit and Liquidity Programs and the Balance Sheet' (federalreserve.gov).

Carlin, Wendy and David Soskice (2015) *Macroeconomics: Institutions, Instability, and the Financial System*, Oxford University Press, Oxford, UK.

Ellis, Joseph (2000) *The Founding Brothers: The Revolutionary Generation*, Vintage, New York.

Federal Reserve System (2021) 'The Fed Explained: What the Central Bank Does,' 11th ed., (federalreserve.gov).

Fuster, Andreas, David Lucca, and James Vickery (2022) 'Mortgage-Backed Securities,' *Federal Reserve Bank of New York Staff Reports*, no. 1001, February, sr1001.pdf (newyorkfed.org).

Greider, William (1989) *Secrets of the Temple: How the Federal Reserve Runs the Country*, Simon & Schuster, New York.

Griffin, G. Edward (2010) *The Creature from Jekyll Island: A Second Look at the Federal Reserve*, 5th ed., American Media, New York.

'Historical Inflation Rates: 1914–2024' (2024) (usinflationcalculator.com).

Kelton, Stephanie (2020) *The Deficit Myth: Modern Monetary Theory and the Birth of the People's Economy*, Public Affairs, New York.

Korten, David C. (1996) *When Corporations Rule the World*, Berrett-Koehler, San Francisco.

Montgomery, John and Mark Van Clieaf (2023) *Net Zero Business Models: Winning in the Global Net Zero Economy*, Wiley, New York.

Paul, Ron (2010) *End the Fed*, Grand Central Publishing, New York.

Piketty, Thomas (2014) *Capital in the Twenty-First Century*, Belknap Press of Harvard University Press, Cambridge, Massachusetts; translated by Arthur Goldhammer.

Piketty, Thomas (2022) *A Brief History of Equality*, Belknap Press, Harvard University.

Preston, Howard (1927) 'The McFadden Banking Act,' *American Economic Review*, Vol. 17, No. 2, pp. 201–218.

Rajan, Raghuram G., and Rodney Ramcharan (2012) 'Constituencies and Legislation: The Fight Over the McFadden Act of 1927,' Finance and Economics Discussion Series 2012-61, Divisions of Research & Statistics and Monetary Affairs, Federal Reserve Board, Washington, DC.

Richardson, Gary, Daniel Park, Alejandro Komai, and Michael Gou (2013) 'McFadden Act of 1927' *Federal Reserve History,* November 22, https://www.federalreservehistory.org/essay

Rothbard, Murray (2021) *The Case Against the Fed*, Ludwig von Mises Institute, Auburn Alabama.

Wessel, David (2024) 'How Will the Federal Reserve Decide When to End Quantitative Tightening?' *Brookings Commentary*, June 4, https://www.brookings.edu/article

Wheellock, David C. (2021) 'Overview: The History of the Federal Reserve,' *Federal Reserve History,* https://www.federalreservehistory.org/essays

Wikipedia contributors (2024) 'Criticism of the Federal Reserve,' In *Wikipedia, The Free Encyclopedia*. June 4, Retrieved July 11, 2024, https://en.wikipedia.org/w/index.php?title=Criticism_of_the_Federal_Reserve&oldid=1232969888

9 Abortion and Reproductive Rights

The Issue: Here in America, no other issue galvanizes the conflict between personal choice, the rule of law, and the general welfare of society like abortion. Since the 1970s, abortion has been "the most controversial political issue in the country" (Gordon, 1991, p. 103). Abortion juxtaposes the rights of the newborn, the rights of the pregnant mother, and the rights of society. Whose rights are preponderant? Who has jurisdiction? Must abortion rights be an 'either/or,' winner take all? The parties in the abortion debate have long since ossified their intransigence with seemingly little room for compromise; not to mention understanding and dialogue. Our objective here is to understand the positions in order to map a way forward.

9.1 Preface: The Process of Determining Reproductive Rights

The Constitution written in 1787 does not specifically address today's problems (Artificial Intelligence, abortion, climate change, Big Tech, surveillance capitalism, etc.) at all. So how should the Court rule on a case with no specific Constitutional reference.[1] Two theories: Originalism, i.e., stick to the meaning/intent of the founders with (2) judges interpret the Constitution, not according to its language, but according to evolving societal standards rewrite, "i.e., a living consitution."

9.2 Historical Context

While today we tend to separate contraception from abortion, historically both were part and parcel of a continuum of an overall mechanism of controlling reproduction. Such a continuum has "characterized virtually all societies of which we have written records" (Gordon, 1991, p. 99).

DOI: 10.4324/9781003591856-11

Here in the United States, abortion has existed since colonial days; it was legal under common law, and before the Civil War, it was uncontroversial,

> people made self-conscious decisions about managing their own fertility on a household and community level, not meditated by doctors, medicines, and new technologies...reproduction in the colonial era was in every way women's work: thinking about pregnancy, birthing, child care, early childhood, and infant care was a landscape of women, their neighbors, and their midwives.
>
> (Aggarwal-Schifellite, 2022)

But during the late 19th century, as abortion was becoming more widespread (with one abortion for every four live births—a ratio similar to today's) (Mohr, 1991, p. 3) opposition began to solidify, largely due to concern over falling birthrates, growing distaste over abortionists' explicit advertising in newspapers; and a growing backlash against a nascent women's right movement with their concomitant neglect of traditional domestic roles (Gordon, 1991, p. 99). In addition, during the late 19th century, the American Medical Association (formed in 1847) began to control medical services by professionalizing both demand and supply, the latter by stifling competitors, many of whom were abortion providers.

By the end of the 19th century, these oppositional factors coalesced to drive abortion services underground. And, as is typical in such situations, while the wealthy could access/afford abortion services, the poor could not, and were forced to find less than palatable providers. Predictably, a political backlash arose over abortion restrictions, so that "...by 1918, birth control leagues [had] developed in every major American city" (Gordon, 1991, p. 101)

During the mid-20th century, primarily due to global concerns over overpopulation, state governments in the United States began calling for a repeal of regulations proscribing abortion. Planned Parenthood, formed in 1942, "originally advocated family stability and neo-Malthusian population control as a cure for poverty" (Gordon, 1991, p. 102). It was not until the 1960s that Planned Parenthood would become a major pro-abortion player. In addition, it was realized that abortion, if done under the proper conditions, was a lot safer than underground.

While the 1960s saw an explosive demand for individual rights, especially from the marginalized and from those whose voices had not been heard, a backlash occurred among conservatives who decried the decrease in law and order, decaying moral standards, and the decline of the traditional paternalistic family. For these conservatives, the increasingly visibility of women's rights and the call for abortion exemplified this decline. This conservative backlash, in turn, helped elect Richard Nixon as President in 1968.

The 1960s ossified the contours of the abortion debate's two main opponents, with ostensibly little hope for compromise. On one side is the Right to Life movement which has sought to protect unborn fetuses; along with the Catholic Church which saw abortion as murder. On the other side, a renewed women's liberation[2] aided by Planned Parenthood, which has shifted reproductive control politics away from family planning and population control to women's self-determination.

While several states began reversing their anti-abortion laws during the 1960s, there was no legislation passed at the federal level, despite attempts to do so. The lack of legislative success would later come back to haunt pro-abortionists.

9.3   Roe v Wade

In 1973, the US Supreme Court, in *Roe v. Wade*,[3] ruled in a 7-2 majority[4] that women could abort in the first trimester.[5] Three months was considered the threshold above which the fetus could be viable outside the womb, and as such, the state had a right in protecting it, whereas before three months, the fetus was the mother's prerogative. Thus, a compromise was struck between the rights of the mother and the right of the state in protecting a viable human being.

Roe v. Wade was "certainly one of the most controversial cases in the Court's history" (Roe v. Wade, 1991). The case was rooted in the constitutional right to privacy formally enshrined in *Griswold v. Connecticut*, 381 U.S. 479 (1965), i.e., that the state could not prohibit married couples from using contraceptives.[6] In turn, this case was based on the US Constitution's 14th Amendment, and explicitly its due process provision, "nor shall any State deprive any person of life, liberty, or property, without due process of law."

Although *Roe v. Wade* ostensibly granted the long sought-after right to an abortion, in retrospect the case "had not resolved the issue at all. Instead, [it] became a rallying point for an emerging New Right coalition that would continue to gain momentum" (Evans, 2003, p. 112).

After *Roe v. Wade*, increasing grassroots opposition made abortion the most severely polarizing issue in American politics, and one of the defining issues of the New Right.[7] Right-wing politicians "at all levels of government began imposing restrictions on accessing abortion, which in turn [generated fears amongst abortion supporters] that Roe v. Wade could be overturned" (Evans, 2023, pp. 182, and 214). Abortion in America became a "divisive and intensely emotional public issue" and has since "quickly evolved into a litmus test for liberals and conservatives" (Roe v. Wade, 1991, p. 952).

In 1992, the Supreme Court in *Planned Parenthood of Pennsylvania v. Casey*,[8] reaffirmed the right to abortion, but declared that the state's interest in fetal life was present from the moment of conception. And, in addition, "Casey authorized states to impose waiting periods and informed consent requirements. Roe and Casey fit neatly into a long line of decisions protecting from government intrusion a wealth of private choices about family matters, child rearing, intimate relationships, and procreation."[9]

Since the late 1970s, abortion opposition has become increasingly violent, especially against the property of abortion providers. Motivated by religious fundamentalism, such violence is an extension of the broader spectrum of far-right violence, ideologically motivated to restore values/practices considered to be part of the USA's historical heritage (Perliger, 2020, p. 28).

In addition, Evangelicals, "who have come to play an increasingly important role in the far fight and Republican politics, view abortion not as a difficult moral choice but as an assault on Women's God-given role, on the family, and on Christian America itself" (Du Mez and Kobes, 2020, p. 69). In the United States, "increased violence against abortion clinics has accompanied a growth in hate crimes overall and a greater tolerance for overt expressions of prejudice" (Evans, 2003, p. 183).

9.4   Dobbs v. Jackson Women's Health Organization

Almost immediately, Roe v. Wade's passage set in motion efforts to overturn it. The effort finally succeeded in 2022, in the Court's *Dobbs v. Jackson Women's Health Organization*.[10] In 2018, the state of Mississippi (where Jackson is based and the state's only abortion provider) outlawed abortions after 15 weeks. Jackson Women's sued. Both a federal court and district sided with Jackson Women's. The state of Mississippi sued, effectively sending the case to the Supreme Court. Thomas Dobbs, by the way, is the chief health officer at the Mississippi State Department of Health.

In a 6-3 majority, the Court ruled that the right to abortion was not provided for by the 14th Amendment. Justice Alito wrote the majority opinion,

> We hold that *Roe* and *Case*y must be overruled. The Constitution makes no reference to abortion, and no such right is implicitly protected by any constitutional provision, including the one on which the defenders of *Roe* and *Casey* now chiefly rely—the Due Process Clause of the Fourteenth Amendment. That provision has been held to guarantee some rights that are not mentioned in the Constitution, but any such right must be "deeply rooted in this Nation's history and tradition" and "implicit in the concept of ordered liberty. Abortion presents a profound moral question. The Constitution does not prohibit the citizens of each State from regulating or prohibiting abortion. *Roe* and *Casey* arrogated that authority. We now overrule those decisions and return that authority to the people and their elected representatives.[11]

The majority adheres to the principle of originalism which we discuss in **The Supreme Court**. In addition to directly criticizing the majority opinion, the Dissent, jointly written by Justices Stephen Breyer,[12] Sonia Sotomayor, and Elena Kagan, noted,

> Abortion is a common medical procedure and a familiar experience in women's lives. About 18 percent of pregnancies in this country end in abortion, and about one quarter of American women will have an abortion before the age of 45. Those numbers reflect the predictable and life-changing effects of carrying a pregnancy, giving birth, and becoming a parent. As *Casey* understood, people today rely on their ability to control and time pregnancies when making countless life decisions: where to live, whether and how to invest in education or careers, how to allocate financial resources, and how to approach intimate and family relationships.

In addition, the Dissent noted that *Dobbs* will directly affect women economically,

> The ability of women to participate equally in the life of the Nation—in all its economic, social, political, and legal aspects have been facilitated by their ability to control their reproductive lives. Without the ability to decide whether and when to have children, women could not—in the way men took for granted—determine how they would live their lives, and how they would contribute to the society around them. But, by taking away the right to abortion, as the majority does today, destroys all those individual plans and expectations. In so doing, it diminishes women's opportunities to participate fully and equally in the Nation's political, social, and economic life. Abortion availability has large effects on women's education, labor force participation, occupations, and earnings.

This is important given the nexus between self-determination over reproductive rights and the self-empowerment of women. The modern-day reincarnation[13] is over

> women's agency, whereby women are no longer the passive recipients of welfare enhancing help, women are seen by men as well as women, as active promoters of change: the dynamic promoters of social transformations that can alter the lives of both women and men.
>
> (Sen, 1999, p. 189; emphasis in original excised)

Dobbs presents a double blow for women: First, the insistence of originalism[14] to decide a case, when, at the time the Constitution was written, women were politically treated as a non-entity with no voice in political life,

> the Constitution was drafted by fifty-five men in 1787. As it happens, there is also nothing at all in that document, which sets out fundamental law,

about pregnancy… There is nothing in that document about women at all. Most consequentially, there were no women among the delegates to the Constitutional Convention. There were no women among the hundreds of people who participated in ratifying conventions in the states. There were no women judges. There were no women legislators. At the time, women could neither hold office nor run for office (except in New Jersey, and then only fleetingly). Legally, most women did not exist as persons.

(Lepore, 2022)

The second blow was the decoupling of self-determination, reproductive rights, and the ability to participate freely in the economic life of the nation. Just like in the late 19th century when attempts were made to restrict abortion access, the effects of Dobbs, as the Dissent notes,

will be felt most severely, as they always have been, on the bodies of the poor. The history of state abortion restrictions is a history of heavy costs exacted from the most vulnerable women… The State will greatly restrict abortion care without addressing any of the financial, health, and family need that motivate many women to seek it.

Indeed, in a nation as wealthy as the United States, we should put "our money where our mouth is and support life by ensuring that no child is poor [while] helping pregnancies become intentional and safer [and] offering free paternal leave and free childcare" (Desmond, 2023, pp. 154–155). Any one of these would go a long way in supporting life in all its fullness, but each requires a functional Congress, which lately, has been anything but.

Additionally, as the *Dobbs* Dissent notes "since *Roe*, nothing has changed to support what the majority does today. Neither law nor facts nor attitudes have provided any new reasons to reach a different result than *Roe* and *Casey* did. All that has changed is this Court."[15] But the Court isn't finished, as the Dissent in Dobbs warned, "we cannot understand how anyone can be confident that today's opinion will be the last of its kind." More specifically, "if the Fourteenth Amendment did not protect abortion, the other civil rights it protected were on the table, including interracial gay marriage, the right to contraception, and perhaps even desegregation" (Richardson, 2023, pp. 158, 250). Look for a Court assault on all of these rights, which many had thought ensconced in the constitutional law.

9.5   Conclusion

Will the United States follow France's lead becoming the first nation to make abortion a constitutional right, which it did March 4, 2024? Most likely not, given that "the French are among the strongest supporters of the legal right to abortion, with 82% in favor, far ahead of the…55% in America" (*The Economist*,

March 9, 2024, p. 48). And it is extremely unlikely that abortion advocates can meet America's constitutional requirement for approving amendments. With the *Dobbs* ruling, abortion rights advocates can either pursue state legislation, or lobby Congress to enact a law supporting abortion. As this book goes to press, the first is being enacted, while we will have to wait on the second. For women who desire an abortion, there is only one option: To pursue abortion services at the state level, which as the Dissent in *Dobbs*, noted calls into question both issues of safety and equity. Currently in the United States, 14 states have near total abortion bans, while four states ban abortion after six weeks of pregnancy.

In the interests of a livable, viable democracy, we need to resolve where to draw the line, a line that equally respects all parties: Mother, unborn, and society. But with such a dysfunctional Congress, this is indeed a herculean task.

Notes

1 For further discussion, see our chapter on **The Supreme Court**; and for one of the earliest cases—a central bank—see our chapter on the **Federal Reserve**.
2 Known as Second Wave Feminism, it developed in the United States and western Europe out of the Civil Rights and antiwar movements as women were disillusioned with their own second-rate status even among such activists.
3 The full citation is *Jane Roe et al. v. Henry Wade*, District Attorney of Dallas, 410 US 113 (1973).
4 Justices William Rehnquist and Byron White dissented, while Harry Blackmun wrote the majority opinion.
5 Roe, i.e., Norma McCorvey, filed a lawsuit challenging Texas' law of allowing an abortion only when the mother's life was at risk. McCorvey was given the pseudonym Jane Roe to protect her privacy. The suit was filed against Henry Wade, the Dallas district attorney. Interestingly, for one of McCorvey's lawyers, Sarah Weddington, this was her first case (Evans, 2003, p. 47). The movie, *Roe v. Wade*, highlights the conflict between the ASCLU and Ms. McCorvey, especially the dilemma of trying the case herself (as a novice) or letting more experienced ASCLU try the case.
6 For a detailed discussion of this case, especially the evolution of Harry Blackmun's drafts, see Schwartz (1993, pp. 337–361).
7 The New Right formed in the mid-1970s appealing to conservative values on abortion, the Equal Rights Amendment, affirmative action, school prayer; as opposed to the Old Right's emphasis on laissez faire economics and anti-communism (Evans, 2003, p. 112).
8 The full citation is Planned Parenthood of Southeastern Pennsylvania et al. v. Robert P. Casey et al. 505 US 833 (1992).
9 This quote is taken from the Dissent in Thomas E. Dobbs, State Health Officer of the Mississippi Department of Health et al v. Jackson Women's Health Organization et al. 597 US 215 (2022).
10 The full citation is Thomas E. Dobbs, State Health Officer of the Mississippi Department of Health et al v. Jackson Women's Health Organization et al. 597 US 215 (2022).

11 The majority opinion is taken from Thomas E. Dobbs, State Health Officer of the Mississippi Department of Health et al v. Jackson Women's Health Organization et al. 597 US 215 (2022).
12 Justice Breyer served on the Court from 1994 to 2022, when he was replaced by Ketanji Brown Jackson, appointed by President Biden.
13 See Nussbaum and Glover (1996).
14 We discuss the pros/cons of originalism in **The Supreme Court**. Here, we can say that Originalists believe that the Constitution should be interpreted to comport with original meaning, i.e., "what the public would have understood [the framers'] words to mean at the time" (Gass, 2021) using contemporary dictionaries and news coverage, among other sources.
15 Interestingly, "five of the justices in the majority are Catholics" (Greenhouse, 2023, p. 9).

References

Desmond, Matthew (2023) *Poverty, By America*, Crown, New York.
Du Mez, Kristen Kobes (2020) *Jesus and John Wayne: How White Evangelicals Corrupted a Faith and Fractured a Nation*, Liveright Publishing, New York.
Evans, Sara M. (2003) *Tidal Wave: How Women Changed America at Century's End*, Free Press, New York.
Gordon, Linda (1991) 'Birth Control,' in *The Reader's Companion to American History*, in Eric Foner and John A. Garraty, eds., Houghton Mifflin, Boston, pp. 99–103.
Greenhouse, Linda (2023) 'Religious Doctrine Drove the Abortion Decision,' *The New York Times*, July 24, Sunday Opinion, p. 9.
Aggarwal-Schifellite, Manisha (2022) 'When Abortion Wasn't a Legal Issue,' *The Harvard Gazette*, May 9, https://news.harvard.edu/gazette/story
Lepore, Jill (2022) 'Of Course the Constitution Has Nothing to Say About Abortion' *The New Yorker*, May 4, https://www.newyorker.com/
Mohr, James L. (1991) 'Abortion' *The Reader's Companion to American History*, in Eric Foner and John A. Garraty, eds., Houghton Mifflin, Boston, pp. 3–5.
Perliger, Arie (2020) *American Zealots: Inside Right-Wing Domestic Terrorism*, Columbia University Press, New York.
Richardson, Gary, Daniel Park, Alejandro Komai, and Michael Gou (2013) 'McFadden Act of 1927' *Federal Reserve History*, November 22, https://www.federalreservehistory.org/essay
'Roe v. Wade' (1991) in Eric Foner and John A. Garraty (Eds.) *The Reader's Companion to American History*, Houghton Mifflin, Boston, pp. 951–952.
Schwartz, Bernard (1993) *A History of the Supreme Court*, Oxford University Press, New York.
Sen, Amartya (1999) *Development as Freedom*, Anchor Books, New York.

10 Guns, Gun Violence, and the Right to Bear Arms

The Issue: On June 25, 2024, the United States Surgeon General declared gun violence a public health crisis. Indeed, no matter how one looks at the data, America does have a gun crisis, unparalleled with any other nation. Besieged Americans look to Congress, which is hog-tied; they look to the Supreme Court, which is hamstrung by the law, albeit tinged with an overly expansive view of gun ownership. Meanwhile, gun control advocates feel powerless, and the spiral of gun violence continues. We need to develop a workable and equitable solution that is palatable to all stakeholders. Let's have a democratic discussion post-2024 in order to solve this public health crisis.

10.1 Introduction

A gun-induced incident elsewhere in the world becomes an invitation to reflect, after which laws are passed, giving some hope that future violence will become less likely. But not here in America. The pattern is disturbingly predictable and all too familiar: A shooting followed by an outpouring of grief and lament, followed by widespread accusations and scolding exhortations to do something. But then as time fades, America returns to business as usual, until the next shooting. Then, the cycle repeats itself, depressing and never-ending, "a polarized doom loop" (Manjoo, 2022, p. 3) if you will. Meanwhile, the proliferation of guns continues, while more and more Americans feel less safe.

Guns and gun culture, probably more than any other issue in America, is deeply woven into the inner fabric of our society; for some, it represents a threat to democracy, while to others, it is the quintessence of democracy itself (Erdozain, 2024). At heart is a deep struggle of how we see ourselves as Americans and how we govern ourselves (Metzl, 2024).

This chapter will explore the United States' worship of the right to own/use guns, why it is a problem, the rights of non-gun owners, as well as equitable solutions.

DOI: 10.4324/9781003591856-12

10.2   Gun Ownership in the United States

America is unique in worshiping the right to own *and* to use guns. The United States, with only 5% of the world's population, possesses 40% of the world's civilian guns—more guns than people (400 million v. 330 million). America's civilian gun ownership rate per 100 people (120.5) is almost double that of #2, the Falklands Islands (Gun Ownership by Country 2023). Numbers which no doubt will keep increasing.

In 2022, according to the Pew Research Center,[1] 40% of US adults live in a household with a gun, including 32% who say they personally own one, unchanged since 2021. Not surprisingly, gun ownership rates differ by political affiliation, gender, and community type:

- Republicans and Republican-leaning independents are more than twice as likely as Democrats and Democratic-leaners to say they personally own a gun (45% vs. 20%).
- 40% of men say they own a gun, compared with 25% of women.
- 47% of adults living in rural areas report personally owning a gun, compared to the suburbs (30%), and urban areas (20%).
- 38% of White Americans own a gun; Blacks (24%), Hispanics (20%), and Asians (10%).
- 58% of US adults favor stricter gun laws; 26% say that US gun laws are about right, and 15% favor less strict gun laws.
- 60% of US adults say gun violence is 'a very big problem', up 9 percentage points from spring 2022, while 62% of Americans say they expect the level of gun violence to increase over the next five years. This is double the share of those who expect it to stay the same (31%). Just 7% of US adults expect the level of gun violence to decrease.

10.3   Setting the Stage for Gun Ownership: The Framing of the USA Constitution

The Constitutional Convention was held in Philadelphia, May 25, 1787, through September 17, 1787, in order to reform the ineffectual Articles of Confederation, especially their inability to raise money for the federal government to carry out its functions.[2] The end result was a new Constitution of the United States offered to the American people, September 17, 1787, "a terse outline of government—seven articles of four thousand words" (Bernstein, 1991, p. 833).

During and prior to the Convention, it was debated whether the Constitution should also contain a Bill of Rights, i.e., explicitly delineated rights to which all citizens would be guaranteed. Alexander Hamilton, co-author of *The*

Federalist Papers, and a staunch advocate of a stronger federal government, argued strongly against a bill of rights, which is,

> not only unnecessary in the proposed constitution, but would even be dangerous. They would contain various exceptions to powers which are not granted; and on this very account, would afford a colorful pretext to claim more than were granted. For why declare that things shall not be done which there is no power to do? Why for instance, should it be said, that the liberty of the press shall not be restrained when no power is given by which restrictions may be imposed...The truth is...that the constitution is itself in every rational sense A BILL OF RIGHTS... And the proposed constitution, if adopted, will be the bill of rights of the union.
>
> (Hamilton et al., No, 84, p. 524, and pp. 525–526; emphasis in the original)

In support of the above statement, Hamilton further noted that 'bills of rights,'

> are in their origin, stipulations between kings and their subjects, abridgements of prerogative in favor of privilege, reservations of rights not surrendered to the prince...It is evident, therefore, that according to their primitive signification, they have no application to constitutions professedly founded upon the power of the people, and executed by their immediate representatives and servants. Here in strictness, the people surrender nothing, and as they retain every thing, they have no need of particular reservations.
>
> (Hamilton et al., No. 84, pp. 523–524)

Implicit in Hamilton's argument is that the separation of powers explicit in the new Constitution would suffice to guarantee the rights of citizens and that the separation of powers would be the best way "to establish Justice, insure domestic Tranquility, provide for the common Defense, promote the general Welfare, and secure the Blessings of Liberty..."

On the other hand, George Mason (among others) insisted that a Bill of Rights was necessary in order to explicitly delineate the rights guaranteed to its citizens. The Constitution was a transformative change consolidating unprecedented power to a new federal government. Americans at the time were split into federalists (those who supported a strong central government) and anti-federalists. The latter felt that the new government was too strong, usurping power from the states where the locus of decision making best belonged. Reconciling the two opposing camps, and especially assuaging the anti-federalists was critical to ratifying the US Constitution.

After the Constitution was approved by the Convention, it still needed to be ratified by at least nine of the 13 states.[3] The Constitution's opponents rallied around the absence of an explicit bill of rights. To ensure ratification, a Bill of Rights was written (principally by James Madison) and formally adopted (as the first ten Amendments to the Constitution) on December 15, 1791.

For many Americans, these ten rights are the workable face of our government. Perhaps best known is the First Amendment:

> Congress shall make no law respecting an establishment of religion or prohibiting the free exercise thereof; or abridging the freedom of speech, or of the press; or the right of the people to peaceably assemble, and to petition the Government for a redress of grievances.

As the reach of the federal government has since expanded, the Tenth Amendment has assumed critical importance and has generated extensive debate over the rights of states vis-à-vis the federal government, "The powers not delegated to the United States by the Constitution, nor prohibited by it to the states, are reserved to the States respectively, or to the people."

The Constitution's framers optimistically understood that the nation would be growing, and as such, a provision/mechanism was needed to amend the Constitution as conditions changed. Article Five of the Constitution accomplishes this objective by allowing Congress to propose and then ratify an amendment (when two-thirds of both houses deem it necessary, or via the conventions of three-fourths of the states). Without Article Five, the original Constitution would have ossified; thus, Article Five has kept the Constitution alive, useful, and relevant.

10.4   The Second Amendment

Probably, no amendment has been (and is) more controversial than the Second (although the 10th gives it a run for its money) and, at the same, "There are few more antiquated constitutional provisions" (Posner, 2008). The Second Amendment reads, "A well-regulated Militia, being necessary to the security of a free State, the right of the people to keep and bear Arms, shall not be infringed."

Despite much written on the Second Amendment,[4] a fundamental (even visceral) disagreement persists over its meaning and ramifications; so much so that we wonder if a reconciliation can ever be worked out. We are not constitutional scholars, although at the same time, as American citizens, this is our Constitution, so we have an interest and a right (like every American) to read and actively comment. Here is our take:

- Perhaps there would have been no ambiguity with two separate sentences, one commencing with 'A well-regulated Militia…,' and the second commencing with 'The Right of the People…' Or even a semi-colon, but a comma implies that the two separate phrases are intricately linked. Sure, shorter sentences would have clarified, but long-winded sentences with multiple clauses that obfuscated subject and verb typified contemporary prose.
- The language of the Articles of Confederation[5] was much clearer on the relationship between a militia and the right to bear arms: "every State shall

always keep up a well-regulated and disciplined militia, sufficiently armed and accoutered, and shall provide and constantly have ready for use, in public stores, a due number of field pieces and tents, and a proper quantity of arms, ammunition and camp equipage."

- Although the Articles mentioned the need for a militia, there was no mention of the right to bear arms. However, several of the state constitutions explicitly did so. For example, the Virginia Declaration of Rights (adopted in 1776) which, by the way, was relied upon by James Madison (a Virginian) in writing the USA Bill of Rights, read, "That a well-regulated militia, composed of the body of the people, trained to arms, is the proper, natural, and safe defense of a free state." And the Massachusetts Declaration of Rights (adopted in 1780) explicitly stated that "The people have a right to keep and to bear arms for the common defense."
- The word 'militia' comes from the Latin, meaning military service. According to the common dictionary, a militia is "an army composed of ordinary citizens rather than professional soldiers, on call for service in an emergency." Given that the United States' armed forces were not (yet) fully developed during the late 18th century, each state's militia was a necessary first step in the bulwark against a foreign invasion, biding time for the regular forces to arrive. In addition, the anti-federalists were worried perpetually that the federal government could usurp the power of the states and invade, a very palpable concern at the time. Thus, a well-equipped militia did double duty: "a first step in protecting against foreign invasion i.e., a valuable and powerful auxiliary" (Hamilton et al., 2003 [1787–1788], No. 27., p. 155); and to protect the states from federal government encroachment/invasion.[6]
- The right for ordinary citizens to bear arms was well-established in the common law, dating to England. The English Bill of Rights of 1689, for example, stated, "subjects, which are Protestants, may have arms for their defense as allowed by law." Colonial America recognized the need for ordinary people to bear arms, especially with "no effective police, with individuals compelled to self-protection [while] hunting was a major source of food, and citizens needed protection against [often] hostile Indians" (Leddy, 1991, p. 477).
- Obviously, it was absolutely necessary for a militia composed of ordinary citizens to be armed; if not, it would be ill-equipped to do its duty; and an un-armed militia would have invited an invasion from a foreign government or even from the federal government, so it was thought at the time. Given their important role in colonial America, the militias would be inspected and assembled, usually on the town square,

Little more can reasonably be aimed at with respect to the people at large than to have them properly armed and equipped; and in order to see that this be not neglected, it will be necessary to assemble them once or twice in the course of a year.

(Hamilton et al., 2003 [1787–1788], No., 29, p. 167)

Alexis de Tocqueville noted that in colonial Connecticut, "citizens of more than sixteen were obliged to bear arms. They formed a national militia which appointed officers, and which was to hold itself in a state of constant readiness to defend the country" (Tocqueville, 2003 [1835, 1840], p. 52). And Thomas Jefferson wrote of the militia in his home state of Virginia during the early 1780s,

> Every able-bodied freeman, between the ages of 16 and 50, is enrolled in the militia. Those of every county are formed into companies, and those again into one or more battalions…the law requires every militiaman to provide himself with the arms usual in the regular service.
> (Jefferson, 1788 [1952], p. 88)

- In the Second Amendment's phrase, 'being necessary to the security of a free State,'[7] notice that the security of the United States or the union is not addressed, but that of a free state. This clearly connects the right to bear arms to the functioning of a militia at the state level, which in turn would be the best way to protect against usurpation and invasion. The United States would soon have its own standing army to protect against foreign invasion, but the state governments would need a militia as a first step and as a necessary bulwark,

> it will be possible to have an excellent body of well trained militia ready to take the field whenever the defense of the State shall require it. This will not only lessen the call for military establishments; but if circumstances should at any time oblige the government to form an army of any magnitude, that army can never be formidable to the liberties of the people, while there is a large body of citizens little if at all inferior to them in discipline and use of arms, who stand ready to defend their own rights and those of their fellow citizens. This appears to me the only substitute that can be devised for a standing army; the best possible security against it, if it should exist.
> (Hamilton et al., 2003 [1787–1788], No. 29, pp. 167–168)

- It is also interesting to note that the First Amendment's opening sentence contains the strong declaratory word 'shall,' i.e., "Congress shall[8] make no law…" (as does the Third Amendment, "No soldier shall…") But the Second Amendment ends with it: "…the right of the people to keep and bear Arms, shall not be infringed."[9]
- We also find it interesting that the Second and Third amendments are grouped together, with an obvious link to *The Declaration of Independence*. Today, when we read *The Declaration* we savor the opening paragraph's lofty language. But nevertheless, the second section, which contained the long list of abuses and usurpations, was considered at the time to be far more important,

providing explicit reasons to sever ties with the mother country. Several of these 'facts' (i.e., 'the facts to be submitted to a candid world') address the tyrannical British government's standing army, e.g., "He has kept among us, in times of peace, standing armies, without the consent of our legislatures. He has affected to render the military independent and superior to the civil power…and quartered large bodies of armed troops among us…." The Constitution's Third Amendment redresses this injustice, while also highlighting the complementary nature of the militia.[10]

10.5   Today's 'Debate' Over Gun Control

Certainly, debate is the wrong word here, since the two sides have ossified their intransigence,[11] with little give and take. The essence of this debate, however intransigent the two sides have become, is "whether the [Second] Amendment protects the right of private individuals to keep and bear arms, or whether it instead protects a collective right that should be exercised only through formal militia units" (History.com editors, 2023).

Each side claims a legitimate reading of the Second Amendment. Gun advocates insist that the Second Amendment affords all citizens, not just militias, the right to own guns for self-protection (History.com editors, 2023). They insist that any attempt to control or even restrict gun ownership infringes on Constitutionally protected rights.

The organization most synonymous with gun advocacy and gun proliferation is the National Rifle Association (NRA). Founded in 1871 to assert the rights of citizens to own and use guns; as well as to encourage target shooting, hunting, safety training, and shooting sports, it has morphed into a gun lobbyist whose efficacy is unequaled, effectively capturing the Republican Party. This underscores the proliferation of special interests and the threat that they pose to a democracy. Today, "to get elected or win reelection, it might be in a politician's self-interest to be more sensitive to one's party or special interest agenda than to the public's collective interests. This is not what we want in a society" (Paul, 2021, p. 150). Of course not.

On the other hand, gun control advocates argue that gun ownership is a *collective* right, pointing to the Second Amendment's 'well-regulated Militia' clause. They argue that the right to bear arms should accrue only to organized groups, like the National Guard, a reserve military force that replaced the state militias after the Civil War. In addition, they argue that their constitutionally protected right "to be secure in their persons, houses, papers, and effects"[12] has been attenuated by gun proliferation.

The lobbying power of gun control advocates is nowhere near that of the NRA. The Handgun Control, Inc, for example, lobbies against gun ownership, arguing that guns are a danger to society, so much so that only police and the military should own firearms. Ironically, the increasingly violent United

States reinforces the gun lobby argument that more firearms are necessary to protect against violence. Alas, more guns beget more guns. And the cycle continues.

Tracing its roots to 1886 as part of the Treasury Department, the Bureau of Alcohol, Tobacco, Firearms, and Explosives (ATF) has since undergone several reorganizations with concomitant name changes. The ATF, headquartered in Washington, DC, is now housed within the Justice Department. According to its web page, its responsibilities include,

> the investigation and prevention of federal offenses involving the unlawful use, manufacture, and possession of firearms and explosives; acts of arson and bombings; and illegal trafficking of alcohol and tobacco products. The ATF also regulates, via licensing, the sale, possession, and transportation of firearms, ammunition, and explosives in interstate commerce.[13]

In a 1968 ATF reorganization, mail order sales of guns were prohibited, as were sales to minors; guns are now required to carry serial numbers, convicted felons are prohibited from gun ownership, and a tracking system was begun. Prior to 1968, "there was no reliable data on gun ownership or production… millions of guns were manufactured, imported or sold as surplus after the wars (Leddy, 1991, p. 478)."

The pro-gun lobby continues to steamroll any effort to curtail gun ownership rights. As just one example, the Firearms Owners Protection Act of 1987 repealed federal restrictions on ammunition sales and out-of-state sales of rifles/ shotguns (because, it was argued, they have no crime reduction value); and today, it is legal to transport unloaded and inaccessible guns across state lines regardless of local restrictions.

In the amorphous, constantly changing far right, violence, guns, White evangelicals, gun culture, and God are all deeply intertwined.[14] Indeed, "From toy guns in childhood to real firearms, guns are seen to cultivate authentic God-given masculinity" (Du Mez and Kobes, 2020, p. 296). The far right, spearheaded by White evangelicals, has engineered a bunker mentality: Tough aggressive men must defend a vulnerable nation, which in turn attracts them to aggressive 'shoot from the hip' 'leaders' like Trump (Du Mez and Kobes, 2020, p. 3).

10.6   Gun Violence in the United States

While gun violence is certainly not unique to America, and here, not all violent crimes are committed with guns, gun-induced violence has been increasing in the United States with no signs of stopping. In a survey of high-income nations with populations over 10 million, the United States had by far the highest rate of capital firearms homicides, 4.52. Compare this to Canada (0.62), Germany

(0.24), France (0.06), and the UK (0.01) (Leach-Kemon et al., 2023). According to the US Surgeon General,

> The rate of firearm-related deaths in our nation has been rising and reached a near three-decade high in 2021. This crisis is being driven, in particular, by increases in firearm-related homicides over the last decade and firearm-related suicides over the last two decades. Across all firearm-related deaths in 2022, more than half (56.1%) were from suicide, 40.8% were from homicide, and the remaining were from legal intervention, unintentional injuries, and injuries of unknown intent.
>
> (The US Surgeon General's Advisory, 2024)

Gun advocates argue that it isn't guns that kill people, it is people who kill people. While superficially not false, it also ignores the disturbing and palpable nexus of the availability of guns, the ease of attainment, and the method of choice in homicides,

> About eight-in-ten U.S. murders in 2021 (20,958 out of 26,031) or 81%—involved a firearm, the highest percentage since at least 1968, the earliest year for which the CDC [the Center for Disease and Control] has online records. More than half of all suicides in 2021 (26,328 out of 48,183) or 55%—also involved a gun, the highest percentage since 2001; and the 48,830 total gun deaths in 2021 reflect a 23% increase since 2019.
>
> (Gramlich, 2023)

Firearms are also the weapon of choice in mass shootings. The exact number of mass shootings depends on which of the following two definitions is used:

- An 'active shooter incident,' defined by the FBI as "one or more individuals actively engaged in killing or attempting to kill people in a populated area." Based on this definition, 103 people—excluding the shooters—died in 2021, the latest year for which data are available.
- The Gun Violence Archive defines a mass shooting as one in which four or more people are shot, even if no one was killed (again excluding the shooters). Using this definition, 706 people died in 2021.

However, both numbers represent only a very small percent of total gun murders. While mass shootings account for only 1% of all gun fatalities, they nevertheless carry a psychological toll, increasing the fear factor here in the United States[15] (Follman et al., 2023). Furthermore, data suggest that USA mass shootings are increasing, although additional data will be needed to ascertain this trend.[16]

104 Questions for America

10.7 Amend the Second Amendment?

Since the gun debate is couched in terms of 'rights,' then any solution(s) should be based on a recognition of competing rights, despite ostensible exclusivity and intransigence. Every right has a limit, and every right obfuscates a right granted. There is no Constitution-based infinite right to own guns. Likewise, there is no infinite right to do whatever one wants with gun ownership. Owning a gun does not give one license to ignore all other stakeholders, especially those with opposing interests.

In the *Federalist Papers*, James Madison wrote,

> The claims of justice, both on one side and on the other, will be in force, and must be fulfilled; the rights of humanity must in all cases be duly and mutually respected; whilst considerations of a common interest, and above all the remembrance of the endearing scenes which are past, and the anticipation of a speedy triumph over the obstacles to re-union, will, it is hoped, not urge in vain *moderation* on one side, and *prudence* on the other.
>
> (*The Federalist*, #43, p. 270, upper case emphasis excised)

While Madison is not addressing gun control in this passage (specifically the relation between those states that will ratify the Constitution and those that do not), we feel it sheds important issues on the gun control debate.

As Madison wrote in the same paper, "But a right implies a remedy; and where else could the remedy be deposited, than where it is deposited by the Constitution?" (*The Federalist*, #43, p. 264). Especially so when the right emanates from the Constitution.

Section V of the Constitution allows it to be amended as conditions change. The deliberately non-easy process "guards equally against that extreme facility which would render the constitution too mutable; and that extreme difficulty which might perpetuate its discovered faults" (*The Federalist*, #43, p. 268). A supermajority (not just a majority) of states or state conventions must ratify the amendment, since "to have required the unanimous ratification of the 13 states, would have subjected the essential interests of the whole to the caprice or corruption of a single member" (Ibid., p. 269). If the Constitution is to remain a living dialogue, it must evolve (via amendments) as conditions evolve; otherwise, it ossifies.

Since 1789, there have been 11848 proposed amendments to the Constitution, with only 27 succeeding, the most recent being #27 (1992), which reads "No law, varying the compensation for the services of the Senators and Representatives, shall take effect, until an election of Representatives shall have intervened." It was intended that the electorate could vote out any corrupt officials before they gave themselves a pay raise.

An argument could certainly be made today that the role of the militia has significantly changed since the Constitution was ratified, giving grounds to at least consider an amendment. Today, the federal government has a large and powerful armed forces,[17] while the United States' defense budget is greater than the next eight nations combined. The National Guard has replaced the militia in providing a wide array of services, e.g., emergency/disaster, first responders. In addition, the threat of the federal government invading the states has all but disappeared except in the minds of far-right fringe groups. Since well-armed citizens are no longer necessary to ensure the militia's efficacy, and militias are no longer necessary to defend the United States, it is time to rethink the basis for claiming that citizens need to be well-armed. It is the armed forces and the National Guard that protect against foreign invasion and domestic insurrection, and the latter provides logistical help during an emergency.

Today, it is hard to see any connection between the militia, a free State, and well-armed citizens. Instead, militias are associated with right-wing fringe groups, which in turn have deep seated, emotional, and irrational fears of conspiracy, federal government takeovers, encroachment by the federal government, and of course threatened usurpation of the much treasured Second Amendment (Bennett, 1995). Gun advocates who have joined the militia movement argue that,

> they are only defending the second amendment, that they are the modern-day Minutemen—like revolutionary heroes of old—protecting threatened individual and local rights from the tyranny of Washington autocrats, that an armed citizenry is the last defense of democracy. But the tone and temper of their response suggests even deeper anxieties.
>
> (Bennett, 1995, p. 465)

It is theoretically possible that the Supreme Court could reverse its pro-gun stance sometime in the future, without any Constitutional amendments. But with a 6-3 conservative majority holding an expansive view on gun ownership, that is not likely any time soon.

In the important case *District of Columbia, et al. v. Dick Anthony Heller,* 554 U.S. 570 (2008), the Court's conservative majority ruled that a Washington DC ban on handguns in one's home violated the Second Amendment; as did DC's law that rifles and shotguns at one's home be unloaded and unassembled. This ruling effactually disengaged the Amendment's two phrases,

> The majority opinion acknowledges that allowing people to keep guns in their homes cannot help the militias, because modern military weapons are not appropriate for home defense (most of them are too dangerous), and anyway the opinion says that the only weapons the Second Amendment entitles people to possess are ones that are not 'highly unusual in

society at large.' Modern military weapons are highly unusual in society at large. By creating a privilege to own guns of no interest to a militia, the Court decoupled the amendment's two clauses.

(Posner, 2008)

However, 'decoupling the two clauses' contravenes the original construction of the Amendment (see our discussion above). If the two phrases did not go together, they would have been separated by either a semi-colon or a period, or even each allocated to their own separate amendments.

While gun advocates have extolled this ruling, it nevertheless underscores the Court's ideological bias. The Court's modus operandi (at least that of the majority) is originalist; and as we have mentioned, the Robert's Court is the most originalist in history, yet originalism was not used in constructing this opinion. If it were, "it would have yielded the opposite results" (Posner, 2008). More specifically,

Originalism without the interpretive theory that the Framers and the ratifiers of the Constitution expected the courts to use in construing constitutional provisions is faux originalism. True originalism licenses loose construction. And loose construction is especially appropriate for interpreting a constitutional provision ratified more than two centuries ago, dealing with a subject that has been transformed in the intervening period by social and technological change, including urbanization and a revolution in warfare and weaponry…The absence of principles supports the hypothesis that ideology drives decision in cases in which liberal and conservative values collide.

(Posner, 2008)

We agree. Posner's last sentence in the above quote applies with equal force to several of the Court cases we discuss in our **Supreme Court** chapter.

In 2023, Governor Gavin Newsome (D. California) proposed an amendment to the US Constitution that would[18]:

- Restrict gun ownership by raising the federal minimum age to buy a firearm from 18 to 21.
- Mandate universal background checks.
- Institute a reasonable waiting period for all gun purchases and ban assault rifles nationally.

Newsome, motivated by incessant mass shootings and a Supreme Court that has rolled back many gun control measures, is aware of the "seemingly unimaginable hurdles" (Cadelago and White, 2023). But at the same time, he lamented that "I don't know what the hell else to do. I don't know what else is the answer" (Cadelago and White, 2023).[19]

10.8   Other Solutions

Aside from the quixotic (yet necessary task) of either amending the Second Amendment, or interpreting it differently, what other options do we have? Any proposed solution depends on which side of the fence one stands. Gun advocates claim that the system works fine, that nothing need be done except vigilantly protecting the Constitutional right to bear Arms. On the other hand, gun opponents proffer a bevy of solutions including recalling guns, offering a cash reward for the voluntary turning in of guns; making gun permits incredibly hard to obtain, and restricting access to firearms.

But in a nation with more guns than people and over 45% of the world's civilian arms, it is hard to say how efficacious stricter access to gun laws will be. It seems like moving sand around the ocean. But doing nothing means surrendering our malls, churches, and schools to metal detectors and security guards.[20] Do we really want to live in such a buttoned-down and stripped-down country, with guards, police and metal detectors? Do we really want to foster "a world of fear and alienation, where people live in a state of heightened awareness… [Bereft] of trust or hope or solidarity or any of the values we need to make democracy work as a way of life, much less a system of government" (Bouie, 2023, p. 3). Do we really want to completely forfeit the rights of gun control advocates? While at the same time, parrying responsibility for the effects of loose gun ownership and liberal access, blaming shootings on mental health,[21] or even LGBTQ—everywhere except where it is due.

10.9   Gun Violence Is a Health Crisis

On June 25, 2024, the USA Surgeon General, Vikay Murthy, declared gun violence in America to be a public health crisis. By doing so, "we have the opportunity to take it out of the realm of politics and put it into the realm of public health" (Barry, 2024).

By declaring gun violence a public health crisis, Dr. Murthy hopes to achieve results similar to when Congress in 1964 voted to print a warning label on cigarettes about smoking's health risks. The percent of American adult smokers decreased from 42% to 11.5% by 2021 (Barry, 2024). Of course, an explicit warning cannot do anything in and of itself but instead needs to take place within a context of "education and awareness campaigns, culture shifts and policies" (Barry, 2024).

Dr. Murthy has offered a bevy of workable solutions within the context of a public health crisis,[22]

- Expand research to examine short-term and long-term outcomes of firearm violence and evaluate specific prevention strategies.
- Conduct research to improve effectiveness of prevention strategies.

- Implement community violence interventions to support populations with increased risk of firearm violence.
- Encourage health systems to facilitate education on safe and secure firearm storage, including child access prevention law.
- Implement universal background checks and expand purchaser licensing laws.
- Ban assault weapons and large-capacity magazines for civilian use.
- Prioritize increased access to affordable, high-quality mental health care, substance use treatment, and other trauma-informed resources.
- Treat firearms like other consumer products.

The last suggestion, a no-brainer, could help galvanize widespread support for reform,

> unlike motor vehicles which have safety standards that are regulated by the National Highway Traffic Safety Administration (NHTSA), pesticides that are regulated by the Environmental Protection Agency (EPA), or prescription drugs that are regulated by the Food and Drug Administration (FDA), there are no federal standards or regulations regarding the safety of firearms produced in the U.S. Therefore, firearms manufactured and sold in the U.S. may not undergo safety testing or include safety features like warning labels related to associated risk or authorized-use technology… for firearm access. Treating firearms as a consumer product could result in changes which may enhance safety.
>
> (The US Surgeon General's Advisory, 2024, pp. 25–31)

If we are to make significant headway against gun violence, it is not enough to label it a public health crisis, which it surely is, it is not enough to look to the Courts for redress, since their hands are tied by interpreting the law as is (at least theoretically) although it is no secret their expansive view of gun ownership. A solution should come from Congress, supported by a strong democratic consensus, along with a transparent debate involving all stakeholders, and not just industry lobbyists and their beholden Republican legislators, but all stakeholders, and even the amorphous public interest, although it is quite obvious that

> …the public good is disregarded in the conflicts of rival parties; and that measures are too often decided, not according to the rules of justice, and the rights of the minor party; but by the superior force of an interested and over-bearing majority.
>
> (James Madison, *The Federalist*, #10, p. 51)

The 2024 Supreme Court ruling on bump stocks is a case in point. After a horrific Las Vegas public shooting in which the perpetrator used a bump stock to convert a semiautomatic weapon (legal in the United States) into a rapid-fire machine gun (illegal in the United States since the 1934 National Firearms Act and the 1968 Gun Control Act), the Trump administration in 2018 outlawed bump stocks. But the Supreme Court in a 6-3 majority (Garland v. Cargill[23]) ruled the ban unconstitutional. Justice Thomas, writing the majority opinion, pointed out that, "there is a simple remedy for the disparate treatment of bump stocks and machine guns. Congress can amend the law. Now that the situation is clear, Congress can act."[24]

Simple in theory, yes; in practice, no. Alas, Justice Thomas ignores that half of Congress, i.e., the Republican Party,[25] is beholden to the NRA, putting self-interest ahead of national interest.

10.10   Conclusion

Today in America, "guns seem to be a permanent part of the American scene" (Leddy, 1991, p. 479). While this placates gun advocates, it makes America less safe, while spreading fear, increasing the need for more guns. The rights of *all* Americans deserve to be recognized and protected. *All* citizens have an inalienable right to persevere in their safety and not to have their life taken by an indiscriminate use of firearms. *All* Americans deserve to be secure in their persons and houses. That is certainly not the case today. As Governor Newsom acknowledged, any workable solution on gun control will "require a national construct, a national frame" (Wiley, 2023). Tall stuff. But this is the only way to garner enough support for federal legislation.

Besieged Americans look to Congress, which is hog-tied; they look to the Supreme Court, which is hamstrung by interpreting the law, albeit tinged with an overly expansive view of gun ownership. Meanwhile, gun control advocates feel powerless, and the spiral of gun violence continues.

Notes

1 Schaeffer (2023) provides the statistics in the following bullets.
2 McDonald (1965, pp. 189–236) provides an interesting play-by-play account.
3 See Article VII of the Constitution.
4 For a representative sample see Cottrol (1993), McClurg et al. (2002), Spitzer (2023), and Skiba (2024).
5 The Articles can be read in full at Articles of Confederation (1777).
6 For further discussion of the contemporary view of militias, see (Hamilton et al. (1787–1788 [2009]), #28).
7 Typical then was to upper-case such nouns, despite not being proper.
8 The common dictionary defines 'shall' as 'an order, promise, or obligation.'
9 The original phrasing had 'shall' at the beginning, but this was reversed in the final draft.
10 The Third Amendment reads, "No Soldier shall, in time of peace be quartered in any house, without the consent of the Owner, nor in time of war, but in a manner to be prescribed by law."
11 A similar ossification has occurred in the rancorous debate over **abortion**.

12 This quote is from the Fourth Amendment's opening line. While this Amendment protects against "unreasonable searches and seizures" and that warrants should only be issued by "probable cause" with very specific particulars, we also read it as that the people have a right to be secure 'in their persons and houses' with 'secure' broadly defined.

13 For more information on the AFT, see its web page, What We Do (aft.gov) | Bureau of Alcohol, Tobacco, Firearms and Explosives. And for a good discussion, see Moore (2001).

14 41% of white evangelicals own guns compared to 30% of Americans overall (Du Mez, 2020, p. 296).

15 Follman (2023) gives an interesting expose on how to spot and possibly prevent a mass shooter.

16 See Follman et al. (2023).

17 As Alexander Hamilton acknowledged in *The Federalist Papers*, "For a long time to come, it will not be possible to maintain a large army…" (2003 [1787–1788], No. 28, p. 163).

18 Taken from Cadelago and White (2023).

19 Governor Newsome is frustrated that his state's gun control restrictions "the most aggressive state in the union on gun control" (Cadelago and White, 2023) including a ballot initiative regulating ammunition sales; bills restricting ghost guns, barring companies from marketing firearms to minors, and preventing people under 21 from purchasing certain weapons, have either been challenged or overturned by the Supreme Court. In September 2023, Governor Newsom signed a bill that tightens the state's concealed-carry rules and another that imposes a new tax on firearm and ammunition sales (Wiley, 2023).

20 This is analogous to our **climate change** policy: Instead of implementing ex-ante solutions that could have averted climate change, we did nothing for so long, and are now seeing the consequences of dereliction. As Governor Newsom lamented about the lack of gun control solutions, "This is insane. It's absolute insanity. And the biggest and most insane thing we can do is the same old BS and just point fingers" (Cadelago and White, 2023).

21 A recent FBI report on mass shootings from 2000 to 2018 discounted the role of mental health (Bouie, 2023, p. 3).

22 For a full discussion, along with additional solutions, see The US Surgeon General's Advisory (2024, pp. 25–31).

23 The full citation: Merrick B. Garland, Attorney General et al., v. Michael Cargill, 602 US 406.

24 Quoted in 22-976 *Garland v. Cargill* (06/14/2024) (supremecourt.gov).

25 A perplexing disconnect exists between the Republican Party's steadfast opposition to illegal immigration and their expansive position on gun proliferation. The two issues are logically connected: Clamping down on illegal immigrants also necessitates clamping down on the proliferation of guns. And not just because the latter can be used as instruments by the former.

References

Articles of Confederation (1777) National Archives, Washington, DC., https://www.archives.gov/

Barry, Ellen (2024) 'Surgeon General Declares Gun Violence a Public Health Crisis,' *The New York Times,* June 25, (nytimes.com).

Bennett, David H. (1995) *The Party of Fear: The American Far Right from Nativism to the Militia Movement*, Vintage, New York.

Bernstein, Richard (1991) '*Philadelphia Convention*' in *The Reader's Companion to American History*, Eric Foner and John A. Garraty, eds., Houghton Mifflin, Boston, pp. 831–833.

Bouie, Jamelle (2023) 'No Dignity in this Kind of America' *The New York Times*, February 12. Opinion | (nytimes.com).

Cadelago, Christopher and Jeremy B. White (2023) 'Gavin Newsom wants 28th Amendment for guns in U.S. Constitution,' *Politico*, (June 8), https://www.politico.com/

Cottrol, Robert (Ed.) (1993) *Gun Control and the Constitution: The Courts, Congress, and the Second Amendment Controversies in Constitutional Law*, Routledge, London.

Du Mez, Kristen Kobes (2020) *Jesus and John Wayne: How White Evangelicals Corrupted a Faith and Fractured a Nation*, Liveright Publishing, New York.

Erdozain, Dominic (2024) *One Nation Under Guns: How Gun Culture Distorts Our History and Threatens Our Democracy*, Crown Publishing, New York.

Follman, Mark (2023) *Trigger Points: Inside the Mission to Stop Mass Shootings in America*, Dey Street Books, New York.

Follman, Mark, Gavin Aronsen, and Deanna Pan (2023) 'US Mass Shootings: Data from Mother Jones' Investigation,' *Mother Jones*, December 6, https://www.motherjones.com/politics/2012

Gramlich, John (2023) 'What the Data Say about Gun Deaths in the US,' Pew Research Center, April 26, https://www.pewresearch.org/short-reads/2023

'Gun Ownership by Country' (2023) World Population Review, Gun Ownership by Country 2024 (worldpopulationreview.com).

Hamilton, Alexander, James Madison, and John Jay (2003 [1787–1788]) *The Federalist Papers*, Bantam Books, New York.

History.com editors (2023) 'The Second Amendment,' July 27, (history.com).

Jefferson, Thomas (1788 [1952]) *Notes on the State of Virginia*, W.W. Norton, New York.

Leach-Kemon, Katherine, Rebecca Sirull, Scott Glenn (2023) 'On Gun Violence, the United States is an Outlier Institute for Health Metrics and Evaluation, (October) Institute for Health Metrics and Evaluation (healthdata.org).

Leddy, Edward F. (1991) 'Guns and Gun Control,' in Eric Foner and John A. Garraty (Eds.) *The Reader's Companion to American History*, Houghton Mifflin, Boston, pp. 447–449.

Manjoo, Farhad (2022) 'We May Be Able to Prevent Some Mass Shootings,' *The New York Times*, Opinion Section, April 10, p. 3.

McClurg, A. J., David B. Kopel, Brannon Denning (Eds.) (2002) *Gun Control and Gun Rights: A Reader and Guide*, New York University Press, New York.

McDonald, Forrest (1965) *The Formation of the American Republic 1776–1790*, Penguin Books, Baltimore.

Metzl, Jonathan M. (2024) *What We've Become: Living and Dying in a Country of Arms*, W.W. Norton, New York.

Moore, Jim (2001) *Very Special Agents: The Inside Story of America's Most Controversial Law Enforcement Agency—the Bureau of Alcohol, Tobacco, and Firearms*, University of Illinois Press, Champaign.

Olasky, Marvin (1988) *The Press and Abortion: 1838–1988*, Routledge, London.

Paul, David L. (2021) *Redesigning America for the 21st Century*, Funding Visions.

Posner, R. A. (2008) 'In Defense of Looseness: The Supreme Court and gun control,' *The New Republic*, August 27, https://newrepublic.com/article/62124/defense-looseness

Schaeffer, Katherine (2023) 'Key Facts about Americans and Guns,' Pew Research Center, September 13, https://www.pewresearch.org/

Skiba, Richard (2024) *Gun Control: International Views, Perspectives and Comparisons*, After Midnight Publishing, London.

Spitzer, Robert J. (2023) *The Politics of Gun Control*, 9th Edition, Routledge, London.

The US Surgeon General's Advisory (2024) *Firearm Violence: A Public Health Crisis in America*, Firearm Violence: A Public Health Crisis in America (hhs.gov).

'The Virginia Declaration of Rights' (1776) George Mason & Historic Human Rights Documents (archive.org).

Tocqueville, Alexis de (2003 [1835, 1840]) *Democracy in America*, Penguin Books, New York.

Wiley, Hannah (2023) 'Newsom signs gun laws that add new taxes and limit where owners can carry firearms,' *Los Angeles Times*, September 26, (latimes.com).

Ziegler, Mary (2020) *Abortion and the Law in America*, Cambridge University Press, Cambridge, UK.

11 Social Security: Will It Go Bankrupt?

The Issue: Social Security is the federal government's largest expenditure and its second largest source of revenue; it is a major government program. In addition, as this manuscript goes to press (October 2024) many Americans fear (and even assume) that the Social Security system will go bankrupt; that despite constant payments into the system, when the time comes to use our money, it will be gone. This issue will discuss the origin, intent, and current functions of Social Security, along with its presumed deficit.

11.1 Introduction

In 1870, Otto Von Bismarck united the separate and often bellicose German territories into a new German state, which turned out to be one of the more consequential decisions for the 20th century. Shortly after becoming chancellor, Bismarck[1] became the world's first leader to offer an income security, or what we now label Social Security. Worried about potential domestic insurrections (and for good reason), his motivation was a tad instrumental: Appease the most economically vulnerable with an income cushion, which in turn will disincentivize rebellion. Interestingly, Bismark set the eligibility age at 65, because only a minority of Germans lived to that age: In 1890, the average German life expectancy at birth was 40 years (O'Neil, 2022).

Other nations followed Bismark's example incentivized by the presence (and threat) of the Soviet Union (Piketty, 2022, p. 14).

11.2 The Development of Social Security in the United States

By the 1930s, the United States was the only Western nation without an income security.[2] However, the Great Depression's widespread poverty and **unemployment** set the ball in motion. Ironically, it was Gerald Swope, General Electric's president, a well-known and well-respected businessperson, who first put the bug into President Roosevelt's ear.[3] We say ironically because Social Security was (and has been) criticized as a socialist ploy

DOI: 10.4324/9781003591856-13

by critics, but Mr. Swope was anything but. An inveterate capitalist—chair of the Business Advisory Council—he was worried (like many contemporary business leaders) of a catastrophic breakdown in the economy. During a luncheon with President Roosevelt on March 8, 1934, Swope proposed a government-sponsored insurance program; impressed, Roosevelt established the Committee on Economic Security to develop a proposal for a social security program.

Not surprisingly, there was fierce debate. Liberals argued that a nation's reputation is determined by how well it treats its citizens, especially the most vulnerable. What does this say about the United States if we refuse to secure the income of the most vulnerable? Conservatives argued that such a program would be the first step along the slippery slope to socialism (a real fear at the time) diminishing the will to work and to self-provide, and who knows what next.

Given the severity of the Great Depression, the liberals won out.[4] Social Security was implemented to decrease the poverty rate of the elderly and to provide a cushion for the most vulnerable citizens (Reardon, 2014). In addition, the increased income of Social Security earners would help the economy by boosting the demand for consumer goods, which in turn would increase optimism, and hence the incentive to invest. On April 20, 1935, the Social Security Act (SSA) was signed into law. Given the visceral controversy surrounding the debate, it should be no surprise that compromises were made in the final bill, leaving both liberals and conservatives not fully satisfied. Conservatives, of course, felt the SSA went too far, and liberals felt that the SSA did not go far enough. Specifically, the latter wanted universal health care. However, the American Hospital Association (AHA) and the American Medical Association (AMA), two powerful lobbying groups, successfully argued that universal health care would change the very nature of health care, increasing prices, reducing profits, and compromising care: All shortchanging consumers.

11.3   Social Security's Intended Vision

When the SSA was passed in 1935, it was assumed that the typical worker upon his/her retirement would be able to enjoy a private pension and a lifetime of savings, with Social Security providing an additional cushion. More specifically, "in 1940, Social Security was designed to replace 20% of a typical worker's income at age 65; today, thanks to augmented benefits, that number is now just under 40%" (Dagher and Tergesen, 2024).

But unfortunately, since then, there has been a whittling away of private pensions and private savings, while shifting the incidence of risk to workers (Reardon et al., 2018, pp. 108–109).[5] Today, for many Americans, Social Security is their only source of income, "roughly one out of seven recipients, age 65 and older depend on [Social Security] benefits for nearly all of their income" (Dagher and Tergesen, 2024).

Social Security was envisioned to play a key role in a rosy vision of retirement for American workers as a capstone to a fulfilling work life in which, thanks to built-up savings and pensions, Americans could enjoy their golden years, pursuing hobbies, traveling, spending time with their children and grandchildren. Today, unfortunately, this is not the reality for many Americans:

> Forty-four percent of households with members ages 55-64 have no savings at all. Their median retirement account balance is $100,000, whereas most middle-class people need $600,000. Workers 75 and older are the fastest growing age segment of the US workforce. [But] at least two-thirds of workers 62 and older are working because they have not enough money to retire.
>
> (Ghilarducci, 2024a)

These statistics "reveal America's severely broken national retirement system. Welcome to retirement American style, where retirement is work" (Ghilarducci, 2024a).

11.4   The Nuts and Bolts of Social Security

Social Security has evolved into a vast array of programs, too numerous to mention here.[6] In the remainder of this chapter, we will focus on the Old-Age Survivors and Disability Insurance (OASDI) which for many Americans is Social Security.

President Roosevelt was intent on making Social Security his legacy and did not want it to be dismantled when he left office. Given visceral Republican opposition at the time, that was a real possibility. Roosevelt reasoned that the only way to ensure Social Security's long-term survival was to institutionalize it, meaning that it had to put down roots, so to speak. So instead of a system where each individual would contribute funds into the Social Security system to be earmarked for his/her use when needed; a pay-as-you-go system was established, whereby each individual's contribution would be used immediately by those in need. In so doing, each individual would trust that his/her contribution would be there when needed. This trust, Roosevelt reasoned, would guarantee Social Security's survival. A pay-as-you-go system incentivizes individuals not to change or even abolish the system for fear of losing their initial contributions.

Today, all wage earners are taxed (currently at 12.4%) divided equally between employee and employer. (A self-employed worker pays the full 12.4%.) Only wage earners pay a Social Security tax. In the United States, income can be earned in one of four ways: Wages and salaries, profits, rent, and interest. Of the four, wages and salaries account for 64.6% of total income (Bureau of

Labor Statistics, 2023). Political opposition explains why only income is taxed for social security: While most wages are earned by workers, rent, profits, and interest accrue mostly to upper income earners. In addition, the maximum level of wages to be taxed is capped, to be increased with the rate of **inflation**, as measured by the Consumer Price Index. In 2023, the ceiling was $160,200 increasing from $147,000 in 2022.

The Social Security tax is regressive, i.e., the preponderant burden is borne by lower-income earners. To illustrate this, take two individuals: One earning wages at the ceiling ($160,200) and the other earning, let's say, five times that amount. Both will pay the same Social Security tax. While some say this is equitable, that everyone should pay the same; others say that a tax should be progressive: The higher the income, the higher the rate.[7]

The first Social Society taxes were imposed in 1937 at 1% of wages, jointly shared by employers and workers. The first Social Security recipient, Ida Fuller, received her first benefits on January 31, 1940, and continued receiving benefits until her death in 1975 (Gruner, 2022, p. 95).

Today, the average monthly SSA benefit is $1710.78 (Social Security Trustees, 2023b). As of 2022, there were 66 million recipients: 51 million retired and dependents of retired workers; 6 million survivors of deceased workers; and 9 million disabled and dependents of disabled workers (Social Security Trustees, 2023a). In addition, 181 million workers paid Social Security payroll taxes (SSA Trustees, 2023a).

11.5   Medicare and Medicaid: Amendments to Social Security

In 1965, as part of Lyndon Johnson's war on poverty,[8] his Administration amended the 1935 Social Security Act[9] with passage of Medicare and Medicaid.[10] The debate on universal health care was revisited, but just like the 1930s it was defeated, largely due to the lobbying efforts of the AHA and the AMA. The resulting Medicare/Medicaid programs were a compromise between liberals (who wanted more) and conservatives (who wanted less).

Neither Medicare nor Medicaid provides direct health care; instead, each provides health care insurance targeted to Americans over the age of 65 (Medicare) or to the poor[11] (Medicaid). While Medicare is exclusively a federal program, Medicaid is jointly run by the states and the federal government.

As the American population has been aging, various programs have been added, e.g., the Medicare Prescription Drug Improvement and Modernization Act of 2003 offers drug coverage under Medicare; the 2023 Inflation Reduction Act enables allows Medicare, the USA's largest drug purchaser, to directly negotiate prescription drug prices.

In 2023, Social Security was the federal government's largest outlay[12] at 22.6% of the federal expenditures, followed by Medicare (14.6%), National Defense (13.4%), Medicaid (9.4%), and Net Interest on the Federal Debt (6.8%).

These programs combined for 66.8% of total government spending. And, as Americans age, the percentage accrued to Social Security and Medicare is expected to increase. On the budget's revenue side, in 2023, Social Security was the second largest source, at 24.4%, sandwiched between the personal income tax (51.1%) and corporate taxes (9.1%).

11.6   Is Social Security in Jeopardy?

With the exception of a brief COVID-induced dip, Americans' life expectancy has steadily increased during the last 100 years, thanks largely to advances in health care and technology, which is all well and good. But increased life expectancy has put additional pressure on Social Security's solvency. Today, the average life expectancy at birth for men is 73.5 years, and for women, 79.3 years. Compare this to 1940 when the average life expectancy was 62.07 years. But a more telling statistic is life expectancy upon reaching 65. Today, men reaching the age of 65 can expect to live 17 additional years, and women 19.7 (Elflein, 2023). And, once an individual begins receiving Social Security, there is no cut-off.

As the USA population ages (along with increased life expectancies), the amount of taxes going into the SS fund is decreasing while the demand for such funds on a pay-as-you basis is increasing. If nothing is done, it is projected that the Social Security trust fund will go into deficit in the year 2035 (Social Security Trustees, 2023a).

This does not mean that the Social Security reservoir will dry up, for as long as taxes on wages provide the source of the incoming funds the system will have funds; rather, the level of the available funds will decrease (think of a reservoir). The problem becomes that unless something is done the Social Security system will only be able to partially meet its obligations. More specifically, in 2035, for every dollar owed to beneficiaries, the Social Security Administration could only pay 76 cents (Social Security Trustees, 2023a). Needless to say, this would be a significant burden for retirees: An individual, for example, with lifetime contributions of $300,000 would only receive $228,000, a loss of $72,000.

11.7   Fixing the Impending Social Security Deficit

Three categories of solutions exist: (1) Chimerical; (2) Pragmatic; and (3) Holistic.

11.7.1   *Chimerical*

These solutions, proffered by ideological partisans, will not be implemented; hence their name. This is because Roosevelt succeeded in his goal of institutionalizing Social Security. Nonetheless, since they are offered as solutions, they deserve brief mention:

- **Abolish Social Security**: Return to pre-1935, with no Social Security tax and no Social Security benefits. This is an anti-government solution, solving the problem by throwing out the baby with the bath water, so to speak. Too many individuals have a stake in the survivability of SS.
- **Partially privatize Social Security:** By allowing an individual to divert a portion of his/tax into an individual discretionary investment account, say stocks or bonds. Proponents argue that the government has no right to coerce saving for a specific purpose, and that the individual should be able to choose where, when, and what to save. Proponents argue that investing in assets offering a higher return will relieve the overall burden on the Social Security system. Critics, however, argue that fund diversion will exacerbate the impending deficit; and will only weaken the whole Social Security edifice, with the intent of eventually collapsing it (Gruner, 2022, p. 480). For us, this solution raises a deeper, more critical issue of what America is as a nation: Are we simply a set of utility maximizers, only caring about our own self-interest, or does America mean something beyond this? something greater? That we have a collective responsibility for the public good, especially for the most vulnerable?

11.7.2 *Pragmatic Solutions*

These solutions either have been implemented or easily (relatively) could be. They are pragmatic, although not necessarily palatable. They tackle the crux of the issue, i.e., the impending deficit, focusing on either the inflow or the outflow, or both:

- **Increase the tax rate on wages**: In small amounts, which, ceteris paribus, will increase the inflow.
- **Raise taxes on the outflow benefits**: Which, ceteris paribus, can be used to increase the trust fund level.
- **Decrease the benefit levels to recipients**: Which, ceteris paribus, increases the trust fund level.
- **Increase the age for full eligibility**: Which, ceteris paribus, will increase the trust fund level. After all, we are living longer:

> From 2010 to 2020, the US older population (over the age of 65) grew at the fastest pace since 1880–1890, [now] constituting 16.8% of the American population. In 1920, 1 in 20 Americans were over 65 years; today 1 in 6. Individuals over the age of 95, currently at less than one

percent of the population, had from 2010 to 2020, the fastest growth rate of all demographic groups, at 48.6%, essentially doubling their numbers.

(Caplan, 2023)

Nevertheless, as recent efforts to reform the French state pension system attest, it is not easy to increase the age of pension eligibility, even for economically sound reasons. Here in the United States, the age for receiving full benefits has been slightly raised, with significant penalties for collecting earlier. For example, a 64-year-old can begin to withdraw now, but if he/she waits until he/she is 70, the benefits received will increase substantially.

While we hesitate to call the next two solutions 'pragmatic,' they are not necessarily chimerical either; rather, they straddle the boundary between the two categories. Although the two are unlikely to be implemented, neither solution would compromise the Social Security System's structural integrity, unlike the chimerical solutions:

- **Abolish the tax ceiling on wages**: Based on our back-of-the napkin calculations, doing so would completely alleviate the SS deficit. But good luck, given likely political and economic opposition.
- **Instead of just wages, tax all income, i.e., profits, rent, and interest**: Once again, efficacious, but little hope of implementation, due to political opposition.

Of course, doing nothing is also a solution, and if nothing is done, when 2035 rolls around the government can reshuffle money from general revenue to Social Security.[13] While doing nothing is a solution, it is not practical and evades the issue.

11.7.3 Holistic Solutions

These solutions recognize that in addition to the practical focus on inflow/outflow, any effective solution to the Social Security problem must look at linkages with the broader economy. We offer two, with each focusing on growth in the labor market as the key driver:

- **Economic growth:** In the late 1990s, **real GDP** increased at 4% per annum, a rate which has not been sustained since. As the economy grows, so does the labor force, which in turn increases the inflow into the SS Trust funds. Such a growth rate could help alleviate the SS deficit, and the federal budget deficit for similar reasons. Of course, the economy must grow **sustainably** and in conjunction with the requirements of **Net Zero**. Economic growth, of course, doesn't just happen; we need an active blend of government and the private sector and public and private capital; and a functional government, unfortunately noticeably absent.

• **Immigration**: Given our aging society (as with all Western nations), increased immigration will increase the labor force, thereby increasing the level of the trust funds, since workers' wages are taxed, all else equal. However, our immigration system is broken, and repairing it is a herculean (but necessary) task requiring a workable, functional government. Nevertheless, fixing immigration by restricting illegal immigrants and easing the flow of legal immigrants, would kill three birds with one stone, so to speak (or as we prefer, give three scones to one bird): (1) attenuate labor shortages, especially in high-skilled positions; (2) more workers means more revenue for the federal government; thus, ceteris paribus, the budget deficit would also decrease, ceteris paribus; and (3) more workers would postpone the impending deficit, even eliminating it.

We can add two quasi-holistic reforms: Fixing our private pension system, and/or increasing private savings, each of which would reduce the undue burden on Social Security. But neither is currently on the horizon right now, and if either were, we would need a functional government to forge solutions. Interestingly, Ghilarducci (2024b) recommends a 'Gray New Deal' in order to strengthen pensions, offer subsidized guaranteed retirement accounts and advance-funded pensions, strengthen the Social Security System, and construct an Older Workers' Bureau at the Department of Labor. A lot to ask, and perhaps given our dysfunctional government, a lot to expect, but her ideas provide a thinking roadmap for moving forward,[14] while, at the same time, acknowledging the holistic type of thinking that is needed.

11.7.4 Discussion

As 2035 looms closer, expect the implementation of all three pragmatic solutions, perhaps in a package deal, and perhaps sooner than later. For precedent, we can look at a similar package deal enacted by the Reagan administration. Faced with an impending Social Security deficit, in 1983, the Administration implemented the recommendations of the Greenspan Commission: Increase the full retirement age, increase the combined tax to the current 12.4%, and increase taxes on SS benefits (Social Security Administration, 1983). Reagan's reforms worked because the sacrifices were, "as equitably as possible, spread across workers, employers, and beneficiaries" (Gruner, 2022, p. 373). Such an equitable, multi-faceted solution would need to be implemented in the near future in order to stave off the impending deficit.

Expect the full retirement age to be increased in the near future. But at the same time, rescuing the Social Security System by coercing Americans to work longer only "exacerbates inequalities in wealth, health, well-being, and retire-ment time" (Ghilarducci, 2024a) while doing little to tackle the overall problem of retirement insecurity.

11.8 Conclusion

President Roosevelt succeeded in institutionalizing Social Security, which be-came his legacy, the hallmark of the New Deal. Social Security succeeded in its original goals of decreasing the poverty rate of the elderly and cushioning the most vulnerable, while being run extremely efficiently (Reardon, 2014). No government program is perfect, nor can one ever expect it. Today, in order to 'save' Social Security, and to keep it working well into the future, we need a functional, bi-partisan government to provide the above-mentioned pragmatic and holistic reforms. It is necessary for our lawmakers to,

> address the projected trust fund shortfalls in a timely way in order to phase in necessary changes gradually and give workers and beneficiaries time to adjust to them. Implementing changes sooner rather than later would allow more generations to share in the needed revenue increases or re-ductions in scheduled benefits. Social Security will play a critical role in the lives of 67 million beneficiaries and 180 million covered workers and their families during 2023. With informed discussion, creative think-ing, and timely legislative action, Social Security can continue to protect future generations.
>
> (Social Security Trustees, 2023a)

We agree.

Notes

1 In the United States, North Dakota's capital is Bismark. It was named not so much for Bismark himself, but for the influx of German immigrants settling in the upper Midwest during the 19th century. Many Germans were fond of a certain type of jelly doughnut, known as a bismark.
2 For a pithy discussion of pre-1935 income security programs in the United States, see (Social Security Administration, 1997).
3 Discussion on Mr. Swope is based on (Gruner, 2022, pp. 88–89). Swope's initial proposal offered a "sweeping national plan to provide life insurance, unemployment benefits, and pensions for workers—a plan too ambitious for even Roosevelt's brain trust to accept" (Gruner, 2022, p. 106).
4 That high wages would benefit the economy helped enact the Fair Labor Stand-ards Act (FLSA) in 1938, which created the **minimum wage**, as well as pro-viding the rationale for the Labor Management Relations Act in 1935, which legalized **labor unions** and collective bargaining. The opposing argument that high wages would cause unemployment was defeated (at the time) by the Great Depression's severity.

5 Also, see Hacker (2006). He writes: "As private and public support erodes, workers and their families must bear a greater burden. This is the essence of the Great Risk Shift. Through the cutback and restructuring of workplace benefits, employers are seeking to offload more and more of the risk once pooled under their auspices."
6 For an interesting discussion of the evolution of these programs, see (Social Security Administration, 1997).
7 A flat tax basically works the same way. Everyone pays the same flat rate, although some versions offer two or three graduated rates.
8 In his State of the Union Address, January 4, 1965, Johnson announced his Great Society's goals, including his War on Poverty.
9 Since initial passage of the SSA in 1935, there have been numerous reforms to increase efficiency and broaden its base. In 1953, for example, coverage and benefits were increased for the self-employed, farmers, domestic workers, and beneficiary descendants. For a full text of the Social Security Act, see (Social Security, n.d.).
10 On July 30, 1965, President Johnson signed the Social Security Amendments of 1965, which created Medicare and Medicaid.
11 While there are several ways to determine who is poor, here in the United States, it is done by income earned vis-à-vis income thresholds which are determined by the Census Bureau. If one's income falls beneath a threshold, then one is officially poor. For 2022, the income threshold for a family of four was $29,950 (Shrider and Creamer, 2023). Each year the thresholds increase with the rate of inflation.
12 The Office of Management and Budget (2023) provides the source for federal outlays/receipts. As of 2022, Medicare has replaced National Defense as the second largest outlay, a position the latter held since the late 1990s.
13 Given the SS Trust Funds' substantial surpluses (due to a greater inflow than outflow), other branches of the federal government typically borrow from the SSA. The substantial borrowed sums have, in turn, "paid for all of George Bush's Middle Eastern wars, much of Ronald Reagan's defense spending and [some] of Bill Clinton's budget surpluses" (Gruner, 2022, p. 95).
14 Disclaimer: Professor Ghilarducci was my (Jack) doctoral thesis advisor at the University of Notre Dame.

References

Bureau of Labor Statistics (2023) A Profile of the Working Poor, (November) U.S. Bureau of Labor Statistics, Washington DC.
Caplan, Zoe (2023) 'US Older Population Grew from 2010 to 2020 at Fastest Rate Since 1880–1890' (May 25), https://www.census.gov/library
Dagher, Veronica and Anne Tergesen (2024) 'Here's What it's Like to Retire on Almost Nothing But Social Security,' *The Wall Street Journal*, January 6, p. A1 and A8.
Elflein, John (2023) 'Life Expectancy—Men at the Age of 65 years in the US 1960–2021,' *Statista*, https://www.statista.com/statistics
Ghilarducci, Teresa (2024a) 'Work longer is no solution for people who can't afford to retire,' *Los Angeles Times,* February 26, Opinion, (latimes.com).
Ghilarducci, Teresa (2024b) *Work, Retire, Repeat: The Uncertainty of Retirement in the New Economy*, University of Chicago Press, Chicago.
Gruner, Ronald (2022) *We the Presidents: How American Presidents Shaped the Last Century*, Libratum Books, Naples, Florida.

Hacker, Jacob (2006) *The Great Risk Shift: The Assault on American Jobs, Families, Health Care, and Retirement, and How You Can Fight Back*, Oxford University Press, New York.

O'Neil, Aaron (2022) 'Life Expectancy in Germany 1875–2020,' June 15, *Statista*, https://www.statista.com/statistics

Office of Management and Budget (2023) *Budget of the US Government*, Budget of the United States Government, Fiscal Year 2023 (whitehouse.gov).

Piketty, Thomas (2022) *A Brief History of Equality*, Belknap Press, Harvard University.

Reardon, Jack (2014) 'Social Security,' in Lindsey K. Hanson and Timothy J. Essenburg (Eds), *The New Faces of American Poverty: A Reference Guide to the Great Recession*, ABC-CLIO Books, Santa Barbara, California, 2014, pp. 481–492.

Reardon, Jack, Maria Madi, and Molly Scott Cato (2018) *Introducing a New Economics: Pluralist, Sustainable, Progressive*, Pluto Press, London.

Shrider and Creamer (2023) *Poverty in the United States: 2022*, US Census Bureau, Washington DC, (census.gov).

Social Security Administration (1983) *Greenspan Commission on Social Security Reform*, Social Security History, Washington, DC (ssa.gov).

Social Security Administration (1997) 'Social Security Programs in the US,' (July) Social Security Programs in the United States (ssa.gov).

Social Security Trustees (2023a) *The 2023 Annual Report of the Board of Trustees of the Federal Old-Age and Survivors Insurance and Federal Disability Insurance Trust Funds*, The 2023 OASDI Trustees Report (ssa.gov).

12 The Student Loan Crisis

The Issue: What to do about the seemingly unbearable burden of student loan debt was a major during the Biden administration and promises to be so post-2024. This is an issue that will not go away. Given the expected rancor, American citizens need to know first of all the data, and then the true reasons for the (escalating) debt. Only then can we map out a workable solution that is equitable for all.

12.1 Introduction

When I (Jack) was an undergraduate, every year I was able to pay for all my tuition, and my room and board, and my books. I graduated in four years without any debt. Was I unusual? An outlier? No, I don't think so. I knew lots of people who did the same. Sure, I had a steady job throughout my four years. And sure, I worked every summer and every Christmas break and every spring break as well (although at times I wish I hadn't so I could join my friends on spring break or sleep late the day after Christmas). My situation was by no means unique: Many of my friends paid for their tuition via a combination of summer/winter work and working during the semester. Back in those days, there wasn't the culture of debt as there is now; I was never solicited with a credit card application of any type, nor were my friends. If anything, there was a stigma attached to debt, not like today when it seems we are awash in an enabling culture of debt.

But when my two kids (Jack) recently attended college (at a comparable school), there was absolutely no way that they could come even close to paying even a tenth of their tuition/room board, no matter how many times I did the math, and no matter how many hours I asked (nicely) them to work.

12.2 The Stats

There are lots of statistics to back this up,[1] which is good, since I know I wasn't dreaming:

- **Tuition has exploded**: From 1970 to 2020, the average annual in-state tuition and fees at a public (non-profit) university increased by 2,580%; and 2,107% at private schools.

DOI: 10.4324/9781003591856-14

- **The tuition increase was far greater than the inflation rate**: During this period, the annual increase in inflation was 3.87%, resulting in a cumulative increase of 567%. This means that the tuition increase was roughly four times that of inflation.
- **Yes, the minimum wage had increased but nowhere near enough**: The federal **minimum wage** (which is what most students would likely have earned) increased by only 353% during this period, not even keeping up with inflation.
- **Today's students need to work far more hours to pay their tuition**: In 1970, a student attending a public university and working full-time during the summer at the federal minimum wage, could earn enough to pay tuition in full with money left over; and would not need to work the rest of the year. In 2021, however, after working full-time during the summer, a student would need to work 24 hours per week for the remainder of the year, which is insane. The numbers for private schools are much worse: In 1970, a student would need to have worked full-time all summer and then 15 hours/week the rest of the year. Whereas today, that student, after working the full summer, would need to work 100 hours per week, for the remainder of the year. Doubly insane!

Just as the demand for health care has become disconnected from its cost/price so has the decision to attend college. And, just like health care insurance which allows many of us to afford health care, the panoply of available loans makes it easier to attend college. Of course, it is assumed that after graduation, one will be earning a much greater wage, enabling the repayment of the loans. After all, attending college is part of the American Dream, with a degree being the ticket to a high-paying job, guaranteeing a comfortable living. Right? Well, not really.

According to an insightful analysis by Beamer and Steinbaum (2023), the genesis of this debt/tuition linkage dates to the 1970s as,

> the fruit of a tacit agreement among state legislatures, college administrators and the federal government: defund public colleges/universities and shift them to a tuition-based revenue model, with the federal government backstopping the system with student debt so that more students can continue to obtain more expensive education. This change was justified by the idea that higher education 'pays off' in the labor market.

Such a linkage, needless to say, masks the real reasons for spiraling tuition.

Today, 45 million student borrowers owe a total of $1.6 trillion (approximately 6% of **GDP**—an aggregate measure of the yearly value of what our nation produces). Student loan debt is now the second largest consumer debt (after mortgages) comprising 9.5% of total debt, and furthermore, 54% of college students graduate with debt (Haughn, 2023). Although the exact figures differ, the consensus on default rates seems to be around 10% (Sherman, 2023). The exact rate differs according to the type of school (for-profits have the highest percentage) and the period of analysis. The latter is due to the moratorium on student loan paybacks implemented during the COVID which expired, September 2023. This has significantly reduced the default rate—if you don't have to pay back, then you can't really default. According to data from Best Colleges, "among all borrowers who entered loan repayment in 2019, 2.3% had defaulted by September 2021. That's a massive drop from prior years" (Welding, 2023). However, there is no reason to assume that defaults will not begin to trek upward.

12.3   Congressional/Presidential/Judicial Responses

During his 2000 campaign for the presidency, Joe Biden promised to relieve this debt burden, calling it an albatross, constricting the standard of living of recent graduates, preventing them from buying houses, starting their own families, putting down roots, and living on their own. Biden pledged to reduce the student debt on all federally funded student loans[2] (if one had borrowed from a private source, then he/she was out of luck).

In August 2022, President Biden implemented his student loan forgiveness program. It specifically allowed individual borrowers who made less than $125,000/year, and married couples or heads of households who made less than $250,000/year to have $10,000 of their federal student loans forgiven. If a qualifying borrower also received a federal Pell grant (based on exceptional financial need) while enrolled in college, the individual would have been eligible for up to $20,000 of debt forgiveness.

Immediately, Republicans filed lawsuits offering a host of reasons why this was bad economics and bad politics:

- It would increase **inflation** (which had already reached the highest levels since the early 1980s) by allowing tuition to continue to increase.
- The amount of the loan forgiveness would de facto act as a stimulus, further pressuring prices at a time when additional stimuli were not needed.
- It would increase the **deficit** and thereby the **debt.**
- President Biden had no constitutional basis to do so.
- It would be unfair for those who never went to college or who did not take out student loans. It would also unfairly discriminate against young people who took out a loan not to attend school but to start a business, or for any other reason.
- Forgiving a student loan debt is a classic example of a moral hazard, i.e., encouraging the very behavior that the policy was designed to prevent.[3]

In other words, debt forgiveness sends the wrong message: If you get into debt, no problem, the federal government will bail you out. Thus, the student is incentivized to take out a loan, since it will (or even might) be forgiven. This is a classic case of an overly paternalistic government: You screw up and get into trouble, then we will help you. Additionally, this moral hazard attenuates the end result of the problem, while not incentivizing the individual to change his/her behavior, thus ignoring the source of the problem.

President Biden argued that not only would debt forgiveness help students attain a better standard of living, but that he was on solid constitutional grounds by connecting his debt cancellation to the 2003 Heroes Act. This Act, passed in the wake of 9/11, allows the Secretary of Education to cancel or alleviate student debt due to a national emergency. And, according to the Biden administration, COVID, along with the rapid accumulation of debt, was a national emergency.

The US Supreme Court disagreed. On June 30, 2023, in Biden v. Nebraska,[4] the Court ruled 6-3 that President Biden had no right under federal law to authorize student loan forgiveness. The Court based its decision on the 'major questions' doctrine, i.e., the courts cannot decide any matters (or implement policy) which have major economic and political impacts, unless Congress has given it express authority.[5]

Generally, Republicans tend to favor limits to student loans as well as imposing a ceiling on how much debt each student is allowed to accumulate.[6] Beamer and Steinbaum (2023) call this "an exclusionary vision that seeks to return higher education to its pre-GI Bill status as a bastion of white privilege for a tiny elite." On the other hand, Democrats propose to make information more symmetric by asking schools to post numbers on their graduates' earnings and debt burden, so that potential students can weigh this information before making their decision. Unfortunately, neither Republicans nor Democrats are attacking the source of the problem.[7]

12.4   The Real Cause(s) of Spiraling Tuition

With or without the student debt cancellation, tuition will continue to increase unabated, for debt cancellation doesn't address its real causes. Perhaps if the student loan forgiveness had anything to do with reducing the spiraling cost of tuition, we would at least have given it due consideration, for getting at the root cause of the problem is long overdue. As college professors ourselves, in a way we wish that the higher tuition went to us, but alas, we have the pay stubs to prove otherwise. For starters, keep in mind that approximately one-third of college professors are adjuncts which means they're teaching a course here and another there at extremely low pay, so that they have to teach a lot just to make ends meet. At the other end of the spectrum, our profession has its superstars that command high salaries, while writing their own ticket to any university. While this certainly puts upward pressure on tuition, whether it outweighs the increasing number of adjuncts is not clear.

The real cause of spiraling tuition is that as the number of college students has long-term declined, colleges and universities compete each other, not by offering lower tuition (why should they, with myriad agencies offering loans?), but by offering state-of-the art student centers, world-class dorms and dining centers (the latter always with several options), impressive intercollegiate and intramural facilities; and the list goes on, with an ever-increasing overseeing bureaucracy to administer and oversee. Schools that cannot compete have no choice but to close their doors or even merge with their rivals. According to an analysis of the USA flagship's public universities by *The Wall Street Journal*,

> the nation's best-known public universities have been on an unfettered spending spree. In the past two decades, they erected new skylines of snazzy academic buildings and dorms. They poured money into big-time sports programs and hired layers of administrators. Then they passed the bill along to students…The spending is inextricably tied to the nation's $1.6 trillion federal student debt crisis. Colleges have paid for their sprees in part by raising tuition prices, leading many students to take on more debt. That means student loans served as easy financing for university projects.. . Through it all, schools operated in a culture that valued unrelenting growth and prioritized raising revenue over cutting costs. Administrators established ambitious strategic plans and tried to lure wealthy students with luxurious amenities. Influential college rankings rewarded those that spent more.
>
> (Korn et al., 2023)

So, what we have here is a system which encourages increased spending and increased revenue, while ignoring costs. Administrators can do this because they are not accountable, with their plans often (but not always) rubber-stamped by the university's board of trustees. And you would think that the ongoing cutback in state funding would restrain university spending, but just the opposite:

> universities generally didn't tighten their belts as a result. Rather, they rais[e] prices far beyond what was needed to fill the hole. For every $1 lost in state support at those universities over the two decades, the median school increased tuition and fee revenue by nearly $2.40, more than covering the cuts.
>
> (Korn et al., 2023)

12.5 Conclusion

Education is one of the most fundamentally important things that we can do as human beings for ourselves, our families, our future, and our planet. Let us get it right. Rising and unaffordable tuition is too important a problem to ignore since it excludes those least able to afford it. If the problem is really about debt relief, perhaps we should relieve other types of debt, and perhaps even offer a debt jubilee. But if the problem is about how to stop spiraling tuition (as it should be), then let's stop beating around the bush, roll up our sleeves (so to speak), and get to work. Let's address the real causes of spiraling tuition and offer effective solutions.

Notes

1 Scatton (2021) provides the statistics in the following bullets.
2 Joe Biden tweeted on March 20, 2020, "We should forgive a minimum of $10,000/person of federal student loans…Young people and other student debt holders bore the brunt of the last crisis. It shouldn't happen again." In April 2020, Biden reiterated (in *Medium*) that if elected, he would "immediately cancel a minimum of $10,000 of student debt per person." And during an October 2020 town hall meeting, he repeated his goal to "make sure everybody…gets $10,000 knocked off of their student debt."
3 Or more formally: the lack of incentive to guard against risk where one is protected from its consequences, e.g., the existence of insurance reduces risk from what it otherwise would be.
4 Only plaintiffs who stand to be directly injured by the defendant have a right to sue before the US Supreme Court. In this case, six Republican-controlled state governments (Nebraska, Missouri, Arkansas, Iowa, Kansas, and South Carolina) sued the Biden Administration that debt cancellation would cost them significant lost revenue.
5 We discuss this doctrine in our chapter **The Supreme Court**. In addition, see the highly readable *Major Questions Doctrine*' (2023). While President Biden contemplated issuing an executive order, his debt forgiveness was directly tied to the Heroes Act passed in 2003, rendering unnecessary such an issuance.
6 This paragraph heavily relies on (Beamer and Steinbaum, 2023) with the exception of our opinion.
7 According to a recent survey of college students, "Most…do not see themselves as Democrats or Republicans. Thirty-four percent identify as strong or weak Democrats and 11 percent claim to be strong or weak Republicans, leaving the majority—54 percent—in the middle, identifying as Independents, Leaners, or something else entirely. While college students are less likely to be Republican and more likely to be centrist, they are by no means more left than the rest of the nation" (Abrams and Suri, 2021).

References

Abrams, Samuel and Jeremy Suri (2021) 'Some Surprising Facts About College Politics,' *Real Clear Policy*, https://www.realclearpolicy.com
Beamer, Laura and Marshall Steinbaum (2023) 'Who Repays Student Loans?' *The New York Times*, July 16, 2023.

Haughn, Raija (2023) 'Student Loan Debt Stats,' bankrate.com, July 18. https://www. bankrate.com/

Korn, Melissa, Andrea Fuller, and Jennifer Forsyth (2023) 'State Colleges Devour Money and Students Foot the Bill,' *The Wall Street Journal*, August 11, pp. A1 and A9.

'Major Questions Doctrine,' (2023) Wikipedia Contributors in *Wikipedia, The Free Encyclopedia*. July 4. https://en.wikipedia.org/w/index.php?title=Major_questions_doctrine&oldid=1163318331

Scatton, Kristen (2021) '1970 vs. 2020: How Working Through College has Changed,' *Intelligent*, https://www.intelligent.com/

Sherman, Emily (2023) 'Student Loan Default: What You Need to Know, *US News & World Report*, April 27. (usnews.com).

Social Security (n.d.a) 'Legislative History: Social Security Act of 1935,' Social Security History (ssa.gov).

Welding, Lyss (2023) 'Student Loan Default Rate: Facts and Statistics,' *Best Colleges*, February 6, https://www.bestcolleges.com/

13 Housing

The Issue: America has a housing problem. No matter how we define or measure it, there is "an acute shortage of affordable housing, resulting in homelessness, excessive rents, and punishingly long commutes" (Block, 2023, p. 30). But why? In the richest nation on earth? How has this come to be? What does this say about our priorities as a nation? What can be done? Any one of these questions would be a challenge to answer; taken together they are formidable but not impossible. The purpose of this chapter is to develop a holistic understanding of this very complex problem and what we can do about it.

13.1 Introduction

A central objective of our economy (and one that should be prioritized) is to build housing that is both affordable and sustainable. In turn, this raises a bevy of pertinent and interrelated questions: Who decides the specifics and on what basis? Should market forces or government be preponderant in housing construction and housing prices? Should housing be constructed as rental units or as homes? How and where should they be constructed? How sustainable should they be? And what exactly is affordable?

This chapter will discuss the essential importance of housing in our economy, our pervasive housing problem, potential solutions, the government's role, and the persistence of homelessness.

13.2 The Importance of Housing for the Individual and the Economy

Every culture has a word for 'house,' which should not surprise us, since housing, or shelter, is a basic human need. We all need protection from the elements. In a June 2024 speech, Treasury Secretary Janet Yellen noted,

> That housing matters is intuitive to many of us. It's the backdrop of our day-to-day lives and the foundation for a better economic future. Quality

DOI: 10.4324/9781003591856-15

housing that is affordable supports good health, saving families from unsafe situations such as lead exposure. It supports education, preventing frequent moves that disrupt learning. And it supports job possibilities, enabling workers to live close to jobs where they'll be most productive. For many Americans, housing is a linchpin of the American Dream and a gateway to the middle class.

(Yellen, 2024)

For many of us, a home is our space, our safe enclave, where we can have some down time, where we can be with our family, and even alone, enjoying some respite from the world. Indeed, "The right to housing and access to housing involves what is most private in each of us. This is the sphere of family life" (Piketty, 2022, p. 37).

Housing is also important for the health of the economy; it "is the wheel within the wheel to move the whole economic engine" (Marriner Eccles, Federal Reserve Chair, 1934–1948; quoted in Mari, 2023, p. 35). Here, we list a few reasons why:

- New housing starts is one of the **leading economic indicators** used by economists to anticipate an upturn/downturn in the economy. A fall in housing starts could signal the start of a recession, especially in conjunction with rising interest rates.
- For many Americans, their home is their preponderant (and perhaps only) source of wealth.
- Housing, and more specifically, its value (and whether increasing/decreasing) affects the health of the economy by affecting both consumption and investment, important macro-economic variables which together explain 86% of America's economic activity.[1]
- Housing is also central to the financial markets (Harnett, 2022). Over the last century, housing has helped define the swings in the economic cycle, being a key driver of investment, employment, and consumption. As one recent research paper exclaimed 'Housing IS the Business Cycle" (Harnett, 2022; emphasis in the original).
- Housing promotes neighborhood stability and reduces crime.
- Housing is intimately connected with sustainability or lack thereof. Cheap oil and gas have fueled the construction of suburbia, as well as the construction of energy-draining McMansions.[2] While increases in new housing starts might presage a stronger economy, at the same time, they should,

> send chills up the spine of a reflective person, because [they] represent monoculture tract developments of cookie-cutter bunkers on half-acre lots in far-flung suburbs, or else houses plopped down in isolation

along country roads in what had been cornfields, pastures, or woods. In any case, you can rest assured that they will only add to the problems of our present economy and of American civilization.

(Kunstler, 1993, p. 147)

- The lack of housing (i.e., homelessness) is a collective failure. If our economy is all about helping all to provision, and if someone is without housing (a most basic and fundamental need) what does this say about our economy?
- And finally, the most recent **inflation** spell was largely driven by housing and more specifically a national housing shortage.

13.2.1   *Housing, Monetary Policy, Inflation, and the Federal Reserve*

Renters and home buyers, especially first-time buyers, bear the brunt of monetary policy: To combat inflation, as the **Federal Reserve** had earlier been doing, they increase interest rates[3] to curtail aggregate demand by effectively making borrowing more expensive. But as interest rates increase so do mortgage rates. And during periods of **inflation,** rent will also increase. For example, the most recent bout of inflation (which began March 2021) renters were particularly hard hit. The median rent for a two-bedroom flat increased from $1,424 at the end of 2020 to $1,713 at the end of 2023. And, according to the USA Treasury, "from 2000 to 2020, median rents increased by more than median incomes in counties covering 97 percent of the U.S. population. The National Low Income Housing Coalition finds that today, not a single state has sufficient housing available for low-income renters" (Yellen, 2024).

Although the Fed has been steadfast in its fight against inflation "Congress has yet to help by addressing our national housing shortfall. If it had, pandemic-era inflation might already be behind us" (Harris, 2024). The preponderant driver of rising housing prices is a severe housing shortage, estimated anywhere between 1.5 million and 5.5. million units (Harris, 2024). Higher prices benefit existing homeowners with fully paid mortgages (e.g., adding $2 billion of wealth to their balance sheets during the recent inflation).

Not surprisingly, the median net worth of US renters is 2.5% of the median worth of homeowners (Mari, 2023, p. 31). Speculation also plays a role, increasing the wedge between the housing haves and have nots: "In 2022, one in four home sales was to someone who had no intention of living in it. These investors are particularly incentivized to buy the sorts of homes most needed by first-time buyers: Inexpensive properties generate the highest rental-income cash flows" (Mari, 2023, p. 31). Homeowners with fully paid mortgages have benefited; renters have not.

Rent has more than doubled since 2000, rising much faster than renters' incomes (Desmond, 2023, p. 65). While the lack of affordable housing is problematic, there is another deeper, more sinister reason: Poor people—and particularly poor Black families—don't have much choice when it comes to where they can live. Because of that, landlords can overcharge, and they do, given that "the ownership of housing involves strategies of extraction and relations of power between landlords and renters" (Piketty, 2022, pp. 36–37). According to Desmond: even after accounting for all expenses, and after accounting for *all* costs, (including missed payments, higher vacancies and more repairs due to older buildings) landlords in poor neighborhoods enjoy profits that are double those of landlords operating in affluent communities (Desmond, 2023, p. 67).

In the United States, post-COVID inflation, easy monetary policy and extravagant fiscal policy has fueled 20% of US housing price inflation (Harnett, 2022). If we factor everything out except housing, then inflation would be well under the **Federal Reserve's** self-imposed target of two percent. Given housing's continued importance, "perhaps it is time for the Fed and other central banks to follow the Reserve Bank of New Zealand, and explicitly add housing into their policy mandates. After all, housing *is* the business cycle" (Harnett, 2022). Not a bad idea.

13.3   The Lack of Affordable Housing and Possible Solutions

13.3.1   *Defining Affordable Housing*

While several affordable housing definitions exist, a common one is for housing costs (whether rent or mortgage) not to exceed 30% of one's income. In turn, an individual is cost-burdened if spending more than 30% on rent, and severely cost-burdened if spending more than half one's income on rent. Given a limited budget,

such burdens often manifest physically. When families are forced to make budgetary tradeoffs, they spend less on food and transportation, and way less on healthcare for seniors and kids. That's not to mention the psychological toll that housing instability itself takes.

(Paul, 2021 p. 77)

13.3.2   *Solutions*

In ordinary times, we could look to Congress for solutions. But these are not ordinary times. Congress, with its ideological rifts has become dysfunctional, abnegating its important role to help the American people. Thus, it is quixotic to look for the federal government to solve the housing crisis. As just one example: In 2022, the House passed a bill that would have channeled $40 billion to the Housing Trust Fund, the Low-Income Housing Tax Credit, and HOME Investment partnerships, but the Senate killed the bill.

Thus, we need to look for more localized and innovative solutions to see how cities/localities have tackled their housing crises, while keeping in mind that "there's no one answer to America's housing crisis" (Kristof, 2023b, p. 3), for example, Tokyo: More flexible zoning laws; New Zealand: Upzoning[4] which allows taller and more denser buildings as well as multi-family dwellings; and Vienna: Gemeindebauten (i.e., social housing).

Space precludes a detailed look at every and all, so we felt it prudent and productive to discuss Vienna's social housing in depth.[5] During the 19th century, Vienna had one of Europe's worst housing crises, but by the early to mid-20th century, it was practically solved. Here are some highlights:

- Today, 43% of Viennese housing has escaped commodification, i.e., rental prices reflect costs/rates set by law and not by what the market will bear or what a person with no other options will pay. Limited-profit housing (charging rents that reflect costs) accounts for half of the city's social housing.
- The government subsidizes affordable housing for a wide range of incomes and not just for the poor. In other nations such as the United States, public housing is only for the poorest, spatially concentrating poverty while stigmatizing those living in such units, while also creating a 'Not in My Backyard' opposition to construction of new subsidized housing.
- Two-thirds of the city's rental housing is covered by rent control and all tenants have just-cause eviction protections.
- Vienna prioritizes the subsidizing of housing construction. Compare this to the USA which subsidizes people and demand.
- Vienna's choice illustrates a fundamental economic reality: A large enough supply of social housing offers a market alternative that improves housing for all.

Can Vienna's experience be applied elsewhere? Can we "imagine a world where individuals are freed from the ordinary struggle to pay rent, where habitation is treated as a right and not a privilege" (Mari, 2023, p. 49). Indeed, imagine if this "staggering burden" (Mari, 2023, p. 49) of housing were to recede for many of us?

The typical American reader will object that Vienna's socialized housing will not work here; after all, this is capitalism where markets rule. But, as Mari points out, any American with a mortgage (now or in the past) is living in subsidized housing:

> the fixed rate 30-year mortgage is only possible because the government insures the debt; and for those affluent to buy homes, they can write off the interest they pay on their mortgages, they can deduct property taxes from their federal taxes, and if they sell their primary residence they can even avoid paying capital gains.
>
> (Mari, 2023, p. 31)

But this is just the tip of the iceberg for government involvement (see the next section).

Here in the United States, a visceral opposition exists to building affordable housing in one's backyard, so to speak. This is due to a fear of increased drugs, crime, and lower property values. Called 'home voters,' these people are,

> a coalition of Americans who—consciously or not— vote to protect their property value, and tend to oppose local development and favor exclusionary zoning…which in turn has transformed the nation's housing stock into an ever—more scarcer and an ever-more expensive class of speculative assert.
>
> (Mari, 2023, p. 37)

Perhaps we can take a lesson from Vienna which offers social housing to a wide range of people across a wide range of incomes, and not just the poor, effectively removing the stigma of public housing.

Problematic in America's housing sector, especially vis-a-vis other sectors/industries, is lagging productivity:

> while most industries have become more productive/efficient, the housing industry still uses the same labor-intensive methods as they have for hundreds of years, i.e., different skills at different stages (e.g., electricians, plumbers, carpenters, masons, etc.) come together to build the product from start to finish.
>
> (Paul, 2021, p. 79)

This suggests the need for 3-D printing, prefab homes (the parts arrive factory-made but installed on-site), and manufactured homes, i.e., built in a factory and transported to site (Paul, 2021, p. 79). Although, the technology exists to expedite affordable housing (Paul, 2021, p. 81) expect formidable opposition from home voters.

Here in the United States, a solution that seems to be working (and gaining momentum) was crafted by PadSplit, a public benefit corporation (i.e., for profit, while advancing a social purpose, but privately funded). PadSplit, founded in 2017, typically takes, "a house that is near public transportation, convert[s] the living room to a bedroom, puts locks on each bedroom door and then rents out each room by the week. This typically means a shared bathroom and kitchen" (Kristof, 2023b, p. 3). This policy is especially effective given that 28% of American households consist of a single person living alone, yet fewer than one percent of housing units are studios" (Kristof, 2023b, p. 3).

Perusing PadSplit's webpage[6] as this issue goes to press (October 2024), one sees (weekly) offers for $145/week in New Orleans, $250/week in Miami, $135/week in Richmond, $129 in Houston, etc. Such rates are cheaper than hotels and Airbnbs, while offering a palatable alternative to homelessness (see below)[7] (Kristof, 2023b, p. 3).

This could work hand-in-hand with land banks, i.e., "a quasi-governmental agency specifically tasked with acquiring blighted properties, clearing their debts, assembling lots and selling them to qualified developers... [which is a] vision of community control" (Bologna, 2023, p. B6). Land banks currently operate in 200 USA cities, typically areas which have experienced population loss, and blighted neighborhoods populated by vacant, abandoned, boarded-up buildings.

13.4   The Role of the Federal Government

The federal government's role in housing is extensive, so much so that we would need a separate book to discuss/evaluate. At best, we can briefly discuss the following key elements, all designed to increase home ownership and expand the creditworthiness of housing consumers:

- The extensive role of the federal government dates to the Coolidge Administration, and specifically, Commerce Secretary Herbert Hoover and Treasury Secretary Anthony Mellon, who began encouraging home ownership.[8] It was also during the 1920s that 'Better Homes in America,' an association of bankers, realtors, and manufacturers formed to promote home ownership and home building.
- During the Great Depression, a concerted effort was made to rescue home ownership; and such policies have continued to this day. By 1933, half of USA mortgage debt was in default. While the Hoover administration preached self-reliance and rugged individualism, "Roosevelt immediately created the Homeowners' Loan Corporation, which among other things bought underwater mortgages in order to stabilize the housing market, while also bundling principal and interest so that borrowers eventually became homeowners" (Mari, 2023, p. 35). Roosevelt also passed the National Housing Act of 1934, creating the Federal Housing Administration which insured mortgage debt.[9]
- Policies that affect housing demand include[10]: (1) the availability of the tax deduction for home mortgages; (2) the 1944 GI bill offering veterans low cost mortgages; (3) the Federal National Mortgage Association (i.e., Fannie Mae) which allowed banks to monetarize mortgages so that they could receive cash immediately rather than wait for the original mortgage to be repaid; (4) The American Dream Downpayment Act (2003) helping first-time home buyers.

- Policies that affect housing supply include: (1) The Federal Housing Administration (1934) provides insurance to protect FHA-approved lenders against losses. This, in turn, effectively extends credit to less than optimal creditors; (2) the Emergency Home Finance Act (i.e., Freddie Mac) reduces interest rate risks for banks; (3) the Government National Mortgage Association (i.e., Ginnie Mae) provides liquidity for mortgage-backed securities (MBS); (4) the development and encouragement of low-income housing; (5) the Community Reinvestment Act mandates the Federal Reserve to funnel credit to low- and medium-income neighborhoods.
- Policies that promote public goods such as constructing the interstate highway system. Begun in 1954 by President Eisenhower[11] "it changed America" (Gruner, 2022, p. 190). More specifically for our purposes, it enabled overall housing prices to fall, as housing was built away from dense, congested urban areas. Spread-out markets, in turn, encouraged the development of low-density housing.
- While both the Reconstruction Finance Corporation and the Home Loan Banks System were developed during the later days of the Hoover administration (January 13, 1932, and July 1932, respectively), "they afforded an important precedent for a much more comprehensive system of loans in the next administration" (Studenski and Kross, 1963, p. 373).
- The procurement of cheap energy (actively pursued by the American government (see **oil industry**) decreased overall energy prices, allowing/enabling suburbia, with its McMansions and long commutes. Cheap gasoline powered the automobile which decreased urban rents and land values by stretching out the available market. This intensified suburbanization, begun during the late 19th century with the development of streetcar lines, allowing workers to live further away from their jobs.

Unfortunately, with the focus on incentivizing home builders, renters, and home buyers. The totality of these policies has not been able to create enough affordable housing to meet our needs (Paul, 2021, p. 77). Incentives are very important in a market economy, aligning the economy's overall objectives with the specific actions/behavior of market participants. The cumulative effects of the federal government's policy have left us with a two-tiered system with "generous support for affluent homeowners and deliberately insufficient support for the lowest-income households" (Mari, 2023, p. 31).

13.5   The Need for Participatory Democracy to Solve the Housing Crisis

Solutions for the housing problem tend to oscillate between the two extremes of market forces and government action. But this 'either/or thinking' ignores a third and potentially very effective option: Participatory democracy (PD). It directly involves citizens and is effectuated at the local level, thus reversing the locus of traditional top-down decision making.

More specifically, PD starts with citizen juries, whereby participants are chosen at random in order to discuss/deliberate an issue (Block, 2023, p. 37).[12] PD requires effort and hard work. PD attacks the problem directly at its source, with solutions (including funding) suggested by people most affected by the problem. It "give[s] people greater ability to collectively control the economy, which in turn requires increasing the resources available at the local, state, and regional levels" (Block, 2023, p. 37).

A persistent argument made by right-wing ideologues is that elites have dominated policy for the benefit of the few. This, in turn, has fomented the rise of populism, as well as the Brexit, and helped elect Trump to the White House in 2016 and 2024. While we don't dispute that "a technocratic/elitist consensus has dominated both the left and the right of American politics in the 20th century" (Earle et al., 2017, p. 153), we feel that more democracy is needed as a solution, not less. PD serves this much-needed purpose by redirecting problems away from "the domain of the elite [to] much wider parts of the population" (Earle et al., 2017, p. 153). By creating "new mechanisms to increase the public's voice" (Block, 2023, p. 37), PD effectively enfranchises the disenfranchised.

Solving problems (especially housing) at the local level is a most effective learning laboratory for citizens of a democracy[13] and can effectively put a stop to runaway populism. Thus, PD effectively kills two birds with one stone, so to speak. And, as an added bonus,

> The kinds of and qualities of skills needed by citizens for a broad democracy to function effectively are learned, not innate, and must be practiced to be mastered. They include listening, compromise, the ability to critically evaluate verbal and numerical argument, and developing independent judgment. They can only come through practical experience of being involved in participatory democratic institutions. In this sense, moving towards a system of broad democracy is a process of learning by doing.
>
> (Earle et al., 2017, p. 152)

No better place to start than tackling the problem of affordable housing.

13.6   The Problem of Homelessness and Possible Solutions

13.6.1   *Introduction*

Is housing a right or a privilege? Should it be available to all, or only to those able to afford it?[14] As social scientists, we are acutely bothered by privation of any type, and especially homelessness—a major problem in America in both rural and urban areas, affecting every major city/region. Its existence underscores our economy's inability to provision adequately for all, and should be a clarion call for immediate action, since "no American should ever need to remain homeless or unsheltered" (Paul, 2021, p. 125).

According to the Department of Housing and Urban Development, in 2023, the USA homeless population was 650,000, a 12% increase from 2022, and the highest number since reporting began in 2007 (Jersey Sure, 2023). By all accounts, this statistic, which is an annual snapshot, undercounts, prompting states and even local governments to better tabulate using real-world data.

13.6.2   Causes

Why are people homeless? The easy but not entirely accurate answer is due to unaffordability, but there is a plethora of additional factors on both the demand and the supply side that abet homelessness: Mental health, drug addiction, unemployment, poor human capital and job skills, having a prison record; and over-government regulation that reduces supply and boosts prices, high rents and lack of availability. A recent study, however, found that high rates of homelessness didn't correlate with high levels of addiction, poverty, or mental illness, but rather to high rents and low availability of rental housing (Colburn and Aldern, 2022).

13.6.3   Solutions

While "homelessness is an American tragedy…it is not hopeless" (Kristof, 2023a, p. 3). While not neglecting other causes of homelessness, solving the housing crisis could go a long way to solving homelessness. Workable solutions abound. To start, ask if a solution is ex-ante or ex-post. That is, should we focus on predictive factors that could lead to eventual homelessness and try to prevent the problem ex-ante; or should we wait until after the problem is manifest and solve it ex-post? Prevention is usually cheaper in the long run (but not always); at the same time, focusing on factors that could lead to eventual homelessness (ex-ante) is a herculean task involving a keen understanding of macro trends (unemployment, inflation, poverty, etc.) and also micro factors (human capital, work ethic).

Which predictive variable should we focus on? And what specific action(s) to take? For example, a typical red flag would be if a renter fell behind on monthly payments (or homeowners on their mortgage). Do we offer counseling or even financial help? If the latter, this sets up a classic moral hazard (i.e., lack of incentive to guard against risk where one is protected from its consequences). If I know financial assistance is available, why be fastidious? This, unfortunately, encourages the very problem that it was designed to solve.

An effective and necessary ex-ante policy is to ensure adequate money/credit. That doesn't mean that everyone should have an unlimited amount, since this would lead to **inflation**, but that allocative mechanisms are in place to ensure an adequate credit supply; and enough jobs exist to ensure that anyone wanting to purchase housing has the means to attain it, i.e., money/credit, and a job. In our **Artificial Intelligence** chapter, we discuss a basic income policy to deal with potential job loss due to automation. Here, Basic Income would go a long way to solving the problem of unaffordability.[15]

Another ex-ante policy is rent control, which establishes a ceiling on rent prices below the existing price, and above which rents cannot rise. Economic theory posits that a price ceiling (implemented for whatever purpose) will result in a shortage since the lower price incentivizes more quantity demanded and less quantity supplied. However, this ignores the underlying power differentials between owner and renter, along with the fact that the renter often has no alternative place to go, which can lead to exploitation.

Another ex-ante policy is a negative income tax which returns money to an individual if his/her income is under a certain threshold. The problem, of course, is that the individual must be working in order to benefit. If done correctly, however, the negative income tax could phase out most, if not all, government assistance programs such as Medicaid, food stamps, housing assistance, and unemployment insurance.

If we focus on ex-post policies to redress/alleviate homelessness, then at what level should solutions be enacted? Federal, state, or local? And who will pay? Local governments regulate via zoning and building codes, while the federal government underwrites most of housing finance, although "these powers have not been used at the scale needed to expand the supply of affordable housing" (Block, 2023, p. 31). At the federal level, it is necessary to create "a national network of agencies committed to building homes that are attractive, environmentally sound, and located in neighborhoods with the full range of needed services" (Block, 2023, p. 38).

None of this is easy, and taken together, one might even say that the problem is intractable. But we are encouraged by local-level solutions that coalesce interested stakeholders to conceptualize and implement solutions.[16] A success story is Houston: Its homeless population has decreased by 60% since 2011. Most effective was establishing an independent 'Coalition of the Homeless' to coordinate the efforts of 100 non-profit housing initiatives, which might have otherwise gone in many different directions and have been at odds with each other.

13.7 The Interrelationship between Housing, Climate Change, and Immigration

For starters, here in the United States, almost one in ten households do not have air conditioning, most in low-income urban neighborhoods, where the paucity of trees and high prevalence of concrete exacerbates urban heat.[17] A study conducted in New York City found that,

> the neighborhoods most unprepared for climate change have a lot in common: They are poor; they have congestion and histories of redlining

or industrial pollution; and for many of their residents English is a second language. [And in addition]: very little tree covering, heavily exposed pollutants and projects and industry that's been zoned to be placed there.

(Howard, 2024, p. 30)

Jeff Goodell tells us that globally "the heat risk in urban areas tripled over the last forty years, putting 1.7 billion people at risk…[and] unless we take dramatic action to reduce CO2 pollution and change how we live, the number of people at risk will grow exponentially" (2023, p. 66).

Here in the United States, state laws do no mandate landlords to provide AC. However, the Biden Administration's Low Income Home Energy Assistance program helps low-income households pay utility bills. In addition, President Biden's Inflation Reduction Act has set aside money for tax credits/rebates to help poorer households install energy efficient cooling.

The influx of immigrants has important economy-wide implications for housing,

Big movements of people have big economic consequences…Nowhere is this clearer than in the case of rental housing, which is in short supply across the anglosphere [and the] supply is strictly curtailed by excessive regulation in many of the same places now experiencing a migration surge. Migrants, like natives, need places to live, which increases the imperative to build. Welcoming new arrivals means a lot more than just letting them in.

(*The Economist*, May 4, 2024, p. 60)

Needless to say, climate change will intensify the migration already underway, both within and between nations, "as the temperature rises, it will drive a great migration—of humans, of animals, of plants, of jobs, of wealth, of diseases" (Goodell, 2023, p. 16).

13.8   Conclusion

It is hard not to disagree that "America's housing crisis is a big problem that requires an equally big solution" (Harris, 2024). But to solve the crisis, multiple solutions are needed; only one solution, no matter how big, will not work. Many causes and factors are intertwined: Immigration, cheap oil, interest rates, government incentives, and climate change. Thus, the solutions need to be holistic and multi-faceted.

Fixing the housing crisis cannot be done overnight, but at the same time, "there is an enormous advantage in waging such struggles when we can present our fellow citizens with a realistic and practical way forward that makes sense of their lived experience" (Block, 2023, p. 40). To successfully transition to **Net Zero**[18] will require a transformational change in our thinking. We will have to think about where we live, where we work, what we produce, how we build our homes, our schools, our workplaces; "we will have to replace a destructive economy of mindless expansion with one that consciously respects earthly limits and human scale" (Kunstler, 1993, p. 275).

Notes

1 A good example is the 2007–2009 **recession**. In late 2005, the **Federal Reserve** (our central bank) began increasing interest rates. This in turn jeopardized many homeowners, especially those whose finances were precarious to begin with. Many homeowners defaulted. As housing wealth declined, so did consumption, plunging the nation into recession. Average home prices decreased from \$305,000 in 2006 to \$257,000 in 2009, a significant decrease (Gruner, 2022, p. 456). See (Gruner, 2022, pp. 454–475) for a superb account of the 2007 housing crisis.
2 In the dystopian novel, *The World Made by Hand* (Kunstler, 2008) war, disease, and climate change have run rampant, so much so that no one even knows if the United States still exists. Empty McMansions evocatively portray an earlier arrogant and profligate age abetted by cheap energy.
3 The Fed only controls two interest rates: the federal funds rate (i.e., the rate of interest one bank charges another) and the discount rate (the rate of interest the Fed charges to a bank). All interest rates affecting consumers and businesses (as well as the government as a major borrower) will rise and fall with the federal funds rate, unless fixed by agreement.
4 Such legislation was necessary to not only increase housing supply but also to attenuate the discriminatory prohibitions that developed during the 19th century to protect white enclaves from minority intrusion.
5 The following draws heavily on Mari (2023).
6 See its webpage PadSplit: Affordable Rooms for Rent, Homes, Weekly Rentals & More (padSplit.org)
7 As Kristof (2023b, p. 3) notes, "Rooming houses, boardinghouses, or single room occupancy hotels [were ubiquitous earlier in our history]. President Thomas Jefferson stayed in a boardinghouse before moving into the White House."
8 Hebert Hoover, quite popular due to the success of his policies as Commerce Secretary during the Coolidge administration, easily won the 1928 presidential election. But his earlier policies did not carry over as the United States slipped into its worst recession. Widespread and record setting unemployment resulted in housing/rental evictions and the hasty construction of shantytowns, or Hoovervilles as they were bitterly called—an evocative image of the widespread suffering during the Great Depression (Gruner, 2022, pp. 63–64).
9 More insidious: a mortgage loan abiding by certain standards, i.e., if the borrower lived in a stable neighborhood, i.e., white enough, it would minimize the probability of default (Mari, 2023, p. 35).
10 While for taxonomic purposes, we differentiate between policies that affect demand and supply, there is a significant overlap.
11 President Eisenhower, who had been personally impressed by Germany's autobahns, outwitted his critics who viewed it as 'creeping socialism' by touting the system's ability to evacuate cities and move military convoys during an atomic war (Gruner, 2022, p. 189–190). Back then, an atomic war was a very palpable fear.

12 Similarly, Earle at al. recommend Citizens' Policy Groups where "each group would consist of a representative cross section of the community which would enable people from all walks of life to have a much more active role in economic and political discussion and debate, with substantial input into the development of government policy" (2017, pp. 168–169).

13 Other problems to be tackled include education, healthcare, childcare, elder services, and financial services (Block, 2023, p. 30); all of which seem to be intertwined with housing.

14 Of course, we can ask this about other goods produced in our economy, especially health care and university education.

15 A preponderant argument against Basic Income is its affordability, which in turn, comes down to the priority society gives to social justice, republican freedom, and economic security. In those terms, not only is a basic income affordable; we cannot afford *not* to afford it" (Standing, 2017, p. 154; emphasis in the original).

16 See *The Economist* (2023).

17 See the US Climate Vulnerability Index (2024); and Goodell (2023, pp. 65–80). Goodell writes "as cities grow and the heat rises, the future…is of a kind of temperature apartheid, where some people chill in a bubble of cool and others simmer in debilitating heat. This is not how you build a just, equitable, or peaceful world" (Goodell, 2023, p. 80).

18 That is, where the earth's net contribution of global warming gases is zero. For further discussion, see our **Net Zero**.

References

Block, Fred (2023) 'The Habitation Economy,' *Dissent,* Vol. 7, No. 3, Fall, pp. 29–40.

Bologna, Giacomo (2023) 'To Remedy Decaying Properties, Housing Advocates Start Land Bank Campaign,' *The Washington Post*, August 25, p. B6.

Colburn, Gregg and Clayton Page Aldern (2022) *Homelessness is a Housing Problem: How Structural Factors Explain US Patterns*, University of California, Berkeley.

Desmond, Matthew (2023) *Poverty, By America*, Crown, New York.

Earle, Joe, Cahal Moran and Zach Ward Perkins (2017) *The Econocracy: The Perils of Leaving Economics to the Experts*, University of Manchester, Manchester, UK.

Goodell, Jeff (2023) *The Heat Will Kill You First*, Back Bay Books, New York,

Gruner, Ronald (2022) *We the Presidents: How American Presidents Shaped the Last Century*, Libratum Books, Naples, Florida.

Harris, Ben (2024) 'Inflation isn't really the problem-housing is,' *Los Angeles Times*, (March 8) Inflation isn't really the problem. Housing is - Los Angeles Times (latimes.com).

Harnett, Ian (2022) 'Why housing is the key to the next Fed pivot,' *Financial Review,* September 4, (afr.com).

Howard, Hillary (2024) 'Storm Clouds in Vulnerable Neighborhoods,' *The New York Times,* May 12, 2024, p. 30.

'Jersey Sure' (2023) *The Economist*, December 23, p. 16.

Kristof, Nicolas (2023a) 'Houston Shows How to Tackle Homelessness,' *The New York Times*, Opinion Section, November 26, p. 8.

Kristof, Nicolas (2023b) 'The Old Way to Provide Cheap Housing,' *The New York Times*, Opinion Section, December 10), p. 3.

Kunstler, James Howard (2008) *World Made by Hand*, Atlantic Monthly Press, New York.

Kunstler, James Howard (1993) *The Geography of Nowhere: The Rise and Decline of America's Mad-Made Landscape*, Touchstone Books, New York.

Mari, Francesca (2023) 'Soaring real estate markets have created a worldwide housing crisis. How can we learn from a city [Vienna] that has largely avoided it?' *The New York Times Magazine*, May 28, pp. 28–37, and pp. 47, 49.

Paul, David L. (2021) *Redesigning America for the 21st Century*, Funding Visions.

Piketty, Thomas (2022) *A Brief History of Equality*, Belknap Press, Cambridge, Mass.

Standing, Guy (2017) *Basic Income: And How We Can Make it Happen*, Pelican Books, London.

Studenski, Herman and Paul Kross (1963) *Financial History of the United States*, 2nd Ed., McGraw Hill, New York.

'The US Climate Vulnerability Index' (2024), (climatevulnerabilityuindex.org)

'Thousands are Flying In,' *The Economist*, May 4, 2024, p. 60.

White, Eugene, Kenneth Snowden and Price Fishback (2014) *Housing and Mortgage Markets in Historical Perspective*, National Bureau of Economic Research, University of Chicago Press, Chicago.

Yellen, Janet (2024) 'Remarks by Secretary of the Treasury Janet L. Yellen in Minneapolis, Minnesota,'.

14 Immigration

The Issue: Probably, no issue is seen as more political now than immigration. And probably, no issue better illustrates the deep divide between Democrats and Republicans. A thorough resolution of immigration requires full understanding of its causes/consequences and, in addition, cooperation between the two parties (albeit practically impossible these days) and between host and home nations.

14.1 Introduction

Perhaps one of the most agonizing decisions that any individual ever will make is whether to leave his/her native country. Often an act of desperation, with all hope lost; when leaving is the only possibility, or at least that's how it may seem. And then, just as difficult is to enter a new nation with a different culture, history, customs, and even language. No wonder so few people have actually left their native land. Specifically: 3.6% of the world's population have emigrated[1] which amounts to 281 million people.

Not surprisingly, the reasons for emigration throughout history have never been trivial: War, famine, persecution, political upheaval, revolution, lack of opportunity, and, increasingly, **climate change** which has brought about excessive heat, flooding, drought, and species depletion, among other problems.[2] History teaches us that the greater the difference in any of these factors *between* countries, the greater the motivation to leave, all else equal. In turn, this suggests that "unless conditions are the same across all countries, or there are strict prohibitions against migration, the will to migrate will always exist" (Reardon et al., 2018, p. 88).

This doesn't mean that everyone leaves who wants to—since not everyone can—it just increases the probability of the marginal person leaving (i.e., that person with more affluence, more resources, better connections, more desperation, or with family members already living in the host nation). It costs money to leave; it also entails a dispiriting opportunity cost, meaning ironically, that many

DOI: 10.4324/9781003591856-16

of the least able, but perhaps the most desperate are not able to emigrate. Lest we put too much faith in economic determinism,

> In many countries long characterized by migration, a dual culture of migration is centered on both indigenous cultures of reciprocity and care, and on a desire for superior skills and their contemporary economic consequences. Migration strategies may therefore be developed and enabled over many years, rather than being short term responses to the catalysts of inadequate wages and poor working conditions…international migration may even have a quasi-autonomous existence, centered on evolving transnational kinship structures.
>
> (Connell, 2010, p. 204)

This is a very important point, suggesting that immigration solutions must involve both the home and host nations; in other words, immigration and emigration are two sides of the same coin.

Globally, the number of migrants has doubled since 1990 and has tripled since 1970. And thanks to **climate change**, it is expected to continue to increase. While the exact numbers are difficult to predict, future migrants (although in many ways the future is already here) will be a function of the extent of global warming and how well we keep the projected global temperature increase under 2 degrees C, which at this point, doesn't look too likely. This raises the important question of what to do in the United States (and globally) about increased emigration/immigration. It is an issue that will not go away; it will actually become more pressing as climate change accelerates.

14.2 The United States' Historical Schizophrenia toward Immigration

The United States has always been schizophrenic toward immigration, despite being the land of opportunity and the land of open borders. On the one hand, there have always been Americans opposed to anyone else coming to America, especially if they were somehow in any way different. This is despite the obvious fact that everyone in America, except for native Americans, was or came from immigrants.

A good example of this early anti-immigration animus is the Native American Party (NAP) founded in 1844 in New York City. The name does not refer to native American Indians, but rather, protecting the interests of the already well-established 'natives' of America, i.e., the Protestants of northern Europe, hence the term 'nativism.' The NAP feared and disparaged immigrants, especially Catholics, assuming that the Pope was conspiring to take over the federal government. Being a secret organization, if a NAP member was caught, they would innocently proclaim that 'I knew nothing.' The NAP's detractors disparaged it as the 'Know Nothings' and the name stuck. (Perhaps the inspiration for Sergeant Schultz on the TV series *Hogan's Heroes*.)

The NAP even ran a slate of candidates in the 1856 presidential election, headlined by former president Millard Fillmore[3] (1850–1853). Although the Party won 21% of the popular vote (with only the state of Maryland in the Electoral College), it lost the election to Franklin Pierce. By 1860, on the eve of the Civil War, it was defunct. Nevertheless, its nativism spirit has lived on, remerging and regrouping.

At the same time, largely due to persistent labor shortages, the United States has always welcomed immigrants.[4] In 1863, President Lincoln, for example, noted that "there is still a great deficiency of laborers in every field of industry, especially in agriculture and in our mines, as well of iron and coal as of the precious metals" (quoted in Chua, 2007, p. 247). This shortage pushed up wages, especially compared to Europe, incentivizing any who could to emigrate.[5] Adding to this was the wide-open Western frontier[6] further encouraging immigration and domestic migration.

Additionally, the United States has always been a land of respite, offering a new life to the oppressed and poor, as evidenced by the Statue of Liberty's heartfelt and welcoming words, "Give me your tired, your poor, your huddled masses yearning to breathe free."[7]

Given the co-existence of anti- and pro-immigration, which have pulled and tugged at America's heart, our immigration policies have been, not surprisingly, wildly erratic. For example, from the nation's founding through the late 19th century, immigration was virtually unrestricted. This abruptly came to an end in 1921 with the passage of the Emergency Quota Act which reduced immigration from countries that would dilute America's perceived racial homogeneity. This was followed by the National Origins Act in 1924, which has been called (by today's standards), "one of the most racist pieces of legislation signed in the last century" (Gruner, 2022, p. 39). It limited annual immigration to each nationality tabulated in the 1890 census when the non-slave USA population was largely British and Western European, while excluding all Asians, and effectively most Jews. Since then, immigration policy has oscillated between restrictive and highly restrictive policies based on hemisphere of origin, country of birth, the presence of family members, and/or skills.

14.3 Today's USA Immigration Stats

Today, the United States is home to 50.6 million immigrants, which represents 18.1% of the world's total migrants, and 15.3% of the USA population.[8] The latter percentage has been steadily trending upward after reaching a low of 4.7%

in 1970, while also challenging the USA all-time record of 14.8% in 1890 and 14.7% in 1910.

The Federation for American Immigration Reform (FAIR) estimates that approximately 15.5 million illegal aliens reside in the United States,[9] significantly higher than the 14.5 million in 2020 (Raley et al., 2022).

Prior to 2016, new immigrants to the United States averaged 1.0 million per year, but with the get-tough policies of the Trump administration (e.g., building a wall along our southern border), and then COVID, the number of new immigrants drastically decreased. But now these numbers are increasing. In 2023, the number of immigrants was 3.3 million, four times the level during the 2010s (*The Economist*, May 4, 2024, p. 59). Immigration is increasing throughout the developed world, with Germany, the UK, Spain, Australia, and Canada, expecting either a record or near-record numbers. This is due to pent-up demand to emigrate left over from COVID, as well as low unemployment rates and a high number of vacancies, and surplus labor in many developing nations.

Here in the United States, the composition of immigrants has changed dramatically over time, from largely northern and western European (17th through the 19th centuries) to southern and eastern European (early to mid-20th century), to India, Asia, Mexico, and Latin America (1960s–present). Today, Mexico, India, China, the Philippines, and the Dominican Republic are the top five countries in terms of immigrants to the United States. Mexico, at number #1, should not surprise, given the proximity of the border and the sharp difference in economic conditions between the two nations. Overall, the reasons immigrants are attracted to the United States are basically the opposite of why they emigrate: A stable political system (relative to other nations); economic opportunity, which in turn offers hope; relative peace; stability; and prosperity. The states with the greatest number of immigrants are California, Texas, New York, Florida, and New Jersey.

14.4   USA Immigration Policy: Legal Immigration

Pertaining to legal immigration, we have three options:

- Allow everyone and anyone to enter, regardless of nationality, skills, and even criminal background. Since 1921, the United States has not endorsed this, and for good reason: Doing so renders moot the concept of a national border and the concept of a nation. In addition, it tells the world that we do not recognize the sanctity of our borders, or the sanctity of the nation; rather, we are content to let our population ebb and flow with the influx of migrants, assimilating their traits and characteristics. By the way, this was the official USA policy until 1921.[10] It is noteworthy that if anyone can legally enter, then by definition, no one enters illegally, and hence, there are no illegal immigrants. Thus, the legality/illegality of immigration is conceptually defined and enforced by law.

- Completely close the borders and deny entry. Since 1921, the United States has rationed the number of annual immigrants, which has ebbed and flowed based on the practical needs of the nation and on policy vicissitudes, but we have never completely shut our borders. And notice that if there is no legal immigration, then everyone who enters does so illegally, which in turn focuses our entire immigration policy on illegal immigrants.[11]
- The middle ground: Restrict or ration the ability to enter. This has been our policy since 1921. By rationing, the United States retains its national integrity and the sanctity of its borders, allowing entrants on the basis of economic and political needs. The problem here is that even in the best of times (and this is certainly not the best), Americans will disagree on what basis to allow immigration, how many per year, from where, and also, just as importantly from *not* where. Since there is no easy recipe for deciding, this leaves old-fashioned political discourse, dialogue, and dialogue, all regrettably in short supply in today's America. No wonder our immigration 'debates' are rancorous, failing to result in any holistic solution.

Nevertheless, despite the drawbacks of the third option, a broad consensus exists that *at this point in time*, this is our only practical policy. The following reasons are given:

- To ameliorate persistent labor shortages by luring the world's best talent. Indeed,

  > Among America's greatest strengths is its ability to lure and assimilate such talent, thereby boosting growth, entrepreneurship, and innovation. H-1B workers also create opportunities for US citizens by enabling companies to invest in domestic operations instead of sending jobs overseas.
  >
  > (Layoffs, 2022)

- Attracting workers increases the dynamic innovativeness of the USA economy, making it the world's most competitive. This is a major reason why America became a global superpower in the first place, "surpass[ing] all its rivals in pulling in and motivating the world's most valuable human capital" (Chua, 2007, p. 338).
- Increased immigration kills several birds with one stone, so to speak; or as we prefer: It offers several scones to one bird. Specifically, more immigrants will mean more workers. In turn, since they pay taxes, the revenue accruing to the federal government will increase, all things equal, which will reduce the **budget deficit,** all else equal. In addition, at least in the short-term, the

additional taxes taken out of immigrants' paychecks for **Social Security** will help replenish the Social Security Trust Fund, thereby forestalling the supposed day of reckoning when the trust funds will be depleted. (The same argument, by the way, applies to the **Medicare Trust Funds.**) However, the budgetary effect differs depending on whether the immigrant is skilled or unskilled:

> High-skilled types make enormous net fiscal contributions. But for low-skilled workers the question is harder to answer, depending if they arrive young (requiring public schooling, and if they stay until old age/retirement whereupon they become a fixed drag on the public coffers.
> (*The Economist*, May 4, 2024, p. 60)

- Immigration brings talent and new ideas. Interestingly, in the United States, immigrants are 80% more likely than native born citizens to start a business (*The Economist*, June 3, 2023, p. 56).
- The United States (and all Western nations, as well as China, India, South Korea, and Japan are facing declining **birth rates**, which are now lower than required for natural population replenishment. Meaning that, all else equal, a declining (and thereby aging) population places a greater burden on the younger population to support a growing percentage of the elderly, diverting resources away from investment and innovation. Immigration can offset this potential decline. In fact, the United States is one of the few major developed nations whose population is expected to increase during the next generation, almost entirely due to immigration.

On the flip side, arguments against this third policy include:

- Immigration ignores the interests of the well-established citizens, thereby weakening America and what it stands for; well, at least according to those already here. This has been a persistent argument since the early 19th century. Similarly, immigration also dilutes perceived racial homogeneity. President Calvin Coolidge's 1924 presidential nomination speech exemplified this thinking:

> Restricted immigration is not an offensive but purely a defensive action. It is not adopted in criticism of others in the slightest degree, but solely for the purpose of protecting ourselves. We cast no aspersions on any race or creed, but we must remember that every object of our institutions of society and government will fail unless *America be kept American.*
> (quoted in Gruner, 2022, p. 39; emphasis added)

- Immigrants take away jobs, which rightfully belong to Americans. But many such jobs are basically unwanted by most Americans. It is hard to sustain that argument today with so many job vacancies.[12]

- Multiplicative effects, associated with increasing immigration, usually manifest locally. For example, one reason that mortgage rates have not declined as expected is that the new immigrants have increased the demand for **housing**. In addition, more immigrants increase the overall demand for goods and services. At the same time however, both of these effects must be seen in conjunction with the historical decline of the **US labor participation rate.** While the effects of immigration on overall wages are not clear, on the positive side they relieve labor shortages, thus attenuating (supply-reduced) growth in wages and hence inflation, but on the negative side, "the people most likely to see their wages fall…are those most similar to the migrants, which is the typically previous generations of foreign workers" (*The Economist*, May 4, 2024, p. 60).
- However, immigration tends to increase the overall size of the economy; specifically, by 2034, the USA **GDP** is expected to be 2% higher than originally forecast, propelled by immigration; GDP per capita,[13] all else equal, will decline, given that most current immigrants are low-skilled, thus taking low-wage jobs (*The Economist,* May 4, 2024, p. 59). Thus, if we measure the standard of living by GDP/per capita, as many nations are wont to do, immigration could decrease the standard of living, all else equal.

A full and complete analysis of the effects of immigration is complex and multi-faceted, requiring the close cooperation of many social scientists.[14] This is missing in the United States. Unfortunately, what passes for immigration policy is often an ideological distillation of the complex issues.

14.5   USA Immigration Policy: Illegal Immigration

Because the United States currently restricts the number of legal immigrants (as do all nations), anyone entering the United States not legally, enters illegally both by definition and by law. This is more than wrestling with semantics; for defining who can legally enter also defines who cannot, and thus who is an illegal immigrant. Thus, in terms of policy and the law, legal and illegal immigration are two sides of the same coin.

America's broken immigration policy is underscored by the huge number of migrants along our southern border. In fiscal year 2022, there were 2.38 million border stops (i.e., encounters). This was a record for the first time topping two million. In 2023, about 2.4 million people entered the United States illegally (*The Economist*, May 4, 2024, p. 60). We say 'about,' because we don't know exactly. By the way, such border encounters are separate and distinct from immigration via official channels, and thus by definition are illegal.

President Biden precipitated this migrant onslaught during the opening days of his administration by encouraging and welcoming all. Most illegals are sent away, either to foreign asylum centers in Mexico or to USA processing stations. But quite worrisome is that in addition to the 2.38 million encounters, approximately 600,000 migrants are not encountered (i.e., they slip in undetected) and enter the USA illegally. This provides fodder for right-wing populism, and for anti-immigration, yet it should be of concern for all Americans, since it evidences the failure of border sanctity.

It has long been acknowledged that "Border control in an age of easy global movement is not a simple policy problem" (Douthat, 2023, p. 3). The proposed solutions for illegal immigration run the gamut from constricting punishment to blanket amnesty:

- Illegal immigrants first and foremost should be punished; after all, they violated the law of the United States. Punishments include rounding up and returning all who entered illegally or imprisoning them. If the law is to have any substance, then its sanctity must be upheld with concomitant punitive damages. Not doing so renders ineffectual any attempt to maintain border integrity. It also sends a loud and clear message that the sanctity of the law is not inviolable and that violation of the law (if caught) will go unpunished. This is hardly a basis for deterrence; and if anything, will incentivize the desire to emigrate.
- Incentivize migrants to not enter illegally, while ratcheting up the penalties for doing so. This assumes, of course, that the decision to emigrate is rational, where the individual weighs the costs and benefits before deciding. But often desperation and emotion are preponderant. The ultimate and probably the most effective penalties are either a prison sentence or immediate deportation, both of which should be clearly articulated and widely disseminated in all prospective home nations. But any punishment in the host nation tugs against the natural human emotion (for most of us) of the reluctance to heap more misery on people who have already suffered.
- De-incentivize illegal immigration by beefing up the southern border and funneling all immigration through pre-determined and well-known ports of entry. The Trump Administration, for example, attempted a wall along our southern border with Mexico. But building a wall is not the same as denying complete legal entrance, as the legal ports of entry are still maintained. History teaches us a lesson: As long as persistent economic, social, and political differences exist between nations then so will the desire to emigrate, wall or no wall.
- Probably, the most effective policy to decrease illegal immigration, yet the least palatable from the host nation's perspective, is to solve the problem at the root, i.e., in the home nation, with both nations working cooperatively. As mentioned earlier, there is always a reason for emigrating. Solve the reason(s) and you reduce emigration, which in turn reduces illegal immigration, ceteris paribus. From the home nation's perspective sustained emigration creates a

brain drain, especially among skilled workers, and especially among health workers.[15] As more workers emigrate, the resulting inequality within the host nation increases, as does inequality between the host and home nations; thus, incentivizing the decision to emigrate,

> The costs of global mobility are unevenly borne by the poorer source countries, with the primary benefits elsewhere. Migration emerges from inequality, contributes to it (especially as skilled migrants ply their skills elsewhere), stimulating an institutionalization of social and economic inequality that may ultimately entrench social problems.
>
> (Connell, 2010, p. 203)

However, two centrifugal forces lessen any chance of home/host nation cooperation. (1) often the home nation favors emigration to let off domestic steam, so to speak. This is especially true for developing nations and for those with high rates of unemployment, e.g., Mexico, Cuba. No outlet leaves the malcontents clamoring for jobs and social services, while increasing social unrest and weakening the government's legitimacy. And (2) to tackle the root problem in this fashion requires significant commitment from both nations in terms of resources and people power; each of which, however, comes with a high opportunity cost.

- Offer amnesty to all (or perhaps just to some). However, doing so sends a clear signal that the sanctity of law is not inviolable, eviscerating any distinction between legal and illegal immigration. This in turn will further encourage illegal immigration. It's like a teacher saying that anyone caught cheating on an exam will be expelled, but then ignoring the policy and giving such a student an A.

Each of the above solutions for solving illegal immigration is fraught with problems, both practically and philosophically. For example, rounding up all illegal immigrants to either imprison or deport, assumes an unlimited federal budget (in terms of personnel and dollars) which is certainly not the case. Today, the United States "doesn't have the agents to conduct interviews to find out whether migrants meet the standards to request asylum, the judges to rule on whether asylum is warranted, or enough beds to house migrants until these things are determined" (*The Washington Post,* May 25, 2024, p. A14).

14.6   USA Immigration Policy Moving Forward?

Immigration/emigration is one of the most complex issues confronting a nation (both home and host), given its interaction among law, politics, economics, living standards, and human emotions. A thorough resolution of this issue requires not only domestic cooperation here in the United States between Democrats and Republicans (practically impossible these days) but also between host and home nations. The United States can never solve its illegal immigration problem without the active cooperation of Mexico and other home nations. Climate change gives immigration an added urgency: It will steadily increase emigration from poor to rich, and from South to North.

An effective immigration policy must combine incentives/disincentives, tight border security, upholding the sanctity of the law, widely publicizing the sanctity of the law, and home/host nation cooperation. None of these are easy, and all suggest a long-term holistic multilateral solution. In sum, an effective immigration policy must send "a credible signal around the world that the US can enforce its rules. Today it can't" (*The Washington Post,* May 25, 2024, p. A14).

Solving immigration is neither a Democratic nor a Republican issue. It is the nation's problem. At the same time, however, neither Party is offering effective solutions. Republicans have persistently blamed the Biden administration for the current border mess, while the Administration has defended its actions, saying the problems are long-standing, while trying to correct the punitive and restrictive measures of the first Trump administration.

14.7   Conclusion

Probably, no issue is more political now than immigration. And probably, no better issue illustrates the deep divide between Democrats and Republicans. Democrats favor enacting policies to accommodate the flow, making it faster and more streamlined and efficient. Republicans advocate reducing and even eliminating illegal immigration, deporting temporary aliens, strengthening border protection, a greater say in who can legally enter, and increasing the use of law enforcement. Nevertheless, the Parties are not able to come together to iron out their differences to construct a workable set of reforms. And worse, both Parties, but especially Republicans, have been engaging in political grandstanding, refusing to do anything to fix the border so that President Biden could accrue the total blame. Such 'showmanship' (*The Washington Post*, May 25, 2024, p. A14) does nothing to solve the real problems of immigration, and worse, deflects from the actual work that needs to be done. No wonder that "immigration is the most difficult and intractable issue in American politics" (York, 2024).

We agree, adding that this 'most intractable issue' is nothing new but goes back several generations. Our broken immigration system (we hesitate to use the word 'system') should at the very least motivate us to redress past inequities and to finally get it right. But, even in the best of times, we would need a herculean effort to bridge the policies of the Republicans and Democrats. And this is certainly not the best of times.

Notes

1 The word 'migrate' originates from the Latin 'migrare' (to wander, to move). The preface 'e' means away; thus, 'emigrate' means wander away from, or officially to leave one's native land. The prefix 'im' means into, so immigrate means wander into, or officially to enter into a nation.

2 This section borrows heavily from (Reardon et al., 2018, pp. 86–90).

3 Perhaps, underscoring the 'Know Nothing' epithet, Fillmore, at least initially, was unaware that the Party placed his name on the ballot, being out of the country at the time. Incidentally, the reason for Fillmore being in office for only three years, is that when President Zachary Taylor (elected the 12th president in 1848) died of food poisoning in 1850, he was succeeded by vice-president Millard Fillmore as the 13th president. Fillmore declined to run in the 1852 election. Interestingly, of the 46 US presidents, eight have died in office: four by natural causes: William Harrison, Zachary Taylor, Warren Harding, and FDR; and four by assassination: Abraham Lincoln, James Garfield, William McKinley, and JFK.

4 Persistent labor shortages were a main reason, but certainly not the only reason for slavery in the United States. The United States was not the only country to experience this scourge upon mankind; indeed, it is evidenced in just about all societies, but it certainly has transformed our nation. We are still feeling its effects today, and the United States has never fully come to grips with its legacy. For a good discussion, see Piketty (2022, pp. 48–94).

5 Americans were not passive in European emigration by any means; they actively recruited across Europe, forcing vehement restrictions by European officials on emigrations, albeit not quite successful (Chua, 2007, pp. 242–244). Chua notes that between 1820 and 1914, more than thirty million people entered the US—the largest human migration in the history of the word (Chua, 2007, p. 248). Of course, this number doesn't include the forced importation of slaves.

6 Although this was the perception offered, the frontier really wasn't open, given the presence of Native Americans. So as the frontier was pushed west, the Indian civilizations were pushed back, forced onto reservations, their way of life destroyed. As de Toqueville noted, " As the native peoples move away and die [albeit not by their own volition], an immense and growing population is taking their place. Never among nations had such an enormous development happened before, nor so swift a destruction (1835 [2003], p. 376; also see pp. 378–379).

7 For an interesting account of the genesis of this phrase, as well as the poem from which it is taken, see (Hermann, 2020).

8 The World Population Review (2023b) provides the source for the statistics given.

9 Given that illegal immigrant is illegal, it is not easy to obtain data. See Raley et al. (2022) for the methodological problems.

10 Notable and important exceptions were restrictions against Chinese immigrants in the late 19th century, and Japanese immigrants under the Theodore Roosevelt administration.

11 The Trump Administration promised to build a wall along our southern border. The Administration only completed one-third, running out of both money, patience, and willpower.

12 See 'Crossing Borders' (*The Economist,* June 3, 2023, p. 56).

13 GDP per capita divides GDP by the number of people living in the nation; it better proxies living standards than GDP.

14 See McConnel et al. (2021, pp. 247–263) for a partial yet informative literature review.

15 Connell (2010) provides an interdisciplinary discussion of brain drain in the context of health care.

References

Chua, Amy (2007) *Day of Empire: How Hyperpowers Rise to Global Dominance—and Why They Fail*, Doubleday, New York.

Connell (2010) *Migration and the Globalization of Health Care: The Health Worker Exodus?* Edward Elgar, Cheltenham, UK.

'Crossing Borders' (2023), *The Economist*, June 3, 2023, pp. 55–56.

Douthat, Ross (2023) 'Why Biden Needs an Immigration Deal, *The New York Times*, (Opinion section, December 10), p. 3.

Gruner, Ronald (2022) *We the Presidents: How American Presidents Shaped the Last Century*, Libratum Books, Naples, Florida.

Hermann, Diane (2020) 'The Truth Behind 'Give me your tired, your huddled masses,' *Independent Sentinel*, October 28.

'How Not to Fix Immigration,' *The Washington Post*, editorial, May 25, 2024, p. A14.

'Layoffs Illustrate the Need for Visa Changes,' (2022) *Bloomberg Opinion*, December 16.

McConnell, Campbell, Stanley Brue, David Macpherson (2021) *Contemporary Labor Economics*, 12th ed., McGraw Hill, New York.

Piketty, Thomas (2022) *A Brief History of Equality*, Belknap Press, Harvard University.

Raley, Spencer, Madison McQueen, and Jason Pena (2022) 'How Many Illegal Aliens Were in the US: 2022,' Federation for American Immigration Reform, https://www.fairus.org

Reardon, Jack, Maria Madi, and Molly Scott Cato (2018) *Introducing a New Economics: Pluralist, Sustainable, Progressive*, Pluto Press, London.

'Thousands are Flying,' (2024) *The Economist*, May 4, pp. 59–60.

Tocqueville, Alexis de (1835 [2003]) *Democracy in America*, Penguin, New York.

World Population Review (2023b) 'US immigration by Country,' US Immigration by Country 2023 (worldpopulationreview.com).

York, Byron (2024) 'Finally, Biden admits there is a crisis at the border,' January 30, *Washington Examiner*, https://www.washingtonexaminer.com/.

15 The Minimum Wage

The Issue: Should wages be determined by the government or the market? Should there be a minimum for wages? If so, how should that be determined? Should the government decide? Or the market? Is the minimum wage some artificial construct which can only worsen the beneficent workings of the market place, or is it necessary to make the market work better?

15.1 Introduction

Is labor merely a cost of production, something to be minimized, like the cost of capital or the cost of energy? Or is labor something more, something unique?[1] Our labor is attached to us, and as human beings, we have needs and wants and aspirations. Our labor and the wages earned determine our ability to provision. But at the same time, labor is a cost to those who hire us, and in some industries, it is the preponderant cost.[2] A firm, if it is to remain competitive and provide jobs, must contain its costs including labor, and the latter at a fair price. But what is fair? And who decides?

Answering these questions requires us to engage, listen, and dialogue with views different from our own. It is from this 'competing' perspective that we discuss the minimum wage. And like many of today's issues, it underscores the pervasive disagreement over not just the facts, but also ideologically—we have different ways of viewing how the world works.

15.2 The Historical Movement for a Minimum Wage

The Industrial Revolution, which began in full force in the United States after the Civil War, transformed how, when, and even why we worked. Work was no longer performed in small and scattered places, but centralized in factories, controlled by a hierarchal management (Edwards, 1979). Companies became larger, and thanks to the telegraph, businesses became national in scope, and even international. **Labor unions** developed to offset

DOI: 10.4324/9781003591856-17

the power of capital and became institutionalized.[3] The workplace and work itself was being transformed and revolutionized (hence the term Industrial Revolution).

In 1891, to make sense of these revolutionary changes, Pope Leo XIII issued a papal encyclical (i.e., an explanatory letter) titled 'Rerum Novarum' (translated 'New Matters'; and subtitled 'Rights and Duties of Capital and Labor'). Today, the Encyclical is an interesting document to read not just for the light it sheds on the late 19th century labor/capital relations but also for insights on today's economy; for many of the issues that the Pope discussed are still with us.

The Encyclical was highly anticipated, being one of the first documents to discuss the ongoing changes and how they were affecting workers; and it was widely read.

The Encyclical begins,

> That the spirit of revolutionary change, which has long been disturbing the nations of the world, should have passed beyond the sphere of politics and made its influence felt in the cognate sphere of practical economics is not surprising. The elements of the conflict now raging are unmistakable, in the vast expansion of industrial pursuits and the marvelous discoveries of science; in the changed relations between masters and workmen; in the enormous fortunes of some few individuals, and the utter poverty of the masses; the increased self-reliance and closer mutual combination of the working classes; as also, finally, in the prevailing moral degeneracy. The momentous gravity of the state of things now obtaining fills every mind with painful apprehension; wise men [sic] are discussing it; practical men are proposing schemes; popular meetings, legislatures, and rulers of nations are all busied with it—actually there is no question which has taken deeper hold on the public mind.
>
> (Pope Leo XIII, 1891)

The Encyclical provides a rationale for a minimum wage, and also for labor unions to strengthen the power of workers vis-à-vis employers.

The Encyclical got the ball rolling in the USA, so to speak, on the minimum wage.[4] By 1923, 12 states had implemented a minimum wage law. Interestingly, they exempted men, while covering women and children. At the time, it was assumed that men had access to labor unions to help redress, while women and children did not—which says a lot about the sexism and racism of contemporary labor unions.[5]

In 1923, the Supreme Court, in *Adkins v. Children's Hospital* (261 U.S. 525), ruled that such state minimum wage laws violated the 'due process clause' of the Constitution's 14th Amendment (Section I)[6] which reads,

"...nor shall any State deprive any person of life, liberty, or property, without due process of law; nor deny to any person within its jurisdiction the equal protection of the laws." The Court argued that the state minimum wage laws restricted the freedom of contract. Specifically, by preventing women to work at dirt cheap wages (if they so wanted), the state laws deprived them of 'life, liberty, or property,' especially in an either/or situation, i.e., either work at a low wage or not work at all. Conversely, such laws, by constricting a firm's ability to offer low-wage jobs, further weakened the worker's freedom to contract.[7] In *Adkins v. Children's Hospital*, the Court argued that state minimum wage laws,

> forbid two parties having lawful capacity...to freely contract with one another in respect of the price for which one shall render service to the other in a purely private employment where both are willing, perhaps anxious to agree. [And with Adkins] freedom of contract reached its apogee, which struck the death knell of not only this legislation, but of kindred social legislation because it laid down a constitutional principle that any kind of change by statute has to justify itself, and not the other way around.
>
> (Schwartz, 1993, pp. 218 and 219)

15.3   The Fair Labor Standards Act (1938)

Talk of a minimum wage was revived during the Great Depression of the 1930s due to two factors: (1) The Roosevelt administration's pro-labor and pro-labor union stance, passing many important pieces of legislation[8]; and (2) a new economic theory was gaining ground, based on John Maynard Keynes' *The General Theory* (1936). Keynes posited that higher wages would boost consumer spending, which, in turn, would increase aggregate demand, thereby business optimism. Higher optimism would incentivize business to hire more workers and increase investment. Thus, not only would a minimum wage help the individual worker, but it would also benefit the macro economy.

But not everyone accepted this argument, then or now. Any minimum wage by setting a floor above the prevailing wage (some would say equilibrium, although we do not (Reardon, 2006)) increases wages and hence the cost of labor, which in turn reduces profits. A firm will then have no choice but to lay off workers. This negative effect would be most strongly felt by smaller businesses.

The FLSA struck a compromise between these two extremes, largely due to the exigencies of the Depression: Small businesses (i.e., earning less than a specified revenue) and/or businesses not engaged in interstate commerce (since the United States Congress cannot pass legislation that only affects one state) would be exempt from FLSA coverage.[9]

15.4   The Specifics of the FLSA[10]

5.4.1   *The Specifics*

While the FLSA covers a lot of ground,[11] here we limit our discussion to the FLSA's provision of the federal minimum wage, and not the Act's other fair labor provisions. The FLSA is enforced by the Wage and Hour Division of the U.S. Department of Labor (DOL).

An enterprise covered under the FLSA must have at least two employees and have an annual dollar volume of sales (or business done[12]) of at least $500,000. Even if a firm is not covered by the above criteria, employees are protected by the FLSA if their work regularly involves them in commerce between states, i.e., interstate commerce. Examples of such employees are those who produce goods (such as a worker assembling components in a factory or a secretary typing letters in an office) that will be sent out of state; and employees who regularly telephone persons located in another state, handle records of interstate transactions, travels to other states on their jobs, or does janitorial work in buildings where goods are produced for shipment outside the state.

5.4.2   *The FLSA and Independent Contractors*

Given today's proliferation of gig workers and independent contractors,[13] whether a worker is classified as an employee, or an independent contractor is important: Only the former is protected under the FLSA. As Secretary of Labor Julie Su testified in 2024: "Misclassifying employees as independent contractors is a serious issue that deprives workers of basic rights and protections" (United States Department of Labor, 2024b).

To clarify this distinction, the DOL promulgated a rule that took effect March 11, 2024.[14] According to Ms. Su, the rule "will help protect workers, especially those facing the greatest risk of exploitation, by making sure they are classified properly and that they receive the wages they've earned" (United States Department of Labor, 2024b) A Department of Labor News Release (2024b) explains,

> the new 'independent contractor' rule restores the multifactor analysis used by courts for decades, ensuring that all relevant factors are analyzed to determine whether a worker is an employee or an independent contractor. The rule addresses six factors that guide the analysis of a worker's relationship with an employer, including any opportunity for profit or loss a worker might have; the financial stake and nature of any resources a worker has invested in the work; the degree of permanence of the work relationship; the degree of control an employer has over the person's work; whether the work the person does is essential to the employer's business; and a factor regarding the worker's skill and initiative.

5.4.3 Tipping

Many minimum wage workers experience tipping as part of their wage. According to the DOL (2024a),

> an employer may pay a tipped employee not less than $2.13 an hour in direct wages if that amount plus the tips received equals at least the federal minimum wage, the employee retains all tips…If an employee's tips combined with the employer's direct wages of at least $2.13 an hour do not equal the federal minimum hourly wage, the employer must make up the difference.

5.4.4 Miscellaneous

Each state can offer a minimum wage for covered workers greater than the mandated federal wage. In 2023, 30 states offered a federal minimum wage above the federal wage of $7.25/hour (Hufford, 2024). In addition, the FLSA allows states to pass their own wage laws for non-covered workers.

Unlike Social Security benefits which annually increase with the rate the **inflation,** there is no provision to automatically increase the minimum wage. Rather, it is increased by an act of Congress, although each state is free to increase its wage as it sees fit. The last federal minimum wage increase was in 2009. The stretch between 2009 and 2024 (as this manuscript goes to press) is the longest without an increase. And, by the way, the FLSA does not mandate a maximum wage rate.

15.5 Characteristics of Minimum Wage Workers[15]

The federal minimum wage only applies to workers receiving an hourly wage; salary workers are not covered. In 2022, 78.7 million workers aged 16 and older were paid at hourly rates, representing 55.6% of all wage and salary workers. Among those paid by the hour, 141,000 workers earned exactly the prevailing federal minimum wage of $7.25 per hour, while 882,000 workers had wages below the federal minimum (the latter worked in firms not covered by the FLSA). Together, these 1.0 million workers with wages at or below the federal minimum comprised 1.3% of all hourly paid workers, little changed from 2021, but far below the 1979 high of 13.4%, when data began to be regularly collected.

Why such a low percentage? Two reasons: (1) a long period without an FLSA increase—not since 2009; and (2) post-COVID, labor shortages among lower-tiered workers, along with hefty pay increases, have rendered minimum wages moot (Hufford, 2024). Specifically, through September 2023, the lowest 10% of workers by income in each state earned hourly wages that were nearly 50% higher than their state's minimum wage—the highest in ten years (Hufford, 2024). While one might conclude that tight labor markets have rendered a government-imposed wage moot, we hold off on this assessment for two reasons: (1) This situation might easily be-reversed especially with the next **recession**; (2) a full assessment of the minimum wage can only come with a more complete and holistic conception and empirical testing beyond the narrow wage–employment nexus, which we briefly discuss below.

Specific characteristics of today's USA minimum wage workers include:

- 44.7% are between the ages of 16–24, while 55.3% are older than 25.
- Women comprise 67.9% of all minimum wage earners, and men 32.1%. The proportion of women over 25 years receiving the minimum wage is triple that of men.
- Part-time workers comprise 53.6% of minimum wage workers, and full-time workers 46.2%.
- Whites comprise 72.6% of minimum wage workers, and blacks 17.5%.
- Over two-thirds of minimum wage workers (72.7%) are in service occupations, with more than half in food preparation and servicing.
- 11.7% have less than a high school education; 36.9% have some college but no degree; 13.1% have a bachelor's degree; and 0.3% have a doctoral degree.
- 11.4% of minimum wage earners over the age of 25 are women who have never been married; while 8.8% of minimum wage earners over the age of 25 are women, divorced, widowed, or separated.

It is difficult to pinpoint exactly how many minimum wage workers are officially in poverty, since poverty status depends on the worker's annual earnings and the number of people living in that household (Shrider and Creamer, 2023). In addition, the actual minimum wage varies by state.[16] Troubling, however, is the number of working poor in the United States. According to the Bureau of Labor Statistics (2023),

> The working poor are people who spent at least 27 weeks in the labor force (i.e., working or looking for work) but whose incomes still fell below the official poverty level. In 2021, there were 6.4 million working poor. And the ratio of the working poor to all individuals in the labor force for at least 27 weeks—was 4.1 percent, unchanged from 2020.

15.6 The Effects of the Minimum Wage

The literature on the effects of the minimum wage is voluminous, so much so that we would need several volumes to fully discuss. Indeed, "more has been written about the minimum wage, than any other economic policy" (Champlain and Knoedler, 2004, p. 78); a statement that remains just as true today.[17] And, although perhaps not surprisingly, there is a lack of consensus as on what the evidence/data actually means (Neumark and Shirley, 2021). Here, we offer our two cents on the literature:

- There is no consensus on the effects of the minimum wage. Whatever your position on the minimum wage, you can proffer a study to back it up.
- By far, the majority of studies have focused on the relationship between a higher wage and employment, largely ignoring other effects (Yu et al., 2023). This is done largely due to the ease in obtaining such data, and the difficulty in obtaining data on non-employment effects. However, this leaves us with an incomplete assessment.
- An ideological rift separates minimum wage studies. At the risk of simplifying, conservatives argue that a labor market can efficiently allocate resources on its own; thus, any interferences, e.g., a labor union or government-mandated wage, distorts the market's beneficent workings. The result, theoretically at least, is unemployment, with economists tasked to empirically measure size. Thus, "a market clearing wage is always preferable" (Champlain and Knoedler, 2004, p. 78). And the assertion "that the minimum wage causes unemployment has become so entrenched in economic literature that it is considered a textbook example of a price floor" (Champlain and Knoedler, 2004). Power differentials between firms and workers are ignored. Liberals, on the other hand, begin with power in the labor market, which ceteris paribus favors firms. A labor union or a government will equilibrate the worker's wage and his/her productivity, thereby providing a service which the market itself cannot do (Reardon, 2006). Important is that we cannot assume that the existing wage is or is not an equilibrium wage without empirical investigation. It could very well turn out that any equilibrium wage might be too low to work in anyone's model.
- Liberals tend to emphasize the positive effects of higher wages: Increasing workplace productivity, reducing quits (i.e., increasing the cost of exit), and increasing the capital/labor ratio.[18]
- In our view, economists have for too long used the wrong methodology for empirical testing, i.e., econometrics. More conclusive testing can be obtained via other methodologies such as system dynamics, while analyzing all effects and not just employment. The minimum wage does not exist in isolation but is holistically connected to other aspects of the labor market (Paul, 2021; Desmond, 2023), and this would take minimum wage studies beyond the narrow wage/employment nexus.

15.7   Conclusion

Perhaps no other issue better illustrates the disagreement over the proper role of the government in the labor market than the minimum wage. Nor a better issue to evidence the visceral ideological disagreements that buttress the competing arguments. Despite good competing arguments on both sides, and voluminous evidence, we have yet to reach an agreement. Blame the ideology.

Notes

1 Prasch makes this point very well (2004).
2 Karl Marx (one of capitalism's most profound critics) wrote that once the worker enters the workplace, the labor is no longer his/hers but belongs to the employer, "Suppose that a capitalist pays for a day's labor-power at its value; then the right to use that power for a day belongs to him, just as much as the right to use any other commodity, such as a horse that he has hired for the day. To the purchaser of a commodity belongs its use, and the seller of labour-power, by giving his labour, does no more, in reality, than part with the use value-that he has sold" (Marx, 1867 [1967], Vol. I, p. 185).
3 Becoming institutionalized meant that labor unions were becoming permanent rather than transient and ad hoc. See our **Labor Unions**.
4 Helping to get the ball rolling was the influential book, *Industrial Democracy* (1897) by Sidney and Beatrice Webb. In addition, Henry George's best seller *Progress and Poverty* (1879 [1948]) caught on with the general public. George wrote, "The association of poverty with progress is the great enigma of our times. It is the central fact from which spring industrial, social, and political difficulties that perplex the world, and which statesmanship and philanthropy and education grapple in vain" (George, 1879 [1948], p. 10). Unlike Marx, George did not blame capitalists, instead blaming landowners. He advocated a land tax which would provide sufficient revenue to eliminate all other taxes, boost wages, and reduce inequality.
5 At the time, there was no national prohibition against child labor; this would come during the Great Depression.
6 The 1937 USA Supreme Court case, *West Coast Hotel Co. v. Parrish*, 300 US 379, overturned *Adkins v. Children's Hospital*. And one year later, the Fair Labor Standards Act (1938) was passed, providing a federal minimum wage. For discussion of the FLSA, see the text.
7 Of the antilabor cases heard under the Taft court, *Adkins v. Children's Hospital* was "the most extreme…so extreme was it, that [Taft] himself could not go along with the majority and issued a dissenting opinion" (Schwartz, 1993, p. 218). And President Taft was certainly anti-labor, for example writing to his brother "the only class which is arrayed against the court…is organized labor" (Schwartz, 1993, p. 218).
8 Such legislation will be discussed in **Labor Unions**.
9 This restriction is based on the Constitution's interstate commerce clause (Article I, Section 8, paragraph 3), "The Congress shall have Power…To regulate Commerce with foreign nations, and among the several States, and with the Indian Tribes." The Constitution envisioned two governments: federal and that of the states. The Clause "is a critical component of the United States Constitution that has evolved over time to address the changing economic and legal landscape. It grants Congress the authority to regulate commerce among the states, providing a framework for federal oversight of economic activities that cross state boundaries. While its interpretation has evolved and been the subject of numerous legal battles, the clause remains a fundamental element of the Constitution, balancing federal and state powers in the realm of commerce" (An Overview to the Interstate Commerce Clause 2023). The careful delineation between state and federal rights is evidenced by the Constitution's 10th Amendment, "The powers not delegated to the United States by the Constitution nor prohibited by it to the States, are reserved to the states respectively, or to the people."
10 This discussion is based on the United States Department of Labor (2024a).
11 The FLSA outlaws child labor (i.e., individuals under the age of 16 must be attending school full-time) and provides an overtime provision: Workers in non-discretionary jobs (i.e., the essentials of the production process are determined by management) must receive a premium after working 42 hours in a week; the latter was reduced to 40 hours in 1940. See United States Department of Labor (2024a).

12 The DOL emphasizes that coverage includes hospitals, businesses providing medical or nursing care for residents, schools and preschools, and government agencies.
13 We don't know have an exact number since there is no universally agreed upon definition. Estimates range from 10% of employment to 33% (Weil, 2023). See (Weil, 2023) for a useful discussion of the conceptual and definitional issues of gig workers.
14 See Federal Register (2024).
15 Data in this section are taken from Bureau of Labor Statistics 2024.
16 A worker receiving the federal minimum wage of $7.25/hr., working full time (46.2% of minimum wage workers do) at, let's say, eight hours/day, five days/week, and 52 weeks/year; he/she earns a yearly income of $15,080 (at 2080 annual hours) slightly beneath the 2022 poverty threshold of $15,230 for a single individual.
17 For an interesting discussion of contemporary minimum wage plans in mid-19th-century Britain, see John Stuart Mill's *Principles of Political Economy* (1965 [1848], Vol. II, Chs. 12, 13; pp. 355–379). The book, published in 1848 was one of the 19th century's most influential books.
18 A groundbreaking text (and still relevant) is Freeman and Medoff (1984, especially pp. 162–180).

References

'An Overview to the Interstate Commerce Clause' (2023) https://constitution.laws.com/.
Bureau of Labor Statistics (2023) A Profile of the Working Poor, (November) U.S. Bureau of Labor Statistics, Washington DC.
Champlain, Dell and Janet Knoedler (2004) 'Wages in the Public Interest,' in Champlain, Dell P. and Janet P. Knoedler (Eds.) *The Intuitionalist Tradition in Labor Economics*, M.E. Sharpe, Armonk, New York, pp. 75–87.
Edwards, Richard (1979) *Contested Terrain: The Transformation of the Workplace in the Twentieth Century*, Basic Books, New York.
Federal Register (2024) 'Employee or Independent Contractor Classification Under the Fair Labor Standards Act,' January 10. https://perkinscoie.com/insights.
Freeman, Richard and Medoff, James (1984) *What Do Unions Do?* Basic Books, New York.
George, Henry (1879 [1948]) *Progress and Poverty*, Robert Schalkenback Foundation, New York.
Hufford, Austen (2024) 'Workers to Get Additional Benefit from Minimum-Wage Hikes, *The Wall Street Journal,* January 2, 2024, p. A3.
Keynes, John Maynard (1936) *The General Theory*, Harcourt, Brace and Company, New York.
Marx, Karl and Frederic Engels, *Capital: A Critique of Political Economy*, Vol. I, International Publishers, New York.
Mill, John Stuart (1965 [1848]) *Principles of Political Economy*, Liberty Fund, Indianapolis.
Neumark, David, and Shirley, Peter (2021) 'Myth or Measurement: What Does the New Minimum Wage Research Say about Minimum Wages and Job Loss in the United States?' National Bureau of Economic Research, Working Paper, 28388. http://www.nber.org/papers/w28388.
Pope Leo XIII (1891) 'Rerum Novarum, St. Peter's, Rome, hf_l-xiii_enc_15051891_rerum-novarum.pdf (vatican.va).
Prasch, Robert (2004) 'How is Labor Distinct from Broccoli? Some Unique Characteristics of Labor and Their Importance in Economic Analysis and Policy,' in Champlin, Dell and Knoedler, Janet, (Eds.) *The Institutionalist Tradition in Labor Economics*, ME Sharpe, Armonk, UK, pp. 146–158.

Reardon, Jack (2006) 'Are labor unions consistent with the assumptions of perfect competition?' *Journal of Economic Issues*, Vol. 40, No. 1, pp. 171–181.

Schwartz, Bernard (1993) *A History of the Supreme Court*, Oxford University Press, New York.

Shrider and Creamer (2023) *Poverty in the United States: 2022*, US Census Bureau, September 12, Report Number P60-280, Poverty in the United States: 2022 (census.gov).

Webb, Sidney and Beatrice Webb (1897) *Industrial Democracy*, Longmans, Green and Co., London.

United States Department of Labor (2024a) 'Questions and Answers About the Minimum Wage,' U.S. Department of Labor (dol.gov).

United States Department of Labor (2024b) 'News Release: 'US DOL Announces Final Rule on Classifying Workers as Employees or Independent Contractors Under the FLSA,' January 9, (dol.gov).

Weil, David (2023) What's a Gig Job? How it's Legally Defined affects Workers' Rights and Protection,' *The Conversation*, January 9, (theconversation.com).

Yu, Qiuping, Shawn Mankad and Masha Shunko (2023) 'Evidence of the Unintended Labor Scheduling Implications of the Minimum Wage,' *Manufacturing & Service Operations Management*, Vol. 25, No. 5, pp. 1947–1965.

16 Inequality

The Issue: The Declaration of Independence opens with the powerful words: "All men are created equal." These words have since acted as a powerful beacon of hope, speaking to, and attracting the disadvantaged in all corners of the globe. But at the same, it was understood then, that 'all men' meant white men: Women were excluded, as were Blacks, and Native Americans. Since the Declaration of Independence, the evolution of the United States has been a concerted effort to broaden the base of equality to cover all Americans. While great strides have been made to achieve equality before the law, the march toward real equality is just beginning and we have a lot of work to do. An unequal America is a discontented America, full of rancor, angst, and distrust. An unequal America is unsustainable. Reducing inequality, while striving to increase equality for all Americans, and especially the marginalized, is a pressing task, post-2024.

16.1 Preface

Of all the issues discussed in this book, this is the most far-reaching and the most open-ended; it seems that no matter how much we wrote, we felt compelled to write more. The reason being is that inequality is inextricably linked with most of the other issues discussed in this book, e.g., **Climate Change**, **Labor Unions**, the **Minimum Wage.** Where does one begin? Where does one end? Given its historical importance, it is impossible to thoroughly review the literature in just a short space—to do so adequately necessitates volumes. Our focus in this chapter will be to conceptualize inequality, to understand why it is a problem, and to discuss possible solutions.

16.2 A Brief Note on Karl Marx, Joseph Schumpeter, Thomas Malthus, John Maynard Keynes, and Mary Wollstonecraft

16.2.1 Introduction

In such a far-reaching chapter, we thought it best to open up by introducing five giant intellectuals whose writings on inequality have set the stage for how most

DOI: 10.4324/9781003591856-18

of us conceptualize/redress the problem. This doesn't mean, of course, that we agree with any or all, only that we find their analysis both stimulative and generative, and highly relevant.

16.2.2   *Karl Marx (1818–1883)*

The Industrial Revolution (beginning in Great Britain around 1800) ripped asunder traditional ways of doing things (especially the how/where/when, and even why we produce). For some, it presented a laboratory in which to understand capitalism as it was developing. One of the most powerful (and earliest) intellectuals to do so was Karl Marx.[1]

Marx saw capitalism peopled by two classes: (1) capitalists (i.e., the bourgeoisie[2]), a minority of the population that owns the means of production (i.e., the factories, buildings, technologies, and land); and (2) proletariats (from the Latin, those who have children), i.e., workers own nothing but their own ability to labor.[3] Given the disparity in ownership, the two classes are inherently unequal.

Due to their inherent superiority, capitalists were assumed to have power over workers, which they use to force them to work longer hours at low pay.[4] Such exploitation enables capitalists to accrue a surplus, i.e., the difference between what the workers produced and the cost of labor. The rich get richer, and they acquire the necessary resources to lobby the government to sustain their position. For Marx, the only solution was to throw out the baby with the bathwater, so to speak: To replace capitalism with a new type of economic system—communism, whereby everyone owned the means of production. With equal ownership, there would be no inequality, and with no inequality, there would be no exploitation.

But unfortunately, this was not just an academic debate, for Marx's ideas provided the fodder for violent socialist revolutions, which, at least titularly, aimed to create a new society based on economic equality.[5] Marx saw socialism (i.e., the state owns most of the means of production) as a temporary expedient between the evils of capitalism and the ideal of communism. For Marx, inequality was intrinsic to the economic system, and the only redress was to develop the new system of.

But socialism failed (e.g., the Soviet Union, the world's first nation to adopt socialism; Cuba and North Korea), and if anything, exacerbated the inequality between nations; more specifically, socialist nations (and there aren't many left) lagged nations that never adopted socialism. And for those of us who lived and worked (or even visited) socialist nations, it was obvious that the so-called inequality existing in pre-socialist systems was never extirpated; it just manifested itself in new and different forms.

16.2.3   *Joseph Schumpeter (1883–1950)*

Joseph Schumpeter emigrated from Austria to the United States. Although not a Marxist, he was steeped in Marxian thought and analysis. And like Marx, he had a pessimistic long-term view of capitalism. This was due to the concept of 'creative destruction,' a quintessentially unique feature of capitalism initially developed by Marx. Specifically, endogenous dynamics spearheaded by the profit motive lead to continuous improvements in technology and know-how; so much so that new ways of doing things continuously replace and destroy the old,

> Capitalism ... is by nature a form or method of economic change and not only never is but never can be stationary. ... The fundamental impulse that sets and keeps the capitalist engine in motion comes from the new consumers' goods, the new methods of production or transportation, the new markets, the new forms of industrial organization that capitalist enterprise creates…that incessantly revolutionizes the economic structure *from within*, incessantly destroying the old one, incessantly creating a new one. This process of Creative Destruction is the essential fact about capitalism. It is what capitalism consists in and what every capitalist concern has got to live in. [Capitalism requires] the perennial gale of Creative Destruction.
>
> (Schumpeter, 1942 [1975], pp. 82–83)

For both Marx and Schumpeter, power was part and parcel of capitalism. For Marx, power was inherent in capitalism's differential ownership of the means of production, while for Schumpeter, power resulted from winning the spoils. With the aggrandizement of power comes the willingness and ability to use it and to further extend it by lobbying the government.

16.2.4   *Thomas Malthus (1766–1834)*

It is hard to write anything about inequality (or equality for that matter) without mentioning Thomas Malthus, a British parson and professor at East India's College at Haileybury. Malthus (at the risk of simplification) is best known for his *Principle of Population*. The title in full: *An Essay on the Principle of Population (1958 [1803]) as it Affects the Future Improvement of Society, with Remarks on the Speculations of Mr. Goodwin, M. Condorcet and Other Writers*[6] whose chilling prognosis still hovers over us. Malthus, a wealthy patrician, unabashedly defended the interests of the wealthy; he firmly believed that the different classes which were inherently unequal were part of God's plan. The essence of his population principle is:

> …that population, when unchecked, goes on doubling itself every twenty-five years [i.e.,] increases in a geometric ratio…It may be fairly pronounced, therefore that considering the present average state of the earth, the means of subsistence, under circumstances the most favorable to human industry could not possibly be made to increase faster than in an arithmetic ratio.
>
> (Malthus, 1958 [1803], Vol. 1, pp. 8 and 10)

Thus, population increases much faster than the required sustenance.

This 'iron clad law' implies that "the limited good which it is sometimes in our power to effect is often lost by attempting too much" (Malthus, 1958 [1803], Vol. 1, p. 258). In other words, any attempt to ameliorate the situation of the poor (by whatever means) will backfire by increasing the number of people, which in turn decreases living standards for all.

Practically speaking, this means that there isn't anything that we can do to change the God-given hierarchal order[7] of which inequality is central, for "no possible sacrifices of the rich, particularly in money, could for any time prevent the recurrence of distress among the lower members off society, whoever they were[8] (Malthus, 1958 [1803], Vol. 1, p. 39). In other words, for Malthus, "the structure of society, in its great features, will probably always remain unchanged" (Malthus, 1958 [1803], Vol. 2, p. 262).

Not only did Malthus advocate against welfare policy and against moral suasion (the latter because the poor are not capable of such virtue, only the upper classes) but he callously recommended policies that would deliberately reduce the population, especially among the poor,[9]

> In our towns we should make the streets narrower, crowd more people into the houses, and court the return of the plague. In the country, we should build our villages near stagnant pools, and particularly encourage settlements in all marshy and unwholesome situations. But above all, we should reprobate specific remedies for ravaging diseases; and those benevolent, but much mistaken men, who have thought they were doing a service to mankind by projecting schemes for the total extirpation of particular disorders.
>
> (Malthus, 1958 [1803], Vol. 2, p 180)

16.2.5 *John Maynard Keynes (1883–1945)*

In 1936, John Maynard Keynes, one of the most influential economists of the 20th century, concluded his *General Theory* noting that "the outstanding faults of the economic society in which we live are its failure to provide for full employment and its arbitrary and inequitable distribution of wealth and incomes" (Keynes, 1936, p. 372). At the same time, Keynes argued that pure equality would stifle investment in capital, which historically, has been a preponderant factor in increasing living standards. Thus, for Keynes, the government is tasked to maintain some level of inequality while redressing its excesses.[10]

Keynes' *General Theory* offers both a rationale and a recipe for ameliorating the worst extent of inequality. His analysis, together with the suffering of the Great Depression, solidified concerted efforts by the federal government to ameliorate the most ostensible accoutrements of inequality—income and wealth. While efforts to do so were underway in most Western nations, around WWI,[11] Keynes' *General Theory* provided a solid rationale for stimulating the economy via government spending and increased consumer spending during recessions.

16.2.6   *Mary Wollstonecraft (1759–1797)*

One of the earliest advocates of women's rights, Mary Wollstonecraft's *Vindication of the Rights of Woman* (1792), makes a passionate plea that women are no different from men and that the ideas of women deserve to be heard. She argued that there is no innate difference in intellect between men and women, but only deliberate decisions by men to deny education to women. Equal access to education would enable husband and wife to be equals, rather than one dependent on the other, and would be best for the nation, especially raising children.

Her other books include: *A Vindication of the Rights of Men* (1790) in which she scathingly critiqued Edmund Burke's *Reflections on the Revolution in France*, especially his defense of the aristocracy and his patriarchal view of women.[12] She also published two interesting novels: *Mary: A Fiction*, and *The Wrongs of Women*;[13] the latter published posthumously. Mary died at the age of 38, less than two weeks after giving birth to her second daughter, Mary.[14]

The economic theories, books, and treatises that were written during the 18th and 19th centuries would provide the economic foundations of the West, especially Great Britain and the United States. Unfortunately, this economic thought was written by men for men, in a society run by men. Women were disenfranchised from thinking and writing about the economy, except in the domestic sphere. And when women did write on the greater economy, they were ignored and disparaged.[15] As a social scientist myself, this was a shameful period in our history.

16.2.7   *Summation*

These five authors focus on the overall economic system and raise some interesting questions that we still wrestle with: (1) Is inequality intrinsic to capitalism? (2) If so, how effective can be government redress? (3) Is capitalism rigged, not so much maliciously, but due to its inherent characteristics?[16] (4) Is there an optimal mix of inequality that will enable adequate capital accumulation *and* the ability of all to provision? (5) How can we address racial, sexual, and religious inequality which today is still preponderant. We will return to this important discussion later in the chapter.

16.3   Have Human Societies Ever Been Equal?

In a chapter on inequality, it is logical to ask if human societies have ever been equal. The answer, at least since the dawn of agriculture some 10,000 years ago, is an unequivocal no,[17] "the struggle over inequality has always been the underlying force that drives the history of humanity… elites have taken practically everything for themselves and left all others with little more than the means with which to survive" (Wisman, 2022, p. 2).

Wisman argues quite convincingly, that striving for inequality is and (has been) hard-wired into our genes,

> The essential driving force for inequality is the biological imperative to send one's unique set of genes into future generations. The genes that exist at any moment are those whose carriers competed successfully for mates. Because high social status results in greater success in mating, humans have evolved to seek status for competitive sexual advantage. The qualities that provide status are predominantly determined by society's cultures and institutions.
>
> (Wisman, 2022, p. 449)

Wisman explains that while,

> this dynamic of sexual selection was extensively developed by Charles Darwin in his *The Descent of Man and Selection in Respect to Sex* (1871), it has been largely ignored by historians and social scientists. Yet this dynamic is critical for understanding social dynamics and history.
>
> (Wisman, 2022, p. 6)

We agree.

Central to Wisman's thesis is the pervasive existence of power and its ubiquitous use, which is constructed by the elites in order to perpetuate their advantage. This predates capitalism and is not part and parcel of any particular economic system. The power differential and the apparent unfairness is camouflaged and obfuscated by ideology, i.e., something that manipulates our sense of fairness, which in turn is "used to hoodwink the losers into seeing conditions that are contrary to their best interests as fair and just" (Wisman, 2022, p. 449).

So if Wisman is correct, and we believe that he is, power, ideology, and inequality are inextricably related in every society. The specific manner in which they relate will differ, which in turn means that politics plays a key role "in resolving the tension between competition and fairness" (Wisman, 2022, p. 449). Politics shapes social institutions and sets the rules of the game for how competition can be conducted, while ideology manipulates our sense of fairness. Always and everywhere according to Wisman, at least, since the dawn of agriculture.

As an historical aside, we find it interesting that a preponderant reason for the United States' Constitution's deliberate separation of powers was the existence of factions, of which the primary cause was inequality. Specifically,

> …the various and unequal distribution of property. Those who hold, and those who are without property, have ever formed distinct interests in society…The regulation of these various and interfering interests forms the principal task of modern Legislation, and involves the spirit of party and faction in the necessary and ordinary operations of Government.
>
> (Hamilton et al., 2003 [1787–1788], No. 10, p. 53)

The separation of powers was the Constitution's way to tame the virulence of factions, which at the same time was inextricably linked to liberty, "Liberty is to faction, what air is to fire, an ailment without which it instantly expires" (Hamilton et al., 2003 [1787–1788], No. 10, p. 51). Our point here is not to expound on this example, but to note that the link between power, ideology, and politics is central to the very formation of the Constitution.

Overall, Wisman provides a provocative way to conceptualize inequality, suggesting that we are looking for causes and solutions in all the wrong places. The cause resides in our innate desire for procreation. But that doesn't mean that we wash our hands and do nothing; on the contrary, as we discuss later in this chapter, solutions abound at both the societal and the individual level.

16.4   Is Inequality a Problem?

Given that inequality has existed since the dawn of agriculture, why is something so intrinsically fundamental considered a problem? Thomas Piketty, a foremost authority on inequality, argues that inequality "is not necessarily bad in itself: the key question is to decide whether it is justified, whether there are reasons for it" (Piketty, 2014, p. 25). At face value, the statement is incontrovertible. However, this immediately raises the question of who decides whether it is justified and what are justifiable reasons. And what type of inequality are we discussing? Piketty's statement also suggests that as a concept, inequality cannot exist on its own, but is defined by time and place (Milanovic, 2023a, 2023b). More specifically,

> The history of inequality is shaped by the way economic, social, and political actors view what is just and what is not, as well by the relative power of those actors and the collective choices that result. It is the joint product of all relevant actors combined.
>
> (Piketty, 2014, pp. 27–28)

Indeed, as Piketty adds, inequality is first of all a social, historical, and political construction. In other words, "for the same level of economic or technological development, there are always many different ways of organizing… These options are political in nature. They depend on the state of power relationships between the various social groups and the worldviews involved" (Piketty, 2022, p. 9).

Arthur Okun (1975) argued that inequality is necessary to attain an efficient economic system, i.e., allocate resources to where they are most needed. Inequality incentivizes both the 'haves' and the 'have nots' to work harder. If everyone earned the same income, or was guaranteed the same, then there would be no incentives to work. Okun's thesis is problematic for two reasons: (1) The optimal inequality can never be specified, rendering it a political judgment; and

(2) efficiency has multiple meanings, in addition to Okun's usage (Fullbrook, 2009).

While some inequality is necessary to incentivize, too much inequality can cause angst and discontent, and even destroy a society from within,

> ...greater inequality corresponds with wider social and political rifts in society. This polarization can weaken democratic institutions and deteriorate trust in government. Research from civil liberties watchdog Freedom House shows that inequality and authoritarianism reinforce each other, as people who find themselves unable to improve their economic situations can believe the deck is stacked against them and support autocratic overhauls to democratic systems.
>
> ('What is Economic Inequality?', 2023)

Unfortunately, this is happening now in the United States. There is no threshold of inequality, above which it becomes a societal problem and below which it is fine; rather, we must look at its evolution over time, i.e., is it worsening or improving, and to ascertain the causal reasons.

Having said this, capitalism has been likened to a footrace, whereby we don't want, nor expect everyone to be equal; nor for all to finish at the same spot/ time, given differences in ability, talent, and even strategy. Our sense of fairness would be is offended if some were offered a head start, practically guaranteeing their success. We consider a race fair if everyone starts at the same position (even offering a handicap to the less advantaged).

In a sense, capitalism is a race: It is a race for riches, success, consumption, high income, wealth,[18] and, in addition, a race to send one's genes into posterity. At the same time, the race analogy is incomplete, for it does not differentiate on the basis of race, gender, or socio-economic background; all of which can affect the outcome. And in real life, when the race ends, the winner(s) will use their winnings to even better their position and then pass on their advantage to their scions, who become advantaged in their own race. Is it fair to pass on accumulated wealth (from winnings) to the next generation? Or should such 'winnings' be taxed by society and redistributed?[19]

On the race analogy, John Stuart Mill, a foremost political economist of the 19th century, questioned if the race was *ever* fair,

> The Social arrangements of modern Europe commenced from a distribution of property which was the result, not of just partition, or acquisition by industry, but of conquest and violence...the laws of property ... have not held the balance fairly between human beings, but have heaped impediments on some, to give advantage to others; they have purposely fostered inequalities, and prevented all from starting fair in the race.
>
> (Mill (1965 [1848]) Vol. II, Chapter 1, p. 207)

Thomas Piketty makes this point in his latest book (2022, pp. 49–67) that the advantages enjoyed by the North were propelled by colonialism, slavery, and hefty military advantage.

In 2015, the United Nations issued their 17 Sustainable development Goals. Two of them directly address inequality/equality: #5 Achieve gender equality and empower all women and girls; and #10 Reduce inequality within and among countries. Nevertheless, the 17 are interrelated, and taken as a group are a powerful antidote to inequality. For example,

> given that women in developing countries are the principal gatherers of firewood, spending an additional 2 to 20 hours per week; as more trees are felled, women spend more time looking for wood—time with a high opportunity cost. But if the global North helps Africa invest in renewable energy (Goal #7) then no need to deforest; which in turn will increase biodiversity (Goal #15) and help increase equality of education (Goal #4), since women and girls do not have to spend time gathering firewood; which will help achieve gender equality and empower all women and girls (Goal #5); which would help make cities more inclusive (Goal #11) and combat climate change (Goal #13); which will promote just, peaceful, and inclusive societies (Goal #16). Of course, whether these Goals are achieved is a function of Goal #17: Revitalize the global partnership for sustainable development.
>
> (Reardon et al., 2018, pp. 18–19)

Sustainability is not just achieving environmental justice, but social and economic justice—a three-legged stool if you will, of which reducing inequality is a central objective.

16.5   Conceptualizing, Defining, and Measuring Inequality

The common dictionary defines 'inequality,' as "the condition of being unequal." The common dictionary defines 'unequal,' as "not the same in any measurable aspect. Asymmetrical. Irregular; variable. Not having the required abilities; inadequate." Inequality can be defined/measured along a number of dimensions: income, wealth, spending power, property ownership, access to education, race, gender, legal status, socio-economic background, with "many individuals often fac[ing] inequalities in common" (Piketty, 2022, p. 2).

Two problems arise in measuring and conceptualizing inequality:

- Inequality's multiple dimensions are interwoven with causes/effects stretching from the micro to the macro,

> the history of inequality has always been chaotic and political, influenced by convulsive social changes and driven not only by economic

factors but by countless social, political, military, and cultural phenomenon as well. Socioeconomic inequalities—disparities of income and wealth between social groups—are always both causes and effects of other developments in other spheres. All these dimensions of analysis are inextricably intertwined. Hence the history of the distribution of wealth is one way of interpreting a country's history more generally.

(Piketty, 2014, p. 343).

This means, of course, that measuring inequality along only one dimension, while ignoring its interconnections is incomplete, and even a tad misleading. At the same time, it is much easier for social scientists to focus on only one dimension rather than investigate their interconnectedness.

- Without an agreed-upon threshold for inequality that tells us unequivocally when it is problematic, we rely on its evolution to ascertain if it is getting better/worse. To ascertain when inequality is problematic, we need a specific conceptualization of inequality, a specific definition, and a specific way of measuring. The conceptualization and its measurement need to be contextualized in a time and place.

16.6   Measuring Income/Wealth Inequality

Social scientists have focused on income/wealth inequality, given the relative ease of measurement and data ubiquity. Such a focus, however, is fundamental and deserves emphasis, since although,

human beings need to live in harmony with nature…they also need housing food, clothing and access to culture…Unless we are capable of measuring incomes, the inequality of their distribution, and their development over time, it is hard to see how we could develop norms of justice…without resolute action to compress socioeconomic inequalities, there is no solution to the environmental and climatic crisis.

(Piketty, 2022, p. 26)

We leave to others the arduous task of discussing precise measurements and definitions which can get quite technical.[20] Here, we offer a few observations/thoughts[21]:

- A useful definition of income/wealth inequality is "the disparity in wealth (one's total assets) and income (the money one receives from activities like work or investment) between people. The higher the disparity, the greater the inequality" (CFR, 2023).

- Is income/wealth a means to an end or an end in itself? Does income/wealth help achieve further goals, or is each an end? Or a little of both? If just a means, then the problem of inequality,

> gets magnified as the attention is shifted from income inequality to the inequality in the distribution of substantive freedoms and capabilities...For example, a person who is disabled, or ill, or old, or otherwise handicapped may, on the one hand, have problems in earning a decent income, and on the other, also face greater difficulties in converting income into capabilities and into living well.
>
> (Sen, 1999, p. 119)

> If income is a means then, "the far-reaching powers of the market mechanism have to be supplemented by the creation of basic social opportunities for social equity and justice" (Sen, 1999, p. 143).

- While most of us would agree perfect equality is not desirable; nor is it attainable for, "no matter what a nation does, it will never succeed in reaching perfectly equal conditions (Tocqueville, 1835 [2003], p. 625), we disagree on what degree of equality is desirable. Just like there is no optimal threshold for inequality, there is no optimal threshold for equality.
- We tend to measure income/wealth inequality by several methods: (1) statistically at one point on time (i.e., how cohort members differ from each other); (2) comparing an individual (or a cohort) over time; and (3) comparing the incomes/wealth going to the poorest 50% versus the richest 10% (Piketty, 2022, p. 29). These techniques utilize, more or less, the same methodology: First divide the population into five equal groups, each containing 20% of the population. Then divide income/wealth earners into five groups, from highest to lowest, with each group containing 20% of income/wealth earners. Perfect equality exists if each cohort receives the same percentage of income/wealth, i.e., 20%. Perfect inequality exists if only one individual earns all the income. Based on this methodology,[22] data for 2022 indicate[23]:

Quintile	Share of USA Aggregate Income
Lowest Quintile	3.0%
Second Quintile	8.2%
Third Quintile	14.0%
Fourth Quintile	22.5%
Highest Quintile	52.1%
Top 5 percent	23.5%

Here in the United States, the richest 20% of income earners (the highest quintile) earn 52.1% of aggregate income, compared to the bottom cohort which earns only 3.0%. And the top 5% of income earners earns 23.5% of aggregate income, more than the bottom 40%. In terms of wealth,

> In 2021, the top 10 percent of Americans held nearly 70 percent of U.S. wealth, up from about 61 percent at the end of 1989. The share held by the next 40 percent fell correspondingly over that period. The bottom 50 percent (roughly sixty-three million families) owned about 2.5 percent of wealth in 2021.
>
> (Siripurapu, 2022)

- One measure of inequality easily grasped is the wealth controlled by the world's billionaires. In 2023, the world counted 2,544 billionaires, with a combined wealth of $12 trillion, i.e., the world's richest 0.00003% earned 15% of its income (Neate, 2023). Incidentally, for the first time in nine years, the next generation of billionaires will have accumulated more wealth through inheritance than entrepreneurship (Neate, 2023, p. 27).
- Another statistic easily grasped is the ratio of CEO compensation to the compensation of the median worker. In 1965, in the USA, this ratio was 20-to-1; in 1989, it had increased to 60-to-1; and in 2023, it was 200-to-1 (Wallace-Wells, 2023, p. 17). This gap has since slightly narrowed due to labor shortages (partly COVID-induced) which in turn has increased the demand for labor and increased wages, especially for those at the bottom (*The Economist,* December 2, 2023, p. 9). Nevertheless, despite this slight contraction, since "1974, the biggest and most important change is the social fact of exploding income inequality" (Wallace-Wells, 2023, p. 16).
- At the other extreme, 712 million people globally live in extreme poverty, i.e., earning less than $2.15 a day (Overview: Poverty, 2024).
- Regardless of who measures income/wealth inequality in the United States: The Government Accountability Office, the Congressional Budget Office, the Bureau of Labor Statistics, or the Census Bureau; or which measurement is used: Cohort, the Gini Coefficient,[24] or the CEO/worker ratio, wage inequality has surged, especially between 1970 and 2006).[25]
- The causes of income inequality are varied and multi-faceted and include: De-industrialization, increased globalization, decreased unionization, increased demand for skilled workers, and the influx of less-skilled baby boomers into the labor force during the 1970s (McConnell et al., 2021, pp. 448–452). Income inequality is also due to discrimination, exhibited directly by one actor toward another, and institutionally, "i.e., unconscious, implicit biases and inertia within society's institutions, rather than intentional choices" (Barocas and Selbst, 2016, pp. 673–674).
- Inequality between nations is a major causal factor of **immigration**, and inequality between areas within a nation is a major cause of internal migration.

- Thomas More's novel *Utopia*, published in 1516, depicts a society without money, property, poverty, and inequality. Reading this makes one wonder if such a society could ever, in fact, exist. The answer is no, and to even suggest so, is to earn the epithet 'utopian,' i.e., one's head is in the clouds.
- Inequality is not the same as poverty (defined as a deprivation and measured either absolutely or relatively). Thus, "the nature of—and causal influences—on inequality may differ somewhat between the problem of persistent deprivation and that of sudden destitution" (Sen, 1999, p. 187). Nevertheless, inequality and poverty share the same underlying and recurring social conditions,[26] so that

> a fuller approach would be reparative with respect to the ongoing reproduction of historic inequalities. These would be systems that take into account ways in which people are differently situated and what we can do to create a more equal playing field while maintaining procedural fairness.
>
> (Marchese, 2023, p. 25)

- Finally, we should mention that since 2021, there has been an explosion in inequality methodologies, research, and findings, which are contained in the *World Inequality Database* (WID.world). This resource is too massive to even begin to discuss, but for anyone interested in the empirical work on inequality this is ground zero.

16.7   Solutions to Income/Wealth Inequality

While it is interesting to discuss utopian conceptualizations of perfect equality and hence the absence of inequality, especially given their importance in contemporary political philosophy (Sen, 2009); at the same time, if the goal is to "identify [and then redress] redressable injustices" (Sen, 2009, p. vii), then it becomes appropriate to make "comparisons between different ways in which people's lives may be led, influenced by institutions but also by people's actual behavior, social interactions and other significant determinants" (Sen, 2009, p. xvi). In other words, begin with actual living conditions and consider practical solutions.

While volumes have been written on practical solutions, here, given limited space, we can only summarize:

- **Redistribute through taxing**: This solution is probably the most familiar. It taxes the rich at an appropriate level and then distributes to the poor. A criticism is that taxing the rich distorts incentives—why should I work more if the fruits of my labor will be taxed away; likewise redistributing to the poor distorts incentives—why should I work with a guaranteed income. (Note: There is no agreed optimal level of taxation.)

- **The Earned Income Tax Credit**: Returns income to working individuals who earn an income below a certain threshold. The credit is phased out once the individual's income surpasses it.
- **Economic Growth**: Which doesn't always lift all boats, but certainly provides more opportunities for lower-income workers than does a lack of growth. We feel that a significant investment in renewable energy infrastructure will help (see **Net Zero**). This in turn will create high-paying middle-class jobs which will decrease income dispersion. At the same time, evidence is mixed on how inequality affects economic growth, largely depending on how inequality is measured, and its extent.[27] But we do know that increased inequality can worsen financial instability. For example, analyzing the first decade-and-a-half of the 21st century, Thomas Piketty found,

> one consequence of increasing inequality was virtual stagnation of the lower and middle classes in the United States, which inevitably made it more likely that modest households would take on debt, especially since unscrupulous banks and financial intermediaries, freed from regulation and eager to earn good yields on the enormous savings injected into the system by the well-to-do, offered credit on increasingly generous terms.
>
> (Piketty, 2014, pp. 372–373)[28]

- **Artificial Intelligence**: While much uncertainty exists over the effects of AI (see our chapter), it is plausible that AI could increase the demand for workers, especially for jobs that do not require a college education. This, in turn, could lessen inequality by boosting wages of the bottom- and middle-tier cohorts.[29]
- **A new type of firm**: Necessary to achieve **Net Zero** that recognizes and enables all the firm's stakeholders (Boyd and Reardon, 2020). Such a firm would "eliminate the core source of exploitation that Marx identified within capitalism—the separation of workers from ownership, control, and ready access to the means of production" (Wisman, 2022, p. 441).
- **A progressive and global tax on capital**: This would complement existing income taxes and inheritance/estate taxes.[30] A global tax on capital,

> would expose wealth to democratic scrutiny, which is a necessary condition for effective regulation of the banking system and international capital flows. A tax on capital would promote the general interest over private interests while preserving economic openness and the forces of competition.
>
> (Piketty, 2014, p. 597)

Another rationale for a global tax on capital is that for the very wealthy, "income is often not a well-defined concept…and only a direct tax on capital can correctly gauge the contributive capacity of the wealthy" (Piketty, 2014, p. 676). Despite the forceful arguments in favor of such a tax, implementing it

> …is a utopian idea. It is hard to imagine the nations of the world agreeing to any such thing anytime soon. To achieve this goal, they would have to establish a tax schedule applicable to all wealth around the world and then to decide how to apportion the revenues. But [even] if the idea is utopian, it is nevertheless useful[31] (2014, p. 663).

- **Basic Income**: At the very least would provide a floor for everyone to have a modicum of income. This would reduce income inequality by compressing the difference between higher and lower echelons. Although a basic income is offered as a solution for income insecurity rather than inequality (Standing, 2017), the two are linked. While critics say that this will stifle initiative and effort, Guy Standing (2017, pp. 179–181, and passim) effectively counters this, arguing that it would unleash creativity and raise productivity while freeing slavish devotion to dead-end jobs. Thomas Piketty argues that a basic income (BI) is simply not enough. He suggests adding guaranteed employment and an inheritance tax for all; the latter's primary objective is to increase the negotiating power of everyone who owns almost nothing (that is, about half the population (Piketty, 2022, p. 162).

16.8   The Drive Toward Real Equality: Race and Gender

Hannah Arendt lamented,

> When Russians have become Slavs, when Frenchmen have assumed the role of commanders of a force noire, when Englishmen have turned into 'white men,' as already for a disastrous spell all Germans became Aryans, then this change will itself signify the end of Western man [sic]. For no matter what learned scientists may say, race is, politically speaking, not the beginning of humanity but its end, not the origin of peoples but their decay, not the natural birth of man but his unnatural death.
>
> (Arendt, 1968, p. 157)

Indeed, race is a relatively modern phenomena dating to European colonialism, where the world's people were classified along racial lines, with white Europeans at the top (Arendt, 1968, pp. 158–266; Alexander, 2012, p. 23).

In the United States, "the idea of race emerged as a means of reconciling chattel slavery—as well as the extermination of American Indians—with the ideals of freedom preached by whites in the new colonies" (Alexander, 2012, p. 23). Slavery was so integral to the new United States that the Constitution itself,

> was based largely on the effort to preserve a racial caste system—slavery—while at the same time affording political and economic rights to whites, especially propertied rights…Federalism—the division of power between the states and the federal government–was the device employed to protect the institution of slavery and the political power of slaveholding states.
>
> (Alexander, 2012, pp. 26–27)

In addition to being denied the right to vote, Blacks were to be counted as three-fifths of a person for purposes of political representation. So, rather than being a land of opportunity, for Blacks, America was a land of forced brutality, where one group of humans was able (on the newly constructed theory of race) to control, direct, exploit, brutalize, and rip another group asunder from its motherland,

> in one fell swoop, oppression has deprived the descendants of the Africans of almost all the privileges due to human beings! The American Negro has lost even the recollection of his [sic] homeland; he no longer hears the language of his fathers; he has renounced their religion, and forgotten their ways. Ceasing, in this way, to belong to Africa, he still has not acquired any rights to the good things of Europe; but he is left suspended between the two societies; he has remained cut off from the two nations, sold by one and rejected by the other.
>
> (Tocqueville, 1835 [2003], pp. 371–372; exclamation in original)

America has never reconciled this conflict between the Declaration's lofty words, and the nation's birth in slavery,[32] despite recently achieving formal equality.

In the global North and South, "Historically women have undoubtedly been subjected to the most massive and systematic discrimination …Nearly all societies have been patriarchal societies" (Piketty, p. 184). Here in the United States, when the Constitution was written, women were a non-entity. Women did not draft the constitution, nor could they vote to ratify it. Women were not allowed to run for office. In the United States, it wasn't until 1920 with the 19th Amendment, that women were given the right to vote. Yet, few today would insist that the sexes are really equal. Just looking at income alone, for example, women today in America earn 75 cents for every dollar that a man earns. A galvanizing and polarizing issue in America (among many others) was the Equal Rights

Act Amendment, which petered out June 30, 1982, due to heavy opposition. The lack of equality between genders has feminized poverty, i.e., women currently have a higher share of poverty, and in addition, the proportion of women among the poor has increased over time. In the formative stages of the United States, and well up to quite recently, "an inflexible opinion prevail[ed] to contain women within the restricted sphere of domestic business and duties and to forbid them to step beyond it" (Tocqueville, 1835 [2003], p. 687).

Piketty offers practical solutions to both race and gender discrimination,[33] cautioning, however, that the causes and attitudes run deep and wide, making any solution arduous at best. For example, quotas, and affirmative action can work, but only superficially, given the deeply held values and biases that support discrimination of all kinds, especially race and gender, "A natural prejudice leads a man [sic] to despise anyone who has been inferior to him a long time after he has become his equal; an imaginary inequality, rooted in custom, always follows the real inequality produced by wealth or the law" (Tocqueville, 1835 [2003], p. 400).

It was well understood that for Blacks, the indigenous, and women, that the Declaration's lofty words were just that, lofty yet empty words that did not ring true to anyone but white men. But since the Declaration,

> Americans who believed in the principles of democracy…have asserted the principles of equality and government by consent even in the face of such repression, even as they died for their beliefs. More often than not, those articulating the nation's true principles have been marginalized Americans who demanded the nation to honor its founding promises. Their struggles have constantly renewed the country's dedication to the principles articulated in the Declaration of Independence. Their fight for equality reveals the true nature of American democracy; it is, and always has been, a work in progress.
>
> (Richardson, 2023, pp. 167–168)

Despite its initial exclusivity, "the Declaration…gave marginalized Americans not just the language but also the grounds to challenge the laws that made them unequal" (Richardson, 2023, p. 189). At the same time, achieving equality before the law can lull us into a self-congratulatory complacency, for it can prevent us from looking beneath the surface to see how things really are,

> Equality of condition, though it is certainly a basic requirement for justice, is nevertheless among the greatest and most uncertain ventures of modern mankind. The more equal conditions are, the less explanation there is for the differences that actually exist between people; and thus all the more unequal do individuals and groups become.
>
> (Arendt, 1968, p. 54)

On the contrary, rather than being content with formal equality before the law, which, nevertheless, is a necessary first step, we must strive for real equality under the law. To do so, we must develop indicators and procedures that will allow us to fight gendered, social, and ethno-racial discrimination, which is in practice endemic nearly everywhere, in the global North as well as in the South" (Piketty, 2022, p. 175).

Many such statistics are generative, i.e., arising only within a specific time/place context. The goal, here, is not to just gather statistics, although this is much needed, but to develop new and more holistic indicators, and to utilize them

> in the service of a genuine antidiscrimination policy, firm and resolute, transparent and reliable, and involving all the actors (labor unions and employers, political movements and citizen associations). So far beyond national models, this has never really been done
>
> (Piketty, 2022, p. 200)

And ideally, change our biases and values in order to obviate the need for discrimination—a herculean task if there ever was one, while developing new modes of democratic and inclusive thinking suitable for the age of sustainability.

This is our next step in the fight for real equality, a fight that will never end.

16.9   Inequality and Climate Change

Jeff Goodell writes that the "heat caused by fossil fuel combustion will cause a great migration within the next 100 years, and not just of humans, but of animals, of plants, of jobs, of wealth, of diseases…it will expose deep fissures of inequity and injustice" (2023, pp. 16 and 17). While all will suffer the effects of climate change, the poor will suffer the most, "the poorest, and particularly the poorest in the poorest countries, are preparing to be subjected, with increasing violence, to climatic and environmental damage caused by the richest people's way of life" (Piketty, 2022, p. 11). The countries of the global South will see increased hunger, increased flooding/droughts and more extreme weather. While the global North "has the economic resources to adapt to many of the effects of climate change, without significant aid poorer countries will be unable to implement preventive measures, especially those that rely on the newest technologies" (Harris and Roach, 2018, p. 327).

Climate justice (where North helps South) needs to be a central policy, post-2024. Climate justice goes hand-in-hand with enabling the countries of the global South, while also constructing a new global architecture that is equitable to all.[34] We owe it to our children and to our children's children to put this issue on the front burner, so to speak.

16.10 Conclusion

Lincoln's 'Gettysburg Address' (November 19, 1863) opens, "Four score and seven years ago our fathers brought forth on this continent a new nation, conceived in liberty, and dedicated to the proposition that all men are created equal" (Fehrenbacher, 1989, p. 536). Since the Declaration, the evolution of the United States has been a concerted effort to broaden the base of equality to cover all Americans. While great strides have been made to achieve equality before the law, in reality the march toward real equality is just beginning and we have a lot of work to do, it "is a battle whose outcome is uncertain, and not a road laid out in advance" (Piketty, 2022, p. 243).

Notes

1 We would be remiss not to mention Friedrich Engels (1820–1895), Marx's good friend, collaborator, and co-author on their principal works, including *Capital* (published in three volumes 1868, 1885, 1894) which dissects and explains capitalism's inequality and exploitation; *The Communist Manifesto* (1848) which introduces socialism to the world and its most important elements; and *The German Ideology* which criticizes Hegel's assertion that ideology is the driving force of human history.

2 Sonenscher (2022) provides an interesting historical discussion of the word 'capitalism' and its evolving meaning.

3 For Marx, these two classes are not mere categories but social classes. This is essential to understand Marx, "it unifies his sociology and his economics by making the same class concept fundamental to both" (Schumpeter, 1954, p. 551). But then Schumpeter rightly adds, "Of course, the question is complicated by another, viz., the question of the validity of the Marxist theory of classes" (Schumpeter, 1954, p. 551, note # 13). As we see it, looking at a system as complicated as capitalism, using only a lens that sees 'classes,' while, in addition, defining class only by the means of production, inevitably distorts. After all, "class is itself plural and multidimensional: status, property, income, diplomas, gender, origin, and so on" (Piketty, 2022, p. 14).

4 Marx, for the most part, ignored the ameliorative role of government, assuming that government would always side with capital.

5 Today, the terms 'socialism' and 'communism' are used interchangeably. For that, we can blame Marx and Engels. In their treatise on socialism, *The Communist Manifesto* (1848), they wanted to distance themselves from contemporary socialists, whom they felt were "intellectually inferior, members of sects that were dying out, and social quacks; so, we opted for the older term communism" Marx and Engels (1992 [1848], p. 55).

6 We include the full title as it evidences Malthus criticism of Goodwin, Condorcet and other writers' endorsement of welfare policies to help the poor. The 'other writers' included Adam Smith and David Hume. By the way, Malthus significantly revised the original text, publishing each revision as a separate edition. Nevertheless, the central message remained basically the same.

7 For Malthus, the rich and the poor each served a central place in God's plan.

8 Hinduism looks at different stations in life as pre-ordained, as well as 'just karma' for performance in a previous life, suggesting that nothing can or should be done for the poor. Protestants assume that the accumulation of wealth was a sign that their souls would be saved, thus enjoying eternal life.

9 This passage conjures up Jonathan Swift's satirical *A Modest Proposal* (1729), in which he suggested that poor people in Ireland could ease their economic troubles by selling their children as food to the upper classes. Swift's '*Proposal*' was satirical parody; unfortunately, Malthus' *Essay* was offered as actual policy.

10 For a perceptive biographical essay on Malthus, see Keynes (1956). Especially, interesting is Keynes' discussion of the correspondence between Malthus and David Ricardo; the latter, instrumental in pushing 19th century economics towards deductive, ahistorical, logical reasoning. Keynes lamented, "If only Malthus, instead of Ricardo, had been the parent stem from which nineteenth-century economics proceeded, what a much wiser and richer place the world would be today!" (Keynes, 1956, p. 36). We fully agree, not so much for his policy prescriptions but for his modus operandi—the antithesis of Ricardo.

11 See Piketty (2022, pp. 121–149) for a good discussion of the causes of the Great Redistribution and its key elements.

12 Wollstonecraft (1997) contains both *Vindications*.

13 For a fascinating biography of Mary Wollstonecraft, see Gordon (2006).

14 Her daughter, Mary (1791–1851), married the Romantic poet Percy Bysshe Shelly. Mary Shelly authored the novel *Frankenstein* (1818).

15 See Madden and Dimand (2019) for a superb attempt to bring to light economic writings since the 18th century. It is a wonderful effort to recapture the past.

16 Indeed, the argument that "capitalism is rigged is so engrained that it is a clarion call for government ameliorative action by the left and the gestating of populism on the right" (*The Economist*, Dec. 2, 2023).

17 An interesting tidbit: The Council on Foreign Relations tells us that, "Augustus—the emperor of Rome from 31 BCE to 14 ACE—controlled one-fifth of the Roman empire's immense wealth, while Mansa Musa—the ruler of Timbuktu from 1280 to 1337 ACE—owned almost half the world's gold" (CFR, 2023).

18 Thorstein Veblen (1857–1929) an American economist, argued that most consumption is wasteful, done merely to keep up with the Jones' so to speak. For Veblen, consumption is motivated by emulation and envy: My neighbor buys a boat, I buy a boat. My neighbor remodels his/her house, so do I; and if I have the resources a bigger and better one. Veblen termed this 'conspicuous consumption' (1899 [1934]), most of which is unsustainable (Reardon et al., 2018, pp. 247–248).

19 Known as estate taxes, their provenance can be traced to the French Revolution when "a tax on estates and gifts was established [shortly after the fiscal privileges of the nobility were abolished]. These were astonishing innovations at their time… [their] purpose…was not only to fill the coffers of the new regime but also to enable the government to record all transfers of wealth whether by bequest (at the owner's death) or gift (during the owner's lifetime) in order to guarantee to all the full exercise of their property rights" (Piketty, 2014, p. 426). Here in the United States, estate taxes comprise less than 1% of total government revenue.

20 Piketty (2014, pp. 57–65) provides a good discussion; as does Piketty (2022, pp. 45–47).

21 For a general overview, see Reardon et al. (2018, pp. 80–83).

22 For elaboration, see Guzman and Kollar (2023).

23 Source: Guzman and Kollar (2023) 'Table A-3: Income Distribution Measures Using Money Income and Equivalence-Adjusted Income.'

24 The Gini coefficient, developed by the Italian sociologist Corrado Gini in 1912, measures the extent to which a distribution of household income deviates from a perfectly equal distribution. See 'What is Economic Inequality?' (2023).

25 For evidence, see McConnell et al. (2021, pp. 447–448; especially footnotes #22–25).

26 Analyzing issues from a systems wide perspective is a major theme of this book.
27 For a representative sample with ample references to the literature, see Panizza (2002) and Topuz (2022).
28 Piketty is quick to add that "it would be altogether too much to claim that the increase of inequality in the United States was the sole or even primary cause of the chronic instability of the global financial system" (Piketty, 2014, p. 374). We agree, but feel that it was a factor.
29 The COVID-induced labor shortages have been partially responsible for decreasing the USA college/noncollege wage premium from two-thirds to one-half (Blue-Collar Bonanza, 2023, p. 9).
30 Piketty writes that "these progressive taxes play distinct and complementary roles. Each is an essential pillar of an ideal tax system" (2014, pp. 675–676).
31 For further discussion, see Piketty (2014, pp. 685–691).
32 In North America, "Slavery…began in the 17th century and ended in the 19th. Approximately half a million slaves were imported into the area that became the United States before the international slave trade was outlawed in 1806. In the southern states—the region to which slavery was largely confined—slaves constituted one-third of the population from 1790 to 1860 despite the cessation of new supplies of slaves from overseas…The rate of increase of the slave population in the absence of imports was the same as the rate of increase of the southern free population" (Temin, 1975, p. 53). Also see de Tocqueville (1835 [2003], pp. 398–426).
33 See Piketty (2022, pp. 175–202).
34 For a good discussion, see (Fraser, 2009).

References

Alexander, Michelle (2012) *The New Jim Crow: Mass Incarceration in the Age of Color-blindness*, The New Press, New York.

Arendt, Hannah (1968) *The Origins of Totalitarianism*, Harcourt, New York.

Auerbach, Alan J., Laurence J. Kotlikoff, and Darryl Koehler (2023) 'US Inequality and Fiscal Progressivity: An Intragenerational Accounting,' *Journal of Political Economy*, Vol. 131, No. 5, pp. 1249–1293.

Barocas, Solon and Andrew D. Selbst (2016) 'Big Data's Disparate Impact,' *California Law Review*, Vol. 104, No. 3, pp. 671–732.

'Blue-Collar Bonanza' (2023) *The Economist*, December 2, editorial, p. 9.

Boyd, Graham and Jack Reardon (2020) *Rebuild the Economy, Leadership, and You: A Toolkit for Builders of a Better World*, Evolutesix, London.

Carpinteyro, Marilyn (2023) 'Precarious May Best Describe Situation,' *DC Journal*, (June 28), https://dcjournal.com/

Fehrenbacher, Don E. (Ed.) (1989) *Abraham Lincoln: Speeches, Letters, Miscellaneous Writings, Presidential Messages, and Proclamations 1859–1865*, The Library of America, New York.

Fraser, Nancy (2009) *Scales of Justice: Reimagining Political Space in a Globalized World,*' Polity Press, Cambridge.

Fullbrook, Edward (2009) The Meltdown and Economics Textbooks,' in Jack Reardon (Ed.) *The Handbook of Pluralist Economics Education*, Routledge, London, pp. 17–23.

Gordon, Lyndall (2006) *Vindication: A Life of Mary Wollstonecraft*, Perennial, New York.

Guzman, Gloria and Melissa Kollar (2023) *Income in the United States: 2022*, Report Number P60-279, September 12, US Census Bureau.

Harris, Jonathan and Brian Roach (2018) *Environmental and Natural Resource Economics: A Contemporary Approach*, 4th ed. Routledge, London.

Keynes, John Maynard (1936) *The General Theory*, Harcourt, Brace and Company, New York.

Keynes, John Maynard (1956) 'Robert Malthus,' *Essays and Sketches in Biography*,' Meridian Books, New York, pp. 11–38.

Madden, Kristen and Robert Dimand (2019) *The Routledge Handbook of the History of Women's Economic Thought*, Routledge, London.

Malthus, Thomas Robert (1958 [1803]) *An Essay on the Principle of Population*, Vol. 1 and 2, Dent Publications, London.

Marchese, David (2023) 'Talk: interview with Colin Koopman,' *The New York Times Sunday Magazine*, March 26, pp. 23–25.

Marx, Karl and Friedrich Engels (1992 [1848]) *The Communist Manifesto*, Oxford University Press, Oxford, UK.

Marx, Karl and Friedrich Engels (1967 [1867]) *Capital: A Critique of Political Economy*, published in three volumes, International Publishers, New York.

Marx, Karl and Friedrich Engels (1947 [1970]) *The German Ideology*, International Publishers, New York.

McConnell, Campbell, Stanley Brue, and David Macpherson (2021) *Contemporary Labor Economics*, 11th ed., McGraw Hill, New York.

Milanovic, Branko (2023a) *Visions of Inequality: From the French Revolution to the End of the Cold War*, Belknap Press/Harvard University Press.

Milanovic, Branko (2023b) 'The Great Convergence: Global Equality and Its Discontents,' *Foreign Affairs*, July/August, Vol 102, No. 4, pp. 78–91.

Hamilton, Alexander, James Madison, and John Jay (2003 [1787–1788]) *The Federalist Papers*, Bantam Books, New York.

Mill, John Stuart (1965 [1848]) *Principles of Political Economy*, Liberty Fund, Indianapolis.

More, Thomas (1516 [1965]) *Utopia*, Penguin, New York.

Neate, Rupert (2023) 'Most New Billionaires Owe Wealth to inheritance, Not Work,' *The Guardian*, November 30, p. 27.

Okun, Arthur (1975) *Equality and Efficiency: The Big Tradeoff*, Brookings Institution Press, Washington DC.

'Overview: Poverty' (2024) The World Bank, https://blogs.worldbank.org/

Panizza, U. (2002) 'Income Inequality and Economic Growth: Evidence from American Data,' *Journal of Economic Growth*, Vol. 7, pp. 25–41.

Petrou, Karen (2023) 'Bidenomics has a Mortal Enemy, and it isn't Trump,' *The New York Times*, Opinion, November 19, p. 10.

Piketty, Thomas (2014) *Capital in the Twenty-First Century*, Belknap Press of Harvard University Press, Cambridge, Massachusetts; translated by Arthur Goldhammer.

Piketty, Thomas (2022) *A Brief History of Equality*, Belknap Press of Harvard University, Cambridge, Massachusetts, translated by Steven Rendall.

Reardon, Jack, Maria Madi, and Molly Scott Cato (2018) *Introducing a New Economics*, Pluto Press, London.

Schumpeter, Jospeh (1954) *History of Economic Analysis*, Oxford University Press, New York.

Schumpeter, Joseph (1942 [1975]) *Capitalism, Socialism and Democracy*, Routledge, London. pp. 82–83.

Sen, Amartya (1999) *Development as Freedom*, Anchor Books, New York.

Sen, Amartya (2009) *The Idea of Justice*, Penguin, New York.

Siripurapu, Anshu (2022) 'The US Inequality Debate,' April 20, Council on Foreign Relations (cfr.org).

Sonenscher, Michael (2022) *Capitalism: The Street Behind the Word*, Princeton University Press, Princeton.

Standing, Guy (2017) *Basic Income: And How We Can Make it Happen*, Pelican Books, London.

Temin, Peter (1975) *Causal Factors in American Growth in the Nineteenth Century*, Macmillan Press, London.

Topuz, S.G. (2022) 'The Relationship Between Income Inequality and Economic Growth: Are Transmission Channels Effective?' *Social Indicators Research*, Vol. 162, pp. 1177–1231.

Tocqueville, Alexis de (1835 [2003]) *Democracy in America*, Penguin, New York.

Veblen, Thorstein (1899 [1934]) *The Theory of the Leisure Class: An Economic Study of Institutions*, The Modern Library, New York.

Wallace-Wells, David (2023) 'Surging Inequality has benefited wealthy Americans above all. But increasingly, the global economy's biggest winners are elsewhere', *The New York Times Magazine*, December 24, pp. 16–17.

'What is Economic Inequality?' (2023) *CFR Education*, July 27, https://education.cfr.org/

Wisman, Jon D. (2022) *The Origins and Dynamics of Inequality*, Oxford University Press, Oxford, UK.

Wollstonecraft, Mary (1997) *The Vindications: The Rights of Men and The Rights of Woman*. (Eds.) D.L. Macdonald and Kathleen Scherf, Broadview Press, Toronto.

17 Labor Unions

The Issue: Labor unions have always been controversial in America. At the same time, they have played a critical role in defining America and in determining who we are. It remains to be seen how effective labor unions can be in the expected revolutionary changes brought about by **Artificial Intelligence**. Labor unions tend to react within the existing contours of the capitalist economy, but since these contours are changing with a high degree of uncertainty, we cannot say for certain what a specific role for labor unions would be. To intelligently discuss the post-2024 role of unions, it is important to understand what labor unions are today, how they have evolved, their current objectives, and how they fit in today's America.

17.1 Introduction

Adam Smith, founder of the discipline of economics here in the West,[1] noted the innate power difference between workers and their employers (i.e., masters),

> The workmen desire to get as much, the masters to give as little as possible… It is not, however, difficult to foresee which of the two parties must, upon all ordinary occasions, have the advantage in the dispute and force the other into a compliance with their terms. The masters, being fewer in number, can combine much more easily…and in all such disputes the masters can hold out much longer.
>
> (Smith, 1776 [1976], Volume One, Book I, Ch. 8, p. 74)

Alexis de Tocqueville, a perspicacious observer of early 19th century America, had a different take,

> workmen almost always have a few sure resources which allow them to withdraw their services when they are not awarded what they consider is the fair payment for their work. In the unbroken struggle over wages between [workmen and masters] power is thus divided and success alternates from one to the other.
>
> (de Tocqueville, 1835 [2003], p. 675)[2]

DOI: 10.4324/9781003591856-19

But hidden in this passage is the underlying power which Smith wrote about: The employers decide and award what is considered fair, and if not met, then workers react. That workmen and masters jointly decide the wage was not apparently an option, for it would interfere with managements' rights (dating from English common law) to determine the contours of the workplace. (Apparently, the lofty ideals of the Declaration of Independence had not entered the workplace.)

However, a few paragraphs later, de Tocqueville offers an exception to his sanguine view: That of an aristocrat expelled from political life who starts an enterprise. He writes,

> …since they are few in number they can league together. Workmen, by comparison, are very numerous and their numbers are constantly on the increase…Now, once men have embarked on this career [i.e., workmen], they soon pick up habits of body and mind which render them unsuited for any other work…These men usually lack education, energy, or resources. They are, therefore, at their master's mercy…Should they choose to strike, the master who is wealthy, is easily able to wait, without risk of ruin, until necessity brings them back since they must work every day so as not to die, for they own almost nothing but the strength of their arms. Oppression has long since reduced them to poverty, and as they become poorer, they are easier to oppress—a vicious circle from which they cannot escape.
>
> (Tocqueville, 1835 [2003], pp. 676–677)

Fast forward to 2023: A strike by 130 mechanics at Telsa (one of the makers of the Electronic vehicles) service stations in Sweden, demanding collective bargain rights and pay commensurate with the autoworkers covered under collective bargaining agreements.[3] Telsa, owned by Elon Musk (although not exactly de Tocqueville's aristocratic prototype, surely fits his description), has assiduously kept unions away from his electric car makers which in turn employ some 127,000 workers in America, China, and Europe.

How one perceives workers, and whether they are employees, associates, or even contractors, determines how one perceives labor unions, and whether they are good or bad, help or hinder. Such has been the history of labor management relations throughout its existence. And this makes us wonder about democracy: Does it only pertain to political life? But even politically, democracy has taken a long time to develop. What about the workplace? Does democracy apply? What exactly does democracy in the workplace mean? What does it look like? Like many issues in this book, these questions are not easy issue to resolve. This chapter will explore labor unions: What they are, how they have evolved, and how they fit into today's America.

17.2   What Is a Labor Union?

A labor union is an organization to better economic conditions, i.e., wages, benefits, and working conditions. Three elements of this definition deserve mention:

- A labor union is an organization, and it organizes workers (or employees if you prefer)
- It is a special interest group looking out for the interests of its members, although sometimes 'special interests' and 'members' are loosely defined.
- This suggests an us-versus-them approach, with the interests of the 'us,' i.e., higher wages/benefits, conflicting with the interests of the 'them,' i.e., higher profits and control of management rights. (Of course you can flip the 'us' versus 'them' depending on your point of view.)

Freeman and Medoff (1984), in their landmark book, argued that in order to really understand labor unions, we must recognize that they have two contrasting aspects (or faces as the authors called them): 'monopoly' (the bad, i.e., raising costs, lowering profits) and 'voice' (the good, increasing wages and benefits, and enabling individual workers to be heard). Each face is part and parcel of what a labor union is and what it does; one cannot be separated from the other. The two faces are a complementary pair,[4] if you will.

The voice face can be best understood in the context of Albert Hirschman's seminal book, *Exit, Voice, and Loyalty* (1970). For example, an individual facing an unpalatable situation, (defined as "a divergence between desired and actual, e.g., an unexpectedly unpleasant meal at a restaurant" (Freeman and Medoff, 1984, p. 7)) has three options[5]:

- **Exit without speaking**, or, and just as effectively, never return. Implicitly this assumes that the patron has other options, and that the decision to exit will negatively affect the firm via reduced revenue.
- **Loyalty**, where the worker remains silent and perseveres through the bad experience, either due to high opportunity costs (shyness) or out of respect/ friendship, or even a dearth of options.
- **Voice,** defined as "any attempt at all to change, rather than escape from, an objectionable state of affairs" (Hirschman, 1970, p. 30). Voice, "is the use of direct communication…It means talking about problems…In a political context, [it] refers to participation in the democratic process, through voting, discussion, bargaining, and the like" (Freeman and Medoff, 1984, p. 8). Only voice directly offers redress. Only voice guarantees that at the least the affected will be heard. And voice is best compatible with democracy.

In the workplace, a labor union protects an individual by the collective strength of the whole. A union, by effectuating voice, can make the workplace more democratic and attenuate (but certainly not eliminate) any Smithian difference in power between workers and management.

Another beneficial aspect of voice is that

> at any workplace there are public goods [i.e., conditions/issues that affect everyone] such as lighting, heating, speed of the production line, grievance procedure, pension plan, etc. [whereby] one individual, might not be willing to act; i.e., if it affects everyone why not let someone else do it, the classic free rider problem.
>
> (Freeman and Medoff, 1984, pp. 8–9)

In this case, the labor union attempts to solve the public good problem, by eliminating free riders.

While we find Freeman and Medoff's 'two faces' argument helpful, at the same time, it raises several troubling yet important questions:

* Does a labor union intrinsically have two faces, or is this to be determined via empirically testing?
* If the voice face restores democracy at the workplace, how can democracy exist if the two sides are at loggerheads? Or is this just a partial democracy? What exactly does democracy at the workplace mean?
* Does the 'us-versus-them' approach help or hinder us today, and especially given **AI**, and our transition to **Net Zero**. Do we need a new type of firm that recognizes all stakeholders? If so, would this render the concept of a labor union moot? In other words, are labor unions a vestige of an earlier age?

17.3   The Historical Development of Labor Unions in America

To understand labor unions today, we need to understand how they evolved. This section categorizes this evolution into four periods: (1) Labor union hostility 1790–1930s; (2) Pro-union and a new social contract 1930s–1970s; (3) Reversal: Anti-union labor 1970s–2022; (4) Today: Perhaps a new direction, 2023–? Granted, this demarcation is a tad arbitrary with anti-union and pro-union sentiment often mixing, but for presentation purposes, it is helpful.[6]

17.3.1   *Hostility 1790s–1930s*

Here, we are reminded of a line from Paul Simon's *Kodachrome*: 'With all the crap I learned in high school, it's a wonder I can think at all.' For during this period, with all the intense and pervasive opposition, it's a wonder that labor unions developed at all. Yes, they did develop, and toward the latter half of the 19th century they survived and became institutionalized as a fixture of the economy, despite ubiquitous opposition, Employers opposed labor unions throughout this period, not just for their monopoly face, but for usurping the deeply held concept of management rights: The manager/master/employer (whatever term we use) has an intrinsic right to control the basic contours of the workplace.

Before the Civil War, labor unions would spring up to redress an unpalatable situation (usually low wages). The first to do so (at least that we have written records) was the Federal Society of Journeymen Cordwainers (shoemakers) formed in Philadelphia in 1791. It was unusual in that it survived. Far more typical was that at the first sign of union activity, management would petition a local judge for an injunction (i.e., a court order prohibiting or requiring a specific action; from the Latin, 'enjoin'). The local judge, being of the same class and temperament, would readily oblige.

Post-Civil War, labor unions developed along two lines: Radical/socialist/reformist, and capitalist. The former wanted to reform/change capitalism and the latter wanted to work within it. Initially, unions of both types flourished, but by the mid-1930s reformist unions were all but extinct.[7] The capitalist unions survived because, at the risk of over-simplification, they gave workers what they wanted: Better wages and working conditions, whereas the reformist unions tried to educate/instill[8] on the bigger picture and/or how socialism offers a better alternative. But for workers, whose immediate concern was putting bread on the table, the opportunity cost of such activities was too high. Today, the objectives of capitalist labor unions resonate with America's workers,

> Unions and collective bargaining are labor responses to the organization of production in a market economy…workers try to gain some control over the conditions under which they make goods and provide services. Collective bargaining functions entirely within the established order of industrial ownership and management... [It] does not threaten the wage system but seeks a more balanced distribution of income; it does not expel supervision from the workplace but restrains the exercise of managerial prerogative
> (Craypo, 1986, p. 2).

In the second half of the 19th century, capitalist labor unions organized workers along a particular skill (i.e., craft) such as bricklayers, cigarmakers, carpenters, cordwainers. An exception was the United Mine Workers of America (UMWA), which would become one of the more important unions in the first half of the 20th century. It was an industrial union, meaning it would organize all workers within the industry (coal) regardless of craft (skill).

To strengthen labor's voice, the American Federation of Labor (AFL) was formed on December 8, 1886, in Columbus Ohio. Samuel Gompers, a member of the Cigar Workers Union was its first president. The AFL was a federation (i.e., a grouping) of capitalist labor unions and would steadily grow in importance and membership throughout this period.

The AFL was formed during a period of **deflation** (i.e., falling average level of prices), and frequent **recessions**, including the United States' longest recession, from 1873 to 1879. During a deflation, as prices fall, so do profits, and as profits fall so does hiring and investment. Unemployment increases with severe pressure to decrease wages, setting the stage for labor management confrontation. As we explain in our issue on **Inflation**, while one might assume that deflation is less harmful than inflation, it is not, for it sets in motion a steep downward spiral of prices, wages and profits, while exacerbating labor/management hostility. The 1880s was certainly no exception.

It was during this deflationary period that the first Labor Day was celebrated (September 5, 1882, in New York City) largely put together by the founding AFL unions. September 5 was chosen as a halfway point between July 4 and Thanksgiving. Disagreement exists over who first proposed Labor Day, although evidence points to Matthew Maguire, a member of the International Association of Machinists Department of Labor (n.d.). On June 28, 1894, President Grover Cleveland made the first Monday in September an official holiday to recognize the contributions of America's workers.

One more thing to mention during this period: The Sherman Antitrust was implemented in 1890 as the first of a series of **Antitrust** Laws to tame the growing monopolization of many important industries at the time, including **oil,** whiskey, linseed oil, and the railroads. But the first case tried under the Sherman Act was against a labor union: In 1893, the US Supreme Court ruled in *United States v. Workingmen's Amalgamated Council of New Orleans* that the participant labor unions (in a city-wide strike) violated the anti-monopoly provisions of the Sherman Act (Primm, 1910).

A lesson learned from this period which is still apropos today is that a labor union always arises for a specific reason: to redress an inequity (or a perceived inequity) at the workplace. An inequity that stands out vis-à-vis other workplaces within sight, or more technically, within their orbit of coercive comparison.[9]

17.3.2   *Pro-labor and a New Social Contract 1930s–1970s*

Beginning in the 1930s, the tide began to turn in favor of unionization, for the following reasons:

- The AFL's growing clout; especially, one of its constituent unions, the UMWA, the day's largest and most important union, given that it organized America's most important energy source at that time.
- The pro-union sentiments of the popular Franklin Delano Roosevelt, elected president in 1932 and remaining in office (with an unprecedent four terms) until 1945.

- The tumult of the Great Depression, which saw record **deflation** and **unemployment**, agitating workers to organize.
- John M. Keynes' widely circulating argument (1936) that high wages benefit the economy. Specifically, high wages, by increasing overall demand will increase business optimism, thereby incentivizing businesses to hire more workers and increase investment.[10] Despite the obvious counter argument that high wages reduce profits, and hence can potentially reduce business investment, the high-wage argument won out given the Great Depression's severity. The high-wage argument led to the passage of pro-union legislation throughout the 1930s.

The first favorable piece of union legislation was the Norris–LaGuardia Act (passed in 1932) which officially forbade the use of injunctions—the hated instrument of the 19th century used by management to extirpate union activity. This Act gave labor unions some breathing room in their organizing efforts and enabled their principal weapon, the strike, to become more effective. Indeed, the Act "clearly strengthened union bargaining power. Because firms could no longer gain legal relief from…a work stoppage, threats by unions to strike now became more credible" (McConnell et al., 2021, p. 357). In addition, the Act strengthened labor union protection against the anti-monopoly provisions of the Sherman Act.

The second piece of favorable legislation was the Labor Management Relations Act (LMRA) passed July 5, 1935; also known as the Wagner Act after its main sponsor, New York Senator Robert Wagner.[11] The LMRA, along with its subsequent amendments, is the main legislation governing/regulating today's labor unions. Still operational today, its major objectives/provisions are as follows:

- To legalize (and protect) the right of workers to form unions, and the right to engage in collective bargaining.
- Establish an election procedure that will ensure an orderly democratic establishment of labor unions. Whereas before, a labor union was established by force, i.e., a contest of the wills.
- Establish a new government agency, the National Labor Relations Board, headquartered in Washington, to oversee the Act's enforcement.
- Delineate a list of unfair labor practices (ULPs) which if committed by management would be illegal, e.g., it is an ULP for management to interfere with the protected right to organize.
- Establish a protected right to strike: A strike is protected if for an economic reason (i.e., wages, fringe benefits, and working conditions) or over an ULP violation.[12] Strikes over other issues are not legally unprotected and can result in immediate firing and/or permanent replacement.[13] At the same time, the labor law recognizes that the firm has a right to continue operating during a strike, thus allowing the hiring of replacement workers. Whether the

strikers can return to their jobs once the strike is over (i.e., permanently re-placed) depends on whether the strike is legally protected or not.
* The law cements/ossifies the assumption that labor and management have opposing interests; and as such, cooperation is precluded. While perhaps appropriate during the 1930s, we question its relevance today, an issue we will return to in **Net Zero**.

In 1935, the Committee for Industrial Organization was formed within the AFL to study the possibility of organizing the unskilled workers of America's growing manufacturing sector, especially in steel, automobiles, tire/rubber, electrical products, and clothing. These industries were ignored by the AFL leadership for many reasons, but mainly that such workers were non-craft (i.e., without a specific skill) and had emigrated from eastern and southern Europe.

The Committee was highly critical of the AFL's lackadaisical organizing efforts and recommended that it was absolutely necessary to begin organizing these workers under the auspices of the AFL. When the AFL rejected the Committee's recommendation, the Committee and its ten unions broke away in 1938 to form the Congress of Industrial Organizations (CIO) as a federation of labor unions. Both the Committee and the Congress (initially) were headed by John L. Lewis, president of the UMWA. He utilized innovative and highly effective organizing tactics such as the sit-down strike (i.e., strikers would occupy the workplace, not allowing management to enter. The UAW (aided by the UMWA and the CIO) used the sit-down strike to successfully organize General Motors, one of America's largest corporations (Sulzberger, 1938). It is now, however, il-legal since management is denied the right to continue operation—a fundamental tenet of the labor law. The law recognizes labor's legal right to strike, while also recognizing management's right to remain open and continue operations.

The CIO rapidly grew in membership, aggressively organizing the auto and steel industries, along with subway workers, machinists, electrical workers, and longshoremen (among others). For the next generation, the AFL and the CIO were rival federations raiding each other's territory.[14] In 1955, with the old guard leadership of each federation now deceased, and recognizing that the membership of each federation had grown similar, the AFL and the CIO merged to become the AFL-CIO. Based in Washington DC., George Meany was its first president.

Today, the AFL-CIO is a federation of labor unions, with a two-fold purpose: (1) to better the conditions of all workers, not just union members;[15] and (2) lobby on behalf of its members. In 2023, the AFL-CIO had 60 member unions representing 12.5 million workers, which is 87% of America's total unionized workers. Liz Schuler is AFL-CIO president (elected in 2022) and its first female head.[16]

Like most pieces of legislation, passage of the LMRA set in motion (almost immediately) forces to either repeal or amend. In 1947, the LMRA was amended by the Labor Management Relations Act, also known as the Taft-Hartley Act, after its two sponsors.[17] While the NLRA was clearly pro-labor, Taft-Hartley restored the balance; it was either restorative in favor of management or neutral depending on one's point of view. Still operational today, its specific objectives/provisions include the following:

- The protected right of employees *not* to join a union.
- The right of unionized workers to decertify their union via an orderly election, i.e., a decertification election.
- The establishment of a set of Unfair Practices which if committed by a labor union is illegal.
- Each state can implement a Right to Work law, i.e., a worker is not obligated to join a labor union even if that union has organized the workplace. More specifically, the Taft-Hartley Act outlawed the union shop, in which all employees must join the union if that workplace is covered by a collective bargaining agreement. Today, 27 states have passed a Right to Work law.[18] This free rider problem is a palpable irritant for labor unions: A typical worker might ask why should I join a labor union in a Right to Work Law state, when I would get the benefits without paying the union dues?
- The lockout—a management equivalent to the right to strike—was established, which prevents employees from entering the place of work.
- A restriction on the types of strikes protected by the law. (This will be discussed more fully later in this chapter.)
- To lessen the economic fallout from a strike, the federal government is allowed to stop for up to 80 days a strike that imperils national health and safety.

According to the labor law, a labor union becomes established (i.e., certified) via an orderly and democratic election procedure. The next step is to engage in collective bargaining (i.e., a process of negotiations) with the employer, with the ultimate goal of jointly writing a contract specifying wages, benefits and working conditions. This explains why unions, during the first stages of the union certification process, will try to sign up as many interested workers as possible. (To conduct an election, the NLRB requires a minimum of 30% of the workers to sign a petition indicating their preference for an election.) But once the union is certified, the employer need not reach an agreement with the union; it is only obligated to negotiate in good faith. Failure to reach an agreement is a preponderant reason why employees will decertify their labor union.

When WWII ended, the United States emerged with the world's strongest economy. With its economy largely intact, its firms were ready to go; looking to do business across the globe.[19] To be successful, however, they needed the active cooperation of their workers, so an implicit quid pro quo was made: In exchange for management conducting its traditional prerogatives (i.e., management rights), employees would enjoy higher wages, more fringe benefits and better conditions, while conceding the right to strike. Known as the Social Contract, it would last until the early 1970s.

In the United States, the post-WWII economic pie was growing, and labor stability/peace would enable a bigger piece for all. The Social Contract was unusual given the preceding conflict and the conflict that came after. Wages steadily increased during the Social Contract, as did productivity. In 1955, the percentage of American workers in a labor union reached 33%, an all-time high. This was the golden age of the American middle class, and of American workers, and of American unions—a unique period in American history.

The Landrum-Griffin Act, passed in 1959, amended the 1935 NLRA. Largely due to the illicit financial activities of the Teamsters and the improper election procedures of the UMWA, the Landrum-Griffin required regularly scheduled union elections, and strict accountability over the union's finances.

The LMRA and the Taft-Hartley did not apply to public sector workers at any level. But this would soon change. In 1962, President Kennedy issued Executive Order 10988 giving federal workers the right to join a union. In 1978, Congress passed the Civil Service Reform Act (CSRA) which expanded EO #10988 to give federal workers almost the same rights as did the LMRA for private sector workers. The rights include: the protected right to join or not to join a labor union; unfair labor practices for both unions and government agencies; and the Federal Labor Relations Authority (tantamount to the NLRB) to oversee and adjudicate the labor law. However, the right to strike, protected under the LMRA, was not extended to public sector workers at the federal level, since they were assumed to be too essential.

At the state level, the labor laws are too varied to discuss here, although we can say that over two-thirds of the states do not allow any state workers the right to strike; and no state allows firefighters and police officers the right to strike.[20] Given their essentiality, it is assumed that withholding labor would jeopardize public health and safety.

17.3.3   *Reversal: Anti-labor 1973–2022*

As the Japanese and West German economies recovered during the late 1960s, their products began to compete with America's, especially steel and automobiles. American wages and profits began to decline, and by the early 1970s, the Social Contract which had worked so well for the previous generation began to disintegrate. A new period of anti-union animus had begun, punctuated by Ronald Reagan's firing of the Professional Air Traffic Controllers Organization (PATCO) strikers. They struck on August 3, 1981, protesting stressful working conditions. The strikers were overly confident that President Reagan would be on their side since he "had been a seven-term

President of the Screen Actors Guild and even led the Guild's first strike during the nineteen-fifties after the studio chiefs refused to negotiate film and television residuals" (Gruner, 2022, p. 347). But they were wrong. After fair warning, all striking PATCO workers who did not return to work were fired and permanently replaced. And not surprisingly, the new workers voted to decertify the PATCO.[21]

During this period, the legal basis of the right to strike—labor's most important tool to achieve its objectives, was gradually weakened (Dubal, 2023). The labor law recognizes the right to strike if conducted over economic conditions and/or an ULP, while also recognizing a firm's right to stay open and conduct its business. A clear recognition that both sides have legitimate objectives. But alas, like many laws, fully recognizing both sides attenuates the full rights of each. Today, strikes that labor unions had once relied on during the tumultuous 1930s are outlawed, including the sit-down strike and the secondary boycott, i.e., withholding labor against a third party (often a retailer/supplier) to put pressure on the targeted firm. The law protects the right for workers to strike against their primary business but not a secondary firm.

The specific conditions of the right to strike (especially if protected) are adjudicated by the NLRB and sometimes by the Supreme Court if necessary. The US Department of Labor maintains data on major strikes, i.e., lasting at least one full day or one work shift, and involving at least 1000 workers. After reaching 400+ in 1975, the number steadily decline until 2017, then has trended upward, although still far below its 1970s level,

> Given that about 700 major collective bargaining agreements are negotiated each year, the number of major work stoppages is surprisingly small…the lost time from major strikes has been consistently far less than one-half of 1 percent of total work time.
>
> (McConnell et al., 2021, pp. 310–311)

That the working time lost is so small is explained by the labor law requiring that management must be pre-warned of a strike and that the union must not harm/destroy the overall business, giving the targeted firm time to prepare.[22] In addition to the time lost, the costs imposed (although, of course the two are intricately related) are quite small, "the costs imposed on the immediate parties to a strike and affected firms and consumers are not as great as one might surmise: A small fraction of 1 percent of total annual output" (McConnell et al., 2021, pp. 312–313).

17.3.4 Unions Today: Perhaps a New Direction?

In 2023, the percent of wage and salary workers[23] who are labor union members was 10.0%, slightly lower than the 10.1% in 2022, and the lowest since

1935. A stark difference exists between the organization rates of public and private sector workers. The former's unionization rate is 32.5%, over five times higher than that of the private sector's 6.0%. In 2023, 7.0 million public sector employees belonged to unions, along with 7.4 million private sector workers, for a total of 14.4 million workers. In 2023, unionization was highest in local government (38.4%), e.g., police officers, firefighters, and teachers (Bureau of Labor Statistics, 2024). One reason for the stark difference is that in the private sector, competition is rife (with monopoly outlawed by the antitrust laws), but not so in the public sector where most agencies have no competition making it easier to grant higher pay (Ohanian, 2019). In addition, many agency 'heads' especially at the local level largely depend on workers to get elected/re-elected, incentivizing the 'heads' to be more cognizant of employee interests.

Post-COVID, labor unions began flexing their muscles in Europe and here in the United States. Precipitated by the highest inflation rates since the early 1980s, tight labor markets, booming profits and increasing inequality, 2023 saw the highest level of strikes since 1979 (Eidelson, 2023). Workers across a broad array of industries have been striking for better pay, better control over working conditions, and a more equitable share of record-setting corporate profits. USA labor unions are also organizing industries and firms that have been traditionally non-union, e.g., Amazon and Starbucks. This union activity is occurring against the backdrop of the public's positive view of labor unions, a trend which is expected to intensify (Bahat et al., 2023, p. 68). Today,

> 55% of Americans have a positive view of labor unions, while 41% say they have a negative impact. A significant partisan difference exists: 75% of Democrats view labor unions positively while only 23% of Democrats view labor unions negatively; whereas 35% of Republicans view labor unions positively, compared to 61% who view unions negatively.
>
> (Pew Research Center, 2024)

Joe Biden was the most pro-labor USA president since FDR (*The Economist*, September 16, 2023), clearly differentiating himself from his predecessors,

> Biden has repeatedly voiced staunch support for workers, argu[ing] that union jobs are good jobs for workers and for America. He has overseen funding commitments, rule changes and personnel appointments that are handing more power to unions—a profound shift after decades in which they were regularly undermined.
>
> (*The Economist*, September 16, 2023)

In April 2021, the Administration established (via executive order) the Task Force of Worker Organizing and Empowerment, chaired by VP Kamela Harris and Labor Secretary Martin Walsh whose objective is self-explanatory.[24] In addition, President Biden's $1 trillion Inflation Reduction Act (see **Net Zero**) will create well-paying and stable middle-class jobs (which are most amenable to unionization). In addition to committing to fair wages under the IRA, the Administration has gone one step further by offering (opponents would say forcing) tax breaks to companies that pledge to remain neutral during a union organizing campaign.[25] Finally, the Biden administration has appointed pro-labor candidates to the NLRB, reversing the pro-management appointments of the previous administration.

This is a dramatic reversal to the anti-union animus of the Trump administration. All this is generating optimism—or concern—depending on which lens one uses: Is this the start of a new labor movement? A resurgence? Or just a flash in the pan?

Fueling this speculation are two high-profile and successful strikes that occurred in the summer of 2023: (1) 150,000 UAW workers struck in Detroit to recoup wage concessions granted earlier during periods of global restructuring; and (2) 340,000 members of the Teamsters Union at UPS struck to reclassify work jurisdictions.

Their success was partly explained by the election of firebrands to their respective union presidencies: Sean O'Brien of the Teamsters, and Shawn Fain of the UAW. However, somewhat ominously, both campaigns focused on existing members by extending their benefits, rather organizing the unorganized, which has been a long-standing problem. It is unlikely that the success of these two high-profile strikes will carry over to the "vast unorganized territory outside the contract campaigns (Elrod, 2023, p. 61).[26] This is an important point and does not bode well for organized labor beyond 2024,

> labor's epochal challenge has been to establish beachheads among the unorganized competition, while at the same time pursuing collective bargaining that protects the profit ability and employment stability of unionized workplaces…while the low organizing budget of most unions evidences the priorities.
>
> (Elrod, 2023, pp. 63 and 64)

Despite these two electrifying campaigns (or maybe because of it), we agree with Elrod's pessimistic outlook that, "the defining characteristic of our era has been organized labor's continued decline, which current business trends and union campaigns indicate will continue" (Elrod, 2023, p. 66). Expect few successful inroads into the unorganized. This is especially true given the severe weakening of the right to strike. However, if labor does not make systematic efforts to organize the unorganized then any uptakes in the unionization rate will only be marginal and ephemeral. Look for continued decline.

17.4   Conclusion

In a perceptive article published in the *Harvard Business Review,* Bahat et al. (2023) suggested that management's old way of perceiving labor unions as an interference with management rights, along with the belief that it is necessary to defeat unions at all costs (e.g., Amazon and Starbucks) is counterproductive and no longer effective. We agree. We need a new approach and a new conceptualization of labor management relations for the 21st century. Our current, ossified vision might have been applicable during the 1930s, but certainly not now. The 'us' v. 'them' modus operandi assumes that labor and managements objectives are mutually exclusive. Cemented by the current labor law, this precludes cooperation. It is outdated and in need of a makeover.

In addition to the traditional topics of wages, fringe benefits, and working conditions, today's workers increasingly want to bargain over public goods, climate change, and company values. As we transition to **Net Zero**, active cooperation between firms and all stakeholders, not just employees, is needed. We need a broad discussion of whether a new type of capitalist firm is needed that can help navigate the treacherous and tricky waters of AI. And if so, what type of labor management relations are needed, and even if this term will become passe and not reflect underlying realities.

Labor unions have always been controversial in America. At the same time, they have played a crucial role in defining America and determining who we are. It remains to be seen how effective labor unions can be in the expected revolutionary changes in the workplace brought about **AI**. Labor unions tend to react within the existing contours of the capitalist economy, but since these contours are changing with a great degree of uncertainty, we cannot say for certain what a specific role for labor unions would be certain what a specific role for labor unions would be. Nevertheless, the role of labor unions post-2024 is critical to discuss.

Notes

1 Islahi (2014) argues quite persuasively that many of Smith's arguments and even specific examples can be traced back to the developing discipline of Islamic economics during the 9th–12th centuries.
2 At the same time, Tocqueville scathingly criticizes the division of labor which was gaining currency, "as [it] is applied more completely, the worker becomes weaker, more limited and more dependent" (1835 [2003]), p. 646).
3 Source on the Telsa strike: 'Musk v. Unions' (2023).
4 This is an important concept, especially when we tend to view things as either one or the other, i.e., good or bad, male or female, black or white, etc. Originally derived from the Eastern religions, and heavily used in quantum physics, a complementary

pair refers to "two apparently different entities (they may even be ostensibly opposites) with a fundamentally deeper relationship" (Boyd and Reardon, 2020, p. 472).

5   While the restaurant meal seems trivial (yet, at the same time, one that resonates), Hirschman discusses a wide range of unpalatable situations: Social mobility, the two-party system, political associations, public schools, Nigerian railroads, etc.

6   For more historical details than we can provide, see Phil Foner's masterful nine volume *History of the Labor Movement in the United States*. We don't list the nine volumes in the references, since as separate volumes, they have separate publishers, although most are published with International Publishers. Unfortunately, they are not available in one collected volume.

7   Today, one socialist/radical union survives—The International Workers of the World (IWW), also known as the Wobblies. Founded in 1906, it is headquartered in Chicago with a membership of 12,000. The preamble to its Constitution states that, "The working class and the employing class have nothing in common…Between these two classes a struggle must go on until the workers of the world organize as a class, take possession of the means of production, abolish the wage system, and live in harmony with the earth" (IWW, 2022).

8   A good example of such a union was the Knights of Labor founded in 1869. It experienced a meteoric rise in membership, peaking at 900,000 members by 1886, making it the largest labor union up until then. But by 1900 it was defunct, although vestiges remained until 1949. Its decline was due to leadership weakness, organizational challenges/difficulties, the loss of several key strikes, and most importantly, a disconnect between purpose/function and membership wants, i.e., better pay and working conditions. Interestingly, unlike today's capitalist unions, management was allowed to join the Knights, although bankers, speculators/gamblers, and bartenders, were excluded as parasites.

9   Coined by Arthur Ross (1948) it means that when workers survey working conditions in other firms, they do not look at all but only those within their locality and/or industry, i.e., those that are strictly relevant.

10   This argument was due to a visceral love for labor unions but recognizing that drastic action was needed (see our **Social Security** chapter).

11   Senator Wagner, a staunch Democrat and FDR supporter, also sponsored the 1935 Social Security Act, and the 1937 Housing Act.

12   The LMRA exempted agricultural and domestic workers.

13   The law on the right to strike is complicated involving many nuances. For clarification see 'The Right to Strike' (n.d.). Incidentally in the 1962 Supreme Court case, *NLRB v. Washington Aluminum*, it was ruled that nonunion workers have the protected right to strike.

14   In addition to Foner's work, see Bernstein (1970).

15   According to the AFL-CIO's webpage, "We strive to ensure *all* working people are treated fairly, with decent paychecks and benefits, safe jobs, dignity, and equal opportunities. We help people acquire valuable skills and job-readiness for the 21st century economy. In fact, we operate the largest training network outside the U.S. military" (AFL-CIO, 2024, emphasis added).

16   Interestingly, this is the first time that the three key positions in organized labor were all held by women: In addition to Ms. Schuler, Jennifer Abruzzo is NLRB general counsel, and Lauren McFerran is chair of the NLRB. Schuler's immediate predecessor, Richard Trumka (AFL-CIO president from 2009 until 2021) from the UMWA, typified the new labor leader: Educated (he had a law degree) and progressively committed.

17   Robert Taft, Republican Senator from Ohio, was the eldest son of William Howard Taft, the 27th USA president and the tenth chief justice on the **Supreme Court** (Taft

was the only US president to serve as chief justice). Fred Hartley, a Republican from New Jersey, served in the US House of Representatives. Incidentally, The Taft-Hartley Act had widespread Democratic support, which was used to overturn President Truman's veto.

18 For specific information see 'Right to Work States Timeline' (2024).
19 For an interesting discussion of the effects of labor unions written during the post-WWII period, see Wright (1951).
20 For a helpful reference on the myriad state laws, see 'State Provisions Regarding Labor Unions and Strikes,' (2023).
21 The then Secretary of State, George Schultz called the PATCO firings, "Reagan's most important foreign policy decision. Since it showed the world, and especially the Soviets, that his tough rhetoric was backed up by tough actions" (Gruner, 2022, p. 349).
22 See Dubal (2023) for an expanded discussion.
23 The data in this paragraph are taken directly from BLS (2024).
24 For elaboration, see Fact Sheet (2021).
25 This says a lot about how non-neutral organizing campaigns are, with approximately one out of eight union supporters fired, a clear violation of the labor law.
26 Of the United States' 1 million autoworkers, the UAW represents just 150,000. And the Teamsters represent 132,000 truckers out of 1.7 million truck drivers (Elrod, 2023, p. 63).

References

AFL-CIO (2024) 'About Us,' About Us | AFL-CIO (aflcio.org).
Bahat, Roy E., Thomas A. Kochan, Liba Wenig Rubenstein (2023) 'The Labor Savvy Leader,' *Harvard Business Review*, July/August, Vol. 101, No. 4, pp. 67–75.
Bernstein, Irving (1970) *Turbulent Years; a History of the American Worker, 1933–1941*, Houghton Mifflin, Boston.
Boyd, Graham and Jack Reardon (2020) *Rebuild the Economy, Leadership, and You: A Toolkit for Builders of a Better World*, Evolutesix, London.
Bureau of Labor Statistics (2024) 'Unions—2023, (bls.gov).
Craypo, Charles (1986) *The Economics of Collective Bargaining*, Bureau of National Affairs, Washington, D.C.
de Tocqueville, Alexis (1835 [2003]) *Democracy in America*, Penguin, New York.
Department of Labor (n.d.) 'History of Labor Day,' History of Labor Day | U.S. Department of Labor (dol.gov).
Dubal, Veena (2023) 'Clipping Away at the Right to Strike,' *Dissent*, Vol. 70, No. 3, pp. 113–118.
Elrod, Andrew (2023) 'A New Class Consciousness,' *Dissent*, Vol. 70, No. 3, pp. 59–68.
Eidelson, Josh (2023) 'America is Barreling Toward a Summer of Strikes' *Bloomberg News*, July 20, https://www.bloomberg.com
Fact Sheet (2021) 'Executive Order Establishing the White House Task Force on Worker Organizing and Empowerment, https://www.whitehouse.gov/
Freeman, Richard and Medoff, James (1984) *What Do Unions Do?* Basic Books, New York.
Gruner, Ronald (2022) *We the Presidents: How American Presidents Shaped the Last Century*, Libratum Books, Naples, Florida.
Hirschman, Albert (1970) *Exit, Voice and Loyalty: Responses to Decline in Firms, Organizations, and States*, Harvard University Press, Cambridge, Mass.

Islahi, Abdul Azim (2014) *History of Islamic Economic Thought: Contributions of Muslim Scholars to Economic Thought and Analysis*, Edward Elgar, Cheltenham, UK.

IWW (2022) 'Preamble to the Constitution of the IWW, Industrial Workers of the World,' Industrial Workers of the World (iww.org).

McConnell, Campbell, Stanley Brue, David Macpherson (2021) *Contemporary Labor Economics*, 12th ed., McGraw Hill, New York.

'Musk v. Unions' (2023) *The Economist*, December 2, pp. 57–58.

Ohanian, Lee (2019) 'At $140,000 Per Year, why are Government Workers in California Paid Twice as Much as Private Sector Workers?' Hoover Institution, April 30, https://www.hoover.org/

Pew Research Center (2024) Americans' views of labor unions, https://www.pewresearch.org/

Primm, C.J. (1910) 'Labor Unions and the Antitrust Law: A Review of Decisions,' *Journal of Political Economy*, Vol. 18, No.2, pp. 129–138.

'Right to Work States Timeline' (2024) The National Right to Work Committee, States Timeline National Right To Work Committee (nrtwc.org).

Ross, Arthur (1948) *Trade Union Wage Policy*, University of California, Berkeley.

Smith, Adam (1776 [1976]) *The Wealth of Nations*, University of Chicago, Chicago.

Sulzberger, Cyrus (1938) *Sit Down with John L. Lewis*, Random, New York.

'State Provisions Regarding Labor Unions and Strikes,' (2023) (uslegal.com).

'The Right to Strike' (n.d.) National Labor Relations Board, The Right to Strike | (nlrb.gov).

'Trade Unions: Striking Times' (2023) *The Economist*, September 16, pp. 21–22.

Wright, David McCord (1951) *The Impact of the Union*, Harcourt, Brace and Company, New York.

18 LGBTQ+

The Issue: Despite the widespread perception that LGBTQ+ is ubiquitous, a recent Gallup Poll estimated the number of American adults who identify as LG-BTQ+ at 7.2% of the population. Nevertheless, there is much hatred, animosity, and violence directed toward LGBTQ+ from individual dislike and distrust to state legislators enacting anti-LGBTQ+ legislation. This issue will try to understand this group from both sides of the debate. A democracy needs to welcome all its citizens, including the marginalized. If the first three words of our Constitution 'We the People' are to mean anything, then all of us must ensure that our democracy includes everyone, endures, and delivers (Carpinteyro, 2023).

18.1 Introduction

If our government is to be for the people and by the people, then it is imperative to know the people, or at least how many and their basic characteristics. Hence, the constitutional requirement for a census (from the Latin, 'to assess') every ten years.[1] The first Census conducted in 1790, counted 3.9 million people, including 697,697 slaves (17.8% of the total population). The original objective of the Census was to obtain an accurate count for purposes of taxation and representation, based on the principle that an effective government needs a number of representatives in Congress to match the number of citizens.[2] But nowadays, the census data are used to understand who we are as a nation; and the data, in turn, are used to conceptualize, measure, and evaluate our health and well-being (Anderson, 1991, p. 156).

Not only does the census help us understand who we are as a nation (literally) but how we are changing over time. Are we becoming more racially diverse, older, younger, etc.? Effective government only happens with an effective enumeration of the population. Thus, it is important for all Americans to be counted.

18.2 LGBTQ+

The term is a concatenation of separate groups of people expressing their preference for gender and/or sexual identity. The term has evolved over time reaching its current usage in the early 21st century[3]: L = Lesbian; G = Gay; B = Bi-sexual;

DOI: 10.4324/9781003591856-20

T= Queer or Questioning; + = additional gender and sexual orientations not covered. Sometimes an I (intersex) or an A (Asexual) is tacked on the end. The LGBTQ+ is a loose federation of ostensibly very different groups. (Transgender people, for example, have very different needs and interests than bi-sexual.) Perhaps the only common denominator uniting the disparate groups is their shared experience of discrimination, hostility, and exclusion. But as Blakemore (2021) writes,

> The acronym has its critics, especially among those who argue that no term can ever encompass the entire spectrum of gender and sexual expression. And it's all but certain the words people use to describe gender expression and sexual identity will continue to evolve.

In the 2020 census, the US Census Bureau counted those living in same-sex households for the first time. Of the 124 million households in the United States, 1.7% are same-sex. Problematic is that same-sex partners only account for 20% of the LGBTQ population, meaning we know nothing about the remaining 80%, at least via our national census, rendering them from this perspective, invisible.[4] And if invisible, their rights can neither be articulated nor enforced, leaving them vulnerable to oppression and exclusion and all the other (negative) rights of invisibility, as Alexander Hamilton noted, "An actual census or enumeration of the people must furnish the rule, a circumstance which effectively shuts the door to partiality or oppression" (Hamilton et al., 1788 [1987] No. 36, p. 238).

Thus, to obtain a full assessment of the LGBTQ+, we must look to other sources for information. A 2022 Gallup Poll estimated the number of American adults who identify as LGBT at 7.2%, a doubling since initial data collection in 2012 (Jones, 2024). The Williams Institute estimates that 1.6 million Americans over the age of 13, or 0.6% of this total age group, identify as transgender (Herman et al., 2022, pp. 5–6).

Nevertheless, due to the widespread media exposure of the LGBTQ (and especially TG), the actual numbers seem to be much higher. But according to the Williams Institute, both the percentage and the number of TG adults has remained constant (Herman et al., 2022, p.1), at least since reasonably comprehensive data began to be collected in 2016. Nevertheless, and quite interesting, the share of the 13–17 group as a percent of the overall TG-identified population has increased from 10% in 2016 to 18% today (Herman et al., 2022, p. 1).

The increased visibility of LGBTQ individuals (and especially TG) has sparked uproars and protests, and a backlash by Republican-led state legislatures. This gives the (false) impression that the LGBTQ presence is new to America and seemingly out of control. But on the contrary, the constituent components of the LGBTQ have been present since antiquity in all cultures; and in the United States, since colonial times (Heyam, 2022).

So why the increased negative attention now? We think a preponderant reason is that for younger people struggling with identity issues (especially TG) there are more resources to help, and more role models (especially high profile). Whereas earlier, such an individual would often feel isolated and alone, on a road less traveled, which in turn, would increase the self-imposed stigma and self-blame. Knowing that there are others who have waged a similar battle is a welcoming sense of community. A community that is growing not from going door-to-door and converting but by welcoming its own, helping, nurturing, and sustaining life. This also explains why LGBTQ members of the (and especially the TG) actively try to make themselves visible to connect and reach out to the heretofore invisible. Thus, many 'successful' or well-established TG individuals (and by this we mean successful with who they are, and not so much their economic station in life) feel that they have an ethical and moral duty to help others.

Every TG (and of course every LGBTQ) wages a two-front battle: (1) To come to peace with the disconnect between one's birth-given body and his/her inner identity; and (2) the battle against society's expectations and the disconnect that comes with self-imposed expectations based on how one should behave and societal expectations.

Although these two battles are intertwined, the first is far more difficult for most. Some choose to rebel, some choose to confirm, while others are torn between the two options and not able to come to a resolution. It is this latter group which is most vulnerable to suicide. Overall, it is no wonder that TG people have the highest suicide rate of any demographic group: TG adults have a past-year suicide ideation 12 times higher than the general population, and past-year suicide attempts 18 times higher. The numbers for TG youth are even higher (Herman et al., 2019). It is assumed that for both groups, the numbers are greater, since for many suicides, the exact reason is never known.

Like other marginalized groups, LGTBQ (and especially TG) long for dignity. Not just from self-satisfaction with their identity, but from society's imprimatur: i.e., despite your differences, you are a person just like me, entitled to the same rights and privileges.

18.3   Criticism toward LGBTQ+

The preponderant argument against LGBTQ is three-fold:

- A visceral belief that men and women were created differently to complement each other, and that these differences are designed and blessed from above (Yarhouse, 2015, pp. 29–46).
- A fear, at least among some people that such 'deviant and abnormal' behavior will not only influence and change America's mores, but also corrupt society's youngest and most vulnerable.
- Supporting the LGBTQ+ (which the political left is wont to do) will weaken and even collapse the natural patriarchal order (Perliger, 2020, p. 130). The patriarchal order has been well-defined in Western societies (although not well-accepted by all) and is a central plank in the far-right ideology (Du Mez

and Kobes, 2020). Thus, according to the right (and especially the far right) toleration and acceptance of the LGBTQ is the first step on a slippery slope of moral degradation and ultimately the collapse of the social fabric of America.

18.4   State and Federal Action

Liberals, in general, favor the inclusivity of all citizens rather than the invidious exclusion of some and will use the federal government as a means to do so, starting with clamoring for more official statistics about LGBTQ+ (Wang and Lin, 2023). Here, it seems an interesting reversal of the conservative/liberal divide. Whereas you would think that conservatives would eschew any heavy-handed government intrusion as to how we live our lives in private, that appears not to be the case.

At the state level, nearly 500 bills targeting the LGBTQ+ community have been introduced in 2023 (Alfonseca, 2023). As of this writing, 19 states have enacted laws either restricting or banning gender-affirming care for TG minors (Beaty et al., 2023). Only Florida has enacted restrictive gender-affirming care for adults, as well as targeting hospitals that offer such procedures.

But for many, even worse than these invidious laws, is the upturned disdain, the self-assured smirk, and the wanton violence—seemingly sanctioned by law and the complicity and intolerance of elected officials on the right.

18.5   Violence against LGBTQ+

Violence against LGBTQ+, although always present, has been increasing, abetted by far-right intolerance. Maggie Astor (2023) offers two supporting studies:

- A report from the Anti-Defamation League (ADL) and the GLAAD (Gay and Lesbian Alliance Against Defamation[5]) cites 350 anti-LGBTQ+ incidents during the period June 2022–April 2023. Astor notes that these numbers are certainly undercounted since many incidents go reported.
- The Study of Hate and Extremism at the University of California-San Bernadino found a 52% increase in anti-LGBTQ+ hate crimes and a 28% increase in anti-TG hate crimes. This study, however, focused only on major cities and on hate crimes.

These two studies don't necessarily overlap since not all ADL/GLAAD incidents are crimes, never mind hate crimes.[6] Nevertheless, very troubling for Astor (2023) is that although half of the ADL/GLAAD incidents were committed by extremist groups, half were not, "suggest[ing] that anti-LGBTQ sentiment is being mainstreamed in society and being picked up on by local church groups, local parents' rights groups, and whatever might be the local grassroots movement for the Republican Party." Unfortunately, "when an idea has seized the mind of the American people, be it correct or unreasonable, nothing is harder than to rid them of it" (Tocqueville, 1833 [2003], p. 217).

18.6   What to Do?

Societies differ in terms of their toleration and inclusivity (or lack thereof) of LGBTQ+ which in turn is determined by the majority's will imposed on the minority. The Founding Fathers warned against this which, for all practical purposes, becomes a "new face of enslavement" (Tocqueville, 1833 [2003], p. 502). As James Madison wrote in *The Federalist Papers*,

> It is of great importance in a republic not only to guard the society against the oppression of its rulers, but to guard one part of the society against the injustice of the other part. Different interests necessarily exist in different classes of citizens. If a majority be united by a common interest the rights of the minority will be insecure.
>
> (Hamilton et al., 1788 [1987] Number 51, p. 321)

One such example (among many) is the June 30, 2023, Supreme Court case, '*303 Creative LLC v. Aubrey Elenis*,' a 6-3 ruling in favor of a Christian graphic designer's refusal to create a wedding website for a same-sex marriage, despite Colorado's anti-discrimination law.[7] Justice Neil Gorsuch, writing the Court's majority opinion, said that "the plaintiff's right to free speech was violated because the state seeks to speak in ways that align with its views but defy her conscience about a matter of major significance." Justice Sonia Sotomayor, writing the Court's minority opinion, noted that "this is the first time in history the Court has granted a business, open to the public, a right to refuse service to members of a particular class, and the act of discrimination has never constituted protected expression under the first Amendment."

In this case, the majority and dissent represent two palpably different views of protected rights. Whose rights should be recognized and protected? And why? Is there any room for conciliation/compromise or does our system of adjudication pre-ordain that rights have to be contested with winners and losers?[8] While this is a difficult issue to resolve, we believe that to deny a person political equality and to allow one's personal beliefs to supersede society's interest in preventing/reducing discrimination is to deny the recipient any chance at self-affirmation and dignity (Bromell, 2021). This in turn, perpetuates a two-tiered or multi-tiered society, which worsens the situation for all.[9] Injustice and inequality before the law, not only harms the recipient, but just as equally, the perpetrator as well.[10] Alexis de Tocqueville wrote,

> no citizen is so obscure that it is not very dangerous to allow him to be oppressed, nor any individual rights so unimportant that they can with impunity be surrendered to capricious government decisions…to violate the right of a private individual…is deeply to corrupt the manners of the nation and to endanger the whole of society because the very idea of these kinds of rights tends endlessly to deteriorate and disappear among us.
>
> (Tocqueville, 1835 [2003], p. 814)

18.7 Conclusion

Equality before the law and democracy is what the United States is all about. It is our distinguishing badge among nations; after all, "'We the people' are the first three words of [our] Constitution. It is up to us to ensure that our democracy includes everyone, endures, and delivers. Together we must stand strong and united because when we the people do so, we win" (Carpinteyro, 2023).

At the same time we recognize a fundamental paradox that has gripped America since birth: "the radical idea that all men were created equal depended on the traditional idea that all men were created unequal and that a few wealthy men should control the government, and therefore the lives, of women and men of color" (Richardson 2020, p. 22). Efforts to extend equality have unfortunately and paradoxically intensified polarization, which "extends beyond policy differences into race and culture" (Levitsky and Ziblatt, 2018, p. 9). While this means that our work is cut our for us, it is not an excuse to hang up our hats, so to speak.

Notes

1 Article I, Section 2: "The actual enumeration shall be made within three years after the first meeting of the Congress of the United States, and within every subsequent term of ten years, *in such manner as they shall by law direct*." We italicized the latter phrase since this constitutionally enables the census to probe and ask data questions beyond the number of inhabitants.
2 Although slaves were counted in full for the census, they were considered three-fifths of a person for apportioning representatives to Congress. This abhorrent provision, reflecting an abominable practice, was excised from the Constitution after the Civil War.
3 Blakemore (2021) discusses the genesis of the full term and its constituent components.
4 Trump, during his first term attempts by the US Census to experiment with mini-surveys about sexual orientation and gender identity (Wang and Lin, 2023).
5 Founded in 1985, it is a LGBTQ advocacy group.
6 Two essential elements for a hate crime: (1) There must be a crime, either overt or threatened, and usually violent like murder, assault, arson, vandalism; (2) there must be a bias directed against individuals or groups with specific characteristics that are defined by the law. More specifically, a hate crime is committed on the basis of the victim's perceived or actual race, color, religion, national origin, sexual orientation, gender, gender identity, or disability (United States Department of Justice, 2023b). Of the 10,530 single-bias hate crimes committed in 2021, 15.9% involved sexual orientation, and 3.2% involved gender identity (United States Department of Justice, 2023a).
7 The information about the case and the quotes therein are based on Alfonseca (2023).
8 See Tang (2023) for suggestions to compromise. Also, for an interesting and practical framework for conceptualizing and resolving legal differences, see Klammer and Scorsone (2022).
9 See Bouie (2023) for a further discussion.
10 A great example is Barry Unsworth's novel *Sacred Hunger* (1991). Winner of the Booker Prize, it offers a superb account of how the inequity of slavery insidiously demoralizes the perpetrator as much as the slave.

References

Alfonseca, Kiara (2023) 'Scotus Ruling prompts fear, criticism from LGBTQ leaders,' June 30, ABC News, https://abcnews.go.com/

Anderson, Margo (1991) 'Census' in Eric Fonner and John A. Garraty (Eds.) *The Reader's Companion to American History*. Houghton Mifflin, Boston, pp. 154–156.

Astor, Maggie (2023) 'Report Cites More than 350 Anti-LGBTQ Incidents Over 11 Months,' June 22, *The New York Times* (nytimes.com).

Beaty, Thalia, Brendan Farrington, Hannah Schoenbaum (2023) 'TG Adults blindsided by new Florida Law,' *Associated Press*, Tallahassee, June 5, https://www.nbcmiami.com/

Blakemore, Erin (2021) 'From LGBT to LGBTQIA+: The evolving recognition of identity,' October 19, (nationalgeographic.com).

Bouie, Jamelle (2023) 'No Dignity in this Kind of America' *The New York Times*, February 12. Opinion | (nytimes.com).

Bromell, Nick (2021) *The Powers of Dignity: The Black Political Philosophy of Frederick Douglass*. Duke University Press, Durham, NC.

Carpinteyro, Marilyn (2023) 'Point: State of the Republic—Precarious,' June 28, DC Journal

Jones, Jeffrey M. (2024) 'LGBTQ+ Identification in US Now at 7.6%,' *Social and Policy Issues,* March 13, https://news.gallup.com

Du Mez, Kristin Kobes (2020) *Jesus and John Wayne: How White Evangelicals Corrupted a Faith and Fractured a Nation*, W.W. Norton, New York.

Hamilton, Alexander, Madison, James, and John Jay (1788 [1987]) *The Federalist Papers*, Penguin, New York.

Herman, Jody, Taylor N.T. Brown, Ann P. Haas (2019) 'Suicide Thoughts and Attempts Among Transgender Adults,' (September), The Williams Institute (ucla.edu).

Herman, Jody, Andrew Flores, Kathryn O'Neil (2022) *How Many Adults and Youth Identify as Transgender in the US?* The Williams Institute, (ucla.edu).

Heyam, Kit (2022) *Before We Were Trans: A New History of Gender*, Seal Press, New York.

Klammer, Sarah, and Eric Scorsone (2022) *The Legal Foundations of Micro-Institutional Performance*, Edward Elgar, Cheltenham, UK.

Levitsky, Steven and Ziblatt, Daniel (2018) *How Democracies Die*, Broadway Books, New York.

Perliger, Arie (2020) *American Zealots: Inside Right-Wing Terrorism*, Columbia University Press, New York.

Richardson, Heather Cox (2020) *How the South Won the Civil War*, Oxford University Press. Oxford, UK.

Tang, Aaron (2023) 'States Can Still Protect LGBTQ Consumers, *New York Times*, July 2, Opinion section, p. 4.

Tocqueville, Alexis de (1833 [2003]) *Democracy in America*, Penguin, New York.

United States Department of Justice (2023a) '2021 Hate Crime Statistics' Facts and Statistics (justice.gov).

United States Department of Justice (2023b) 'Learn About Hate Crimes,' (justice.gov).

Unsworth, Barry (1992) *Sacred Hunger*, W.W. Norton, New York.

Wang, Hanoi Lo and Connie HanZhang Jin (2023) 'What the 2020 Census Can – and Can't Tell Us About LGBTQ+ people,' National Public Radio, May 25 (NPR.org).

Yarhouse, Mark, A. (2015) *Understanding Gender Dysphoria*, IVP Academic, Downers Grove, Illinois.

Part III
Power and Technology

19 Big Tech

The Issue: The five companies designated Big Tech: Apple, Amazon, Microsoft, Google/Alphabet, and Facebook/Meta are all big; they are all relatively new, and they all innovate. Overall, consumers like what they are getting, but on the other hand, there is growing concern that Big Tech is too big and too influential. The question is what should be done about Big Tech, if anything. But first, we must understand what Big Tech is and what they do.

19.1 Introduction

Admittedly, the term 'Big Tech' is somewhat arbitrary in both subject and scope given that technology has always been a significant driver of economic growth. The word 'big' is also subjective: How big is big, and measured by what metric? And if there is a 'big tech' shouldn't there also be a 'small tech'?

In this chapter, we follow the standard classification of Big Tech (BT) to include Apple, Amazon, Microsoft, Google/Alphabet, and Facebook/Meta.[1] Although these five straddle different industries,[2] they are, "the defining institutions of our day, dominating our political economies, societies, and polities as Big Oil or Big Banks did in their time…They are becoming the watchword for corporate surveillance, monopoly, and market power" (Birch and Bronson, 2022).

Apple was formed in 1976; Amazon in 1994; Microsoft in 1975; Google in 1998, renamed Alphabet in 2015; and Facebook in 2002, renamed Meta Platforms, or just Meta in 2021. This chapter will dissect these companies to try to understand their modus operandi, their importance in America's economy, and why they are under the gun, so to speak.[3]

19.2 The Big Tech Companies Are Big

While all BT companies are big no matter the metric, not all big companies are BT, e.g., General Motors, Exxon Mobil, Walmart, Chevron, MacDonalds, just to name a few. While there are many ways to measure bigness, a traditional means is by revenue, and a traditional metric is the Fortune 500.[4] The five BT firms are (not surprisingly) among the 100 largest in the world, ranked by revenue[5]: Amazon, #2

DOI: 10.4324/9781003591856-22

(revenue \$469bn); Apple, #7 (revenue \$365bn); Alphabet, #17 (revenue \$257bn); Microsoft, #33 (revenue \$168bn); and Meta, #71 (revenue \$469bn).

Each BT company operates in an industry structure known as an oligopoly, defined as an industry with a few large firms each producing a similar but not identical product (e.g., the beer industry, the breakfast cereal industry, the oil industry, and the cigarette industry). A more specific (yet more technical) definition of an oligopoly is that it has a four-firm concentration (i.e., sales of the industry's largest four firms as a percentage of industry sales) over 40%. Economic theory suggests that firms in such an industry can act interdependently and with power—the two defining characteristics of an oligopoly.

Interdependence means that one firm will not act without estimating/predicting a rival's reaction—a direct result of the fewness in number. Power here means,[6] "the generalized potentiality for getting one's own way or for bringing about changes [at least some of which are intended] in other people's actions or conditions" (Benn, 1967, p. 426). Power is contextual, involving a specific time and place, and specific actors; and it is relational, occurring between two or more parties. Indeed, the essence of power is one actor forcing another to act contrary to its wishes in order to enforce its will.

While the USA **Antitrust Laws** have narrowly construed power as the ability to raise prices and hence decrease consumer welfare, the BT firms have flexed their power in myriad and novel ways, which has attracted attention. While we will discuss the BTs use of power later in this chapter, here we note that like most large companies, the BTs have used their power to lobby, which in turn has abetted their own power, allowing more favorable laws/regulations and hence more growth. In 2022, Apple, Microsoft, and Amazon broke their previous lobbying spending records, "as they fended off heightened scrutiny of their business models and power over the US economy" (Birnbaum, 2023). In 2023, the overall top 20 lobbyists in the United States included Amazon (#7), Meta (#9), and Alphabet (#16) (Top Spenders, 2024).

All large firms (not just BT) have obtained, currently enjoy, and use economies of scale for their benefit, which we define as declining costs as output increases. In other words, firms enjoying economies of scale can produce more output cheaper. Achieving economies of scale was a preponderant driver in the formation of some of the United States' well-known firms: US Steel (1901), General Electric (1892), General Motors (1907), and Exxon Mobil (1997), just to name a few. Merging to achieve economies of scale is also the modus operandi in today's pharmaceutical industry, banking, oil, and health care. Once achieved (often via horizontal mergers, i.e., firms merging within the same industry), economies of scale are then used as a formidable entry barrier to discourage entry. Simply put, the big get bigger in order to stay big, by creating formidable entry barriers based on economies of scale, while accruing sufficient revenue and power. As we discuss in the next section, economies of scale have been crucial in the growth of BTs.

19.3 Platform Capitalism: The Quintessence of Big Tech

19.3.1 Defining Platform Capitalism

All BT firms use platform capitalism, and as we use the term here, they are in effect platform capitalism firms (PC), but not all PC firms are big tech, e.g., Uber, Airbnb, Lyft, Siemens, Salesforce (Srnicek, 2017, p. 49). Srnicek writes that, "The platform has emerged as a new business model, capable of extracting and controlling immense amounts of data…" (2017, p. 6). More specifically:

> Platforms, in sum, are a new type of firm; they are characterized by providing the infrastructure to intermediate between different user groups, by displaying monopoly tendencies driven by network effects, by employing cross-subsidization to draw in different user groups, and by having a designed core architecture that governs the interaction possibilities. Platform ownership, in turn, is essentially ownership of software … By providing a digital space for others to interact in, platforms position themselves so as to extract data from natural processes … production processes … and from other businesses and users…they are an extractive apparatus for data.
>
> (Srnicek, 2017, p. 48)

You might be thinking that that platform firms are no different from ordinary market firms and that platform capitalism is just traditional capitalism[7] with a different twist and an added emphasis on data. Yes, and no. Platforms are capitalist since they are privately owned and are incentivized by the profit motive, but at the same time, platforms differ from traditional/ordinary markets on three counts:

- No one owns a traditional market: It exists for anyone to use, including new and emergent firms, whereas a platform is owned by a firm and, as such, can control its accessibility and on what terms.
- Whereas traditional markets have all sizes of firms (depending on firm life cycle, i.e., birth, maturity, fade, death), platform firms are very large to begin with and will use the platform to only grow larger.
- In a traditional market, buyers and sellers are (at least in theory) symmetrical in power and leverage; and in situations where this isn't so, the government will redress. But platform capitalism is typified by asymmetric information, "They know everything *about us*, whereas their operations are designed to be unknowable *to us*. They accumulate vast domains of new knowledge *from us*, but not *for us*. They predict our futures for the sake of others' gain, not ours" (Zuboff, 2019, p. 11; emphasis in original).

19.3.2   *Platform Capitalism as Surveillance Capitalism*

Zuboff defines/explains surveillance capitalism:

> Surveillance capitalism unilaterally claims human experience as free raw data for translation into behavioral data. Although some of these data are applied to product or service improvement, the rest are declared as a proprietary behavioral surplus, fed into advanced manufacturing processes known as 'machine intelligence,' and fabricated into *prediction products* that anticipate what you will do now, soon, and later. Finally, these prediction products are traded in a new kind of marketplace for behavioral predictions that I call behavioral futures markets. Surveillance capitalists have grown immensely wealthy from these trading operations, for many companies are eager to lay bets on our future behavior.
>
> (Zuboff, 2019, p. 8; emphasis in original)

Surveillance capitalism is distinguished by its ability to collect surplus data (i.e., data that is generated as a by-product of the firm's intended objectives) and to analyze it via algorithms, which in turn enables more and better data usage. Surveillance capitalism is a new process inherent in a new type of capitalist firm, "Just as surveillance capitalism is not the same as technology, this new logic of accumulation cannot be reduced to any single company or group of companies." (Zuboff, 2019, p. 8).

Surplus is key. All economies, firms, and individuals, BT or otherwise, need a surplus in order to save, invest, and grow; without a surplus, there is no future. A surplus is defined as,

> that part of the total output ... in excess of what is needed for reproducing and replenishing the labor, tools, materials and other inputs used in production. There is no reason why a surplus must exist, but it does exist and has existed in all but a few human societies... It can take the form of cathedrals, palaces, luxury goods, military spending, more or better equipment, higher levels of education, improved health, and many other things.
>
> (Bowles et al., 2005, p. 94)

A critical task for political economists[8] is to understand how and why a surplus originates, and its generating process,

> how the surplus arises, the size of the surplus, who controls it, and how it is used are the most important issues to be considered when analyzing the structure of any society, tracing a society's evolution over time, or determining the extent to which its economy allows for and supports a flourishing life for all of its people.
>
> (Bowles et al., 2005, p. 94)

For platform capitalists, the surplus is data.[9] That surplus data could be used for profit was discovered by Google and Facebook early in the first decade of the 21st century and quickly spread to firms as diverse as automobile makers, telecoms, insurance and companies. Indeed, "surveillance capitalists have extended and elaborated across every human domain" (Zuboff, 2019, p. 195).

A traditional firm's size is limited by transaction costs within and outside the firm i.e., whether it is cheaper and more efficient/reliable to task within the firm or outside.[10] But for the platform firm, there is no upper limit on size: "the extraction imperative produces a *relentless* push for scale in supply operations" (Zuboff, 2019, p. 128; emphasis added). Known as network effects (i.e., economies of scale) the more users the better the product, and the better the product the more users, and the more users the more and better the data, and the more data, the more effective the algorithm. This cycle continuously increases the value of the product—which is not the same as the product's price which is more associated with a declining marginal cost—with no end in sight. Thus, the size of the platform capitalist firm is not limited to the efficiency of transaction costs; hence, the sky is the limit. It is no wonder that the BT firms are all among the top 75 in the Global Fortune 500.

In addition to economies of scale, economies of scope (i.e., variation) play a critical role, "in addition to behavioral surplus being vast, it also must be varied. These variations are developed along two dimensions. The first is the extension of extraction operations from the virtual world into the real world…[and] the second…is even more audacious. The idea here is that highly predictive, and therefore highly lucrative, behavioral surplus would be plumbed from the intimate patterns of the self…at your personality, moods, and emotions, your lies and vulnerabilities" (Zuboff, 2019, p. 201).

19.4 Why Big Tech Is under the Gun, so to Speak

In general, we can offer several reasons, but not all BT firms are guilty on every count.

19.4.1 *Surveillance without Permission*

This gets to the heart of BT: "The main difference between ordinary capitalism and surveillance capitalism is that an ordinary capitalist firm collects behavioral data with permission and solely as a means of product or service improvement" (Zuboff, 2019, p. 23), whereas the latter does not. This violates the rights of users, although as Zuboff acknowledges, most users are unaware of the very concept of surplus data and unaware that they are the primary instrument for data collection.[11]

Nevertheless, numerous lawsuits have been filed against the BT firms (and others[12]) for conducting such operations. One example among many: GoodRx, a prescription app service, was slapped with a $1.5 million dollar fine for its data policies that violated customers' right to know how and why/how their data will be used (*Los Angeles Times*, 2023). By the way, it is the first time that the Federal Trade Commission has used the Health Breach Notification Rule (passed in 2009; Public Law 111-5, 123 Stat.115) which is designed for data privacy protection, especially guarding against a breach of data security[13] not covered by the Health Insurance Portability and Accountability Act of 1996 (HIPPA, Public Law 104-196, 110 Stat.1936).

Levying fines on guilty firms raises a question of equity: While the BT companies have deep pockets to fend off/finance lawsuits, small firms do not; hence, the big companies might simply write it off as a cost of doing business.

19.4.1.1   Are BT firms liable for their platform content?

This issue applies primarily to the social media BTs. Section 230 of the Communication Decency Act (CDA), passed in 1996, clarifies (somewhat) the obligation/liability pertaining to content, "no provider or user of an interactive computer service shall be treated as the publisher or speaker of any information provided by another information content provider." The CDA was designed to promote competition in broadcasting and telecommunications, while also encouraging the Internet. Section 230 also offers the provider some protection and hence immunity from content; while allowing providers the good-faith opportunity to moderate/delete posted content.[14]

Section 203's provenance dates to the 1950s when a bookstore owner was sued and held liable for selling books containing obscenity. In 1957, the Supreme Court in *Roth v. United States* (354 US 476) ruled that holding a store liable for someone else's content created a chilling effect.[15] In 2023, the US Supreme Court, in *Gonzalez v. Google*, declined to rule on Section 230 immunity, remanding the case to district court. Briefly: The family of a young student killed in Paris by an ISIS terrorist act sued Google (owner of Facebook) claiming that it was a tool used by ISIS to aid and abet terrorism.[16]

The content issue will pop up again and again, but rather than rely on the Supreme Court for protection/liability,[17] the initiative should remand to Congress. It is time for Congress to revisit the 1996 Act along with Section 230, given the vast changes in the internet since then, along with changes in the users and producers of information. For starters, none of the social media companies existed in 1996, nor did social media, for that matter.

How free is free speech if it can be used to snuff out the life of innocents through no fault of their own, but only because someone has used a medium explicitly designed to accomplish something quite different. To paraphrase our discussion on **Gun Control**: Every right has a limit, and every right will obfuscate a right granted. But there is no infinite right to use the internet to post anything. All rights need to be recognized and all effects on all stakeholders should be calibrated in terms of the public good.

19.4.2 *Anti-Competitive Behavior*

As we discuss in our **Corporate Power and Antitrust** chapter, the Clayton Antitrust Act (1914) makes actions illegal that could lead to the formation of a monopoly: Price discrimination; exclusive-dealing contracts (i.e., tying contracts); the acquisition of competing companies via stock purchases, and interlocking directorates.[18] The BTs are not immune from prosecution nor should they be. For example, in September 2023, the US Dept of Justice sued Google claiming illegal its efforts to make it the default search engine on various domains including Amazon. Another example: In 2020, Epic Games, a game studio, sued Google for stifling competition by striking deals with smartphone makers such as Samsung and LG to give prime placement in exchange for a percentage of the revenue.

Traditional antitrust theory argues that monopolies (or the movement toward monopoly) restricts competition, enabling the firm to raise prices, thereby increasing its prices/revenues while reducing consumer welfare. But the problem with platform capitalism is not price per day, but that,

> There is no monetary price for the user to pay, only an opportunity for the company to extract data. Cornering [user-derived raw-material-supplies] are not designed to protect product niches but rather to protect critical supply routes for the unregulated commodity that is behavioral surplus…The corporation unfairly impedes competitors in search in order to protect the dominance of its most important supply route, not primarily to fix prices
> (Zuboff, 2019, p. 133; emphasis in original)

As we discuss in **Corporate Power and Antitrust**, we need a thorough reconceptualization of the antitrust law, from top to bottom, to recognize new configurations of capital (especially platform capitalism), with a greater understanding of how such a firm affects all stakeholders and not just the consumer. It is imperative that "our antitrust laws should move away from focusing solely on pricing and avoiding economic harm to encompass data privacy protection and security" (Boghosian, 2024). Antitrust regulators, public policy officials, and economists alike were caught napping at the wheel during BT's formative stages, when action could have been taken. Now, it is perhaps too late, and the resources of the BTs are too large to break up, and furthermore, the BT firms are not unpopular with consumers who perceive a tangible benefit.

But even if antitrust officials did (or could) break up social media companies,

> it would result in establishing multiple surveillance capitalist firms, though at a diminished scale, and thus clear the way for more surveillance capitalist competitors. Similarly, reducing Google and Facebook's duopoly in online advertising does not reduce the reach of surveillance capitalism if online advertising market share is simply spread over five surveillance capitalist firms or fifty, instead of two.
> (Zuboff, 2019, p. 23)

19.4.3   *The Deleterious Effects of Social Media on Users*

According to the USA surgeon general,[19] Dr. Vivek Murthy:

> Social media use by youth is nearly universal. Up to 95% of youth ages 13–17 report using a social media platform, with more than a third saying they use social media almost constantly. Although age 13 is commonly the required minimum age used by social media platforms in the U.S., nearly 40% of children ages 8–12 use social media... Adolescents who spend more than three hours a day on social media face double the anxiety and depression symptoms.
>
> (The U.S. Surgeon General's Advisory, 2023, pp. 1 and 6)

Writing in 2019, Shoshana Zuboff surveyed the 302 most significant quantitative studies on the relationship between social media use and mental health. She found,

> that the psychological process that most defines the Facebook experience is what psychologists call social comparison. It is usually considered a natural and virtually automatic process that operates out of awareness, effectively forced upon the individual by [his/her] social environment as we apply evaluative criteria tacitly internalized from our society, community, group, family, and friends.
>
> (Zuboff, 2019, p. 461)

While invidious comparison has always been a part of human society, at the same time,

> social media marks a new era in the intensity, density, and pervasiveness of social comparison processes, especially for the youngest among us, who are almost constantly online at a time of life when one's own identity, voice, and moral agency are a work in progress ... One consequence of the new density of social comparison triggers and their negative feedback loops is a psychological condition known as FOMO (fear of missing out). It is a form of social anxiety defined as the uneasy and sometimes all-consuming feeling that...your peers are doing, in the know about, or in possession of more or something better than you. It's a young person's affliction that is associated with negative mood and low levels of life satisfaction.
>
> (Zuboff, 2019, pp. 462 and 463)

In a conversation with adolescents during the fall of 2023, Dr. Murthy found that social media abetted an,

> endless comparison with other people that shredded their self-esteem, the feeling of being addicted and unable to set limits and the difficulty having

real conversations on platforms that too often fostered outrage and bullying. There was a sadness in their voices, as if they knew what was happening to them but felt powerless to change it.

(Murthy, 2024)

At the same time, social media is not all deleterious. It can provide certain benefits, especially for marginalized teenagers,

The buffering effects against stress that online social support from peers may provide can be especially important for youth who are often marginalized, including racial, ethnic, and sexual and gender minorities. For example, studies have shown that social media may support the mental health and well-being of lesbian, gay, bisexual, asexual, transgender, queer, intersex and other youths by enabling peer connection, identity development and management, and social support.

(The U.S. Surgeon General's Advisory, 2023, p. 6)

Additional benefits of social media include: (1) Positive community and connection with others who share identities, abilities, and interests; (2) access to important information; (3) creating a space for self-expression; (4) forming and maintaining friendships online and developing social connections, especially among more diverse peer groups (The U.S. Surgeon General's Advisory, 2023, p. 6).

Recognizing the good and the bad, Dr. Murthy proposes a surgeon general's warning on social media use,

It is time to require a surgeon general's warning label on social media platforms, stating that social media is associated with significant mental health harms for adolescents. A surgeon general's warning label, which requires congressional action, would regularly remind parents and adolescents that social media has not been proved safe. Evidence from tobacco studies show that warning labels can increase awareness and change behavior.

(Murthy, 2024)

Murthy admits that a warning label by itself will not make social media safer; at best it can draw attention to the problem and perhaps change behavior at the margin. To help effectuate greater safety and less harm for social media, Murthy offers a bevy of solutions[20]:

- **For children and adolescents**: Create boundaries to help balance online and offline activities; don't keep online harassment or abuse a secret.
- **For parents and caregivers**: Create a family media plan, create tech-free zones, and encourage children to foster in-person friendships.

- **For tech companies**: Create effective and timely systems and processes to adjudicate requests and complaints from young people, families, educators, and others; be transparent and share assessment findings and underlying data.
- **For policymakers:** Support the development, implementation, and evaluation of digital and media literacy curricula in schools and within academic standards; and require a higher standard of data privacy for children.
- **For researchers:** Investigate the impact of social media on youth mental health as a research priority and develop a shared research agenda; evaluate best practices for healthy social media use.

19.5   Should Big Tech Be Regulated and If so, How, and by Whom?

Who controls information in an age of information, how that information is produced and generated, associated privacy violations, as well as the adverse well-being effects of social media should be the issues addressed post-2024, not the ability (or lack thereof) to raise prices; the latter being largely irrelevant. As Zuboff writes, "surveillance capitalists [are taking] command of the essential questions that define knowledge, authority, and power in our time: *Who knows? Who decides? Who decides who decides?*" (Zuboff, 2019, p. 175; emphasis in original). Shouldn't this be a wake-up call? A call to action?

But in order to regulate and to govern, the regulators (whoever they may be) need a modicum of understanding of the underlying issues. US Supreme Court justice, Elena Kagan acknowledged during *Gonalez v. Google*[21] (2/21/23) that "we don't really know about these things. These are not like the nine greatest experts on the Internet" (Elliot and Cameron, 2023). A refreshingly candid assessment. But what should we make of it? Is this a defect of our judiciary system? A defect in the much-lauded separation of powers? Should the Supreme Court justices develop an acumen/specialty in Big Tech, given its importance today? If so, then why not **Artificial Intelligence**, or **Net Zero**? Or **Climate Change**?

No, not all. With knowledge explosion, the days of polymaths are over. And besides, asking justices to do so contravenes their objective, as laid out in the US Constitution (Article III, Section 1), "the judges both of the supreme and inferior courts, shall hold their offices during good behavior." This permanency in office, based on the standard of good behavior is, according to Alexander Hamilton, "one of the most valuable of the modern improvements in the practice of government" (The Federalist #78, p. 472). Of the several reasons given (we fully explain in our **Judiciary** chapter) one in particular is relevant here,

a voluminous code of laws is one of the inconveniences necessarily connected with the advantages of a free government. To avoid an arbitrary discretion in the courts, it is indispensable that they should be bound by strict rules and precedents, which serve to define and point out their duty in every particular case that comes before them; and it will be readily conceived … that the records of those precedents must unavoidably swell to a very considerable bulk, and must demand long and laborious study to acquire a competent knowledge of them.

(Hamilton et al., 2003 [1787–1788], #78, pp. 478–479)

Notice that the rationale for good behavior is to develop an acumen in "rules and precedents" and not so much in developing an expertise in the day's general topics. It wasn't expected then, nor now, that judges would become polymaths. The preponderant objective of the courts, both inferior and supreme, then and now is to "declare all acts contrary to the manifest tenor of the constitution void" (Hamilton et al., 2003 [1787–1788], #78, p. 473).

In defense of Justice Kagan, most Americans do not have a workable knowledge of **BT**, **Artificial Intelligence**, or **Climate Change**. Hence, the purpose of our book. The Congress has an important role in discussing, formulating and studying issues of the day so that laws can be enacted if need be. But this requires a functioning Congress. In lieu of this, we look to participatory democracy, or citizens' councils to understand and debate, and have a say on policy. Yeah, this is a lot to ask, and we sound a tad quixotic, but what are our alternatives? The purpose of this book is to provide an understanding of the issues so that the right questions can be asked and hopefully answers provided. We return to this discussion in our Conclusion.[22]

Complicating any proposed regulation is that the typical user does not perceive BT as inherently malevolent, nor producing an economic bad. Rather, he/she sees a well-defined good delivered at a reasonable price. Although the actual process is murky, it is not exactly of interest to the typical user. Thus,

politicians and regulators need to be careful not to kill the golden goose. AI and other emerging technologies are key to developed countries escaping the growth malaise they have experienced since the Global Financial Crisis. Big Tech firms mustn't be too stifled in their attempts to help us all achieve that escape.

(Lilico, 2024)

Srnicek suggests transforming (and even creating) platform capitalism into public platforms, "owned and controlled by the people…This would mean investing the state's vast resources into the technology necessary to support these platforms and offering them as public utilities" (Srnicek, 2017, p. 6). While thought-provoking, today's BTs are too big, too powerful, and have amassed far too much wealth to change or to be changed. Srnicek, however, offers another solution which would not break up the companies, but instead would regulate the surplus data in the public interest (Srnicek, 2017, p. 128). If the surplus data is about us and is generated by us, shouldn't we have a say in how it is used? Isn't this what democracy is all about?

19.6 Conclusion

To fashion a workable solution for all BT stakeholders, and not just the public, Congress must roll up its sleeves, so to speak, and get to work, with full and active participation from all stakeholders. A fruitful first step for the Congress is to revisit the 1996 Communication Decencies Act, and especially Section 230. Focus on the importance of privacy and its nexus with surveillance capitalism. To do so requires a functional Congress, willing to put aside ideological differences for the public good. Quixotic indeed. But a necessary first step.

A potential Big Tech policy, as well as **Artificial Intelligence**, that deserves discussion post-2024 is federal chartering to comport the public objectives and obligations of such firms more closely with their modus operandi. After all,

> companies reaching unprecedented sizes and valuations in the trillions control digital infrastructure that people depend on at least as much as the mail and trash pickup. Tech companies now run or help run communications, commerce, and other services more nimbly than do federal agencies. But they do it with less regulation and public oversight—as well as a profit motive.
>
> (Boghosian, 2024)

We discuss this proposal at length in our **Corporate Power and Antitrust** chapter.

Notes

1 As to be expected, not all researchers agree on which firms to include. Some include Telsa, Alibaba, or Nvidia. Some advocate for including Zoom. While we appreciate that this sector is very dynamic and innovative and thus continuously evolving, we will stick with the consensus definition of BT.
2 Brock (1990) and Irwin (1990) provide an interesting discussion of the origins of the computer and telecommunications industry, respectively. Each account is interesting given its perspective from an earlier point in time.
3 We could have easily combined **Corporate Power and Antitrust, Artificial Intelligence,** and **Big Tech**. While acknowledging any delineation as artificial, we chose to present these issues as separate chapters.

4 Other metrics include profits, capitalization, number of employees, etc. As the world transitions to **Net Zero**, other metrics focusing on sustainability, and effective transitioning will become prevalent.

5 Source: Global 500 (2023).

6 See our discussion on power in our chapter Corporate **Power and Antitrust.**

7 Traditional capitalism is an economic system whereby individuals and firms own their means of production, and are incentivized by the profit motive. As such BT firms are capitalist, although they have adapted into a new form. Constant adaptability is capitalism's trademark, "Capitalism is a learning organism: It adapts constantly, and not just in small increments. At major turning points, it morphs and mutates in response to danger, creating patterns and structures barely recognizable to the generation that came before" (Mason, 2015, p. xiii). Surveillance capitalism is capitalism's latest adaptation.

8 In the late 19th century, the discipline of political economy divorced itself from the messy field of politics and renamed itself economics. In doing so, it turned inward, becoming more mathematical, deductive, and ahistorical. Many of us today would like to resuscitate the term political economy, along with its more holistic scope and overview, "because one cannot understand contemporary societies very well unless politics, economics, psychology, and the other social science disciplines are all brought together to study the complexities of modern life. Another way of describing the political economy approach, then, is to say that it is interdisciplinary" (Bowles et al., 2005, p. 51). Indeed, this is a major theme of our book.

9 While the five BTs are often regarded as a single entity with similar strategy and interests, their use of surveillance capitalism markedly differs (Zuboff, 2019, p. 8). For a full, in-depth discussion see Zuboff (2019).

10 For an interesting example, see Casadesus-Masanell and Spulber (2000). For a discussion of the relationship between transaction costs and firm size, see Coase (1937).

11 In a study on the decision to join a new online service, "74 percent of 543 participants opted for the 'quick join' procedure, bypassing the terms-of-service agreement and the privacy policy. Among those who did scroll through the abusive contracts, most went directly to the 'accept' button. The researchers calculated that the documents required at least forty-five minutes for adequate comprehension, but for those who looked at the agreement, the median time they spent was fourteen seconds" (Zuboff, 2019, p. 237). These terms of service agreements tend to be "oppressively long and complex in part to discourage users from actually reading the terms" (Zuboff, 2019, p. 49). One legal scholar calls these agreements "a unilateral seizure of rights without consent…a moral and democratic degradation of the rule of law and the institution of a contract, a perversion that restructures the rights of users granted through democratic processes, substituting for them the system that the firm wishes to impose… recipients must [then] enter a legal universe of the firm's devising in order to engage in transactions with the firm (Margaret Radin quoted in Zuboff, 2019, p. 49).

12 This underscores Zuboff's point that although the BT firms initiated surveillance capitalism, its practice has spread throughout the economy.

13 The Rule defines breach of security as acquisition of pertinent information without the authorization of the individual.

14 For an excellent discussion of Section 230's provenance see Koseff (2019)

15 Although Samuel Roth, a book seller and publisher, was found guilty sending pornography via mail, the Supreme Court loosened its definition of obscenity. In 1973, the main ruling of Roth v. United States was overturned by Miller v. California.

16 In a similar case issued on the same day, *Twitter, Inc. v. Taamneh* (598 US 471 2023), the defendants sued Twitter for aiding and abetting an ISIS-backed terrorist

in an Istanbul nightclub. The Court ruled that Twitter did not knowingly provide assistance to ISIS and thus could not be held liable.

17 The role of the US Supreme Court vis-à-vis Congress is restricted to "declare all acts contrary to the tenor of the constitution void" (Hamilton et al., 2003 [1787–1788], # 78, p. 473). Article Three, Section Two, of the US Constitution, elaborates the Court's purview and prerogatives. See our **The Supreme Court** chapter.

18 As noted in **Corporate Power and Antitrust**, these actions are prohibitive only if the effect is to lessen competition.

19 The US surgeon general directs the US Public Health Service Commissioned Corps, and is the nation's top doctor explaining to Americans how to improve health and reduce risk of illness/injury (HHS.gov.)

20 These suggestions are only a representative sample. For additional solutions, see 'The U.S. Surgeon General's Advisory' (2023, pp. 14–18). The Surgeon General issued a similar warning for gun usage. See our **Guns and Gun Violence** chapter.

21 This case involved an ISIS attack in Paris in which a woman was killed. Her relatives sued claiming that algorithms abetted ISIS' objective of mass destruction. The Court refused to apply Section 230 and instead remanded the case to the 9th Circuit of Appeals for further review.

22 Also see Boghosian (2025), Kemp (2023), and Koopman (2019).

References

Benn, Stanley (1967) 'Power,' in Edwards, Paul, *The Encyclopedia of Philosophy*, Vol. 6, Macmillan, New York, pp. 424–426.

Birch, Kean and Kelly Bronson (2022) 'Big Tech,' *Science as Culture*, Vol. 31, No. 1, pp. 1–14.

Birnbaum, Emily (2023) 'Tech Giants Broke Their Spending Records on Lobbying Last Year,' *Bloomberg News*, February 1, (bloomberglaw.com)

Boghosian, Heidi (2024) 'The CrowdStrike outage shows the danger of depending on Big Tech overlords,' *The Los Angeles Times*, July 23, (latimes.com)

Boghosian, Heidi (2025) *Cyber Citizens: Saving Democracy through Digital Literacy*, forthcoming.

Bowles, Samuel, Richard Edwards, and Frank Roosevelt (2005) *Understanding Capitalism: Competition, Command, and Change*, Oxford University Press, Oxford, UK.

Brock, Gerald W. (1990) 'The Computer Industry,' in Adams, Walter (Ed.) *The Structure of American Industry*, 8th ed., MacMillan, New York, pp. 161–182.

Casadesus-Masanell, Ramon and Daniel F. Spulber (2000) 'The Fable of Fisher Body,' *The Journal of Law & Economics*, Vol. 43, No. 1, pp. 67–104.

Coase, Ronald (1937) 'The Nature of the Firm,' *Economica*, Vol. 4, No. 16, pp. 386–405.

Elliot, Vittoria and Dell Cameron, (2023) 'The US Supreme Court Does Not Understand the Internet,' *Wired*, February 22, https://www.wired.com

'FTC crackdown on GoodRx sends a message that private consumer data must be protected,' *Los Angeles Times*, editorial, February 10, 2023, https://www.latimes.com

Global 500 (2023) *Fortune*, Global 500, https://www.fortune.com

Hamilton, Alexander, James Madison, and John Jay (2003 [1787–1788]) *The Federalist Papers*, Bantam Books, New York.

Irwin, Manley R. (1990) 'The Telecommunications Industry,' in Adams, Walter (Ed.) *The Structure of American Industry*, 8th ed, MacMillan, New York, pp. 244–263.

Kemp, Tom (2023) *Containing Big Tech: How to Protect Our Civil Rights, Economy, and Democracy*, Fast Company Press, Austin, Texas.

Koseff, Jeff (2019) *Twenty-Six Words that Created the Internet*, Cornell University Press, Ithaca New York.

Koopman, Colin (2019) *How We Became Our Data: A Genealogy of the Informational Person*, University of Chicago Press, Chicago.

Lilico, Andrew (2024) 'Big Tech firms are powering the US economy. Politicians shouldn't stop them,' *The Telegraph*, June 25 https://www.telegraph.co.uk.

Mason, Paul (2015) *Postcapitalism: A Guide to Our Future*, Farrar, Straus and Giroux, New York.

Murthy, Vivek (2024) 'Surgeon General: Why I'm Calling for a Warning Label on Social Media Platforms,' *The New York Times*, June 17, Opinion section (nytimes.com).

Reardon, Jack (2020) 'Platform Capitalism, Big Data, and Data Ethics,' *JKAU: Islamic Econ.*, Vol. 33, No. 1, pp. 59–69.

Reardon, Jack, Maria Madi, and Molly Scott Cato (2018) *Introducing a New Economics*, Pluto Press, London.

Srnicek, Nick (2017) *Platform Capitalism*, Cambridge, UK, Polity Press.

The U.S. Surgeon General's Advisory (2023) *Social Media and Youth Mental Health*, Social Media and Youth Mental Health (hhs.gov)

'Top Spenders,' (2024) Open Secrets, Top Spenders • OpenSecrets.

Zuboff, Shoshana (2019) *The Age of Surveillance Capitalism: The Fight for the Future at the New Frontier of Power*, Profile Books, London.

20 Artificial Intelligence

The Issue: Artificial Intelligence (AI) juxtaposes words that ostensibly do not go together: How can intelligence—the defining characteristic of our civilization be artificial? It also sends alarm bells that anything artificial can and will be used malignantly, perhaps beyond our control; conjuring images of robots gone wild unleashing massive destruction. We have all watched such dystopian movies; is this what in store for us? At the same time AI promises to do a lot of good from developing new cures for disease to attenuating the worst effects of climate change. This issue will sift through the pros and cons of AI to understand what it is, its potential for good and bad, as well as how we can democratically safeguard against misuse.

20.1   Introduction

On May 24, 1844, Samuel Morse, co-inventor of the telegraph,[1] sent its inaugural message from New York to Washington DC. Of all the phrases to use, he selected a pithy passage from the Bible,[2] "What hath God wrought?" (Numbers 23:23) expressing both awe over the technological breakthrough, but also a sense of wariness over this new double-edge sword. Would the telegraph "eliminat[e] misunderstanding between nations and usher in a new era of world peace" (Standage, 1998, p. 207). Or would it be used as an instrument of war, insurrection, and malicious intent.

A century later, when the atom bomb was first detonated, Robert Oppenheimer, the director of the Manhattan project (which developed the bomb) thought of two Hindu phrases from the sacred scripture *Bhagavad Gita* as most apropos, "Now I am become Death, the destroyer of worlds"; and "if the radiance of a thousand suns were to burst at once into the sky, that would be like the splendor of the mighty one." Both phrases describe the awe-inspiring creative destructiveness that humans now possess, thanks to this new technology.[3]

For both these inventions, there was a sense that thanks to human ingenuity, their discovery was inevitable; yet, at the same time, a sense of forlorn—that perhaps humans in all their frailties and moral foibles cannot cope with the awesome responsibility of this forbidden knowledge, enabling control over life and death itself.

DOI: 10.4324/9781003591856-23

While no similar religious analogies have been used with AI (at least on the public record), its mere existence conjures the same fears of the atom bomb, and a century earlier the telegraph. In researching this chapter, we also found ourselves repeating Morse's words of awe, 'what hath God wrought.' We can't help but wonder if there is any knowledge that is forbidden or should be forbidden.[4] Should the laws of physics that eventually led to the building of the atom bomb have been forbidden knowledge?[5] Should the knowledge of mathematics, computers, algorithms and such, which eventually led to the discovery of AI have been forbidden?

No. Absolutely not.

While we are aware of the adverse effects of discovery, we are adamantly opposed to forbidding knowledge of any kind. To do so, raises severe questions of practical ethics: (1) If knowledge is to be forbidden, how do we know what to forbid? and (2) who will do the forbidding? It seems to us that forbidding knowledge has more severe consequences and raises more critical ethical concerns than not doing so. Instead, rather than extirpating the technology (and the requisite knowledge to do so) we must fully use our intellectual capacity to harness it for social good, while doing our best[6] to prevent the worst effects from actuating and to channel its use for peaceful purposes.

Roger Shattuck writes, "the knowledge that our many sciences discover is not forbidden in and of itself. But the human agents who pursue that knowledge have never been able to stand apart from or control or prevent its application to our lives" (1996, p. 225). The laws of physics, while providing its intellectual foundation did not lead automatically to the construction of the atom bomb. We have developed institutional controls (albeit imperfect) to prevent nuclear annihilation.

As human beings we are naturally curious and inquisitive, and we implicitly assume that our inquisitiveness produces knowledge that will do more good than harm; we firmly believe that we can devise cultural and institutional controls to contain the genie, once out of the bottle. But Shattuck brings us back to reality, "At the end of the second millennium, I believe we have arrived at a crisis in our lengthy undertaking to reconcile liberation and limits" (Shattuck, 1996, p. 6).

Surely, with AI, one might think so. But it is impossible to put the genie back in the bottle, nor is it possible to put a lid on our curiosity and on our quest for knowledge. Artificial intelligence is with us. It is not going away. We need to democratically discuss how to nurture and control this technology so that it does not get out of hand.

20.2 Defining Artificial Intelligence

Artificial intelligence (AI) touches the lives of all of us from,

> simple systems like text autocorrect to complex algorithms capable of setting prices, driving cars, and writing essays. As commonly used, AI is a catch-all phrase for many specific technologies that are rapidly becoming familiar:

CHAT GPT; algorithms recommending where to eat or how to finish a sentence or even writing a book; on the spot language translation, etc. The possibilities for applications are limitless.

(Economic Report of the President, 2024, p. 343)

While we see how AI can benefit humanity, however, at the same time we can see with alarming clarity its potential for mass destruction.

The common dictionary defines AI as "the theory and development of computer systems able to perform tasks that normally require human intelligence, such as visual perception, speech recognition, decision-making, and translation between languages." The US Copyright Office gives a slightly nuanced definition: "A general classification of automated systems designed to perform tasks typically associated with human intelligence or cognitive functions" (Federal Register, 2023, p. 59944).

AI technologies use different techniques; one of the better known is machine learning, "a technique for building AI systems that is characterized by the ability to automatically learn and improve on the basis of data or experience, without relying on explicitly programmed rules" (Federal Register, 2023, p. 59948). The word 'systems' frequently appears with AI and refers to the software plus model, i.e., "A software product or service that substantially incorporates one or more AI models and is designed for use by an end-user" (Federal Register, 2023, p. 59948).[7]

AI is a general-purpose technology like electricity and computers with expectations that it will improve over time and lead to complementary inventions (*Economic Report of the President*, 2024, p. 255).

Its genesis can be traced to a conference held at Dartmouth College, June 18–August 17, 1956. Organized by John McCarthy, Marvin Minsky, Claude Shannon, and Nathaniel Rochester, "it brought together a few dozen of the leading thinkers in AI, computer science, and information theory to map out future paths for investigation" (Solomonoff, 2023).

The terms 'generative AI' and 'non-generative AI' are frequently used. The former is an

> application used to generate outputs in the form of expressive material such as text, images, audio, or video. Generative AI systems may take commands or instructions from a human user, i.e., prompts. Examples of generative AI systems include Midjourney, OpenAI's ChatGPT, and Google's Bard.
>
> (Federal Register, 2023, pp. 59948–59949)

Whereas non-generative AI,

also known as discriminative AI or analytical AI, encompasses a wide range of techniques with tasks of classification, prediction, and decision-making. Some common examples of non-generative AI include spam filters; recommendations systems, e.g., used by Amazon or Netflix to recommend another item based on a previous item purchased; and fraud detection to identify suspicious transactions and prevent fraudulent activities.

(Valenzano, 2024)

The difference between the two terms is that "While non-generative AI excels at making predictions and decisions based on patterns in data, Generative AI takes it a step further by creating entirely new content" (Valenzano, 2024).

20.3   Distinguishing Features of AI

Two key factors distinguish AI: Its multi-faceted use of data in novel ways; and its ability to predict.

20.3.1   *Multi-Faceted Use of Data*

In addition to the traditional data well familiar to social scientists and scientists, AI obtains data from myriad sources, including "digitally encoded text, images, sound, video, information on real-time human input, simulation feedback, and many other categories of information. AI systems can integrate multiple sources of data, often at different points and for different purposes" (Economic Report of the President, 2024, pp. 246 and 249). Similar to the data obtained by surveillance capitalism,[8] AI systems (and especially generative AI) generally obtain data from "from users, e.g., the words they publish in books or on social media, as well as records of the things they do, typically captured by now ubiquitous electronic devices" (*Economic Report of the President*, 2024, p. 250).

20.3.2   *Prediction*

Using mathematics and algorithms, AI systems will make predictions based on data obtained. Indeed, some have called them "prediction machines" (Agrawal et al., 2018). AI systems share this emphasis on prediction with surveillance capitalism,

whose master motion is the accumulation of new sources of behavioral surplus with more predictive power. The goal is predictions comparable to guaranteed outcomes in real-life behavior. Extraction [of data] begins online, but the prediction imperative increases the momentum, driving extraction toward new sources in the real world.

(Zuboff, 2019, p. 131)

There is no upper limit to the data extraction/prediction nexus. With AI systems,

> predictions are used to inform recommendations or determine how other components of the system will act. For example, AI systems have been developed to solve challenging scientific problems, and they are widely used to set prices and rank job candidates. In other cases, as with some generative AI models, these predictions themselves are simply aggregated to form an output. In this context, predictions are far broader than forecasting the future, and can indeed be about practically anything for which reliable data can be obtained...AI may partially or entirely eliminate the need for products that exist primarily due to insufficient prediction capabilities.
>
> (*Economic Report of the President*, 2024, pp. 245 and 247)

An illustrative example is inventories stored in warehouses: AI can improve prediction capabilities resulting in less need to hold large inventories, reducing the requisite need for land and infrastructure as smaller warehouses can be built (if at all).

20.4   Benefits of AI

20.4.1   *AI Boosting Productivity*

Productivity is critical in any economic system (although its consequences and effects—some of which can be quite far-reaching—are not well understood). In simple terms, productivity measures output produced per worker. Increasing productivity allows workers to enjoy higher wages without adding to inflation. High (and increasing) productivity enables high and increasing living standards. Simply put economic growth cannot occur without productivity increases.[9] Indeed, the preponderant factor explaining America's strong growth in wages (especially in the middle class) during the 1950s–1970s (America's golden age for workers) was strong productivity, increasing at least three percent annually. When productivity growth is sluggish, as now,[10] this reduces living standards (or at best prevents them from increasing) often leading to conflict between different stakeholders, especially labor and management.

Economists have heavily researched the factors affecting productivity and its role as a lynchpin in economic growth. Spectacular increases in productivity, and hence, living standards have been touted as the preponderant benefit of AI. According to the McKinsey Global Institute, generative AI could add more than $4 trillion annually to the global economy, on top of $11 trillion annually added by non-generative AI, with the causal effect being gains in productivity (Manyika and Spence, 2023, p. 70). Let us discuss a few specific cases:

20.4.1.1   *Increasing productivity by trisociation*

In just about everything we do, we are hobbled and even straight-jacketed by traditional ways of thinking (i.e., by what we know) effectively limiting our potential for creativity. In a way, this is expected, since after all we are creatures of habit; so that we look at the new by seeing how it comports with the old. When we want to change the new, we naturally begin with what we know. Trisociation, however, combines two ideas with a third; the latter, usually random. Trisociation can,

> Lead to solutions that humans might never have imagined using a traditional approach, where the functions are determined first, and the form is designed to accommodate them. These inputs can help overcome biases such as design fixation, an overreliance on standard design forms, functional fixedness (a lack of ability to imagine a use beyond the traditional ones and the Einsteining effect, where the individual's previous experience impede them from considering new ways to solve problems…and even new ways of communicating that go beyond written or visual form.
>
> (Eapen et al., 2023, p. 60)

20.4.1.2   *Merging the consumer and producer into the prosumer*

Traditional production separates consumers from producers. The latter innovates and produces what they hope consumers will demand, while consumers vote with their dollars. But AI will integrate consumers and producers into one, which in turn can innovate improvements and new products. It is part and parcel of a process known as democratizing innovation (von Hipple, 2006).

Generative AI will radically change how we design, invent, implement; along with the mutual relationship between firm's stakeholders, heretofore separated. Generative AI can facilitate collaboration between designers and users (Eapen et al., 2023, p. 62), so that the locus of creativity is diffused, residing within multiple stakeholders.

20.4.1.3   *Increasing productivity with large language models*

Large language models (LLMs) are supported by a deep learning architecture (i.e., multilayered neural networks that simulate the way neurons send and receive signals in the human brain) that provides the basis for generative AI.[11] The LLMs connect between words, enabling the model itself to learn, while having the capability to operate across disciplines, generating human-like responses.

As a pluralist who has constantly inveighed against the traditional silo-based education, I (Jack) find the AI-driven connection across disciplines fascinating, with untold potential. But as a novelist, I am both intrigued and a little worried that "the artist could be eventually replaced by AI" (Manyika and Spence, 2023, p. 82). Is this possible since a novel (and art itself) is based on unique emotional factors that make up the individual? It is not yet clear (to us anyway) how LLMs can connect to human emotion, which almost by definition is irrational.

20.4.1.4   *Increasing productivity via automation*

At the workplace, generative AI can potentially automate activities that currently comprise 60–70% of a worker's time; while also accelerating on-the-job training, thereby boosting employee performance and hence productivity. It can also speed up routine report writing and even help with key decisions to be made.

A good example is AI's ability to write scientific papers. According to *The Economist*, "at least one in ten new scientific papers contains scientific material produced by an LLM. That means over 100,000 papers in 2024 alone" (June 29, 2024, p. 66) The cited benefits of doing so include:[12] Help with editing/translation, especially for non-native English speakers; easier coding; ease in trawling the literature; and a faster overall writing process, "thereby freeing up time for scientists to develop new ideas, collaborate or check for mistakes in their work" (June 29, 2024, p. 10).

But, as we discuss in the next section, for every positive aspect of AI, there is always a negative risk. And here, the risks of AI scientific writing are myriad:

- Purloin the words of others without attribution.[13]
- The inability (as of yet) to wrestle with the important concept of uncertainty, so important in many scientific papers, and so foundational in fiction.
- Hallucinations, i.e., a tendency to assert fantasies, and/or palpable non-truths.
- Preferentially citing papers that themselves are highly cited, thus stifling the development of new ideas.
- Possibly churning out high-volume, low-quality papers.

20.4.1.5   *Increasing productivity in science and medicine*

Perhaps the area with the greatest potential from AI is science and medicine. If done right,

> AI can turbocharge scientific progress and lead to a golden age of discovery [somewhat similar to the 17th century with a rich array of inventions with far reaching potential including the microscope and the telescope] and could help humanity solve its biggest and thorniest problems by radically accelerating the pace of scientific discoveries especially in medicine, climate change, and green technology.
>
> (*The Economist*, September 16, 2023, p. 11)

Specifically, *The Economist* highlights two promising areas: (1) Analyzing scientific literature looking for new hypotheses, connections, or ideas, missed by humans, which could stimulate interdisciplinary work and foster innovation at the boundaries between fields; and (2) robot scientists, "who unlike human scientists are less attached to previous results, less driven by bias, [so that] they could develop unexpected theories and explore avenues that human investigators might not have considered" (*The Economist*, September 16, 2023, p. 11).

In medicine, two expected benefits from AI: (1) Reduced medical errors, more robust diagnoses, and an infinitely quicker process of information at a lower cost and much less time" (Jacobson and Jokela, 2024); and (2) unexpectedly (at least for us) more time and more patience for patients (Jacobson and Jokela, 2024, p. 11).

20.5   Potential Negative Effects

20.5.1   *Introduction*

Should we work out *all* the negative aspects of AI before the technology is fully released, or is it too late for that? (Too late.) Should we anticipate all unintended effects, ironically using AI to do so? (Impossible). Or is the genie out of the bottle, so to speak? (Yes). As AI evolves exponentially, there will always be unintended effects, which cannot be ascertained now. (True.)

So how can we make a decision today based on what we do know, which itself is incomplete? Should we cease and desist until complete information is worked out, or do we proceed as is? Is AI evolving too fast (even assuming a life of its own) without adequate human input? And how can we properly guide AI so that it produces the greater good. How can "we ensure that knowledge/ technology produced now will not result in its use for destructive ends in the future?" (Reardon et al., 2018, p. 28)

These are important questions to be asked about any new technology, and especially AI, and especially post-2024. All are being currently asked and will continue to do so. Not only will our responses affect AI's evolution, but so will the questions asked. Thus, in the AI context,

> it is important to ask generative questions, i.e., questions that generate new understanding, that neither entrench one's current understanding, nor create misunderstanding…[However] The questions one asks and the answers one pursues are created by the lenses one wears. This means that there are limits to what one knows and can know.
> (Boyd and Reardon, 2020, pp. 27–28)[14]

This is why asking AI questions should take place via a pluralist dialogue while including all relevant stakeholders. We need to be constantly vigilant of

AI's unintended consequences, its potential negative effects, and its risks, all of which are evolving within a context of high uncertainty.

AI proponents, while aggressively touting the good, also readily acknowledge its potential for harm. The good and the bad are both couched in terms of 'awe-inspiring.' Sam Altman, for example, who cofounded OpenAI in 2015, a company that for some "holds the fate of humanity in its hands" (Bajekal and Perrigo, 2023, p. 59) and is currently its CEO,[15] considers AI to be,

> the most important technology in history. [It] could turbocharge the global economy, expand the frontiers of scientific knowledge, and dramatically improve standards of living for billions of humans—creating a future that looks wildly different from the past…Having more access to higher quality intelligence and better ideas…could help solve everything from climate change to cancer…[getting] abundant intelligence and abundant energy will do more to help people than anything else.
> (Bajekal and Perrigo, 2023, pp. 61 and 62)

While at the same time, Altman worries that "advanced AI could pose existential risks on the scale of global pandemics and nuclear war" (Bajekal and Perrigo, 2023, p. 61). Let's take a look at some of the negative effects:

20.5.2   Fear

We acknowledge that, "anything that cannot be easily understood may elicit fear. AI certainly qualifies. In a world filled with uncertainty and risk, AI systems of all kinds offer tremendous benefits. Yet the uncertainty and risk that surrounds us will not miraculously go away with AI" (Jacobson and Jokela, 2024). The fear of the unknown is to be expected, and there is a lot that is unknown about AI; and since AI will develop/evolve exponentially, the fear factor will never be alleviated.

20.5.3   Learning the Right Set of Human Values

Known more formally as the 'alignment problem,' i.e., ensuring that AGI adheres to human values (Bajekal and Perrigo, 2023, p. 61). This is yet to be solved, although doing so is just a matter of time. This is more difficult than ostensibly appears: Exactly what are the right human values? And who gets to decide? Two of the many yet unanswered AGI questions.

20.5.4   The Possibility of Global Annihilation

Elon Musk, co-founder of OpenAI, warned in a 2023 Fox News interview that AI "has the potential of civilizational destruction" (*The New York Times*, June 2, 2024, p. 2). Indeed, the greatest fear of AI is that this could very well happen.

Perhaps due to a mistake in learning/assessing, or even a dystopian situation where computers take on a life of their own, threatening to conquer and annihilate humanity. This could happen if, for example, the AI system learns the wrong type of human values, or even where a Machiavellian self-interest becomes paramount, excluding the rights/values of all others. We need to guide AI away from such dystopian tendencies.[16]

Relatedly, and not surprisingly, AI is already changing how wars are conducted and warfare itself, potentially "making war faster, more opaque, and less humane" (*The Economist* June 22, 2024, p. 16). Thanks to today's

> greater computing power, whizzier algorithms and more data, owing to the proliferation of sensors, the result is not just more or better intelligence… but a blurring of the line between intelligence, surveillance reconnaissance, and command and control—between making sense of data and acting on it.
> ('Model major general', 2024, p. 17)

And, according to Kenneth Payne of King's College London, "AI will transform not just the conduct of war, but its essential nature: this fused machine-human intelligence would herald a genuinely new era of decision-making in war" (Model major general, 2024, p. 19).

20.5.5 *AI Usurped by Evildoers*

While we implicitly assume that AI technology develops under the aegis of human direction, in a way, new developments suggest that this might not always be so—that AI technology can develop on its own. New research shows that large language models (LLMs) by working in teams can better solve complex problems,

> known as multi-agent systems (MAS) … [they] can assign each other tasks, build on each other's work or deliberate over a problem in order to find a solution that any one, on its own, would have been unable to find. And all without the need for a human to direct them at every step.
> (*The Economist*, May 18, 2024, p. 68)

Now the bad news: In addition to multi-agent systems being both computationally intensive and consuming a lot of energy, they can be conditioned with dark personality traits. This could enable them to bypass any blocking mechanisms for 'bad' behavior, while instructing other agents to carry out harmful tasks. Research indicates that MAS are much more successful at convincing fellow agents to behave nefariously than are humans (*The Economist*, May 18, 2024, p. 69). Thus, "a team of agents in the wrong might, therefore, be a formidable weapon" (*The Economist*, May 18, 2024, p. 69).

20.5.6   *Potential for Discrimination*

Combine data with prediction[17] and AI could be used discriminatorily. More specifically if we can predict, we can prevent and/or punish. Unfortunately, discrimination is still with us; it is exhibited directly by one actor toward another, and institutionally, "i.e., unconscious, implicit biases and inertia within society's institutions, rather than intentional choices" (Barocas and Selbst, 2016, pp. 673–674). Data mining, absolutely essential for AI generative learning, might either unintentionally or unintentionally result in discrimination. Here's an example of how it might happen,

> Data mining allows employers who wish to discriminate on the basis of a protected class to disclaim any knowledge of the protected class in the first instance while simultaneously inferring such details from the data... It is possible that some combination of musical tastes, stored 'likes' on Facebook, and network of friends will reliably predict membership in protected classes. An employer can use these traits to discriminate by setting up future models to sort by these items and then disclaim any knowledge of such proxy manipulation.
>
> (Barocas and Selbst, 2016, p. 712)

In terms of solutions to possible discrimination, as probably expected, they aren't easy to come by: "The problems that render data mining discriminatory are very rarely amenable to obvious, complete, or welcome resolution" (Barocas and Selbst, 2016, p. 722).

20.5.7   *Job Loss*

Since the Industrial Revolution, economists and others have written about the effects of technological change on unemployment.[18] AI is the latest embodiment. As AI significantly increases productivity, then overall that means since we are producing more with the same number of workers, we can reduce the number of workers. History is filled with resistance to technological change for this very reason.

But this 'fear' incorrectly assumes that "demand is fixed (or inelastic) and hence insensitive to price and cost changes" (Manyika and Spence, 2023, p. 84). Whereas productivity-enhancing changes in prices and costs can set in motion a positive and favorable chain reaction across the global economy. In other words, more might be demanded of both complementary goods/services and new ones. Indeed, research suggests that in most scenarios the AI net-job effect will be positive[19] (Manyika and Spence, 2023, p. 85). Although it isn't exactly clear which industries will benefit and which ones will not.[20]

In 2016, Sam Altman, at the time president of Y Combinator,[21] launched a pilot basic income[22] project in Oakland, California (Standing, 2017, pp. 268–269). During the launch, Altman told the press, "I'm fairly confident that at some point in the future, as technology continues to eliminate traditional jobs and massive new wealth gets created, we're going to see some version of Basic Income (BI) at a national scale" (quoted in Standing, 2017, p. 107). Thus, BI could be implemented in conjunction with AI, either regionally, by industry or nationally, such that it could be "a way in which all would benefit from economic gains resulting from technological advance" (Standing, 2017, p. 107).

Speaking of job loss, as an author (both fiction and non-fiction) I wonder about my profession? Could AI capture the emotion and the passion that goes into writing a good book? Would there still be a role for a human author? Would a reader have a preference for an AI-written story or one by a human author? How would the reader know? Should AI authorship require an imprimatur? What if AI only assists in the writing? But what would be the defining threshold? Could AI write a memoir, or a biography? Can an AI system develop to become self-reflexive, i.e., understanding itself enough to critically reflect on itself? Does that mean that AI could evolve into creating a machine (or actual human being) with a conscious? If so, could the AI system evolve into something far more complex, even capable of procreation? These generative questions are only a drop in the bucket. Partly out of fear. Partly out of ignorance. And partly out of curiosity.[23]

20.5.8   *Worsening Income Inequality*

Given the potential for discrimination, automation, and job loss, income inequality could worsen. While the specific effects are uncertain, studies suggest that,

> AI may be a skill-biased technology, increasing relative demand for workers with high levels of education in high-earning occupations. They also suggest that AI could exacerbate aggregate income inequality if it substitutes for employment in lower-wage jobs and complements higher-wage jobs.
> (*Economic Report of the President*, 2024, p. 254)

20.5.9   *AI Overtaking Student Research*

If used properly, AI can be a wonderful learning device, especially connecting research across the disciplines and generating novel ideas—which, by the way, we need for our transition to **Net Zero**. If used properly, AI can become an important tool in education and knowledge acquisition. On the other hand, it is feared that students are using AI to write research papers, jeopardizing the integrity of out-of-class writing assignments. (By the way, the Internet generated, more or less, the same ethical concerns.) As academics, we use the advent of AI as a teaching moment to explore how and when it can be used in order to achieve maximum learning/teaching benefits. We have also substituted short in-class writing assignments, where AI cannot be used for out-of-class assignments.

20.5.10   *Copyright Infringement*

According to the USA Copyright Office,[24]

> Generative AI…is capable of producing outputs such as text, images, video, or audio (including emulating a human voice) that would be considered copyrightable if created by a human author. The term 'author,' used in both the Constitution and the Copyright Act, excludes nonhumans. In the context of generative AI, this means that [i]f a work's traditional elements of authorship were produced by a machine, the work lacks human authorship, and the Office will not register it.
>
> (Federal Register, 2023, p. 59944)

Generative AI systems need to be trained,[25] i.e., they must be exposed to relevant data; that is the only way that generative AI systems can learn. But how does this work with copyrighted material? Does a copyrighted author have a right to say no to AI training, and if so, exactly how can this be done? How would the author even know that such training was underway? And what constitutes fair use?[26]

In August 2023, in *Thaler v. Perlmutter*,[27] the federal district court for the District of Columbia upheld the Copyright Office's position that a machine cannot receive a copyright if authoring a work. This ruling however far from settles the issue for the following two reasons[28]:

- The decision is not binding nationwide and will do little to slow the spread of AI, or the stream of products, works, and services created or enhanced by AI.
- Unlike Thaler v. Perlmutter where a machine produced the work, many situations will be a mix of human and machine, so the question becomes what is the amount of human creativity required to qualify as enough to secure a copyright, or how to locate the line between human and non-human contributions?

20.6   The Need to Regulate AI: But How and Exactly What?

We are not sure if the word regulate is appropriate in the context of AI. The classic concept of regulation[29] starts with accumulated knowledge upon which government officials (well familiar with the knowledge) will prevent/maintain based on a specific criterion such as price and/or cost. It also assumes that regulators are cognizant of risks/benefits and are able to make appropriate judgments.

With AI, it is not clear that government (or anyone for that matter) has the requisite knowledge. And, even if one did at some point, given AI's exponential change, any accumulated knowledge would quickly become outdated. In April 2024, for example, South Korean president Yoon Suk Yeol and British Prime Minister Rishi Sunak noted that "It is just six months since world leaders met at Bletchley, but even in this short space of time, the landscape of AI has changed dramatically. The pace of change will only continue to accelerate, so our work must accelerate too" (Quoted in NPR, 2024).

Bletchley refers to the inaugural AI Safety Summit, November 2023, at Bletchley Park, UK,[30] where participating countries agreed to work together to contain potentially catastrophic risks posed by 'galloping advances' in AI (NPR, 2024). In 2025, a global AI conference will be held in France to discuss a wide range of issues, including regulation, although the exact time/place has yet to be announced.

What AI needs is not regulation per se,[31] but "a new policy framework and a new mindset toward AI" (Manyika and Spence, 2023, p. 72). Or what we label/ define as Regulation Plus (RP): To democratically ensure, nurture, prevent, and guide, on the basis of rapidly changing technology within a context of high uncertainty, the process of which includes all relevant stakeholders.

The process of RP is just as important as the object of regulation. How and what we 'regulate' will determine how AI evolves and what it becomes. RP needs to rapidly evolve and change/adapt as does technology, as does AI itself. Alfred Kahn, a foremost thinker on traditional regulation, noted that "a politically free society will insist on exercising some control over its economic destiny... [and despite] the inescapable imperfections of regulation, the only available remedy is to try to make it work better" (Khan, 1988, Vol. II, pp. 328 and 329). We agree. We also feel that expanding regulation to RP is an admirable endeavor along these lines.

Regulation Plus must address/answer the following questions/items/issues:

- What exactly should we regulate: The development of the technology, its use(s), its effects, and/or traditional antitrust concerns such as industry structure and competition?[32]
- Who possesses the requisite knowledge to participate in RP, and how is such knowledge obtained?
- Should we be content with insiders deciding the rules of the game?
- Who should be invited to the RP table and who should do the inviting? What is the role of the ordinary citizen in RP?
- At what level should AI be regulated? Globally, nationally, state/local?
- What about self-regulation? (Given its importance today, coupled with AI's unique characteristics we have allocated this topic to a separate subsection.)

Sam Altman, CEO of OpenAIg, acknowledged that "building superintelligence is going to be a society-wide project…it's not going to be something that one company just does" (Bajekal and Perrigo, 2023, p. 68). We agree, only adding that it is going to be a global project, and not just society wide. Thus, the RP governance system should also be global, "a new form of international governance…one that will ensure that all areas of the globe (both within and between nations) receive the full benefits of AI, rather than just funneling AI to the already prosperous regions" (Manyika and Spence, 2023, p. 85). We would add that a new global governance system is needed to protect equally all areas of the globe from catastrophic risks.

Perhaps RP's first task would be to investigate what seems to be the development of an economic 'arms race' among the major AI firms: Microsoft, Amazon, Alphabet, and Meta to such an extent that "all signs are that big tech has succumbed to irrational exuberance" (*The Economist,* May 18, 2024, p. 12).[33] An economic 'arms race' suggests wasted resources with a high opportunity cost that society could be better off with the resources re-allocated. Should this be the private sector's purview (i.e., the firms themselves) or does RP have a role to play? As with any economic arms race, there might come a point in time of overabundance, in which case the industry must take a step back to reconfigure.

20.6.1   Self-Regulation?

In July 2023, the leading AI companies, Anthropic, Google (owner of UK-based DeepMind), Microsoft, and OpenAI formed the Frontier Model Forum[34] to advance the "safe and responsible" development of frontier AI models. This was a form of self-regulation. Microsoft's president, Brad Smith said, 'Companies creating AI technology have a responsibility to ensure that it is safe, secure, and remains under human control…This initiative is a vital step to bring the tech sector together in advancing AI responsibly and tackling the challenges so that it benefits all of humanity'" (Milmo, 2023).

In addition, the United States, the United Kingdom, Japan, South Korea, and Canada have each established an AI safety institute. The US AI Safety Institute (AISI),

> exists to help advance the understanding and mitigation of risks of advanced AI so that we may all harness its benefits. AISI is housed within the National Institute of Standards and Technology (NIST), the federal government's premier body for developing and promoting science-based technological standards. AISI's research, testing, and guidance will enable more rigorous assessment of AI risk; more effective internal and external safeguards for AI models, systems, and agents; greater public confidence; and ultimately wider and more responsible development and adoption of

AI. AISI will prioritize community engagement; publication of usable tools, benchmarks, and guidance; and encouragement of new national and global networks for the evaluation.

(USAI: Vision, Mission, and Strategic Goals, 2024)

In May 2024, the AISI released its three-pronged strategic vision:

- Advance the science of AI safety.
- Articulate, demonstrate, and disseminate the practices of AI safety.
- Support institutions, communities, and coordination around AI's safety strategic vision (USAI: Vision, Mission, and Strategic Goals, 2024, p. 3).

These strategic visions are based on the AISI's two foundational principles:

- Beneficial AI depends on AI safety,
- AI safety depends on science (USAI: Vision, Mission, and Strategic Goals, 2024, p. 2).

In July 2023, seven AI companies: Amazon, Anthropic, Google, Inflection, Meta, Microsoft, and OpenAI, agreed to voluntary safeguard their AI products in response to White House urging. Later that year eight companies were added: Adobe, Cohere, IBM, Nvidia, Palantir, Salesforce, Scale AI, and Stability. Their Agreement[35] covers issues of cybersecurity, discrimination, and watermarking.[36] According to the *Economic Report of the President*, this

demonstrated not only the industry participants' interest and willingness to work toward the common good, but also their belief that it is possible to make progress through open dialogue, unilateral action, and social norms. Still, the agreements are unlikely to be a long-term solution.

(2024, p. 283)

This is because all interested and affected stakeholders must actively participate in order for a long-term agreement to be effective and viable. To date, this has not been the case.

In May 2024, the leading AI companies: Amazon, Google, Meta, OpenAI, Samsung, Microsoft, xAI, IBM, Cohere, Zhipu.ai [China], G42 [UAE], and Mistral AI [France][37] met in Seoul to discuss future plans/possibilities for regulation. They agreed to voluntary safety commitments and "to hit the kill switch and stop developing or deploying their models and systems if they can't mitigate the risks" (Milmo, 2023). Antonio Guterres, UN Secretary General, addressing the Conference via video said, "We cannot sleepwalk into a dystopia future where the power of AI is controlled by a few people—or worse, by algorithms beyond human understanding" (Milmo, 2023).

The obvious problem with self-regulation is the conflict of interest between profit making, which every AI company has a right to pursue, and public safety. If the two come into conflict which one will be chosen? And without some basis of transparency, how would the public know about the conflict, and which road was taken?

Has too much oversight been ceded to the private sector? Andrew Rogoyski, of the Institute for People-Centered AI at the University of Surrey argues yes,

> oversight of artificial intelligence must not fall foul of regulatory capture, whereby companies' concerns dominate the regulatory process. I have grave concerns that governments have ceded leadership in AI to the private sector, probably irrecoverably. It's such a powerful technology, with great potential for good and ill, that it needs independent oversight that will represent people, economies and societies which will be impacted by AI in the future.
>
> (Milmo, 2023)

His point is well taken and should be the focal point of post-2024 discussion: All stakeholders need to participate.

20.6.2   *The Federal Government Must Have a Role in RP and Not Just R*

The federal government as guardian of the public interest (at least in theory) must, along with all other stakeholders, have a place at the RP table to help nurture and guide AI to effectuate its positive attributes, while minimizing and even eliminating its negative. The federal government should also continue its more traditional objectives of tempering increased **inequality** (both income and wealth) and to help those who lose their jobs due to AI (Acemoglu, 2021; *Economic Report of the President*, 2024). The federal government should also dialogue with other nations on **tariffs and trade** and develop a workable fiscal and monetary policy in conjunction with AI, and to continue its work on copyright infringement and violations of trust. Additionally, the federal government should ensure that the good that AI can do does "not come at the price of civil rights or democratic values—foundational American principles" (White House, 2023, p. 3). In 2023, the White House promulgated its AI handbill of rights, emphasizing five safeguards:

- Protection from unsafe or ineffective systems.
- Eliminate discrimination by algorithms: Systems should be used/designed in an equitable way.
- Protection from abusive data practices with individual agency over data usage.

- The right to know when an automated system is being used; and understand how and why it contributes to impactful outcomes.
- The right to opt out, where appropriate, and have access to someone who can quickly consider/remedy any encountered problems.

While these are well and good and represent an important first start, we are concerned that an individual acting within a specific context, might not be cognizant of any rights violation(s), thus incapable of redress. This is not to disparage or downplay the federal government's role, for we feel that it is absolutely necessary; but at the same time, government regulation cannot be exclusionary but must occur with an enlivened RP.

The Biden administration was exemplary in their AI approach.[38] Secretary of Commerce Gina Raimondo, appointed in 2020 (she was Rhode Island's first female governor, and a former venture capitalist) was "the point woman for AI, as it has rocketed up the government's priority list" (Henshall, 2024, p. 14). On October 2023, President Biden's executive order, made Commerce the go-to department on AI, although the decision was largely "due to Congress's failure to confer legal authority elsewhere" (Henshall, 2024, p. 14). The Commerce Department under Raimondo's leadership is also oversaw the CHIPS Act (passed August 2022), which among other objectives provides funding for the production of specialized chips[39] needed for AI, as well as imposing export restrictions on chips and chip making technology.

We argue in our chapters on **Big Tech**, and **Corporate Power and Antitrust**, that the traditional antitrust focus on competition to reduce costs and prices in order to enhance consumer welfare seems quaintly out of place and a tad naïve. We need social scientists to build an empirically based understanding of how AI firms work, how they operate, how they compete; and how they affect all stakeholders, not just the consumer. And once done, we can reconceptualize antitrust to comport with the transformational changes brought about by AI.

20.7   Conclusion

Artificial intelligence is already a game changer with radical implications for how we live and work; and even how we conceptualize and solve our problems. While the potential from harm is menacingly real, we believe that AI "can enhance rather than undermine human potential and ingenuity" (Manyika and Spence, 2023, p. 72). At the same time, we, respectively, must disagree with Mr. Rhodes' overly optimist assessment, that "far from threatening civilization, science, technology, and the prosperity they create will sustain us well in the centuries to come" (Rhodes, 2018, p. 343). Science and technology, and especially AI, is a double-edged sword, so much so that it is not really an overstatement to claim that "AI holds the fate of humanity in its hands" (Bajekal and Perrigo, 2023, p. 58).

In the late 1980s, Edwin Fredkin, a pioneering computer scientist,[40] said that in the whole of cosmic history, AI is the third great event, following the creation of the universe, and the appearance of life (quoted in Rifkin, 1995, p. 60.) Writing in 1995, Rifkin disagreed, saying that "most computer scientists would hesitate to put AI on the same par" (1995, p. 61). But in 2025 we have no choice *but* to put AI on the same par. While AI can and will do a lot of good, it can also become 'death, the destroyer of worlds.' This is why it is so important to first understand AI and then to democratically guide and nurture its evolution: The stakes are too high. Successfully harnessing the positive aspects of AI while mitigating its negative effects/risks, might very well be humanity's biggest challenge, right up there with the herculean efforts to transform to **Net Zero**.

Notes

1 The phrase 'tele' originates from the Greek 'tele' meaning far off; and 'graph' originates from the Greek 'graphein,' 'write.' The phrase 'tele' prefaces many common-use words today: e.g., television, telemarketing, telephone, telethon, telescope. For an interesting discussion of the telegraph's invention, see (Standage, 1998).
2 The biblical passage was suggested by Annie Ellsworth, the young daughter of a friend of Morse.
3 Reading this poem, it is easy to see why Oppenheimer selected from it. Its prose is magical, so much so that every time I read it, the words speak to me in different ways, depending on my mood. Not only is the poem the centerpiece of the Hindu religion, but it also a universal masterpiece.
4 For a wonderfully intoxicating discussion of forbidden knowledge spanning the disciplines, see Shattuck (1996)
5 For a fascinating tale, see Bodanis (2000).
6 Even doing our best, there is no guarantee. No better example than Thomas Midgley, a mechanical engineer at General Motors who "had more impact on the atmosphere than any other single organism in earth history" (McNeil, 2000, p. 111). In the early 1930s, he thought he had solved the perennial problem of refrigerators exploding due to using ammonia or sulfur dioxide as a cooling agent, by replacing them with Freon, a chlorofluorocarbon (CFCs). Being non-toxic, non-flammable, and non-reactive with other substances, Freon was hailed as the ideal gas. In addition to refrigeration, it made air conditioning possible and was also used in spray propellants. During the 1960s, it was discovered that CFCs were the preponderant cause of ozone depletion, leading to global conferences that eventually outlawed them. By the way, Midgely had earlier solved the problem of automobile engine knocking (i.e., premature fuel ignition) by adding tetraethyl lead. By 1963 more than 98% of US gasoline was leaded, despite its well-known, ill-health effects (Rhodes, 2018, pp. 236–237).
7 While computers and computer power/technology are central to AI, they do not stand alone, but are part of a much larger system. For an interesting discussion of the development of the computer and its antecedents see Brock (1990, pp. 161–182) and Rifkin (1955, pp. 60–68). Brock notes "the electrical digital computer was born out of the critical military requirements for computation during WWII and the early cold war" (1990, p. 161).
8 See our **Big Tech** chapter.

9 Of course, causation runs both ways: Sustained economic growth can foster new ideas/innovations which in turn increase productivity.

10 After a peaking at a relatively high of 3.5% in 2005, USA annual increases in productivity have since trended downward: 0.53% annually in the decade before the pandemic.

11 This paragraph relies heavily on Manyika and Spence (2023).

12 The discussion of benefits/risks heavily relies on *The Economist* (June 29, 2024, pp. 66–67; and an accompanying editorial, June 29, 2024, p. 10).

13 We discuss this later in this chapter; see the section on copyrights.

14 Ernest Rutherford, Nobel laureate and a pioneer in nuclear physics, was befuddled every time he asked, 'where is the electron,' since he always got a different answer, "this told him that something was fundamentally wrong with classical mechanics. Eventually, he began questioning the question, realizing that asking where the electron is prevented him from seeing and understanding its true nature: it has no place" (Boyd and Reardon, 2020, p. 27).

15 Altman was appointed CEO in 2015. On November 17, 2023, the board fired Altman, citing issues of trust, only to reinstate him five days later after a public backlash from both investors and employees (Bajekal and Perrigo, 2023).

16 By 'we' we mean all AI stakeholders, and not just the government. AI is now (or will soon become) ubiquitous. Given that all of us are affected, then all of us should have a hand in how AI evolves. We expand on this concept of 'participatory democracy' in our conclusion.

17 This assumes that the predictions are correct, but "predictions can be wrong [and thus] AI systems introduce an additional kind of risk" (Economic Report of the President, 2024, p. 254).

18 For a helpful article see (Mokyr et al., 2015). Also see Rifkin (1995).

19 In our **Tariffs and Trade** chapter, we use similar reasoning to impugn the misguided argument that higher tariffs will increase federal revenue, thereby reducing the budget deficit. This assumes, quite naively, that tariffs will not change the behavior of buyer/seller, and that no retaliation will occur. The evidence, however, is overwhelming otherwise.

20 See the *Economic Report of the President* (2024) for speculative scenarios.

21 Y Combinator, an incubator company, was founded in 2005. Altman was president from 2014 to 2019, stepping down to focus on OpenAI, while remaining on the Board.

22 A BI is defined as "a modest amount of money paid unconditionally to individuals on a regular basis" (Standing, 2017, p. 3). For a comprehensive assessment of BI, and even how to implement one, see Standing (2017, p. 3).

23 My disclaimer: I hereby swear that we have used no generative AI in the writing of this book, except for the (sometimes frustrating) auto text correct, which, more often than not, does not capture the nuance of what we want to say.

24 The relevant Constitutional provision is Article I, Section 8, "The Congress shall have power… to promote the progress of science and useful Arts, by securing for limited times to authors and inventors the exclusive right to their respective writings and discoveries." The 'Copyright Act' refers to the 'Copyright Law of the United States and Related Laws, contained in Title 17 of the United States Code' (2022).

25 According to the USA Copyright Office, "training material includes a combination of text, images, audio, or other categories of expressive material, as well as annotations describing the material. An example of training material would be an individual image and an associated text label that describes the image" (Federal Register, 2023, p. 59949).

26 For a good discussion, including a representative sample of federal cases, see the *Economic Report of the President* (2024, pp. 274–275).
27 The citation is *Thaler v. Perlmutter*, 1:22-cv-01564-BAH WL 5333236 (D.D.C., Aug. 18, 2023).
28 The bulleted material is taken entirely (word-for-word) from Reinhart (2023).
29 For a classic discussion of regulation, see Kahn (1988). Later in this chapter, we argue that effective AI regulation must move away from the narrow focus of traditional regulation (i.e., competition, price, cost) to embrace broader, more holistic objectives; nevertheless, knowledge of traditional regulation is absolutely essential.
30 For more information on Bletchley's purpose/objectives/results see Allen and Adamson (2024).
31 Language is critical to convey and effectuate the precise meaning of words; it has "a pervasive influence in camouflaging assumptions…while actively shaping our world" (Madden, 2020, pp. 41 and 169). Here, regulate (from the Latin 'regula' meaning, rule, ruler, straight piece) means to control or direct according to rule, principle or law; to adjust or regulate. Today, its usage connotes heavy-handed state oversight. As we explain in the text, in the context of AI, we need a more holistic word for 'regulate,' one that will facilitate/enable/foster/govern. This is especially so since "the words we use implicitly promote separation of subject versus object, and organism versus environment" (Madden, 2020, p. 41).
32 For further discussion, see our **Corporate Power and Antitrust** chapter.
33 These companies have pledged to invest $200bn in 2024 on data centers, chips, and other gear for building, generating, and employing generative AI models (*The Economist,* May 18, 2024, p. 12).
34 Facebook/Meta joined the group in May 2024.
35 For further discussion, see White House (2023) and(White House (2022). AI watermarking is the process of embedding a digital code/image/text as an authenticity imprimatur.
36 Perhaps Zoom Communications might be the next invitee. Founded in 2011, in 2024, it launched Zoom Workplace to directly compete with Microsoft by providing an AI collaboration platform. Zoom's stock price took a beating post-Covid, falling from $559/share in late 2020 to $58/share as this book goes to press (October 2024). But perhaps more significant, its revenue stream has continued increasing since 2020 and is now at just over $1billion/quarter (Zoom Video Communications Annual Report 2024).
37 Elon Musk founded xAI in July 2023. In late May 2024, it raised $6 billion, "putting it in a position to compete with OpenAI and Anthropic, which have secured funding from Microsoft and Amazon" (*The New York Times*, June 2, 2024, p. 2). Musk, a co-founder of Open AI, quit the company due to his concerns that the company was putting profits before safety.
38 This paragraph relies heavily on Henshall (2024).
39 A chip is a tiny electric circuit made of silicon; it is comprised of microscopic transistors that transmit electrical data signals.
40 Pioneering is an understatement. A college dropout, Fredkin became a professor of computer science at MIT. His ideas fascinate us, and we wish we could write a chapter just on him. For a tantalizing flavor of his ideas see Chandler (2023).

References

'$6B: The Amount Raised by Elon Musk's Intelligence Company,' (2024) *The New York Times*, June 2, Business section, p. 2.
Acemoglu, Daron (2021) 'Harms of AI,' NBER Working Paper 29247, NBER, Cambridge, MA.

Agrawal, Ajay, Joshua Gans, and Avi Goldfarb (2018) *Prediction Machines: The simple Economics*

Allen, Gregory and Georgia Adamson (2024) 'The AI Seoul Summit,' Center for Strategic and International Studies, May 23, (csis.org).

Bajekal, Naina and Billy Perrigo (2023) 'CEO of the Year: Sam Altman,' *TIME*, December 25, pp. 58–68.

Barocas, Solon and Andrew D. Selbst (2016) 'Big Data's Disparate Impact,' *California Law Review*, Vol. 104, No. 3, pp. 671–732.

Bodanis, David (2000) *E=MC²: A biography of the world's most famous equation*, Berkley Books, New York.

'Can you make this clearer,' (2024) *The Economist*, editorial, June 29, p. 10.

Chandler, David (2023) 'Is the Universe a giant (quantum) computer?' *Nature*, Vol. 620, August 31, pp. 943–945.

'Copyright Law of the United States and Related Laws Contained in Title 17 of the United States Code' (2022), December, circular 92, https://copyright.gov.

Economic Report of the President, (2024) The White House, Washington, DC.

Eapen, Tojin, Daniel Finkenstadt, Josh Folk, Lokesh Venkataswamy, (2023) 'How Generative AI Can Augment Human Creativity,' *Harvard Business Review* (July-August), Vol. 101, No. 4, pp. 56–75.

Federal Register (2023) 'Artificial Intelligence and Copyright' Vol. 88, No. 167, August 30, 2023, Docket No. 2023-6 AGENCY: U.S. Copyright Office, Library of Congress, pp. 59942–59949, 2023-18624.pdf (govinfo.gov)

'Generative AI: A Trillion Dollar Arms Race,' (2024), *The Economist,* May 18, p. 12.

'Generative AI: Two Bots are Better than One' (2024) *The Economist*, May 18, pp. 68–69.

Henshall, Will (2024) 'How U.S. Commerce Secretary Gina Raimondo is navigating America's AI future.' *TIME,* June 24, pp. 14–16.

'How AI Can Revolutionize Science,' (2023) *The Economist,* editorial, September 16, p. 11.

Jacobson, Sheldon, and Janet Jokela (2024) 'Opinion: What should we fear with AI in medicine?' May 28, (medicalxpress.com)

Khan, Alfred (1988) *The Economics of Regulation: Principles and Institutions*, Vol. I and II, MIT Press, Cambridge, Mass.

Madden, Bartley J. (2020) *Value Creation Principles*, Wiley, Hoboken, New Jersey.

Manyika, James and Michael Spence (2023) 'The Coming AI Economic Revolution,' *Foreign Affairs*, Vol. 102, No. 6, pp. 70–86.

McNeil, J.R. (2000) *An Environmental History of the Twentieth-Century World*, W.W. Norton, New York.

Milmo, Dan (2023) 'Tech companies say Frontier Model Forum will focus on 'safe and responsible' creation of new models,' *The Guardian,* July 26. https://www.theguardian.com/technology

'Model major general' (2024) *The Economist*, June 22, pp. 16–19.

Mokyr, Joel, Chris Vickers, and Nicolas Ziebarth (2015) 'The History of Technological Anxiety and the Future of Economic Growth: Is This Time Different?' *Journal of Economic Perspectives*, Vol. 29, No. 3, pp. 31–50.

'Only Humans can be authors of copyrightable words' (2023) Reinhart, September 7, Only Humans Can Be Authors of... | Reinhart Boerner Van Deuren s.c. (reinhartlaw.com)

Oremus, Will and Elahe Izadi (2024) 'AI's future could hinge on one thorny legal question' *The Washington Post,* January 4, https://www.washingtonpost.com/technology

Reardon, Jack, Maria Madi, Molly Scott Cato (2018) *Introducing a New Economics*, Pluto Press, London.

Rifkin, Jeremy (1995) *The End of Work: The Decline of the Global Labor Force and the Dawn of the Post-Market Era*, Putnam, New York.

Rhodes, Richard (2018) *Energy: A Human History*, Simon and Schuster, New York.

'Scientists, et al.,' (2024) *The Economist*, June 29, pp. 66–67.

Shattuck, Roger (1996) *Forbidden Knowledge: From Prometheus to Pornography*, Harcourt Brace and Company, San Diego.

Solomonoff, Grace (2023) 'The Meeting of the Minds that Launched AI,' *IEEE Spectrum*, May 6, https://spectrum.ieee.org

Standage, Tom, (1998) *The Victorian Internet*, Berkley Publishing, New York.

Standing, Guy (2017) *Basic Income: And How We Can Make it Happen*, Pelican Press, London.

'USAI: Vision, Mission, and Strategic Goals' (2024) The United States Artificial Intelligence Safety Institute, May 21.

Valenzano, Jason (2024) 'Unveiling AI's Secrets: The Interplay of Generative and Non-Generative Techniques,' *Medium*, March 23, https://medium.com/

Von Hipple, Eric (2006) *Democratizing Innovation*, MIT Press, Cambridge, Mass.

White House (2022) *Blueprint for an AI Bill of Rights: Making Automated Systems Work for the American People*, https://www.whitehouse.gov/wp-content/uploads/2022/10/Blueprint-for-an-AI-Bill-of-Rights.pdf

White House (2023) 'Biden-Harris Administration Secures Voluntary Commitments from Eight Additional Intelligence Companies to Manage the Risks Posed by AI,' https://www.whitehouse.gov

'World leaders seek unity on AI at virtual summit co-hosted by South Korea, U.K.' (2024) National Public Radio, (May 21). https://npr.org.

Zoom Video Communications, Inc. (2024) Annual Report, 50e0c380-f4bd-4a16-80e3-da56b64017ce (zoom.us).

Zuboff, Shoshana (2019) *The Age of Surveillance Capitalism: The Fight for the Future at the New Frontier of Power*, Profile Books, London.

21 Corporate Power and Antitrust

The Issue: A basic tenet of economics is that more competition is better than less. But how much competition is enough? How big should firms be allowed to be? Is there an ideal firm size? Does bigness beget power? Should the government regulate businesses? If so, how? And why? These questions have long been asked, but now have greater urgency with the rise of **Big Tech**. This chapter will explore how USA policymakers have tried to answer these questions, and why such discussion is important post-2024.

21.1 Introduction

We ask of our economic system to produce the goods and services that we all need; and to provide us with jobs and hence an income to be able to purchase these products. Indeed, this is a fundamental task of all economic systems, no matter capitalist or socialist,[1] and no matter rich or poor. Different economic systems have different ways of meeting this fundamental task. Under the old USSR, the first socialist nation, the government mandated all aspects of production, from where firms obtained their resources, to the technology used, to the final outlet. In a market economy, however, like that of the United States, the government refrains from such micromanagement and for good reason—no socialist nation has ever provided an adequate living standard for its people. But that doesn't mean that our government doesn't take an active role in our economy—it does, but not in producing goods and services.

While it is easy to understand how the government can effectively mandate the production of goods and services under socialism (by decree), it isn't so obvious under capitalism. Adam Smith (1976 [1776]) told us more than three centuries ago, that to ensure that needed goods/services are produced, entrepreneurs and firms must be incentivized via the profit motive, then minimize regulation and ensure ample competition. Then voila!

While competition benefits consumers via lower prices, and incentivizes firms to adopt the most efficient technology, competition means that some firms will succeed and others fail. Firms that succeed will capture a competitive

DOI: 10.4324/9781003591856-24

advantage resulting in economies of scale, i.e., the successful firms will get bigger. Successful firms succeed because they have either directly responded to consumer needs, or nurtured new consumer needs so that they are best able to satisfy. The new supplants the old, and the profit motive incentivizes adopting/creating the new; a process that Joseph Schumpeter called 'creative destruction,'

> Capitalism … is by nature a form or method of economic change and not only never is but never can be stationary. … The fundamental impulse that sets and keeps the capitalist engine in motion comes from the new consumers' goods, the new methods of production or transportation, the new markets, the new forms of industrial organization that capitalist enterprise creates. The opening up of new markets, foreign or domestic, and the organizational development from the craft shop and factory to such concerns as U.S. Steel illustrate the process of industrial mutation that incessantly revolutionizes the economic structure from within, incessantly destroying the old one, incessantly creating a new one. This process of Creative Destruction is the essential fact about capitalism. It is what capitalism consists in and what every capitalist concern has got to live in… [capitalism requires] the perennial gale of Creative Destruction.
>
> (Schumpeter, 1994 [1942], pp. 82–83)

So in this way, bigness becomes a badge of honor, if it can deliver the goods. But paradoxically, both success and bigness can lessen competition, consolidating and increasing market power, subverting the beneficial aspects of competition.

What to do?

To surf through possible options is what this chapter is all about, while at the same time discussing the necessary role of government to enable and sustain creative destruction. Just like a game of football, an economy needs a set of rules/procedures to ensure fair and adequate competition, while preventing/minimizing the abuses of bigness, while at the same time trying to capture its positive benefits.[2]

In a market economy, the government is tasked with establishing the rules of the game. Without government, we have anarchy, and without a market economy, we have no production. It is not a question of either the government or the market, as people are sometimes wont to say, since both are needed for the economy to successfully provision.[3] A good example is so-called 'market instruments,' such as cap-and-trade; established to attenuate **climate change**, which requires active government support from start to finish.[4] Corporate power and antitrust is a good example: We look to the government to provide the right incentives for firms to produce, while simultaneously curtailing the abuses of bigness.

21.2 Competition and Corporate Power—A Complementary Pair[5]

21.2.1 Introduction

Economic theory posits that competition benefits consumers by reducing the price of products and increasing the array of possible goods, while incentivizing firms to adopt the most efficient technology, thereby reducing overall cost. The profit motive will incentivize firms to develop new products and to serve new markets. It is the profit motive that actualizes creative destruction. Even Karl Marx and Friedrich Engels—two of capitalism's most cogent critics lauded capitalism's powerful ability to produce,

> The bourgeoisie, during its rule of scarce one hundred years, has created more massive and more colossal productive forces than have all the preceding generations together. Subjection of Nature's forces to man, machinery, application of chemistry to industry and agriculture, steam-navigation, railways, electric telegraphs, clearing of whole continents for cultivation, canalization of rivers, whole populations conjured out of the ground…
>
> (Marx and Engels, 1848 [1960], pp. 7–8)

While competition might seem beneficial from the vantage of consumers and even society, from the firm's perspective it is not.[6] Competition implies that any firm is content with engaging with similar firms producing similar products. But most firms (we would say all) want to offer a unique product with a significant competitive advantage. A comfortable niche, if you will. Ideally: Enjoy a monopoly with no competition.

21.2.2 Defining Power and Corporate Power

Power is a multi-faceted word, much like freedom, democracy, and sustainability; hence, it should not be surprising that several definitions exist.[7] One that we like for its simplicity, defines power as, "the generalized potentiality for getting one's own way or for bringing about changes (at least some of which are intended) in other people's actions or conditions" (Benn, 1967, p. 426). Or more simply, "what is a power, but the ability or faculty of doing a thing?" (Hamilton et al., (2003 [1787–1788]) #33, p. 186).

From this definition, it is clear that power is contextual (i.e., it involves a specific time, place, and actors) and it is relational, i.e., occurring between two or more parties. Indeed, the essence of power is one person, firm, or nation forcing another to act contrary to its wishes in order to enforce one's will. Needless to say, the ability to exercise power "is supported by specific underlying rules, values, and institutions which, if changed, could tilt the balance of power in another direction" (Hamilton et al., (2003 [1787–1788]) #33, p. 60). Recognizing corporate power—in all its manifestations—is an important purview of economics.

Corporate power[8] has been traditionally (and unfortunately, somewhat narrowly) defined as a firm's ability to raise prices. A firm with market power can increase its price, thereby increasing profits, all else equal, which in turn reduces consumer welfare. The ability of a firm with market power to raise prices and reduce consumer welfare has been the preponderant driver in both the enactment and enforcement of USA antitrust laws.

But corporate power to raise prices only tells part of the story. In many sectors of the economy, we are witnessing a decline in the marginal cost of production, especially firms using the internet order to produce and allocate, i.e., platform capitalists.[9] As marginal cost decreases, so should price (at least theoretically). But that doesn't mean that corporate power dissipates; rather it becomes manifest in other areas, and against other stakeholders. This is the crux of the **Big Tech** problem, which we discuss in a separate chapter.

To define corporate power, we need a broader definition of the firm,[10] which we define as a "focal point for a set of transactions among interested stakeholders (e.g., managers, owners, financiers, employees, customers, retailers, suppliers, and the community) in the production of goods and services." Thus, the firm, at any point in time, is a function of the interactions with everyone it comes into contact with.[11]

Inherent power can only be ascertained by empirically investigating the embeddedness and mutual dependencies among all stakeholders at a specific point in time, as well as a more dynamic analysis of how the mutual dependencies are evolving. Conducting such a stakeholder analysis requires: (1) Identifying all stakeholders; (2) prioritizing them by constructing a power grid; and (3) mapping the strategies for each stakeholder.[12] Excluding relevant stakeholders gives an incomplete picture of the firm. While we tend to think of stakeholders as defined by hard and fast boundaries, the boundaries are instead fluid and constantly evolving[13] (Boyd and Reardon, 2020, p. 69). This is a result of creative destruction.

Reflecting on Machiavelli's *The Prince* (1532 [1988]), one assumes that power is used negatively (and unethically) to subvert another's will.[14] But power (especially soft power, i.e., leading by example) can be used positively against[15] one or more stakeholders. Power can also be used positively to enable fulfilling one's potential; however, we define 'one' and 'potential.' Here it is "power to, rather than power over" (Boyd and Reardon, 2020, p. 110). The positive use of power is especially apropos in the transition to **Net Zero**.

In studying power, and especially corporate power, one must ascertain its genesis, its enabling conditions, and how it is used. This is a preponderant task for economists and all social scientists. At the very least, understanding power in all its dimensions can elucidate how our economy functions and how it is evolving. It can also help us recognize and thus overcome any vested interests in maintaining the status quo, i.e., obstacles (Boyd and Reardon, 2020, pp. 104–107). Government's role should not be to extirpate all sources of power, since power can be used to achieve objectives that comport with the public interest; rather, it must distinguish between malevolent and benign sources of power. Not an easy task.

Firms with power will try to protect their power source. Typically, this is done by erecting entry barriers to prevent others from directly competing. So, for example, if I own a restaurant, I will hire a unique cook, one with a special flare that no one else can replicate; or hire unique staff; situate it on property with a unique view, etc.

An effective entry barrier is to produce more output at a declining cost, i.e., economies of scale, effectively prohibiting all but very large firms from entering. In many situations economies of scale are achieved via mergers and acquisitions, e.g., US Steel (1901) and GM (1908). But that doesn't mean that new entrants will not enter, especially if they can compete on a non-price basis. A good example is the beer industry long dominated by giants whose sheer size precludes price competition, but new entrants can compete on quality—a better tasting beer, albeit more expensive, while only serving a fraction of the market.

Competition and corporate power are often assumed to be opposites, i.e., competition will prevent corporate power. But not necessarily so: The latter forms from the former, and both must be studied and analyzed together, i.e., a complementary pair, if you will.

A business can also use its power more nefariously to subvert the political process, especially by convincing the public that it is too big to fail. Ironically, this is a preponderant reason for mergers and acquisitions; using its economies of scale to ultimately protect itself, by convincing both the public and policy makers that it is too big to fail.

21.3 The Government's Role in Maintaining Competition and Reducing Corporate Power

21.3.1 *Introduction*

Many concepts, measures, and definitions (e.g., **unemployment, GDP, and inflation**) used to conceptualize, define, and assess our economy were constructed from the late 19th century to the mid-20th century. They were intended to measure and assess a very different economy, i.e., "an industrial economy producing physical standardized commodities... [to be produced, bought and sold] in a single moment in time" (Block, 2023, p. 30). But while such products are still produced today, more of our products are

> de-standardized and produced with differentiated technologies, ranging from beer and bread to automobiles, mattresses, appliances, clothing, and pharmaceuticals. Such production requires a collaborative network organization where success depends on the confluence of many skills and jobs, and the expertise of many different employees…Such a…network opens up the space for smaller firms, cooperatives, ethical firms organized as beneficial corporations, and publicly owned entities.
>
> (Block, 2023, pp. 32 and 38)

Unfortunately, the conceptualization of corporate power used by today's economists is still ensconced in that earlier age. A good example is the antitrust laws, designed to restrict monopoly while augmenting consumer welfare, while ignoring the effects of power on *all* the firm's stakeholders.

Since a market economy can adequately produce private goods (e.g., any good where the producer reaps the full profits and the user pays the cost, such as an automobile) the government does not micromanage such production. Instead, it takes a more indirect approach by influencing the industry structure, i.e., the number of firms, the relative size of each firm, and entry barriers. Every firm belongs to an industry (defined as a set of firms producing a similar product).

Industry structure will determine firm behavior and firm performance, e.g., prices, profits, and technology. Thus, a firm operating in a monopoly (i.e., an industry with only one firm) will behave differently than a firm operating in an industry with lots of small firms.

The federal government attempts to influence industry structure and hence firm behavior indirectly via the antitrust laws: A broad body of law which prevents monopoly while encouraging competition. In the following subsection, we briefly discuss the major antitrust laws.

21.3.2   The Antitrust Laws

The US antitrust laws are:

- **Sherman Antitrust Act (1890)**
  After the Civil War, monopolies were becoming more widespread in basic industries, e.g., whiskey, linseed oil, sugar, railroads, and oil. As we discuss in our chapter on the **oil industry**, it was Standard Oil's ruthless monopolistic actions that convinced many Americans of the need for government action. The result was the Sherman Act.[16]

  Section 1 prohibits "every contract, combination in the form of trust or otherwise, or conspiracy, in restraint of trade or commerce among the several

States, or with foreign nations." Section 2 prohibits actions that "shall monopolize, or attempt to monopolize, or combine or conspire with any other person or persons, to monopolize any part of the trade or commerce among the several States, or with foreign nations." In other words, the Sherman Act made the existence of monopoly illegal. The Act also made illegal firms colluding to act as a monopolist (e.g., dentists in town conspiring to set prices, thus, de facto performing and acting as one).

The Sherman Act's two provisions have one important proviso: Monopoly is only illegal if its effect is to lessen competition. In practice, this means that the litigant must prove that a monopoly reduces competition and hence adversely affects consumer welfare. Sometimes this is easy and other times not. An analogy is to make driving over 70 mph illegal only if the effect is to lessen the welfare of others. In some cases, this would be easy to prove (e.g., an accident), while in other cases it would be quite difficult. No wonder antitrust cases can be both expensive and time consuming.

While there are many firm stakeholders, the Sherman Act (and the entire body of antitrust law) primarily focuses only on one: The consumer. It is presumed that greater competition will result in more efficient use of resources and hence lower prices, thus increasing consumer welfare. Even the word 'efficiency' is constructed to focus on consumer welfare; yet, it "is only one conceptualization of efficiency heavily imbued in ideology, and a narrow one at that" (Fullbrook, 2009, p. 21). But why not calibrate efficiency to sustainability, or all citizens reaching their full potential? Or even jettisoning the use of efficiency altogether in favor of another yardstick? (Reardon et al., 2018, p. 175).

An illustrative example is the 1997 Exxon and Mobil merger; two large well-established firms and incidentally the two largest remnants of the original Standard Oil corporation.[17] In testimony before Congress, supporters argued that the merger would increase economies of scale, reduce oil prices, reduce corporate overhead, boost energy supplies, and enhance domestic energy security. Opponents, on the other hand, raised significant objections.[18] For example, former US Senator (D. MN) Paul Wellstone warned that the oil industry is setting a pattern of consolidations that ultimately will leave only a few 'megacompanies.' And, Athan Manuel of the US Public Interest Research Group: "The proposed mergers set up a lose-lose situation. With less competition, consumers will lose. And the increased political power of these new megacompanies means that democracy and the environment will lose too."

- **Clayton Antitrust Act 1914**
  A major loophole in the Sherman Act was its inability to prevent actions that might lead to a monopoly. Nipping a monopoly in the bud, so to speak, would be easier (especially financially) than dealing with a full-fledged monopoly. Thus, passage of the Clayton Act. This act outlawed the following practices,

which, if implemented, could eventually lead to a monopoly: Price discrimination; exclusive-dealing contracts (i.e., tying contracts); the acquisition of competing companies via stock purchases[19]; and interlocking directorates. These practices are illegal if the effect is to reduce competition. For example, if a firm deliberately prices below its average total cost to drive out competitors (thereby reducing competition), it is illegal under the Clayton Act. This was Standard Oil's modus operandi throughout the late 19th century, while also notoriously negotiating favorable rates with railroad companies, lessening the competition's ability to compete.

The passage of the Clayton Act (like all pieces of legislation) was influenced by special interest groups, and as such, deserves a modern reexamination,

> After more than eight decades, the Clayton Act continues to influence much of the organization and structure of American corporations. Many of the government regulatory agencies' decisions regarding allowance (or disallowance) of mergers today rest on bureaucrats' interpretation of antitrust laws. To the extent that the enactment of these laws was influenced by interest groups, their imposition must have resulted in a much more inefficient allocation of resources. The aggregate long-term effects of passing inefficient antitrust legislation have been, and continue to be, enormously costly for society.
> (Ramirez and Eigen-Zucchi, 2001, p. 177)

Point well taken. All laws need to be continually reexamined in order to remain relevant and effective.[20]

Today, the federal government's close scrutiny of a company via the Clayton Act, allows others to escape from being watched, enabling them to grow and prosper. For example, the government's focus on Microsoft abetted the fast rise of Google ('The Trustbusters of Tech,' 2023).

- **1914 Federal Trade Commission Act**
This Act created the Federal Trade Commission (FTC), which along with the US Dept. of Justice, enforces the Antitrust Laws. The FTC also monitors unfair methods of competition and unfair/deceptive acts or practices. So, for example if a firm claims it uses real maple syrup in one of its products, but does not, then the FTC will investigate if the matter is brought to its attention.

- **Robinson-Patman Act (1936)**
This Act amends the Clayton Act to make it illegal to charge a price discount to another business, unless based on cost. As with the other laws, it is only relevant if the effect is to lessen competition. The law does not apply at the retail level, only at the wholesale. Behavior not illegal under the Clayton Act: If a book publisher, for example, sells copies of a best-seller at a heavily discounted price to a large bookstore, but not to a smaller one. This is legal since the larger bookstore will sell more copies, so it is

beneficial for the publisher to ship in bulk and thus offer a discount based on lower shipping costs. The Robinson-Patman Act would be violated if the two bookstores were of equal size, and one received a discount and the other did not.

- **The Celler-Kefauver Act (1950)**
  The impetus for this law was the rise of fascism in Germany, in which large firms dominated key sectors of the economy. It was thought that they facilitated Hitler's rise to power, by subjugating the German economy to Hitler's wartime aims.

  The Act filled two loopholes in the Clayton Act: (1) The illegal practice of competing companies purchasing stock said nothing about acquiring physical assets; (2) the Sherman and Clayton Acts only applied to intra-industry horizontal mergers (e.g., the Edison General Electric Company and the Thomson-Houston Electric Company merging in 1892 to form General Electric) and to vertical mergers (a firm merging with either its retailer or supplier, e.g., Amazon and Whole Foods 2017; AT&T and Time Warner 2018; CVS Health and Aetna 2018). But the Acts were silent on conglomerate mergers, i.e., a merger of two or more unrelated firms in different industries (e.g., Berkshire Hathaway and Burlington Northern Santa Fe, 2009; United Technologies and Goodrich, 2011). So, hypothetically, without the Celler-Kefauver Act, if Walmart and Exxon Mobil wanted to merge, the federal government would be powerless to stop it.

- **Hart-Scott-Rodino Antitrust Improvements Act (1976)**
  This Act amends the Clayton Act (Section 7) and requires that companies planning significant mergers notify the government in advance. It also requires a waiting period and a filing fee. Sounds basic, and you would have thought this law would have come first, but it did not.

21.3.3   *Brief Evaluation of the Antitrust Laws*

The Acts do not prohibit every restraint of trade, only those that reduce competition. The latter, in turn, must be proven by the plaintiff, which is typically not easy. In the 2001 case, United States of America v. Microsoft Corporation,[21] the federal government sued Microsoft for violating the Clayton's Act prohibition against tying contracts, i.e., selling one product that customers wanted, while forcing them to buy another. More specifically, Microsoft was accused of tying its Web browser to its internet operating system, thus disadvantaging competitors selling only one product (i.e., Netscape).[22] Microsoft, however, argued that it was giving consumers what they wanted, enhancing the system's overall usability; thus enhancing consumer efficiency and improving consumer welfare. Although initially the federal government intended to break up Microsoft, it did not, eventually settling with Microsoft on very minor Antitrust violations.

Speaking of breaking up companies, one can count on one hand the number of breakups ordered by the federal government; so much so, that one wonders why there haven't been more. In 1911, the US government under the Sherman Act broke up the Standard Oil Corporation. Founded by John D. Rockefeller, Standard was a notorious monopoly, at one time controlling 90% of America's refining capacity, while striking deals with railroad companies to subvert the competition. Also in 1911, the US government broke up the American Tobacco Company into R.J. Reynolds; Liggett and Myers; and Lorillard. More recently, in 1974 the federal government sued AT&T for violating the Sherman Act, by monopolizing 80–85% of phone lines, both local and long-distance, and with "most of the telephone equipment…produced by AT&T's subsidiary Western Electric, which gave AT&T almost complete dominion over telephone service and equipment" (Archer-Ventures, 2023). On January 8, 1982, fearing it would lose, AT&T voluntarily agreed to divest itself of its local telephone service firms, while keeping its long-distance. The dissolvement, by the way, unleashed a torrent of technological development in the telecommunications industry resulting in the formation of large, household name companies (e.g., T-Mobile, Comcast, Verizon[23]) who themselves have been merging.[24]

On January 17, 1969, the Justice Department filed a lawsuit against IBM alleging that it had violated Section 2 of the Sherman Act. On January 8, 1982, the Justice Department withdrew the case claiming it was without merit.

21.4 Monopoly Exemptions

There are two exemptions to the Antitrust Laws' prohibition against monopoly: (1) Natural Monopoly, and (2) intellectual property rights. Each will be briefly explained.

21.4.1 *Natural Monopoly*

Defined as a single firm that can supply a product to an entire market at a lower Average Total Cost (ATC), i.e., fixed plus variable costs, than two (or more) firms.[25] Natural monopolies have high fixed costs i.e., the costs to get up and running, but a very low marginal cost (MC) (i.e., the extra cost of servicing an additional customer). A good example is an electrical utility, which must first build a generator and lay transmission lines before any electricity can be produced. But once production begins, a unit of electricity can be produced cheaply, with total costs decreasing over the entire range of output. Other examples include waste management systems, water and sewage systems, as well the platform capitalists, Facebook, Amazon, and Google. (See our **Big Tech** chapter.)

Since a natural monopoly's ATC doesn't reach a minimum until well past total market demand, it is best that demand be serviced by one firm with a declining ATC (i.e., economies of scale). A natural monopoly can produce the same output cheaper than two firms (assuming that each would equally sub-divide the market). Thus, conventional thinking suggests that one firm should produce the entire output to take advantage of economies of scale. If an additional firm enters this market, then each firm will now produce one-half the output at a much higher ATC and hence a much higher price. Competition in this case is considered wasteful (think of multiple competing generators and multiple competing lines of distribution to produce electricity) resulting in an unnecessary replication of fixed costs, which are always high with a natural monopoly.

Awarding a natural monopoly comes with the stipulation that the government will regulate its price. Then, the question becomes at what price. At the socially optimal price (where consumer demand equals MC), then the business suffers a loss, which is unfair. The monopoly price is ruled out (charging whatever the market will bear) since it is too high. A fair return price is usually chosen, where the business is allowed to charge a break-even price and allowed to enjoy a per unit profit. This raises the obvious catch-22: For a business to be allowed to charge a fair return price, its ATC must be known, but for it to be known, it must be proffered by the firm, which in turn has a built-in bias to inflate its costs.

Economists assume that without regulation the firm would not act in the public interest and would take advantage of its monopoly by charging higher prices, thereby reducing consumer welfare. An interesting case is AT&T during WWI.[26] In 1918, the telecommunications industry was briefly nationalized (for national security purposes). Theodore Vail, AT&T's president, requested,

> government regulation, hoping it would make his own company the 'natural monopoly' the government was looking for…As soon as the ink was dry on the contract, AT&T applied for significant rate increases for service connection charges and received them…Within [six months] of being taken over by the federal government, the company had secured a 20% increase in its long-distance rates, a far greater return than it had enjoyed when still wrestling with the competitive free-enterprise marketplace.
>
> (Rifkin, 2014, pp. 50–51)

Not all economists agree that regulation of a natural monopoly is the best solution. Some propose cooperatives (either producer or consumer) especially in the energy sector.[27] Others suggest redesigning the firm so that it comports with the public interest to encompass all stakeholders, not just the consumer (Boyd and Reardon, 2020).

Today more and more companies are producing with high fixed costs and declining and very low marginal costs, giving them an ability to service the entire market. Especially platform capitalists (e.g., Google, Facebook Uber, and Lyft) which we will discuss in our **Big Tech chapter**. In addition, declining (and near zero) marginal costs are becoming common across the economy, and not just natural monopolists. From,

> using the Internet to secure information to the cost of harvesting the sun and wind and other abundant resources, the 3D printing of 'things' and online courses in higher education. [In fact] the Internet of Things is the first general purpose technology platform in history that can potentially take large parts of the economy to near zero marginal costs. And that's what makes the marginal cost controversy so pivotal to humanity's future.
>
> (Rifkin, 2014, p. 138)

This suggests the federal government's antitrust policy is using the wrong lens to see the wrong problem, which is the firm's ability to use its power to affect any and all stakeholders, not just the consumer, whereas the government should be investigating how government power is used in all its manifestations against all the firm's stakeholders. It is this myopic focus on consumer welfare at the expense of other stakeholders that has led to a new Gilded Age (Wu, 2018). Time for a refocus.

21.4.2   *Intellectual Property Rights*

The Founding Fathers recognized the rights of Americans to enjoy the benefits of new technology as well as works of art, music, and books. At the same, they recognized that authors, artists, and entrepreneurs need to be incentivized in order to produce. The US Constitution compromised the competing interests of society versus the innovator/inventor by awarding a brief monopoly to the innovator after which the innovations would remand to the public interest, "The congress shall have power… to promote the progress of science and useful arts, by securing for limited times to authors and inventors the exclusive right to their respective writings and discoveries" (Article 1, Section 8).

Of course, innovators could forego monopoly protection if they so choose. Ben Franklin, inventor of the lightning rod, the Franklin stove, bifocals, and many other inventions, was famous for never applying for a patent, saying that he had benefited from humanity's largeness and would like to return the favor. Likewise, Tim Berners-Lee, inventor of the World Wide Web in 1989 offered his invention for the public good. And, Gerald Holton, who developed the ubiquitous peace symbol[28] "insisted that [it] remain forever in the public domain" (Rock, 2024 p. 10).

Intellectual property rights (IPRs) include:

- **Patents**: The federal government grants the sole right to produce for a specified period, usually for at least 20 years.

- **Trademarks**: Protecting a name, symbol, or anything else identifying a product. It can last indefinitely.
- **Copyrights**: The legal right to exclusive publication, production, distribution, and sale of a literary or artistic work, which lasts for the author's lifetime, plus an additional term, usually 70 years.[29]

Advocates argue that IPRs are necessary to incentivize innovators and ensure technological progress, thereby promoting societal welfare. Detractors argue that they "are the ultimate entry barrier, representing a "political choice by a government...to grant monopolies over knowledge to private interests, allowing them to restrict public access to knowledge and to raise the price of obtaining it or of products and services embodying it" (Standing, 2016, p. 50). Standing also notes that most patents are used for purposes other than rewarding/supporting innovation, instead to "gain or protect a monopoly, acting as a deterrent, not a spur to innovation" (2016, p. 61). *The New York Times* agrees at least with prescription drugs,

> Twelve of the drugs that Medicare spends the most on are protected by more than 600 patents in total...Many...contain little that's truly new. But the thickets they create have the potential to extend product monopolies for decades. In so doing, they promise to add billions to the nation's soaring health care costs—and to pharmaceutical coffers... [while consumers] are still struggling to afford it. The United States Patent and Trademark Office is in dire need of reform...not only is legal trickery rewarded and the public's interest overlooked, but innovation—the very thing that patents were meant to foster is undermined.
>
> (Save America's Patent System, 2022, p. 8)[30]

Also problematic with IPRs is its policy to award on a first-come basis, rather than rewarding a group effort or even multiple founders. The latter more accurately reflects the reality that innovators benefit from humanity's largeness, and that innovativeness reflects a more widespread intellectual achievement.[31]

21.5 Conclusion

American capitalism, known for its adaptability, continues to evolve to fit changing conditions. Yet, unfortunately, economics and its conceptualization of corporate power has not; it remains ensconced in late 19th century/early 20th century thinking. Rather than more vigorous antitrust, we need a thorough reconceptualization of the antitrust law, from top to bottom. The law must recognize new configurations of capital (especially platform capitalists) and it must focus on all stakeholders rather than just the consumer.[32]

The law must come to grips with firm bigness and corporate power,[33] which contrary to traditional antitrust thinking, can manifest in myriad ways. The traditional antitrust law does not help us to deal with **Artificial Intelligence, Climate Change**, and transitioning to **Net Zero**, which all require transformational thinking, rather than thinking that emanates from narrowly based solos.[34]

We are not demanding more government regulation, especially when it would be based on 19th century thinking, but rather, something like participatory democracy where all stakeholders can offer input in forging policies to move forward. And, in addition, as we will discuss, the three issues in bold above demand participatory democracy.

An interesting proposal is to address corporate power by requiring all firms that engage interstate commerce to be federally chartered. So doing recognizes "the large modern corporation for what it is—an essentially public institution" (Mueller, 1990, p. 345). The federal government should do the chartering rather than the state governments "which have become increasingly framed to suit the interests of corporate enterprises" (Mueller, 1990, p. 344). The federal charter would require a contract between the corporation and all stakeholders, and especially the public interest, something which tends to be forgotten. The contract would detail strict guidelines of accountability and disclosure and would require the corporate board to represent all stakeholders, especially the public interest. The goal is not to straightjacket corporations but to recognize their vast influence over all aspects of lives, while harnessing the profit motive so that capitalism works for all us,

> During this critical historical moment, in which one of the most fundamental challenges our species faces is to rediscover the purpose and unity of life, we must decide whether the power to govern will be in the hands of living people or will reside with corporate entities driven by a different agenda.
>
> (Korten, 1996, p. 66)

No better example than the corporations developing **Artificial Intelligence**. While this technology will do a lot of good, it also has the potential for cataclysmic destruction. Likewise with the **Big Tech** firms, many of whom are also developing **AI** along with surveillance capitalism, which is invidiously affecting how we live and work and the choices we make. The development of **AI**, as well as **Big Tech's products**, is forcing us to ask an age-old question that really gets to the heart of capitalism:[35] "is all wealth collective in origin? [Especially since wealth creation] depends on the international division of labor, the use of worldwide resources, and the accumulation of knowledge since the beginnings of humanity" (Piketty, 2022, p. 9).

If yes, then should private property serve the common good, via a balanced set of institutions and rights making it possible to limit individual accumulations, to make power circulate, and to distribute wealth more fairly? If yes, then this logically leads to federal chartering—how else could the corporate interest be aligned with the public interest? How we answer these questions will, to a large extent, determine how our future unfolds, and all deserve consideration post-2024.

Notes

1 Under socialism the government owns most of the means of production, and hence decides how to use them; under capitalism individuals and businesses own most of the means of production, while under communism everyone owns the means of production. Many people today use the word communism to refer to socialist.
2 Alas, the words 'fair,' 'adequate,' and 'abuses' are subjective. This issue will attempt to objectify them. Of course, these are just a few of the rationales for government involvement; others include redressing externalities; attaining full employment; reducing poverty; mitigating climate change; and providing public goods. In addition, as Adam Smith noted, the market cannot produce public goods (i.e., something that we all benefit from, but no one has the incentive to produce, e.g., national defense) necessitating by default government production.
3 Karl Polanyi (1944) makes such an argument.
4 Another good example of the interplay between government and the market is the Securities and Exchange Commission established June 6, 1934. Its mission is three-fold: Protect investors; maintain fair, orderly, and efficient markets; and facilitate capital formation. It was designed to restore much-needed trust in the markets after the 1929 stock market crash. Without trust, markets do not work. Ironically, we look to the government to maintain/restore trust in the market, so that markets can do their job, i.e., produce needed goods and services.
5 A complementary pair is defined as "two apparently different entities (and even presented as mutually exclusive) that have a deeper relationship" (Boyd and Reardon, 2020, p. 472). Complementary pairs are central to eastern religion and quantum physics.
6 We say 'might' because it isn't obvious that this will happen: Competition could result in low wages, and/or exploitation of workers or other stakeholders of the firm. Competition is used here as both a noun—the number of firms competing in an industry, and as a verb—the process of competing and developing a competitive advantage.
7 This discussion relies heavily on (Reardon et al., 2018, pp. 60–64).
8 We use the terms 'firm' and 'corporate' interchangeably, even though there is a definitional distinction.
9 For a classic discussion of corporate power, see Edwards (1955).
10 This definition is widespread, with an unknown genesis.
11 For a further discussion, see Boyd and Reardon (2020, pp. 68–70).
12 For a detailed presentation, see Reardon et al. (2018, pp. 177–179). Conducting a stakeholder analysis logically leads to game theory and system dynamics, both beyond the confines of this book.

13 A "hard distinction is not something that nature itself recognizes, where the distinction is soft and fluid, and everything is in constant flux shaping and morphing into everything else" (Boyd and Reardon, 2020, p. 69).

14 From Machiavelli, we obtain the word 'Machiavellian' whereby craft and deceit are justified in pursuing and maintaining political power. In the context of stakeholder analysis, "a firm's ethical behavior can be judged by how it deals with its less powerful stakeholders" (Reardon et al., 2018, p. 179).

15 Here, we use the word 'against' since the traditional essence of power is to force another party to act contrary to its wishes.

16 Named for its primary Congressional sponsor, Senator John Sherman (Republican, Ohio).

17 See our **Oil Industry** chapter.

18 These points are taken directly from 'Consumer groups voice opposition to Exxon-Mobil merger' (1999).

19 In addition, under the Clayton Act, "mergers and acquisitions accomplished through the purchase of physical assets, such as plant and equipment, were not restricted [so that] this legislation affected companies of different size disproportionately" (Ramirez and Eigen-Zucchi, 2001, p. 159). This loophole was filled by the 1950 Kefauver Act.

20 A good example is David Ricardo's 'Theory of Comparative Advantage', which was developed to maintain Great Britain's dominant position during the early stages of the Industrial Revolution. Despite being constructed entirely by special interests, it is now treated as sacrosanct by both policymakers and economics professors (Yu, 2009).

21 See our discussion in **The Oil Industry** of the specific firms involved in the breakup, and their evolution.

22 The full citation is: *United States of America v. Microsoft Corporation*, 253 F.3d 34 (D.C. Cir. 2001).

23 Verizon is a member of the 30-firm **Dow Jones Industrial Average**, invited April 8, 2004. AT&T, invited way back on October 4, 1916, was dropped from the Dow, March 19, 2015.

24 For an interesting discussion, see Archer-Ventures (2023).

25 For a classic discussion of natural monopoly, see Kahn (1988 II, pp. 113–171).

26 The telephone was invented in 1876 by Alexander Graham Bell; American Telephone & Telegraph was incorporated in 1885.

27 For a further discussion, see Reardon et al. (2018, pp. 188–194).

28 The peace symbol defined an era like no other, "Originally designed as a symbol for the British antinuclear proliferation movement…the divided circle mark—derived by overlapping the flag-semaphore signals for the letters N and D to stand for nuclear disarmament—itself proliferated as an open-source logo for global antiwar and counterculture movements" (Rock, 2024, p. 10).

29 For a helpful discussion, see Birch et al. (2017, especially, pp. 274–289).

30 This *New York Times* editorial offers several proposals for so doing.

31 One of history's better-known examples: On February 14, 1876, Alexander Graham Bell and Elisha Gray separately applied for patents for the telephone. The US Supreme Court awarded the patent to Mr. Bell for applying first. Ironically, Mr. Gray was delayed due to a snowstorm traveling to Washington from Philadelphia.

32 For an interesting and provocative discussion of contemporary antitrust, spanning the ideological spectrum, see Bork (2021), Klobucha (2021), and Posner (2021).

33 Concerns about corporate bigness have been continuously raised since the Civil War. For example, in his 1888 State of the Union Address, Benjamin Harrison, the United States' 23rd president, said "Corporations, which should be the carefully restrained creatures of the law and servants of the people, are fast becoming the people's masters" (quoted in Richardson, 2023, p. 223).
34 For a discussion of transformational thinking, see our **Net Zero** chapter.
35 This question very closely paraphrases Piketty's declarative statement (2022 p. 217).

References

Archer-Ventures (2023) 'The Breakup of AT&T: What Happened to the Baby Bells?' *Medium*, June 13, https://npr.org.

Birch, Kean, Mark Peacock, Richard Wellen, Caroline Shenaz Hossein, Sonya Scott, and Alberto Salazar (2017) *Business and Society: A Critical Introduction*, Zed Books, London.

Block, Fred, (2023) 'The Habitation Economy,' *Dissent*, Vol. 7, No. 3, Fall, pp. 29–40.

Brown, H. Claire (2023) 'A Game of Chicken,' *The New York Times Magazine*, December 3, pp. 36–39, pp. 60–63.

Bork, Robert (2021) *The Antitrust Paradox: A Policy at War with Itself*, Bork Publishing.

Boyd, Graham and Jack Reardon (2020) *Rebuild the Economy, Leadership, and You: A Toolkit for Builders of a Better World*, Evolutesix, London.

'Consumer groups voice opposition to Exxon-Mobil merger' (1999) *Oil & Gas Journal*, October 25, (ogj.com).

Edwards, Corwin (1955) 'Conglomerate Bigness as a Source of Power,' in *Business Concentration and Price Policy*, National Bureau of Economic Research/Princeton University Press, Princeton, N.J, pp. 331–351.

'Free Exchange: Internet Monopoly,' (2023) *The Economist,* October 21.

Fullbrook, Edward (2009) 'The Meltdown and Economics Textbooks,' in Jack Reardon (Ed.) *The Handbook of Pluralist Economics Education*, Routledge, London, pp. 17–23.

Kahn, Alfred (1988) *The Economics of Regulation: Principles and Institutions*, The MIT Press, Cambridge, Mass.

Klobucha, Amy (2021) *Antitrust: Taking on Monopoly Power from the Gilded Age*, Knopf, New York.

Korten, David C. (1996) *When Corporations Rule the World*, Berrett-Koehler, San Fransisco.

Machiavelli, Niccolo (1532 [1988]) *The Prince*, Oxford University Press, Oxford, UK.

Marx, Karl and Frederich Engels (1848 [1960]) *The Communist Manifesto*, Oxford University Press, Oxford, UK.

Mueller, Willard F. (1990) 'Conglomerates: A Non-Industry,' in Adams, Walter (Ed.) *The Structure of American Industry*, 8th ed, MacMillan, New York, pp. 318–348.

Piketty, Thomas (2022) *A Brief History of Equality*, Belknap Press, Cambridge, Mass.

Polanyi, Karl (1944) *The Great Transformation: The Political and Economic Origins of Our Time*, Beacon Press, Boston.

Posner, Eric (2021) *How Antitrust Failed Workers*, Oxford University Press, Oxford, UK.

Ramirez, Carlos D., and Christian Eigen-Zucchi (2001) 'Understanding the Clayton Act of 1914: An analysis of the interest group hypothesis, *Public Choice*, Vol. 106. No. 1 / 2, pp. 157–181.

Richardson, Heather Cox (2023) *Democracy Awakening: Notes on the State of America*, Viking, New York.

Rifkin, Jeremy (2014) *The Zero Marginal Cost Society*, Palgrave MacMillan, New York.

Rock, Michael (2024) 'A Sign Battered by Time,' *The New York Times*, March 31, The Sunday Opinion section, p. 10.

'Save America's Patent System' editorial (2022) *The New York Times*, April 16, The Sunday Opinion section, p. 8.

Schumpeter, Joseph A. (1994 [1942]) *Capitalism, Socialism and Democracy*, Routledge, London.

Smith, Adam (1976 [1776]) *The Wealth of Nations*, University of Chicago Press, Chicago.

Standing, Guy (2016) *The Corruption of Capitalism: Why Rentiers Thrive and Work Does Not Pay*, Biteback Publishing, London.

'The Trustbusters of Tech' (2023) *The Economist*, November 18, p. 62.

Wu, Tim (2018) *The Curse of Bigness: Antitrust in the New Gilded Age*, Columbia Global Reports, New York.

Yu, Fu-Lai Tony (2009) 'A Human Agency Approach to the Economics of International Trade,' *International Journal of Pluralism and Economics Education*, Vol. 1, Nos. 1–2, pp. 22–36.

Part IV
International Governance

22 The United Nations

The Issue: The United Nations is part of a rules based global order, established at the end of WWII, that has provided stability and predictability. Like any institution, the UN is not perfect and can surely be criticized on a host of issues; but at the same time, it serves a useful purpose in a violent and chaotic world. At the very least, the UN has prevented the outbreak of a global war, and it has been instrumental in steering the world toward sustainability with the publication of its 17 Sustainable Development Goals in 2015. That doesn't mean that we should view the UN's mission and presence as set in stone; rather, like any institution, it can be modified as times change. Whether or not the UN needs modification is a worthy issue to discuss post-2024. Needless to say, the United States would be best positioned as an insider, rather than an outsider.

22.1 Historical Origins

The UN traces its lineage to the League of Nations (formed in January 1920 in Geneva). As part of Woodrow Wilson's 14 Points, the League was an ambitious plan to maintain peace after WWI.[1] However, the US Senate, and specifically, Henry Cabot Lodge (R., Mass.), chair of the Senate Foreign Relations Committee, was instrumental in rejecting USA membership. The Senate exhorted the United States to safeguard its own interests rather than eagerly engage in an international conflict.

The United Nations was officially conceptualized during a 1945 conference in San Francisco. On June 26, 1945, 50 nations signed a declaration creating the Charter of the United Nations, with Poland adding its signature in October. In an excellent book, *The Shield of Achilles: War, Peace and the Course of History* (2002, p. 356), author Philip Bobbitt, discussing the UN's provenance wrote, "the international society that we have today, manifested in the UN General Assembly...has been shaped by the Long War (1914–1990), which he defined as "an epochal war fought to determine whether the 19th century imperial constitutional order would be replaced by nation states governed by communism, fascism, or parliamentarianism" (Bobbitt, 2002, p. 24).

DOI: 10.4324/9781003591856-26

The UN charter took effect October 15, 1945. New York was chosen as host of the United Nations for four interconnected reasons (Mires, 2015):

- A reluctance for a European headquarters, given the former presence of the League of Nations (Geneva).
- America was equidistant (more or less) between Europe and Asia.
- It was hoped that locating the UN in the United States would jar the United States out of its 1930s isolationism, which was thought by many Europeans to have abetted the rise of German fascism.
- John D. Rockefeller's gift of $8.5 million to purchase land along the East River, where the present headquarters is located.

22.2   The UN's Mission

Since 1945, the UN's overall mission has remained constant: To be the one place on Earth where all the world's nations can gather, discuss common problems, and find shared solutions that benefit all of humanity. According to the UN Charter's preamble, signed 1945,

> We the peoples of the United Nations, determined to save succeeding generations from the scourge of war, which twice in our lifetime has brought untold sorrow to mankind, and to reaffirm faith in fundamental human rights, in the dignity and worth of the human person, in the equal rights of men and women and of nations large and small, and to establish conditions under which justice and respect for the obligations arising from treaties and other sources of international law can be maintained, and to promote social progress and better standards of life in larger freedom.
>
> (United Nations Charter, n.d.)

Since 1945, the UN has added 142 nations for a total of 193. The following nations are not (yet) fully recognizable members: Vatican City and Palestine, which are admitted as observer states; along with Kosovo, Taiwan, and Western Sahara (World Population Review, 2024). (We will discuss the special nature of **Palestine** and **Tiawan** later in the book). Here, we can say that Palestine and China are in a classic catch-22, since "It is actually quite unusual for a country to exist without becoming a UN member, simply because one of the required steps in becoming a country is to be recognized by the United Nations" (World Population Review, 2024).

As enshrined in the UN charter "nations seek to renounce the use of force as a means of international policy while pledging to respect the independence, sovereignty, and territorial integrity of all countries" (Scholz, 2023, p. 27).

The UN's mission covers five broad areas[2]:

- **Maintain international peace and security**: A principal objective following the devastation of WWII and WWI. To fulfill its mission, the UN assists parties to make peace, as well as deploying peacekeepers and envoys.
- **Protect human rights:** Centered by the UN's Universal Declaration of Human Rights and the Human Rights Council, based in Geneva. On February 24, 2022, UN Secretary General Antonio Guterres launched a clarion 'Call to Action for Human Rights.'
- **Deliver humanitarian aid**: To help with natural and human-made disasters, coordinated through its office, 'Coordination of Human Affairs.'
- **Support sustainable development and climate action**: This is conducted along three avenues: (1) The dissemination of the 17 sustainability goals, which is a recipe for sustainable living. Central to these goals is the idea that sustainability comprises three dimensions: Environmental, social, and economic. Each dimension is part of the whole, which functions like a three-legged stool[3]; (2) the Intergovernmental Panel on Climate Change, which assesses research on climate change (see **Climate Change**); and (3) the Conference of the Parties (COPs) which brings nations together in order to coordinate policy on climate change. Note: The Paris 2015 COP decreed that we should prevent the global temperature from rising more than 1.5 degrees Celsius since 1800.
- **Uphold international law:** Focusing on disarmament, human rights, migration, international crimes, and the conduct of war. The UN operates the International Court of Justice, its principal judicial organ, located in the Hague, Netherlands.

According to Article 7 of the UN Charter, the UN's principal organs shall be a(n):

- **General Assembly:** Open to all members (i.e., nations) with each nation receiving one vote.
- **Economic and Social Council**: Which may make/initiate studies and reports on international economic, social, cultural, educational, health, and related matters and may make recommendations with respect to any such matters to the General Assembly and/or to its specialized agencies.
- **Trusteeship Council**: Guarantees that former territories are administered fairly and offered an efficacious road to statehood and independence.
- **International Court of Justice**: Explained above.
- **Secretariat:** Comprising "the Secretary-General and tens of thousands of international UN staff members who carry out the day-to-day work of the UN as mandated by the General Assembly and the Organization's other principal bodies. The Secretary-General is Chief Administrative Officer of the Organization, appointed by the General Assembly on the recommendation of the Security Council for a five-year, renewable term (UN, 2023b)."

- **Security Council:** Composed of 15 members: Five permanent and 10 non-permanent elected on a rotating basis. The Security Council is primarily responsible for the maintenance of international peace and security. The five permanent members, China, France, Russia, the United Kingdom, and the United States, have a veto over matters that come before the Security Council, but not over matters in the General Assembly. Interestingly, the Charter does not explicitly use the term veto, instead relying on the language of Article 27, "Decisions of the Security Council on all other matters shall be made by an affirmative vote of nine members including the concurring votes of the permanent members." Nevertheless, the language's effect is the same. This passage recognizes that if one of the five permanent nations abstains, then the resolution under discussion will not be affected. Interestingly, "in order to support the 1945 UN Charter, the USSR insisted on a unanimous vote [of the Security Council] to authorize UN military intervention, a decision which seemed sound at the time, but today is seen as crippling" (Gruner, 2022, p. 140).

22.3   The UN Today

Given its multifaceted objectives, it should be no surprise that today, member nations will emphasize different objectives based on their own interests. For example, here in the West, and especially the United States, we point to the UN's emphasis on human rights, while Russia and China, for example, point to the UN's unambiguous emphasis on national sovereignty, non-interference in internal affairs, territorial integrity, and the right of the people to determine their own future, i.e., Article 2(Section 7) of the UN charter,

> Nothing contained in the present Charter shall authorize the United Nations to intervene in matters which are essentially within the domestic jurisdiction of any state or shall require the Members to submit such matters to settlement under the present Charter.

This pledge of non-interference is a vestige of the League of Nations' attempt to create a world comprised of sovereign nation states based on the covenant of law (Bobbitt, 2002, p. 477). Obviously, international order would be impossible if every state considered itself entitled to arrange the internal affairs of any other state. But at the same time, a palpable disadvantage is to oblige "the international community to turn a blind eye to anything, no matter how awful, that a government does within its borders" (Mandelbaum, 2003, pp. 190–191). Indeed, Bobbitt quips tongue-in-cheek that "Perhaps we should be grateful that Hitler invaded Poland, for otherwise we might have been treated to the spectacle of the society of states standing by while the Holocaust efficiently preceded as an internal matter" (Bobbitt, 2002, pp. 471–472).

In a survey of 26 nations, the Pew Research Center (Fagan, 2023) found that "a median of 63% across 24 countries see the UN in a positive light, while 28% view it in a negative light." At the positive end are Poland, Kenya, South Korea, and Sweden, all over 80%, while Israel and Japan are at the negative end (62% and 50%, respectively).

Here, in the United States, 58% of Americans positively view the UN, down from 61% in 2022, while 40% have a negative view. In the United States, a sharp difference exists between Democrats and Republicans: 79% of Democrats express a favorable view, compared to only 34% of Republicans. Reasons to be in favor, according to the Survey, include the global effort to promote peace, human rights, and economic cooperation. While reasons to be against include a belief that the UN is antagonist toward the interests of the United States; that its best interests would not be served multilaterally by engaging with other nations; that America should come first; that the United States is the preponderant contributor to the UN (the US contributes 22% of UN total operating costs) without receiving concomitant benefits; and among the MAGA fringe, a belief that the UN is part of a global conspiracy.

22.4 Conclusion

The UN is part of a rules-based global order, established at the end of WWII, that has provided stability and predictability, and has prevented the outbreak of a global war. But, today as nations have turned inward, ensconced in a zero-sum world view that incentivizes raw power where might is right ('*The New Economic Order*,' 2024, p. 14.), the institutions which established the contours of the post-WWII global order have been eroded both in trust and in efficacy. Like any institution, the UN is not perfect and can surely be criticized on a host of issues, but at the same time, it serves a useful purpose in a violent and chaotic world, and it has been commendable in steering the world towards sustainable living. That doesn't mean that we should view the UN's mission as set in stone; rather, like any institution, it can be modified as times change. Whether it needs modification is an issue to be discussed post-2024. The United States would be best equipped to do so as an insider, rather than as an outsider.

Notes

1 Given the ubiquity of war throughout human history, it is interesting to ponder why such a proposal was not made earlier. Of course, we needed the development of nation states, which were a rather late development in human history. Immanuel Kant gets the ball rolling, so to speak; see Milicic (2021).
2 This discussion is based on United Nations 2023a and 2023b.
3 For a discussion of these goals and their interrelationships, see Reardon et al. (2018, pp. 17–19). This book, which aligns economics and economics education with the SDGs, was motivated by the UN's publication of the 17 SDGs.

References

Bobbitt, Philip (2002) *The Shield of Achilles: War, Peace, and the Course of History*, Anchor Books, New York.

Fagan, Moira (2023) 'People across 24 countries continue to view UN favorably' Pew Research Center, UN viewed favorably among people in 24 countries | Pew Research Center

Gruner, Ronald (2022) *We the Presidents: How American Presidents Shaped the Last Century*, Libratum Press, Naples, Florida.

Mandelbaum Michael (2003) *The Ideas that Conquered the World: Peace, Democracy, and Free Markets in the Twenty-First Century*, Public Affairs, New York.

Milicic, Nenad (2021) 'Kant on Just War and International Order, *Philosophy and Society*, Vol. 32, No. 1, pp. 105–127.

Mires, Charlene (2015) *Capital of the World: The Race to Host the United Nations*, New York University Press, New York.

Reardon, Jack, Maria Madi, Molly Scott Cato (2018) *Introducing a New Economics: Pluralist, Sustainable, Progressive*, Pluto Books, London.

Scholz, Olaf, (2023) 'The Global Zeitenwende: How to Avoid a New Cold War in a Multipolar Era,' *Foreign Affairs*, Jan/Feb, Vol. 102, No. 1, pp. 22–38.

'The New Economic Order' (2024) *The Economist*, May 14, p. 7.

United Nations (2023a) 'Our Work,'. https://www.un.org/

United Nations (2023b) 'About Us,' https://www.un.org/

'United Nations Charter' (n.d.) https://www.un.org/

World Population Review (2024) 'Countries Not in the United Nations,' (worldpopulationreview.com).

23 NATO

The Issue: The North Atlantic Treaty Organization (NATO) was established in 1949. It has since served the United States, Canada, and Europe reasonably well. At the heart of NATO is the principle of collective defense—meaning that an attack against one nation is considered as an attack against all. Needed questions to ask post-2024: Is NATO still relevant? If so, what is its purpose/mission? And is there a role to play for the United States?

23.1 Historical Foundations

On April 16, 1939, Joseph Stalin, the leader of the USSR, proposed to Neville Chamberlain, Britain's prime minister, that the three World War I Allies, the UK, the USSR (formerly Russia), and France, should form a triple alliance to counter Germany's European aggression (Bullock, 1991, pp. 603–609; pp. 617–618). At that time, Germany had already annexed Austria and partitioned Czechoslovakia. Anyone who understood Hitler or even read his autobiography knew that he was just getting started: His longstanding and unwavering goal was expanding east to obtain living space for Germany's growing population. Chamberlain, however, abruptly refused Stalin's overture. Rebuffed, Stalin, increasingly worried about a potential German invasion (for good reason), approached Hitler for a deal. Germany responded affirmatively and within months, the two nations had signed the Ribbentrop-Molotov Non-Aggression Pact—one of the most significant treaties of the 20th century. Signed on August 22, 1939, in addition to secretly carving up eastern Europe, its essence was a mutual non-aggression pledge. Ten days later, with the Treaty in hand, Germany invaded Poland, starting World War Two.

Had the Triple Alliance been formed, it would be interesting to speculate how history might have evolved. Surely, the United States would have been invited as a logical choice, perhaps not immediately but certainly after Pearl Harbor? And who knows if Germany would have invaded Poland, especially

DOI: 10.4324/9781003591856-27

as recent documents reveal a potential Soviet presence along the Polish border large enough to forestall/discourage any attack (Gruner, 2022, p. 433).

Speculation is just that: Speculation.

Let's fast forward to 1944, when it was evident to all but the most stalwart (and blinded) ideologues that Germany would lose the war in Europe. While the allies were meeting in **Bretton Woods** (July 1944) to carve out a new post-WWII global economic order, thoughts began to circulate about what to do about Germany after the War, specifically, how to prevent future German aggression. After all, Germany was critical in precipitating two world wars.

At the Potsdam Conference (July 17–August 2, 1945) held after the defeat of Germany, the United States, the UK, and the USSR agreed to partition Germany into four occupation zones. The Soviet zone eventually became East Germany, and the other three zones eventually coalesced into West Germany. Berlin, Germany's capital, despite being entirely in what would become East Germany, was partitioned into East and West.

Thanks to the Marshall Plan[1] (begun in 1948) which funneled millions of dollars into rebuilding Europe, and particularly, Germany, West Germany, and West Berlin were growing and prospering. Worried that East Germany would be outshone by the west, the Soviets ordered an ill-conceived blockade of West Berlin beginning June 24, 1948. Confident that the blockade would weaken the West and its resolve, it had the opposite effect. Almost immediately, the United States began successfully airlifting food and supplies into West Berlin. The USSR was forced to capitulate on May 12, 1949. Looking back, the airlift, "in its resistance to a tyrannical adversary, in its logistical success, and its magnanimity to a defeated enemy…was one of America's finest moments" (Gruner, 2022, p. 138)

It became clear to all that the USSR, rather than Germany, was the new aggression threat in Europe. In direct response to the Soviet blockade, on April 4, 1949, the North Atlantic Treaty Organization[2] was signed in Washington, D.C. by Belgium, Canada, Denmark, France, Iceland, Italy, Luxembourg, the Netherlands, Norway, Portugal, the UK, and the United States.[3] With an eye toward the USSR, the members pledged mutual military support if one member was attacked,[4] while also trying to wean a more prosperous West Germany into a new western Europe.

However, not all Americans supported the NATO; there were significant misgivings which still persist to this day. Walter Lippman, for example, perhaps America's best-known journalist at the time, if not the most influential, wrote,

> I am convinced that the question of war or peace hangs upon the strength of the local defenses…the attempt to create [NATO] will not only exhaust western Europe and strain the US but would throw western Europe into political convulsions… [*The] expansion of NATO to Russia's frontier would provoke and seal the division of the Continent.*
>
> (Quoted in Steel, 1981, p. 504; emphasis added)

And Senator Robert Taft[5] (R. Ohio) warned that NATO and its mutual protection provision would give the USA president vast powers to send American troops to war abroad without Congressional approval[6] (Steel, 1981, p. 460).

In 1954, the USSR applied for NATO membership, although the USSR's sincerity is not entirely known. In retrospect, if accepted, it could have changed the evolution of the mid-20th century. But the application was rejected, largely for ideological reasons; after all, the USSR was socialist, and the NATO nations were capitalist. Then, rubbing salt in the wounds of a rejected USSR, the NATO accepted West Germany as a member.

Infuriated and worried about their own safety given a rearmed West Germany (the USSR lost 20 million citizens during WWII), the USSR countered with the formation of the Warsaw Pact. It was signed in Warsaw, Poland, on May 14, 1955, with eight signatories: Albania, Bulgaria, Czechoslovakia, East Germany, Hungary, Poland, Romania, and the USSR. Like NATO, the eight nations pledged defensive mutual support, but unlike NATO, which was democratically run, the Warsaw pact was spearheaded by Moscow, which was determined to use the Pact nations as a territorial buffer zone against NATO aggression.

The USSR had now become the preponderant threat to European peace and security. The United States was worried about further Soviet expansion into eastern Europe, while the USSR resented the United States' international aggressiveness. Fueled by mutual distrust and enmity, a cold war developed which thankfully never developed into an open direct war.[7]

The Cold War had unofficially begun February 22, 1946, with George Kennan's 5363-word telegram to James Byrnes, the USA Secretary of State. In the telegram, Kennan, an American diplomat stationed in Moscow, warned of the Soviet threat and the necessary to understand our adversary and to be able to respond as needed. His telegram became the basis of USA policy toward the USSR, cementing a policy of adversarial strength and containment. Kennan wrote,

> Soviet power, unlike that of Hitlerite Germany, is neither schematic nor adventuristic. It does not work by fixed plans. It does not take unnecessary risks. Impervious to logic of reason, it is highly sensitive to logic of force. For this reason it can easily withdraw—and usually does when strong resistance is encountered at any point. Thus, if the adversary has sufficient force and makes clear his readiness to use it, he rarely has to do so. If situations are properly handled there need be no prestige-engaging showdowns.
>
> (George Kennan's Long Telegram, 1946)

The Cold War was a geopolitical and militarily contest between East and West, more specifically between the United States and the USSR, during which the United States, "had committed the greatest portion of their military, scientific, and technological resources…and an incalculable amount of their psychic energy" (Johnson, 2002, p. 2).

23.2   The End of the Cold War

The Cold War officially ended December 25, 1991, with the dissolution of the USSR.[8] Logically, with the dissolution of its major adversary, along with its historical raison d'être, NATO could have ceased and desisted, but that did not happen. Economically, logistically, and ideologically (at least from the United States' perspective), it did not make sense to disband. NATO was too large, too institutionalized, too cemented among friends, and too wedded to American defense spending,

> America, the world's exporter of weapons and supported by $100 billion of defense spending and viewing itself as the world's peacekeeper… contributed to a continuation rather than a de-escalation of America's cold war and associated military spending.
>
> (Gruner, 2022, pp. 431–432)

NATO was also committed to protecting the smaller nations of eastern and central Europe under threat from Russia. But, at the same time, to justify its continued existence, NATO needed a new ideological enemy. If a major provision of the NATO treaty was to provide mutual military protection, then who was it protecting against? Who was the enemy? The choice was made to turn against Russia. At the time, however, there was no good reason. Russia was economically and militarily a basket case. It was not really capitalist but not really socialist, and certainly too weak to be a threat to anyone.

It was one thing for the EU to retain and keep its modus operandi and modus vivendi; and in a way, this could be justified, especially vis-à-vis any future unknown threats; and to protect smaller nations (e.g., the Baltic states who since the Great Depression were occupied first by the USSR, then by Germany, then by the USSR) who were inherently worried about their big neighbor to the east. But it was another matter to deliberately expand east all the way to the Russian border. While this could be justified in terms of providing security for Europe's smaller nations, at the same time, it was seen by Russia as deliberately provocative.

During the early to mid-1990s, applications for NATO membership surged from nations of Eastern Europe, from former members of the Warsaw Pact, and even former members of the USSR such as Latvia, Lithuania, and Estonia. George Kennan who, at the time, was enjoying his reputation as one of the 20th century's most erudite and perspicacious statesmen, warned against NATO expanding east. Kennan knew Russia and understood its people probably better than anyone else. As the architect of the Cold War doctrine of containment (i.e., containing Russia), he was certainly no Russian dove. He argued that expanding east was not only gratuitous but needlessly provocative,

> Expanding NATO would be the most fateful error of American policy in the entire post-cold-war era....Such a decision may be expected to inflame the nationalistic, anti-Western and militaristic tendencies in Russian opinion; to have an adverse effect on the development of Russian democracy; to restore the atmosphere of the cold war to East-West relations, and to impel Russian foreign policy in directions decidedly not to our liking... It is, of course, unfortunate that Russia should be confronted with such a challenge at a time when its executive power is in a state of high uncertainty and near-paralysis. And it is doubly unfortunate considering the total lack of any necessity for this move. Why, with all the hopeful possibilities engendered by the end of the cold war, should East-West relations become centered on the question of who would be allied with whom and, by implication, against whom in some fanciful, totally unforeseeable and most improbable future military conflict?
>
> (Kennan, 1997)

NATO rejected Kennan's warning. Instead, NATO aggressively (and inexorably) marched east, even inviting all former members of the Warsaw Pact to join. Russia as the largest emerging entity from the USSR was humiliated and angered.

23.3   NATO and Russia

In 2000, newly elected Russian president, Vladimir Putin approached George Robertson, then the NATO leader (1999–2003) with possible feelers to join NATO. Putin later told David Frost on a BBC interview (March 5, 2000) that he "would not rule out joining NATO if and when Russia's views are taken into account as those of an equal partner.. Russia is part of European culture. And I cannot imagine my own country in isolation from Europe and what we often call the civilized world" (Rankin, 2021).

But this would soon change. In 2004, NATO extended membership to Romania, Bulgaria, Slovakia, Slovenia, Latvia, Estonia, and Lithuania, all part of the former Soviet sphere; the latter three part of the USSR itself. And just as Kennan predicted, this kindled Putin's anger, who was already simmering at the dissolution of the Warsaw Pact and the USSR. This provocation (among others) turned Putin inward, setting Russia on a nationalistic, restrengthening, and defensive posturing vis-à-vis Europe, which eventually would turn offensive with the invasion of Ukraine. Putin's bellicosity toward the West was crystallized in a speech (February 12, 2007) at the Berlin Security Conference in which he criticized the existing US-based global order, informing the world that Russia was going to challenge it (it had already begun so earlier that year) and re-make the world to better comport with Russia's interests.[9]

It is interesting to speculate that if Russia was extended membership (or invited to join) which by the way could never have happened,[10] if today's events would have turned out differently. Would Russia have retained its hatred and distrust toward the West? How would have the smaller nations reacted to being in the same organization as the former occupier? It is hard to say. Although what we do know is that Russia has used the NATO threat to consolidate power, to direct the threat to the motherland against the belligerent West.

23.4   Today's NATO

According to its web page, NATO's preponderant objective is,

> to secure a lasting peace in Europe, based on its member countries' common values of individual liberty, democracy, human rights and the rule of law. These shared values unite a diverse group of Allies on both sides of the Atlantic, and NATO embodies the transatlantic bond between them, whereby the security of Allies in Europe and North America is inextricably linked. The principle of collective defense – meaning that an attack against one Ally is considered as an attack against all Allies – is at the heart of NATO. This means that no single member country is forced to rely solely on its national capabilities to meet its essential national security objectives. The resulting sense of shared security among NATO members contributes to stability in the Euro-Atlantic area.
>
> (North Atlantic Treaty Organization, 2023)

The Treaty derives its authority from Article 51 of the United Nations Charter (see United Nations), which reaffirms the inherent right of independent states to individual or collective defense. NATO also works beyond its borders to help further peace via diplomacy in an increasingly volatile world,

> Since the outbreak of crises and conflicts beyond Allied borders can jeopardise this core objective, the Alliance also contributes to peace and stability through crisis prevention and management, and through partnerships with other organisations and countries across the globe. Essentially, NATO not only helps to defend the territory of its members, but also engages – where possible and when necessary – to project its values further afield, prevent and manage crises, stabilise post-conflict situations and support reconstruction.
>
> (North Atlantic Treaty Organization, 2023)

These core principles are reiterated in NATO's Strategic Concept, adopted in Madrid, June 29, 2022,

> Our new Strategic Concept reaffirms that NATO's key purpose is to ensure our collective defence, based on a 360-degree approach. It defines the Alliance's three core tasks: deterrence and defence; crisis prevention and management; and cooperative security. We underscore the need to significantly strengthen our deterrence and defence as the backbone of our Article 5 commitment to defend each other.
>
> (North Atlantic Treaty Organization, 2022a)

In addition, NATO is actively working to solve today's pressing problems. Specifically, "the Strategic Concept emphasises the cross-cutting importance of investing in technological innovation and integrating climate change, human security and the 'Women, Peace and Security' agenda across all our core tasks" (North Atlantic Treaty Organization, 2022a).

NATO acknowledges that today's Europe is volatile (a volatility that it, ironically, helped to create) with Russia as the EU's principal threat but certainly not the only one. At the same time, NATO's aggressive expansion cast has "restore[d] the atmosphere of the cold war to East-West relations, and [has] impelled Russian foreign policy in directions decidedly not to our liking" (Kennan, 1997). At least for the near future, this East West confrontation is set in stone. We don't see any path forward other than active containment and adept diplomacy—easier said than done. In the meantime, the current geopolitical instability will continue.

As this book goes to press (October 2024), NATO voted to initiate accession meetings with Ukraine. It takes several years for an accession to turn into a formal acceptance/admittance. The vote was almost unanimous with Hungary abstaining, claiming that Ukraine wasn't ready. To ensure the NATO-mandated unanimity for accession, the Hungarian rep was asked to leave the room when the voting took place.

It was Ukraine's overtures toward the West, specifically the NATO and the EU, that factored in **Russia's** 2022 invasion of Ukraine.[11] Russia considered Ukraine to be in its sphere of influence, with cultural, linguistic, and historical ties too close to sever. And, Ukraine, for the most part, looked west to Europe and away from the East, although of course like other former republics of the USSR, there were sections of Ukraine that continued looking East.

In addition to NATO's 12 founding members, 20 nations have been added via ten rounds of enlargement:[12] Albania (2009), Bulgaria (2004), Croatia (2009), Czechia (1999), Estonia (2004), Finland (2023), Germany (1955), Greece (1952), Hungary (1999), Latvia (2004), Lithuania (2004), Montenegro (2017), North Macedonia (2020), Poland (1999), Romania (2004), Slovakia (2004), Slovenia (2004), Spain (1982), Sweden (2024), and Turkey (1952). Ironically, the Russian invasion of Ukraine has pushed many nations into NATO's arms, most notably Finland and Sweden.

After Russia's annexation of Crimea in 2014, NATO members agreed to spend 2% of their GDP on defense by 2024. In a June 17, 2024, speech at the Wilson Center (in Washington), NATO Secretary General Jens Stoltenberg noted,

> When we made the Pledge to invest 2% of GDP in defence back at the Wales Summit of NATO in 2014, only three Allies met that mark – and that was the United States, Greece, and the United Kingdom. Just five years ago, there were still less than 10 Allies that spent 2% of GDP on defence. But later today when I see President Biden, I will announce new defence spending figures for all Allies. And I can already now reveal that this year more than 20 Allies (out of 32 nations) will spend at least 2% of GDP on defence.
>
> (Stoltenberg, 2024)

Spurred by Russia's aggression, and the possibility of a Trump victory in November 2024, NATO is sharply kicking up its ante. As of NATO's 75th anniversary, July 2024, the number of nations meeting their 2% target is now 23 out of 32.

23.5   Conclusion

NATO is in the center of foreign affairs, global peace, and geopolitical security. It is at the center of how to counter Russian aggression. In our increasingly volatile world, the United States cannot afford to divorce NATO, and likewise, NATO cannot afford to divorce the United States. The United States needs NATO and the NATO needs the United States. Given the increasing importance of **Artificial Intelligence**, especially its potential for catastrophic annihilation, NATO and the United States need to work together. Likewise with the systemic challenges posed by **Climate Change**—some of which pose security threats—NATO and the United States need to work together to construct effective solutions.

Notes

1 George Marshall, a former general who played a key role in the Allied victory during WWII, was Secretary of State under President Truman. Worried about possible Soviet activity in Europe, Marshall, speaking at Harvard University's commencement, June 5, 1947, proposed a plan with USA dollars to rebuild Europe (largely in the image of the United States), "it is logical that the United States should do whatever it is able to do to assist in the return of normal economic health in the world, without which there can be no political stability and no assured peace"

(George C. Marshall Speech at Harvard: Marshall Plan,' 1947). Officially known as the European Recovery Program, and eventually the Marshall Plan, it went into effect in 1948. Incidentally, according to his biographer, Marshall's associates, "have placed him in the company of George Washington and Robert E. Lee, as one who served his country selflessly without ambition or reward" (Pogue, 1991, p. 703).

2 For the founding treating and historical discussion, see (North Atlantic Treaty Organization, 2022b).

3 On March 14, 1948, Belgium, France, UK, Luxembourg, and the Netherlands signed the Brussels Treaty, which in turn, grew out of the Dunkirk Treaty signed in 1947 by France and the UK.

4 Article 1 of the Treaty states that member parties "settle any international disputes in which they may be involved by peaceful means in such a manner that international peace and security, and justice, are not endangered, and to refrain in their international relations from the threat or use of force in any manner inconsistent with the purposes of the United Nations."

5 Robert Taft was also the co-author of one of the most important pieces of labor union legislation, the Taft Hartley Act (see **Labor Unions**). Taft was the nephew of William Howard Taft, the 37th president of the United States, and Supreme Court chief justice, 1921–1930.

6 Alexander Hamilton wrote in *The Federalist Papers,* "It is of the nature of war to increase the executive at the expense of the legislative authority" (Hamilton et al., 2003 [1787–1788], No. 8, pp. 40–41).

7 Although "America fought two indirect Cold War conflicts: Korea and Vietnam [together] costing nearly 100,000 American lives" (Johnson, 2002, p. 3). For a classic history of the Cold War, see Lukacs (1966).

8 One might look to the fall of the Berlin Wall in November 1989 as the end of the Cold War. But given events in Moscow, we think it more accurate to label the late 1980s as the beginning of a thaw in Cold War. Incidentally, the Berlin Wall, separating East and West Berlin, was constructed in August 1961 to prevent millions of refugees from leaving East Berlin to settle in the much more prosperous West Berlin.

9 We discuss this important speech in our chapter, **Iran, Russia, and North Korea**.

10 Then again, we are not sure: the USSR's NATO request during the 1950s was rejected ideologically. But Russia during the 1990s was at least moving (or perhaps slumbering would be more apt) toward capitalism. At the time, Western economists (along with representatives of the IMF and World Bank) were flocking to the former members of the USSR (especially Russia) preaching the virtues of shock therapy, i.e., a quick and abrupt, yet painful pathway to a market economy. For a discussion of Russia's market economy tribulations, see Jha (2002), who compares Russia's attempted transition with that of China and India.

11 For other factors, especially Putin's megalomania, see Ponomarenko (2024).

12 Source: North Atlantic Treaty Organization (2024).

References

Bullock, Alan, (1991) *Hitler and Stalin: Parallel Lives*, Alfred K. Knopf, New York.

'George C. Marshall Speech at Harvard: Marshall Plan,' (1947) National Archives: Harry S. Truman Library/Museum, Independence, MO. (trumanlibrary.gov).

'George Kennan's Long Telegram' (1946) George Washington University, Washington, DC (gwu.edu).

Gruner, Ronald (2022) *We the Presidents: How American Presidents Shaped the Last Century*, Libratum Press, Naples, Florida.

Hamilton, Alexander, James Madison, and John Jay (2003 [1787–1788]) *The Federalist Papers*, Bantam Books, New York.

Jha, Prem Shankar (2002) *The Perilous Road to the Market*, Pluto Press, London.

Johnson, Haynes (2002) *The Best of Times*, Harcourt, Orlando.

Kennan, George F. (1997) 'A Fateful Error,' *The New York Times*, February 5, (Opinion) (nytimes.com).

Lukacs, John (1966) *A New History of the Cold War*, 3rd ed., Anchor Books, New York.

North Atlantic Treaty Organization (2022a) 'NATO 2022 Strategic Concept' Madrid June 29, 290622-strategic-concept.pdf (nato.int).

North Atlantic Treaty Organization (2022b) 'NATO Founding Treaty,' September 2, NATO - Topic: Founding treaty.

North Atlantic Treaty Organization (2023) 'NATO's purpose,' July 4, 'NATO - Topic: NATO's purpose.

North Atlantic Treaty Organization (2024) 'NATO Member Countries,' March 11, NATO - Topic: NATO member countries.

Ponomarenko, Illia (2024) *I Will Show You How it Was*, Bloomsbury, London.

Pogue, Forrest (1991) 'George C. Marshall' *The Reader's Companion to American History*, Eric Foner and John A. Garraty, (Eds.) pp. 702–703.

Rankin, Jennifer (2021) 'Ex-NATO head says Putin wanted to join alliance early on in his rule, *The Guardian*, November 4, Ex-Nato head says Putin wanted to join alliance early on in his rule | Nato | The Guardian.

Snell, Jukka (2016) 'The Trilemma of European Economic and Monetary Integration, and its Consequences,' *European Law Journal*, Vol. 22, No. 2, pp. 157–179.

Steel, Ronald (1981) *Walter Lippman and the American Century*, Vintage Books, New York.

Stoltenberg, Jens (2024) 'Speech at the Wilson Center Auditorium,' June 17, NATO - 17-Jun.-2024, https://www.nato.int

24   The European Union

The Issue: The European Union (EU) is comprised of 27 countries, with a combined **GDP** of $14.5 trillion, making it the third largest economy after the United States and China. The EU is a union of free, sovereign, democratic states based on the rule of law. It shares many common interests with the United States. Given the multiplicity of today's global problems that need dialogue and common cooperation, e.g., **Artificial Intelligence**, **Climate Change, Immigration**, the transition to **Net Zero, Russia**, and **China**, it is in the best interest of the United States to work with the EU.

24.1   Introduction

I (Jack) taught Latvia during the USSR's final year in 1991, as well as throughout the 1990s. It was exciting both for me and for my students yet steeped in uncertainty. The eventual goal was to build a new state from the ruble of the USSR.[1] I frequently saw cadres of government officials commuting between Riga and Brussels; their briefcases stuffed with papers and memos, detailing the requisite rules, regulations, and institutions to make Latvia amenable for membership in the NATO (for mutual protection, given its tenuous border with Russia) and the European Union (EU) to begin repairing a broken-down economy, due to generations of Soviet misrule. Lativa, like its sister Baltic republics (Lithuania and Estonia) looked West with little interest in looking East (toward Russia).

Most of my students were in favor of Latvia joining NATO and the EU, although a handful lamented that Latvia, by devising its rules/institutions to comport with EU requirements, was selling its soul to become part of a greater whole. Perhaps this was the price to pay for a small nation bordering a restless giant? To retain independence only by forfeiting its uniqueness? But for many Latvians, and especially those working to form a new government based on the rule of law, freedom, and democracy, there was no choice.

DOI: 10.4324/9781003591856-28

24.2   The Birth of the EU

The Scottish philosopher David Hume, looking back at the frequent European wars of the 17th century, advocated commerce as a great recipe for peace, dramatically reducing the reasons for going to war. His advice remains true today.

The immediate impetus for the EU stemmed from the death and destruction brought about by the two world wars, both principally fought on European soil. By integrating economically, the goal was to prevent such wars from happening again. In addition, post-WWII, the high protectionism of the 1930s, was still fresh in everyone's mind,[2] as a causal factor (among many) that led to WWII.

The formal process of European economic integration began in 1951 with the Treaty of Paris which created a common market for the coal and steel industries.[3] The Treaty was signed by Belgium, France, Italy, Luxembourg, the Netherlands, and West Germany. The Treaty of Rome, signed in 1957, established a customs union[4] while renaming the Common Market the European Economic Community (EEC). The Maastricht Treaty (1992) formally established the European Union. The EU, like **NATO,** was determined to expand east and to include former members of the Warsaw Pact and former members of the USSR.[5]

As any organization expands, it brings to the fore the tension between strength in numbers and balancing the competing (and sometimes disparate) interests of its members in order to forge a common yet supra identity, while maintaining the supremacy of the laws of the greater association to which the member nations subscribe,

> If a number of political societies enter into a larger political society, the laws which the latter may enact, pursuant to the powers entrusted to it by its constitution, must necessarily be supreme over those societies, and the individuals of whom they are composed. It would otherwise be a mere treaty…
>
> (Hamilton et al., 2003 [1787–1788], No. 33, p. 188)

A not so easy balancing act for the EU, although as the manuscript goes to press (October 2024) the EU is evolving toward "towards deeper…integration," (*The Economist*, May 4, 2024, p. 46).

24.3   Today's EU

Today, the European Union is comprised of 27 countries, with a combined GDP of $14.5 trillion, making it the third largest economy after the United States and China.[6] The EU accounts for 14% of global trade, and has 448.4 million inhabitants, spread over 4 million km^2. Twenty of the 27 nations use the EURO, which formally debuted January 1, 1999, with coins and notes circulating on January 1, 2002. Germany's former chancellor, Olaf Scholz, extolled the EU as,

> a union of free sovereign, democratic states based on the rule of law… It will set global standards on trade growth, climate change, and environmental protection and will host leading research institutions and innovative businesses—a family of stable democracies enjoying unparallel social welfare and public infrastructure.
>
> (Scholz, 2023, p. 32)

The EU's objectives are as follows[7]:

- Offer freedom, security, and justice without internal borders, while also taking appropriate measures at its external borders to regulate asylum and immigration and prevent and combat crime.
- Establish an internal market.
- Achieve sustainable development based on balanced economic growth and price stability and a highly competitive market economy with full employment and social progress.
- Protect and improve the quality of the environment.
- Promote scientific and technological progress.
- Combat social exclusion and discrimination.
- Promote social justice and protection, equality between women and men, and protection of the rights of the child.
- Enhance economic, social and territorial cohesion and solidarity among EU countries
- Respect its rich cultural and linguistic diversity.
- Establish an economic and monetary union whose currency is the euro.

The EU has very strict and detailed rules for membership: The candidate nation must have political democracy, rule by law, and a free market. Croatia was the most recent nation admitted to the EU (2013). But thanks to the Russian invasion of Ukraine, nine additional nations have applied to join: Ukraine, Moldova, Bosnia-Herzegovina, Georgia, North Macedonia, Serbia, Montenegro, Albania, and Turkey; with Ukraine, Moldova, and Bosnia-Herzegovina cleared to start formal accession[8] (*The Economist*, May 18, 2024, p. 48).

The EU has also laid out strict requirements for a nation to exit. To date, only the UK has done so. In a national referendum, June 2016, the UK formally voted to leave the EU. While we do not have a crystal ball (and we are glad that we do not), we cannot say which EU nation (if any) might soon exit. As this manuscript goes to press, however, the desire to exist has decreased significantly (Henley, 2023). And, additionally "recent polling suggests that citizens in all 27 member states think of [the EU] positively, and want their country to remain in the club" (*The Economist*, May 4, 2024, p. 46).

24.4   Institutional Problems of the EU

From its inception, the EU has wanted to be much more than a financial union and a customs union, "the aim was ultimately to speak with a single voice and act as a single unit on political and monetary issues" (Mandelbaum, 2023, pp. 369–370). As such, the EU has developed global standards on trade, growth, climate change, and environmental protection. But at the same time, it has been handicapped since birth by a fundamental and inconvertible problem: An EU member nation that subscribes to the euro as a monetary unit, cannot use monetary policy to redress economic problems such as unemployment and inflation. It can only use fiscal policy (i.e., changes in government spending and/or taxation). This is problematic for the nation since

> The power to issue its own money, to make drafts on its own central bank, is the main thing which defines national independence [i.e., sovereignty]. If a country gives up or loses this power, it acquires the status of a local authority or colony.
>
> (Godley, 1992)

Forced to use only fiscal policy to solve economic problems will in turn increase government spending which, ceteris paribus, increases the deficit, the debt and interest rates (Reardon et al., 2018, p. 292). Take Greece, for example, where,

> The Euro changed everything. All of the Greek government's existing debt was redenominated into euros, a currency that the Greek government could not issue. From that point on, anyone who bought bonds from the Greek government was taking on a new kind of risk—default risk...The problem, as Greece quickly discovered, was that lenders weren't willing to buy Greek government bonds unless they got a substantial premium for the obvious risk they were taking in lending billions of euros to a currency user[9] who might have trouble paying it back. From 2009 to 2012, the interest rate on ten-year Greek government bonds rose from less than 6 percent to more than 35 percent.
>
> (Kelton, 2020, pp. 84 and 85)

When the institutional structure of the European Central Bank (roughly equivalent to the United States' Federal Reserve System) was designed/conceptualized during the late 1980s, it was assumed that after the awful inflation of the 1970s, a central bank's only job would be to control inflation, while being independent of political control, "hence Europe created a currency without a state and a currency without a government" (Piketty, 2014, p. 723).

A second institutional problem of the EU is procedural in that "public discussion of [the Maastricht proposals] was curiously impoverished" (Godley, 1992). An important problem then as now, as it provides fodder for antielitists who argue that today's institutions such as the EU have ignored the plight of the common person.[10] A broader and more democratic discussion of the strengths/weaknesses of the proposed EU could have led to a broader acceptance, and perhaps could have even led to a solution preventing the latter recessionary events (e.g., in Greece) that were to follow.

This anti-elitist view remains in full force today; and if anything, is gaining strength. In addition to precipitating the Brexit, this anti-elitism has led to the rise of right-wing populist governments in Europe and the United States.[11] And, while at this time, the EU has widespread support from citizens, that could change, due to a number of possible factors, including another global crisis.

24.5   Conclusion

The NATO and the GATT/WTO have made possible the economic relationships that became possible under the EU. But these institutions have been eroding.[12] It remains to be seen whether the EU can successively buffer this trend and survive as a global/regional institution. Perhaps, to ensure the EU's longevity, a continental-wide political authority can be established capable of reasserting control over patrimonial capitalism and private interests and of advancing the European social model in the 21st century (Piketty, 2014, pp. 730–731; Rodrik, 2011). In other words, there should be some type of progression from monetary, fiscal and even budgetary union to closer cooperation among member nations, but that doesn't look like that is happening now, nor any time soon[13] (Piketty, 2014, p. 723).

The EU and the United States share many common interests. Given the multiplicity of today's global problems that need dialogue and common cooperation, e.g., **Artificial Intelligence, Climate Change, Immigration**, the transition to **Net Zero, Russia**, and **China**, it is in the best interest of the United States to work with the EU. Nevertheless, the typical America might say that this is America, so why should we be concerned with Europe? Let them handle their own affairs. This is wrong-headed reasoning (if 'reasoning' is the right word); for the issues affecting the United States are also affecting Europe and the rest of the world. With **AI, Climate Change**, the transition to **Net Zero**, etc., there is no 'us' versus 'them.'

Notes

1 For a fascinating contemporary account, see Lieven (1994). He skillfully weaves together the past, present, and future to establish a workable and viable Baltic identity.
2 For a discussion, see our **Tariffs and Trade** chapter.
3 Information in this paragraph is taken from European Union (2024a).
4 A customs union has a common external tariff for participatory nations, whereas a free trade area (like the North American Free Trade Agreement between Canada, the United States, and Mexico) allows participatory nations to set their own tariffs (Mandelbaum, 2003, p. 488, note 42).
5 We discuss this move east and the ensuing problems in our **NATO** chapter.
6 Source for this paragraph's statistics: European Union (2024b).
7 See European Union (2024c).

8 The Maastricht Treaty signed in 1992, allows any European state to apply for EU membership that respects liberty, democracy, human rights and fundamental freedoms, and the rule of law. Any EU nation, however, can block the accession of a new nation. (*The Economist*, May 18, 2024, p. 48).

9 Countries that can issue their own currency and thus enjoy economic sovereignty are called currency issuers; all others are currency users (Kelton, 2020, pp. 17–18).

10 In addition to Godley, critics of both the EU and the EU Euro Zone abound. For a representative sample see (Patomaki, 2012; Rodrik, 2011).

11 For a cogent argument, see Snell (2016).

12 See our discussion in **The NATO and the UN.**

13 For a helpful discussion, see Van den Berg (2012, pp. 461–468).

References

'Charlemagne: In Search of European Demos' (2024) *The Economist*, May 4, 2024, p. 46.

European Union (2024a) 'Founding Agreements,' (europa.eu).

European Union (2024b) 'Key Facts and Figures,' (europa.eu).

European Union (2024c) 'Aims and Values,' Aims and values (europa.eu).

'Europe's Phoney Enlargement' (2024), *The Economist*, May 18, 2024, p. 48.

Godley, Wynne (1992) 'Maastricht and All That,' *London Review of Books*, Vol. 14, No. 9, October 8, (lrb.co.uk).

Hamilton, Alexander, James Madison, and John Jay (2003 [1787–1788]) *The Federalist Papers*, Bantam Books, New York.

Henley, Jon (2023) 'Support for leaving EU has fallen significantly across bloc since Brexit,' *The Guardian* (January 12), https://www.theguardian.com/

Kelton, Stephanie (2020) *The Deficit Myth: Modern Monetary Theory and the Birth of the People's Economy*, Public Affairs, New York.

Lieven, Anatol (1994) *The Baltic Revolution: Estonia, Latvia, Lithuania and the Path to Independence*, 2nd ed., Yale University Press, New Haven.

Mandelbaum, Michael (2003) *The Ideas that Conquered the World: Peace, Democracy, and Free Markets in the Twenty-First Century*, Public Affairs, New York.

Patomaki, Heikki (2012) *The Great Eurozone Disaster*, Zed Books, London.

Piketty, Thomas (2014) *Capital in the Twenty-First Century*, Belknap Press of Harvard University Press, Cambridge, Massachusetts; translated by Arthur Goldhammer.

Reardon, Jack, Maria Madi, Molly Scott Cato (2018) *Introducing a New Economics: Pluralist, Sustainable, Progressive*, Pluto Books, London.

Rodrik, Dani (2011) *The Globalization Paradox: Why Global Markets, States, and Democracy Can't Coexist*, Oxford University Press, Oxford, UK.

Scholz, Olaf, (2023) 'The Global Zeitenwende: How to Avoid a New Cold War in a Multipolar Era,' *Foreign Affairs*, Jan/Feb, Vol. 102, No. 1, pp. 22–38.

Van den Berg, Hendrick (2012) *International Economics: A Heterodox Approach*, M.E. Sharpe, Armonk, N.Y.

25 Tariffs and Trade

The Issue: Republicans and Democrats agree on few issues today, except perhaps for imposing tariffs, particularly on China which "is the closest thing we have to a bipartisan consensus" (Wallace-Wells, 2024, p. 18). China is the bogeyman, and both Republicans and Democrats largely agree that we should restrict trade with China. But sometimes politicians forget that a tariff is a tax. Like any tax, a tariff which increases the cost of goods, reduces the incomes of those using the goods, while distorting the allocation of resources. Although tariffs are in the news now, they are not new to America; indeed, they have played a long and critical role in our history. This issue will discuss the historical foundations of tariffs, as well as who wins/loses, and why they have been imposed. Are tariffs the best way forward for America?

25.1 Introduction

From 1866 until 1893, the USA federal government ran a budget surplus (i.e., receipts greater than spending) every year (Gordon, 1997, p. 208)—a record that most likely will never be broken, although if economic history teaches us anything, it is to never say never.[1] During that time the United States was also the world's most protectionist nation (i.e., high tariffs); the USA industrialized, with many large firms (e.g., General Electric) becoming established.[2]

Looking back, this elixir of protectionism, industrialization, and budget surpluses seemingly worked—after all America industrialized, and soon became a global power. Today, some politicians want to re-apply tariffs hoping to restore America's greatness. Donald Trump, for one, calling himself the 'tariff man' vows implement a 20% tariff across the board; a significant scale up from his first term when he imposed tariffs on a wide array of goods. President Joe Biden, who inherited the Trump tariff-economy and largely kept tariffs intact, argued that they are needed to nature and sustain America's renewable industries.

We believe, however, that even though the elixir seemed to have worked during the late 19th century, it will not again. The world is different, and the United

DOI: 10.4324/9781003591856-29

States is different. To make America's future great for all Americans we need a different set of prescriptions—one that recognizes the specific needs of the 21st century, and not of the 19th.

25.2   Defining a Tariff

The word 'tariff' comes from the Arabic meaning 'notification.' A tariff is a tax/duty (from the French 'due') on goods produced abroad and sold domestically. In discussing tariffs, it is important to remember that it is a tax, and like all taxes, some segments of the economy will be burdened (e.g., consumers, they must pay a higher price; and firms who use the tariffed good) while others benefit (i.e., protected import-competing sectors, and the government receiving the revenue). Perhaps in our political discourse we should call a tariff for what it really is—a tax. Since a tariff protects workers/firms in the import competing sector, it is also called protectionism,[3] even though it does not protect consumers from being taxed, nor workers/firms from paying higher costs for inputs in exporting sectors, nor does it protect the nation from retaliation by the target nation.

25.3   A look at 19th-Century Tariffs

Tariffs have been imposed since ancient times and throughout the world to regulate trade, to collect revenue, and to keep out foreign competition. Tariffs played a key role in the early history of the United States. Not only were they a preponderant instigator of the Revolutionary War, but the inability of the Articles of Confederation to raise money for the needed functions of government pointed to the necessity of a new constitution with the tariff as the preponderant source of revenue (Studenski and Kross, 1951, pp. 33–44). Alexander Hamilton explained in *The Federalist Papers*,

> it is evident from the state of the country, from the habits of the people, from the experience we have had on the point itself, that it is impracticable to raise any very considerable sums by direct taxation. Tax laws have in vain been multiplied—new methods to enforce the collection have in vain been tried—the public expectation has been uniformly disappointed, and the treasuries of the States have remained empty…In America, it is evident that we must a long time depend, for the means of revenue, chiefly on duties [i.e., tariffs on imported articles].
> (Hamilton et al., 1787–1788 [2009], #12, p. 67)[4]

Tariffs have also been used to exert power and to influence other nations. A good example from modern times is China tariffing 12 Taiwanese petrochemical products in 2024,[5] as a warning to what might happen if Tiawan did not vote pro-Chinese in the January 2024 presidential election ('Trading Threats,' 2024). The Taiwanese, however, parried the threat as the anti-unification Democratic Progressive Party won the election.[6]

Theoretically, a tariff can be implemented on either imports or exports but Article I, Section 9, Clause 5 of the US Constitution prohibits taxes on exports.[7] The clause was insisted by southern states, fearing that northern states would control Congress and raise a disproportionate amount of federal revenue via taxes on Southern exports.

During the 19th century, Henry Clay (1777–1852) was one of the best-known tariff advocates (of whom there were many). Representing (Kentucky) in both the House and the Senate, he was respected for his erudition and economic understanding. In 1824, Clay proposed a high tariff wall to protect and nurture American industry (Glass 2019). The tariff proceeds would fund roads and canals to help prosper American agriculture and bring its proceeds to market, with a central bank helping to allocate funds (Smith, 2018).

Thanks to Clay's clarion tariff call[8] (along with those made by others), tariffs became ubiquitous in the United States during the 19th century,[9] serving three different but inter-related purposes:

- Raise revenue: Throughout the 19th century, tariffs were deliberately designed as the preponderant source of federal revenue. Fast forward to today when income taxes are the largest source,[10] comprising 51.1% of total revenue, while tariffs account for less than 1.7%.
- Protect American firms in export-competing sectors, giving them a chance to take root and grow vis-à-vis Great Britain's more dominant and established firms.
- Control the evolution of the economy.

25.4 Tariffs and the 19th-Century South

Tariffs, which were inextricably connected with slavery, played a major role in dividing the South and the North. Their economies were based on radically different methods of production: Free labor vs. slave labor.[11] The North was relatively self-sufficient in terms of inputs, while the South, with little industry, needed to import manufactured goods from Europe, while relying on Europe as its primary export market for agricultural goods. Whereas tariffs bolstered the North's industry, they hurt the South. As the 19th century progressed, tariffs (both their imposition and the threat to impose) attenuated whatever economic bonds remained between North and South.

An interesting and perhaps foreboding case was the nullification crisis of 1832, precipitated by the federal government slapping tariffs of 38% on almost all imported goods. The South was very much against the high tariffs which disadvantaged its slave-based economy. South Carolina asserted its rights to nullify the previous tariffs,

> When the rights reserved to the several states are deliberately invaded, it is their right and duty to interpose for the purpose of arresting the progress of the evil of usurpation, and to maintain, within their respective limits, the authorities and privileges belonging to them as independent sovereignties.
> (Tocqueville, 1835 [2003], p. 460, Note #1)

While South Carolina "armed its militia and prepared for war" (Tocqueville, 1835 [2003], p. 460), President Andrew Jackson saw the crisis for what it was—a deliberate attempt to weaken the Union, and actively intervened. Congress also reduced the tariffs, tempering subduing the discontent.[12]

25.5   Why Nations Trade[13]

Trade between individuals, firms, and nations is a basic human instinct prompted by curiosity, wants, and needs. Few nations have ever cut themselves off completely from trade (North Korea is the only modern nation that comes to mind). The annals of human history are replete with tales of trade and exploration. We trade for following reasons[14]:

- To augment both the array and the amount of goods/service available domestically, especially those that the nation cannot grow/produce.
- To lower prices, benefiting consumers.
- To benefit workers/firms in exporting industries: As more markets are served, jobs, profits, and wages, tend to increase, all else equal. Global superpowers (e.g., Great Britain in the 19th century, and the USA post-WWII) favor free trade to obtain cheaper resources and inputs, and to sell their products to a global market.
- To integrate nations economically, reducing the probability of going to war. The Scottish philosopher David Hume (1711–1776) heralded this benefit, reflecting on the war-torn 17th century (at least in Europe). Hume's argument also provides the underlying rationale for the **European Union**—an economic union of 27 nations, with free trade between members.

25.6   Why Tariffs?

- Under free trade, workers/firms in import-competing sectors will lose as other nations can produce more cheaply, and in some situations, better, causing prices, profits, jobs, and wages to fall. The affected workers will pester the government to redress, and if the government listens, tariffs/quotas will be imposed. Paradoxically, the greater the extent of free trade, the more likely to petition for redress, since nations will tend to produce and export what they do best, and no nation can produce the best of everything. This is probably why no nation has ever enjoyed complete free trade, and why protectionism is an inevitable by-product of free trade.

- Free trade makes a nation vulnerable in sectors/industries essential for domestic security, e.g., national defense, energy; or industries/sectors essential for development, e.g., finance.
- Ideological: To dis-engage with nations that it disagrees with ideologically, or to promote its self-sufficiency in what it perceives to be a hostile world, e.g., the USSR, North Korea.

25.7   The Political Economy of Tariffs[15]

The economics profession has established a wide-ranging body of evidence-based theory on tariffs[16] and protectionism[17]:

- A tariff, regardless of its rationale *is* a tax. As such, it redistributes welfare from one group to another (i.e., consumers to producers in the import-competing sectors, and to the government) and it distorts behavior, i.e., nudges consumers and producers away from their optimal behavior.
- The price of the tariffed good will increase, increasing the burden on consumers and domestic producers using that product as an intermediate input.
- A tariff can nurture and protect a new industry.
- A tariff protects domestic producers in the import-competing sector, enabling them to remain in business. It could also lead to higher wages and more jobs in the import-competing sector, assuming that other nations will not retaliate, which is quite unlikely.
- Businesses in the protected sector will tend to raise prices on their final products. And, why not? The cheaper foreign competition has been eliminated.
- Higher prices will permeate throughout the import-competing sector, and depending on the tariffed goods could affect the rest of the economy; and affected workers could demand/bargain for higher wages leading to (or abetting **inflation**).
- Like any tax, the government will accrue revenue, ceteris paribus.[18]
- The targeted nation, seldom if ever will remain passive. It will retaliate by imposing its own tariffs, which harms domestic exporting firms/workers. Tit-for-tat tariffs can often lead (and usually so) to a tariff war. No better example than the Smoot Hawley Tariff Act, passed June 17, 1930. Lobbied by farmers suffering from overproduction and dwindling prices, the Act increased tariffs 14%, on top of already-high tariffs of 42% (Gruner, 2022, p. 62). Over a thousand economists petitioned President Hoover not to sign, but he ignored

their advice and even broadened the tariff's scope. Predictably, other nations retaliated and by the end of the 1930s, global trade was a trickle of what it was in 1930. The tariff war was partly responsible for the escalation of global tensions[19] during the latter half of the 1930s and was a cause (although certainly not the preponderant) of WWII.

- Tariffs increase economic nationalism, i.e., the nation looks inward rather than outward, although the causal mechanism between tariffs and nationalism can go both ways, i.e., nationalism can nurture and incubate tariffs.
- Given the higher costs imposed on consumers and firms/workers in the exporting sectors (due to retaliation), it is nonsensical and disingenuous to claim that a tariff war could ever be won. All sides lose.
- It is also nonsensical/disingenuous to claim that tariffs will reduce the trade deficit (i.e., the difference between exports and imports). Actually, the effect is the opposite: As the targeted nation retaliates, the domestic nation's exports will fall, while higher domestic prices make exports less competitive.
- Today, it is also nonsensical/disingenuous to claim that increased tariffs will reduce the **federal budget deficit** (whereby federal outlays are greater than federal receipts). Three reasons: (1) Given that tariffs today comprise 1% of federal receipts, even a tripling of tariffs will have a miniscule effect on the deficit; (2) tariffs reduce consumer spending, and if severe/widespread can reduce economic growth and/or cause a recession; and (3) given that domestic consumption decreases so will investment, since a preponderant factor incentivizing investment is business optimism, which is largely determined by expected consumer spending. Tariffs reduce consumer spending and increase uncertainty, which reduces investment.

25.8   Look to the Real Causes of Trade Deficits

Today, tariffs offer a simple yet misleading solution to a country's economic problems, by pointing the blame at others, while parrying the real cause of the problem. As a form of populism[20] it works, by subsidizing a simplified solution for a complex reality.[21] But effective solutions for today's economic problems need to move beyond populism to examine the real causes, especially with the trade deficit.

The United States' trade deficit (the difference between the value of a nation's exports and imports) has been consistently negative since 1972, with only a brief positive blip in 1991.

The populist approach assumes that taxing imports will, by making imports more expensive, reduce import demand and thus the trade deficit. And given that about 40% of our trade deficit is with China, China becomes the number one target for vented populism. Not only will tariffs reduce our trade deficit, according to populist rhetoric, imposing tariffs will teach these nations a lesson: Play by the rules and don't mess with us.

But this ignores the real cause of the trade deficit. Firstly, since the trade deficit is a relationship between exports *and* imports; increasing tariffs while ignoring the effect on exports is disingenuous. Increasing tariffs to reduce the trade deficit will always backfire given that the targeted nations will retaliate. So for example, when Trump imposed tariffs of $360 billion dollars on Chinese products in 2018, China did not sit idle, but slapped tariffs on USA agriculture outputs. Secondly, increasing exports—the other end of the equation—is always difficult in and of itself, since it assumes that other nations are willing and able to purchase what the United States is offering. Rather than slapping tariffs, the most effective way to increase exports without any negative repercussions is to produce what other nations need. This, in turn, is a function of our ability to produce such goods better and cheaper than anyone else.

Economists believe that the major reason for our trade deficit is a lack of domestic savings and high consumer spending. And interestingly China, which is often blamed by populists for our trade deficits woes, has the mirror image problem: High domestic savings and low consumer spending, whereby "excess savings and depressed aggregated demand lead to very little or no economic growth" (Solis, 2024). And more generally speaking, "countries that have low savings rates (both public and private) relative to their investment rates run trade deficits, and countries that have the opposite pattern run surpluses. In addition, strong economies tend to have increased trade deficits due to greater investment and lower savings"[22] (Clausing and Lovely, 2024, p. 17).

But don't expect a Chinese stimulus any time soon. Xi Jinping, China's leader "frowns on government handouts to ordinary citizens [and] refuses to spark the economy with a big consumer stimulus" (Shelter from the Storm, 2024, p. 9). This is a sharp contrast with the fiscal largess of the United States. Nevertheless, China has other options to stimulate its economy: Lower taxes, liberalizing rural land sales; opening up the services sector; improving/increasing state pensions and health care to reduce consumer over saving; and allowing rural migrants to obtain public services (Shelter from the Storm, 2024, p. 9).

Redirecting USA consumer spending toward savings, which can then be used for domestic investment, is by no means an easy task. For starters, it goes against consumer decisions/actions, which in a free-market economy is difficult to do. And conversely, looking to China, "the defining macroeconomic challenge…is for its citizens to stop holding onto their savings and start spending again" (Larry Summers quoted in Solis, 2024). Also difficult to do since this goes against the inveterate fear of the Chinese (especially the elderly living in rural areas) in not having enough resources to support their old age.

Here, in the United States, the populist solution to the trade deficit is to blame other nations rather than take a close look at its own economy, with "internal imbalances being four times larger than its global imbalance...the place to look for the solutions of certain problems may be more within the United States than in China or other countries" (Piketty, 2014, p. 374)

Given the inherent mutual causation of any trade deficit (or conversely of any trade surplus) effectuating a workable solution requires active dialoguing, negotiating, and listening. It requires looking at the problem from a mutual perspective. Alas, such hard but necessary work, i.e., politics, is missing from the populist playbook, which looks instead for simplistic solutions in order to garner the most votes.

25.9   The USA China Trade War (March 2018–?)

New technological developments during the 1990s, including the internet, more efficient ways of communication, and faster and more voluminous shipping ushered in a new age of globalization and trade interdependence. Optimists felt that global trade could benefit all, by boosting wages and reducing poverty. Indeed, during the early 2000s, "a wave of imports from China and other emerging economies helped push down the cost of video games, T-shorts, dining tables, home appliances and more" (Tankersley, 2024, p. 6). While consumers enjoyed increased discretionary spending due to lower import prices, there was a concomitant dark side to cheaper imports, which

> drove some American factories out of business, and they cost more than a million workers their jobs. Discount stores and online retailers, like Walmart and Amazon, flourished selling low-cost goods made overseas. But voters rebelled. Stung by shuttered factories, cratered industries and prolonged wage stagnation, Americans in 2016 elected a president who vowed to hit back at China on trade. Four years later they elected another one.
>
> (Tankersley, 2024, p. 6)

In an interesting and provocative article, Khanna (2023) blames the loss of 5 million manufacturing jobs and 70,000 factory closures on open markets and particularly the rise of China, writing that "the trade deficit is an important proxy for the decline of the US industrial base" (2023, p. 143).

Gone today is the subdued bipartisan optimism in free trade. Rather than constructively engage with China, and to embrace free trade, China is pointed to as the bogeyman. And unfortunately, "true believers in free trade—especially with China—are now a vanishing breed in Washington, not to mention other global capitals" (*The Economist,* May 18, 2024, p. 63).

The US accuses China of:

- Artificially devaluing its currency to favor exports, while disincentivizing imports.
- Unfairly subsidizing its own exporters in order to increase exports, and hence achieve a favorable trade balance.
- Copying/imitating/stealing western technology.
- Restricting imports via non-tariff means, such as "nontransparent trade barriers on customs regulation, heavy documentation requirements, and randomly applied product certification requirements" (Yu and Kwan, 2023, p. 168).

China does not deny these accusations, for the evidence is plainly available for all to see (Yu and Kwan, 2023, pp. 167–169). China implements tariffs mainly to attain a favorable trade balance as part of its neo-mercantilist strategy (Yu and Kwan, 2023, p. 168).[23] In addition, China feels that "when American firms enjoy a clear competitive edge in world markets, they will lobby their government to push for free trade. When the United States loses its competitive advantage, it returns to tariffs and protectionism in the name of fair trade" (Yu and Kwan, 2023, p. 190).

The Tariff War officially began on March 22, 2018, when Donald Trump, calling himself the 'Tariff Man,' raised tariffs more than any other USA president in the last 100 years,[24] slapping $50–$60 billions of dollars of tariffs on steel, aluminum, washing machines, solar panels, and on most Chinese goods.[25] Steel, an important good in any manufacturing economy, used primarily as an intermediate, was slapped with a 25% tariff.

Of course, China retaliated.[26] On April 2, 2018, China imposed tariffs on a host of USA goods ranging from automobiles, soybeans, aluminum, automobiles, and aircraft. As expected, the USA trade deficit increased, from $481 billion in 2016 to $654b in 2020. (As this manuscript goes to press, the trade deficit stands at $1.1 trillion.) The tariffs' negative effects offset the positive effects of Trump's 2017 tax cut—after all, a tariff is a tax. Trump's tariffs, reduced consumption, increased global uncertainty, and slowed investment and economic growth (in 2019, real GDP decreased from 3.2% in Quarter One to 1.9% by Quarter IV, causing many business economists to predict a recession by 2020 (and this was before the onslaught of COVID). In a definitive investigation of the Trump tariffs, it was found that,

> The net effect of import tariffs, retaliatory tariffs, and farm subsidies on employment in locations exposed to the trade war was at best a wash, and it may have been mildly negative. US import tariffs had either insignificantly negative or insignificantly positive employment effects; retaliatory tariffs had a consistent and significant negative employment impact; and only a minor part of these adverse effects was offset by agricultural subsidies.
>
> (Autor et al., 2024)

The authors argue that the main salutary effect of the Trump tariffs was political, which

> ...appears to have been successful in strengthening support for the Republican party. Residents of tariff-protected locations became less likely to identify as Democrats and more likely to vote for President Trump. Although retaliatory tariffs were more effective in reducing employment than import tariffs were in boosting employment, retaliatory tariffs were less effective in reducing Republican electoral support than import tariffs were in boosting Republican electoral support. Voters thus appear to have responded favorably to the extension of tariff protections to local industries despite their economic cost.
>
> (Autor et al., 2024)

Trump II has vowed to continue getting tough China, ratcheting up his vitriol. He favors a drastic turn inward, revoking 'most favored nation status,' bestowed on China in 2000. He has pledged to raise tariffs on all Chinese imports, banning some goods, and imposing tariffs on imports from other nations (especially Canada and Mexico) while also severely cutting down commercial ties between China and the United States (Tankersley, 2024, p. 6). In a May 2024 interview with *TIME* magazine, Trump promised that if elected, he will raise tariffs by 10% across the board, and even 100% on some Chinese goods (Cortellessa, 2024, p. 34).[27] This would boost tariffs to the highest level since WWII. He has since upped the ante to 20%.

Trump's rationalization is that the tariffs "will liberate the US economy from being at the mercy of foreign manufacturing and spur an industrial renaissance" (Cortellessa, 2024, p. 34). It is estimated that such a policy would cost each American household $2000/year and reduce GDP by 1% (*The Economist*, November 4, 2023). All else equal, such high tariffs could tilt the United States toward a recession.

Not all Republicans are on board with Trump's 2024 proposal. The more traditional[28] free traders,[29] e.g., Kent Lassman of the Competitive Enterprise Institute, strongly disagree. Gramm and Boudreaux (2024) remind us that the "high cost of protectionism has long been documented." They cite an influential CATO Institute study documenting that the average annual cost to American consumers of each tariff-saved job from 1950 to 1990 was $620,000 in 2017 dollars. And, not surprisingly, tariffs hurt import-competing American manufactures, given that "one-half of US imports are raw or intermediate goods used as inputs in production; and unlike tax cuts or regulatory relief, which stimulate production, tariffs do the opposite" (Gramm and Boudreaux, 2024).

If Trump were to implement his broad-based tariffs, the effects would be most acutely felt by the bottom and middle of the USA income distribution,

> A lower-bound estimate of costs to consumers indicates that the tariffs would reduce after-tax incomes by about 3.5 percent for those in the

bottom half of the income distribution; tariffs would cost a typical house-hold in the middle of the income distribution at least $1,700 in increased taxes each year.

(Clausing and Lovely, 2024, p. 2)

Just like the earlier Trump tariffs, the burden of the proposed tariffs will fall on ordinary Americans, while doing little to help USA exporters (actually mak-ing their situation worse, given expected retaliation) while annoying our allies (*The Economist*, November 4, 2023). It is a no-win situation.

As further folly, Trump assumes that higher tariffs will reduce the budget deficit by increasing revenue, which in turn could allow for a reduction in in-come taxes. This is dead-wrong for two reasons:

- Tariffs are an inefficient way to raise revenue because they generate losses to domestic buyers that exceed the sum of benefits to producers and tariff revenues (Clausing and Lovely, 2024, p. 3).
- There is so much uncertainty in the causal relationship between imposing tariffs and raising revenue that we cannot predict the precise effect. It de-pends on how consumers and producers react to the higher prices, how im-ports and exports change, how consumption changes, how tariffs affect the value of the dollar, thereby making exports/imports cheaper/more expensive (Clausing and Lovely, 2024, p. 17, note #33); and the increased uncertainty hovering over investment (Clausing and Lovely, 2024, p. 7). And don't for-get the inevitable retaliation, which will reduce exports and hence GDP, all else equal.[30]

The Democrats reject the Trump plan as too broad, preferring to focus on a set of strategic industries, i.e., renewables, electric vehicles, and semicon-ductors, along with strategic subsidies to firms in such industries. But rather than fully distancing himself from Mr. Trump's high tariff policy, President Biden instead codified and even escalated some. In 2024, the Biden Admin-istration raised tariffs on Chinese semiconductors and solar cells from 25% to 50%; syringes and needles from 0 to 50%; lithium batteries from 7.5% to 25%; and electric vehicles from 25% to 100% (*The Economist*, May 18, 2024, p. 62).

The Democrats' policies are a "one-size-fits-all, policy-and-politics tool–a recipe for addressing the climate crisis, the postindustrial secular stagnation of the US economy, domestic manufacturing decline, white working-class resent-ment, and for the geopolitical challenge posed by China" (Wallace-Wells, 2024, p. 18). Ostensibly, this was done "to level the playing field in industries vital to the United States' future, but like all tariffs, it is American consumers who will pay the price" (*The Economist*, May 18, 2024, p. 62).

While economists are not of one position regarding such policies, we offer the following criticisms against today's bipartisan protectionism:

- Contrary to Trump's assertion that the Chinese will bear the brunt of the tariffs, both economic theory and evidence suggests the opposite: That USA consumers will pay the brunt. After all, no matter how you look at it, a tariff is a tax, and all taxes burden the consumer. But not everyone understands this, even some members of the Trump team, "There have also been questions in the Trump administration about what tariffs really are. Former Treasury Secretary Steven Mnuchin claimed: 'Tariffs are a tariff on imports. They're not a tax.' However, the very definition of a tariff is a tax on imports…Tariffs are a consumption tax, albeit a particularly distortionary type of consumption tax" (*Economic Report of the President*, 2024, p. 2, footnote #4).
- Competition from any source is often a spur to innovation. Yes, competition usually begets collateral damage, i.e., lost jobs (just as its absence does) but take away competition and it is not clear if domestic companies will continue to innovative or will just increase prices while enjoying all the benefits of protection. Under protectionism, where is the incentive to produce better and cheaper goods?
- Here, in the United States, with restrictive trade forestalling rather than encouraging the adoption of electric vehicles, solar panels, and batteries, we are sacrificing long-term environmental stewardship for short-term political expediency.
- Protection results in higher prices, contributing to inflation.[31]

We fully agree with the Cato Institute that the best approach to solving our economic problems, including the trade deficit, "remains an open American economy and active multilateral engagement. A rejection of free trade and an embrace of protectionism would not benefit the United States or correct its real economic problems. In fact, it would only make things worse" (Lincicome and Obregon, 2022). The best way to attack trade deficits is to recognize their real causes, and the mutuality with other nations. Clausing and Lovely argue that,

> tariffs should be rejected on both fiscal policy grounds and on traditional trade policy grounds. Tariffs are a regressive[32] and distortionary source of public finance, and they do not help the groups they are intended to help. They instead introduce new economic inefficiencies and collateral damage, and they make it more difficult to work cooperatively with allies and partners to solve our most vexing international problems.
>
> (2024, p. 18)

Trump assumes that his tariffs will make America Great Again.[33] Such slogans are empty unless backed up by realistic solutions, which in turn are based on an accurate conceptualization of the problem, of which his prognosis is clearly not. We agree with *The Wall Street Journal* that, "the way to create prosperity for the forgotten man [sic] is to compete and innovate, not to have the government mandate hidden inefficiencies to punish some and favor others" ('Tariffs and the Common Man,' 2024). Let's implement policies that will benefit all Americans. Increasing tariffs doesn't do the trick.

25.10 Conclusion

Abraham Lincoln, the presidential candidate of the newly formed Republican Party, in a campaign speech in New Haven, Connecticut (March 6, 1860) said,

> If the Republican Party of this nation shall ever have the national house entrusted to its keep, it will be the duty of that party to attend to all the affairs of national housekeeping …[And] the old question of [the] tariff… will remain one of the chief affairs of national housekeeping to all time.
>
> (Fehrenbacher, 1989)

Indeed, despite the overwhelming economic evidence, as a political issue the tariff is as unresolved as it was during Lincoln's day. But, at the same time, the economic effects are much clearer and less ambiguous. It is time to listen to what economists have to say about the real causes of the trade deficit and about the self-destructiveness of tariffs, rather than lend our ears to simple and mis-leading populist slogans.

Open markets, globalization, and China are convenient populist scapegoats, while tariffs are an ill-conceived cave-in to voters, re-directing attention away from real causes of real economic problems. This is not to say that the United States should sit back and passively accept the vicissitudes of market forces, and/or be passive vis-à-vis other nations. Rather, the United States needs to assert its interests both domestically and globally within a context of multilat-eral dialogue, and not by bullying, threatening, and intimidating with sterile bravado.

At the same time, though, as the world is undergoing several "great trans-formations" (Montgomery and Van Clieaf, 2023, p. 3) simultaneously (e.g., the transition to **Net Zero**, **Climate change**, and **Artificial Intelligence**), we need to rethink what global treaties on tariffs and trade are all about, and how they are negotiated. Instead of constructing treaties premised on the unrestricted move-ment of global capital, perhaps think instead of "treaties that promote genuine, sustainable, and equitable co-development. [They] would set explicit, binding social and environmental goals…[which] would address, for example, tax rates for multinationals, the distribution of wealth, the volume of carbon emissions, and biodiversity" (Piketty, 2022, p. 219). Such co-development treaties have never been done; instead, treaties have been often imposed on less developed nations in order to benefit the developed nations, "with the treaties negotiated vertically without any democratic input" (Piketty, 2022, p. 219).[34]

Notes

1 Today, with projected budget deficits over $1 trillion annually for the remainder of the decade, we will be lucky to see *one* budget surplus in the near future.
2 For a helpful discussion of tariffs, revenue, the budget, and the economy see Gordon (1997).
3 While tariffs are in the news, they are not the only instrument of protectionism. Another is the quota, i.e., a country-specific restriction on the amount of a product that can be exported to the domestic market. In the 1980s, the Reagan administration, for example, imposed quotas on Japanese automobile makers to protect and resuscitate the USA auto industry.
4 Hamilton strongly disapproved of the Articles' lack of revenue provisions, "A nation cannot long exist without revenue. Destitute of this essential support, it must resign its independence and sink into the degraded condition of a province. This is an extremity to which no government will of choice accede. Revenue therefore must be had at all events" (Hamilton et al., 1787–1788 [2009], #13, p. 70).
5 In 2010, China and Taiwan negotiated the Economic Co-operation Framework covering 539 Taiwanese products and 267 Chinese goods, "as one of many economic carrots offered by China …in the hope of bringing Taiwan closer to the mainland" (*The Economist,* January 13, 2024, p. 32).
6 See our chapter on **China** for a brief discussion on the importance of this election.
7 Article I Section 10 reads "No state shall, without the consent of the congress, lay any imposts or duties on imports or exports, except what may be absolutely necessary for executing its inspection laws…" James Madison explained the clause's rationale, "The restraint on the power of the states over imports and exports is enforced by all the arguments which prove the necessity of submitting the regulation of trade to the federal councils" (The Federalist, #44, p. 274).
8 In a letter to Edward Wallace, dated May 12, 1860, presidential candidate Abraham Lincoln wrote "In the days of Henry Clay, I was a Henry-Clay-tariff-man; and my views have undergone no material change upon that subject" (Fehrenbacher, 1989, p. 156).
9 For an extended discussion, see Studenski and Brooks (1951, esp. pp. 45–160).
10 The source for these statistics is Budget of the US Government (2023). Not surprisingly, the amount of tariff revenue doubled from 2021 to 2022 thanks to the Trump/ Biden tariffs, although as a percentage of total revenue, tariffs remained low.
11 For a vivid contemporary picture of the North/South differences, both culturally and economically see de Tocqueville (1835 [2003], pp. 404–421).
12 See Studenski and Kross (1951, pp. 97–99) for a detailed discussion.
13 For a detailed discussion, see Irwin (2020) and *The Economic Report of the President* (2024, pp. 173–174).
14 Based on the following reasons, but especially the first two, global institutions such as the **WTO**, **World Bank**, and the **IMF** have promoted free trade and reduced protectionism.
15 Economics was originally known as political economy, but during the late 19th century, to emulate the physical sciences, the discipline jettisoned the messy field of

politics and renamed itself economics. Many of us would like to return to the former appellation, signifying that economics and politics are always intertwined.

16 The converse holds for reducing/abolishing tariffs.

17 For a helpful discussion of tariffs and quotas from a theoretical, empirical, and historical perspective, see (Van der Berg, 2012, pp. 201–234).

18 A slight difference between a tariff and quota: whereas the revenue from a tariff will accrue to government; the revenue from a quota accrues to the firm.

19 Of course, the causation usually runs both ways: a poor economic relationship between nations can also result in increased tariffs.

20 See Longley (2022) for an interesting and historical look at populism in the United States. Longley explores different meanings of the term, tracing it back to Andrew Jackson, America's first populist president (1829–1837). For Longley, populism is a cosmic struggle between the morally good 'people' and a corrupt and self-serving group of conspiring elites.

21 In a 2023 survey, "66% of Americans believe that the government should implement tariffs in order to protect American jobs at home" (Tariff Man: Part Two,' 2023).

22 For elaboration, see Clausing (2019).

23 For a discussion of neo-mercantilism, see our chapter on **China**.

24 See 'Tariff Man: Part Two,' (2023).

25 The Trump administration cited Section 232 of the Trade Expansion Act. For a discussion, see: Platzer and Peters (2021). In December 2022, the WTO ruled against the United States, noting that the United States was not in a state or war or emergency.

26 For a detailed description of the tariff wars begun during the Trump administration and continued under the Biden administration, see Yu and Kwan (2023, pp. 177–181).

27 This movement is spearheaded by Robert Lighthizer, Trump's former US trade representative and Peter Navarro, Trump's economic advisor. For specifics of the proposal, and a more in-depth rationale, see Lighthizer (2023). His book de-emphasizes the positive effects of trade on consumers, while emphasizing the positive effects of tariffs (i.e., protectionism) on domestic producers. He argues that production is the desired end and not consumption. Not only is this unabashed mercantilism, but "it ignores retaliation by other nations" (Tankersley, 2024, p. 6).

28 We must be careful with word 'traditional.' In the 19th century, the Republican Party was vigorously pro-tariff claiming that American businesses needed protection. In the early 20th century, however, it was the Democrats, particularly Woodrow Wilson and FDR, who espoused free trade, claiming that it would benefit American workers. Eisenhower dissented from Republican dogma, but it wasn't until the Reagan administration that the Republican Party reversed their long-standing pro-tariff position.

29 We can even add Bill Clinton, an ardent free trader. In fact, from 1980 to 2008, a bipartisan consensus existed on the benefits of free trade. This consensus fell apart during the 2007–2009 recession, as many workers lost their jobs and the unemployment hovered near 10%.

30 This is because GDP is defined as Consumption + Investment + Government Expenditures + Net Exports. Where Net Exports = Exports – Imports.

31 For inflation to occur, prices must be rising, not just high.

32 Regressive means "tax payments relative to income fall as income increases; a tax is progressive if tax payments relative to income increase as income increases" (Clausing and Lovely, 2024, p. 1, note #1).

33 Such slogans go back more than a century in America. Warren Harding, the 29th USA president (1921–1923) had first use. His 'America First' resonated with voters, especially following WWI, the influenza pandemic, as well as double digit **inflation** and **unemployment**. Both FDR and Ronald Reagan used variations of the slogan, with Trump being the most recent (Gruner, 2022, pp. 17–18, 107–108).

34 Piketty (2022, pp. 220–221) provides the groundwork for a new organization of globalization based on transnational democracy; although as he admits, "obviously, the passage from one kind of treaty to the other will not happen overnight" (Piketty, 2022, p. 219). In moving from Situation A to Situation B the vested interests, i.e., those who benefit from the current structure/system pose a formidable obstacle. Thus, any detailed map of the transition requires fully understanding the vested interests.

References

'American Trade Policy: 100% Trouble,'(2024) *The Economist,* May 18, pp. 62–63.

Autor, David, Anne Beck, David Dorn, Gordon H. Hanson (2024) 'Help for the Heartland? The Employment and Electoral Effects of the Trump Tariffs in the United States,' Working Paper 32082, National Bureau of Economic Research, Cambridge, Mass., http://www.nber.org/papers/w32082

Budget of the US Government (2023) Office of Management and Budget, Washington D.C. (whitehouse.gov).

Clausing, Kimberly (2019) *The Progressive Case for Free Trade, Immigration, and Global Capital*, Harvard University Press, Cambridge, MA.

Clausing, Kimberly A. and Mary E. Lovely (2024) 'Why Trump's Tariff Proposals Would Harm Working Americans,' Peterson Institute for international Economics pb24-1.pdf (piie.com).

Cortellessa (2024) 'If He Wins,' *TIME,* May 27, pp. 30–38.

Economic Report of the President (2024) The White House, Washington DC.

Fehrenbacher, Don E., (Ed.) (1989) *Abraham Lincoln: Speeches and Writings, 1859–1865*, Library of America, New York.

Glass, Andrew (2019) 'Henry Clay Calls for a High Tariff Wall,' *Politico* (March 30)

Gordon, John Steele (1997) *Hamilton's Blessing: The Extraordinary Life and Times of Our National Debt*, Penguin Books, New York.

Gramm, Phil and Donald J. Boudreaux, (2024) 'The High Cost of the Trump-Biden Tariffs, *The Wall Street Journal,* (January 18), p. A15.

Gruner, Ronald (2022) *We the Presidents: How American Presidents Shaped the Last Century*, Libratum Press, Naples, Florida.

Hamilton, Alexander, James Madison, and John Jay (1787–1788 [2009]) *The Federalist Papers*, Bantam, New York.

Irwin, Douglas (2020) *Free Trade under Fire*, 5th ed., Princeton University Press, Princeton.

Khanna, Ro (2023) 'The New Industrial Age: America Should Once Again Become a Manufacturing Superpower,' *Foreign Affairs*, Vol. 102, No. 1, pp. 141–154

Lighthizer, Robert (2023) *No Trade is Free: Changing Course, Taking on China, and Helping America's Workers*, Broadside Books, New York.

Lincicome, Scott and Alfredo Carrillo Obregon (2022) 'The Updated case for Free Trade,' Cato Institute, Policy Analysis No. 925, April 19, https://www.wita.org

Longley, Robert (2022) 'What is Populism: Definition and Examples,' ThoughtCo. (January 26), (thoughtco.com).

Montgomery, John and Mark Van Clieaf (2023) *Net Zero Business Models: Winning in the Global Net Zero Economy*, Wiley, New York.

Piketty, Thomas (2022) *A Brief History of Equality*, Belknap Press of Harvard University, Cambridge, Massachusetts, translated by Steven Rendall.

Platzer, Michaela and Peters, Heidi (2021) 'U.S. Aluminum Manufacturing: National Security and Tariffs.' (March 11) (fas.org).

Solis, Marie (2024) '5.2% Reported growth of China's Economy Last year,' *The New York Times*, (January 21), p. 2, Business section.

'Tariff Man: Part Two,' (2023) *The Economist*, November 4, pp. 61–63.

'Tariffs and the Common Man' (2024) *The Wall Street Journal*, Editorial, January 2, p. A14.

Tankersley, Jim (2024) 'With New Tariffs on China, Preparing for a Steep Price, *The New York Times*, May 19, Sunday Business Section, p. 6.

Tocqueville, Alexis de (1835 [2003]) *Democracy in America*, Penguin, New York.

'Trading Threats,' (2024) *The Economist,* January 13, pp. 32–34.

'Shelter from the Storm: Some Advice for Xi Jinping ahead of the Communist Party's third plenum,' *The Economist*, editorial, June 29, 2024, pp. 9–10.

Smith, Ryan, P. (2018) 'A History of America's Ever-Shifting Stance on Tariffs,' (April 12), *Smithsonian Magazine*, At the Smithsonian| Smithsonian Magazine.

Studenski, Paul and Herman Edward Kross (1951) *Financial History of the United States* BeardBooks, Washington, DC.

Wallace-Wells, David (2024) 'Post-Normal,' *The New York Times Sunday Magazine*, May 26, pp. 18–19.

Yu, Fu-Lai Tony and Diana S. Kwan (2023) *China's Long and Winding Road to Modernization: Uncertainty, Learning, and Policy Change*, Lanhan, Maryland.

26 The BRICS

The Issue: During the **Bretton Woods** conference in 1944, the United States put forward a new global rules-based order, centered by the World Bank, the International Monetary Fund, and the US dollar as the global currency. As the emerging superpower, the rules and institutions favored the US and its allies. Nations from the developing South have since challenged this order, claiming that it does not serve their interests. The BRICS organized in 2001 to channel this opposition to reform the Bretton Woods system. While the current institutions/rules remain dominant, that could very well change.

26.1 Introduction

In 2001, Jim O'Neil, an investor banker at Goldman Sachs coined the term BRICs, referring to the fast-growing (at the time) emerging markets of Brazil, Russia, India, and China. Goldman Sachs "reckon[ed] that China may very well become the world's largest economy before 2030, and [that] the BRIC economies could well surpass output in the Group of Seven wealthy nations by 2032" (Beattie, 2010).

In 2010, at the behest of China, South Africa was invited to join, and the BRICs became the BRICS. In addition to being fast growing (although the growth rates of China, Brazil, Russia, and South Africa, have since considerably slowed) the BRICS want to construct a new, non-western global order that reflects the interests of all nations, especially those in the global South.[1] Their main complaint is that as nations they were either not invited to the 1944 Bretton Woods conference, and/or did not actively exist at the time. The Prime Minister of Barbados, Mia Motley, has gone so far as to disparage Bretton Woods (and its pro-western global order) as imperialist since many of their colonies had not yet achieved independence (Porter, 2023); yet today, they must live under their global agreements.

On the point of fairness, it is hard to *not* take seriously this argument. International institutions are never sacrosanct. As times change, institutions should be reexamined, and if warranted and agreed by all nations, changed.

DOI: 10.4324/9781003591856-30

26.2 Examining the BRICS

Since its founding, the BRICS' economic clout has increased considerably,[2] from 8% of global GDP in 2001 to 26% in 2022, while, at the same time, the global share of the G-7 has declined from 65% to 43%. China is the BRICS' workhorse, accounting for 70% of its total output today, up from 47% in 2001, while accounting for 69% of all BRICS trade, up from 55% in 2001.

Like its Western counterpart, the G-7, the BRICS is an informal organization without a charter or formal membership criteria.[3] Its main task is providing its members a forum to criticize the Western-dominated global order, while also encouraging and enabling more input from the global South. In addition, the BRICS offers financial benefits somewhat similar to **the IMF** and **the World Bank**: (1) The Contingent Reserve Arrangement, established in 2014 allows member central banks to obtain hard currency if needed; and (2) the New Development Bank, established in 2015 provides money for development projects, although a nation need not be a member to apply.

The BRICS are politically, economically, and militarily quite heterogeneous. As Alan Beattie (2010) quipped in *The Financial Times*, "like a boy band or a street gang, the BRICS might almost have been chosen for their disparate abilities rather than their similarities." To illustrate: Russia and Brazil are oil exporters, while the others are oil importers; GDP per capita differs significantly between the poorest and richest (India and China, respectively); Russia and China are autocracies while the other three are 'messy' democracies; Russia and China are surplus nations with the other three, debtor nations. And the list goes on.[4]

26.3 The Seeds for Change

While Bretton Woods has served the Western world reasonably well— especially the United States[5]; at the same time, when "the political world is changing; henceforth we must seek out new solutions to new disorders" (de Tocqueville, 1840 [2003], p. 816). Indeed, the political world is changing, and today, there is growing agreement for a new and much more inclusive Bretton Woods. History teaches us that "economic institutions are not unchanging. They are constantly redefined according to crises and power relationships, within unstable and precarious compromises" (Piketty, 2022, p. 240). Currently, the world is in one of these moments, although it remains to be seen how these changes will play out.

In November 2022, Prime Minister Motley (Barbados) sketched out a plan/proposal for financial reform[6] and perhaps a new Bretton Woods. She focused on the developing countries that are most susceptible to climate change, yet least able to redress: Nations whose crippling debt precludes accessing much-needed capital to transition away from fossil fuels. The world's existing institutions are unable to solve this interwoven complexity of underdevelopment, debt, and climate change. In June 22–23, 2023, urged by Prime Minister Motley, leaders from both developed and developing nations gathered in Paris to discuss and negotiate. The conference provided a rallying cry to redress the injustice of climate change.

The Paris meeting was followed by the BRICS' 15th summit in Johannesburg (August 22–25, 2023) hosted by South African president Cyril Ramaphosa. In attendance were the leaders of India (Narendra Modi); Brazil (Luiz Inacio Lula da Silva); **China** (Xi Jinping); and of course, South Africa. **Russia's** president, Vladimir Putin, participated virtually, since he would have been arrested if he had physically attended. (South Africa, as a member of the International Criminal Court, would have been obligated to arrest him.)

Such summits provide ample opportunity for the leaders (and underling officials) to get to know each other and to discuss strategy. A significant outcome of the 15th summit was the addition of six new member nations, effective January 2024: Argentina, Egypt, Ethiopia, Iran, Saudi Arabia, and the United Arab Emirates. In the context of current events, the motivation to expand is obvious: As the United States aggressively curries Western allies, "China is seeking an equal and opposite reaction via the BRICS, which is the only counterweight to the G-7" (*The Economist*, August 19, 2023). The (expanded) BRICS fancies itself as "a robust counterweight to Western global dominance [and even] as a kind of anti-hegemonic vehicle" (Shepherd, 2023).

China has been instrumental in the BRICS expansion. This is logical given that "China has been looking at developing nations for strategic partnerships, currying favor with emerging markets at the same time that the United States has shifted its focus to the G-7" (Shepherd, 2023).

In line with China's objective "to become an active leader of the global economy" (Yu and Kwan, 2023, p. 170), in 2013, it launched its 'Belt and Road Initiative,' a coordinating and developing strategy focusing on steel, oil, and coal among the countries along the Old Silk Road. The goal is to integrate China's economic development with the peripheral (developing) nations. To provide the financing, China, also in 2013, founded the Asian Infrastructure Investment Bank (AIIB). China is determined to have a greater voice in finance, especially in the global South, thus bypassing the western-dominated International Monetary Fund and the World Bank, and the Japanese-dominated Asian Development Bank (Yu and Kwan, 2023, p. 170).

The Economist (August 19, 2023) mused that "expansion would make a motley crew even motlier… although the BRICs could criticize the Western-led international order with a louder voice, they would struggle even more to articulate such an alternative." Indeed, "the BRICS complaining about USA hegemony [even with more members][7] doesn't extend to a coherent plan to replace it" (Beattie, 2023). A good example is the lack of agreement on which currency to replace the US dollar. A necessary task for the BRICS but made difficult given the dollar's continued importance. However, this could change, especially with the United States' fiscal imprudence, and its dysfunctional Congress. Nevertheless,

> judging by the world's previous reserve currency—the pound sterling, which declined for decades before being superseded by the dollar—such changes are likely to proceed at a glacial pace. That is, unless the ...global financial system...is supercharged by a new crisis.
>
> (*The Economist*, May 10, 2024)

Although heterogeneity isn't automatically an obstacle to group performance per se, at the same time, "enlarging a grouping doesn't automatically make it more powerful. The G-20 [for example] is beset by entrenched differences" (Beattie, 2023).

26.4   Conclusion

The United States needs to assume an active role in constructing a new Bretton Woods that enables all voices (rich and poor) to be heard. To do so is in the bests interests of all nations and our planet. At the very least, global dialogue is necessary for the United States to safeguard its own interests and to have a say in how this new institution unfolds. It is better for the United States to do so while on top—not that we believe that the dollar is any immediate danger, nor that the United States will lose its number one position. But that could change, if for example, the next time the debt ceiling is approached and we endure the same tempest as in May 2023, this might be enough to incentivize change. It is also noteworthy that three of the BRICS (**Russia, China, and Iran**) pose an existential threat to the United States and its interests, and are determined to change the US influenced global order.

Notes

1 The term 'global South' was first coined by the political activist Carl Oglesby in 1969; it "refers to countries that are sometimes described as 'developing,' 'less developed' or 'underdeveloped.' Many of these countries—although by no means all—are in the Southern Hemisphere, largely in Africa, Asia and Latin America" (Heine, 2023). An emerging market is an 'up and coming', non-rich nation (usually middle income) making a name for itself on the global stage.
2 *The Economist* (August 19, 2023) provides the source for this paragraph's statistics.
3 The Group of Seven (G-7) is comprised of seven pro-democracy/pro-capitalist nations: the United States, Japan, the UK, Canada, France, Italy, and Germany. Originally founded in 1973 by the United States, the UK, France, and West Germany in order to discuss the world's pressing macro problems (largely precipitated by **the OPEC's** price increases) by 1976, the group had expanded to its current seven members.
4 For a further discussion, see Reardon et al. (2018); and *The Economist*, August 19, 2023.

5 The 1944 Bretton Woods conference was silent on three important issues (at least by today's standards): gender, race, and the environment. On this score alone, it is time for a change (Helleiner, 2022).
6 This section relies heavily on Porter (2023).
7 *The Economist* (August 19, 2023) has identified 40 nations that have either applied for BRICS membership or have expressed an interest in doing so.

References

Beattie, Alan (2023), 'The Brics Don't Stack Up as a Committee to Run the World,' *Financial Times*, August 23, (ft.com).

Beattie, Alan (2010) 'BRICS: The Changing Faces of Global Power,' *Financial Times*, January 17, (ft.com).

Heine, Jorge (2023) 'The Global South is on the Rise—but what exactly is the Global South?' *The Conversation,* July 3, (theconversation.com).

Helleiner, Eric (2022) 'Silences of Bretton Woods: gender inequality, racial discrimination and environmental degradation,' *Review of International Political Economy*, DOI: 10.1080/09692290.2022.2144408

'Is the Bigger Party a Better One?' The Economist, August 19, 2023, pp. 50–52.

Piketty, Thomas (2022) *A Brief History of Equality*, Belknap Press of Harvard University, Cambridge, Massachusetts, translated by Steven Rendall.

Porter, Catherine (2023) 'Leaders Look to Remake IMF, World Bank,' *The New York Times*, June 23, (nytimes.com).

Reardon, Jack, Maria Madi, and Molly Scott Cato (2018) *Introducing a New Economics: Pluralist, Sustainable, Progressive*, London, Pluto Press.

Shepherd, Christian (2023), 'Six Nations to join BRICS, Bolstering Group as a Counterweight to the West', *The Washington Post*, August 25, p. A15.

'The Fight to Dethrone the Dollar' (2024) *The Economist*, May 10, Special Report: Deglobalization of Finance, pp. 10–11.

Tocqueville, Alexis de (2003 [1835, 1840]) *Democracy in America*, Penguin Books, New York.

Yu, Fu-Lai Tony and Diana S. Kwan (2023) *China's Long and Winding Road to Modernization*, Lexington Books, Lanham, Maryland.

27 Bretton Woods: Setting the Global Rules of the Game

The Issue: In July 1944, with the defeat of Germany inevitable, the United States and its allies met in Bretton Woods, New Hampshire to devise a new global, rules-based system, centered on free trade and capital mobility, powered by the US dollar. The system worked for the United States and the West. But today, developing nations (especially China, India, and Russia) are clamoring for a different global system, one that better addresses and meets their needs. In addition, the Bretton Woods system is being attacked from within, and especially from the United States, as it has been turning inward and becoming more protectionist. Is Bretton Woods still needed? Or are we better off with each nation fending for its own? Should a new Bretton Woods system be developed, one based on **Climate Change**, the transition to **Net Zero**, and the complexities surrounding **Artificial Intelligence**? Is the old system capable of addressing such issues?

27.1 Introduction

Imagine traveling back in time to the 1870s to London when it was the center of the world, and the United Kingdom was at the height of its empire.[1] Let's stop for a pint in the Docklands overviewing the Thames, in view of ships from every part of the globe. Given your prescience, you might be tempted to say (with a touch of self-conceit) to your new-found pub friends: 'You know, in another 50 years or so, the UK will no longer be a global superpower.' If you did, most likely you would have been accused of smoking something illicit, with your mates reminding you that you are in London, the capital of the British Empire, where the sun never sets.[2]

But one of the inexorable facts of history is that empires rise *and* that they also fall. No global empire has ever not done so. Indeed, within 50 years after your London visit, the United States usurped the UK's position as the world's largest economy, a distinction that it has held since; while for all intents and purposes, the UK's glory days were fast fading into the sunset.[3]

Being the world's largest economy is much more than just bragging rights, for it comes with a bevy of privileges, rights, and responsibilities; the most

DOI: 10.4324/9781003591856-31

important being the unilateral privilege/right to determine the global rules of the game. Carlos Escude explains,

> the world order as a whole is hierarchical. Superpowers are rule-makers who set the rules of the world order…on the other hand, the peripheral states …are rule takers. Developing countries accept the rules as long as the rules do not damage their economic interests. It is crucial to know that rule takers can emerge as rule makers as their economic and political powers grow.
>
> (Quoted in Yu and Kwan, 2023, p. 184)

Indeed, rule takers become rule makers as superpowers rise and fall.[4]

27.2 Bretton Woods Conference, July 1944

The changing of the guard between the United States and the UK took place during the Bretton Woods Conference, officially known as United Nations Monetary and Financial Conference. It was held July 1–22, 1944, at the Mount Washington Hotel in Bretton Woods, New Hampshire. The 19th-century hotel, iconic and beautiful at the base of Mount Washington—the highest peak east of the Mississippi—hosted 730 delegates from 44 allied nations to plan the financial and monetary post-WWII landscape.[5]

At Bretton Woods, the United States was in the driver's seat, so to speak. As the world's major economy, with its economy running full steam, it was emerging practically unscathed from World War II. Indeed, it is fascinating to read the dialogue between the UK (its empire fading) and the United States (its empire rising), which at times, degenerated into diatribe, with the US delegates rebuffing any attempt (usually with a touch of arrogance) at proposed institutions at odds with the United States' interests.[6] One example (of which there are many) was John Maynard Keynes' proposal for a new world currency, the Bancor, which unlike the dollar or the UK's pound would have been unattached to any nation.[7] This proposal, which made sense at the time and probably would have worked, was haughtily rejected by the United States, which wanted its own currency—the dollar as the global currency.[8] Not surprisingly, the United States got its wish.

27.3 The Global Institutions Established at Bretton Woods

In addition to the dollar as the global currency, the United States insisted on free markets, liberalization of **trade**, and a democratic world order. To effectuate this, Bretton Woods also gave birth (with the United States' blessing) to the. The General Agreement on Tariffs and Trade (GATT). It was formally established in 1948 to reduce tariffs and promote trade.[9] In 1995, the GATT was replaced by the World Trade Organization (WTO) with the same objectives but with greater enforcement powers and oversight. Both the GATT and the WTO were established according to the free-market interests of the United States, spearheaded by its pro-market businesses who were determined to become world leaders. Both were/are headquartered in Geneva. Overall, "it has allowed the rich countries [especially the US and its allies] to keep the upper hand and to impose their conditions on sensitive questions right down to the present day" (Piketty, 2022, p. 207).

Bretton Woods wanted to construct a rules-based system for global integration that "would prevent the economic chaos and protectionism of the 1930s and would create an environment that would provide stability and predictability to international trade" (Garten, 2021, pp. 6, 7). Central to achieving this objective was establishing a gold standard. As we discuss in our issue on the **Gold Standard**, during the 19th century many of the world's developed nations were on the gold standard, thanks to Great Britain's prodding.[10] During the **Great Depression**, however, all nations went off of it. After WWII, it was thought/ hoped that reestablishing the gold standard (or some variation) would stabilize the world economy—very much welcomed after the tumultuous Depression and World War.

As the emerging global superpower, the US dollar played a key role in the new gold standard. Starting in 1944, any foreign government or central bank holding US dollars could exchange them for gold at the fixed price of $35/ ounce. Other currencies could also be exchanged for dollars at the fixed price. Exchange rates[11] were held fixed to the dollar which in turn was fixed to the price of gold. They could only fluctuate within a narrow 1% band. Doing so (it was thought) would provide a stable background for countries "to sell their grains, food, machinery, and other products" (Garten, 2021, p. 5).

The problem with fixing exchange rates is that they must be fixed at a specified price, regardless of underlying market forces. To illustrate, let's say the world wants little of a nation's goods and services, say Mexico. This would in turn decrease the demand for that nation's currency, the peso. Thus, the peso's price should fall relative to that of the dollar (just like if no one wants to buy a piece of land, its price must decrease). More specifically, an American buying peso would need fewer dollars when the peso's price falls. But given that the exchange rate is fixed, then something must be done to maintain that price. To do so, the central bank would buy pesos on the world market to boost its price. To obtain the funds, Mexico would have to sell either gold, dollars, or another currency.

If the reduced demand for pesos is sustained, then Mexico could run out of assets trying to maintain the artificially high price. To prevent this, and without any other means of redress (as during the 1930s), Mexico could either depreciate its currency (by selling pesos, if it had access) which in turn would make exports cheaper (denominated in pesos) or erect trade barriers which would reduce the demand for imports. This is exactly what nations did during the 1930s. Known as 'beggar thy neighbor' policies, they would invariably result in tit-for-tat retaliation. Hence, the steadily declining trade during the 1930s

The International Monetary Fund (IMF) was designed to prevent such protectionist policies by providing loans for countries experiencing exchange rate problems. The IMF would also provide technical experts to help redress the underlying structural problems. Thus, the IMF provided the requisite funds for promoting trade and reducing protection.

The IMF's sister organization, the World Bank, provides development funds for all nations (especially from the global South) for infrastructure investment. Both the IMF and the World Bank were (and still are) headquartered in Washington, DC, where President Roosevelt reputedly was to have said their location was deliberate so that he could keep an eye on both.[12]

The economic and financial framework established at Bretton Woods helped propel the United States into global dominance, with New York replacing London as the world's financial capital. Additionally, the "gold-dollar link was a critical underpinning of America's political/military alliances in the heat of the Cold War" (Garten, 2021, p. 9).

27.4   Bretton Woods Unraveling?

The gold standard was the first Bretton Woods institution to go. The gold-dollar link contains the seeds for its own destruction. Given that the United States needed to run trade deficits to inject dollars into the global economy, a greater supply of dollars decreased its value, which in turn incentivized nations to redeem their dollar holdings for gold (Garten, 2021, p. 7). Given that the United States was running out of gold in the early 1970s, it had no choice but to go off the gold standard.[13]

Today, the United States remains in the driver's seat in terms of setting the global rules of the game, although other nations are knocking on the door (most noticeably the **BRICS**) urging for a new Bretton Woods. The clamor for reform, however, started well before. In 1976, for example, Mahbub ul Haq (1979, p. 183), wrote that,

> the debate on the establishment of a new economic order has only recently begun…the poor nations have only a pro forma participation in the economic decision making of the world. Their advice is hardly solicited when the big ten industrialized nations get together to take key decisions on the world's economic future; their voting strength in the Bretton Woods institutions … is less than one-third of the total; and their numerical majority in the U.N. General Assembly has provided no real influence so far on international economic decisions.

As this manuscript goes to press, it appears that the Bretton Woods institutions are breaking down,[14] and even "on the verge of collapse" (*The Economist*, May 11, 2024, p. 7). Three reasons[15]:

- Despite tariffs remaining low, nations around the world (including the United States, China, and India) have collectively imposed trade sanctions more than four times that during the 1990s. The United States, for example, has imposed significant trade restrictions on **Russia** (to punish aggression) and **China** (to forestall direct competition).
- The rise of industrial policy which is fostering/nurturing the strategic industries of the present/future, e.g., renewable energy, computer chips, electric vehicles by implementing protectionism: "By one count governments adopted over 1500 policies to promote specific industries in both 2021 and 2021 compared with almost none in the early 2000s" (*The Economist*, May 11, 2024, p. 14). This has created an "industrial subsidies' arms race, evidenced by a 74% probability that one big nation subsidy will beget another within a year" (*The Economist*, May 11, 2024, p. 14).
- The IMF has redirected its focus away from promoting sound macroeconomic policy toward climate change and income inequality. And the WTO is today, for all practical purposes, impotent, thanks to the United States refusing to appoint more personnel.

The Bretton Woods rules-based global institutions which played a key role in the promotion of trade and the reduction in global poverty is now being replaced by an inward focus of 'might is right.' This has, not surprisingly, increased 'trade policy uncertainty' an empirical measure tracked by **the Federal Reserve**.

27.5   Pathways to Reforming Bretton Woods

Reforming Bretton Woods can take one of three pathways[16]: (1) Do nothing, and let the existing institutions atrophy; (2) completely dismantle the current system and build a new one from scratch; or (3) work within the existing system and enact needed reforms. Given the momentum and the **BRICS'** clarion call for change, #1 is not realistic, although paradoxically, it very well might happen. And, given the vested interests of the **IMF, the World Bank**, and **the WTO** to continue the current global order, #2 is not likely. That leaves option #3. This doesn't mean that radical reform is not possible, or that new institutions cannot be established, but for all practical purposes, reform (if it is to happen) will have to work within the current system.[17] This doesn't mean that there aren't any obstacles to reform; on the contrary, the obstacles are significant. One in particular is the global financial network (the central banks, private sector banks and finance corporations) which over the years "has reproduced inequality, increased international tensions, and blocked more effective responses to environmental crises" (Block, 2023, p. 39).

Unlike in 1944, all nations must participate, especially from the global South. At this point, it remains to be seen how this will play out. Of the BRICS nations, currently **China** is in the best position to effectuate change, while its relationship with the United States is probably one of the world's most critical.

27.6 Conclusion

The world is facing multiple challenges including "rebuilding the American economy so that it benefits all citizens, dealing with China and Russia/Iran/North Korea, the road to Net Zero, getting off our addiction to fossil fuels, and a rapidly growing AI which threatens to change our very way of life" (Garten, 2021, p. 326). Taken together, these changes will "put severe stress on the operation of the global economy and the international currency/monetary systems… suggesting a new set of global arrangements" (Garten, 2021, p. 326).[18] That the world needs more cooperation and not less is a major theme of our book, which we will return to in our conclusion. It is time to consider a new Bretton Woods,

> for the redefinition of international rules is critical not only for the global North, but also for the global South and the entire planet. The current economic system, based on the uncontrolled circulation of capital, goods, and services, without social or environmental objectives, is akin to a neo-colonialism that benefits the wealthiest.
>
> (Piketty, 2022, p. 174)

Notes

1 Some Americans confuse the United Kingdom, Great Britain, and England. But they are distinct. Great Britain is England, Scotland, and Wales. It was formed in 1707 when England (containing Wales) merged with Scotland. The United Kingdom was formed in 1801 with the union of Great Britain and Ireland. When Ireland formally succeeded in 1922, six northeastern counties remained with the UK, becoming Northern Ireland (capital Belfast), while the rest of Ireland (capital Dublin) in 1949 became the Republic of Ireland. In 2016, a UK-wide referendum voted to secede from **the European Union**. This formally occurred in February 2020, which in turn has accelerated talks of Scottish independence.
2 Francis Bacon first uttered this phrase in 1626 referencing the Spanish empire, the global superpower of his day. In 1773, Earl McCartney, a colonial administrator, first used this phrase in reference to the Great Britain. Source: 'Phrase Finder,' https://www.phrases.org.uk
3 You would think that measuring how much stuff each nation produces and then comparatively ranking it, would be a piece of cake. Perhaps so if every nation used the same currency. But since that is not so, we must first decide which currency to use.

And then figure out what stuff to measure. Like many issues in economics, there is disagreement. We will return to this in **Basic Economic Indicators**.

4 For a good discussion of the rise and fall of superpowers, see Chua (2007) and Phillips (2002, pp. 171–200).

5 It was also the site of my (Jack) first relationship (as a high school student) with a member of the opposite sex. This happened on a CYO (Catholic Youth Organization) ski trip. I grew up in Massachusetts and Bretton Woods was about a three-hour drive north. Unfortunately, for me (or perhaps, looking back, very fortunate) the parish priest (our moderator) randomly selected me for his ski trip roommate.

6 For the full transcripts and proceedings, see United States Department of State (1944).

7 Keynes (1883–1946) was perhaps the most important economist of the 20th century. His *Theory of Employment, Interest, and Money* (1936) revolutionized the relationship between the government and the economy, endorsing an active role for the government in ending recessions. His *The Economic Consequences of the Peace* (1919) excoriated the peace agreement which had ended WWI, especially the punishing reparations inflicted on Germany, as unworkable and unenforceable, which as he predicted, sowed the seeds for future conflict.

8 The dollar as the global currency means that for other nations to be able to buy global commodities such as oil and medical supplies (which are expressed in dollars), they must have access to dollars. While there are many ways to inject dollars into the global economy, the way chosen was for the United States to run trade deficits, i.e., buying more from abroad then selling. To do this, the United States must purchase other currencies (say pounds if it wants to buy from the UK) by selling dollars, hence the increased supply of dollars.

9 We will discuss this in our **Tariffs and Trade**.

10 The sun really never set on the British Empire. Thus, its merchants wanted uniform and stable prices throughout the Empire, which could only be accomplished via a gold standard.

11 An exchange rate is the price of one currency in terms of another. For example, if I want to go to London, I must exchange my dollars for British pounds. Given that both currencies are limited in supply (although at times it doesn't seem so with the dollar) their price (i.e., how much of one is given up to obtain the other) will vary according to market forces, i.e., demand and supply. So, an increased demand for dollars vis-à-vis pounds, would increase the price of dollars per pound, all else equal.

12 For a discussion of the historical evolution of these institutions, see Reardon et al. (2018, pp. 278–284).

13 We discuss this in our **Gold Standard** chapter.

14 One common measure of global trade, 'Exports as a percent of global GDP,' after doubling from 1970 to 2010 (12–30%) have since stagnated, as has cross border investment (*The Economist*, May 11, p. 7).

15 This paragraph relies heavily on *The Economist* (May 11, 2024, p. 7).

16 For an in-depth discussion of these options, see Reardon et al. (2018, pp. 286–290); and Van der Berg (2012, pp. 474–497).

17 The Nobel laureate, Amartya Sen strongly endorsed working within the present system to redress injustice, arguing that most people when clamoring for justice don't want a "perfectly-just society, but merely… the eliminations of some outrageously unjust arrangement" (Sen, 2009, p. 26).

18 A global tax on financial transactions has been suggested as a means of killing two birds with one stone: (1) help finance needed changes; and (2) reduce the profitability of speculating on currency (Block, 2023, p. 39).

References

Block, Fred, (2023) 'The Habitation Economy,' *Dissent*, Vol. 7, No. 3, Fall, pp. 29–40.

Chua, Amy (2007) *How Hyperpowers Rise to Global Dominance and Why They Fail*, Doubleday, New York.

Garten, Jeffrey (2021) *Three Days at Camp David: How a Secret Meeting in 1971 Transformed the Global Economy*, Harper, New York.

Haq, Mahbub ul (1979) 'The Inequities of the Old Economic Order,' in Charles K. Wilber, (Ed.), *The Political Economy of Development and Underdevelopment*, Random House, New York, pp. 179–187.

Keynes, John Maynard (1919) *The Economic Consequences of the Peace*, Macmillan & Co., London.

Keynes, John Maynard (1936 [2010]) *The General Theory of Employment, Interest, and Money*, Martino Publishing, Mansfield Center, Connecticut.

Phillips, Kevin (2002) *Wealth and Democracy*, Broadway Books, New York.

Piketty, Thomas (2022) *A Brief History of Equality*, Belknap Press of Harvard University, Cambridge, Massachusetts, translated by Steven Rendall.

Reardon, Jack, Maria Madi, and Molly Scott Cato (2018) *Introducing a New Economics*, Pluto Press, London.

Sen, Amartya (2009) *The Idea of Justice*, Penguin, New York.

'The Great Recession' (2024) *The Economist,* May 11, pp. 13–15.

'The New Economic Order' (2024) *The Economist,* May 11, p. 7.

United States Department of State (1944) 'Volumes I and II,' in *Proceedings and Documents of the United Nations Monetary and Financial Conference, Bretton Woods, New Hampshire, July 1–22, 1944* (July 1–22). https://fraser.stlouisfed.org/title/430#7569

Yu, Fu-Lai Tony and Diana S. Kwan (2023) *China's Long and Winding Road to Modernization*, Lexington Books, Lanham, Maryland.

28 The Gold Standard

The Issue: Gold by definition is scarce and its scarcity provides its value. Linking the paper money that circulates in the economy for everyday use to a scarce commodity like gold subdues inflation, but at the same time constricts economic growth. Not surprisingly, given today's recent bout of *inflation* (the highest in the United States since the early 1980s, a call for return of the gold standard has been made. A gold standard pits those in favor of low prices against those who favor growth. It is an issue that won't go away.

28.1 Preface

One of my favorite movies (Jack) is *The Wizard of Oz*, although my kids refuse to watch it with me because they dislike the opening tornado scene (we live in Wisconsin where tornadoes are not uncommon). The movie, starring Judy Garland, was released in 1939. It was based on the book, *The Wonderful Wizard of Oz*, published in 1901, and written by L. Frank Baum. While intended primarily as a children's book, the author included the economic and political controversies of his day as backdrop, including the gold standard.

28.2 Defining a Gold Standard

A gold standard links the amount of money that people and firms use for everyday purchases with the amount of gold in the economy. A global gold standard has three main characteristics (Temin, 1991, p. 6):

- Free flow of gold between individuals and countries.
- Maintaining fixed values of national currencies in terms of gold and each other.
- The absence of any international coordinating mechanism.

DOI: 10.4324/9781003591856-32

28.3   A Brief History of the USA Gold Standard

To understand the role of gold in the United States, we can divide USA history into five periods[1]:

- **1792 to 1862**: The dollar was backed by a bimetallic system of gold and silver. The Coinage Act of 1792, which established the US Mint, fixed the dollar to 24.75 grains of fine gold and 371.25 grains of fine silver. An obvious problem was that the exchange rate of dollars for either gold or silver was susceptible to frequent changes in supply, forcing Congress to revalue, but not before speculators could profit.
- **1862 to 1879:** To finance the Civil War, Congress went off the gold standard, relying on fiat money.[2] "During this time, the Union printed $450 million in paper currency and inflation rose by 80 percent. By the end of the Civil War, the national debt had reached $2.7 billion." During this time, the nation went off the silver standard as well in order to reign in inflation. While inflation was bad in the North, it was even worse in the South.
- **1879 to 1933**: Considered the classic period of the gold standard and even 'the most perfect one ever' (Lewis, 2013). During this period, the gold standard was ideologically attractive, since

> it is part and parcel of a laissez-faire and free trade economy. It links every nation's money rates and price levels with money rates and price levels of all the other nations that are 'on gold.' It is extremely sensitive to government expenditure and even to attitudes or policies that do not involve expenditure directly…and, in general, to precisely all those policies that violate the principles of economic liberalism [i.e., of free markets].
>
> (Schumpeter, 1954, pp. 405–406)

During the Great Depression, the United States, like all other nations, was forced to go off the gold standard.

- **1933–1944:** A period of transition. Private citizens could not hold gold,[3] nor could they redeem paper currency for gold. Gold during this period could only be used in transactions with foreign governments.[4] In 1934, the price of gold was increased from $20.67/ounce to $35/ounce. The higher price allowed the **Federal Reserve** to inflate the economy by increasing the supply of dollars.[5] As the 1930s progressed, all nations went off the gold standard.
- **1944–1971:** President Roosevelt worked with leaders across the globe to create a new gold standard in which the dollar was pegged to gold and the price of gold was maintained at $35 per ounce. Any nation, firm, bank, or individual could exchange dollars for gold at the fixed price.

- **1971–present:** The United States went off the gold standard, due to a mismatch been the United States' supply of dollars vis-à-vis gold: Specifically, the supply of dollars increased to a much greater extent than did USA gold holdings. In 1955, for example, the United States held $21.7 billion in gold deposits vis-à-vis $13.5 billion in dollars. By 1971, USA gold had dwindled to $10.2 billion vis-a-vis $40 billion in dollars, meaning that the United States could not honor its full convertibility commitment (Garten, 2021, p. 9). In addition, US inflation was increasing, interest rates were being increased and the nation was running both budget deficits and trade deficits. Since 1971, the dollar is backed up only by full faith in the federal government and the **Federal Reserve**. Incidentally, today no countries are on the gold standard.

28.4   The Politics of the Classical Gold Standard 1879–1933

Thanks to the gold standard, deflation was rife during this period, especially before 1900. Wages and prices fell. **Unemployment** increased. **Recessions** became longer and more frequent. Ordinary farmers and laborers suffered. This led to a movement to back the dollar with a commodity more plentiful than gold, such as silver.[6] This in turn would reflate the economy causing prices and wages to increase. Others, however, questioned the need to link money with any commodity, be it gold, silver, or platinum. Why not have a central or national bank dispense money as needed? Eventually, this happened but not until 1913. We will return to this when we discuss **The Federal Reserve**.

The gold standard created a sharp rift between the Democrats (who advocated a silver standard, given that silver was much more plentiful than gold) and the Republicans who advocated a gold standard to ensure economic stability, especially no inflation. The Republicans won this battle, with newly elected President William McKinley[7] (1897–1901) severing any connection of silver to paper currency with passage of the 1900 Gold Standard Act.[8]

In *The Wonderful Wizard of Oz* (the book) and *The Wizard of Oz* (the movie), gold and silver symbolism abound.[9] For example, in the movie, Dorothy's slippers were ruby, but in the book they were silver; the yellow brick road symbolized the gold standard; gold is measured in ounces and is abbreviated oz; the scarecrow represented the suffering farmer who was hit hard by deflation[10]; the Tin Man represents the industrial worker whose joints were rusted from high unemployment[11]; and the cowardly lion represents the great orator and populist, William Jennings Bryan, who unsuccessfully ran as the Democratic Party candidate in the presidential elections of 1896, 1900, and 1908. The contemporary press sometimes called him a lion and sometimes criticized him for having a loud roar with no bite. Incidentally, at 36 years old in the 1896 election, he was the youngest presidential candidate ever of a major political party, and the youngest person to ever win an electoral vote.[12]

Bryan strongly advocated a silver standard. He gave his famous 'Cross of Gold Speech,' a passionate plea for moving off the gold standard in favor of silver at the 1896 Democratic Convention. The speech propelled him to national fame, and it remains one of the most studied and influential speeches in American history.

28.5   Arguments in Favor of a Gold Standard

- A gold standard has a simplistic appeal: Money can only increase as the amount of gold increases. And since gold is scarce, **inflation** will not be a problem.
- Linking the money supply to a scarce commodity is the best preemptive solution for inflation.
- Without inflation, when a banker establishes a loan to a customer, the repaid loan will have the same purchasing power as before (i.e., it can buy the same quantity of goods and services). Inflation benefits the borrower since the repaid loan will have less value than before (in terms of its purchasing power), while deflation benefits the lender since the repaid loan will have greater value than before.
- A gold standard renders the discretion of a central bank moot since it isn't necessary for the purpose of regulating the supply of money. Indeed, during the late 19th century, the United States had no central bank.
- While one might posit that the recent bout of inflation would not have happened if the United States was on a gold standard, such a statement cannot be made out of context. Certainly inflation would have been much less, but at the expense of a much longer and deeper recession, possibly rivaling the United States' most severe recession (August 1929–March 1933). As is, the COVID-induced recession (from February 2020 to April 2020) was the shortest on record. At the same time, a preponderant reason for the severity of the August 1929–March 1933 recession was the stubborn tenacity to the gold standard,[13]

> The Depression was not even inevitable in 1929. Had policymakers been able to free themselves from the straightjacket of the gold standard, they could have instituted countercyclical policies [i.e., inflate and spend, rather than deflate and cut spending]. But without the change, the rules of the gold standard mandated deflation…[which] was about the worst thing that could have been done.
>
> (Temin, 1991, p. 34)

28.6   Arguments against a Gold Standard

- Given that the money supply is linked to a scarce commodity, i.e., gold, there isn't enough money for all. The result is **deflation**. This was evident throughout the period of the classical gold standard, in addition to high

unemployment, and frequent and severe **recessions**, including the longest in our history[14] (October 1873–March 1879).

- A gold standard links the movement of prices to the supply of gold. Specifically,

> if the global stock of gold [is] static but global output increased, the price level has to fall (since the same money stock now has to support a larger volume of commercial exchange…If large deposits of gold or silver were suddenly discovered, as in Spanish America in the 16th and 17th centuries or California in the mid-nineteenth century, prices could skyrocket [bringing] undeserved windfalls to some (Piketty, 2014, p. 711).

- Today, most of the world's gold is produced overseas. Three guesses as to today's largest gold producer. If you guessed China, you get a gold cigar.[15] If you guessed Russia, you get a bronze cigar, since Russia is the world's third largest producer. In 2022, China produced 10.6% of global gold production, followed by Australia, and Russia, both at 10.3%. The United States is fifth at 5.5%. So why link our money supply to a commodity over which we have little control? In this spirit, in 1923, John Maynard Keynes, a citizen of Great Britain, which at the time was on the gold standard, noted that given,

> the existing distribution of the world's gold, the reinstatement of the gold standard means, inevitably, that we surrender the regulation of our price level and the handling of the credit cycle to the Federal Reserve Board of the United States…it would make us too dependent on the policy and on the wishes of the Federal Reserve Board.
>
> (Keynes, 1931 [2010], pp. 181–182)

- An argument made today (but not so much in the 19th century, since many believed that the economy was self-regulating) is that the gold standard severely constricts the nation's discretion to deal with emergencies and unforeseen events. Thus, if the United States was on the gold standard during Covid, the government's hands would have been tied; there would have been nothing it could have done.[16] Yes, a gold standard would have prevented inflation, but at a devastating cost.

28.7 Conclusion

In every presidential election, a gold standard is usually proposed by the Republican Party's far-right, sometimes even becoming part the Republican platform. The argument is made that only a gold standard can temper what seems to be an arbitrary and explosive growth in the money supply. Conversely, those who prefer discretionary control over monetary policy do not advocate a gold standard which straightjackets monetary policy.

We cannot say with certainty that the absence of a gold standard will always result in inflation; nor conversely, that a gold standard will automatically result in deflation. This is because it is the relationship between the amount of money and the level of economic activity that determines the movement of prices. The greater the mismatch, the greater the probability for either inflation or deflation, depending on the context.

Notes

1 Studenski and Kroos (1963) is indispensable as background.
2 Fiat, from the Latin 'let it be done.' Fiat money has no intrinsic value; nor is it directly tied to any commodity; it only exists by government order. Only trust in the issuing agency gives fiat money its value.
3 This executive order was rescinded in 1974 by President Ford.
4 Keynes celebrated the UK going off the gold standard, "There are few Englishmen who do not rejoice at the breaking of our gold fetters. We feel that we have at last a free hand to do what is sensible. The romantic phase is over, and we can begin to discuss realistically what policy is for the best" (Keynes, 1931 [2010], p. 245).
5 For an explanation, please see our **Federal Reserve** chapter. When the Federal Reserve was created in 1913, it was allowed to print money, while keeping 40% of the value of the paper currency in gold.
6 Without getting too technical, some people also argued for a bi-metallic standard, i.e., linking gold *and* silver to dollars, which also would have increased the amount of money available for everyday use.
7 McKinley, first elected in 1896, and then re-elected in 1900, was assassinated in 1901 barely into his second term. His vice president, Theodore Roosevelt, assumed the presidency in September 1901. At 42 years of age, he was the youngest to assume the presidency. In 1960, JFK at 44 years of age was the youngest to be elected president. Incidentally, McKinley defeated William Jennings Bryan twice for the presidency: 1896 and then again in 1900.
8 Studenski and Kroos (1963, pp. 243–248) discuss the specifics of this Act, as well as its immediate effects.
9 Yes, Baum wrote a children's book intended for children, but the symbolism in his book came from his world. Whether it was deliberate or inadvertent is irrelevant, and to even ask, ignores the subtle yet dynamic and evolving relationship between reader and author. A reader might not see something exactly the same way as the author intended and vice versa, and different readers from different times/places will see different things.
10 Most farmers at the time were in debt. During deflation, the nominal value of one's debt does not change, but given that prices and wages are lower, the debt becomes a greater burden, as the lower prices make it hard to repay.
11 The word 'unemployment' was coined during the 1880s.
12 The US Constitution mandates a minimum age of 35 for a person elected to the presidency (Article II, Section 1, Clause 5). Interestingly, there is no prohibition against a person *running* for office under the legal age, only that he/she cannot be elected. There is no constitutional maximum age for the presidency. Donald Trump, at 78 is the oldest elected president, elected in 2024.
13 Studenski and Kroos (1963, pp. 352–376) provide a good foundational background

14 Specifically, "in the United States from 1865 to 1895, falling prices were a normal part of life. The cost-of-living index (as calculated by the Federal Reserve Bank of NY; with 1913 = 100) fell from 103 in 1886 to 73 in 1895" (Gunderson, 1976, p. 349).

15 Pistilli (2023) provides the statistics on gold ownership.

16 The United States experienced its shortest recession on record in 2020 (February–April), only lasting two months. Compare this with the longest recession 1873–1879, lasting 65 months. The main difference was that during the COVID recession, the federal government (both the Trump and Biden Administrations) vigorously implemented effective solutions, whereas when the United States was on the gold standard, there was no active intervention.

References

Garten, Jeffrey (2021) *Three Days at Camp David: How a Secret Meeting in 1971 Transformed the Global Economy*, Harper, New York.

Gunderson, Gerald (1976) *A New Economic History of America*, McGraw-Hill, New York.

Keynes, John Maynard (1931 [2010]) 'Essays in Persuasion,' *The Collected Writings of John Mayard Keynes*, Volume 9, Cambridge University Press, Cambridge, UK.

Lewis, Nathan (2013) 'The 1870–1914 Gold Standard: The Most Perfect One Ever Created, *Forbes,* January 3 (forbes.com).

Piketty, Thomas (2014) *Capital in the Twenty-First Century*, Belknap Press of Harvard University Press, Cambridge, MA; translated by Arthur Goldhammer.

Pistilli, Melissa (2023) '10 Largest Producers of Gold by Country', *INN Gold Investing News*, June 15 (investingnews.com)

Schumpeter, Joseph (1954) *History of Economic Analysis*, Oxford University Press, New York.

Studenski, Paul and Herman E. Kroos (1963) *Financial History of the United States*, 2nd ed., McGraw Hill, New York.

Temin, Peter (1991) *Lessons from the Great Depression*, The MIT Press, Cambridge, MA.

Part V
International Trouble Spots

29 The People's Republic of China

The Issue: Here in the United States, both Democrats and Republicans share a get-tough attitude toward China, with little significant difference between the two. Indeed, it seems that the only agreement across the aisle today is the bipartisan 'China is the bogeyman.' China is viewed as America's greatest threat, and not just economically (as with Japan during the 1980s) but also ideologically, geopolitically, and militarily. The future of the 21st century will be determined by how this multi-faceted rivalry will play out. Thus, it is of the utmost importance for China and the United States to dialogue. Uncertainty, dislike, and distrust are always a breeding ground for war. The purpose of this chapter is to provide a foundational understanding upon which constructive dialogue can occur.

29.1 A Brief Pre-1949 History

China is an ancient nation going back thousands of years. Qin Shi Huang, who ruled China from 221 to 210 BC (and gave himself the epithet of emperor), unified China (largely along its present-day borders) while building the Great Wall to protect against marauding invaders from the North. He died in 210 BC, but not before ordering the building of a vast mausoleum, guarded by the now-famous Terra Cotta warriors.

Like **Russia** and **Iran**, China has reinvented itself over the years. Its latest incarnation, the People's Republic of China (PRC), dates only to October 1, 1949, following a tumultuous civil war. On one side was the Nationalists tracing their roots to 1894 and to Sun Yat-Sen. When the Qing Dynasty fell in 1912, ending 2000 years of imperial rule, the Nationalists became a political party (the Kuomintang, or KMT) led by Chiang Kai-shek. The KMT wanted a representative constitutionally based government, as well as international recognition and integrity. They governed China from 1928 to 1949. On the other side of the civil war was the Chinese Communist Party (CCP) led by Mao Zedong. The CCP[1] was founded July 23, 1921, with a different vision for China than the KMT, one that would bring China under socialist rule.

DOI: 10.4324/9781003591856-34

The KMT and the CCP cooperated in the early 1920s, and then again (although reluctantly) after Japan invaded China, July 7, 1937. But the ideological rifts were too strong, and after Japan surrendered in 1945, they resumed fighting. Mao and the CCP ultimately won, forcing the Nationalists to flee to Taiwan.

29.2   A Brief Note on Mao Zedong[2]

It is impossible to understand modern day China without understanding Mao Zedong (1893–1976), a revolutionary leader who founded communist China. And it is impossible to gloss over Mao's ideological-driven tragedies which killed millions of his own people.

The Great Leap Forward (1858–1960) (GLF) was designed to 'overtake Great Britain and outperform the USA,' by imposing communes and denigrating the family as a stabilizing unit (Yu and Kwan, 2023, p. 43). It was an unmitigated disaster,

> resulting in shortages of food and industrial products, overproduction of poor-quality goods, deterioration/mismanagement of industrial plants, and exhaustion and demoralization of the peasantry and intellectuals… millions of people died of starvation.
>
> (Yu and Kwan, 2023, p. 49)

But rather than admit defeat and self-blame, Mao blamed others. He was also convinced that GLF failed because its reforms did not go far enough.[3] So in 1966, he launched the ideological Cultural Revolution, "to purge the nation of anti-revolution sentiments, while destroying the 'four olds,' "old customs, culture, habits, and ideas" (Yu and Kwan, 2023, p. 70). The Cultural Revolution was even more devastating than the GLF. By the time, it ended in 1976 (with Mao's death) millions of people had died from starvation.[4]

Not surprisingly, Chinese living standards were no different October 1, 1949, when Mao came to power then on September 9, 1976, when he died. During Mao's tenure, China remained "one of the poorest nations of the world" (Yu and Kwan, 2023, p. 43), along with untold suffering and millions of deaths.

29.3   A Quick Look at Taiwan

The war between the Nationalists and the Peoples Republic of China (PRC) was never formally concluded. Hence, the visceral (and ongoing) disagreement over whether Taiwan (officially known as the Republic of China, i.e., ROC) belongs to the mainland as the PRC claims, or is an independent nation, as Taiwan claims. Each side claims historical legitimacy to the 'real' China.

The PRC has long maintained a non-negotiable goal: the reunification of the mainland with the three islands of Macau, Hong Kong, and Taiwan. Macau, taken by the Portugal in 1557 was returned to China in 1999; Hong Kong taken by the British in 1841, was returned in 1997. Now, China insists on the non-negotiable return of Taiwan, making it clear that the nation will go to war over this issue.[5] Here in the United States, Taiwan's independence has bipartisan support, which at this point, would be the issue most likely to precipitate a war between China and the United States. Ostensibly, it appears that there is little room for compromise between China and Taiwan, but this is where the art of statecraft becomes so important.

Since 1949, the history of Taiwan can be divided into two periods[6]:

- **Sinicization, 1949–1988**: To strengthen the unity between Taiwan and mainland China. Education, the media, universities, and cultural life were all Chinese focused. Taiwan was ruled "according to China's image…as a miniature of mainland China…through strong government policies and education, people in Taiwan were socialized as Chinese, and Taiwan was socially constructed as China" (Yu and Kwan, 2023, p. 225). Only Mandarin was taught in schools.
- **Americanization: 1988–present**: This period begins with the death of Chiang Ching-Kuo (the eldest son of Chiang Kai-Shek[7]) who ruled Taiwan from 1978 until his death in 1988. During this period, Taiwan adopted a western political system and assimilated Western values, while modeling its university system after America's. Three factors account for this Americanization[8]: (1) An increasing number of Taiwanese students returning home after being educated in the West, especially the United States. Incentivized by attractive packages from the Taiwanese government, once home they were offered top jobs in sectors throughout the economy, especially in Information Technology; (2) an increasing nationalist identity encouraging Taiwan to look west, rather than to China; and (3) the increasingly important defense relationship between the United States and the ROC.

A centerpiece of the United States/Taiwan relationship is the Taiwan Relations Act (TRA) of 1979. Its main objectives include the following[9]:

- To preserve and promote extensive, close, and friendly commercial, cultural, and other relations between the people of the United States and the people on Taiwan.
- Peace and stability in the area.
- The United States' decision to establish diplomatic relations with the PRC rests upon the expectation that the future of Taiwan will be determined by peaceful means and that any effort to determine its future by other than peaceful means, including by boycotts or embargoes is considered a threat to the peace and security of the Western Pacific area and of grave concern to the United States.

- The United States shall provide Taiwan with arms of a defensive character and shall maintain the capacity to resist any resort to force or other forms of coercion that would jeopardize the security, or social or economic system, of the Taiwanese people.

Noteworthy, and a key point of concern, is that the Act does not obligate the United States to defend the ROC in the event of an attack, although it is hard to imagine otherwise (Campbell, 2024, p. 46).[10] Only that the United States "shall maintain the capacity ... to resist any resort to force." This passage poses a strategic ambiguity: Will the USA defend the ROC given an attack by the PRC or not? What does 'maintain the capacity' actually mean? Given this strategic ambiguity,

> Some members of Congress want to clarify…in the positive in order to strengthen deterrence vis-à-vis an increasingly more belligerent PRC. But others state that the ambiguity kills two birds with one stone: it tempers Chinese belligerence, while encouraging Taiwan to strengthen its own defense forces.
>
> (Campbell, 2024)

As this manuscript goes to press (October 2024), the US House of Representatives approved a US$500 million military aid package for Taiwan, along with US$2 billion in supporting loans and loan guarantees. The US Senate is working on its variation.[11] Finally, we should mention that in January 2024, Lai Ching-Te of the Democratic Progressive Party (center of left, nationalist) was elected president of Taiwan.[12] He is adamantly opposed to any reunification with the mainland (as is the DPP) citing "substantial differences between the two economies" (Campbell, 2024, p. 48). Interestingly, earlier polls indicate (September 2023) that 76.7% of Taiwanese respondents see themselves as Taiwanese, rather than Chinese or some mix (Campbell, 2024, p. 48). Meanwhile, evidence indicates that China wants to seize Taiwan by 2027 (Campbell, 2024, p. 47). Stay tuned.

29.4   China Today

29.4.1   *The Reforms of Deng Xiaoping*

Following a tumultuous two years of internal bickering and posturing, after Mao's death, Deng Xiaoping (1904–1997) assumed China's leadership in 1978, holding that position until November 1989. Deng retreated from Mao's overt political/ideological activities in order to modernize China.[13] The goal was to introduce market forces and market reforms, open up to the West, minimize ideology, while maintaining tight political control, i.e., "socialism with Chinese characteristics" (Yu and Kwan, 2023, p. 50).[14]

Deng introduced his 'Four Modernizations': agriculture, science and technology, industry, and defense. The specifics included abolish collectivized agriculture; incentivize peasants to be self-sufficient while allowing them to sell their surplus on market; reduce central planning; use technology to increase productivity; and enter joint ventures as a preponderant way of learning by doing (Yu and Kwan, 2023, p. 50).

Deng's modernization reforms were implemented gradually,[15] i.e., 'groping for stones to cross the river.' From 1988 to 2002, China's GDP increased 9.4% annually (on average) (Yu and Kwan, 2023, p. 43). A key factor explaining China's GDP success is its large, internal markets, enabling its firms to achieve economies of scale (i.e., produce more output at a declining unit cost) just as the United States did during the 19th century. In 2001, China became a member of the **World Trade Organization** (WTO) a move which, at the time, was applauded by the West as a sign of openness and more reliance on markets.[16]

29.4.2 *China Today*

China, with 1.4 billion people, is the world's second most populous nation, having been overtaken by India in 2019. China possesses 24% of the world's population, but only 10% of its arable land, while producing 20% of global output, second only to the United States' 24%.

Since the late 1970s, China has used market incentives in order to reform its economy, but that doesn't make it a market economy. China is best described as neo-mercantilism, defined as an economic system where "government officials, policymakers, and merchants seek to increase wealth and power via state action...by subordinating private interests to national interests" (Yu and Kwan, 2023, p. 164). Mercantilism was practiced widely throughout the Western world during the period 1500–1800, hence the term neo-mercantilist. Mercantilists, then as now, believe that global wealth is fixed, so that one nation's wealth accumulation comes at the expense of another. This is unlike capitalism which assumes that wealth creation has no upper limit.[17] Under mercantilism, producers benefit while consumers are treated as instruments for the greater gain of the nation.[18] Other modern-day nations practicing neo-mercantilism include Meiji Japan (1868–1912), Taiwan, and Singapore. All have done quite well, and China is using its success to model for Latin American and African nations.

Politically, China is authoritarian, ruled by the Chinese Communist Party. Authoritarianism means that no one else politically runs the show. Being a one-party state gives the government the ability to control, influence, direct, and nudge the economy, one way or another. Certainly, democracy is not in the cards: China, like **Russia**, has no experience with democracy, making it highly unlikely, but not impossible, that it will ever move in that direction.

China has ample access to cheap coal, which it relies on for 73% of electricity production—much like the United States during the 19th century. It has a much higher savings rate than the United States, both per capita and overall. Thanks to its indulgence in **fossil fuels**, its major cities have long been among the world's most polluted (although now sharing that distinction with India), which explains its major investment in renewable energy.[19]

29.4.3 Xi Jinping, China's Leader Since 2012

Born in 1953, Xi is currently the general secretary of the Chinese Communist Party, chairperson of the Central Military Commission; and since 2013, the president of the People's Republic of China. Xi Jinping,[20] as a perspicacious student of history, has studied why and how empires unravel (both at home and abroad, especially the USSR in 1991). He understands China's long history, and especially, the palpable connection between famine and instability.[21] Thus, for Xi, China must become self-reliant in food production for political and national stability and to attain superpower status.[22] This explains China's vigorous stockpiling of crops (as the world's largest producer and consumer of wheat, for example, it maintains half the world's wheat reserves), purchasing overseas farmland, and developing climate change-resilient crops.[23]

29.5 Will China Overtake the United States?

Just a decade ago, the consensus was that China would overtake the United States as the world's largest economy sometime during the 2030 (Pillsbury, 2016). Today, the consensus has been downgraded: "China and the USA will approach parity and remain locked in that position for decades to come" ('Peak China,' 2023). However, the consensus is by no means unanimous. Thomas Piketty for one: "barring an unexpected collapse, over the coming decades the [PRC] is likely to become the greatest economic power on the planet even if no one can predict how soon and for how long" (Piketty, 2022, p. 230).[24] But then three pages later Mr. Piketty acknowledges that, "the anticipated demographic decline and accelerated aging of the population are also going to constitute major challenges for the regime, and in the course of the second half of the twenty-first century may lead to the replacement of China by India as the world's primary power" (Piketty, 2022, pp. 233–234). It is to these anticipated problems that we now turn.

The consensual downgrade is due to China's projected slowdown, what some have called 'Peak China' (Beckley and Brands, 2022) and others 'The Great Maturation,' (*Editorial: Peak China,* 2023). Whatever we term China's slowdown, it is due to several factors:

- **Declining and aging population**: China officially ended its one-child policy in 2016 (begun in 1980)[25] and is now encouraging more births, however, with little tangible luck. As China ages, its labor force decreases, as does its GDP; with more resources allocated to the elderly. Unlike the United States, which has looked to **immigration** to expand its economy, China has had an extremely restrictive immigration policy, "Chinese citizenship [is] the most difficult to acquire in the world" (Yu and Kwan, 2023, p. 173). Mainly because China "wants a population of pure Chinese blood so that the government can convey Chinese nationalism to people effectively…and to make it easier for China to control and govern" (Yu and Kwan, 2023, pp. 173–174).

- **Declining productivity:** (defined as output per worker, a key economic variable for any society).[26] After years of high-profile investment (high-speed rails, airports, bridges, etc.), the returns to new investment are diminishing, although China's productivity is still increasing at a respectable 3% annual rate. Lower growth combined with China's aging population will set the stage for conflict over dwindling resources.
- **Over Savings and Under Consumption:** China is currently over-investing (40% of its GDP), while its citizens are over-saving and under-consuming. (Conversely, the USA is under-investing, only 16% of GDP, while under-saving and overconsuming.[27]) This needs to be reversed.
- **Deflation**: Beginning in 2023, manifest in falling export prices, declining food prices (especially pork, very popular in China), declining producer prices, and a real estate glut, causing property prices to fall with multiplicative effects on the construction and household appliance sectors. As discussed in our chapter **Economic Indicators,** deflation leads to reduced demand, unemployment, and possible recession. Hence, "if China's policymakers do not do more to dispel deflation, China's growth will be needlessly slow" (*The Economist*, August 12, 2023, p. 11). The best antidote for deflation is economic stimulus, directed at increasing consumer spending, decreasing the savings glut, while stimulating investment in green infrastructure.

In March 2023, Xi Jinping visited Heilongjiang, located in China's northeast, an economically laggard province in the grip of deep deflation. In a talk to provincial leaders, Xi urged the cultivation of 'new productive forces.' This has become China's new buzzword; reminding us of Deng's 'reform and opening up.' Xi recognizes that China's once vibrant economy is stagnating, bordering on deflation,

Its workforce is now shrinking and demand for property has slumped: fewer people are moving to China's cities, speculative gains on real estate are no longer assured and potential homebuyers are reluctant to buy flats in advance in case distressed developers run out of cash before building is complete. The property downturn has hurt consumer confidence and deprived local governments of crucial revenue from land sales. Even after China abandoned its strict Covid-19 controls, the economic recovery has been muted and uneven. Spending has not been strong enough to fully employ China's existing productive forces.

(The Economist, April 6, 2024, p. 57)

For a nation accustomed to double digit growth rates, lackluster growth has been quite a setback. As a solution,[28] Xi Jinping has vowed to 'reinvent China's economy' by:

- Upgrading traditional industries (such as agriculture).
- Breaking foreign strangleholds on existing technologies (primarily caused by USA blockades, especially **Artificial Intelligence** technology, thanks to the August 2022 CHIPS Act), including lithography machines and aviation-grade stainless steel).
- Develop the industries of tomorrow, e.g., photonic computing, brain–computer interfaces, nuclear fusion, and digital twins—simulacra of patients that doctors can monitor for illnesses that might arise in their real-life counterparts.

This 'cultivating new productive forces' comports nicely with China's goal to become "the leader of the next industrial revolution" (*The Economist*, April 6, 2024). However, its lofty goals are coming up against significant problems[29]:

- Excessive bureaucratic interference with private enterprise firms.[30] In China, state enterprises account for approximately 40% of total output. Despite their well-known inefficiency vis-à-vis privately held firms, state enterprises are viewed as a bulwark of party rule and an important pillar of the economy (*The Economist*, May 13, 2023, p. 19). However, a broader measure of state control/influence in the economy is the share of public capital (all levels of government and all collectivities): In 1978, this share was about 70%; and since the middle 2000s has stabilized at 30% of national capital (Piketty, 2022, p. 230).
- Weak consumer spending.
- A tenuous and inadequate social security system forcing many Chinese, especially in rural areas, to over-save for their retirement.
- Overcapacity in infrastructure and especially in the property sector, which has depressed prices while reducing revenue received by local governments, making their situation more financially precarious.
- An antiquated household registration system that denies migrant workers equal access to public services.

These problems must all be adequately addressed in order for China to successfully cultivate 'new productive forces.'

The jury is still out on how China will react to its predicted declining power. Will China turn inward to increase the living standards of its people, whose income per capita is less than half of America's? Or will it become more belligerent to deflect domestic discontent, and try to unite Taiwan with the mainland? (*The Economist*, May 13, 2023). It is hard not to discount China turning more belligerent, given that "autocratic regimes sometimes respond to domestic difficulties by trying to distract the population with foreign adventurism" (Krugman, 2023).

29.6 The United States and China: Cooperation or Conflict?

Historically, there has never been a bi-polar cooperative relationship among superpowers (among nations, yes; among global powers, yes; but not among superpowers, or what Any Chua calls hyperpowers.[31] Instead, one nation has always maintained global dominance. While history teaches us that superpowers rise and fall, problematic are the transition points, i.e., one nation rising as another is falling; or when the dominant nation senses another rapidly gaining ground.

Thucydides,[32] whom many consider to be the father of history, notes such a transition in his *The History of the Peloponnesian War*,[33] "The real cause [which plunged the Hellenes into a war of such magnitude] I consider to be the one which was formally most kept out of sight. The growth of the power of Athens, and the alarm which this inspired in Lacedaemon, made war inevitable." At the time, Athens was the rising power and Sparta the existing power.

Based on this passage, Graham Allison (2018) developed the concept of 'the Thucydides Trap,' finding that of 16 such transition points in history, i.e., when a rising power threatens to displace an established power, 12 have resulted in war. This is not a causal effect, nor does it offer guidance in the current relation between the United States and China, other than suggesting the Trap as an historical possibility.[34] However, what we can say with confidence is that the two nations are "struggling for hegemony in world affairs" (Yu and Kwan, 2023, p. 181), and that there exists a high degree of mutual mistrust and suspicion.

Nevertheless, we see three compelling reasons for a closer, even bi-polar superpower relationship between China and the United States:

- They are the world's two largest economies,[35] together producing almost half of global output. Neither nation can act on its own without affecting the other.
- The two economies are intricately linked. As the world's largest surplus nation, China has lent trillions of dollars to the USA Treasury to finance its **budget deficit** and **trade deficits**. And the United States, the world's largest deficit nation needs China's surplus funds. Such a practical relationship cannot be terminated quickly by either side, although China has signaled its intention to slowly ease away. In one sense, China feels that it is enabling the United States to live beyond its means.[36]

- China and the United States are the largest global emitters of global green-house gas emissions, with China at 27% and the United States at 11% (although per capita, the United States emits four times China's amount). This suggests, at a very basic level, the need to cooperate, and for all practical purposes, the world cannot attenuate the effects of **climate change** without the active cooperation of these two nations.[37]

There is no reason why the United States and China should be belligerent toward each other, never mind becoming mortal enemies, especially with the above-mentioned centripetal forces toward cooperation. We feel that failure to develop a more cooperative relationship was (and is) a lost opportunity, not easily recoverable.

At the same time, however, several factors are causing both nations to disentangle, decouple, divorce, de-risk; or as Charles Hutzler (2023) suggests, "choose your [own] D word." The United States, post-COVID, wants to reduce its over-reliance on global supply chains dominated by China. The United States is also worried of a possible war with China over Taiwan. Add to this each nation's struggle for hegemony, along with a self-focus on economic and national security, and we have a ready-made recipe for the 'D word.'

Other nations, which ironically rely on Chinese imports, jump at the chance to process intermediate goods and sell the finished product to the United States. Ostensibly, this circumvention bi-passes the official links with China, but in reality, the United States' reliance on Chinese goods remains intact, so much so that "much of the decoupling is phony," and even worse, "it has been deepening the economic links between China and other exporting nations pitting their interests against America's" ('Costly and Dangerous,' 2023).

A complete decoupling is out of the cards (at least right now) given current economic and political entanglements, but it remains to be seen how much of a partial decoupling will occur, and if the momentum to decouple will be enough to undo the ties that bind and the factors pushing for cooperation.[38] Stay tuned.

Yes, both nations possess nuclear weapons. And their conventional armies globally are ranked #1 (USA) and #2 (China).

29.7   What to Do About China?

This, of course, is a very narrow question, tinged with self-serving arrogance, assuming that China is only to be used instrumentally. Having said that, let's look at the United States' options:

- Do nothing and ignore China as if it doesn't exist. Impossible. The United States and China are locked in an inextricable bilateral relationship on many levels.

- Bide for time, during which Taiwan can strengthen its defenses, and the United States can attenuate its dependence on China (Alperovitch and Graff, 2024).
- With America's left and the right advocating putting America first, we should relegate China to the back burner and focus on America. Impossible. Not only is China too big to ignore, but each nation's policies will affect the other.
- Be belligerent. Why? What possible benefit would the United States obtain? This is not a playground where the provocative bully wins, but the real world where actions have consequences.
- Constructively engage with each other, work on solving mutual problems, while accepting and living with mutual differences. Although this option is the most practical and the only logical one, it nevertheless isn't easy. For one thing, China's emphasis on national rights and economic development, puts it at odds with America's emphasis on human rights underlined by a liberal democratic order. At the same time, cooperation with China could drive a wedge between it and **North Korea, Iran, and Russia**; the nations currently posing an existentialist threat to the United States. Perhaps the United States could take a page from the Nixon playbook, when President Nixon reached out to China in 1972.[39] Nixon and Kissinger (his Secretary of State) understood the big geopolitical picture and how mutual cooperation could benefit the strategic interests of the United States,[40] while at the same time, driving a wedge between China and the USSR.

It isn't just the national leaders that should engage, but also citizens, businesspeople, students, mayors, etc. This is a most effective way to chip away at stereotypes and to forge deeper connections and understanding.[41] The relations between nations should be established by what the polity thinks, rather than just between leaders and/or elites.

29.8   China's Push for a New World Order

China's approach for a new world order is three-pronged:

- A true global multilateralism as envisioned in the inaugural United Nations Charter, which was (and is) to help *states* co-exist and trade peacefully, while legitimizing opposing values.[42] This is opposed to the current global order's (spearheaded by the United States) almost exclusive focus on individual human rights. China would also like to see states cooperate over broader economic issues and on issues of national security.
- As a founding member of the **BRICS**, China would like to expand it, so that it includes the voices of developing nations. China feels that a remake of the

USA-imposed global order is long overdue, an interest that it shares with **Russia**.

• To replace the US dollar, currently the global currency, with its own currency, the RMB; or at the very least, to replace the US dollar with an artificial currency such as the Bancor. Incidentally, this was suggested as a possibility by Great Britain during the 1944 **Bretton Woods** conference but rejected by the United States.

29.9   The Deepening Friendship between China and Russia

A major development has been the coalescing of Russia's interests with that of China.[43] This has developed into a full-fledged friendship between the two nations, and between the two leaders Xi Jinping and Vladimir Putin. In February 2022 (in Moscow), the two leaders pledged that "their friendship has no limits, that there are no forbidden areas of cooperation"[44] (*The Economist*, May 18, 2024, p. 34). At the meeting, Mr. Putin noted that the two countries have "a profound mutual trust and were strengthening their foreign policy coordination in the interests of building a just multipolar world order" (*The Economist*, May 18, 2024, p. 34). Significantly, this meeting was held just a few days before Russia's invasion of Ukraine in February 2022.

The friendship has deepened economic and military ties. For example, "China has been supplying Russia with 'dual use' goods, i.e., goods that can be used for both military and civilian purposes such as ball bearings, electrical machinery and parts, and metalworking machine tools" (*The Economist*, May 18, 2024, p. 35). While Russia, in turn, has been supplying China with oil and natural gas; and with overland gas pipelines in the works. Given their mutual desire to lessen the US dollar's global influence, China and Russia have been engaging in bilateral trade deals that bypass the dollar (Yu and Kwan, 2023, p. 166). Russia has become an ever more important partner in China's push against American might. Indeed, this strengthening friendship[45] "is not a marriage of convenience, but is one of vital, long-term necessity" (*The Economist*, May 18, 2024, p. 36).

29.10   Conclusion[46]

As this manuscript goes to press (October 2024), tensions remain high between the two nations, fueled by mutual distrust and uncertainty, and spearheaded by each nation's differing strategic objectives and different world visions. It is, however, of the utmost importance for China and the USA to dialogue.[47] Uncertainty, dislike, and distrust are always a breeding ground for war,

> rival powers must find ways to communicate—particularly when tensions are high…simply talking will not make America and China friends, either.

But [communication] reduces the risk of miscalculation, which is no small thing when both powers are nuclear-armed giants.

('Great Powers Must Talk,' 2022)

Reducing the risk of miscalculation is critical and is reason alone for regular dialogue.

How we reconcile our differences and how we navigate our conflict with China, will largely determine what the new global order will look like. It will also determine how we transition to the future; and, to a large extent, the future itself. It will also determine whether and if we can avoid war with China, with the most likely provocation being China's invasion of Taiwan.

There is a lot to be said for statesmanship and for geopolitical strategy, especially in the context of today's multi-faceted tensions. This doesn't mean that we jettison our scruples and our values—after all, it is scruples and values that give every nation its defining character. Quite the contrary, we need to accept our differences (which in turn are built on different visions of the how the world works, although not necessarily mutually exclusive) and negotiate and dialogue on this basis. Sounds easy, but it is not, involving a lot of diplomacy. But this is what the art of politics is all about.

Notes

1 For an insightful commentary on the CCP's role in China, see Chang et al. (2021). Incidentally, Mao was a founding member. Pipes (2003) offers a classic discussion of communism, stretching back to ancient Greece.
2 We found (Yu and Kwan, 2023) most helpful. Their interdisciplinary approach is unique in explaining China's long and winding road to modernization, emphasizing culture, literature, history, entrepreneurship, hermeneutics, and phenomenology (Yu and Kwan, 2023, p. ix). Also recommended is Hsu (1999).
3 Mao's personality disorders were a central cause of the Cultural Revolution, "the bi-polar co-existence of intense paranoia and grandiose fantasies exhibited in the last ten years or so of his life, testified to Mao's deteriorating narcissistic disorder, which, in turn, translated into China's chaotic and frenzied politics of the Cultural Revolution" Yu and Kwan (2023, p. 62).
4 China shares this policy of self-induced killings with Russia and North Korea. See our chapter, **Iran, North Korea, and Russia**.
5 Taiwan, a nation of 23 million, lies approximately 100 miles from mainland China. The island was under Japanese occupation (1895–1945); Chinese occupation during the Qing Dynasty (1883–1895); the Dutch and Portuguese during the Age of Exploration. For a detailed history of Taiwan, see Rubinstein Murray (2018).
6 Diep-Nguyen (2020) discusses the formation of post-1949 Taiwan, with interesting parallels to the creation of the state of Israel.
7 Chiang Kai-Shek ruled Taiwan from 1949 until his death in 1975. Yen Chia-Kan, a Chinese chemist, served as president from 1975 to 1978. Chiang Ching-Kuo ruled until his death in 1988.
8 This discussion is heavily based on Yu and Kwan (2023, pp. 225–227).
9 Source: H.R.2479—Taiwan Relations Act (96th Congress 1979–1980).

10 This paragraph heavily relies on (Campbell, 2024).
11 For further discussion, see 'US House passes military aid for Taiwan' (2024).
12 The DPP lost control of the legislature in the same election to the KMT and the pro-China Taiwan's People Party (Campbell, 2024, p. 49). So, it will be interesting to see how the relationship between the two nations evolves.
13 For an informative account of Deng and Mao, see Salisbury (1992).
14 Interestingly, there is discussion in China about whether a Cultural Revolution could happen again (Yu and Kwan, 2023, pp. 73–74).
15 See Jha (2002) for a detailed discussion of China's gradual reforms vis-à-vis the reforms of India and China.
16 The Clinton administration at the time favored China's WTO accession as a means to influence its trade and development (Yu and Kwan, 2023, p. 186).
17 For a classic read on mercantilism, see Hecksher (1935).
18 Adam Smith (1723–1790) founded the discipline of economics (at least here in the West). His *The Wealth of Nations* (1776 [1976]) is a scathing critique of European mercantilism: "It cannot be very difficult to determine who have been the contrivers of this whole mercantile system; not the consumers…whose interest has been entirely neglected, but the producers, whose interests have been so carefully attended to…it has not been very favorable to the revenue of the great body of the people, to the annual produce of the land and labour of the country … [nor] to the revenue of the sovereign; so far at least as that revenue depends on the duties of customs" (Smith (1776 [1976] Vol II, Book IV, Ch. VIII, p. 180 and Vol. II, Book V, Ch. II, Article IV, p. 411).
19 We expand on China's energy situation in our chapters, **Fossil Fuels**, and **Climate Change**.
20 For a good biography of Xi, see Wong (2023). In addition, see Bougon (2018), and Tsang and Cheung (2024).
21 Since Emperor Huang unified China more than 2000 years ago, it has been ruled by different family-controlled monarchies, hence the term 'dynasty'. The succession of monarchal dynasties ended abruptly with the 1911 Revolution, toppling the Qing dynasty.
22 This paragraph relies on Hong (2023).
23 In addition, China buys 1/5 of the world's oil, half its refined copper and zinc; and 3/5 of its iron ore. China also has the world's largest navy and the largest shipbuilding industry. And, thanks to massive investment in electric vehicles, China is the world's largest automobile manufacturer, and soon to be its largest exporter.
24 One reason for Mr. Piketty's optimism is that "the Chinese state has considerable assets that far outweigh its debts, and this gives it the means to pursue ambitious policies, both domestically and internationally, particularly concerning investments in infrastructure and in the transition to new forms of energy. In contrast…the main Western states' share of public property is almost nil or even negative" (Piketty, 2022, p. 234). One such asset stands out: China has $3.2 trillion worth of foreign exchange reserves, far more than any other nation, and double that of Japan, the second highest holder. The People's Bank of China holds these reserves, funneling them out to various development projects.
25 Mao aggressively pursued pro-natal polices, assuming that high population would beget economic growth. China's population doubled between 1949 and 1976. In 1979, realizing that high population was a problem (it was a tad under 1 billion) China imposed its harsh one child per couple policy. This in turn decreased the birthrate to well under fertility replacement, while increasing the male/female ratio. On

October 29, 2015, China rescinded this policy, allowing all families to have two children (Yu and Kwan, 2023, p. 173).

26 We further discuss this important variable in our chapter on **Artificial Intelligence**.

27 We discuss this important relationship in **Tariffs and Trade**.

28 This paragraph relies heavily on *The Economist*, April 6, 2024.

29 The following bullets are taken from *The Economist*, June 29, 2024.

30 This is despite contrasting rhetoric. For example, Yi Gang, a former governor of China's central bank said, "Both theory and practice have proven that the market is the most efficient way to allocate resources… [but alas] equal treatment is easier said than done" (*The Economist*, June 29, 2024, p. 33).

31 See Bobbitt (2002). Chua defines a hyperpower as a nation that has "amassed such extraordinary military and economic might that they essentially dominate the world" (2007, p. xxi). She also discusses the historical evolution of economic superpowers.

32 Thucydides (460 BC–400 BC) whose fastidious and impartial attention to detail, evidencing points with interviews and factual documents, while avoiding any gratuitous appeal to the gods, earned him the nickname, the father of history.

33 The war occurred from 431 BC until 404 BC and was fought between Sparta and Athens, with Sparta eventually winning.

34 For an extended discussion, see Chan (2020)

35 Of the world's 197 nations (albeit the total is disputed by two, based on the exact definition of a nation) most use their own currency. Interestingly, the UN does not view Taiwan as a separate nation, but rather as part of China; thus, Taiwan is not a member of the World Bank or the IMF. Only 12 other nations recognize Taiwan as a separate nation; the United States does not. We briefly discuss the methodology used to compare the output of nations in our chapter, **Economic Indicators**.

36 I (Jack) would always get an earful on this score (as if I had anything to do with the United States' macro policies) during my frequent lectures in China.

37 With so many once-in-a-lifetime climate events becoming more common, how efficacious is a unipolar world? Today, global cooperation is most needed over a range of issues discussed in this book, e.g., **Artificial Intelligence**, **Net Zero**, **Fossil Fuels**, and **Trade and Tariffs**.

38 In an important speech, May 26, 2022, USA Secretary of State Anthony Blinken noted that China is engaged in asymmetric decoupling, i.e., making China less dependent on the world and the world more dependent on China (Blinken, 2022). No doubt the United States' position will change, rendering it difficult to accurately read the somewhat ambiguous tea leaves to see in which direction this important relationship is heading.

39 For an interesting account of Nixon's China visit, see Salisbury (1992, pp. 306–314).

40 It is not our intention to whitewash Nixon. No president is without criticism; after all we are all human beings, and as human beings we all have faults, although, admittedly, Nixon had more than most. See (Kissinger 2012).

41 A helpful guide on Chinese culture is Balcikonyte-Huang and Flowerr (2021). Also, see Yu and Kwan (2023, especially pp. 195–208), and Yu and Kwan (2024). In addition, highly recommended is the novel *Soul Mountain* (2000) by the Nobel laureate Gao Xingjian.

42 This discussion relies heavily on (Peak China, 2023). For further discussion, see our chapters **NATO**, and **the UN**.

43 This paragraph relies heavily on *The Economist*, May 18, 2024.

44 The phrase 'has no limits' intrigues. Is there any possible act committed by either side that could limit?

45   Xi Jinping was instrumental in convincing Russia not to use nuclear weapons against Ukraine.
46   A major point of contention between the United States and China is tariffs. We thought it better to discuss in our chapter **Tariffs and Trade**.
47   Alas, the same advice holds for our domestic factions and squabbles.

References

Alperovitch, Dmitri and Garrett Graff (2024) *World on the Brink: How America Can Beat China in the Race for the Twenty-First Century*, Public Affairs, New York.

Allison, Graham (2018) *Destined for War: Can America and China Escape Thucydides's Trap*, Mariner Books, Boston.

Balcikonyte-Huang, Indre and Kathy Flowerr (2021) *China - Culture Smart!: The Essential Guide to Customs & Culture*, 4th ed., Kuperard Publishing, London.

Beckley, Michael and Hal Brands (2022) *Danger Zone: The Coming Conflict with China*, W.W. Norton, New York.

Blinken, Anthony (2022) 'The Administration's Approach to the People's Republic of China,' Speech delivered at George Washington University, Washington DC, May 26, 2022. https://www.state.gov/

'Blowing Against Ill Economic Winds' (2024) *The Economist*, June 29, 2024, pp. 32–33.

Bobbitt, Philip (2002) *The Shield of Achilles: War, Peace, and the Course of History*, Anchor Books, New York.

Bougon, François (2018) *Inside the Mind of Xi Jinping*, Hurst, London.

Campbell, Charlie (2024) 'Straight Talk,' *TIME,* June 24, pp. 45–49.

Chan, Steve (2020) *Thucydides's Trap? Historical Interpretation, Logic of Inquiry, and the Future of Sino-American Relations*, University of Michigan Press, Ann Arbor.

Chang, Ailsa, Sarah Handel, and Ashish Valentine (2021) 'Unpacking The 100-Year History Of The Chinese Communist Party, NPR: All Things Considered, July 5, (npr.org).

'China and Russia: An autocratic bromance' (2024) *The Economist*, May 18, pp. 34–36.

Chua, Amy (2007) *Day of Empire: How Superpowers Rise to Global Dominance and Why They Fail*, Doubleday, New York.

'Costly and Dangerous: Joe Biden's China Strategy is Not Working' (2023) *The Economist*, Editorial, August 12, p. 9.

Diep-Nguyen, Luke (2020) *Taiwan: The Israel of the East: How the US, China, and Japan Influenced the Forming of a New Nation*, Pacific Atrocities Education, San Franscico.

'Editorial: Peak China,' (2023) *The Economist,* May 13, p. 7.

'Great Powers Must Talk' (2022) *The Economist*, Editorial, November 12.

Hecksher, Eli (1935) *Mercantilism*, 2nd ed., London, Allen & Unwin.

Hong, Nicole (2023) 'Extreme Floods and Heat in China Ravage Farms,' *The New York Times*, June 25, p. 4.

H.R.2479 - Taiwan Relations Act) H.R.2479 - 96th Congress (1979–1980). https://www.congress.gov.

Hsu, Immanuel C. Y. (1999) *The Rise of Modern China*, 6th ed., Oxford University Press, Oxford, UK.

Hutzler, Charles (2023) 'US, China Poised to Drift Farther Apart,' *The Wall Street Journal,* August 11, p. A7.

Jha, Prem Shankar (2002) *The Perilous Road to the Market*, Pluto Press, London.

Kissinger, Henry (2012) *On China*, Penguin, New York.

Krugman, Paul (2023) 'Why is China's Economy Stumbling?' *The New York Times*, Opinion Section, August 13, p. 3.

'Peak China,' *The Economist* (2023), May 13, pp. 14–20.

Piketty, Thomas (2022) *A Brief History of Equality*, Belknap Press of Harvard University, Cambridge, Massachusetts, translated by Steven Rendall.

Pillsbury, Michael (2016) *The Hundred-Year Marathon: China's Secret Strategy to Replace America as the Global Superpower*, St. Martin's Griffin, New York.

Pipes, Richard (2003) *Communism: A History*, The Modern Library, New York.

'New Productive Forces: Hype and Hyperopia,' *The Economist* (2024), April 6, pp. 57–59.

Rubinstein Murray A. (2018) *Taiwan: A New History*, Routledge, London.

Salisbury, Harrison (1992) *The New Emperors: China in the Era of Mao and Deng*, Avon Books, New York.

Smith, Adam (1776 [1976]) *An Inquiry into the Nature and Causes of the Wealth of Nations*, The University of Chicago Press, Chicago.

'The Chinese Economy: Straight-Forward' (2023) *The Economist*, Editorial, August 12, p. 11.

Thucydides (404 BC) *The History of the Peloponnesian War*, The Internet Classics Archive, http://classics.mit.edu//Thucydides/pelopwar.html, translated by Richard Crawley.

Tsang, Steve and Olivia Cheung (2024) *The Political Thought of Xi Jinping*, Oxford University, Oxford.

'US House passes military aid for Taiwan' (2024) *Taipei Times*, June 30,

Xingjian, Gao (2000) *Soul Mountain*, Perennial, New York.

Wong, Chun Han (2023) *Party of One: The Rise of Xi Jinping and China's Superpower*, Simon and Schuster, New York.

Yu, Fu-Lai Tony and Diana S. Kwan (2023) *China's Long and Winding Road to Modernization*, Lexington Books, Lanham, Maryland.

Yu, Fu-Lai Tony and Diana S. Kwan (2024) 'A Cultural Interpretation of the World's Two Most Tragic Dramas: Romeo and Juliet and 'The Flower Princess,' *The International Journal of Pluralism and Economics Education*, Vol. 15, No.1, pp. 33–53.

30 Iran, Russia, and North Korea

The Issue: Four nations pose an especially vexing existentialist threat to the interests of the West, and especially the United States: Iran, Russia, North Korea, and China. Why? How did this come to be? What are the drivers of this deep-seated animosity? What can be done? How should the United States react? These questions are necessary to discuss post-2024. This chapter will discuss Iran, Russia, and North Korea, while **China** will be discussed in a separate chapter.

30.1 Preface

During my freshman year, I (Jack) took a really interesting seminar on revolutions. It was the quintessential course taught by the quintessential professor at the quintessential liberal arts campus. We read widely, and the erudite teacher exposed us to new ways of thinking. Since then, I've retained a keen interest in revolutions and have read as much as I can on the subject.[1] Of the four nations that pose the most trouble for the USA post-2024, three were born of revolution (Russia, China, and Iran) with the post-regime starkly different than before. These four nations pose an especially vexing and troubling existentialist threat to the interests of the West, and especially the United States. An entire book could be written on each, but our objective is to cogently describe why each nation is a threat—the quintessence if you will, and the United States' best response, post-2024.

30.2 Iran

30.2.1 Brief History

Once known as Persia, the ancient kingdom was part of the Fertile Crescent stretching from Iraq, Israel, Jordan, Lebanon, Palestine, Syrai, northern Kuwait, southeastern Turkey, and western Iran. The Fertile Crescent originated during the transition of humans from wanderers to sedentary farmers, settling humans

DOI: 10.4324/9781003591856-35

into one place. Many of the staple crops that have since sustained humanity also developed in this region (Diamond, 1999, pp. 94–113).

Like many ancient nations (e.g., India, China, and Russia), Persia has reinvented itself over the millennia, and "like Afghanistan, Persia had been a target of foreign ambitions since Alexander the Great" (Gruner, 2022, p. 394).[2] During the 7th century, Islam developed first in Saudi Arabia and then spread outward. Very early on, a dispute arose over the proper successor to Muhammad (570–632 CE), Islam's founder. This dispute has caused a rift within Islam which remains to this day. Given that this rift affects our story, we need to explain[3]

> the main historical difference is between the mainstream Sunnis (traditionalists from sunnah, tradition) who comprise 87 percent of all Muslims, and the Shi'ites (literally partisans of Ali, Muhammad's son-in-law, whom Shi'ites believe should have directly succeeded Muhammad but was thrice passed over and who, when he was finally leader of the Muslims was assassinated). Geographically, the Shi'ites cluster in and around Iraq and Iran, while the Sunnis flank them to the West (the Middle East, Turkey, and Africa) and to the East (through the India subcontinent, which includes Pakistan and Bangladeshi) on through Malaysia, and into Indonesia.
>
> (Smith, 1991, p. 258)

Although the substantive differences are minor, the two camps are quite wary of each other and mutually belligerent. This difference is still important today as Islamists tend to portray today's events within this divide.

Discussion of today's Iran often begins with December 7, 1979, when Shia fundamentalists overthrew the Shah (literally, 'king') of Iran. The Iranian revolution is assumed to demarcate past Iran from the present. But to fully understand today's Iran and its relation to the United States, we must start at the beginning of the 20th century. Not surprisingly, the events involve oil.[4] In 1908, largely due to British exploration efforts, the Anglo-Persian Oil Company was formed with the backing of the Shah of Iran. The British ruthlessly exploited Iran's oil while only allotting a pittance in remuneration, which became a long-standing and simmering Iranian[5] grievance over several decades. Iran insisted on a 50–50 split much like that negotiated by Saudi Arabia and the United States with the Arabian Oil Company. Britain refused, and on May 2, 1952, the newly elected and immensely popular Prime Minister of Iran, Mohammad Mosaddegh[6] nationalized the Anglo-Persian company.

This, of course, angered both Britain and the United States.[7] British intelligence combined with the newly formed CIA[8] to overthrow Mosaddegh in August 1953. He was replaced by Mohammad Reza Pahlavi, who ruled as Shah until the 1979 Revolution. The Anglo-Persian Oil company was renamed the British Petroleum Company[9] in 1954 and was forced to operate within a consortium of eight western oil companies (Yergin, 1992, pp. 470–478).

Until the 1979 Revolution, Iran was pro-west, emulating Western consumerism along with freedom for women, "but at its core, the country was a harsh dictatorship run by the Shah and maintained by SAVAK, the Shah's secret police" (Gruner, 2022, p. 181). It was also corrupt with stark differences in wealth/income abetted by one's connections, all brutally enforced—a sure ticket to a revolution. Indeed, "almost all the revolutions which have changed the shape of nations have been undertaken to reinforce or destroy inequality" (de Tocqueville, 2003 [1835, 1840], p. 738).

In addition to the long-simmering and widely held anti-USA sentiment, the Shah's western reforms were deeply resented by Iran's conservative Shiite clergy. Furthermore, the Shah's nationalism was "directly hostile to Islam, since it tried to sever the country's connection to Shiism and base itself on the ancient Persian culture of the pre-Islamic period" (Armstrong, 2002, p. 160).

Between January 7, 1978, and February 11, 1979, a theocratic revolution, led by Islamic Shiite clerics, established the Islamic Republic of Iran. The Revolution's objectives were three-fold:

- Remake Iran from top-to-bottom on the basis of religion, i.e., "to provide a Shia alternative to the secular nationalism of the Shah" (Armstrong, 2002, p. 173).
- Reduce Western power in Iran, and to eliminate it in the Middle East.
- To export its revolution to other Arab Islam states in the Middle East. At the time, Iran considered many of these states illegitimate given their pro-west leaning and their non-committance to principled Islam (Mandelbaum, 2003, p. 206).

Meanwhile in neighboring Iraq, Saddam Hussein, on July 16, 1979, officially assumed power, quickly centralizing control. Iraq borders Iran, and although Iraq is mainly Sunni, it has a sizeable Shiite minority. Hussein viewed himself as the Arab world's leader, assuming the mantle of Nasser's pan-Arab nationalism,[10] of which Iran's theocracy was a primary threat. Not taking any chances with Iran's Revolution spreading, and sensing USA geopolitical weakness (Gruner, 2022, p. 335), Hussein attacked Iran on September 22, 1980.

The Iran/Iraq War "stalemated until August 8, 1988, [and became] the longest conventional war of the 20th century" (Gruner, 2022, p. 335). The War weakened Iran (and Iraq) and successfully diminished Iran's ability to export its revolution, although as we discuss below, it has continued to sow chaos in the region. The Iranian Revolution also destabilized the Middle East since other Sunni regimes didn't want the Iranian revolution exported.

30.2.2   *Iran Today*

Since the 1979 revolution,[11] "training and arming non-state militia groups have been pillars of Iran's foreign and security policy" (MacFarquhar, 2023, p. 11). Calling its proxies the Axis of Resistance,[12] its 'Shiite Crescent' is actively involved in,

- Yemen: Arming the militant Houthi Shiite movement and targeting international vessels in the Red Sea.
- Syria: Assisting the Assad family and attacking US military targets in the region.
- Iraq: Which has a sizeable Shiite minority. Iran has attacked US troops stationed in Iraq. The USA presence ostensibly ensures that the defeated ISIS stays defeated, but also keeps an eye on Iran.
- Lebanon: Where it funds and heavily arms the Shite Hezbollah (the Party of God). It is Iran's most advanced (at least militarily) group. But unlike other militias, Hezbollah is also a political party seeking to govern, while offering substantial social services to citizens.[13]
- Hamas: A Sunni organization which controls Gaza. It was Gaza that invaded Israel on October 7, 2023. It is agreed that "Iran at least provided the means, motivated to disrupt an incipient peace agreement between Israel and Egypt" (MacFarquhar, 2023, p. 11) while also putting the Palestinian situation back on the front burner.[14] While it is uncertain if Iran directly ordered 10/7, "it is clear that Iran's Islamic Revolutionary Guard Corps (the regime's elite military force) clearly helped Hamas to acquire the capabilities needed to mount it, especially the jamming of Israel's defenses and drone attacks" (*The Economist*, December 16, 2023; 'Iran: A Tamer Troublemaker', March 16).

Several events/developments are coalescing to perhaps change Iran's focus to make it less of a troublemaker, although it remains to be seen how events will play out:

- Iran's current supreme leader, Ayatollah Ali Khamenei, at 84 years old, is setting up a possible succession crisis.[15] This is forcing Iran to focus inward to worry about its own stability and keeping its hold on power by bettering the economy, and thus augmenting domestic support. It is not clear to us how genuinely widespread is Khamenei's base of support.
- Iran is hesitant to fully antagonize the United States and incur a regional war involving the United States. Iran's long-term goal has been to foment crisis but at a distance and not within Iran, and directly with the United States.
- Domestic discontent over deteriorating economic conditions. As this manuscript goes to press, Iran's currency, the Rial, has declined precipitously vis-à-vis the dollar. It is currently at a record low of 627,000 Rials to the dollar.

Compare this to 2015, when the Nuclear Accord was signed, when the Rial stood 32,000 to the US dollar (Stevenson, 2024). Since then,

> the rial's decline has been relentless; with the exchange rate now exceeding hundreds of thousands of rials per dollar. The impact of the currency crisis extends beyond the financial realm, affecting various aspects of daily life for Iranians. Inflation has soared approximately 42- 46%. Prices have skyrocketed, and access to imported goods has become increasingly constrained...The erosion of purchasing power has heightened economic uncertainty and social unrest, compounding the existing challenges faced by the Iranian population.
>
> (Stevenson, 2024)

- The poverty rate is now 30% and money is often stashed abroad; inflation has outpaced wage growth while food prices increased 40% from 2022 to 2023. Middle-class discontent had been directed toward former president Ebrahim Raisi and his ministers, who are largely viewed as ill-equipped and incompetent ideologues, with reformers and pragmatists having long been purged. Iran's middle class has "fumed at the flow of money to foreign militias" (*The Economist*, December 16, 2023). The upper class can still live comfortably and travel to London and Toronto, but the middle class is taking a hit and turning their wrath toward the regime,

> Iranians are dismayed that while they suffer economically, the theocratic regime continues to spend billions backing Bashar al-Assad in Syria, the Houthi rebels in Yemen, the Shi'ite militias in Iraq, and the terrorist groups Hezbollah in Lebanon and Hamas in Gaza. The IRGC [the Islamic Revolutionary Guard Corps, established May 1979 as the official guardians of the Revolution] controls more than 70% of the Iranian economy, pays no tax and is answerable only to the autocratic Supreme Leader, Ayatollah Ali Khamenei. Its leaders are venally corrupt, enriching themselves at the expense of the poor, while increasing suppression at home, sponsoring terrorism and waging proxy-wars abroad. Repeated nationwide uprisings have been met with lethal force. Iran is now a powder keg waiting to explode.
>
> (Stevenson, 2024)

- In May 2024, Iranian President Ebrahim Raisi, a hardliner, was killed (along with several senior officials) when his helicopter crashed in a remote, mountainous region. Complicating matters is that Raisi was also seen as Khamenei's possible successor, despite his deep unpopularity. In a July 2024 election to replace Mr. Raisi, 69-year-old Masoud Pezeshkian, a moderate reformist defeated conservative Saeed Jalili.[16] Mr. Pezeshkian, a former heart surgeon and deputy speaker of the Iranian Parliament, has his work cut out for him with, "an ailing economy debilitated by years of sanctions, a frustrated electorate and geopolitical tripwires that have brought Iran close to war twice this year [and a third time as this book goes to press]" (Fassihi, 2024, p. 7). While Iran's president helps shape domestic policy and the direction of foreign policy, ultimate power in Iran resides with the Supreme leader.

30.2.3   *Iran and Nuclear Weapons*

The United States and other Western nations have been worried of Iran attaining nuclear weapons.[17] On July 14, 2015, the Joint Comprehensive Plan of Action Agreement (also known as the Iranian Nuclear Deal) was signed between the United States, Iran, the EU, France, Germany, UK, China, and Russia. The Deal, officially due to expire in 2030, ensures that Iran will not be able to attain/develop nuclear weapons. The Deal,

> was considered a first step. But rather than attempt to extend the agreement, Trump terminated it on May 8, 2018, and instead imposed strict sanctions and even threatened US allies who fail to wind down their activities with Iran…Trump was convinced that he could force Iran to the negotiating table. It didn't work.
>
> (Gruner, 2022, pp. 555 and 556)

And not surprisingly, Iran has since resorted to uranium enriching, which defeats the Deal's original purpose. Bullying doesn't work. But neither does capitulation. Politics involves dialogue, listening, give-and-take, and negotiating. This is hard work and time-consuming. It ostensibly is much easier for ideologues (right-wing or left-wing) to blame and bully. But this does not solve the problem.

As this manuscript goes to press (October 2024), Iran is approaching the enriching threshold of 90% (currently at 60%), which will enable it to produce nuclear weapons. Doing so puts Iran in a delicate situation: It has pledged to use nuclear energy only for peaceful purposes, i.e., producing electricity; yet, the only reason for enriching uranium to 90% is to produce a nuclear weapon (it already claims a stockpile of uranium enough for several bombs). If Iran does develop nuclear weapons (which at this point looks inevitable), three guesses as to who the target is.

The USA State Department has already warned Iran, which in turn puts Iran in a bind: with its economy already suffering from US-imposed sanctions, does it risk further sanctions, and further deterioration of its currency, the Rial? At least outwardly, Iran has said that it will not bow to pressure, especially from the United

States. Iran, a signatory of the Treaty on Non-Proliferation of nuclear weapons, has also pledged to open its nuclear facilities to inspectors from the International Atomic Energy Agency. Mr. Pezeshkian, Iran's newly elected president, has promised to negotiate the lifting of sanctions, acknowledging that they are inextricably linked with Iran's failing economy (Fassihi, 2024, p. 1).

30.2.4   *Iran and Energy*

Iran is a major player in the global oil and natural gas industries.[18] As of 2023, Iran is the third largest natural gas producer (6.4% of global total) following the United States and Russia; and the world's second largest natural gas reserve owner (17.1%) following Russia. Iran is the third largest petroleum reserve owner (17.2%) following Venezuela and Russia. Today, it pumps more than 3.4 million barrels per day, a five-year high. It has been exporting to China and India. This is despite the USA imposing sanctions,[19] although with energy exports, the United States has basically looked the other way. Nevertheless, the sanctions have made it more difficult to repatriate profits.

Finally, like many developing nations, Iran is bearing the ill effects of climate change: Extreme heat, desertification, and water shortages could by 2050 force out 70% of the population (*The Economist*, December 16, 2023). Redressing climate change promises to be a major issue (if it isn't already) which in turn will require significant regional and global cooperation. This partially explains Iran's decision in August 2023 to join the **BRICS**, a global organization designed to counter and supplant Western (i.e., the United States) power and dominance.

30.2.5   *Conclusion*

Iran is facing a bevy of domestic problems. Whether or not the cumulative effect is enough to pacify Iran's bellicosity is not clear. But jettisoning its bellicosity means relinquishing its long-established foreign policy, which in turn requires a fundamental reconstruction of its identity as a nation. To so, at least at this point, looks highly unlikely. Iran remains a theocracy and a militant one at that. In November 2023, for example, widescale protests emerged after a woman, who had been arrested for having her hair too long, was killed. And today, headscarves and the Habib are officially required. Whether this will be maintained with the election of the new president remains to be seen.

Notes

1 Still my two favorite books on revolutions: Arendt (1965) and Brinton (1965).
2 It is impossible to fully discuss Iran's rich history in such a short space, nor is it our intention. See Axworthy (2016).
3 For a good discussion, see Armstrong (2002, pp. 56–58).

4 This discussion relies on Blair (1978) and Yergin (1992). For further discussion, see our **Oil Industry** chapter.

5 On March 21, 1935, Persia officially changed its name to Iran.

6 Elected Prime Minister April 28, 1951, he was the immensely popular among Iranians. He promoted Iran for Iranians and was *Time's* Man of the Year in 1951 (Gruner, 2022, p. 180). For further discussion of this critical period in Iranian history, see Yergin (1992, pp. 456–470).

7 We rely on Kinzer (2008) for this account.

8 President Truman signed the National Security Act of 1947 on September 18, creating the Central Intelligence Agency, "as an independent, civilian intelligence agency within the executive branch. The Act charged the CIA with coordinating the Nation's intelligence activities and, among other duties, collecting, evaluating, and disseminating intelligence affecting national security…In 1949 President Truman signed the Central Intelligence Agency Act, enabling the CIA to secretly fund intelligence operations and develop personnel procedures outside standard US government practices" (CIA, n.d.)

9 British Petroleum traces its roots to 1901, when William D'Arcy, an Australian, obtained a 60-year concession, covering five sixths of present-day Iran, which established the Anglo-Persian Oil Company (Blair, 1978, pp. 29 and 31). During WWI, it acquired British Petroleum from the British government (Yergin, 1992, p. 174).

10 On April 18, 1954, Egypt's Gamal Abdel Nasser (1918–1970), an army colonel, seized power and led Egypt until 1970. For a good understanding of Iraq, Saddam Husain, and contemporary events in a historical context see Committee Against Repression and for Democratic Rights in Iraq (1989).

11 The spiritual leader of the 1979 Iranian Revolution, Ayatollah Ruhollah Khomeini died June 3, 1989, which incidentally (and nothing more than coincidentally) was the same day that China's army began to quash the pro-democracy demonstrators in Beijing.

12 This bulleted section is heavily based on MacFarquhar's (2023, p. 11) pithy and cogent summary of the Axis of Resistance.

13 For a good Hezbollah primer, see Yee (2024).

14 We will discuss further in our **The Palestine Question.**

15 For a discussion of possible successors, see *The Economist*, December 16, 2023.

16 This discussion relies heavily on Fassihi (2024).

17 In the Middle East, only Israel is a member of the nuclear club. The Middle East club should never be expected to remain at one, since one nation attaining nuclear weapons, incentivizes other nations to do so, as both a means of defense and as an imprimatur of modernity.

18 For an expansion of this discussion, and the source for these statistics, see our **Fossil Fuels**.

19 Donald Trump re-imposed sanctions in 2018 when he pulled out of a deal to lift them in exchange for Iran's agreement not to build nuclear weapons.

References

Arendt, Hannah (1965) *On Revolution*, Penguin Classics, New York.

Armstrong, Karen (2002) *Islam: A Short History*, The Modern Library, New York.

Axworthy, Michael (2016) *A History of Iran: Empire of the Mind*, Basic Books, New York.

Blair, John (1978) *The Control of Oil*, Vintage Books, New York.

Brinton, Crane (1965) *The Anatomy of Revolution*, Vintage, New York.

Committee Against Repression and for Democratic Rights in Iraq (1989) *Saddam's Iraq: Revolution or Reaction*, 2nd ed., Zed Books, London.

Central Intelligence Agency (n.d.) Legacy: History of CIA, History of CIA - CIA.

Diamond, Jared (1999) *Guns, Germs, and Steel: The Fates of Human Societies*, Norton, New York.

Fassihi, Farnaz (2024) 'Iranians Elect Reform Leader to Presidency,' *The New York Times*, July 7, pp. 1 and 7.

Gruner, Ronald (2022) *We the Presidents: How American Presidents Shaped the Last Century*, Libratum Press, Naples, Florida.

'Iran: A Tamer Troublemaker' (2023) *The Economist*, December 16, pp. 37–39.

'Inside Putin's Russia,' (2024) *The Economist,* Editorial, March 16, p. 10.

'Lock and Load: Financing Conflict,' (2023) *The Economist*, December 16, p. 60.

Kinzer, Stephen (2008) *All the Shah's Men: An American Coup and the Roots of Middle East Terror*, 2nd ed., Trade Paper Press, New York.

MacFarquhar, Neil (2023) 'A Shiite Crescent: The Proxy Forces Iran has Assembled Across the Mideast,' *The New York Times*, October 29, p. 11.

Mandelbaum, Michael (2003) *The Ideas that Conquered the World: Peace, Democracy, and Free Markets in the Twenty-First Century*, Public Affairs, New York.

Smith, Huston (1991) *The World's Religions*, Harper San Francisco, San Francisco.

Stevenson, Struan (2024) 'The Plunge of Iran's Rial, and Its Cruel Impact On the People,' RealClear Markets, April 5, https://www.realclearmarkets.com.

Tocqueville, Alexis de (2003 [1835, 1840]) *Democracy in America*, Penguin Books, New York.

Yee, Vivian (2024) 'A Primer on Hezbollah, Potent Ally of Hamas and Enemy of Israel,' *The New York Times*, July 7, p. 9.

Yergin, Daniel (1992) *The Prize: The Epic Quest for Oil, Money & Power*, Simon & Schuster, New York.

31 Russia

31.1 Brief History

Like Iran, Russia has a deep history of re-inventing itself. To understand today's Russia, it is necessary to take a look at Russia's immediate predecessor: the Union of Soviet Socialist Republics (USSR). It originated during the Russian Revolution[1] begun in 1917, which overthrew Czar Nicholas II. The USSR officially formed on December 30, 1922, after a brutal Civil War.

The union was fifteen formally independent nations, with Russia and the Ukraine, the two largest in population and area. While the word 'Union' is part of its formal name, the USSR was never a voluntary union; rather, the union was ruthlessly coerced, with constituent parts to fit a not-so-congruent whole. Indigenous cultures were ruthlessly exterminated, regions were played off against one another, and even gravestones manipulated. As a student of the USSR, (Jack) and a frequent lecturer there, one particular event needs to be explained which in turn will help us understand Russia and Ukraine: The enforced and self-inflicted famine during the 1930s.[2]

In 1931–1932, Joseph Stalin (the USSR premier) began a policy (and yes it was a policy, however brutal and inhumane) to transfer food and grain from Ukrainian peasants to Moscow. Ukraine was and still is one of the richest bread baskets in the world. It was "a brutal way of enforcing collectivization and "a vicious backlash against Ukraine's independent farmers whom Moscow felt were too greedy" (Golinkin, 2022, p. 3). These actions were also accompanied by "a wide-ranging attack on all Ukrainian cultural and intellectual centers and leaders, and on the Ukrainian churches…dealing Ukrainian nationalism a numbing blow"[3] (Conquest, 1986, pp. 4 and 334)

This was part and parcel of Stalin's two-fold objective of "*dekulakization* (i.e., killing/deporting peasants, especially the better off, most influential and recalcitrant) and *collectivization* (the abolition of private land ownership and the concentration of the remaining peasanty into the collective farms)" (Conquest, 1986, p. 4).

DOI: 10.4324/9781003591856-36

Today, the enforced famine is known as 'Holodomor' (Death by Hunger). Ukrainians officially honor its memory the fourth Saturday of November. Although we don't know exactly the number of Ukrainians who died, it is estimated between 3 and 5 million (Conquest, 1986).

Most incomprehensible is the internal looting and plundering—especially from the Ukraine—that was typical during Stalin's reign (1924–1953). Hannah Arendt explains that,

> like a foreign conqueror, the totalitarian dictator regards the natural and industrial riches of each country, including his own, as a source of loot and a means of preparing the next step of aggressive expansion...this economy or systematic spoilation is carried out for the sake of the movement and not of the nation...The fact that the totalitarian dictator rules his country like a foreign conqueror makes matters worse because it adds to ruthlessness an efficiency which is conspicuously lacking in tyrannies in alien surroundings.
>
> (Arendt, 1968, p. 417)

Mikhail Gorbachev (1931–1991) was the USSR's last leader. In 1985, he assumed the position of General Secretary of the Communist Party and held that until the USSR's dissolution in 1991. During this last chapter of Soviet history, it was evident to all that the Soviet Union was economically a basket case, in desperate need of reform.[4] It was unable to produce enough goods for its people, and the consumer products that it did produce were shoddy. The living standards of Soviet citizens were well below western standards; and thanks to CNN's weekly broadcasts and contacts with the west, most people were acutely aware of the difference. Indeed, "perhaps in no other society, at a comparable level of per capita income [was] the impact of an ongoing economic malaise so oppressive as in the Soviet Union" (Desai, 1989, p. 3).

In an attempt to save the Soviet Union, Gorbachev implemented two policies which sui generis made sense, especially vis-à-vis the option of doing nothing[5]: Glasnost (literally, 'opening up') to encourage freedom of speech and the press; and perestroika (literally 'restructuring') which transferred economic decision making to local units, away from Moscow's stifling bureaucracy.[6] But given the context of the USSR, especially that the so-called Union since its inception was only held together by brutal force[7] (as every Soviet leader knew) Gorbachev's two policies were a disaster, at least in terms of his original stated objectives.

Together, the policies unleashed the powerful forces of nationalism, which had long been seething beneath the surface. Throughout the mid to late 1980s, nationalism was percolating throughout the USSR and especially in the Baltic republics of Latvia, Lithuania, and Estonia.[8]

Gorbachev gravely underestimated the presence, role, and effects of nationalism. Inexplicably, during his time in office, he did not include any policies for dealing with nationalism; nor did he anticipate the ethnic ramifications of political change until it was too late, admitting that "we underestimated the forces of nationalism and separatism that were hidden deep within our system…creating a socially explosive mixture" (Smith, 1990, p. 296). Writing in 1989, Padma Desai warned, "Ethnic strife and demands for secession are threatening to break the Soviet Union apart. The deepening economic crisis partly reflects and, in turn, contributes to that possibility" (Desai, 1989, p. 126).

On August 18, 1991, Soviet hardliners, intent on saving the USSR, staged a futile coup in Moscow. Boris Yeltsin (who was elected president of the Russian federation just one month before in July 1991) famously stood atop a tank to deliver a scathing speech, effectively arresting the coup. The USSR unraveled on December 25, 1991.

While Gorbachev is revered in the west for ending the Cold War relatively peacefully and for promoting economic and political freedoms within the USSR (for his efforts at both, he was awarded the Nobel Peace Prize in 1990), many Russians (including Vladimir Putin) to this day lament the breakup of the empire and how it cascaded the former USSR off the world stage. For many Russians, December 25, 1991, was surreal, cruel, and inexplicable.

31.2   Putin's Metamorphosis

Vladimir Putin (1952–) assumed the presidency of Russia on December 31, 1999, after Boris Yeltsin unexpectedly announced his resignation. After working as a KGB foreign intelligence officer for 16 years, Putin resigned in 1991 with the rank of lieutenant colonel to begin his political career. First in the mayor's office in his native Leningrad (now St. Petersburg); he then moved to Moscow in 1996, joining Boris Yeltsin's administration. Putin rose quickly through the ranks, eventually assuming the position of director of the Federal Security Service, the KGB's successor. He was elected president in 2001 and served two terms. Due to Russia's two-term presidential limit, Putin took a brief hiatus (2008–2012) and then retook the presidency. He has since continued in that capacity.[9]

Prior to 2007, Putin ostensibly adhered to a conciliatory global system, pledging to work within it; although deep down inside most of us believed that "he may have harbored hatred of the West, and contempt for rules-based order" (Fix and Kimmage, 2023, p. 20). That would have been more consistent with his character; after all, Putin did refer to both the dissolution of the USSR and the Warsaw Pact (i.e., a group of European socialist nations largely mirroring the NATO)[10] as the "biggest geopolitical catastrophe of the [20th] century (Scholz, 2023, p. 24).

But whatever his inner thoughts really were, his outer thoughts and actions dramatically changed in a 2007 speech given at the Munich Security Conference. Perhaps at least externally and at least initially, Putin tried to fit into a

Western-dominated world. But it was inevitable that his true passions would eventually show through, after all "the passions of men [sic] will not conform to the dictates of reason and justice without constraint" (Hamilton et al., 2003 [1787–1788], p. 86).

In Munich, Putin laid out his plans for a new Russia and its changed involvement in world affairs, "while deriding the rules-based international order as a mere tool of American dominance" (Scholz, 2023, p. 24). Indeed, since his speech,

> Russia has been a revisionist power. It has redrawn borders, annexed territory, meddled in elections, inserted itself in various African conflicts and altered the geopolitical dynamics of the Middle East by propping up Syrian dictator Bashar al-Assad.
>
> (Fix and Kimmage, 2023, p. 11)

Putin has also been "undercutting arms control treaties, poisoning and murdering Russia dissidents, [while] cracking down on civil society" (Scholz, 2023, p. 25). In addition, as part of his effort to promote traditional values, Russia's rubber-stamp supreme court, "has labelled LGBTQ+ as extremists subject to lengthy prison sentences while also banning medical intervention and LGBTQ+ as part of a strategy to create imaginary enemies at home" (Saver, 2023, p. 26).[11] And as a true authoritarian, he has vigorously clamped down on the press, even American journalists working in Moscow.

Today, Vladimir Putin's Russia is exactly that: Vladimir Putin's Russia. All dissenting voices have been exiled or killed (sometimes both). There is no dissent, no alternative leaders; nor is there even any grooming for succession. Writing in 1996, Figes accurately prognosticated post-USSR Russia,

> Perhaps even more worrying, authoritarian nationalism has begun to fill the vacuum left by the collapse of Communism, and in a way has reinvented it, not just in the sense that today's nationalists are, for the most part, reformed Communists, but also in the sense that their violent rhetoric with its calls for discipline and order, its angry condemnation of the inequalities produced by the growth of capitalism, and its xenophobic rejection of the West, is itself adapted from the Bolshevik tradition.
>
> (Figes, 1996, p. 824)

Russian history has always fascinated me. While teaching and living in the old USSR, and then in Lithuania and Latvia, I read everything I could to understand the nexus between Russia's Tsarist past, its Bolshevik revolution, and Putin's autocracy. I have always assumed that democracy was never in the cards for Russia post-USSR, despite (or maybe in spite of) Yeltsin's effusive predilections—that Yeltsin's Russia was a temporary aberration bound to fail; that autocracy in Russia was inevitable. McFaul, however, disagrees,

> Russia's present system of government did not result inevitably from historical structures—that is, from cultural, geographic, or socio-economic inheritances from its Soviet or tsarist past. Russia's hundreds of years of autocratic traditions made democratic consolidation in the 1990s harder, but not impossible. Rather, individual choices at pivotal moments pushed Russia towards a more autocratic path and then produced a reordering of preferences and power in favor of continuity within this new autocratic arrangement. Actors, not structures, were the drivers of these changes—both towards democracy and then away from it.
>
> (McFaul, 2018, p. 307)

I would, however, add, that individuals acted in a historical context where democracy was largely absent; there was never a deep well of democratic experience or democratic thought to draw from, while conceding that Putin's actions post-Yeltsin have been critical in evolving Russia to where it is today.

31.3   Putin's War with Ukraine

Putin assumed that the war with Ukraine (begun February 24, 2022) would be his crowning achievement, solidifying his place on the world stage (and in world history) as a major global player along with China and the United States, in a new multipolar world. A successful conquest would have been Putin's first step in reconstructing the Russian empire (Fix and Kimmage, 2023, p. 8). Putin had envisioned dividing Europe and the world into zones of influence based on blocs of the Great Powers of which Russia would assume its rightful role along with China and the United States (Fix and Kimmage, 2023, p. 32). Each would rule their periphery, while respecting the rights of the others.

Great powers have traditionally worried that a defeat anywhere on its periphery would start an adverse chain reaction ultimately reaching the core. To prevent this, the country would invade and conquer buffer states to afford a modicum of protection. For example,

> the Athenians invaded Corcyra in the 5th century BC...to prevent it from coming under the control of their rivals the Spartans. The ancient Romans expanded their imperial sway to create buffers between their territories and those of rival empires.
>
> (Mandelbaum, 2003, p. 96)

In 1946, George Kennan, an American diplomatic, stationed in Moscow, perceptively portrayed the USSR's geopolitical insecurities, which, in turn, can shed light on Russia's insecurity today,[12]

> At bottom of the Kremlin's neurotic view of world affairs is traditional and instinctive Russian sense of insecurity. Originally, this was the insecurity of a peaceful agricultural people trying to live on a vast exposed plain in a neighborhood of fierce nomadic peoples. To this was added, as Russia came into contact with the economically advanced West, fear of more competent, more powerful, more highly organized societies in that area. But this latter type of insecurity was one which afflicted Russian rulers rather than Russian people; for Russian rulers have invariably sensed that their rule was relatively archaic in form, and fragile and artificial in its psychological foundation, unable to stand comparison or contact with political systems of Western countries. For this reason, they have always feared foreign penetration, feared direct contact between the Western world and their own, feared what would happen if Russians learned the truth about the world or if foreigners learned the truth about world within. And they have learned to seek security only in a patient but deadly struggle for total destruction of rival power, never in compacts and compromises with it.
>
> (George Kennan's Long Telegram, 1946)

Putin's war was also motivated by Russia's border states tilting toward the west. In addition, Putin claimed a rich historical bond between Russia and Ukraine, along with a common linguistic, cultural, and religious identity, which would be ripped asunder by Ukraine's affiliation and identification with the West.[13]

With parallels to the USSR's earlier harsh repression of everything Ukrainian, for Putin, the invasion of Ukraine "is much more than a physical war, he denies that Ukraine is a sovereign nation, and is working to erase the very concept of Ukraine from existence" (Golinkin, 2022, p. 3). An eerie replication of Stalin, who couldn't tolerate any ethnic identity that challenged Soviet dominance.

Instead of Russia achieving its lofty goals, "it has…strayed further from Europe and a cooperative peace order while retuning imperialism to Europe" (Scholz, 2023, p. 26). Rather than remake Europe in his image, he has isolated himself while concomitantly strengthening the **EU**, **NATO**, and the G-7. Putin's war has nudged Europe move away from **fossil fuels** (and especially Russian-based natural gas) and in the direction of renewable energy (Scholz, 2023, p. 30). Norway, for example, is now Europe's largest supplier of natural gas, replacing Russia.

31.4   Will Putin Use Nuclear Weapons?

This question has been perplexing many policymakers, not to mention Ukrainian citizens. Putin has threatened to use nuclear weapons, but it is not clear if this is strategic rhetoric rewrite. Fix and Kimmage argue that "threatening to use nuclear weapons is of greater utility than actually doing so and if so, this would surely catapult Russia over the rogue nation threshold which might set well with Putin, but not so much Russian citizens" (Fix and Kimmage, 2023, p. 15). **China,** by the way, has convinced Russia not to use nuclear weapons against Ukraine, although it is not clear if Putin would have used nuclear weapons otherwise.

Of course, if Russia decides to use nuclear weapons, in addition to catastrophic destruction, the United States will have to respond, while keeping in mind the effect that both actions (i.e., Russia and the United States) will have on other rogue nations.

31.5   Russia's Energy and Economy

Like Iran, Russia, is a major player in fossil fuels.[14] It relies on fossil fuels for over half of its budget revenue. In 2023, the United States, along with the G-7, introduced a price cap on Russian oil exports of $60/barrel. This was designed to limit the oil revenue going into Russia's war chest, while minimizing any global disruptions in the oil market. It is not clear to us the efficacy of the sanctions, since Russia appears to be able to circumvent via a network of traders and vessels (with opaque ownership) mostly in India and China (Wilson and Cook, 2023, p. 4).

Finally, we should mention the current strength of Russia's economy. For us, this is most surprising given the contrary predictions at the invasion's start. The IMF projects growth rates higher than initially predicted at the war's onset; thus, "predictions of an economic collapse made almost entirely by western economists have proved thumpingly wrong" (Lock and Load,' *The Economist*, December 16, 2023, p. 60). Worrisome, though, is increasing inflation brought about by significant increases in government spending. Russia has boosted defense spending to 6% of GDP, its highest since the collapse of the USSR, with fiscal spending amounting to 5% of GDP. Russia has also increased wages, which will only increase future inflation, especially with Russia's ongoing brain drain, along with a shortfall reduction in foreign investment (Lock and Load,' *The Economist*, December 16, 2023, p. 60). As this book goes to press (October 2024) Russia is facing a housing bubble: Housing prices have soared by 172% in Russia's biggest cities between 2020 and 2023, spearheaded by heavily government subsidized mortgages, especially for individuals buying new-builds (*The Economist,* July 27, 2024, p. 64). Such a bubble is to be expected, given that with war sanctions, higher wages have really no place to go. It remains to be seen how and if Russia can weather this housing bubble.

It remains to be seen how Russia will deal with impending inflation, although "as in so many previous occasions, in Russia there are more important things than economic stability" (*The Economist,* July 27, 2024, p. 60). But as the world transitions to **Net Zero** and away from **fossil fuels**, Russia's budget and future economy will become more precarious.

31.6   Future Conflicts?

Russia has set its sights on other former Soviet republics, especially Moldova, Belarus, Estonia, Latvia, and Lithuania. Whether it attacks will largely depend on the outcome of its invasion of Ukraine. But if Russia loses its "disastrous war of choice" (Fix and Kimmage, 2023, p. 10) it could devolve into a rogue even a failed state. (Of course, it could even do so if it defeats Ukraine). Then, what would stop Mr. Putin from invading other nations, or from using nuclear weapons? Win or lose, Russia has "morphed into a nihilistic and unpredictable foe of the global order bent on disruption and sabotage. It is like North Korea or Iran on steroids, armed with thousands of nuclear warheads" (*The Economist*, February 16, 2024, p. 10).

Notes

1 For a fascinating read, see Figes (1996).
2 Amarta Sen wrote that "famines, are, in fact, so easy to prevent that it is amazing that they are allowed to occur at all. The sense of distance between the ruler and the ruled—between us and them—is a critical feature of famines" (Sen, 1999, p. 175). While tens of millions of people have died in famines across the globe, since the end of World War II, "no major famine has ever occurred in a functioning democracy with regular elections, opposition parties, basic freedom of speech and a relatively free media (even when the country is very poor and in a seriously adverse food situation" (Sen, 2009, p. 342). It is interesting that three of the nations that we investigate in this book: China, Russia, and North Korea, all have suffered debilitating famines where tens of millions have died. Each precipitated by its own leaders—the ultimate betrayal of a nation toward its people. For further discussion of famines, see Sen (1981).
3 For the definitive account of this tragic event, which today remains seared into the minds of all Ukrainians, see Conquest (1986).
4 Waiting in line to buy groceries was a daily event; and worse, one never knew what would be there and what wouldn't be on any given day. In 1990, vodka was rationed as was gasoline (two staples of Soviet life) along with countless other items. I (Jack) remember my first visit to the USSR, relaxing one night watching TV with friends. After I had asked why they tended to sit in the back of the room, they explained that Soviet TVs sometimes exploded, and since one never knew when, it was prudent to sit back. I had also noticed that upon meeting someone for the first time, a Soviet would glance at the person's shoes, which would tip off if he/she was a foreigner. Given my preference for wingtips, I was a dead giveaway. To assimilate in Soviet society, I bought a pair of Soviet-made shoes, less comfortable, and far less stylish.
5 As late as January 1991, most of my students saw secession and the dissolution of the USSR as inevitable, although five or ten years off. No one expected (or predicted) that the USSR would be moribund by the end of the year. My students were also worried that any immediate dissolution would be catastrophic in terms of lives lost, so Gorbachev's policies were preferred to doing nothing and or doing something more radical.
6 For a cogent (and contemporary) explanation of both perestroika and glasnost, see Desai (1989).

7   In addition to brute repression, dispossession, and forced internal migration, the So-
    viet Union implemented a gulag system, more commonly known as 'the camps.' It
    was a brutal instrument of political repression, begun during the Russian Revolution
    and not formally abolished until 1960. While mortality estimates vary, the consensus
    is at least six million, although the actual number is most likely much higher. A book
    that everyone should read at least once in their lives is Aleksandr Solzhenitsyn's The
    Gulag Archipelago (1973) for its depiction of such a sheer, brutal system of terror.
    A fictional account (and much briefer) is Solzhenitsyn (1963). He was awarded the
    Nobel Prize in Literature in 1970.

8   Writing in 1986, Robert Conquest noted that "the resuscitation of Ukrainian na-
    tionalism was well underway, "regaining much of its power" (Conquest, 1986,
    p. 335).

9   His quick and almost inexorable rise to power fascinates. See Gessen (2013) and
    Sakwa (2004).

10 See our **NATO** chapter.

11 Ruth Ben-Ghiat in her very interesting book, *Strongmen: Mussolini to the Present*
    (2020), draws strong parallels between Trump and Putin. For example, both men
    view the MeToo movement as an anathema. Not surprisingly, Trump's "prominent
    appointees have included men who have been accused of sexual harassment or do-
    mestic abuse" (Ben-Ghiat, 2020, p. 140). In addition, each man's "own political and
    financial interests prevail over national ones in shaping domestic and foreign policy
    (Ben-Ghiat, 2020, p. 7). In addition, "propaganda, virility, corruption and violence
    are all key elements uniting these 'strongmen" (Ben-Ghiat, 2020, p. 7). Thus, it
    should be no surprise that Trump and Putin have taken a liking to each other: they
    have a lot in common.

12 This quote is taken directly from George Kennan's famous long telegram sent from
    Moscow in 1946 to James Byrnes, the USA Secretary of State. It was instrumental
    in laying the intellectual groundwork for establishing NATO. Since it literally is a
    telegram, we took liberty to polish the prose a tad without disturbing its meaning.

13 For an interesting account of the origins of Putin's war and what might lie ahead, see
    Ponomarenko (2024). The author, incidentally, is co-founder of the *Kyiv Independent*.

14 For further discussion, see our **Fossil Fuels** chapter.

References

Arendt, Hannah (1968) *The Origins of Totalitarianism*, Harcourt, New York.

Ben-Ghiat, Ruth (2020) *Strongmen: Mussolini to the Present*, W.W. Norton, New York.

Conquest, Robert (1986) *The Harvest of Sorrow: Soviet Collectivization and the Terror-Famine*, Oxford University Press, New York.

Desai, Padma (1989) *Perestroika in Perspective: The Design and Dilemmas of Soviet Reform*, Princeton University Press, Princeton.

Figes, Orlando (1996) *A People's Tragedy: The Russian Revolution: 1891–1924*, Penguin, New York.

Fix, Liana and Michale Kimmage, (2023) 'Putin's Last Stand: The Promise and Peril of Russian Defeat,' *Foreign Affairs*, Jan/Feb, Vol. 102, No. 1, pp. 8–21.

'George Kennan's Long Telegram' (1946) George Washington University, National Security Archives, George Kennan's "Long Telegram" (gwu.edu).

Gessen, Masha (2013) *The Man Without a Face: The Unlikely Rise of Vladimir Putin*, Riverhead Books, New York.

Golinkin, Lev (2022) 'Ukraine's History is Being Erased,' *The New York Times*, March 6, Opinion Section.

Hamilton, Alexander, James Madison, and John Jay (2003 [1787–1788]) *The Federalist Papers*, Bantam Books, New York.

'Iran: A Tamer Troublemaker' (2023) *The Economist*, December 16, pp. 37–39.

McFaul, Michael (2018) 'Choosing Autocracy: Actors, Institutions, and Revolution in the Erosion of Russian Democracy,' *Comparative Politics*, Vol. 50, No. 3, pp. 305–325.

Ponomarenko, Illia (2024) *I Will Show You How it Was*, Bloomsbury, London.

Sakwa, Richard (2004) *Putin: Russia's Choice*, Routledge, London.

Saver, Pjotr (2023) 'Russia Steps Up Anti-gay agenda as Top Court Bans LGBTQ Movement,' *The Guardian*, December 1, p. 26.

Scholz, Olaf, (2023) 'The Global Zeitenwende: How to Avoid a New Cold War in a Multipolar Era,' *Foreign Affairs*, Jan/Feb, Vol. 102, No. 1, pp. 22–38.

Sen, Amartya (1981) *Poverty and Famines: An Essay on Entitlement and Deprivation*, Clarendon Press, Oxford.

Sen, Amartya (1999) *Development as Freedom*, Anchor Books, New York.

Sen, Amartya (2009) *The Idea of Justice*, Penguin, New York.

Solzhenitsyn, Alexander (1963) *One Day in the Life of Ivan Denisovich*, Signet, New York.

Solzhenitsyn, Alexander (1973) The Gulag Archipelago, Harper and Row, New York.

Smith, Hendrick (1990) *The New Russians*, Random House, New York.

'War and Prices,' *The Economist*, July 27, 2024, p. 64.

Wilson, Tom and Chris Cook (2023) 'White House Aims to halve Russia's Energy Revenues by 2023,' *The Financial Times*, December 2/3, p. 4.

32 North Korea

32.1 An Inexplicable Birth

United for over thirteen centuries, Korea's division in the 1950s was not only unanticipated but came about largely due to 'astonishing' blunders and mishaps,

> no division of a nation in the modern world is so astonishing in its origin as the division of Korea; none is so unrelated to conditions or to sentiment within the nation itself at the time the division was effected; none is to this day so unexplained; in none does blunder and planning oversight appeared to have played so large a role.
>
> (Mandelbaum, 2003, p. 445, note 55)

Here's how it happened[1]: Japan invaded Korea in the last year of WII, which precipitated the USSR to invade and establish a presence. The US felt compelled likewise, claiming the 38th parallel as the northern border. A communist regime established itself in the North with a non-communist regime in the South. On June 25, 1950, the North backed by the USSR (and eventually China) invaded the South to reunite the peninsula, claiming it as the legitimate ruler. The War ended in a stalemate in 1953, creating a demilitarized zone with the 38th parallel separating the two nations. Although an Armistice was signed July 27, 1953, between North and South, no peace treaty has been signed. The stalemate between the two countries, once unified and now separate, has continued to this day, with little hope of reunification.

The Korean War was brutal and, "the physical destruction and loss of life on both sides was almost beyond comprehension, but the North suffered the greater damage, due to American saturation bombing and the scorched-earth policy of the retreating UN forces" (Fifield, 2017). Similar to the Soviets conceptualizing the German invasion as the Great Patriotic War in order to rally its people; North Korea, has convinced its citizens that they fought a great patriotic war against

DOI: 10.4324/9781003591856-37

American intruders (Fifield, 2017). North Korean leaders use the war both to rally the people and to deflect blame for dire economic conditions.

32.2   North Korea Today

North Korea (capital, Pyongyang) was initially led by Kim Il-Sung from the nation's birth in 1948 to his death, July 8, 1994. Under his bizarre cult-like dictatorship, North Korea became heavily militarized and isolated with a narcissistic determination for self-survival. South Korea (capital Seoul) with the United States as its patron, adopted Western institutions, including a market economy. South Korea thrived while North Korea stagnated. Starting out relatively equal in 1960, by 2000 the South had pulled far ahead economically[2] (Mandelbaum, 2003, pp. 175–176).

The increasing economic (and political and social) difference between North and South has attenuated (and possibly extirpated) any desire for reunification. The South feels that reunification would inflict massive assimilation costs, preferring instead detente. Neither does the North favor reunification, assuming that it would be de facto dissolved into the South, erasing its own much-contrived identity. Quite telling, the North refers to the South as the 'permanent enemy' (*The Economist*, March 9, 2024, p. 33).

After Kim Il-sung's death in 1994 he was replaced by his son Kim Jong-Il who ruled until his death in 2011, with his son Kim Jong Um, now North Korea's hereditary dictator.

Understanding today's North Korea involves three words,[3]

- **Juche**: 'Self-determination or going it alone.' Largely due to the experiences of North Korea's founder, Kim Il-sung, during his formative years, as well as during WWI and the Cold War. He learned that the world is dangerous, peppered with deceptive and not always trustful allies.
- **Songun**: Putting the military first, or 'maintaining power with military might.' The military is North Korea's number one institution. In addition to providing national defense, it provides many of the functions of government. In a country of 24 million people, more than 1 million are active members of the military, and the institution has a compulsory 10-year service requirement. By 1965, North Korea's budget for national defense was 30 percent of GDP, compared to just 4.3 percent in 1956.
- **Byungjin**: 'Parallel Paths to Butter and Bombs.' A multi-faceted policy of arming with nuclear weapons (which they did in 2006) in order to show the world that they are able to defend themselves; and that regime change is not on the table. It is also North Korea's realpolitik acknowledgement of how countries fare that do not develop nuclear weapons, like Iraq and Libya. Developing and maintaining nuclear arms is a central policy in portraying strength. And to buttress domestic legitimacy, North Korea has focused on producing consumer goods.

32.3   North Korea and Nuclear Weapons

North Korea's decision to arm is important to its national identity, while also underscoring the precariousness and instability of a nuclear armed world. As North Korea has learned, the history of the 20th century shows that of the nations that have obtained nuclear weapons, "none was made an international outcast. None found itself markedly less secure than before" (Mandelbaum, 2003, p. 222). (However, perhaps Russia in the 21st century might be the first.) Nations that have developed nuclear weapons have also attained their geopolitical goals, a lesson not lost on North Korea,

> The destruction of Hiroshima and Nagasaki did help to persuade Japan to surrender in 1945. Nuclear weapons also helped the Soviet Union to become the military equal of the United States. [Nuclear weapons] helped China avoid a military assault…Their unacknowledged possession conferred advantages on Israel. The threat to join the nuclear club brought North Korea political attention and economic assistance. Absent that threat [it] might have joined the world's other Marxist-Leninist regimes in the dustbin of history…
>
> (Mandelbaum, 2003, p. 222)

It is estimated that North Korea has enough fissile material for 35 to 63 nuclear devices (*The Economist,* March 9, 2024, p. 33). It is not clear how far their current saber rattling will go. But since regime change is out of the question, North Korea might have "fewer reservations about starting a war that would lead to its demise if it were on the point of expiring anyway" (Mandelbaum, 2003, p. 179) Are the leaders of North Korea, sufficiently fanatical, unstable or disconnected from reality to embark on a suicidal mission? It is really hard to say. North Korea is openly thwarting the West and remains a palpable danger. Unknown at this point is if its belligerent rhetoric will be actualized.

33.4   Conclusion

How should the United States treat Iran, Russia, and North Korea, each openly hostile and have vowed to change the global rules of the game? Should the United States threaten and bully aka Trump, while cozying up to dictators aka Trump? Should it directly hold talks with each nation, perhaps even to isolate and cooperate, as the United States has been doing off and on with China? Or should it negotiate with other nations that are also worried. There is obviously no easy solution. And this is why politics is never easy, but to eschew dialoguing, and negotiating and listening—the quintessence of politics—does not work either.

As a final point, we should say that logically China belongs in this section, after all it has made no secret of its bellicosity toward the United States, while looking toward Russia as "an indispensable partner in its campaign to dismantle the American-led order" (*The Economist*, May 18, 2024, p. 11). China shares an 840-mile border with North Korea, and a 2615-mile border with Russia. But we feel that the United States/China relationship is the world's most important in terms of economics, climate change, and geopolitical stability, and as such, deserves a separate chapter.

Notes

1 This discussion is largely based on (Mandelbaum, 2003, pp. 174–175).
2 South Korea's success is partly due to its mercantile economy (like that of Taiwan, Hong Kong, **Singapore** and **China**: Encouraging work, while subsiding housing, capital, and education; encouraging high accumulations of capital, while expanding output (Bobbitt, 2002, pp. 672–673). We discuss mercantilism further in our **China** chapter.
3 The following relies heavily on Boissoneault (2017).

References

'Armed and Autocratic' (2024) *The Economist*, March 9, pp. 33–34.
Bobbitt, Philip (2002) *The Shield of Achilles: War, Peace, and the Course of History*, Anchor Books, New York.
Boissoneault, Lorraine (2017) 'Why North Korea Needs an Enemy Like America to Survive,' *Smithsonian Magazine,* July 28, https://www.smithsonianmag.com
'China and the World: The Challenge of Xi Jinping' (2024) *The Economist*, May 18, p. 11.
Fifield Anna (2017) 'Why does North Korea hate the United States? Let's go back to the Korean War,' *The Washington Post*, (May 17), https://www.washingtonpost.com
Mandelbaum, Michael (2003) *The Ideas that Conquered the World: Peace, Democracy, and Free Markets in the Twenty-First Century*, Public Affairs, New York.

33 The Question of Palestine

The Issue: Here in the United States, there is a palpable asymmetry between our knowledge of Israel and that of Palestine, so much so that Palestine and the Palestinians are contemptuously dismissed as a non-entity; an invisible and insignificant other. This deliberate misunderstanding amplifies and perpetuates distrust, dislike, and conflict. Addressing the longstanding 'Question of Palestine,' is a central task, post-2024. But this can only occur with a full understanding of Palestine, the land and its people, hence the purpose of this chapter.

33.1   Introduction

This chapter was our most difficult to write. Not because of the intricate complexity of the issues, e.g., colonialism, Zionism, oil, Arab nationalism, the USSR, imperialism, the Holocaust, anti-Semitism, the United Nations, the Middle East, and Palestine. For as scholars, we welcome the challenge. Nor was it difficult because every facet of the Palestinian question is suffused with emotion, with tragedy, with anger, with the worst of the human spirit. Rather, what made this chapter so difficult is that there is no common ground. Absolutely none. Edward Said, a foremost intellect and a Palestinian himself, said it best,

> the most demoralizing aspect…is the almost total opposition between mainstream Israeli and Palestinian points of view. We were dispossessed and uprooted in 1948; they think they won independence and that the means were just. We recall that the land we left and the territories we are trying to liberate from military occupation are all part of our national patrimony; they think it is theirs by biblical fiat and diasporic affiliation. Today, by any conceivable standards, we are the victims of violence; they think they are. There is simply no common ground, no common narrative, no possible area for genuine reconciliation. Our claims are mutually exclusive. Even the notion of a common shared life in the same small piece

DOI: 10.4324/9781003591856-38

of land is unthinkable. Each of us thinks of separation, perhaps even of isolating and forgetting the other.

(Said, 2001, p. 41)

Menachem Begin, Israeli Prime Minister, 1977–1983, and co-founder of Israel's right-wing Likud Party said,

> When you recognize the concept of 'Palestine,' you demolish your right to live in Ein Hahoresh [a kibbutz in central Israel]. If this is Palestine, and not the Land of Israel, then you are conquerors and not tillers of the land. You are invaders. If this is Palestine, then it belongs to a people who lived here before you came.
>
> (quoted in Barghouti, 2001, p. 176).[1]

And Joseph Weitz, director of the Jewish National Land Fund, wrote in his diary, December 19, 1940, "It must be clear that there is no room for both peoples in this country...There is no room for compromise on this point! There is no other way out" (quoted in Said, 1992, pp. 99 and 100; emphasis excised).

This lack of a common ground made even choosing the chapter's title problematic: should it be Palestine/Israel, or Israel/Palestine? The last-put would have surely taken umbrage, and immediately criticized us for unabashed bias. We also thought about 'Palestine,' but felt that incomplete. We chose the title 'The Question of Palestine,' for three reasons:

- We like the word 'question.' Not only does it chip away at the hierarchy between reader and author, but asking the right questions can "develop new understanding...that neither entrench current understanding nor create misunderstanding, and can lead to more answers and more questions in unexpected ways" (Boyd and Reardon, 2020, p. 27).
- We borrow the title from Edward Said's book, *The Question of Palestine.* His goal was "to put our matter...before the ...reader...not as something watertight and finished, but as something to be thought through, tried out, engaged with..." (Said, 1992, p. xii). Exactly our approach in this book, as well as this chapter.
- In order to understand the Palestinian conflict, we have to understand Palestine; in order to understand Israel, we have to understand Palestine; and in order to understand the Palestinians, we have to understand Palestine.

Finally, we should mention that given the complexity of Palestine Question, it is impossible to discuss everything; especially given our constricted space. The best that we can do, and the objective of this chapter, is to get a handle on the question of Palestine—its quintessence, if you will. We start by introducing the major players leading up to the creation of the state of Israel in 1948.

33.2   Introducing the Major Players: The Palestinians and Palestine; Zionism and the Search for a Jewish Homeland

Emily Bazelon, in a perceptive article for *The New York Times Sunday Magazine*, wrote, "one year matters more than any other for understanding the Israeli Palestinian conflict: 1948" (Bazelon, 2024, p. 26). We, respectively, disagree. While 1948 matters to understand the most recent chapter in the Israeli–Palestinian conflict, to understand the question of Palestine and to understand Palestine itself one must go back to the 5th-century BC. For it was then that Herodotus (484 BC–425 BC), considered the father of the discipline of history, first coined the concept 'Palestine' to refer to an area comprising "the whole region between the Phoenicia and Egypt" (Masalha, 2022, pp. 72–74).

Thus, the starting point is, and has to be, Palestine itself. The land and the people, which has existed for over two millennium. This is the only way to understand the whole story,

> The Palestinians are the indigenous people of Palestine; their local roots are deeply embedded in the soil of Palestine and their autochthonous identity and historical heritage long preceded the emergence of a local Palestinian national movement in the late Ottoman period [late 19th century] and the advent of Zionist settler-colonialism before the First World War.
> (Masalha, 2018, p. 1)

Over the millennia, Palestine has gone through many reincarnations, so much so that its history, "unlike the myth narratives of the Old Testament, has multiple beginnings [from which] the idea of a Palestine has evolved over time into a geo-political concept and a distinct territorial polity" (Masalha, 2018, p. 22). Indeed, "there are multiple beginnings and multiple meanings to the idea of Palestine" (Masalha, 2018, p. 8). It is impossible to discuss here a detailed history of Palestine, nor even a brief outline; the best that we can do is to emphasize the following points:

- One of the most striking characteristics of Palestine throughout its history is that "multifaith and polytheism want hand in hand, for millennia the country was a multifaith/polytheistic polity with a multitude of religions and cultures" (Masalha, 2018, p. 14).
- This richly textured history "cannot be an appendage to the Israel-Palestine conflict or subsidiary to the debates on identity politics in Palestine-Israel" (Masalha, 2018, p. 14).
- Contrary to myth, Palestine was always a land with a people, with a rich history of trade, architecture, urbanization, literature, libraries, culture, seats of learning.
- Contrary to another myth propagated by British colonialism in the early 20th century, that Palestine was bereft of any administrative unit of governance, (Masalha, 2018) fastidiously documents the contrary dating back over 1000 years.

33.2.1 Zionism

Zionism is "an unchanging idea that expresses the yearning for Jewish political and religious self-determination—for Jewish national selfhood—to be exercised on the promised land" (Said, 1992, p. 57). Its goal is to provide a Jewish homeland for the Jewish people independent of citizenship; in addition, "it was the only political answer that the Jews have ever found to antisemitism as well as to answer against the overwhelming odds of dispersion and to provide a home" (Arendt, 1968, pp. 355, 120, and xv).[2]

The first Zionist Congress was held in 1897 in Basel. David Herzl, founder of the Zionist movement, noted in his diary that at that meeting he had founded the Jewish state. Palestine was among several locations looked at for a possible homeland, including Australia, Egypt, the USSR, Argentina, East Africa, Madagascar, and New York.[3] But ultimately Palestine was chosen, because "in addition to being the place where there existed a spiritual bond in the form of a covenant between God and the Jews, Palestine had the further advantage of being a backward province in an even more backward empire" (Said, 1992, pp. 23–24). This latter point is extremely important. It is at the root of the Palestine question, and why there is no common ground, as we will shortly explain. For Jews, "Israel had always been there, an actuality for the natives to perceive. Zionism therefore reclaimed, redeemed, repeated, replanted, realized Palestine, and Jewish hegemony over it. Israel was a return to a previous state of affairs" (Said, 1992, p. 87), i.e., the promised land of the Bible.

Zionism also coincided with unparalleled European territorial acquisition in Africa and Asia" (Said, 1992, p. 69).[4] At the time, "British colonialists often saw large parts of the earth as 'terra nullius,' i.e., nobody's land" (Masalha, 2018, p. 307), readily available for possessing. Thus, Zionism was part and parcel of colonialism but with a specific religious purpose. Zionism, which had begun in the West comported very nicely with the objectives of colonialism which had also begun in the West.

The first Zionist settlement in Palestine was Ptah Tikva, named after the biblical prophecy of Hosea. The settlement replaced the destroyed Palestinian village of Mlabbis. The colony was purchased from absentee landlords living in Jaffa (Masalha, 2018, p. 330). This settlement was established quite typical of others: Land was purchased from an absentee landlord, the original Palestinian village was destroyed, the indigenous inhabitants were expelled, and a settlement was built. Another typical settlement was Rehovot (after a name in the Hebrew Bible), founded in 1890. It was bought from land purchased by Arab landlords, displacing the Palestinian village of Khirbet Duran (Masalha, 2022). In 1901, the Jewish National fund was established to buy land either for incoming Jewish immigrants or to develop the land.

But here's the problem: Rather than accepting the Palestinians and try to live among them; after all, they were living on the land for millennia, the Zionists denied the existence of the indigenous, dispossessed the villagers, and expropriated their land. This was a deliberate policy to "first minimize, then to eliminate, and then, all else failing, finally to subjugate the natives as a way of guaranteeing that Israel would not be simply the state of its citizens (which included Arabs, of course) but the state of the whole Jewish people" (Said, 1992, p. 84).

Part and parcel of this was to assume and then treat the natives as if they weren't there, as if there was no nation, as if there were no people. Not too dissimilar to how "white Europeans in Africa, Asia, and the Americas believed that natives of those places [were] nonexistent and their lands uninhabited, neglected, and barren" (Said, 1992, p. 150).[5]

Thus, the Zionist slogan 'a land without a people, for a people without a land.' For the Zionists, this slogan epitomized their attempt to connect the present to their own fabled past, while ignoring those living on the land for millennia.[6]

33.3 Palestine pre-1948

In 1516, Palestine was incorporated into the Ottoman Empire (mostly Arab) in which it remained until 1918, when the Empire was defeated by the British and the allies, and its empire dismembered. After the Prophet Muhammad died in 672 AD, Islam began a forceful conquest of much the region. Palestine was one of the first to be included. It thrived both culturally and economically, under the Ottoman Empire and Islam, although its noted polytheism became monotheistic. But nevertheless, minorities were tolerated.

On November 2, 1917, British Foreign secretary Arthur Balfour promised a Jewish home in Palestine. Known as the Balfour Declaration its provenance was an admixture of domestic and imperial considerations,[7] along with lobbying by both Christian and Jewish Zionists. It set the fate of Palestine, and that the evolution of Palestine and Israel would be intricately related, although unfortunately, not as equals. Interestingly, and perhaps not surprising "the Declaration was made by a European power, about a non-European territory, in flat disregard for both the presence and the wishes of the native majority, [while] promising the territory to another foreign group, the Zionists" (Said, 1992, pp. 15–16). Keep in mind that at the time, Great Britain was the world's reigning superpower.

In 1918, the League of Nations[8] formally awarded Great Britain a Mandate for Palestine, i.e., a protectorate, with the goal of keeping Palestine under its wings until was ready to be on its own. Incidentally, the Mandate's territory was based on administrative divisions created by the Ottoman empire in 1872, which in turn date back to the 18th century (Masalha, 2022, pp. 262–263).

After the Mandate was created, immigration increased, especially from eastern Europe and Soviet Russia: "between 1922 and 1946 the Jews in Palestine were increasing at an average of 9.0% annually, helped by the British policy of forcing a Jewish majority on the country" (Said, 1992, pp. 17–18).

The immigration would intensify during the Nazi Holocaust. While the atrocities committed against the Jewish people were horrific and represent one of the darkest chapters in human history, at the same time they elicited increased world sympathy (especially from the West) in favor of a Jewish homeland.

It should be pointed out that during the Mandate, the Palestinians did not take any concerted action to either limit or cease the settlement activity. It was not that the Palestinians did not know what was happening, but they had no idea that the land could and would be taken; after all, it was their land; land that they had lived on for millennia.

33.4   1948: Nakba

In 1939, the British government issued its White paper, calling for the establishment of a Palestinian state by 1948, at which time Britain would remand its Mandate to the UN. In 1947, the UN passed Resolution 181 which would have partitioned Palestine to allow for the creation of a Jewish and an Arab state, with international control over Jerusalem. However, on May 14, 1948 (the very day that the British mandate ended) David Ben-Gurion (1886–1973) Israel's first prime minister, declared Israel a new nation and an independent state. The next day, Transjordan, Egypt, Syria, Iraq, and Lebanon, having no toleration for an independent Jewish state in their backyard, or even 'two states' attacked Israel, a war which they decisively lost. For the Arab peoples of the Middle East "Israel's very existence [was] another chapter in the Western assault…and humiliation" (Mandelbaum, 2003, p. 208).[9]

Israel expropriated most of what was historical or Mandatory Palestine, "destroying and depopulating 531 Arab villages in the process. Two-thirds of the population were driven out…and the West Bank and Gaza went to Jordan and Egypt respectively" (Said, 2001, p. 32). More than 700,000 Palestinians were forced from their homes, some at gunpoint, an event remembered in Arabic as Nakba—the catastrophe. Today the Palestinian diaspora numbers six million, with 2.4 million in Jordan, 584,000 in Syria, and 491,000 in Lebanon (Davis, 2024).

33.5   The 1967 Six Day War

In 1967, Egypt, Syria, and Jordan attacked Israel, in what became known as the Six Day War. It was a devastating (and humiliating) defeat for the aggressors, with ramifications still felt today. The immediate precipitating factor was Egypt's closing of the Straights of Tiran to Israel shipping. The Straights, sandwiched between the Sinai Peninsula and Saudi Arabia, connect Eilat, Israel's southernmost city to the Red Sea. Egypt, the largest nation in the region and riding high on Arab nationalism, was confident in victory. Israel decimated Egypt's air force (helped immensely by USA weapons). Israel seized Syria's

Golan Heights, Jordan's West Bank (including East Jerusalem), Egypt's Sinai Peninsula, and the Gaza Strip. In 1988, Jordan surrendered its claim to the West Bank, and no longer recognized its residents as citizens (Casey, 2023, p. 32). In 1992 the Sinai Peninsula was returned to Egypt. Today, Israel maintains control over the West Bank, the Gaza Strip and East Jerusalem, i.e., the Occupied Territories.

33.6 Israel Policy Post-1948 toward Palestine and the Palestinians

Since 1948, Israel's policy has been to de-Arab Palestine, to dispossess the original inhabitants, to construct a nation of Jews rather than a nation of citizens, and to erase the memory of Palestinians being on the land. To accomplish these objectives, they have pursued a set of interrelated policies:

33.6.1 *Hebraization of Names, Places, Towns, Cities*

The objective of Hebraization was/is to "erase the history of one people in order to write that of another over it" (Masalha, 2022, p. 360). This was part and parcel of a broader systematic and racist ethnic cleansing: to cleanse the new nation of all Palestinians and even their memory, to get the point across that this is now Israel connecting to its biblical past.

As one prominent example, immediately after the 1948 war, David Ben-Gurion, Israel's founder and first prime minister, mandated as state policy to Hebraicize surnames. This policy provided "many Zionist settlers in Palestine with a prototype for emulation in a process of self-invention and self-indigenization" (Masalha, 2022, p. 343). Ben-Gurion was born in what is now Poland, then part of the Russian Empire. He emigrated to the United States and then to Palestine where he changed his name from David Grün. His new Hebraicized name was "biblical-sounding, lionized and predatory, literally meaning son of the lion cub" (Masalha, 2022, p. 343). He named his daughter a biblical-sounding name (Geula, i.e., redemption) and his son, Amos, after a minor Hebrew prophet.

Other well-known examples of Hebraicized surnames were: Golda Meir, born Golda Mabovitch in Kiev, 1898; Yitzhak Shamir, born Icchak Jeziernicky in Poland in 1915; Menachem Begin, the founder of the Likud Party born Mieczyslaw Biegun, in Brest-Liovsk; and Amos Oz, the well-known Israeli novelist, born named Amos Klausner.[10]

Village names were also Hebraicized to root out the original Arabic, along with all vestiges of Palestinian life. When Jewish settlements were constructed on what used to be Palestinian villages, the original name was twisted into something Hebrew sounding. For example, the Jewish settlement replacing the Palestinian village Beit Dajan was renamed Beit Dagon; and the Palestinian village Hittin[11] was renamed Kfar Hittim.[12]

This renaming was systematically part of

> a massive appropriation of Palestinian heritage [which in turn] provided support for the European Jewish colonizers' claim to represent an indigenous people returning to their homeland after 2000 years of exile. [And, in addition] to prevent future claim to the villages [while] returning to the map something that resembled ancient Israel.
>
> (Masalha, 2022, p. 361)

To construct a direct nexus between the present and a fabled past, use was made "of Biblical studies, Holy Land archeology, cartography, and scriptural geography" (Masalha, 2022, p. 360). Central was the Hebrew Bible, which "became not a religious document or a repository of theological assertions; it was reinvented as a nationalized and racialized sacred text central to the modern foundational myths of secular Zionism" (Masalha, 2022, pp. 343 and 373). Simply put, the Bible was read as factual history to connect Israel's fabled past to its sole claim on Palestine, i.e., "a retrospective colonizing of the past" (Masalha, 2022, pp. 343 and 373).

But intensive archeological work did not substantiate any of the major Zionist myth-making episodes. Specifically, "the patriarchs' acts are legendary, the Israelites were never in Egypt, they did not wander in the desert, nor exodus out of Egypt; and David and Solomon had only a small tribunal kingdom" (Masalha, 2022, pp. 27–29).

33.6.2   *Settlements, Closure, and Bypass Roads*

One reason for the lack of a common ground is the relentless building of settlements, both in the occupied territories after the 1968 war, and dating to the late 19th century on what was Palestinian land. The most recent count indicates 465,000 Israeli settlers on the West Bank, along with the 222,000 in East Jerusalem.

The policy of closure (and it is a policy) around Palestinian villages in the West Bank, prohibits the free movement of Palestinian goods and persons in and out of the occupied territories. First implemented in 1994 as a security measure, and enforced by bureaucratic checkpoints, it has since remained part of official Israeli policy. The result has been recession, unemployment, poverty and a disfigurement of the Palestinian land, "resulting in an economy becoming more atavistic, disarticulated, and fragmented" (Roy, 2001, p. 92, passim). Israel's closures and bypass roads violate Article 13 of The Universal Declaration of Human Rights: "Everyone has the right to freedom of movement and residence within the borders of each State; and Everyone has the right to leave any country, including his [sic] own, and to return to his country."

Bypass roads have been constructed effectively, enabling Israel to seal off the Palestinian villages while allowing the Jewish settlers "transport to key destinations in the West bank without having to pass through Palestinian areas" (Pacheco, 2001, p. 205, note #26). The roads form "moats strategically placed around most Palestinian populated and agricultural areas, cutting off nearly all semblance of Palestinian territorial contiguity" (Pacheco, 2001, p. 193). The result is not too dissimilar from the South African Bantustans,[13] i.e., forced racial segregation of blacks into isolated geographical areas, a key element of South Africa's apartheid.

33.7   UN Resolutions

In the immediate aftermath of WWII, the United Nations passed a series of resolutions to protect people from human rights abuses. One in particular is relevant here to help us understand the Question of Palestine: 'The Fourth Geneva Convention Relative to the Protection of Civilian Persons in the Time of War.' It was signed August 12, 1949, and adopted October 1950. Its purpose was, as its name implies, to protect civilians, "who are for all practical purposes stateless and remain vulnerable to the mercy of the occupier to protect them" (Pacheco, 2001, p. 182). The Convention's many provisions are designed to prevent human rights abuses against individuals under occupation; prevent the occupier from making a temporary presence permanent; prohibit house demolition, deportation, and the construction of occupier settlements; while also allowing free civilian movement. But, unfortunately,

> Since 1967, the Israeli military has consistently violated nearly every provision: torture of Palestinians, annexation of East Jerusalem, construction of Jewish settlements, illegal transfer of Israeli civilians into occupied territories, repeated collective punishment, demolition of homes/villages, pillage of Palestinian natural resources including water, quarries and trees; and the appropriation of 70% of the occupied territories. [And] most if not all of these violations continued unabated during the Oslo peace process!
>
> (Pacheco, 2001, pp. 184–185; exclamation added)

To the international community, Israel justified its flouting of the Resolution by convoluted reasoning that the areas are administered, not occupied and therefore outside the Convention purview; and in addition, that Israel was not bound by the Convention since it was not incorporated into Israeli law (Pacheco, 2001, p. 183). While Israel is to be blamed, the Palestinian Authority (see below) is also criticized for its failure to prevent this gross violation of the UN Convention,

> The PA failed to make use of its rights under the Convention and failed to prevent this grave breach... The PA did not actively stop the roads or support the legal and grassroots resistance to them. Once the roads were paved, the PA did not demand control over them, compensation for the

extensive destruction, or criminal indictments against those who carried it out. By fall 2000, it accepted the roads as a fait accompli and focused its negotiations on other areas.

(Pacheco, 2001, p. 193)

While space precludes a full discussion of Israel's international treaty violations,[14] one more deserves mention: UN Resolution 194, which protects the right of refugees to return home,

refugees wishing to return to their homes and live at peace with their neighbours should be permitted to do so at the earliest practicable date, and that compensation should be paid for the property of those choosing not to return and for loss of or damage to property which, under principles of international law or equity, should be made good by the Governments or authorities responsible.

Palestinians insist on the return of refugees as a sine qua non of any lasting peace agreement, while Israelis adamantly oppose any return since it would corrupt the Jewishness of the state of Israeli and impose upon Israel the necessity of recognizing a legitimate Palestinian claim to the land. Ideologically, Israel refuses to do the latter, given that ridding the land "of the native inhabitants of Palestine has long been one of the tenets of Zionism" (Sitta, 2001, p. 299).[15]

33.8   The Role of the United States

The United States' first contact with what is now the Middle East was during the late 18th century as missionaries to spread Christianity and establish educational institutions. The Syrian Protestant College, for example, was established in 1866 and renamed the American University of Beirut in 1920. Interesting was the United States' role in the 1914 King Crane Commission, dispatched to Syria and Palestine to ascertain the people's views as to how they can be helped to achieve independence and which major global power they preferred. We mention this now because its paternalistic, non-obtrusiveness would contrast sharply with the United States' role later in the century.

The British Mandate ended the same time that the Cold War was heating up. For the next half-century, the United States would be focused on containing the USSR.[16] With the passing of the baton of global leadership from Great Britain to the United States, the United States focused on preempting Soviet incursion. It passed the Truman Doctrine proclaiming the Middle East a zone of American influence, followed by the 1957 Eisenhower Doctrine committing the United States to aid any state threatened by international communism; the Nixon Doctrine which upgraded military and economic support to regional allies, and the Carter Doctrine in which the United States stated that the Gulf is vital to United States interests.

The United States was the first to recognize the new nation of Israel (not wanting the honor to go the Soviets), doing so the very same day that Israel declared its new existence. However, in a prescient warning, Secretary of State George Marshall,[17] counseled against, at least

> until the Arab issues were resolved, believing Israeli independence would only lead to more conflict and threaten Arab oil production. Marshall argued instead for a UN compromise to establish a neutral trusteeship in Palestine to oversee the Arab and Jewish regions.
>
> (Gruner, 2022, p. 152)

Good advice but rejected by President Truman.

During this time, America emerged as Israel's most stalwart supporter, propelled by its own vocal and large Jewish population (the world's largest) which had been "lobbying vigorously the USA government to support the establishment of a Jewish state and for USA aid" (Goren, 1991, p. 596).

This unabashed support partly explains why "the American public has long lacked understanding of the region which has often complicated the task of US policymakers" (Khalidi, 1991, p. 731). Indeed, there is an asymmetry between understanding Israel and understanding Palestine, which in turn has,

> suppressed the values and the history of troubles animating the Palestinians…since most Americans seem unaware that the Palestinians actually lived in Palestine before Israel came into existence. Yet only if those values and history are taken account of, can we begin to see the bases for compromise, settlement, and finally peace.
>
> (Said, 1992, p. 118)[18]

Unfortunately, what information has been received by the American public has been grossly skewered reflecting a strong pro-Israel bias. In a survey of major news outlets during the Second Intifada,[19] the authors found,

> gross distortion and naked partisanship [which] does an enormous disservice to readers and the public at large. [And, unfortunately] the day when the US press provides evenhanded coverage and balanced commentary to its readers, viewers, and listeners, is still a long way off.
>
> (Abunimah and Ibish, 2001, pp. 235 and 254)

33.9 The Oslo Peace Process: A Structural Failure

On September 14, 1993, long-time and bitter enemies, Yitzhak Rabin (the Israeli Prime Minister) and Yasser Arafat (the chair of the Palestine Liberation Organization) shook hands on the White House lawn to celebrate the Oslo Accord, the first of several treaties intended to bring peace to the Middle East.[20] The peace process, however, ended in bitter failure just seven years later with the Second Intifada. Lots have been written on the failure (Bazelon, 2023) but essentially,

> Oslo's fatal flaw is that it is neither an instrument of decolonization, nor a mechanism to apply international legitimacy to the Israeli-Palestinian conflict, but rather a framework that changes the basis of Israeli control over the occupied territories in order to perpetuate it. As such, the process is constitutively incapable of producing a viable or durable settlement and will ultimately result in more conflict...the imbalance of power inherent in Oslo guaranteed its distorted outcome.
>
> (Rabbani, 2001, p. 75)

Three central issues of concern to the Palestinians: the cessation of settlements; return of the refugees to land that was once theirs, and return of East Jerusalem,[21] were deliberately put off until the final negotiations of the peace process. The thinking was that negotiating/discussing smaller issues would create a positive (and trustworthy) momentum enabling the tackling of the more difficult issues. In retrospect this was a logistical and strategic blunder. Ruminating over Oslo's failure during the Second Intifada, one commentator wrote,

> There will never be a fair solution as long as Israel refuses to agree to a complete withdrawal from the territories occupied in 1967—including East Jerusalem—refuses to recognize its moral and historical responsibility for the Palestinian refugee problem, and insists on an intolerable level of control over Palestinian lives.
>
> (Andoni, 2001, p. 218)

Evidencing Oslo's inefficacy and the pervasive lack of trust, settlement construction continued unabated during the peace process,

> during the seven years of the Oslo process, Israel doubled its Jewish settlement population in the West Bank and Gaza to almost 200,000. In East Jerusalem it grew to 170,000. More than 18,330 new housing units were constructed...and thousands of dunams of Palestinian land were confiscated to expand the settlements.
>
> (Pacheco, 2001, p. 181)[22]

33.10 Solutions to the Palestine Question

There are two elements: (1) An immediate end to the most recent war which began October 7, 2023; and (2) an equitable solution to the Palestinian question. Both are interconnected, with one unattainable without the other. After all, Hamas justified its 10/7 aggression in order to put the Palestinian question back on the world burner. But even if a peace agreement is reached between Hamas and Israel,[23] it can only be tentative as long as the larger Palestinian question still looms. Thus, we would like to devote the remainder of this chapter to discussing the solutions for the Palestinian question.

It is an underestimation to say that there is no easy solution, for this is an existential conflict with ostensibly no common ground: Israel claims it needs Palestine for its existential survival and to connect its present to its Biblical past free from terrorist threats; while the Palestinians advocate a sense of self-agency, wanting full sovereignty to return to a land that is rightfully theirs.

Much-talked about is (or perhaps we should say 'was,' since this has fallen by the wayside) a two-state solution, i.e., Israel and Palestine in two states living side-by-side. This would involve a Palestinian state in Gaza and the West Bank (around 22% of the area of historic Palestine). The West Bank is 130 kilometers long and ranges from 40 to 65 kilometers in width; and the Gaza Strip is 45 kilometers long and ranges from 5 to 12 kilometers in width. The distance by road between them is approximately 120 km.

Ironically, in 1947, the UN initially proposed a two-state partition plan with international control over Jerusalem. The plan was initially backed by the United States but rejected by the Arab states. So, Israel immediately declared independence and the Arab neighbors attacked. For most of the past quarter-century a two-state solution was preferred, but now has fallen out of favor among both sides. Before 10/7, only one-third of Palestinians and one-third of Israel's Jews supported such a solution; now, post-10/7, the support on both sides is much lower.

But even if support existed, a two-state solution would be non-viable for the Palestinians. Not only would a Palestinian state be a fraction of the original British mandate, but the West Bank has been bantustanized to such an extent that the Palestinian enclaves would be isolated within a larger Israeli state. How could they effectively function? How could matters of state be conducted? As an economist I cannot see any way that a functioning economy could be constructed.

An equally formidable problem is integrating the two territories politically. The Gaza Strip (population 2 million) has been governed by Hamas since 2007. Hamas, an acronym of Harakat-al-Muqawamah, or in English: The Islamic Resistance Movement, is a Palestinian Sunni organization. It was founded in 1987 during the first Intifada by Ahmed Yassin as an offshoot of the Muslim Brotherhood. Today, Hamas, considered a terrorist organization, is supported economically and militarily by Iran to the tune of $1 billion annually, plus ammunition and military expertise ('What Does Hamas Want,' 2023, p. 37). Hamas has sought to de-incentivize Israelis from peace and the peace process itself via suicide bombings. This, in turn, has created a rift between Hamas and ordinary Palestinians.

Like any active organization, Hamas has its own rifts/schisms. The 10/7 aggression marked the ascendancy of Hamas' extremists ('What Does Hamas Want,' 2023, p. 37) which explains Israel's reluctance to conclude any peace since it would be rewarding aggressive behavior by extremists.[24] One of Israel's goals in the current war is to exterminate Hamas; while as of this writing, Hamas sees no choice but to continue its opposition.

The Palestinian Authority[25] governs the West Bank (population 3 million, administrative capital Ramallah). It was formed during the Oslo Peace process and is currently led by Mahmoud Abbas, along with his nationalist political party, Fatah (founded in 1959 and headquartered in Ramallah; Fatah's name literally means opening, conquering). The PA is a government of sorts, albeit with limited power and jurisdiction over only a part of the occupied territories.[26] Today, the PA is widely seen as corrupt, ineffectual, and bereft of any credibility (Freedman, 2023, p. 15). The Islamic terrorist organization, Hezbollah, based in Lebanon and largely funded by Iran, is active in the West Bank.

The preponderant problem/obstacle for a two-state solution, is of course, the plethora of Israeli settlements. The settlements are illegal, violating international treaties and UN conventions. The only effective way to create a two-state solution would be to dismantle the settlements. But this is logistically impossible, given that "once Jewish settlements are built and peopled, and once they are hooked into the state network, they become properly extraterritorial, emphatically Jewish and non-Arab" (Said, 1992, p. 99). And even if logistically possible, a two-state solution could never happen politically: (1) it contravenes everything that the Israeli state stands for and its raison d'être; and (2) the almost rabid determination of Israel's far right to *not* only *not* dismantle existing settlements but to continue building.[27]

Politically, dismantling is a no-gainer. Currently, Benjamin Netanyahu[28] serves as Israel's prime minister. Not only is he the longest serving, but the most conservative, far-right leader in Israel's history, which says a lot.[29] To get elected in 2022, Netanyahu had to invite the ultra-far-right parties (Jewish Power, and Religious Zionism) who are, not surprisingly, adamantly opposed to freezing/dismantling settlements to form a governing coalition. If Netanyahu even looks in the direction of dismantling, which ideologically he is very much opposed to, it will disintegrate his coalition, and possibly end his political career.

Another discussed solution is a democratic secular state which would guarantee full equality, dignity, and freedom for both Palestinians and Israelis (Pacheco, 2001, p. 203). However, it would need to be "constructed through the process of decolonization, whereby a transnational identity evolves, an actual fusion of horizons…uniting the Jews of Palestine and the Palestinians and therefore not allowing for the exclusion or hegemony of either group" (Barghouti, 2001, p. 176). At this point, this solution sounds a tad quixotic.

33.11   Conclusion: Which Way Forward?

The Palestine question needs to be solved equitably. This should be a priority of the United States post-2024. Problematic, however, is that the United States is not seen as credible; it is perceived as exceptionally biased, and justifiably so given its longstanding and unabashedly pro-Israel stance. But, at the same time, the United States as a global superpower should use its clout to actively work for a peace that is equitable for both parties. This would be quite a change for the United States, which might not be entirely believable. The United States could actively support other nations, especially those in the Middle East, and maybe even cooperate with China.

Additionally, there is a visceral, long-standing lack of trust between Palestinians and Israel, so much so that it is not clear to us how to get that back. Perhaps the only way for Israel to restore trust is to reason that if it wants to be a democracy and a beacon to the world, and be secure in its state, free of terrorism, it must find a solution to the Palestinian question. Doing so would create a modicum of common ground that can form the foundation for a broader and more sustainable peace process leading eventually to an equitable peace. There is no other option.

Notes

1 Prior to the creation of the state of Israel in 1948, Begin was head of the Irgun terror organization.
2 Arendt presents a detailed and well-argued historical development of antisemitism (1968, pp. 3–120).
3 For a good discussion of the places considered as well as the reasons for/against, see Wikipedia contributors (2024).
4 In 1918, "European powers were in colonial occupation of about 85% of the globe" (Said, 1992, p. 3).
5 How white Europeans treated the native Americans, is almost identical to how the Zionist's viewed 'empty' Palestine, "Although the vast country we have just described [America] was inhabited by ventless native tribes, it is justifiable to assert that, at the time of its discovery, it formed only a desert. The Indians took up residence there but did not possess it. It is only through agriculture that man takes ownership of the soil and the first inhabitants of North America lived off the products of hunting…These shores so ready for commerce and industry, these deep rivers, this inexhaustible Mississippi Valley, this entire continent thus appeared like the still empty cradle of a great nation" (Tocqueville de, 1835 [2003], p. 36).
6 This important propagandist slogan was coined by Israel Zangwill, one of Britain's earliest Zionists, in the mid-19th century (Masalha, 2022, p. 308).
7 For example, in 1905, when Balfour was UK Prime Minister, he passed the Aliens Act to restrict the immigration of Eastern European Jews into the UK; "keeping Jews out of Britain and packing them off to Palestine were two sides of the same coin" (Masalha, 2022, p. 310). In addition, "Protestant Zionists and British imperialists believed that Jewish Palestine would be convenient for a British protectorate along the main route to India" (Masalha, 2022, p. 314). For illuminating background on Balfour, see Dangerfield (1935 [1961], pp. 11–18). For a good discussion of the interplay of the Bible and sword in the formation of Palestine, see Tuchman (1982 [1956]).
8 The League was a predecessor of sorts to the UN; see our **UN** chapter.
9 Also see Said (1979).
10 Masalha (2022, pp. 347–354) provides a detailed list of the surname changes which includes "almost the entire political, military and intellectual Israeli elite, left, right and center" (Masalha, 2022, p. 347).

11 Saladin defeated the Crusaders in 1187 at the Battle of Hattin, in the village of Hittin (Masalha, 2022, p. 361).

12 Masalha (2022, pp. 258–369) provides a wealth of examples.

13 The genesis of the term stems from 'Bantu' people, and 'stan' land. See Phillips (2017) for a good discussion; and Masalha (2022, p. 312). For additional confirmation of the similarity, see Rabbani (2001, note #29, pp. 87–88).

14 For an extended discussion, see Pacheco (2001).

15 See Masalha (1992) for an expanded discussion. Sitta (2001, p. 316) doesn't buy these arguments: "the Israelis have no legal, ethical, practical, demographic, or economic reason to persist in denying the refugees' rights. Israel's position is solely derived from racist policies, the only one left in the world and thus condemned by the rest of the world." Sitta (2001) presents a workable, practical, and equitable plan to return the refugees to Palestine.

16 We discuss this further in our **NATO** chapter.

17 We discuss Marshall in our **NATO** chapter.

18 This asymmetry motivated Edward Said to write his *The Question of Palestine* (1992).

19 The Arabic word 'Intifada' literally means 'shaking off.' Its Palestinian use connotes an uprising, rebellion, resistance. In Palestine, there have been two intifadas: the first during the late 1980s, and the second during the early 2000s. They have arisen about of frustration with the Israeli occupation, and the failure of the Oslo peace process; see Andoni (2001). The two Intifadas are a reaction to and a reflection of "the vastly asymmetrical conflict between an eliminationist European settler-colonialist movement, backed by major Western powers (first Britain, and then the US), and the indigenous people of Palestine" (Masalha, 2022, p. 44).

20 Pacheco (2001, pp. 181–182) tersely discusses the Oslo Treaties.

21 Both Palestinians and Israelis claim historical ties to Jerusalem, and the city contains holy sites for both. In the 1968 War, Israel occupied East Jerusalem, formerly held by Jordan. In 1980, Israel claimed East Jerusalem part of its unified capital and has since increased its settlements, disconnecting East Jerusalem from the West Bank, and rendering any two-state solution impractical. See Boshnaq et al. (2017) and Masalha (2022, passim).

22 As a unit of measurement, the dunam originated during the Ottoman Empire to approximate the amount of land a team of oxen could till in one day. Although the specific measurement has varied over time, today 1 dunam = 0.24711 acres.

23 We agree with *The Economist*, that "peace has never seemed so far away" ('Despite the War in Gaza, talk of a two-state solution will not go away,' December 9, 2023, p. 17). And, given two back-to-back Israeli killings in late July 2024 (Hamas' top political leader, Ismail Haniyeh in Tehran; and Hezbollah commander Fouad Shukur, in Beirut, whom Israel accused of masterminding a rocket attack on an Israeli soccer field) there is a real possibility of a significant escalation. Incidentally, Haniyeh was in Tehran to attend the inauguration of Iran's newly elected president, Masoud Pezeshkian.

24 Iran provided funds, training, and logistical support for Hamas in its 10/7 aggression. We discuss Iran in our chapter, **Iran, Russia, and North Korea.**

25 Not to be confused with the Palestine Liberation Organization (PLO) founded by the Arab League in 1964 "as a way of institutionalizing (perhaps even containing) Palestinian energies" (Said, 1992, p. 134). For an interesting discussion of the PLO's early years see Said (1991, pp. 134–141).

26 The PA, although a government (with administrative headquarters in Ramallah) is not a nation, which means it cannot join the UN, since the latter requires nationhood. Likewise, it is not able to join the World Bank/IMF.

27 See Bergman and Mazzetti (2024). The authors write that "the long arc of harassment, assault and murder of Palestinians by Jewish settles is twinned with a shadow history, one of silence, avoidance, and abetment by Israeli officials" (Bergman and Mazzetti, 2024, p. 28). And some of these very officials are currently in the highest echelons of Israeli government. Quite revealing is that for "many members of the ultraright in Israel [settlers and lawmakers] …war might just be the goal…they want intifada…because it is the ultimate proof that there is no way of making peace with the Palestinians and there is only one way forward—to destroy them" (Bergman and Mazzetti, 2024, p. 53).

28 Benjamin Netanyahu, leader of Israel's Likud Party, returned to office in 2022, after first being elected in May 1996. If driven out of office, perhaps due to a collapsed coalition, Mr. Netanyahu would most likely be prosecuted for longstanding corruption charges.

29 The Knesset, Israel's Parliament, votes for a new prime minister among its members. Israel also has a president, currently Issac Herzog, elected in 2021.The next presidential election is scheduled for 2026.

References

Abunimah, Ali and Hussein Ibish (2001) 'The US Media and the New Intifada,' in Carey Roane, (Ed.) *The New Intifada: Resisting Israel's Apartheid*, Verso, London, pp. 233–256.

Andoni, Ghassan (2001) 'A Comparative Study of Intifada 1987 and Intifada 2000,' in Carey Roane, (Ed.) *The New Intifada: Resisting Israel's Apartheid*, Verso, London, pp. 209–218.

Arendt, Hannah (1968) *The Origins of Totalitarianism*, Harcourt, New York.

Barghouti, Omar (2001) 'Palestine's Tell-Tale Heart, in Carey Roane, (Ed.) *The New Intifada: Resisting Israel's Apartheid*, Verso, London, pp. 165–178.

Bazelon, Emily (2023) 'Why the Oslo Accord Failed,' *The New York Times*, November 20, (nytimes.com).

Bazelon, Emily (2024) 'The Long Shadow of 1948,' *The New York Times Sunday Magazine*, February 4, pp. 24–39.

Bergman, Ronen and Mark Mazzetti (2024) 'Israel's Extremist Takeover,' *The New York Times* Sunday Magazine, May 19, 2024, pp. 26–53.

Boshnaq, Mona, Sewell Chan, Irit Pazner Garshowitz, and Gaia Tripoli (2017) 'The Conflict in Jerusalem Is Distinctly Modern. Here's the History,' Dec. 5, (nytimes.com).

Boyd, Graham and Jack Reardon (2020) *Rebuild the Economy, Leadership, and You: A Toolkit for Builders of a Better World*, Evolutesix, London.

Casey, Nicholas (2023) 'We Will Never Forget Palestine,' *The New York Times Sunday Magazine*, December 23, pp. 30–47.

Dangerfield, George (1935 [1961]) *The Strange Death of Liberal England*, Capricorn Books, New York.

Davis, Elliot (2024) 'Palestinians are the world's largest stateless community. Here's everything you should know about their complicated plight as refugees,' *US News & World Report*, https://www.usnews.com

'Despite the War in Gaza, talk of a two-state solution will not go away,' (2023) *The Economist*, December 9, pp. 17–19; and accompanying editorial, 'How peace is possible,' p. 11.

Freedman, Lawrence, (2023) 'The only way out of the Gaza impasse requires global effort,' *The Financial Times,* December 2/3, p. 15.

Goren, Arthur (1991) 'Jews' in Eric Foner and John A. Garraty (Eds.) *The Reader's Companion to American History*, Houghton Mifflin, Boston.

Gruner, Ronald (2022) *We the Presidents: How American Presidents Shaped the Last Century*, Libratum Press, Naples, Florida.

'Israel is Strangling the West Bank's Administration,' (2023) *The Economist*, December 9, pp. 43–44.

Khalidi, Rashid, (1991) 'Middle East-US Relations,' in *The Reader's Companion to American History*, in Eric Foner and John A. Garraty, (Eds.) Houghton Mifflin, Boston, pp. 729–732.

Mandelbaum, Michael (2003) *The Ideas that Conquered the World: Peace, Democracy, and Free Markets in the Twenty-First Century*, Public Affairs, New York.

Masalha, Nur (1992) *Expulsion of the Palestinians: The Concept of 'Transfer' in Zionist Political Thought, 1882–1948*, Institute for Palestine Studies, Washington DC.

Masalha, Nur (2022) *Palestine: A Four Thousand Year History*, I.B. Tauris, London.

Pacheco, Allegra (2001) 'Flouting Convention: The Oslo Agreements, in Carey Roane (Ed.) *The New Intifada: Resisting Israel's Apartheid*, Verso, London, pp. 181–206.

Phillips, Laura (2017) 'History of South Africa's Bantustans,' African History, Oxford Research Encyclopedias, July 27, https://oxfordre.com

Rabbani, Mouin (2001) 'A Smorgasbord of Failure: Oslo and the Al-AQSA Intifada' in Carey Roane, (Ed.) *The New Intifada: Resisting Israel's Apartheid*, Verso, London, pp. 69–89.

Roy, Sara (2001) 'Decline and Disfigurement: The Palestinian Economy after Oslo,' in Carey Roane, (Ed.) *The New Intifada: Resisting Israel's Apartheid*, Verso London, pp. 91–109.

Said, Edward, W. (1979) *Orientalism*, Vintage, New York.

Said, Edward, W. (1992) *The Question of Palestine*, Vintage, New York.

Said, Edward, W. (2001) 'Palestinians Under Siege,' in Carey Roane, (Ed.) *The New Intifada: Resisting Israel's Apartheid*, Verso, London, pp. 27–42.

Sitta, Salman Abu Sitta (2001) 'The Implementation of the Right of Return,' in Carey Roane, (Ed.) *The New Intifada: Resisting Israel's Apartheid*, Verso, London, pp. 299–319.

'The Irrelevant Prime Minister' (2023) *The Economist*, December 2, p. 44.

'The Israeli Hamas War: Tough Love' (2023) *The Economist*, December 2, p. 11.

Tocqueville, Alexis de (1835 [2003]) *Democracy in America*, Penguin, New York.

Tuchman, Barbara (1982 [1956]) *Bible and Sword: How the British Came to Palestine*, MacMillan, London.

'What Does Hamas Want,' (2023) *The Economist,*' December 2, pp. 37–39.

Wikipedia contributors (2024) 'Proposals for a Jewish state,' *Wikipedia, The Free Encyclopedia*. https://en.wikipedia.org/w/index.php?title=Proposals_for_a_Jewish_state&oldid=1233171636

Part VI

Energy and Climate Change

34 Fossil Fuels: America's Addiction

The Issue: Preventing the global temperature from increasing more than 1.5°C since 1,800 will require a dramatic reduction in fossil fuel usage. Doing so will not be easy since fossil fuels currently account for 78% of America's total energy consumption. Yet, if we are to successfully transition to **Net Zero** and thereby stave off environmental catastrophe, we have no choice. This chapter provides a thorough discussion of fossil fuels from their origin to their current usage, to the major players, and to expected obstacles in our transition to sustainability.

34.1 Introduction

A global consensus has emerged that the world must become **Net Zero** by 2050 to attenuate the worst effects of **climate change** and to avoid cataclysmic and irreversible changes. Given our current over-reliance on fossil fuels (some would say addiction), we have our work cut out for us. It is a herculean task, but certainly not impossible.

34.2 Fossil Fuels: Overview

34.2.1 Origins—They Really Are from Fossils

During the Carboniferous period (aptly named as we shall see), approximately 360–290 million years ago, the Earth was much warmer, more humid, and wetter than today; with carbon dioxide preponderant in the atmosphere. This was the perfect environment for plants, and they took advantage, growing tall and broad and exotic looking. For example,

> the lepidodendron—which grew to 175 feet tall, and the Sigillaria—some with a long trunk forking near the top like a two-headed monster, each head crowned with a large spray of strap-like leaves; others with unbranched trunks six feet wide; and ferns that reached 30 feet high.
>
> (Freese, 2003, p. 18)

Given the oxygen-poor environment, and that the Earth's surface was mostly water, natural decomposition was difficult—as plants died and

DOI: 10.4324/9781003591856-40

layered, they could only partially decompose. This "spongey mass of carbon-rich plants first became peat and over millions of years hardened into coal" (Freese, 2003, p. 20).

Oil and natural gas developed somewhat differently, with their genesis in the ocean. Algae and plankton floating near or at the surface, when they died (if they weren't eaten) drifted to the ocean bottom and over millions of years were compressed by the Earth's heat and pressure, as layers and layers fell to the ocean floor, eventually forming oil and natural gas (tending to form deeper underground, although they also formed with coal deposits on land (EIA, 2022a).

The fossil fuels (coal, oil, and natural gas) differ in their chemical composition, but all are carbon-based, which should not be surprising given their provenance. Crude oil, a liquid, is mainly composed of complex hydrocarbons (i.e., molecules of hydrogen and carbon), along with some sulfur, nitrogen, and oxygen. Natural gas (a gas, obviously), is mainly composed of methane[1] (one carbon atom and four hydrogen atoms), along with ethane, propane, and butane. And coal is mostly carbon (albeit, much more than the other two) with secondary elements hydrogen, sulfur, oxygen, and nitrogen.

The hydrocarbons in oil and natural gas are less dense than the rocks and water in the Earth's crust, so they tend toward the surface, unless trapped by rock where they form into pools or reservoirs.

Coal is the 'dirtiest' fossil fuel since it contains far more carbon than the other two. Natural gas is sometimes mistakenly referred to as 'clean energy' because it contains less carbon,[2] but this is disingenuous since as a fossil fuel it is composed of carbon and methane. The latter is more potent as a global warming gas, with 20 times the effect of CO_2.

34.2.2   *The Gaia Hypothesis*

In our solar system, Earth is the only planet with life (as we know it), and in our galaxy, Earth is the only planet with life (as we know it). The reason is the unique combination of carbon, sunlight, and water, which for millions of years has been more or less self-regulating. Richard Lovelock termed this the Gaia hypothesis, or simply Gaia,[3]

> a complex entity involving the Earth's biosphere, atmosphere, oceans and social; the totality constituting a feedback or cybernetic system which seeks an optimal physical and chemical environment for life on this planet. The maintenance of relatively constant conditions by active control may be conveniently described by the term homeostasis...It is an alternative to that pessimistic view which sees nature as a primitive force to be subdued and conquered.
>
> (Lovelock, 1979 [1982], pp. 10–11)

Indeed, "life on Earth is like a finely calibrated machine, one that has been built by evolution to work very well within its design parameters" (Goodell, 2023, p. 20).

The Earth's atmosphere is comprised of 78.1% nitrogen, 20.9% oxygen, 0.93% argon, 0.04% carbon dioxide, and 0.03% trace gases such as helium, methane, and krypton. ('Earth's Atmosphere Composition: Nitrogen, Oxygen, and CO_2', 2023). Any slight deviation of any gas in either direction would make life much more problematic. This is what Gaia is all about: This unique, life-giving mixture of gases that we should treasure and hold sacred. Keeping Gaia intact is the most important gift that we can give to our children, to our children's children, and to our planet.

34.2.3   Global Warming Gases

When fossil fuels are combusted, carbon (along with other constituents) is released into the atmosphere. Carbon likes to bond with other elements, principally oxygen, forming CO_2. It is the preponderant global warming gas, blanketing the Earth's warmth, preventing its escape into outer space. Without sufficient CO_2 our atmosphere would resemble that of Mars; and too much would turn our planet into something resembling Venus, with scorching surface temperatures.

Of the global warming gases[4] (GHG), CO_2 is by far the most preponderant (accounting for 79.4% of the total) followed by Methane (11.5%), Nitrous Oxide (6.2%), and fluorinated gases emitted from household and industrial applications.[5] When GHG are released into the atmosphere, they tend to remain, although with differing lifespans: CO_2 much longer than methane, although the latter is more potent, doing more damage during its shorter atmospheric stint.

Today, methane is responsible for 45% of global warming, and during any 20-year span, methane has 80 times the potency of CO_2 ('Methane's Moment' 2023). In addition, "Methane is the primary contributor to the formation of ground-level ozone, a hazardous air pollutant and greenhouse gas, exposure to which causes 1 million premature deaths every year" (UN Environment Programme, 2021) Quite worrisome is that melting permafrost can potentially unleash methane into the atmosphere, and "accelerate methane emissions from wetlands—a potentially huge problem" ('Methane's Moment' 2023).

This illustrates the importance of mutual interactions—seemingly separate events that can coalesce into something worse, potentially creating tipping points of no return. This is what climate change is all about and the importance of embarking on our transition to **Net Zero**.

To attenuate the worst effects of climate change Denmark became the first nation to tax livestock, at 16 Euros a head. Livestock manure and gastroenteric releases account for 32% of human-caused methane emissions. Such emissions can be reduced by targeting what animals eat and how they digest,[6] and by "alternative types of feed to reduce the methane produced by cows and…ways to manage manure more efficiently by covering it, composting it, or using it to produce biogas" UN Environment Programme (2021).

Certainly, GHG can be released naturally, e.g., volcano eruptions, cow flatu-lence,[7] but fossil fuel combustion is increasing the presence of CO_2 and thus altering this special atmospheric mix, and disrupting the delicate Gaia balance. The heat from fossil fuel combustion "disrupts how cells function, how proteins unfold, and how molecules move" (Goodell, 2023, p. 20).

We are already seeing the effects, as once-in-a-lifetime climate events are happening with all too much frequency. **Climate change** is not some distant event to prepare for (or ignore) but it is happening now with the heat generated by fossil fuel combustion as the preponderant cause. This effect, known as the greenhouse effect, was first documented by Eunice Foote (1856),

> An atmosphere of that gas [carbonic acid gas, i.e., a common name for CO_2] would give to our earth a high temperature; and if as some suppose, at one period of its history the air had mixed with it a larger proportion than at present, an increased temperature from its own action as well as from increased weight must have necessarily resulted.
>
> (Foote, 1856, p. 383).

While CO_2 levels have fluctuated throughout Earth's history,[8] today, CO_2 con-centration is twice that at the beginning of the Industrial Revolution, and the high-est in 14 million years.[9] Given that CO_2 and the other global warming gases remain in the atmosphere for quite some time, even if we cease all carbon combustion immediately, the Earth will continue to warm. This doesn't mean that we throw up our hands in despair; rather this gives us added urgency, for the time to act is now.[10]

34.3   Coal, the Dirtiest Fossil Fuel, Helped Launch the Industrial Revolution

Coal was used in ancient civilizations for heating and fuel, for smelting; and it was also burned to heat Roman baths. Coal was used especially in times/places where it was easily available on the surface and firewood was scarce.[11] The modern age of coal began in England in the 17th century, precipitated by a wood shortage. At that time, wood was the major source of energy and central to all aspects of English life,

> Elizabethan England was a country built of wood...London was a wooden city, peaked-roofed and half timbered, heating itself with firewood ... But wood was growing dear, its price increasing as London's population in-creased and woodcutters carted firewood into the city from farther and far-ther afield...Besides making charcoal to smelt iron, the English cut down timber to build houses, barns, and fences; to produce glass and refine lead; to build bridges, docks, canal boats [and of course ships for the royal navy].
>
> (Rhodes, 2018, pp. 4, 5, and 7)

The bottom line: Wood, the preponderant and the quintessential mainstay of the Elizabethan way of life, was becoming scarcer and more expensive. And like the history of oil and natural gas in 19th and 20th centuries, "the final failure of the woodlands…was the result of constant neglect and abuse" (Rhodes, 2018, p. 7).[12]

As an alternative fuel, England turned to coal. Because of its combustibility coal became the preponderant source of heating and lighting.[13] But its mining was never easy. Once the easily accessible surface deposits were 'mined,' and it became necessary to mine deeper to access the coal, a host of problems emerged. Two deserve mention:

- Water seepage which necessitated inventing something to continuously suck water out of the mine. This problem eventually led to the steam engine, first developed by Thomas Newcombe in 1712, and greatly refined by James Watt in 1774. In addition to drying out mines, the steam engine acquired myriad other uses; and was most instrumental in powering the Industrial Revolution.[14]
- Transporting coal. Coal deposits were at some distance from the urban areas where they were most needed. Given their bulky weight, transporting over land was not the best option (given England's notoriously poor roads). So canals were dug and the railroad was developed in order to quickly and easily transport coal.[15] On September 27, 1825, George Stephenson, opened the first railway between Darlington and Stockton (in Durham County; the latter on the River Tees). As Freece writes:

> the difficulty of hauling coal has always been one of its greatest drawbacks as a fuel, but now through the locomotive, coal could haul itself; similarly, through the stream engine, coal could pump the mines that contained it. The patterns were the same: Coal created a problem, then helped power a solution, and that solution would have revolutionary consequences far beyond the coal industry.
>
> (Freese, 2003, p. 91)

For both of these problems, human ingenuity first conceptualized the problem and then led to a practical solution. Each solution enabled the next set of problems to be solved,[16] all occurring within an economic system that incentivized profits and extolled private ownership. In addition, there was an intense excitement as the new coal energy regime was unfolding,

> In imagining possible futures, it's important to factor in one last critical energy source: excitement. There was a time when coal was actually fun—not the mining which was never fun, but the building of a powerful new coal-fired world, which inspired distinct bursts of imagination, enthusiasm, and daring at various historical moments.
>
> (Freese, 2003, p. 246)

Lesson for today as we transition to **Net Zero**: Let's harness the same type of 'bursts of imagination, enthusiasm, and daring.'

Lest we give coal too much credit, the Industrial Revolution "was fueled by the large-scale extraction of raw materials (especially cotton [which in turn was largely produced via slave labor in the American South] all within the framework of a coercive [highly militarist] and colonialist organization scheme" (Piketty, 2022, p. 49).

By 1900, the United States was the world's leading coal producer, surpassing Great Britain. Coal "was the unrivaled foundation of US power, providing 71% of the nation's energy, with wood 21%, oil, natural gas, and hydro providing the remainder" (Freese, 2003, p. 137). Sure coal was dirty and difficult to mine, but at the same time, it was emblematic of progress over nature; coal evidenced wealth, progress, and increased living standards.[17] An imprimatur of human ingenuity.

As the United States (and the world) industrialized, more and more uses were found for fossil fuels. Today, coal is primarily used for steel making and cement; and for heating and lighting. Oil is mainly used for transportation, distilled into gasoline, diesel, jet fuel, and heating oil.[18] Natural gas is primarily used as a feedstock for fertilizer and chemicals, as well as for heating and cooking.

In addition, fossil fuels (especially oil and natural gas) are unsuspectingly (at least from the consumer's perspective) used in a multitude of everyday products: Gum, candies, toothpaste, deodorant, antiseptics, lipstick, nail polish, golf balls, housepaint, ballpoint pens, yarn, ink, dyes, CDs, eyeglasses, hand lotion, pantyhose, computer monitors and keyboards, coffee makers, etc. (USDE, 2023). How, when, and if we transition to **Net Zero** will be determined by how well we reduce our reliance on fossil fuels, which means finding effective substitutes of the above-mentioned products, and/or developing new products which effectively serve the same purpose.

34.4 Fossil Fuels in 2024

Table 34.1 presents data on global primary energy consumption[19] by fuel for the year 2023:

Table 34.1 Global energy consumption as a % of total (by fuel type)

Petroleum	33%
Coal	28%
Natural gas	25%
Fossil fuels	86%
Renewables	9%
Hydro	3%
Nuclear	2%

Source: Global Direct Primary Energy Consumption (2023).

Table 34.2 USA 2022 primary energy consumption as a % of the total (by fuel type)

Petroleum	36%
Natural gas	33%
Coal	10%
Fossil fuels	79%
Renewables	13%
Nuclear	8%

Source: US EIA (2023a)

Table 34.2 presents data on USA primary energy consumption by fuel type: Two points about the above data:

• The preponderant energy source in the United States and the world is fossil fuels.
• The world relies on coal almost three times as much as does the United States, while the United States has a greater mix of nuclear and renewable energy.

The United States has significantly reduced its usage of coal over the last half century and will continue to do so (as will Europe). At the 2024 meeting of the G-7 held in Turin, participants agreed to cease using coal plants that do not capture emissions by 2035, with financial assistance to developing nations. Italy's Minister of the Environment and Energy Security noted that, "it is the first time that a path and a target has been set on coal. It is a very strong signal from industrialized countries. It is a big signal to the world to reduce coal" (Bocca, 2024).

Asian nations, however, are ignoring this signal. Strong economic growth and a keen desire for energy independence are increasing Asian coal demand,

China, India, Indonesia, Viet Nam and the Philippines—which together represent more than 70% of global coal demand—will more than offset decreases by [western nations]. In China and India …rising coal consumption is driven by robust growth in demand for electricity and low hydropower output.

(Coal, 2023)

Today, China is the main player in the global coal market,

The dominance of China in coal markets is stronger than any other country for any other fuel. [China] consumes more than half of the world's coal and produces half of it, and it is the largest importer, accounting for close to one-third of the global coal trade. But India and ASEAN also exert a growing influence—helping further shift the focus of the coal market towards Asia.

(Coal, 2023)

China relies on coal for illumination, heating, industry, and overall energy security. It turns to coal when its hydro sources become scarce, which has been happening with increasing frequency, ironically due to climate change. Increased fossil fuel consumption has reduced China's hydro supplies, making them less reliable as an energy source, which in turn forces more fossil fuel combustion, abetting global warming which further depletes hydro supplies, forcing China to burn more coal, etc. China knows such behavior is unsustainable and even irrational in the long-term (it is the world's largest solar and renewables 'investor') but certainly not in the short term as energy security and economic development take priority. So when is irrational behavior rational? Apparently when there is a palpable difference between short- and long-term interests. But even this is not necessarily rational.

As of 2023, the world's five largest petroleum-producing nations[20] are the United States (25.1%), Saudi Arabia (15.0%), Russia (13.5%), Canada (7.1%), and China (6.3%). The world's top five petroleum reserve owners[21] are Venezuela (19.6%), Russia (17.2%), Iran (13.5%), and Iraq (9.4%).

A few remarks about these oil nations[22]:

- Saudi Arabia is the world's largest petroleum exporter.
- China is the world's largest oil consumer, followed by the United States. These two nations account for 45% of global oil demand.
- In 2023, China eclipsed Iraq to take the 5th slot of the largest global oil producers.
- In response to Russia's invasion of Ukraine, the United States, the UK, and Australia have banned imports of Russian oil. It is not clear the embargo's efficacy, given that India and China have largely filled the gap. We will discuss this further in **Iran, Russia, and North Korea**.
- Nearly all of Canada's oil reserves are in Alberta in the form of oil sands, which requires a significant amount of energy to extract.

As of 2023, the largest natural gas producers[23] (by nation) are the United States (23.1%), Russia (17.4%), Iran (6.4%), China (5.2%), and Qatar (4.4%). The largest natural gas reserve owners[24] are Russia (19.9.%), Iran (17.1%), Qatar (13.3%), the United States (6.7%), and Turkmenistan (7.2%).

A few remarks about these important gas nations[25]:

- The world's largest natural gas field is the North Field shared by Iran and Qatar.
- China has incentivized transitioning from coal to natural gas to reduce GHG.
- In order to boost its natural gas production to meet increased demand from Europe, Iran needs a massive infrastructure investment.

- The United States has increased its natural gas production by one-third by increased fracking and transitioning away from coal.
- Norway, the world's fourth largest exporter of natural gas, is now the EU's largest supplier, replacing Russia.

Given that natural gas is a gas, over land it is best transported by pipelines. But overseas, constructing pipelines is not practical. As an alternative, the gas is supercooled to $-260°F$, at which temperature the gas is liquefied; this in turn reduces the volume of the gas by 600 times, allowing the economic transport of Liquefied Natural Gas (LNG) via ships (EIA, 2023c). From port to port requires either liquefying or re-gasifying.[26]

In 2023, the United States replaced Qatar as the world's largest LNG exporter. The United States' top five LNG export markets are France (15% of total LNG exports), the UK (12%), Spain (11%), the Netherlands (10%) and South Korea (8%) (EIA, 2023c).

USA production of LNG has skyrocketed: In 2015 (the last year when the United States was a LNG net importer) it produced 28.4 billion cubic feet (bcf); in 2022 the United States produced 3,865.4 bcf (EIA, 2023c). The United States' increased LNG production has "helped Europe wean off Russian energy and [has] reduced global gas prices" (The WSJ, 1/23/24).

As of 2023, the largest coal producers by nation are[27] China (51.5%), India (9.4%), Indonesia (7.6%), the United States (6.5%), and Australia (5.8%). And the largest coal reserve owners are[28] the United States (23.2%), Australia (14.0%), China (13.3%), India (10.3%), and Germany (3.3%).

These fossil fuel national ownership statistics are important for two reasons:

- They represent significant obstacles in transitioning to **Net Zero**, since such deposits literally represent money in the ground. One study estimated potential lost assets at $11 trillion, a highly variable number, depending upon the transition speed and extent (Watts et al., 2021).
- A central lesson from Jared Diamond's *Collapse* is that vested interests block reform, even when the dangers are explicitly known, "if the elites can insulate themselves from the consequences of their actions, they are likely to do things that profit themselves regardless of whether these actions hurt everybody else" (Diamond, 2005, p. 430). The attempt to preserve fossil fuel usage is no different. Minimizing or even preventing such vested-interest actions is key to an equitable and successful transition to **Net Zero**.

34.5 The United States and China: The Fossil Fuel Kings That Hold the Key to When and How We Transition to Net Zero

In November 2023, the United States (the world's largest oil producer) set an all-time high (until then) for (weekly) oil production at 13.2 million barrels per day; and China (the world's largest coal producer) set an all-time record for coal production. Apparently, both nations are moving in the opposite direction of sustainability and **Net Zero**, at least in the short term, which is troubling. And not surprisingly, China and the United States are world's largest two emitters of GHGs, accounting for 42% of the total.

How and when the world transitions away from fossil fuels will depend on the short-term behavior of the United States and China. On China, Paraskova (2024) writes, "The outlook for coal in China will be significantly affected in the coming years by the pace of its clean energy deployment, weather conditions, and structural shifts in the Chinese economy." And, as we see it, China is able and willing to revert to hydro if weather allows (i.e., ample rain); and its long-term movement is clearly in the direction of renewables and nuclear energy. But for the United States we see no lessening of record-breaking oil production and consumption (along with natural gas) at least in the short run.[29] Obviously, the United States does not possess the long-term resources to sustain such behavior (as the world's largest importer of oil, it only possesses four percent of global oil reserves). Today, a bi-partisan consensus[30] has emerged in the United States that high oil consumption is necessary to maintain our standard of living, and that any transition to an alternative energy regime will take time. Hence, the thinking: We must make do based upon our current strengths.

Somewhat encouraging is that the United States and China reached an agreement at the 2023 COP28 in Dubai to reduce GHGs, especially methane emissions—a major commitment from China (Nilsen and Paddison, 2023). While China is doing its best to substitute away from coal (as is the United States), we don't know how to interpret that against its 305 coal-fired electrical generators coming online in 2023, other than that energy security comes first. Today, China relies on coal for 71% of its total electricity, a significant reduction from its peak of 81% in 2007 (Slotta, 2024). But given that China's coal production is surging ahead, with 2023 setting a record, China is producing more coal than it did in 2007. This highlights the urgency to switch from coal to natural gas, at least in the short term, and then from fossil fuels to renewables/nuclear in the long term.

Switching from coal is desirable, given its greater emissions, but using more natural gas is problematic given its higher concentration of methane. The best answer for both nations: Substitute away fossil fuels.

34.6   Electricity: The Imprimatur of Modernity

As an exercise in my 'Introduction to Economics' classes I (Jack) ask students to list the occasions that they use electricity during the course of a day. It is an eye-opening exercise, to say the least. Yet, despite its ubiquity in everyday use, electricity is not well understood. Is it an energy source? Is it a source of power?

Is it used to produce to energy? Is it a current to carry energy? Is it used to produce work?[31] It turns out that electricity is a little of each,

> Electricity is the flow of electrical power or charge. Electricity is both a basic part of nature and one of the most widely used forms of energy. The electricity that we use is a *secondary* energy source because it is produced by converting primary sources of energy such as coal, natural gas, nuclear energy, solar energy, and wind energy into electrical power. Electricity is also referred to as an *energy carrier*, which means it can be converted to other forms of energy such as mechanical energy or heat. Primary energy sources are renewable or nonrenewable energy, but the electricity we use is neither renewable nor nonrenewable.
>
> (USA EIA, 2023b, emphasis in the original)

Electricity[32] is "the most compact and fastest form of power in widespread use –it pushes power density and speed far beyond the turbine [gas] that generates it" (Huber and Mills, 2005, p. 32). Electricity is used for a host of needs, so much so, that it is an imprimatur of modern life. Electricity runs our computers, lights our homes/businesses, and powers our washing machines, dryers, dishwashers, furnaces, refrigerators, etc. Indeed, the demand for electricity is synonymous with development,

> Demand for electricity has been rising without interruption since Thomas Edison invented the lightbulb over a century ago…Economic growth marches hand-in-hand with increased consumption of electricity—always, everywhere, without significant exception in the annals of modern industry.
>
> (Huber and Mills, 2005, pp. 169–170)

Here in the United States, our electricity is primarily generated from fossil fuels (Table 34.3):

Table 34.3 Source of USA electricity generation[33]

Natural gas	39.8%
Renewables[34]	21.5%
Coal	19.5%
Nuclear	18.2%
Fossil fuels[35]	59.3

Source: US EIA (2023b)

Table 34.4 Sources of global electricity generation

Coal	35.2%
Natural gas	22.5%
Renewables	15.9%
Hydro	15.0%
Nuclear	9.2%
Oil	3.2%
Fossil fuels	60.9%

Source: US EIA (2023b).

Compare this with the global sources of electricity generation (see Table 34.4). Coal is used twice as much in the rest of the world, while nuclear energy is used half as much. In 2023, for the first time in history, renewables provided 30% of all global electricity. This is an achievement worth noting, suggesting that strong momentum will be pushing us forward and not backward, and that achieving Net Zero by 2050 will be in our reach,

> In 2023, growth in solar and wind pushed the world past 30% renewable electricity for the first time. Renewables have expanded from 19% of global electricity in 2000, driven by an increase in solar and wind from 0.2% in 2000 to a record 13.4% in 2023. China was the main contributor in 2023, accounting for 51% of the additional global solar generation and 60% of new global wind generation. Combined with nuclear power, the world generated almost 40% of its electricity from low-carbon sources in 2023. As a result, the CO_2 intensity of global power generation reached a new record low, 12% lower than its peak in 2007.
>
> (Global Electricity Review, 2024)

Post-2024, the world could use some good news and solar power, or more accurately the dramatic growth in solar powered by an equally dramatic fall in price, could be it,

> Installed solar capacity is doubling every three years...solar power is on track to generate more electricity than all the world's nuclear power plants in 2026, than its wind turbines in 2027, than its dams in 2028, its gas-fired plants in 2030, and its coal-fired ones in 2032...and it becomes humankind's largest source of primary energy—not just electricity— by the 2040s.
>
> (*The Economist,* June 22, 2024, p. 42)

Wow! The reason, according to *The Economist* (*The Economist,* June 22, 2024, p. 42) is economies of scale: More is produced (thanks largely to subsidies), its price falls, increasing demand, resulting in more produced, decreasing its cost, further decreasing price. The whole process of economies of scale can creatively find new uses for energy,

> One way to drastically reduce the speed of airborne disease is to speed up the rate at which air in the world's buildings is vented and refreshed. If energy is expensive this is not feasible. But what if?…That human ingenuity finds useful things to do with better access to energy is one of the clearest messages of the past 200 years.
>
> (*The Economist,* June 22, 2024, p. 46)

Richard Rhodes in his book, *Energy: A Human History* (2018) would certainly agree.

Due to falling prices,

> America's low-carbon economy has gained a momentum of its own. Even without subsidies, adding power to the grid with a solar farm is cheaper these days than doing so with a new coal-powered plant. Over 90% of the additional power generation capacity coming online in America in 2024 will be carbon-free.
>
> ('A Fossil-fuel Fantasy' 2024, p. 54)

Not surprisingly, global demand for electricity is expected to increase steadily through 2050, but what is surprising is, at least at first glance, only by 1% total (2022b). This is because electrical appliances, heating, ventilation systems, cooling units, and capital equipment have all become more energy efficient (EIA, 2022b).

When (and if) we transition to **Net Zero** our cars will be electric vehicles which is all well and good. Thus, it is important to remember that today (in 2024) electricity production preponderantly relies on fossil fuels, which, of course, needs to be dramatically curtailed. We will return to this issue in **Net Zero**.

34.7   Conclusion

Barbara Freece noted that coal "has always been both a creative and a destructive force" (2003, p. 14). Indeed, we can say the same about fossil fuels: A gift from nature which has helped us industrialize and has significantly raised living standards everywhere it has been used. Yet, at the same time, its environmental consequences have always been destructive, now reaching a tipping point. A study published in November 2023, just as the COP 28 was underway, found that of the 8.3 million deaths in 2019 due to air pollution, 61% were directly related to fossil fuel combustion; a statistic notably higher than previously thought (Lelieveld et al., 2023). And a statistic that will most likely increase as long as we continue using fossil fuels, adding extra urgency to transition to **Net Zero**.

As if that wasn't bad enough:

the atmospheric heat created by fossil fuel combustion "lowers children's test scores; raises the risk of miscarriages in pregnant women, increases death rates from heart and kidney disease, increases international conflict as well as civil wars, increases suicides, gun violence, rape and violent crime.

(Goodell, 2023, p. 18)

What are we doing to ourselves and to our planet? The time for inaction is past; the time for action is now.

Notes

1   Methane, colorless and odorless, is extremely dangerous in underground coal mines, and can (and often does) lead to explosions. In the early days of coal mining, miners would bring caged canaries with them underground; if the bird died, that would indicate the presence of methane, or coal damp, or simply damp, as it was called. Today, we use more sophisticated methane detectors, although it is an always-present danger, in addition to being a major contributor to **climate change**.

2   The origin of the word 'natural' in 'natural gas' is not clear. Obviously, natural gas is no more natural than coal or oil, but the word natural seems to have originated in a 1930s marketing campaign (Leber, 2022). The strategy worked as, today, most Americans do not associate natural gas as a pollutant or even as a fossil fuel (Leber, 2022).

3   Lovelock (1979 [1982], p. 10) explains, "Gaia, more simply known as Ge, was a Greek Earth goddess, from which geography and geology derive their names."

4   GHG: Greenhouse Gases, which, for our purpose is the same as Global Warming Gases.

5   Source: (EPA, 2023a). We also discuss the contributing factors of GHG in **Climate Change**.

6   For a thorough discussion of various solutions within a cost/benefit context, see United Nations Environment Programme and Climate and Clean Air Coalition (2021).

7   We can debate what is natural. Eating meat is considered an imprimatur of economic development. As income increases so does the demand for meat, which means more farmlands must be cleared and developed, and that means more cows. So, if we are raising more cows given our increased demand for meat, is this really natural?

8   The data in this paragraph are obtained from (Wikipedia, 2023).

9   CO_2 has ranged from 4,000 ppm, 500 million years ago to 180 ppm during the last two million years. The atmospheric presence of CO_2 is measured in parts per million (ppm). Effectively, it means concentration by volume of one part of an entity per million parts of another entity. One ppm approximates five liters of material in an Olympic size swimming pool (Reardon et al., 2018, p. 17).

10   For a helpful and urgent 'to-do' book, see Thunberg (2023).

11   Ramani and Evans (2024) provide the source for these three sentences.

12   See our **Oil Industry** chapter.

13   Goodman (2020) provides an interesting discussion of the socioeconomic effects of switching from wood to coal in England.

14   For a discussion of the development of the steam engine, see Rhodes (2018, pp. 37–42, pp. 49–60).

15 The coal coastal trade necessitated the building of ports and ships not only for transport but to guard against piracy. As the coal trade grew so did England's shipping fleet. Coal was a central impetus in developing England into a maritime power (Freece, 2003, p. 85).

16 This is the major theme of Richard Rhodes' excellent book, *Energy: A Human History* (2018).

17 Perhaps better than no one else, Charles Dickens captured the intricacies of British life during the 19th century, especially income insecurity and the differences between classes. His *Hard Times* (1854 [1985]) masterfully depicts the role of coal, and especially its ambivalent effects, both as an accoutrement of progress and as a tool of subjugation and exploitation. For an interesting and detailed account of conditions in Manchester during the coal-fired Industrial Revolution, see Engels (1845 [1999]).

18 The **oil industry** is discussed later in this book.

19 This data can either be presented by production or consumption. Production of course means that some part may be exported/imported, whereas consumption gives a better picture of domestic use. There is no hard and fast rule for which is preferable. The data for USA energy use as a percent of total production: Natural gas (36%), Petroleum (31%) Coal (12%), Renewables 12%, and Nuclear (8%) (US EIA, 2023a).

20 Source: Pistilli (2023).

21 Source: 'Oil Reserves by Country,' (2024).

22 Unless otherwise stated these remarks are taken from Pistilli (2023).

23 Source: 'Top 10 Countries for Natural Gas Production' (2023).

24 Source: 'Top Ten Countries with the Largest Natural Gas Reserves' (2024).

25 Source: 'Top 10 Countries for Natural Gas Production' (2023).

26 Obviously, both liquefying and re-gasification require energy; according to the EIA (2023c) approximately 14% of the total shipment is needed.

27 Source: 'Coal Production by Country' (2024).

28 Source: 'Coal Reserves by Country' (2024).

29 Fracking has been instrumental in vaulting the United States to the top position. Fracking is used "on shale and other types of sedimentary rock formations by forcing water, chemicals, and sand down a well under high pressure. This process…breaks up the formation [and] releases the natural gas from the rock" (EIA, 2022a).

30 President Biden acknowledged in his 2023 State of the Union address, "we're still going to need oil and gas for a while" (State of the Union 2023); a statement sharply different from his earlier ones. For further discussion, see the **Oil Industry**.

31 According to physics, work is the application of a force to displace an object.

32 Amber was called 'elektron' in Greek and 'electrum' in Latin for its ability to attract small particles after rubbing with a cloth. For the development of electricity in modern times, see Rhodes (2018, pp. 168–206) where many scientific luminaries took an active part: Ben Franklin, Thomas Edison, George Westinghouse, Nikola Telsa, Michael Faraday, Hans Oersted, etc. Reading Rhodes drives home the point that the development of electricity, and of energy in general, is a collective endeavor spearheaded by human ingenuity, along with, of course, the desire for fame and fortune.

33 Both Tables 3 and 4 reflect 2022 Electricity Production by Source (2023); full data for 2023 were not available at press time.

34 More specifically, according to the EIA (2023b) wind accounts for 10.2% of total electricity generated in the United States, hydro (6.3%), solar (3.4%), biomass (1.3%), and geothermal (0.4%). While hydro (i.e., producing electricity by a dam) has been traditionally categorized as renewable, with climate change drying traditional supplies, we are not sure how hydro should be classified. By consensus, as a separate type.

35 Oil is much more preponderant in transportation and industry, although nil in electricity production.

References

'A fossil-fuel fantasy,' *The Economist,* July 27, 2024, pp. 53–54.

Bocca, Roberto (2024) "World Economic Forum, May 8, G7 countries agree 2035 exit for unabated coal plants | World Economic Forum (weforum.org).

'Coal 2023' International Energy Agency, Executive Summary, Executive summary – Coal 2023 – Analysis – IEA.

'Coal Production by Country' (2024) World Population Review, Coal Production by Country 2024 (worldpopulationreview.com).

Diamond, Jared (2005) *Collapse: How Societies Choose to Fail or Succeed,* Penguin, New York.

'Earth's Atmosphere Composition: Nitrogen, Oxygen, and CO2' (2023) Earth How (September 23) Earth's Atmosphere Composition: Nitrogen, Oxygen, Argon and CO_2 - Earth How.

Dickens, Charles (1854 [1985]) *Hard Times,* Penguin, New York.

Engels Friedrich (1845 [1999]) *The Condition of the Working Class in England,* Oxford University Press, Oxford.

Electricity Production by Source (2023) *Our World in Data,* Electricity production by source, (ourworldindata.org).

'Essay: Solar Power' (2024) *The Economist,* June 22, pp. 41–46.

Environmental Protection Agency (2023) 'Greenhouse gas emissions,' July 14, Greenhouse Gases US EPA.

Freese, Barbara (2003) *Coal: A Human History,* Perseus Publishing, Cambridge, Mass.

Foote, Eunice (1856) 'Circumstances Affecting the Heat of Sun's Rays', in *American Journal of Art and Science, 2nd Series,* Vol. 22, No. 66, November 1856, pp. 382–383.

'Global Direct Primary Energy Consumption,' (2023) Our World in Data, (ourworldindata.org).

Global Electricity Review (2024) *Ember,* Report-Global-Electricity-Review-2024.pdf, London.

Goodell, Jeff (2023) *The Heat Will Kill You First: Life and Death on a Scorched Planet,* Back Bay Books, New York.

Goodman, Ruth (2020) *The Domestic Revolution: How the Introduction of Coal into Victorian Homes Changed Everything,* Liveright Publishing, New York.

Huber, Peter and Mark Mills (2005) *The Bottomless Well: The Twilight of Fuel, the Virtue of Waste, and Why We Will Never Run Out of Energy,* Basic Books, New York.

Leber, Rebecca (2022) 'The End of Natural Gas Has to Start with its Name', *Vox,* (February 10).

Lelieveld, Jos, Andy Haines, Richard Burnett, Cathryn Tonne, Klaus Klingmüller, Thomas Münzel, Andrea Pozzer (2023) 'Air pollution deaths attributable to fossil fuels: observational and modelling study' *British Medical Journal,* Vol. 383, p. e077784.

Lovelock, James (1979 [1982]) *Gaia: A New Look at Life on Earth,* Oxford University Press, Oxford, UK.

'Methane's Moment,' (2023) *The Economist,* editorial, December 2, p. 11.

Nilsen, Ella and Laura Paddison (2023) 'Takeaways from COP28: What Does the Climate Deal Say?' CNN, December 13.

'Oil Reserves by Country' (2024) World Population Review, Oil Reserves by Country 2024 (worldpopulationreview.com).

Paraskova, Tsvetana (2024) 'China's Coal Production Hit a Record High in 2023,' *OilPrice.com* (January 17).

Piketty, Thomas (2022) *A Brief History of Equality,* Belknap Press of Harvard University, Cambridge, Massachusetts, translated by Steven Rendall.

Pistilli, Melissa (2023) 'Top 10 Oil-Producing Countries,' *Investing News Network*, (November 2) (investingnews.com).

Ramani, Raja Venkat and M. Albert Evans (2024) 'Coal Mining' *The Encyclopedia Britannica.*

Reardon, Jack, Maria Madi, and Molly Scott Cato (2018) *Introducing a New Economics*, Pluto, London.

Rhodes, Richard (2018) *Energy: A Human History*, Simon and Schuster, New York.

Slotta, Daniel (2024) 'Electricity Generation Share from Coal in China from 2000 to 2022,' *Statista*, (January 3).

'State of the Union Address,' Joe Biden, February 7, 2023, The White House.

Thunberg, Greta (2023) *The Climate Book: The Facts and the Solutions*, Penguin Press, New York.

Top 10 Countries for Natural Gas Production (2023) *Fresh Trader Insider*, August 15.

'Top Ten Countries with the Largest Natural Gas Reserves (2024) *World Population Review*, Natural Gas by Country 2024 (worldpopulationreview.com).

United Nations Environment Programme and Climate and Clean Air Coalition (2021) *Global Methane Assessment: Benefits and Costs of Mitigating Methane Emissions.* United Nations Environment Programme, Nairobi

United Nations Environment Programme (2021) 'Methane emissions are driving climate change: Here's How to Reduce Them,' August 20, (unep.org).

United States Department of Energy (2023) 'Products Made from Oil and Gas' (energy. gov).

United States Energy Information Administration (2022a) 'Natural Gas Explained' (December 27).

United States Energy Information Administration (2022b) 'Outlook: Electricity,' (eia. gov).

United States Energy Information Administration (2023a) 'US energy consumption as a percent of total,' U.S. energy facts - data and statistics - U.S. Energy Information Administration (EIA).

United States Energy Information Administration (2023b) 'Electricity Explained.'

United States Energy Information Administration (2023c) 'Natural Gas Explained: LNG,' Liquefied natural gas - U.S. Energy Information Administration (EIA).

Watts, Jonathan, Ashley Kirk, Niamh McIntyre, Pablo Gutiérrez, Niko Kommenda (2021) 'Half of world's fossil fuel assets could become worthless by 2036 in net zero transition.' *The Guardian*, November 4.

Wikipedia (2023) 'Carbon Dioxide in the Earth's Atmosphere,' Carbon dioxide in Earth's atmosphere - Wikipedia.

35 The Oil Industry

The Issue: Today, oil is the United States' largest energy source as well as the world's. Oil has played a central role in the United States' historical development—it is no exaggeration to say that cheap oil has made the United States into a global superpower. Yet, given the exigencies of **climate change** and the inevitable transition to **Net Zero**, we must radically decrease our oil consumption. An admittedly difficult task, especially given oil's central importance. But how should this be done? Who will make the decisions? We all have a right to participate in this debate, which will ultimately transform how we live. But to participate, we must first understand how oil has evolved into the United States' most important energy source, our oil dependency, and how oil is used today.

35.1 Introduction

Although we could have combined the **Oil Industry**, **Fossil Fuels, Climate Change**, and **Net Zero** into one chapter, we decided that, given the importance of each, to discuss each separately. Oil is "the keystone of the standard of living in the US and to a large degree its rank as a world power" (Wall, 1991, p. 807). Cheap oil has transformed how and where we live, how we travel, and how/what/where we produce and consume.[1] If we are to successfully transition to **Net Zero** by 2050 (i.e., our energy usage produces net zero emissions of greenhouse gases); and if we are to avert the worst effects of climate change, we must radically decrease our oil consumption. Not only is this going to be difficult given the importance of oil in our daily lives, but the obstacles to transition are formidable.

35.2 The Genesis of the Oil Industry[2]

Although oil was used in ancient times for lighting, weapons, and even medicine,[3] the modern oil age commenced on August 27, 1859, in Titusville, Pennsylvania. Then, Edward Drake drilled for oil beneath the earth's surface to tap it at its source. Oil's importance for heating and lighting

DOI: 10.4324/9781003591856-41

was recognized immediately and the industry rapidly developed. The first oil company, Pennsylvania Rock Oil[4] Company (later to become Seneca) was formed; and the barrel became oil's ad hoc container and ubiquitous measurement.[5]

When oil oozes out of the ground or gushes out of a derrick, it is a thick glob. But to be useful, it must be refined and distilled. Kerosene was the first such product,[6] with the process receiving two patents in 1852 and 1854. Before the age of oil, kerosene was distilled from coal and oil shale, and initially used for illumination. It replaced whale oil which had become scarcer and more expensive due to ferocious hunting[7] (Yergin, 1991 pp. 22–25). Kerosene lamps were developed, and kerosene street lighting became ubiquitous during the latter 19th century. Cleveland, Ohio became the initial center of the fledgling USA oil industry, due to its well-developed transportation infrastructure.

35.3   Standard Oil—The Grandfather of Today's Oil Companies

Standard Oil became the first superstar oil company, founded by John D. Rockefeller in 1870. While Standard was instrumental in transforming the fledgling oil industry into a national (and international) powerhouse, it was a ruthless predator. It would typically enter new markets, destroying and gobbling up the competition. A favorite tactic was to charge below cost, forcing rival firms who could not compete to fold; then Standard would acquire their assets at bargain basement prices. Standard would also use its power to strike favorable rates with railroads (the dominant means of transportation at the time), effectively foreclosing competition.

Standard's ruthless predation did not sit well with the public or the federal government.[8] The latter responded by creating the Interstate Commerce Commission in 1887 to regulate the railroads' unsavory practices. In 1890, Congress, largely as a reaction to growing monopoly in the American economy, and especially the oil industry, passed the Sherman Antitrust Act, the first of several **antitrust** laws. While the Act's objective was to make an existing monopoly illegal, a glaring weakness was its inability to prevent a monopoly from forming. To rectify, the Clayton Act was passed in 1914, which prohibited certain actions (such as pricing below cost, and tying contracts) which might lead to the formation of a monopoly. All such actions were taken straight from Standard Oil's playbook.[9]

In 1904, Standard controlled 91% of USA oil production and 85% of final sales.[10] In 1911, under the Sherman Act, the Supreme Court ordered Standard to be divested into 34 separate companies, despite its industry market share falling to 64% from 91% in 1904, and the existence of 147 refining competitors (Desjardins, 2017). Not all 34 were equal in size but given Standard's deliberate policy of horizontal and vertical integration, they remained quite connected post-divestiture (Blair, 1976, pp. 147–151).

The post-1911 evolution of the Standard companies maps out the genesis and the evolution of today's major players in the oil industry. Here are the highlights[11]:

- Standard Oil of California, also known as SoCal, acquired the Gulf Oil Co in 1984, which at the time, was the largest merger in US history to date. In 1984 it changed its name to Chevron,[12] then acquired Texaco in 2000 and Unocal in 2005. Today, it is the tenth largest firm in the United States by revenue.
- Standard Oil of Indiana was renamed Amoco in 1929. In 1998 it was acquired by BP.
- Standard Oil Company of Ohio, renamed Sohio, was acquired by BP in 1987.
- The Ohio Oil Company was renamed Marathon Oil, and now Marathon Petroleum is the 16th largest US corporation.
- Standard Oil of New Jersey, with almost half of Standard's net value (Yergin, 1991, p. 110) renamed Esso, acquired Humble gas in 1959.
- Standard Oil of New York, with 9% of Standard's net value (Yergin, 1991, p. 110) was renamed Mobil.
- In 1999, Exxon (previously known as Esso, i.e., S.O.) Mobil merged to form (at the time) the United States' largest corporation, but now third after Walmart and Amazon.
- Continental Oil became part of Conoco; and Atlantic became part of ARCO and eventually part of Sun.

Other divested companies among the 34 included Vaseline, eventually acquired by Unilever in 1987; Pennzoil acquired by Shell in 1999; and UTLX (a railroad tank company) acquired by Berkshire Hathaway in 2013.

35.4   The Oil Industry Shifts to the Middle East

By 1909, the dawning of the age of gasoline, the United States was the epicenter of the world's oil industry. Not only was the United States the world's largest oil consumer and producer but it "drilled more oil than the rest of the world combined" (Wall, 1991, p. 805). The USA oil industry at the time was extremely profligate and its practices wasteful. Wallace Pratt, for example, a senior oil official with Standard Oil looking back at that time, wrote in the late 1980s, "the poor production techniques as well as the practice of releasing natural gas that often underlay oil pools wasted at least 75% of the oil and gas found to date in the USA" (Wall, 1991, p. 807). At the same time, consumers enjoying plentiful supplies were not incentivized to conserve.

One such wasteful drilling practice was the 'Right of Capture,' a legal concept based on common law. Simply put, land ownership carried the rights to subsoil minerals. In the industry's early days, it was very difficult to estimate the underground pool size (oil collects in pools trapped between layers of rock) while the underground oil didn't respect the topsoil property rights. Under the 'Right of Capture', if a landowner drills for oil, he/she can legally capture all the oil underneath, even if underlying another's property; and even if such drilling disturbs the geological properties needed to extract the oil.

Given the high fixed costs of oil exploration, the Right of Capture led to an excessive number of oil wells, and a high incentive to maximize output and hence revenue. The high exploitation rates also meant that large amounts of oil had to be left in the ground, given the lack of geological pressure to bring it to the surface (van der Linde, 1991, p. 67; Yergin, 1991, p. 23). This practice was somewhat tempered during the 1920s, when state governments and state commissions began prorationing to conserve oil supplies by well-spacing and rationing drilling output.

Nevertheless, thanks to the industry's profligacy, during the 1920s alarm bells were raised that the United States was running out of oil. During the Coolidge administration (1923–1929)[13] Secretary of State Charles Hughes and Commerce Secretary Hebert Hoover exhorted oil companies to search for overseas supplies. The call was initially allayed due to massive oil strikes in Texas during the 1930s (the Joiner Strike) but gained momentum during WWII when it became clear that if the United States was to maintain its high oil consumption and its high standard of living, it would need overseas supplies.

American oil companies, along with their European counterparts turned their sights to the Middle East where geologists were discovering prodigious deposits.

35.5 The OPEC

The Organization of Petroleum Exporting Countries (OPEC) was officially founded at the Baghdad Conference, September 10–14, 1960. The founding members were Iran, Iraq, Kuwait, Saudi Arabia, and Venezuela. The OPEC formed because separately each nation was powerless to control prices and output vis-à-vis the large multinational oil companies. Awash in surplus oil during the 1950s, the powerful oil companies used their leverage to frequently reduce the posted price to oil exporters and hence their profits (Yergin, 1991, pp. 519–522). Drilling for Middle Eastern oil was always about money, power, and greed.[14] But then again, when was the oil industry ever not?

While this deceit was long-simmering, the immediate precipitating factor for OPEC'S formation occurred on August 9, 1960,

> with no direct warning to exporters, [Standard Oil of New Jersey] announced cuts of up to fourteen cents a barrel in the posted prices of Middle Eastern crudes—about a 7 percent reduction. The other [western oil] companies followed suit though without any enthusiasm, and in some cases with a good deal of alarm.
>
> (Yergin, 1991, p. 521)

In addition to wrestling control away from the multinational oil companies, then as now, OPEC's objectives (according to its web page) were/are:

> to coordinate and unify the petroleum policies of its member countries and ensure the stabilization of oil markets in order to secure an efficient, economic, and regular supply of petroleum to consumers, a steady income to producers and a fair return on capital for those investing in the petroleum industry.
>
> (OPEC, 2024)

The OPEC is a cartel, and as such, manages members' supply in order to maximize prices and hence profits.[15] After being relatively quiescent during the 1960s, the OPEC began flexing its muscles in the 1970s. On the Jewish holiday of Yom Kippur, October 6, 1973, to retaliate for the 1967 Six Day War, OPEC's Arab members placed an oil embargo on the United States. Oil imports were reduced by one-third, which sky-rocketed oil prices four-fold. In addition to the long lines and gasoline rationing, the embargo triggered the following events, which eventually coalesced to restructure the contours of the global economy[16]:

- The longest and most severe **recession** since the Great Depression (1973–1975), up until that time.
- President Nixon implemented price controls (against the advice of most economists), which effectively disincentivized consumption and dissuaded producers from developing alternative energy sources.
- Oil companies cut back on full-service gasoline stations (where attendants would fill the tank, check oil and tires, and even wash windows) replacing them with self-service.
- To save oil, year-round daylight savings time began on January 5, 1974. It continues to this day, although parts of Indiana and Arizona have chosen not to abide.
- The embargo underscored the world's interconnectedness. The Group of Seven (G-7) formed to discuss the oil embargo and other international issues. Originally four nations: The United States, the UK, West Germany, and France. In 1976, Italy, Japan, and Canada were added. In 1977 the European Union was invited as a permanent guest. The G-7 makes suggestions to coordinate policy. Although the seven are not the world's richest nations, "they share similar values of democracy, human rights, and the rule of law…and foster international understanding, cooperation, and development" (Gruner, 2022, pp. 307–308). In 1999, the G-7 was complemented by the much larger G-20.
- **The BRICS** was formed to counter the G-7 while providing its members a common forum to criticize/change the global architecture established during **Bretton Woods.**[17]

- Congress passed the Energy Policy and Conservation Act (EPCA), December 22, 1975. In addition to creating fuel mileage standards, and the Energy Conservation Program for Consumer Products, the EPAC also created the Strategic Petroleum Reserve as an emergency buffer.[18] Today, the Reserve has a capacity of 714 million barrels—enough to last about a month, given current consumption of 20 million barrels per day. The oil is stored in underground caverns along the Texas and Louisiana coasts. The EPCA enables the president to tap the reserves if needed. Most recently in 2023, President Biden tapped the Reserve to help ease oil prices after the Russia invasion of Ukraine.

In 1979, a second global oil crisis was triggered by supply reductions during the Iranian Revolution (see **Iran, Russia, and North Korea**) which led to steep price increases; and here in the United States, gas lines and rationing.

On the demand side, the Carter administration started the United States on the road to energy conservation, which to date has been instrumental in reducing oil demand,

President Carter started America's energy transformation on a televised speech [February 5, 1977] wearing a beige cardigan sweater and sitting in front of a crackling fire. Warning Americans that the energy crisis is the greatest challenge in our lifetimes…many scoffed, mocking Carter's cardigan sweater and refusing to turn down their thermostats. But Carter was right. For decades, America's per capita energy consumption had been growing at an unsustainable rate of 1.6% annually. America had become addicted to cheap foreign oil. But a year after Carter's speech, America's energy appetite began a steady decline. Today, the average American consumes 15% less energy than she did in 1977.

(Gruner, 2022, pp. 317 and 321–322)

Massive new oil discoveries in Alaska and the North Sea, along with non-OPEC producers increasing production, helped reduce the price of oil during the 1980s. Cheap oil ushered in long and vigorous economic growth between 1982 and 2007, interrupted by the brief and relatively mild recessions of 1991 and 2001. In addition, new technology, specifically fracking, allowed more oil to be obtained by literally squeezing and pressuring rocks to surrender their oil. Fracking has enabled the United States to become the world's largest oil producer, while the cost of getting oil out of the ground "has decreased by 1/3 since 2014" ('Oil Prices: Fissures', 2023).

Today, the OPEC, headquartered in Vienna, is comprised of Iran, Iraq, Kuwait, Saudia Arabia, Venezuela, Gabon, Equatorial Guinea, Nigeria, UAE, Libya, Algeria, Angola, and the Congo. One would assume that the OPEC would be in full denial of climate change, but it is not. In a speech just prior to the 2023 COP28 in Dubai, OPEC's Secretary General said,

> OPEC Member Countries are investing heavily in renewables technology, as well as in hydrogen projects, carbon capture utilization, and storage and direct air capture facilities, and the circular carbon economy. The OPEC Pavilion at COP28, the first ever for OPEC at a COP meeting, will showcase many of these initiatives and actions, providing visitors with specific details. The UAE has adopted a holistic, practical, and inclusionary approach in the build-up to the COP28. It is an approach that OPEC wholeheartedly endorses, as together, we all work towards an emissions-free future.
>
> (al-Ghais,[19] 2023)

Like any organization, it is difficult for the OPEC to sift through its member preferences to develop a policy that satisfies all. Not only do the OPEC members differ by income, but their ownership of reserves differs dramatically. Saudi Arabia, for example, possesses 25% of global oil reserves and prefers a long-term pricing strategy that maintains consumer demand. Whereas low-reserve nations (e.g., Gabon, Congo) prefer a high price in order to maximize short-term revenue. But in the long run, such short-term policies might kill the goose that lays the golden egg, hence the intra-OPEC conflict.

OPEC members tend to over-rely on oil revenue for their federal budgets.[20] Saudia Arabia, for example, with its surge in development spending, needs oil to be at least $85/b to balance its budget, assuming that a balanced budget is a goal ('Oil Prices: Fissures,' 2023).

35.6   The OPEC+

In 2016, the OPEC+ formed as a semi-quasi joint venture between the OPEC and ten oil-producing nations: Russia, Mexico, Kazakhstan, Oman, Azerbaijan, Malaysia, Bahrain, South Sudan, Brunei, and Sudan.[21] Of the ten (Russia, the world's third largest oil producer after the United States and Saudi Arabia) is by the most important, producing 10.3 million barrels of oil per day (mbpd) in 2022. Mexico, the second largest of the ten, by contrast, produces 1.7 mbpd; with the remaining eight nations producing 4.6 mbpd collectively. Thus, the actions of the OPEC+ are largely driven by OPEC and Russia. Today, OPEC controls 79.5% of global oil reserves and accounts for 42% of global production. The OPEC+ accounts for 90% of global oil reserves and 59% of total global production.

In 1977, the share of USA imports from OPEC peaked at 70%, and has continually trended downward, reaching 12.1% of total imports in 2022.[22] Today, the United States imports from Canada (52% of total imports), Mexico (10%) Saudia Arabia (7%), Iraq 4%, and Colombia (3%).

As the world transitions to **Net Zero** and is producing more renewable energy, the conventional thinking is that OPEC's (and likewise OPEC+) power will diminish, but this is only if OPEC does nothing. However, we think it is too smart to do nothing. It already has established a presence at the COP meetings, which we expect to be ramped up in the future. Look for the OPEC to be a major player, one way or another in the transition to sustainability.

35.7 Today's Oil Industry

In 2023, of the ten largest global corporations, six are oil companies[23]: Saudi Aramco ($603.7b in revenue), State Grid China ($530b), China National Petroleum ($483.1b), Sinopec Group ($471.2 b), Exxon Mobil ($413.7b), and Shell ($386.2), respectively. In addition, two of the top ten corporations, Walmart ($603b, the world's largest) and Amazon ($514b) have a transportation infrastructure and modus operandi built on cheap oil.

The United States, Saudi Arabia, and Russia are the main national oil players, collectively accounting for one-third of global oil production. The United States, as the world's largest oil importer, has a conflict of interest with the other two major producers (Siripurapu and Chatzky, 2022). While OPEC's short-run strategy (and OPEC+) is to restrict output in order to boost prices, their wishes are being outflanked by non-OPEC producers, particularly the United States which has been ramping up production. The United States is currently the world's largest oil producer.[24] In 2023, it produced a record 12.92 mbpd. The Energy Information Administration (EIA) forecasts that in 2024 and 2025, the United States will break its 2023 record at 13.21 mbpd and 13.44 mbpd, respectively (EIA, 2023a).

The United States also is the world's largest oil consumer. In 2022 it consumed 20.18 mbpd, with the difference made up by 8 mbpd of imports. But here's the tricky/confusing part often reported in the news: In 2020, the United States became a net oil exporter for the first time since 1949, which has now continued three years in a row. But how can this be if the United States is a substantial importer of oil? If we compare 2022's exports at 9.52 mbpd to its 8.1 mbpd of imports, then the positive net difference means that the United States is a net exporter. As to why the United States exports *and* imports oil, we will let the EIA explain,

Because of logistical, regulatory, and quality considerations, exporting some petroleum is the most economical way to meet the market's needs. For example, refiners in the U.S. Gulf Coast region frequently find that it makes economic sense to export some of their gasoline to Mexico rather than shipping it to the East Coast because lower-cost gasoline imports from Europe may be available to the East Coast.

(EIA, 2023a)

While 2024 is forecasted to be a record demand for global oil, and despite OPEC's supply reductions, global demand will easily be met (according to the EIA) thanks to the United States' increased supply. This in turn will keep domestic gasoline prices stable, if not actual falling, ceteris paribus, forecasted at $3.36/gallon in 2024, and $3.24/gallon in 2025 (EIA, 2024).

The Biden administration was initially hostile to the oil industry calling it yesterday's fuel, while exhorting an immediate switch to fossil fuels. But the Russian invasion of Ukraine, which saw oil prices double, changed his tune. In 2023 not only did President Biden tap oil from the Strategic Petroleum Reserve, but the Administration approved the Willow oil drilling project (Conoco Phillips) in Alaska that had been stalled for decades (Egan, 2023).

President Biden has been rebuked by some Democrats, especially those on the far left for reneging on his anti-oil campaign rhetoric, while Republicans berate him for obstructing the oil industry. While such obstruction might have been true in the early days of his Administration, today's facts don't support such rhetoric: In 2023,

> oil and gas production was greater than any year during Mr. Trump's term, the Biden administration issued more licenses for drilling than his predecessor…exports have soared…The profits and dividends of America's oil giants have grown fatter under Mr. Biden. The Dow Jones US Oil and Gas Index sputtered on Mr. Trump's watch. It has more than doubled under Mr. Biden's, helped by a surge in prices.
>
> (*The Economist*, July 27, 2024, p. 53)

And besides, there isn't that much that the president can do to increase oil production, which is the result of cumulative decisions by the private sector, "it's not like President Biden or any president has a dial in the Oval Office to increase production" (Egan, 2023).

The Biden administration was short-term pro-oil, but long-term pro-renewable energy, which is not necessarily a contradiction, especially given that the United States only possesses four percent of global oil reserves. A Republican win in the 2024 election would most likely continue the emphasis on oil (possibly resuscitating coal, which is the dirtiest of the **fossil fuels**) while at the same diminishing America's commitment to fight climate change. We think this is a mistake for two reasons:

- America would miss out on the technological changes spawned by the new energy transition, along with the spillover effects. Why not unleash the entrepreneurial spirit and let business do what they do best: Invent and in-novate? If we don't, other nations will.

• An energy transition is inevitable and should be the focal point of current debate. A sobering statistic: Given current energy use and technology, the world has only 41 years of oil left.[25] In other words, expect a collision course between environmental constraints and our lifestyles. How (and if) to use the oil we have left and how to transform to a world of **Net Zero** are critically important and must be post-2024 discussion issues.

35.8   Conclusion

We cannot cease and desist our use of oil and fossil fuels immediately, for any energy transition takes time (see **Fossil Fuels**). Only by actively committing to a long-term **Net Zero** future can we begin to lessen the effects of climate change, or more accurately, temper its worst effects. Otherwise, will have to answer to our children and to our children's children why we continued using fossil fuels when we knew of its deleterious consequences, and why we shortchanged the health of our plant for a short-term monetary gain.[26]

Notes

1   We discuss this further in our **Housing** chapter.
2   Unless stated otherwise the historical discussion relies on Wall (1991) and Yergin (1991).
3   Here in the United States, early colonists had spotted oil slicks off both coasts; they also used oil for wagon grease (Wall, 1991, p. 804).
4   In the mid-19th century, oil was called 'rock oil.' The word 'petroleum' is derived from the Latin word for 'rock.'
5   Yergin explains: "when oil first started flowing out of the wells in western Pennsylvania in the 1860s, desperate oil men ransacked farmhouses, barns, cellars, stores, and trashyards for any kind of barrel—molasses, beer, whiskey, cider, turpentine, salt, fish, and whatever else was handy. But as coopers began to make barrels specially for the oil trade, one standard size emerged, and that size continues to be the norm to the present. It is 42 gallons. The number was borrowed from England, where a statute in 1482 under King Edward IV established 42 gallons as the standard size barrel for herring in order to end skullduggery and 'divers deceits' in the packing of fish" (1991, p. 796).
6   Interestingly, at first, gasoline was burned off as a useless by-product during the refining process, given its high volatility. It would, however, find a use early in the 20th century as the perfect fuel for the spark-induced piston carburetor (Rhodes, 2018, p. 167, and pp. 234–239). Gasoline was key in making the automobile a leading industry.
7   During the 19th century, coal was the main source of heating. See Freese (2003, pp. 35–39, pp. 142–146) for an interesting description of coal's ubiquitous smoke and soot in domestic households.
8   Ida Tarbell's, *The History of Standard Oil Company*, is a fascinating read of the formation and modus operation of Standard Oil. First serialized in the nationally known *McClure's* magazine, it was published in book form in 1904, and "arguably, …was the single most influential book on business ever published in the United States"

(Yergin, 1991, p. 105). Tarbell, a premier journalist and justifiably "…probably the most famous woman in America" (Yergin, 1991, p. 105). She grew up in Titusville, and her father was one of many independent oil men harmed by Rockefeller's predations (Goodwin, 2013, pp. 325–347).

9 We discuss the Sherman and Clayton Acts in our **Corporate Power and Antitrust** chapter.

10 The declining market share was due to significant increases in supply, most notably, the Beaumont Texas, Spindletop discovery, which was "one of the largest and most significant oil strikes in American history which ended any monopolization by Standard Oil. The Gulf Oil company survived out of this" (Wall, 1991, p. 805).

11 These two paragraphs are based on Desjardins (2017) and Yergin (1991, p. 110).

12 From the 1970s, renaming companies with the suffix '-on' was in vogue, portraying a future aura, e.g., Chevron, Raytheon, Exxon, and of course Enron.

13 President Warren Harding (1920–1923) died of a heart attack August 1923, upon which his vice president, Calvin Coolidge assumed the presidency.

14 Hence the title of Daniel Yergin's book, *The Prize: The Epic Quest for Oil, Money, and Power* (1991).

15 Given that the demand for oil is relatively price inelastic in the short run, i.e., a rise in price will not result in a concomitant decrease in demand (given the lack of short-term substitutes), a price increase will increase short-run revenue. In the long run, however, consumers can take action, including conserving/substituting away.

16 For a fascinating day-by-day (almost) account of the 1973 embargo and its immediate aftereffects, see Blair (1978, pp. 261–275).

17 We discuss the **BRICS** and **Bretton Woods** in separate chapters.

18 During WWII, Secretary of the Interior Harold Ickes first proposed such a reserve. For a discussion of the history of the Strategic see (Department of Energy 2015).

19 Haitham al-Ghais, from Kuwait, is OPEC's Secretary General as this book goes to press. He assumed the three-year position on January 3, 2022.

20 For an earlier study but still relevant is Looney (1992) which highlights the intricate relationship between oil prices, development, and federal budgets.

21 EIA (2023b) provides this paragraph's statistics.

22 Data source for this paragraph's statistics: EIA (2023a).

23 Data source: Fortune Global 500. The companies are ranked by revenue. State Grid, is an electrical utility company. China, by the way, relies on coal for 70% of its electricity.

24 Data source for this paragraph's statistics: EIA (2023a).

25 Source: Our World in Data (2023b). One would assume that we know exactly how much oil is left, but we don't. However, the odds of a major find are quite slim, although not improbable.

26 Diamond (2005, pp. 419–440) offers a helpful explanation for why people persevere in such situations. Our thoughts in this paragraph mirror Fresse's speculative condemnation by future generations of our stubborn coal use, "Some of our descendants may simply see coal as a strangely primitive fuel and wonder how we tolerated it for as long as we did" (Freese, 2003, p. 248).

References

'A Fossil Fuel Fantasy, *The Economist,* July 27, 2024, pp. 53–54.
al-Ghais, Haitham (2023) 'COP28 on the horizon: focusing on holistic approach to the energy system,' (OPEC.org).
Blair, John M. (1976) *The Control of Oil*, Vintage Books, New York.

Desjardins, Jeff (2017) 'Chart the Evolution of Standard Oil,' (November 24) ' (visual-capitalist.com).

Department of Energy (2015) 'History of the Strategic Petroleum Reserve,' (DOE.gov).

Diamond, Jared (2005) *Collapse: How Societies Choose to Fail or Succeed,* pp. 419–440.

Egan, Matt (2023) 'The United States is producing more oil than any other country in history' *CNN Business*, December 19.

Freese, Barbara (2003) *Coal: A Human History*, Perseus Publishing, Cambridge, Mass.

Goodwin, Doris Kearns (2013) *The Bully Pulpit: Theordore Roosevelt, Willaim Howard Taft and the Golden Age of Progressive Journalism*, Simon & Schuster, New York.

Gruner, Ronald (2022) *We the Presidents: How American Presidents Shaped the Last Century,*' Libratum press, Naples, Florida.

Looney (1991) 'Fiscal Stress in Saudi Arabia: Budgetary Adjustments in an Era of Declining Oil Revenues,' in Siamack Shojai and Bernard Katz (Eds.): *The Oil Market in the 1980s—A Decade of Decline*, Praeger, New York, pp. 59–67.

'Oil Prices: Fissures,' (2023) *The Economist,* December 2, 2023, pp. 63–64.

OPEC (2024) 'Brief History' OPEC: Brief History.

Siripurapu and Chatzky (2022) 'OPEC in a Changing World, Council on Foreign Relations, (March 9) (cfr.org).

Tarbell, Ida M. *The History of the Standard Oil Company*. New York: McClure, Phillips & Co. 1904.

U.S. Energy Information Administration (2023a) 'Oil and Petroleum Products Explained: Oil Imports and Exports' (October 2).

U.S. Energy Information Administration (2023b) 'What is OPEC+ and How is it Different from OPEC?' (May 9).

U.S. Energy Information Administration (2024) 'Short-Term Energy Outlook' (January 9).

van der Linde, Coby (1991*) Dynamic international Oil Markets: Oil Market Developments and Structure: 1860–1990*, Kluwer Academic Publishers, Dordrecht, Netherlands.

Wall, Bennett H. (1991) 'Oil Industry,' in (Eds:) Foner, Eric and John Garraty, *The Reader's Companion to American History*, Houghton Mifflin, Boston, pp. 804–807.

Yergin, Daniel (1991) *The Prize: The Epic Quest for Oil, Money, and Power*, Simon & Schuster, New York.

36 Net Zero

The Issue: In 2015, the United Nations (UN) told the world that in order to prevent cataclysmic and irreversible change to our climate and environment, we must keep the global temperature from rising more than 2.0°C (now revised to 1.5°C) from 1,800 (i.e., roughly beginning of the Industrial Revolution). Also in 2015, the UN issued its 17 Sustainable Development Goals (SDGs)—a helpful recipe for sustainable living.[1] Two goals directly pertain to this chapter: Goal #7: Ensure access to affordable, reliable, sustainable, and modern energy for all; and Goal #13: Take urgent action to combat climate change and its impacts.[2] Recent climatic events have given these goals a newfound sense of urgency.[3] A global consensus has emerged that is not enough to reduce usage, but that we must achieve net zero emissions by 2050. Unlike previous energy transitions (e.g., wind, wood, coal, oil, gas, nuclear) Net Zero is the first to be mandated by changes in the Earth's climate. How successful we transition will determine what type of planet we leave to our children and to our children's children. How we transition will affect all of us; thus, we all should have a say in how this transition unfolds. Net Zero is not only a practical consideration, but a moral one as well.

36.1 Defining Net Zero

Net Zero's genesis is traced to Farhana Yamin, a London-based environmental lawyer and climate negotiator, who, in December 2014 said at the UN Climate Talks in Lima, "In your lifetime, emissions have to go to zero. That's a message people understand" (Morgan, 2024). The term was also used in a 2014 speech by World Bank President Jim Yong Kim, "we must achieve zero net emissions of greenhouse gases before 2100" (Morgan, 2024). Since then, papers have been written, seminars held, and environmental groups and policymakers have echoed the call.

While different nuanced definitions of Net Zero exist, an authoritative one gaining currency is "an economy or a business model that produces no net Greenhouse gas (GHG) emissions" (Montgomery and Van Clieaf, 2023, p. 12).

DOI: 10.4324/9781003591856-42

Net Zero includes all emissions such as water vapor, methane, etc., and not just CO_2. Broadly speaking, "Net Zero is achieved by reducing and eliminating absolute emissions across an entire value chain to support the target to limit the rise in global temperatures to 1.5°C. Any remaining GHGs are offset with offsets and carbon capture" (Montgomery and Van Clieaf, 2023, p. 12).

Central to Net Zero is that we must reduce our addiction/usage of fossil fuels *while* also taking away existing stock of fossil fuels; doing one without the other cannot be successful in achieving Net Zero.[4] At the same time, it is becoming clear that a net zero policy may not be enough, given that emissions remain in the atmosphere for quite some time.[5] While Net Zero is a first and necessary step to mitigate the worst effects of climate change, it

> will probably not be enough to stabilize the climate. This is because the economy will continue to emit billions of metric tons of heat trapping GHGs into the atmosphere each year until it achieves net zero in 2050. Ultimately, the economy will need to transition from a net zero economy to a negative one.
>
> (Montgomery and Van Clieaf, 2023, pp. 12–13)

We agree, but first things first.
Net Zero is,

> intrinsically a scientific concept. If the objective is to keep the rise in global average temperatures within certain limits, physics implies that there is a finite budget of carbon dioxide that is allowed into the atmosphere, along-side other greenhouse gases. Beyond this budget, any further release must be balanced by removal into sinks. The acceptable temperature rise is a societal choice, but one informed by climate science. However, net zero is much more than a scientific concept or a technically determined target. It is also a frame of reference through which global action against climate change can be (and is increasingly) structured and understood.
>
> (Fankhauser et al., 2022, p. 15)

Thus, Net Zero is inextricably linked with sustainability, energy use, **fossil fuels**, and **climate change**.

No matter how we define Net Zero, we have our work cut out for us: Today, the United States relies on **fossil fuels** for 79% of its total energy consumption and the world, 82%. Here in the United States, we are ensconced in a fossil fuels mentality. Thus, a successful transition to Net Zero will require a transformational change, i.e., "a shift in paradigm," which,

> comes from innovation, maximum stakeholder commitment and engagement, and new ways of thinking and doing things. [It] demands

breakthroughs in conventional wisdom…And it requires new leadership mindsets, strategies, and skills.

(Montgomery and Van Clieaf, 2023, p. 223)

If history is any indication, a quick transition to renewable energy, however, will be difficult,

> …all of the Industrial Age energy sources follow a similar trend when entering the market. It takes 40 to 50 years for an energy source to go from 1% to 10% percent of market share, and an energy source that eventually comes to occupy half of the market will almost take a century to do so, from the epoch when it reaches 1%.

(Rhodes, 2018, pp. 338–389)

But for the first time in human history, we are under the environmental gun so to speak, to transition as quickly as possible.

36.2   Net Zero Requires Interdisciplinary and Transdisciplinary Thinking

Any transformational change is inherently interdisciplinary and even transdisciplinary,[6]

> [Achieving] Net Zero requires operationalization in varied social, political and economic spheres. There are numerous ethical judgements, social concerns, political interests, fairness dimensions, economic considerations and technology transitions that need to be navigated, and several political, economic, legal and behavioural pitfalls that could derail a successful implementation of net zero. [It will] require large-scale changes in the way economies are run, the skills they demand, and the capital assets they require. It will also require input from many disciplines from climate science, biology and geology to anthropology, law, and economics.

(Fankhauser et al., 2022, pp. 16 and 19)

Transformational change doesn't just happen but requires the active cooperation of all interested and affected stakeholders, which might be the most difficult element in the transition to Net Zero. One of the most difficult tasks for a policymaker or an academic is leaving the comfort of one's long-established silo (which has provided comfort, wisdom, and status) to work with another discipline on an interdisciplinary perspective, "disciplines are like tribes, they have a specific culture and specific habits, norms and rules, and they do not easily accept outsiders. This poses problems for cooperation between disciplines, both in research and in education" (Weehuizen, 2007, pp. 165–166).[7] Nevertheless, learning and assimilating both interdisciplinary and transdisciplinary thinking is absolutely necessary for our Net Zero transition since,

> The shift from a fossil fuel-based economy to a net zero emission one is the biggest transformation project in human history (the Great Transformation) [which] will require $275 trillion of cumulative investments in physical assets alone by 2050. The Great Transformation is huge, but humanity has successfully transformed the basis of the economy before. The global economy previously transitioned its primary energy from wood to coal and from coal to oil. Such transitions, however, were gradual and haphazard. The necessity to preserve a habitable planet for our children and grandchildren provides special urgency to the Great Transformation.
>
> (Montgomery and Van Clieaf, 2023, pp. 3–4)[8]

Is our education system up to the task?

No one discipline has (or even pretends to have) all the answers. But in order to reach out and dialogue with those we might disagree with (a necessary first step for both interdisciplinary and transdisciplinary thinking) one's level of adult development must reach a certain elevated stage which enables he/she to differentiate between different ways of thinking, to be cognizant of the 'other,' and to be able to listen and dialogue. Otherwise, one remains at a lower stage, where one's self-value is determined by the imprimatur of group approval and peer collaboration. Approximately half of adults are stuck at this stage. Yet, less than 10% of adults ever reach the higher level of development, enabling one to be self-aware and self-transforming. But this is what we need for the success of Net Zero.[9]

Transformational change is hard to accept and even harder to effectuate, especially given our acclimation to the benefits of fossil fuels, e.g., living standards, cheaper goods etc.

36.3   A Process for Net Zero

While the Net Zero goal has been set: 2050 (although not accepted by all), as this manuscript goes to press (October 2024), there "is no official yardstick against which the adequacy, ambition, or fairness of nationally determined contributions is measured. Instead, the [2015] Paris Agreement relies on process" (Fankhauser et al., 2022, p. 16). Thus, we[10] need to "turn Net Zero into a useful frame of reference for decision-makers [and to] translate into individual decarbonization *pathways* for nation states, sub-national entities, companies, and other organizations" (Fankhauser et al., 2022, p. 16; emphasis added).

Given the dearth of a uniform global (nor national) effort to transition to Net Zero, it might be tempting to dismiss any and all individual action as inconsequential. But as we discuss in our **Climate Change** chapter, there is much that an individual can do, including decisions over consumption, housing, and transportation. Individual action is important regardless of actions at any other level. Not only can individual action help assimilate the necessary values for a Net Zero economy, but one's action can positively influence the same action by another. Indeed, this is why all energy revolutions take time since, "society is a learning system. It works by cultural diffusion—the spreading of ideas from one person to another" (Rhodes, 2018, p. 339). This is the multiplier effect which comes from seeing and emulating others and learning by doing; all critical in the transition to Net Zero.

36.4 Key Elements of an Effective Net Zero Transition

As this manuscript goes to press (October 2024) Net Zero "governance, accountability, and reporting mechanisms are currently inadequate. Long-term ambition is not backed up by sufficient near-term action…with some advocates accusing heretofore pledges as amounting to nothing more than greenwashing" (Fankhauser et al., 2022, p. 17). But at the same time, there is "the need for clear guardrails to ensure the robustness of net zero as a framework for climate action. [Net Zero, if] interpreted right and governed well, can be an effective frame of reference for climate action"(Fankhauser et al., 2022, pp. 17 and 19). In so doing, the authors offer seven attributes of an effective Net Zero transition framework[11]:

- **Front-loaded emission reductions**: Reduce emissions as much and as fast as possible.[12] Given that emissions are cumulative and long-staying, quickness in reducing emissions matters.[13]
- **A comprehensive approach to reducing emissions**: i.e., tackling all emissions and not just the most visible or the lowest hanging fruit; with broad-based support across all stakeholders.
- **Cautious use of carbon dioxide removal:** Widespread reliance on carbon removal can lead to moral hazard risks, enabling 'business as usual' rather than the drastic scaling back of fossil fuels, which is most needed.
- **Effective regulation of carbon offset**: Defined as an action to compensate for the emission of carbon dioxide. Thus, "the scaled-up use of carbon offsets will have to be accompanied by a radical enhancement of their quality and scaled-up regulatory scrutiny" (Fankhauser et al., 2022, p. 18).
- **An equitable transition to net zero**: This goes without saying. Developing nations need financial, technological, and personnel support. The fairness of Net Zero depends on how the burden of meeting the global target is shared across countries and within countries—a long-standing challenge for any climate action. Today, a deep rift exists between developing and developed nations. The former rightly claim a prerogative to develop just as the developed nations once did; and that is hypocritical for the rich nations to exhort the

developing nations not to use fossil fuels, when the preponderance of GHGs is due to rich nations' heavy historical use. Active cooperation between rich and poor might prove the most difficult task of all in achieving Net Zero, as it has been with every climate action undertaken. We advise that each nation should chart its own circumstantial path; at the same time, some countries may need to reach Net Zero faster to create room for laggards. The goal is to anchor net-zero in the principle of sustainable development,[14] which balances social, economic, and environmental objectives.[15]

- **Align net zero with other socio-ecological objectives**, such as biodiversity and land-use change.
- **Net zero is not a zero-sum game**; rather it can be seen as an economic opportunity, and in the long run, "zero-carbon innovation can unleash a virtuous cycle of investment, renewal, and growth" (Fankhauser et al., 2022, p. 19). This is also the central theme of Montgomery and Van Clieaf (2023).

How quickly we transform to renewable energy will determine our success in transitioning to Net Zero. Helpful is a three-pronged approach offered by The International Energy Administration[16] (2023):

- Deploy a wide portfolio of clean energy technologies, with deployment decisions driven by costs, technology maturity, market conditions, and policy preferences.
- All countries must contribute to the pathway to net zero emissions by 2050, with advanced economies taking the lead and reaching net zero emissions well before others. Global collaboration is necessary to facilitate ambitious policies, reduce the costs of clean energy technologies, create bigger and more international markets for those technologies, and support emerging market and developing economies to achieve emissions reductions and the energy-related UN SDGs.
- Safeguard energy security through rapid deployment of clean energy technologies, energy efficiency, and demand reduction

Alas, while the broad brushstrokes are clear, the devil is in the details.

36.5   The Pivotal Role of the Corporation

While all stakeholders (e.g., consumers, employers, communities, financiers, retailers, suppliers, firms, policymakers, and the government) must cooperatively work together to achieve net zero, a special responsibility rests with the firm. In a market economy, we look to the firm "to build knowledge, create value, and generate progress" (Madden, 2020, p. 238).[17] Of course, the government provides the enabling and supporting institutions (e.g., protection of private property, the judiciary, monetary system, etc.) Today, "the firm's purpose, including its social role and responsibilities is at the center of a worldwide debate about capitalism" (Madden, 2020, p. 24). Thus, designing a conceptual framework for the firm to help achieve Net Zero is critical.

Montgomery and Van Clieaf (2023) offer such a framework. The authors offer four pathways depending on the firm's current carbon usage/technology:

- **Pathway One:** e.g., Weyerhaeuser, Microsoft, Canada Goose, JAB/Panera Bread, Exxon Mobil. Such firms can achieve Net Zero by maintaining their existing business model. In addition, by implementing eco-efficiency process improvements, along with carbon offsets/carbon capture.
- **Pathway Two**: e.g., Walmart, Shell, Nestle, Roll-Royce Holdings, Orsted, Vattenfall, General Motors. For these firms, a significant change in their strategies and business models is needed to achieve Net Zero.
- **Pathway Three:** e.g., QuantumScape, Ecolibri Srl, Nuscale Power, Celsius Energy, Carbon Cure, Universal Hydrogen, ZeroAvia. These firms do not have a legacy business; in other words, from the start they have not been carbon intensive. Rather they are creating new Net Zero business models from scratch. Tesla in its early years was Pathway Three.
- **Pathway Four:** Such firms are participating in, and possibly leading, an industry-wide transformation. Telsa is the prototype, although it began as Pathway Three. Such companies,

> are out to change the world with a new low or no-carbon product or service and business model and transform their industry to net zero in the process. [These] companies have business models that inherently conform to a net zero economy and are already doing business in it.
> (Montgomery and Van Clieaf, 2023, p. 199)

For all firms, regardless of their pathway, active cooperation is necessary not just between stakeholders, but across industries, and sectors. This calls into question both the efficacy of current firm structure and its modus operandi, along with the federal government's outdated **antitrust policy**.[18] As I have argued in a previous book, the only way to achieve sustainability and Net Zero is to replace the shareholder corporation (which maximizes short-term profits for shareholders) in all its variations with the stakeholder corporation (which creates long-term value for all stakeholders) in all its variations (Boyd and Reardon, 2020, pp. 379–400. Also see Montgomery and Van Clieaf, 2023, pp. 307–317).

36.6   Carbon Pricing: An Instrumental Panacea?

Carbon pricing (CP) sets a price for emitting carbon-based GHG emissions, incentivizing the reduction of GHG, by changing the price of using carbon. Given that our economy is based on incentives, higher/lower prices will change consumer behavior, so that ideally CP "in one stroke, would recalibrate consumer demand, set the market in motion, reduce emissions and spur innovation" (Forester, 2023).

CP is seen by many economists as the best way to redress a negative externality,[19] i.e., an unintended negative effect on a third party, and the most effective way to reduce GHG emissions and transition to Net Zero. Accordingly, CP will, "align the incentives of consumers, businesses, and government to decarbonize industry, and finance green technology [so that] carbon will be reflected in all company balance sheets, income statements, earning reports and strategic plans" (Forester, 2023).

Critics of CP, however, argue that while the instrument is important, it is only one,[20] and that "no single type of policy is likely to be the best in all circumstances. Incentive-based policies are no exception" (Field and Field, 2009, p. 233). And furthermore, given that the market and the market mindset caused the problem (i.e., the negative externality) then market solutions which emphasize change in relative prices are narrowly ineffective since they ignore the deeper and more systemic (and interconnected) causes. Conceptualizing climate change as a market failure due to a disconnect between relative prices ignores the fact that climate change is a systems-wide failure, and as such requires systems-wide solutions,

> core societal functions, such as heating and mobility are met through large and deeply entrenched sociotechnical systems made up of interconnected technologies, infrastructures, regulations, business models, and lifestyles. Over many decades these systems have become increasingly locked into the combustion of fossil fuels and the associated release of GHG emissions. Design of cities developed along the diffusion of gas cars; and norms about comfort/attire are intertwined with energy intensive indoor temperature and attire regulation; and how important political/economic interests have become entrenched with fossil fuel-based resource development or electricity provision…[thus solutions to climate change] entail profound and interdependent adjustments in sociotechnical systems that cannot be reduced to a single driver such as shifts in relative market prices.
>
> (Rosenbloom et al., 2020)

We agree.[21] Montgomery and Van Clieaf (2023, p. 53) add that "climate change is more than just a carbon-centric issue. At the core, it is a business model design, business strategy, and long-horizon risk management that belongs in the boardroom and C-Suite." At the same time, CP can play a role in the transition to Net Zero as long as it is not viewed as an end-all and the only instrument of change.

Adding credence to our recommendation, a meta-analysis of 21 of the 70+ carbon pricing schemes implemented around the globe found that,

> despite more than three decades of experience with carbon pricing and more than 70 implementations of both carbon taxes and cap-and-trade schemes around the world at national, regional and sub-national levels, there remains no consensus in science nor policy as to how effective such policies are in reducing greenhouse gas (GHG) emissions.
>
> (Döbbeling-Hildebrandt, 2024)

At the same time, due to its ostensible simplicity, the widespread implementation of a carbon tax remains a distinct possibility (although hopefully within a greater holistic context), especially with a sharp deterioration in the environment. As such, "companies need to be prepared for carbon taxes" (Montgomery and Van Clieaf, 2023, p. 49). Unfortunately, they are not. Montgomery and Van Clief analyzed the effects of a hypothetical (yet potentially realistic) carbon tax of $100/ton, on over 18,000 publicly traded companies and found that every industry sector had a negative return on capital (Montgomery and Van Clieaf, 2023, pp. 50 and 325).

Like most issues in economics, we need more research on CP, especially within a systems-wide context,

> we need a range that recognizes the unique institutional context of different industries with more concentrated fixed sources such as electricity versus more spread-out sources (agro-food, transport, and heavy industry). And more specifically, we need 'decline' policies for carbon-intensive industries and 'innovation' policies for low carbon industries.
>
> (Rosenbloom et al., 2020)

36.7   Conclusion

Alfred Marshall wrote that "economic conditions are constantly changing and each generation looks at its own problems in its own way" (Marshall (1946 [1890], p. v). Our generation indeed has its share of problems, but unmistakenly, "climate change has emerged as perhaps the greatest environmental threat of our time" (Harris and Roach, 2018, p. 3) and perhaps the greatest problem of all time.

Future generations will and should have a right to hold us accountable for our longstanding and stubborn delay in cutting our ties with fossil fuels. Needless to say,

> our excuses for continuing to burn coal [and oil and natural gas] while ignoring the threat of climate change for so many years—our lack of

scientific certainty, our desire to keep our electric rates low, our fear of a slowed economy, and our reluctance to make sacrifices others are not forced to make—will ring hollow to those coping with the catastrophic consequences of our actions.

(Freese, 2003, p. 248)

Transitioning to Net Zero is a great transformation, and perhaps the greatest and most daunting in the history of humanity. But if done right, it might very well be the greatest gift that one generation could give another.

Notes

1 See Reardon et al. (2018, passim; and especially pp. 17–19) for a full discussion. My book is the first to reconceptualize economics and economics education around the 17 SDGs.
2 The 17 SDGs and their rationale can be found at (un.org).
3 For further discussion, see our **Climate Change** chapter.
4 Net Zero is not to be confused with 'carbon neutral,' i.e., "a corporation may claim to be carbon neutral when it offsets its emissions by purchasing carbon credits or paying to remove carbon from the atmosphere without necessarily reducing or eliminating any of its own GHG emissions" (Montgomery and Van Clieaf, 2023, p. 223). The Net Zero consensus is that we must reduce emissions as much as we can, say up to 90%, and only then use offsets (i.e., carbon neutral) for the remaining 10%.
5 Archer (2005) notes that "the carbon cycle of the biosphere will take a long time to completely neutralize and sequester anthropogenic CO_2 ... For the best guess case, we expect that 17–33% of the fossil fuel carbon will still reside in the atmosphere 1 kyr [1 kyr = 1000 years] from now, decreasing to 10–15% at 10 kyr, and 7% at 100 kyr. The mean lifetime of fossil fuel CO_2 is about 30–35 kyr." This gives Net Zero an added sense of urgency, suggesting that a negative sequestration might be necessary. Time is of the essence.
6 While lumped together, there are important differences: "**multidisciplinar**y is cooperation between different disciplines aimed at the same business activity or research topic, but applying the theories, methods, and tools of each discipline separately; **interdisciplinary** integrates the different theories resulting in a theoretical foundation of a new discipline; and **transdisciplinary** combines the theory of one discipline with the empirical findings of another" (Lemstra, 2007, pp. 146–147), in effect creating a new discipline.
7 Lest one thinks that tribal loyalty and myopic self-service is unique to our day and age, Francis Bacon, writing at the dawn of the Scientific Revolution lamented, "For after men [sic] have joined a sect and committed themselves (like obsequious courtiers) to one man's opinion, they add no distinction to the sciences themselves, but act like servants in courting and adorning their authors" (Bacon, 1626 [2000], p. 7).
8 As far as we know, the term 'Great Transformation' as used in Montgomery and Van Clieaf (2023) has no intimacy with Karl Polanyi's 1944 *The Great Transformation;* nor Karen Armstrong's 2007 *The Great Transformation: The Beginning of Our Religious Traditions.* Neither author was cited anywhere in Montgomery and Van Clieaf (2023).

9 In my earlier book (Boyd and Reardon, 2020, passim; especially pp. 167–254) we discuss in detail how to effectuate change to higher levels of development. Not an easy process by any means (and too complex to even briefly discuss), but at the same time, absolutely necessary for the transition to Net Zero.
10 'We' refers to all of us collectively, acting in all capacities as consumers, employees, businesses, policy makers, and the government.
11 See Fankhauser et al. (2022) for a more in-depth discussion.
12 Since 2020 the world has made surprising progress, thanks to a significant increase in solar power (Global Electricity Review, 2024). We discuss this further in our **Fossil Fuels** chapter.
13 According to scientific evidence: Every year of delay before initiating emission reductions decreases the remaining time available to reach net-zero emissions by two years (Fankhauser et al., 2022, p. 17).
14 For discussion/elaboration, see (Reardon et al. 2018, pp. 13–17).
15 For elaboration on Sustainable Development, see Daly (1996) and Daly (1997). In addition, see Tim Jackson's important book *Prosperity Without Growth* (2009).
16 The text discussion follows very closely International Energy Administration (IEA) (2023). Also see IEA (2021).
17 We use the term 'firm' rather loosely to include entrepreneurs, partnerships, sole proprietorships, and corporations, along with the specific variations thereof.
18 We discuss antitrust in our **Corporate Power and Antitrust** chapter.
19 For a discussion of the genesis of the term externalities, see Boudreaux and Meiners (2019).
20 See, for example, Rosenbloom et al., (2020).
21 For a good discussion, see Roodman (1997).

References

Archer, David (2005) 'Fate of fossil fuel CO2 in geologic time,' *Journal of Geophysical Research*, Vol. 110, p. C09S05, doi:10.1029/2004JC002625.

Bacon, Francis (1626 [2000]) *The New Organum*, University of Cambridge, Cambridge, UK.

Boudreaux, Donald J. and Roger Meiners (2019) 'Externality: Origins and Classifications,' *Natural Resources Journal*, Vol. 59, No. 1, pp. 1–34.

Boyd, Graham and Jack Reardon (2020) *Rebuild the Economy, Leadership, and You: A Toolkit for Builders of Better World*, Evolutesix, London.

Daly, Herman (1996) *Beyond Growth: The Economics of Sustainable Development*, Edward Elgar, Cheltenham, UK.

Daly, Herman (1997) *Ecological Economics and Sustainable Development: Selected Essays of Herman Daly*, Edward Elgar, Cheltenham, UK.

Döbbeling-Hildebrandt, Niklas; Klaas Miersch; Tarun M. Khanna; Marion Bachelet; Stephan B. Bruns; Max Callaghan; Ottmar Edenhofer; Christian Flachsland; Piers M. Forster; Matthias Kalkuhl; Nicolas Koch; William F. Lamb; Nils Ohlendorf; Jan Christoph Steckel; and Jan C. Minx (2024) 'Systematic review and meta-analysis of ex-post evaluations on the effectiveness of carbon pricing' (2024) *Nature Communications*, Vol. 15, p. 4147, https://doi.org/10.1038/s41467-024-48512-w.

Fankhauser, Sam; Stephen M. Smith; Myles Allen; Kaya Axelsson; Thomas Hale; Cameron Hepburn; J. Michael Kendall; Radhika Khosla; Javier Lezaun; Eli Mitchell-Larson; Michael Obersteiner; Lavanya Rajamani; Rosalind Rickaby; Nathalie Seddon;

and Thom Wetzer, (2022) 'The meaning of net zero and how to get it right,' *Nature Climate Change*, Vol. 12, January, pp. 15–21.

Field, Barry and Martha Field (2009) *Environmental Economics: An Introduction*, 5th ed., McGraw Hill, New York.

Forester, Lynn de Rothchild (2023) 'Why the World Must Set a Price on Carbon,' *TIME*, December 20, https://time.com/6549163

Freese, Barbara (2003) *Coal: A Human History*, Perseus Publishing, Cambridge, Mass.

Harris, Jonathan M. and Roach, Brian (2018) *Environmental and Natural Resource Economics: A Contemporary Approach*, 4th ed. Routledge, London.

International Energy Agency (2021) Net Zero by 2050: A Roadmap for the Global Energy Sector, May 18.

International Energy Agency (2022) *World Energy Outlook*, (iea.blob.core.windows.net).

International Energy Agency (2023) *Net Zero Roadmap: A Global Pathway to Keep the 1.5 Degrees Celsius Goal in Reach,* September, https://www.iea.org/reports

Jackson, Tim (2009) *Prosperity Without Growth: Economics for a Finite Planet*, Earthscan, London.

Lemstra, Wolter (2007) 'A Practitioner's Perspective on Interdisciplinarity in Education: The MBT Case,' in Groenewegen, John, (Ed.) *Teaching Pluralism in Economics*, Edward Elgar, Cheltenham, UK, pp. 140–154.

Madden, Bartley J. (2020) *Value Creation Principles*, Wiley, New York.

Marshall, Alfred (1946[1890]) *Principles of Economics*, MacMillan and Co., London.

Montgomery, John and Mark Van Clieaf (2023) *Net Zero Business Models: Winning in the Global Net Zero Economy*, Wiley, New York.

Morgan, Ruth (2024) 'What is 'net zero,' anyway? A short history of a monumental concept,' *Phys.Org*, May 23, 2024–05-net-short-history-monumental-concept.pdf

Reardon, Jack, Maria Madi, and Molly Scott Cato (2018) *Introducing a New Economics*, Pluto Press, London.

Rhodes, Richard (2018) *Energy: A Human History*, Simon & Schuster, New York.

Roodman David (1997) *Getting the Signals Right: Tax Reform to Protect the Environment and the Economy*, Worldwatch Institute, Washington DC.

Rosenbloom, Daniel, Jochen Markard, Frank W. Geeks, and Lea Fuenfshilling (2020) 'Why Carbon Pricing is Not Sufficient to Mitigate Climate Change and How Sustainability Transition Policy can Help,' *Proceedings of the National Academy of Sciences*, Vol. 117, No. 16, pp. 8664–8668.

Weehuizen, Rifka (2007) 'Interdisciplinarity and Problem-based Learning in Economics Education: The Case of Infonomics,' Groenewegen, John, (Ed.) Teaching Pluralism in Economics, Edward Elgar, Cheltenham, UK, pp. 155–188.

37 Climate Change

The Issue: Climate change is not something that is off in the future, but it is happening now. We no longer have the option of averting climate change, for it is too late. The best we can do is to ameliorate its worst aspects. But how to do so is contentious—it cannot be anything but—for it means drastically curtailing our use of fossil fuels while developing alternative substitutes, and re-examining our way of life. For some Americans, this is a welcome challenge, for others unacceptable, and even an anathema.

37.1 Introduction

I (Jack) have always been interested in science, especially meteorology and deep space exploration. While I've always had an affinity for scientific lingo and frequently read beyond narrowly prescribed silos, try as I might, I could never keep straight the different geological eras, (e.g., the Proterozoic and the Phanerozoic)[1] Perhaps, because, never in my wildest imagination did I think that I would live through a transition. Didn't that only occur with violent, radical, abrupt transformation/revolutions in geological time? But here we are, entering the Anthropocene (from the Greek, 'human' + 'new').

However, like most major human epochs, there is disagreement over the exact start date, while some even question whether we are actually in a new era or have been in the same era since the dawn of agriculture some 10,000 years ago, e.g.,

> rather than focusing on a relatively sudden planetary wide change—a line in a sedimentary deposit where one could plant a golden spike as is traditionally done to mark an epoch—archaeologists [have] outlined an unbroken chain of human influence stretching far back into prehistory.
>
> (Balter, 2013, p. 261)

Point well taken. There is of course merit in delineating the Anthropocene to commensurate with the adverse effects of climate change, stretching its genesis

DOI: 10.4324/9781003591856-43

to the dawn of agriculture. But until that happens, we will stick with the conventional thinking that we have entered a new geological age—the Anthropocene—officially beginning around 1950–1954.[2]

Entering a new age, and especially the Anthropocene, is not something to light a cigar or pop a champagne cork; rather, it is a wakeup call to finally do something. Yes, the Earth has warmed and cooled several times in the past, all due to natural causes (Westerhold et al., 2020) but this is the first time that human beings have abetted such a change. And unlike previous changes, which have occurred slowly over thousands of years, conditions during the Anthropocene are rapidly changing, not giving us (and other species) adequate time to adapt. This is our doing. Thus, it is our responsibility to do something about it: A responsibility to ourselves, future generations, and the Earth itself. A responsibility that we must take very seriously.

Welcome to the Anthropocene.

This chapter is surprisingly short, only because many of the issues usually discussed with climate change such as **Fossil Fuels, Oil, Net Zero**, etc., are allocated their own chapters. The specific purpose of this chapter is to understand what climate change is, its probable causes, and how best to adapt.

37.2   Climate Versus Weather

The common dictionary defines weather as "the state of the atmosphere at a given time and place with respect to temperature, moisture, wind velocity, and barometric pressure. It defines climate as "the average course or condition of the weather at a place, usually over a period of years as exhibited by temperature, wind velocity, and precipitation." Simply put, climate is a long-term phenomenon, while weather is short-term.

While day-to-day events are preponderant in explaining immediate changes in our weather, long-term factors are also important, with a mutual evolution between short-term events and long-term factors. In trying to forecast day-to-day weather (i.e., meteorology) we must be cognizant of long-term changes. But, as Friederike Otto of London's Imperial College warns "Every heat wave that is occurring today has been made more likely and is hotter because of human induced climate change" (Borenstein, 2024).

Welcome to the Anthropocene.

37.3   Why Our Climate Is Changing and Why It Matters

Our economy provides the goods and services that we all need to survive and to live decent lives. But to adequately provision, our economy needs energy. While humans have used various types of energy over the centuries, e.g., wood, water, wind, coal, oil, natural gas, solar and natural gas (Rhodes, 2018); today, our preponderant energy source is **fossil fuels**, i.e., coal, natural gas, and oil.

Fossil fuels account for 86% of total *global* energy consumption, and 79% of USA energy consumption.

Fossil fuels are primarily composed of carbon (i.e., dead plant/sea life). When combusted, the freed carbon unites with oxygen to form carbon dioxide, the preponderant global warming gas,[3] also called greenhouse gases (GHG) since they prevent the lower atmosphere's heat to escape into space. This greenhouse effect is a natural phenomenon that has been operating for millions of years. Without it, the Earth would be too cold to support life as we know it. It is well-established in both theory and measurement that the greenhouse gases (including carbon dioxide, methane, nitrous oxide, and chlorofluoro-carbons) in the atmosphere keep the Earth's mean surface temperature at an average of 15°C. Without the greenhouse effect the mean temperature would be −18°C. While "the greenhouse effect is a naturally occurring phenomenon, it is anthropogenic changes to the composition of greenhouse gases that has caused concern in the scientific community, the public, and policy makers" (Moffat, 2004, p. 13).

No energy source is completely without ill effects, and the deleterious secondary effects of fossil fuel combustion have long been understood.[4] Today, they are responsible for once-in-a-lifetime events becoming all too frequent. Records are continuously being shattered. As this book goes to press (October 2024) the year 2023 was the warmest on record, breaking the 2016 record, while the summer of 2024 is forecast to be the hottest ever, "the last time the Earth was hotter than it is today was 125,000 years ago…The ten years between 2014 and 2023 were the hottest on record…in 2023 the ocean was the hottest ever recorded" (Goodell, 2023, p. 19)

Greater atmospheric heat is responsible for more frequent and more intense storms, with more rainfall in some areas and less in others. Greater heat means that the atmosphere has more energy and can hold more water. In the oceans, warmer water expands, resulting in rising sea levels. Thanks to fossil fuel consumption, "the ocean absorbs the equivalent of the heat released from three nuclear bombs every second" (Goodell, 2023, p. 15). As oceans warm and sea levels rise, they become more violent, with waves becoming taller and more powerful, increasing coastal damage (Borenstein, 2024). Today, GHG emissions are at record levels, sea levels are rising, while Antarctica's sea ice is at a record low.

The heat released from fossil fuel combustion "is the engine of planetary chaos, the invisible force that melts the ice sheets that will flood coastal cities… it dries out the soil and sucks the moisture out of trees until they are ready to ignite. It revs up the bugs that eat the crops and thaws the permafrost that contains the bacteria from the last ice age…" (Goodell, 2023, p. 15). Heat is the first-order effect of climate change, whereas the changes in sea level, the droughts, the wildfires, the ice melting, etc., are the secondary effects (Goodell, 2023, p. 15). We know the cause of the effects, but we cannot seem to stop it.

Welcome to the Anthropocene.

Not only is fossil fuel combustion accelerating climate change, but it is causing more deaths. A 2023 study in the *British Medical Journal* (published just before COP28), found that of the 8.3 million annual deaths due to air pollution, 61% were directly related to fossil fuel combustion, with the aging populations of "North America, Europe, and East Asia, more susceptible to risk from long term exposure" (Lelieveld et al., 2023). The authors concluded,

> Air pollution continues to be a leading public health risk, and the annual number of attributable deaths exceeds the cumulative number of covid-19 deaths to date, according to WHO estimates. A major proportion is potentially avoidable, caused by anthropogenic emissions, of which globally 82% is attributable to using fossil fuels in industry, power generation, and transportation. Given the Paris Climate Agreement's goal of climate neutrality by 2050, the replacement of fossil fuels by clean, renewable energy sources would have tremendous public health and climate co-benefits.
>
> (Lelieveld et al., 2023)

A clarion call to action if there ever was one.[5]

37.4 How Should We Respond to Climate Change?

When I (Jack) first began writing/researching about climate change way back in the 1990s, I was optimistic that there would be a window of opportunity during which we could avert climate change.[6] This was not to parry responsibility on my part, but to savor the luxury of not having to work in haste, affording us some time to increase our knowledge and to gather more individuals able and willing to help ameliorate/redress. But sadly, that window has long passed. We are no longer able to avert climate change; the best we can do is ameliorate its worst effects, while adapting to new conditions.[7]

The Intergovernmental Panel on Climate Change (IPCC), in its most recent report, wrote,

> Human activities, principally through emissions of greenhouse gases, have unequivocally caused global warming, with global surface temperature reaching 1.1°C above 1850–1900 in 2011–2020. Global greenhouse gas emissions have continued to increase over 2010–2019, with unequal historical and ongoing contributions arising from unsustainable energy use, land use and land-use change, lifestyles and patterns of consumption and production across regions, between and within countries, and between individuals. Human-caused climate change is already affecting many weather and climate extremes in every region across the globe. This has led to widespread adverse impacts on food and water security, human

health…and related losses and damage to nature and people. Vulnerable communities who have historically contributed the least to current climate change are disproportionately affected.

(IPCC, 2023, p. 4)

The time to act is now. First, by limiting the overall increase in global temperature to 1.5°C (about 2.7°F) since the start of the Industrial Revolution[8]; a goal adopted at the COP18 held in Paris, November 2015.[9] Failure to meet this goal will exacerbate climate change's worst effects, while inviting more severe/extreme weather. Unfortunately, unless something radical happens now, we are on pace to breach this limit sooner rather than later. According to the World Meteorological Association, at the end of 2023, the global temperature had risen by 1.4°C. Being so close to our limit increases the urgency and reduces the timeframe for action. So, for example, given our present closeness, GHGs need to be reduced by 43% by 2030 relative to today and 60% by 2035 (*The Economist,* December 16, 2023, p. 49).

Yes, we have our work cut out for us. But rather than lulling in complacency as an excuse for inaction or engaging in psychological denial,[10] we need global actions, interdisciplinary thinking, and effective strategies now.

The most logical first step to "staying under 1.5 requires a full, fast, and funded phase out of fossil fuels starting now" (Harvey et al., 2023b, p. 15). However, our high dependence on **fossil fuels** (some would say addiction) evidences a lock-in, rendering it difficult to cease and desist our fossil fuels usage immediately,

Although clean energy has made vast strides, it is unlikely to displace fossil fuels fully by 2050, fossil fuels are likely to remain part of the energy mix for decades to come. Even optimistic forecasts suggest a substantial role for oil and gas, balanced by technologies that remove their [GHG] emissions.

(*The Economist*, December 16, 2023, p. 11)

This comports with Richard Rhodes' sobering analysis of past energy transitions,

All of the Industrial Age energy sources follow a similar trend when entering the market. It takes 40 to 50 years for an energy source to go from 1% to 10% of market share, and an energy source that eventually comes to occupy half of the market will take almost a century to do so… [and the slowness is explained by the fact that] society is a learning system. It works by cultural diffusion—the spreading of ideas from one person to another.

(Rhodes, 2018, pp. 338–339)

Perhaps given the urgency, this change to a new energy regime can and will be expedited.

Welcome to the Anthropocene.

37.5 The Disproportionate Effect of Climate Change on Developing Nations

Developing nations justifiably claim that they have a right to develop. But given today's global energy contours, the cheapest and most reliable energy source is fossil fuels, and especially coal. India, China, Vietnam, and Indonesia have ample coal supplies which they mainly use to produce electricity. Developing nations point out the developed nations' hypocrisy in calling an end to fossil fuels usage, especially since they are most responsible for the preponderance of GHGs: "the global North… with only 15 percent of world population has produced nearly 80 percent of the carbon emissions that have accumulated since the beginning of the Industrial Age" (Piketty, 2022, p. 228–229). And, to make matters worse, given their greater reliance on agriculture, and their proximity to the oceans/tropics, developing nations are (already) bearing the brunt of climate change.[11]

Developing nations are requesting financial/technical aid from developed nations, and specifically, a loss and damage fund. As we elaborate in our issue on **Net Zero**, the transition costs to a new energy regime are staggering, "just to retire coal early from the global energy mix, for example, will require $25 billion–$50 billion per year from the rich world" (The Economist, December 16, 2023, p. 11).

A start was made at the December 2023 COP28 to help developing nations cushion the irreversible impacts of climate change, and to help pay the cost/damage of extreme events such as ocean acidification, sea level rise, and melting glaciers (Harvey et al. 2023a). It remains to be seen how this will work out. A concomitant policy goal is debt relief to developing nations, given that "the world's poor nations pay more than 12 times as much to global creditors as they spend on tackling climate change" (Elliott and Inman, 2023, p. 18). The IPCC elaborates,

> Climate resilient development integrates adaptation and mitigation to advance sustainable development for all and is enabled by increased international cooperation including improved access to adequate financial resources, particularly for vulnerable regions, sectors and groups, and inclusive governance and coordinated policies. The choices and actions implemented in this decade will have impacts now and for thousands of years.
>
> (IPCC, 2023, p. 23)

Inaction on the part of developed nations has been abetted by self-interest and partisan politics. Speaking of the latter, there is a reluctance to outright ban the use of fossil fuels because of its widespread use and importance. Add the political clout and lobbying power of the world's oil companies, and that the world's economically most important nations are either major producers or major consumers of fossil fuels, e.g., the United States, China, India, and Russia,[12] and we have the contour of rich world opposition. The parties came close to outright banning fossil fuels during COP28, but it is admittedly difficult to balance the competing interests of such a large and diverse group especially when it comes to oil.

37.6 The US/China: A Special Climate Relationship?

While we discuss US/China relationship from a number of different angles in our **China** chapter, here we would like to touch on climate. The United States and China are the world's largest users of energy, the largest users of fossil fuels, and the largest emitters of GHG emissions (see **Fossil Fuels**). As such, both nations need to work together to mitigate the worst effects of climate change. The time for posturing is past.

Admittedly, China and the United States have become increasingly at odds over a broad range of issues (see **China**), however, working together on this issue can proffer a workable model for all nations, while jumpstarting them to action.[13] And, not to be discounted: a cooperative climate change relationship can possibly lead to a more peaceful and more fruitful overall relationship. Complicating matters, however, is China's argument that as a developing nation, it has the right to emulate the developed nations in using fossil fuels to achieve high standards of living. This is not just idle debate, for

> in U.N. lingo, this concept is called 'common but differentiated responsibility.' It means that rich countries must contribute more to fighting climate change because they have polluted for a longer time, as rooted in the 'polluter-pays principle.' Conversely, developing countries are allowed to pollute relatively more today to allow prioritization of pressing issues like poverty alleviation.
>
> (Larsen, 2021)

While granted there was a time when China could effectively make this argument, today, that is no longer possible, since

> China will graduate from a middle-income to a high-income country in a few years. Its GDP per capita has grown explosively from $150 in 1978 and is on course to surpass the World Bank's high-income country threshold...Consequently, any reason for China to be treated as a developing country on climate ambitions is gone.
>
> (Larsen, 2021)

Although as of 2024, the World Bank officially classifies China as 'Upper-Middle Income' (Hamadeh et al., 2023).

A hopeful first step for increased climate cooperation between the United States and China occurred during the COP28, with both nations pledging to triple deployment of renewable energy by 2030 (*The Economist,* December 16, 2023, p. 49). The two nations also pledged to jointly reduce their production of methane, "the blowtorch that is boiling the planet" (Harvey et al., 2023b, p. 15). Methane is a GHG 80 times more potent than carbon dioxide.[14]

China, the world's largest coal producer, has pledged to reduce methane from its coal production[15]; and the United States, the world's largest oil and natural gas producer, pledges to reduce methane from such production. Significant cuts of methane and other short-lived pollutants could reduce global temperature by 0.30°C (*The Economist,* December 16, 2023, p. 49). Worrisome, however, is China's coal dependence. Not only is it the world's largest coal user, accounting for over half of the global total, but in 2023, 305 coal-fired plants came online in China. While internationally,

> China is the largest financier of fossil fuel infrastructure. Through its massive Belt and Road Initiative (BRI) China has built or is planning to build hundreds of coal-fired power plants in countries around the world. More than 60 percent of BRI-specific energy financing has gone toward nonrenewable resources. Greenhouse gas emissions in more than a dozen BRI countries have soared.
>
> (Maizland, 2021)

Equally worrisome, in the United States, as we discuss in **Fossil Fuels**, a bi-partisan consensus has emerged that high oil consumption is necessary to maintain our standard of living, and that any transition to an alternative energy regime will take time. Hence, the thinking in the United States: We must make do based upon our current strengths, i.e., oil and natural gas production.

37.7   What Can Individuals Do to Mitigate the Worst Effects of Climate Change?

We need to use our imagination for a wide range of effective solutions at all levels of action, and not just at the global/state level. Individual action does matter,[16] especially when coordinated action between nation states has been less than forthcoming. For example, one action that any individual can do is to eat less meat (Grunwald, 2022). Producing beef is 100 times more land intensive than cultivating potatoes.[17] Livestock uses 80% of all agricultural land while only producing 20% of all calories. Cattle, along with soybeans, is the leading driver of Amazon deforestation.

Unfortunately, as nations develop, and poor nations emulate the rich, meat consumption is expected to increase dramatically. Nevertheless, the benefits of reducing meat consumption are significant,

> Plant-based foods tend to have a much smaller emissions footprint than meat: for example, the volume of GHG released per gramme of protein from peas is on average around 17-times less than for a gramme of protein from pork, and 110-times less than for beef... We estimate that, if sustainable and healthy diets were adopted worldwide and food waste halved, GHG emissions would be reduced by around 700 million tonnes of carbon-dioxide equivalent annually. Around 90% of this reduction would come from lower nitrous oxide and methane emissions in agriculture, with the remainder from reduced deforestation and the planting of new forests on agricultural land no longer needed for livestock feed production. About 240 million hectares (one-third the size of Australia) of pasture and cropland would be freed up, and fertiliser demand would be around one-fifth lower in 2050 than would otherwise be the case.
>
> (World Energy Outlook, 2022, p. 162)

In addition to eating less meat, Flannery (2005, p. 316) provides a helpful 'Climate Change Checklist': Install a solar hot water system; install solar panels; use energy-efficient appliances; use a triple A-rated showerhead; use energy-efficient lightbulbs; check fuel efficiency of your next car; walk, cycle, or take public transportation; calculate carbon footprint; suggest a workplace audit; write to a politician about climate change. Another workable suggestion for the individual is to,

> Imagine yourself one year in the future. Write a letter to someone important to you about what you have done in the past 12 months to promote sustainable living. It's vital to write in the past tense...and not in the form of a resolution of what you will do in the next 12 months.
>
> (Boyd and Reardon, 2020, p. 425)

There is no one-size-fits-all appropriate unit of redress; effective solutions must come from all levels, ranging from the individual to the global. Having said this, we wonder if the nation state with its insular, nationalist purview is the most effective unit to redress climate change. It really hasn't worked to date, and with the world turning more nationalist and inward, it doesn't look hopeful for the future. At the same time, many interesting solutions have come from mayors, community leaders, and activist individuals. To us, this looks like a promising avenue for reform. And, it goes without saying that at every level, we need networking, cooperation, and effective dialogue—all currently in short supply.

37.8   Conclusion

As the new age of coal unfolded during the mid-19th century in the UK, there was an enthusiasm for a new way of life and for the opportunity of "building a powerful new coal-fired world, which inspired distinct bursts of imagination, enthusiasm, and daring at various historical moments" (Freese, 2003, p. 246). Certainly, back then, there were detractors of the new energy regime, along with vested interests wedded to the old way of life. But overall, there was an optimistic gung-ho attitude to forge ahead with the creations of this new energy world.

We also see the same optimism now, although unfortunately, it is much more pronounced in other parts of the world than in the United States. Granted,

> climate change is difficult for people to evaluate dispassionately because it entails deep political and industrial implications, and because it arises from the core processes of our civilization's success. This means that, as we seek to redress this problem, winners and losers will be created. The stakes are high, and this has led to a proliferation of misleading stories as special interests argue their case.
>
> (Flannery, 2005, p. 4)

And for some, global warming (as distinct from climate change) is seen as somewhat beneficial and even welcoming,

> If scientists were predicting the imminent return of the ice age, I'm certain that our response would be more robust. 'Global warming' creates an illusion of a comfortable, warm future, that is deeply appealing, for we are an essentially tropical species that has spread into all corners of the globe, and cold has long been our greatest enemy. From the beginning we have associated it with discomfort, illness, and death, while warmth is the essence of everything good—love, comfort, and life itself.
>
> (Flannery, 2005, pp. 237–238)

But at the same time, the opposition in the USA runs deeper and is more viscerally intertwined with anti-elitism and anti-science (among some segments of the population), along with ever-present partisan politics.

And for some, the overwhelming inevitability of climate change forces one to bury one's head in the sand, to become despondent, and even to deny the possibility. Obviously, this doesn't solve the problem and will only make it worse. Today, we have a golden opportunity to make the world better for us and for our children; a world that is sustainable and able to provision for all. In our transition to **Net Zero** and away from **Fossil Fuels** we must turn despondency into hope, and hope into effective action.[18]

Welcome to the Anthropocene.

Notes

1 For a helpful guide, see 'Geological Time Scale' (2023).
2 The decision was made in 2016 by the 'Subcommission on Quaternary Stratigraphy' (SQS), which is, according to its web page, "a constituent body of the International Commission on Stratigraphy (ICS), the largest scientific organisation within the International Union of Geological Sciences (IUGS). It is also the only body concerned with stratigraphy on a global scale for the whole geological column. Its most important major objective is the establishment of a standard, globally-applicable stratigraphical scale, which it seeks to achieve through the co-ordinated contributions of a network of Subcommissions and Working Groups with a specific, limited mandate" Subcommission on Quaternary Stratigraphy.
3 For a discussion of global warming gases and their importance, see our **Fossil Fuels** chapter.
4 Eunice Foote (1856) first documented the greenhouse effect of fossil fuel combustion.
5 In our **Inequality** chapter we discuss how heat-induced climate change worsens inequality.
6 I wrote my doctoral dissertation on the bituminous mining industry becoming very familiar with the deleterious effects of combustible carbon.
7 For a brief discussion of the difference between mitigation and adaptation especially for developing nations, see Reardon et al. (2008, pp. 55–57) and Harris and Roach (2018, pp. 336–339).
8 If the limit is breached for a short amount of time, that is OK (although, obvious not ideal); the main objective is to keep the long-term trend under $1.5°C$. Although $1.5°C$ is the global limit, regional temperatures are expected to vary considerably.
9 For a good discussion of the 2015 Paris Agreement, its significant achievements, and the scientific basis for the targets, see Harris and Roach (2018, pp. 355–360).
10 A technical term meaning "if something that you perceive arouses in you a painful emotion, you may subconsciously suppress or deny your perception in order to avoid the unbearable pain, even though the practical results of ignoring your perception may prove ultimately disastrous" (Diamond, 2005, p. 435).
11 For a helpful discussion, see Markandya and Halsnaes (2004).
12 For discussion, see our **Fossil Fuels**, and **Oil Industry** chapters.
13 And as we argue in our **Iran, North Korea, and Russia** chapters, reaching out to China can drive a wedge between the three nations—all hostile to the US and intent on remaking the global order—and thus dilute their cooperative relationship.
14 Durwood Zaelke, president of the Institute for Governance and Sustainable Development, said "Turn it [methane] off and you immediately turn down the heat" (quoted in Harvey et al., 2023b, p. 15). For more discussion of methane, see Jones et al. (2023).
15 Li and Shapiro (2020) report on China's progress in mitigating the effects of climate change.
16 At the corporate level, Montgomery and Van Clieaf (2023) provide detailed and differentiated road maps, based on a company's fossil fuels emission. We discuss these in our **Net Zero** chapter.
17 These statements are based on Grunwald (2022).
18 For a how-to discussion, see Boyd and Reardon (2020, especially pp. 3–25, 255–274, and 417–425).

References

Balter, Michael, (2013) 'Archaeologists Say the 'Anthropocene' Is Here—But It Began Long Ago,' *Science*, Vol. 340, No. 6130, pp. 261–262.
Borenstein, Seth (2024) 'Earth Shattered Global Heat Record in '23 and is Flirting with warming limit, European Agency says,' *AP Science Record*, January 10.

'Climate Change: Green Shots,' (2023) The Economist (editorial), December 16, p. 11.

'COP28 Concludes: The Long Goodbye?' (2023) The Economist, December 16, pp. 49–50.

Elliott, Larry and Phillip Inman (2023) 'Climate Crisis: Fight Hampered by debt burden of poorest countries,' *The Guardian*, November 30, p. 18.

Flannery, Tim (2005) *How Man is Changing the Climate and What it Means for Life on Earth*, Atlantic Monthly Press, New York.

Freese, Barbara (2003) *Coal: A Human History*, Perseus Publishing, Cambridge, Mass.

'Geological Time Scale' (2023), June 12, Geologic Time Scale: Divisions, Periods and Eons » Geology Science.

Goodell, Jeff (2023) *The Heat Will Kill You First: Life and Death on a Scorched Planet*, Back Bay Books, New York.

Grunwald, Michael (2022) 'It's time to put down that burger,' *The New York Times*, December 18, Opinion section, p. 7.

Hamadeh, Nada, Catherine Van Rompaey, and Eric Metreau (2023) 'World Bank group country classifications by income level for FY24,' June 30, https://blogs.worldbank.org/

Harvey, Fiona; Nina Lakhami, Rowena Mason, (2023a) 'Deal Agreed at COP28 to help poor countries cope with climate crisis' (December 1), *The Guardian*, p. 1 and p. 6.

Harvey, Fiona; Oliver Millman, and Damian Carrington (2023b) 'Biggest Rise in Greenhouse Gas Emissions since 2015 due to US, China, and India,' *The Observer* (December 3), p. 15.

Intergovernmental Panel on Climate Change (2023) *Climate Change 2023: Synthesis Report*, in Core Writing Team, H. Lee and J. Romero (Eds.) Contribution of Working Groups I, II and III to the Sixth Assessment Report of the Intergovernmental Panel on Climate Change, IPCC, Geneva, Switzerland, 184 pp., doi:10.59327/IPCC/AR6-9789291691647.

Jones, Matthew, Glen P. Peters, Thomas Gasser, Robbie M. Andrew, Clemens Schwingshackl, Johannes Gütschow, Richard A. Houghton, Pierre Friedlingstein, Julia Pongratz, Corinne Le Quéré (2023) 'National contributions to climate change due to historical emissions of carbon dioxide, methane, and nitrous oxide since 1850,' *Scientific Data*, Vol. 10, Article No. 155.

Michael, (2013) 'Archaeologists Say the 'Anthropocene' Is Here—But It Began Long Ago,' *Science*, Vol. 340, No. 6130, pp. 261–262.

Larsen, Mathias Lund (2021) 'China Will No Longer Be a Developing Country After 2023. Its Climate Actions Should Reflect That', *The Diplomat*, July 3, https://thediplomat.com.

Lelieveld, Jos, Andy Haines, Richard Burnett, Cathryn Tonne, Klaus Klingmüller, Thomas Münzel, Andrea Pozzer (2023) 'Air pollution deaths attributable to fossil fuels: observational and modelling study' *British Medical Journal*, Vol. 383, p. e077784.

Li, Yifei and Judith Shapiro, Jos Lelieveld, Andy Haines, Richard Burnett, Cathryn Tonne, Klaus Klingmüller, Thomas Münzel, and Andrea Pozzer (2023) 'Air pollution deaths attributable to fossil fuels: observational and modelling study' *British Medical Journal*, (November 29), 383 doi: https://doi.org/10.1136/bmj-2023-077784.

Li, Yifei and Judith Shapiro (2020) *China Goes Green: Coercive Environmentalism for a Troubled Planet*, Polity Press, Cambridge, UK.

Maizland, Lindsay (2021) 'China's Fight Against Climate Change and Environmental Destruction,' Council on Foreign Relations, May 19, (cfr.org).

Markandya, Anil and Kirsten Halsnaes (2004) 'Developing counties and climate change' in Owen, Anthony D. and Nick Hanley (Eds.) *The Economics of Climate Change*, Routledge, London, pp. 239–258.

Moffat, Ian (2004) 'Global Warming,' in Owen, Anthony and Nick Hanley (Eds.), *The Economics of Climate Change*, Routledge, London.

Piketty, Thomas (2022) *A Brief History of Equality*, Belknap Press of Harvard University, Cambridge, Massachusetts, translated by Steven Rendall.

Reardon, Jack, Maria Madi, Molly Scott Cato (2018) *Introducing a New Economics: Pluralist, Sustainable, Progressive*, Pluto Books, London.

Rhodes, Richard (2018) *Energy: A Human History*, Simon & Schuster, New York.

Westerhold, Thomas, Norbert Marwan, Anna Joy Drury, Diederik Liebrand, Claudia Agnini, Eleni Anagnostou, James S. K. Barnet, Steven M. Bohaty, David de Vleeschouwer, and James C. Zachos (2020) 'An astronomically dated record of Earth's climate and its predictability over the last 66 million years,' *Science*, Vol. 369, No. 6509, pp. 1383–1387.

World Energy Outlook (2022) *International Energy Agency*, World Energy Outlook 2022 (iea.blob.core.windows.net).

Conclusion

In a 1964 graduation speech at the University of Michigan, President Johnson said "we have the power to shape the civilization that we want. But we need your will, your labor, your hearts, if we are to build that kind of society" (quoted in Richardson, 2023, p. 242). Today, we have the power to shape the America that we want post-2024. But our nation needs a citizenry knowledgeable about the issues that are affecting all of us. After all, "today's issues are too important to be left to others. Citizens' *reappropriation* of this knowledge is an essential stage" (Piketty, 2022, p. 244; emphasis added).

In addition, there is a deeper, more visceral need for a knowledgeable citizenry: It is the best weapon to ward off autocracy. The latter with its,

> terrible, demoralizing fascination in the possibility that gigantic lies and monstrous falsehoods can eventually be established as unquestioned facts, that man [sic] may be free to change his own past at will, and that the difference between truth and falsehood may cease to be objective and become a mere matter of power and cleverness, of pressure and infinite repetition.
>
> (Arendt, 1968, p. 333)

History abounds with nations that followed the seductive path of autocracy with nothing but tragic results, with most citizens (but certainly not all) unaware of what was happening until it was too late (Livitsky and Ziblatt 2018). For tyranny

> often advertises itself as the cure of all sufferings, the supporter of just rights, the upholder of the oppressed and the founder of order. Nations are lulled to sleep amid the brief period of prosperity it produces and when they do wake up, wretched they are indeed.
>
> (Tocqueville de, 1835 [2003], p. 280)

Orlando Figes, in his monumental study of the tragedy of the Russian Revolution, warned citizens of today's democracies "As we enter the [21st] century

DOI: 10.4324/9781003591856-44

452   *Questions for America*

we must try to strengthen our democracy, both as a source of freedom and of social justice, lest the disadvantaged and the disillusioned reject it again" (1996, p. 824). And, lest we get too complacent here in America, Alexis de Tocqueville presciently warned, "what I find most repulsive in America is not the extreme freedom that prevails there but the shortage of any guarantee against tyranny" (1835 [2003]), p. 294.

What happens to America, and how America evolves is the responsibility of all of us, and thus, "we all have a role in strengthening our democracy" (Carpinteyro, 2023). And, lest we forget, " American democracy was built on the principle of human self-determination for all" (Richardson 2020, p. 203).

It is hoped that this book will do its small part in enabling human self determination and knowledge to strengthen our nation and to prevent it from slipping down the path toward autocracy. So doing will help us construct an America that provisions for all. It is this process that begets the participation of all, that will keep the embers of democracy burning.

References

Arendt, Hannah (1968) *The Origins of Totalitarianism*, Harcourt, New York.
Carpinteyro, Marilyn (2023) 'Point: State of the Republic—Precarious,' June 28. Point: State of the Republic — Precarious – DC Journal – InsideSources.
Figes, Orlando (1996) *A People's Tragedy: The Russian Revolution: 1891–1924*, Penguin, New York.
Levitsky, Steven and Ziblatt, Daniel (2018) *How Democracies Die*, Broadway Books, New York.
Piketty, Thomas (2022) *A Brief History of Equality*, Belknap Press, Harvard University.
Richardson, Heather Cox (2020) *How the South Won the Civil War*, Oxford University Press. Oxford, UK.
Richardson, Heather Cox (2023) *Democracy Awakening: Notes on the State of America*, Viking, New York.
Tocqueville, Alexis de (1835 [2003]) *Democracy in America*, Penguin, New York.

Index

For Product Safety Concerns and Information please contact our EU
representative GPSR@taylorandfrancis.com
Taylor & Francis Verlag GmbH, Kaufingerstraße 24, 80331 München, Germany

www.ingramcontent.com/pod-product-compliance
Lightning Source LLC
Chambersburg PA
CBHW070710280326
41926CB00089B/3361